UNPRECEDENTED
POWER

UNPRECEDENTED
POWER

Jesse Jones, Capitalism,
and the Common Good

STEVEN FENBERG

Texas A&M University Press ▪ *College Station*

LIBRARY OF CONGRESS CATALOGING-IN-PUBLICATION DATA

Fenberg, Steven.
Unprecedented power : Jesse Jones, Capitalism, and the common good /
Steven Fenberg. — 1st ed.
p. cm.
Includes bibliographical references and index.
ISBN-13: 978-1-60344-434-7 (cloth : alk. paper)
ISBN-10: 1-60344-434-3 (cloth : alk. paper) 1. Jones, Jesse H. (Jesse Holman), 1874–1956.
2. Capitalists and financiers—Texas—Houston—Biography. 3. Philanthropists—
Texas—Houston—Biography. 4. Houston Endowment Inc.—History. 5. Reconstruction
Finance Corporation—History. 6. Houston (Tex.)—Biography. I. Title.
E748.J764F46 2011
973.917092—dc22
[B]
2011006491

"In all the U.S. today there is only one man whose power is greater: Franklin Roosevelt."

— *Time* magazine

January 13, 1941

Contents

Acknowledgments   ix

Introduction: The Most Powerful Person in the Nation   1

HOUSTON
1850–1898: We Had a Good Table   7
1898–1914: The Town Pump   35

THE NATIONAL STAGE
1914–1918: Give Until It Hurts   59
1919–1924: The Family Won't Discuss It   90
1924–1928: Draped and Drowned in Decorations   119

THE GREAT DEPRESSION
1928–1932: Never Rope a Steer Going Downhill   169
1933: At the End of Our String   199
1934: Go Directly to the RFC   215

CONTENTS

1935: Friendly, Industrious, Intelligent Dollars   236

1936: No Actual Ultimate Cost   251

1937: We Are Not Going Haywire   274

1938: Spenders and Lenders   300

WORLD WAR II

1939: An Avalanche of Orders   325

1940: Just Another Loan   343

1941: You'd Better See Jesse   375

1942: A Material More Precious than Gold   399

1943: Ask God to Stop Him from Lying   443

1944: Jump When the Gong Sounds   475

1945: A Very Difficult Letter to Write   505

HOME

1946–1956: It Has Grown Out of Bounds   527

Bibliography   585
Index   591

Acknowledgments

FIRST AND FOREMOST, I want to thank Sheryl Johns, Larry Faulkner, and H. Joe Nelson III, along with Houston Endowment's current and past board and staff, who understood the value of telling Jesse Jones's unvarnished story and who made this book possible through their unwavering support. I also want to thank Joe Pratt, NEH-Cullen Professor of History at the University of Houston, for promoting this book to the Texas A&M University Press and for leading me to believe I could write it. I thank them all for giving me the time, space, and assurance that encourage thinking, creativity, and confidence.

I began my journey with Jesse Jones in 1992 when I was asked to write a biographical sketch about him for Houston Endowment—the philanthropic foundation established by the Joneses in 1937. Once I finished that task, I had the pleasure of helping architectural historian Barrie Scardino assemble a massive collection of Jones's personal and business papers into an archive for Houston Endowment; grant officer Ann Hamilton had previously seen some of the papers in an old safe, asked about them, and unknowingly initiated a progression of projects to renew and maintain knowledge about Jesse Jones. With my involvement and direction, exhibitions, oral histories, and (in collaboration with filmmaker Eric Stange) a documentary film came after the archive and preceded this book. At this rate, *Jones: The Musical* may follow.

In addition to Houston Endowment's archive, other major collections of Jesse Jones's papers are housed at the Dolph Briscoe Center for American History at the University of Texas at Austin; at the Library of Congress and the National Archives in Washington, D.C.; and at the Houston Public Library and Rice University in Houston. I used them all and owe a huge debt of gratitude to Don Carleton, Ralph Elder, and the wonderful staff at the Briscoe Center for American History; to Susan Bischoff, Kemo Curry, Steve Hill, Mary McMillen, Tim Ronk, Sondee Weiss (who showed me how to access invaluable digitized newspapers), and the Houston Metropolitan Research Center's Texas Room staff at the Houston Public Library, who patiently helped me maneuver microfilm machines and access decades of the *Houston Chronicle*; to Lee Pecht at Rice University for sharing materials; and to the United States Government for preserving our national heritage at the Library of Congress and the National Archives, and for providing knowledgeable and accommodating staff who know how to quickly find and deliver requested materials. I would also like to acknowledge the American University Archives and Special Collections for digitizing Drew Pearson and Robert Allen's *Merry-Go-Round* newspaper columns, which added depth to Jesse Jones's story.

I'd like to thank the Sneed and Fuqua families for inviting me inside Jones's Robertson County, Tennessee, childhood homes; Yolanda Reid for helping me learn about Robertson County during Jones's 1870s childhood; and Carol Roark at the Dallas Public Library for finding useful information about Dallas when Jones moved there from Tennessee as a young man. Sherry Adams, former *Houston Chronicle* librarian, gave me access to photographs and verified obscure information. Historian Terry Tomkins Walsh shared facts she uncovered while assembling the John T. Jones Jr. and Audrey Jones Beck archives for Houston Endowment. Author Betty Chapman, and Ramona Davis and David Bush at the Greater Houston Preservation Alliance verified what I wrote about early Houston. Steven and Jean Waldman Shulman and Linda and Bernie Ceilly, formerly with the American Red Cross Historical Resources Department, provided insight about the organization during Jones's World War I service. And Sam Houston State University history professor James Olson reviewed the chapters that deal with the Great Depression. I am grateful to them and to Flo Crady, Jay Fenberg, Ann Hamilton, Thomas P. Lee Jr., and Emily Todd for their guidance and feedback throughout the writing process. I thank Patrick Cox at the University of Texas at Austin and Joe Pratt for reviewing the completed manuscript and for providing their insights, knowledge, and suggestions for improvement.

I thank Polly Koch for her copyediting skills and Tom Nall for his technical expertise, along with their readiness to help despite my demanding nature. I thank designers Alan Krathaus and Fiona McGettigan for their elegant and precise presentations of Jesse Jones in exhibitions, annual reports, and websites. I thank Laura Azevedo for obtaining permission from a variety of sources to publish the pictures found in this book. I thank Terry Tomkins Walsh, Debbie Harwell, and Tomiko Meeks for jumping in at the last minute to find missing footnote information. I thank publicist Gene Taft for his commitment and expertise. And I thank Graphic Composition Inc. for polishing my language and designing this book.

Throughout the years, Jones family members, including Ida J. (Dede) Wingfield Broyles, George Grainger, Jesse (Jay) Jones II, Melissa Jones, Susan Booth Keeton, Anne Butler Leonard, Ida Jo Butler Moran, and Garrett Wingfield have told stories and contributed perspective that have added a personal touch to Jones's story. The countless and enjoyable hours I spent with Audrey Jones Beck—the Joneses' granddaughter, who became my dear friend—turned Jesse and Mary Gibbs Jones into real people. I feel Audrey smiling down on me, along with her "Muna" and "Bods."

University presses publish books that often reveal obscure or forgotten aspects of history that are important to know so we can move forward armed with facts. James Olson's book about the Reconstruction Finance Corporation's activities during the Great Depression, Gerald T. White's book about the corporation's contributions during World War II, and David Kennedy's book about both events were indispensable to my efforts (see the bibliography for more information). All were published by university presses, and contain facts about government, economics, and development that are relevant and vital to know today. I am particularly indebted to the Texas A&M University Press staff for the informative, beautiful, and compelling books they publish—particularly Joe Pratt and Walter Buenger's book about early Houston banks—and for the support and guidance they have provided to this extremely grateful author.

UNPRECEDENTED
POWER

The Most Powerful Person in the Nation

THE MOST POWERFUL PERSON IN THE NATION during the Great Depression and World War II—next to Franklin Roosevelt—was not a member of the president's Brain Trust; he was not a Wall Street figure, a military man, or a college graduate. He was Jesse Jones, an entrepreneur from Texas with an eighth-grade education who built the bulk of Houston's downtown during the first half of the twentieth century and who became such a uniquely powerful appointed official that he was rightly known by many as the "fourth branch of government." Roosevelt even called him "Jesus Jones." Although now largely forgotten, Jones's remarkable accomplishments redefine Franklin Roosevelt's presidency by contradicting common notions about the New Deal, shedding new light on World War II mobilization, and offering perspective on, and possible solutions for, some of today's intractable problems.

In 1931 Jones spent three days and nights cajoling fellow Main Street bankers into rescuing and stabilizing all of Houston's tottering banks. This feat caught the attention of President Herbert Hoover, who then appointed him to the bipartisan board of the Reconstruction Finance Corporation (RFC), the agency that was the president's last-ditch effort to save the nation's drowning economy. Jones thought Hoover's RFC did not go far enough, complaining that it was "entirely too timid and slow." In a stunning observation with compelling relevance for today, he lamented, "A few billion dollars boldly but judiciously lent and invested by such a government agency as the RFC in 1931 and 1932 would have prevented the failure of thousands of banks and averted the complete breakdown in business, agriculture and industry."[1]

After assuming office, President Roosevelt quickly made the wily and talented Texan the RFC's chairman, and Jones showed everyone what he meant as he began turning the agency into the world's largest bank and biggest corporation to address the calamity of the Great Depression. Soon after Roosevelt's first inauguration, Jones and the RFC began buying stock in the nation's banks, intent on recapitalizing them so they could lend again. When the banks hoarded the cash instead, Jones used the RFC to make government loans as a last resort, understanding that flowing credit was essential to turn the frozen wheels of the economy. Many accused Jones, Roosevelt, the RFC, and other New Deal agencies of socialism, but their only aim was to save the capitalist system and help the desperate people of the United States.

To be sure, Jones set limits on the salaries of executives whose banks had received government funds, restricted dividend payments to stock-holders until government loans were repaid, and installed new management when necessary. In doing so, he helped salvage the country's financial system from complete collapse. The banks eventually repurchased all of their stock, no institution was permanently nationalized, and notably the federal government made money on the rescue. Just as Jones had hoped and planned, capitalism and democracy prevailed.

During the Great Depression, Jones and his RFC colleagues established, financed, and managed many New Deal agencies. Their efforts saved thousands of homes, farms, and businesses, and transformed the nation with new aqueducts, bridges, and other consequential infrastructure. Like the bank rescue, these Depression-era RFC programs also made a substantial profit for the United States government while they helped millions of citizens and thousands of businesses.

In 1936 Vice President John Nance Garner, a fellow Texan and Jones's close friend, impressively declared in a national radio broadcast that Jones "has allocated and loaned more money to various institutions and enterprises than any other man in the history of the world." Knowing that Jones had done so at a profit, the colorful vice president added, "Now, to

---

1. Jones, *Fifty Billion Dollars*, 46.

have done the biggest job, and to have done it well, is some accomplishment, and that is what your Texas man, Jesse Jones, has done."[2]

At the end of the 1930s, as countries in Europe and the Pacific fell to aggressors and while Congress and the public dithered over intervention, Jones turned his attention, power, and non-ideological common sense management style from domestic economics to global defense. Fully a year and a half before the attack on Pearl Harbor, he unleashed the unlimited RFC bank account to construct gigantic factories, accumulate vital materials necessary to wage world war and overcome dependence on other nations for essential resources. By then Jones was an almost universally revered public servant, and despite his unprecedented position and power, he was affectionately called "Uncle Jess" by many. He never lost the common touch or forgot the values he learned growing up on a Tennessee tobacco farm after the Civil War and during the time's severe nationwide economic panic. His down-home personality and his disarming turn of phrase—not to mention the substantial profits he made for the U.S. government and the help he provided to millions of people during the nation's most catastrophic economic meltdown—endeared him to Congress, the public, the press, and sometimes to Roosevelt. In 1941, as the rattled nation emerged from the Great Depression and began to prepare for war, *Time* magazine reassured its readers: "To many a U.S. citizen great or small, if Jesse Jones says O.K., O.K."[3]

In 1898, Jones arrived in Houston as an ambitious twenty-four-year-old when the city's banks, newspapers, and insurance companies were all locally owned. He learned early on that he would prosper only if his community thrived; to succeed he would need to wear two hats. As a businessman (and card player), he was a merciless competitor and a fierce negotiator who always intended to win. As a civic leader and a public servant, however, he bent over backwards to help others, enhance Houston, and nurture the common good. He promoted reciprocal win-win situations, like the dredging of the Houston Ship Channel, to simultaneously build his city and his businesses. He would go on to combine capitalism and public service to help save nations.

Jones first stepped onto the national stage during Woodrow Wilson's administration when he organized battlefield and home-front medical aid through the American Red Cross during World War I, becoming "big

2. *Houston Chronicle*, October 31, 1936.
3. "National Affairs: The Cabinet—Emperor Jones," 10–12.

brother to four million men in khaki."[4] A step ahead of Wilson, Jones was also an early advocate for women. In 1918 he beseeched the President to grant Army nurses military rank in order "to attract the very best class of women who go in for professional careers, such as teaching, medicine and law."[5] Jones was one of Woodrow and Edith Wilson's most ardent supporters and created a pension for the financially strapped president after he left office.

As chairman of the finance committee, Jones went on to erase the Democratic Party's persistent debt, changed the scope and length of political campaigns with his colleague "Frank" Roosevelt, and brought the 1928 Democratic National Convention to Houston, the first held in the South since before the Civil War and one of the first to be widely followed over radio.

After fifteen years of arduous public service in Washington, D.C. during the Great Depression and World War II, Jones returned to Houston in 1947, where he focused on philanthropy, added to the city's skyline and its sprawl, and lived long enough to see his adopted hometown grow from 40,000 to over one million inhabitants by 1956.

Jones went from living in the isolated frontier farms and towns of the nineteenth century, where community members supported and regulated one another, to operating in an interconnected global community in the twentieth century, where government promoted the general welfare when private initiative was unwilling or unable to do so. Jones saw government as a catalytic force for progress and as a means to protect citizens from damaging conditions and dangerous threats. He never thought government was the enemy or disparaged it—he would have considered it unpatriotic and counterproductive to do so—but he had clear limits. Jones inserted government into the private sector to an unprecedented degree to save the economy during the Great Depression and to defend nations during World War II; but he also wanted government out as fast as possible. Even so, he might wonder why people now look askance when government offers help or intervenes to improve matters. Jones would wonder because he knew firsthand that government can help people and make money at the same time.

4. *American Red Cross Bulletin*, December 16, 1918, Jesse H. Jones Collection [HE].
5. Jesse Jones to Woodrow Wilson, November 4, 1918, Jesse H. Jones Collection [LOC].

Houston

1850–1898

◆

We Had a Good Table

TOBACCO AND WHISKEY fueled the economy of Robertson County, Tennessee. In 1886, a noted historian wrote, "In nothing is Robertson County more distinguished than in the making of whiskey. From an early period in the history of the State, this brand has been sought after, and it now has a worldwide reputation."[1] The first settlers in the area—Jesse Jones's ancestors included—knew how to distill whiskey and likely were thrilled with resources they found in Robertson County.[2] Jones's ancestors first arrived in North America from Wales in the 1650s, settling in Virginia. They joined a group of pioneers who settled on the Chowan River in North Carolina, and for more than a hundred years, the family prospered there.

In 1774, brothers Eli and Jesse Jones headed west and stopped at an elevated plateau in northwest Tennessee called the Highland Rim, where they found fertile soil and cool, dry air. The brothers bought land, began to farm, helped build a community in what became Robertson

1. Gaston, "Robertson County Distilleries," 49.
2. Ibid., 51.

County, and raised their families on the Tennessee frontier. Two of Eli's children, William and Nancy, stayed on in Tennessee.[3]

William Jones had been born in 1829, and a year after the Civil War ended, he married Laura Anna Holman, a girl who lived on the farm next door. The Joneses and Holmans were self-sufficient farmers. With help from their slaves before the war, they grew their own food, wove their own cloth, and made their own bricks. Farming families in the area were independent, but if anyone in the community was in need, neighbors helped. If the man of the house was sick and needed to till his soil, his neighbor plowed his field. If a birth was imminent, women kept food on the table and stayed to help with the delivery. Self-reliance was the norm, yet help was readily available and reciprocated. Intermarriage among the large families of the close-knit community was common.[4]

William and Laura raised five children on their hundred-acre tobacco farm. Their fourth child, Jesse Holman Jones, named for his pioneer great-uncle, was born on April 5, 1874. Jesse and his siblings (John, Elizabeth, Ida, and Carrie) grew up in the midst of Reconstruction when blacks and whites were struggling with old ways in a new world.[5] A banking panic the year before Jesse was born ushered in a severe national depression.

Cultivating tobacco, as William Jones did, was a year-round, hands-on industry that had always depended on slave labor for its survival and growth, so abolition of slavery brought change. After the war, many freed slaves in Robertson County became laborers and sharecroppers, and, as the county's black population rapidly expanded, a few eventually bought land of their own. Black men had won the right to vote and by the time Jesse was born, a few had been elected to the state legislature. On the Jones farm, shacks belonging to black families dotted the rolling hills behind Jesse's house, giving the rural landscape a greater density of people and buildings than it has today. The black children who lived there in comparative poverty were Jesse's playmates and he called them his best friends even though he did not know their last names.[6] Still, segregation and the poll tax had also become law, the Ku Klux Klan was growing, and lynching "kept order," most notably in 1880 when six black men accused of murder were hanged from the second-floor balcony of the county courthouse in Springfield, the closest town to the Jones farm.[7]

---

3. John T. Jones Jr. to Margaret Bailey, March 30, 1956, John T. Jones Jr. Collection [HE].
4. Reid and Gregory, *Robertson County, Tennessee*, 55.
5. Timmons, *Jones: Man and Statesman*, 13.
6. Ibid., 15.
7. Reid and Gregory, *Robertson County, Tennessee*, 75; Law, *Tennessee Geography*, 221.

Jesse Jones's parents, William Hasque Jones and Laura Anna Holman Jones. Jones said his father's "standards and principles" guided him throughout his "business and public life" (Timmons, *Jones: Man and Statesman*, 51).

Springfield was the social center of the area. On Saturdays families and their horses and wagons packed the robust little town as people came from surrounding farms to shop, to see friends, and to take care of business, whether personal, commercial, or political. The hubbub of town linked the county's citizens, especially those visiting from farms, to a larger world. Stores were busy, saloons were popular, and the only bank in town boomed with business from the quality tobacco and whiskey produced in the county.[8] The bank, Springfield's first, had opened only two years before Jesse's birth, and as abolition of slavery had earlier, this commercial conduit dramatically changed the way things worked in Robertson County.[9] The most immediate improvement was that people needing a bank's services no longer had to ride to Nashville, traveling in defensive groups on horseback or in wagon trains, and risking run-ins with bandits, hostile Native Americans, or bands of Confederate guerillas.[10] Besides providing a safe, convenient place to transact business, the bank also extended credit to the distillers and tobacco farmers, whose high-grade products enjoyed international acclaim.[11] Easy access to credit and the ability to conduct business safely helped area industries grow, which offset the economic panic that gripped the region and nation at the time of Jesse's birth.[12]

By the time Jesse was five, Springfield's prosperity was apparent to anyone who approached—a new, towering county courthouse was being built in the center of the square at a cost of $21,000 ($478,000 in current dollars, which reflect 2009 values). The first institutions of higher education had also opened in the area. And resorts advertising warm mineral water and a drier, cooler climate attracted people from lower-lying cities, bringing with them everything from musical ensembles to croquet.

As a young boy, Jesse knew there was a world beyond the farm. The new bank surely must have been a topic of discussion at home as his father's tobacco business flourished, and riding into Springfield on the back of his family wagon, Jesse would have seen the town's newest building growing toward the sky. It is easy to imagine that he was touched by the poverty and injustice he saw and was aware of the contrast between his life and that of others. Those early experiences may have influenced Jones's later life, but what is certain is that his mother's death dramatically changed

8. Reid and Gregory, *Robertson County, Tennessee*, 80.
9. Ibid., 78.
10. Ibid., 66.
11. Reid and Gregory, *Robertson County, Tennessee*, 76.
12. Gaston, "Robertson County Distilleries," 63.

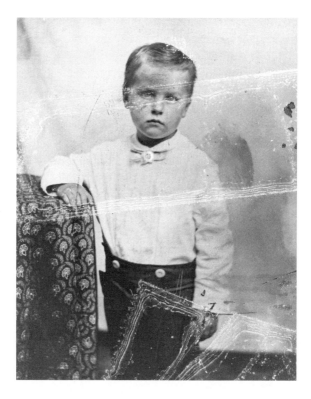

Jesse Jones as a young boy was, according to one of his teachers, "a typical example of the rural boy of his time who was not without a goodly amount of devilment in him" (Timmons, *Jones: Man and Statesman*, 16).

his childhood. On April 22, 1880—just seventeen days after Jesse's sixth birthday—Laura Anna Holman Jones died from tuberculosis at the age of thirty-eight. She was buried in the family cemetery down the dirt road from their home. William's widowed sister, Nancy Jones Hurt, moved in to take charge of the house and five motherless children. Including her own two sons, "Aunt Nancy" now had seven rowdy children to care for. She was a small woman without much education, but her shrewd, loving personality gave her stature.[13]

Aunt Nancy, whose husband had died fighting for the Confederacy during the Civil War, was the "guide, physician, and clothes-maker of all the Jones children, who paid her the tribute of saying no children ever had a better mother. She was a famous cook, preparing all sorts of edibles without benefit of cookbook; set a much-talked-of table for the family and friends who dropped in; and exported the products of her culinary art to neighbors for miles around when sickness overtook them. Of all the

13. Timmons, *Jones: Man and Statesman*, 13.

members of the family, it was Aunt Nancy for whom [Jesse] manifested the greatest affection."[14]

Jones would later recall life on the farm, saying, "My jobs included looking after the chickens and turkeys, feeding the pigs, wiping the dishes, helping with the churning, bringing in wood and kindling, building fires, taking out the ashes, sweeping and doing generally the things necessary to farm life where there was no hired help for housework."[15] He continued, "In summer we liked to 'go washin'—more properly stated 'in swimming.' We also went barefoot in summer and the woe of my existence was having to wash my feet every night before going to bed. I would sit up as long as I could, because I liked to hear the grown people talk. There were no bathtubs in the country homes, and all the bathing we got was in washtubs or in large wash pans. By the time I was ready to go to bed, I was usually sleepy enough to try to skip the foot-washing chore, and sometimes succeeded, only to get a scolding the next day from Aunt Nancy."[16]

Jesse tried to get away with whatever he could at home and at school. As J. B. Farthing, one of Jesse's teachers, remembered, "Jesse Jones in school as a youngster was not particularly bright nor did he differ greatly from the boys of the countryside who attended old Hopewell. If I was impressed by any different trait of Jesse Jones as a youngster, it was his genius for getting into scraps which his brother, John, always seemed to pull him safely out of." Farthing went on, "He never seemed to study very hard nor did he seem to need to. His lessons were always fair and his grades averaged high enough not to cause him any worry from me. It can be said with truth and without discredit to the man that Jesse H. Jones was a typical example of the rural boy of his time who was not without a goodly amount of devilment in him." Farthing concluded, "So far as I have been able to learn, Jesse Jones missed grammar and its use completely. Although a victim of the rural school system, which prevailed at that time, in so far as grammar was concerned, he was to later develop the art of self-expression to a fine degree."[17]

Jones recalled, "I attended Howard School one session, then old Hopewell, another one-room school near home, for two years. I did not learn very easily. The children were punished for slight infractions of the

14. Ibid.
15. Ibid., 15.
16. Ibid., 16.
17. Ibid.

rules, sometimes with the switch, but more often by standing in the corner of the schoolroom, facing the wall. I had my share of this kind of punishment, largely as a result of playing pranks on the other children when I should have been studying."[18]

Everyone knew school was about to resume in the fall when they smelled tobacco. At summer's end, bundled leaves of burley tobacco hung upside down in the old, weathered barns that lined the sides of the roads. Smoldering fires on the floors of the closed-up barns cured the fresh leaves, and smoke escaped through the split wood, shrouding the structures in a fragrant haze. The scent of curing tobacco did not mean the same thing to all the children, though, because only half of them went to school,[19] and for those who got to go, schools were not that good. The public school system, which was divided by race into separate black and white schools, had been established only a year before Jesse's birth and had next to no money. For a good time after, schools were locally run with no coordinated requirements or accreditation.[20] There were, however, pockets of improvement: Neophogen College opened in Robertson County in 1873,[21] and Vanderbilt University and Peabody State Normal School opened in Nashville in 1875.[22] Even so, primary education out in the country was patchy, and the pupils less than healthy. Jones remembered, "Almost every day the teacher told some pupil to stay at home next day for a delousing."[23]

William and Nancy wanted more for their children. Their brother, Martin Tilford (M. T.) Jones, had moved from Tennessee to Illinois, and then to the town of Terrell, Texas, where he established what would become an exceptionally successful lumber business. With M. T.'s encouragement, William and Nancy moved to Dallas in 1883. Jones remembered, "When I was nine, my father sold the little farm for, I think, about $5,000 [$114,000] and took the family to Dallas, Texas. He thought the five children could get better schooling there than in the country schools where we lived. Moreover, M. T. Jones had been urging my father to come to Texas and go into business with him."

He recalled the day clearly, saying, "When the man who bought Father's farm went with him around the fence lines to see where the boundaries

18. Ibid., 15.
19. Reid and Gregory, *Robertson County, Tennessee*, 74.
20. Ibid.; Law, *Tennessee Geography*, 222.
21. Reid and Gregory, *Robertson County, Tennessee*, 74.
22. Law, *Tennessee Geography*, 223.
23. Jesse Jones to Blanche Babcock, October 9, 1944, Jesse H. Jones Collection [LOC].

were, I went along. There were no abstracts of title in those days in the country where we lived. When we got back to the house, my pet pig greeted us as he always did when I came into the yard."

Jones continued, "Father said to the man, 'I cannot sell you the farm unless you buy Jesse's pig.' The man looked at the pig, then looked at me and asked, 'What do you think your pig is worth?' I told him, 'About $4.25.' He then asked what I thought it would weigh, and I told him, 'About eighty-five pounds.' The market price of hogs was five cents a pound, which made $4.25. The gentleman replied, 'I think you are about right, and I will buy your pig.'"

Jones concluded, "It was my biggest money transaction up to that time. I was very proud to have $4.25 all my own. But a great shock and sorrow came to me when I realized that the friendly pig had gone from me forever."[24] Much later, he would feel that way about skyscrapers in Texas.

The large family moved into a home on Leonard Street near Ross Avenue in Dallas.[25] In 1883, about 19,000 people lived in the city, which was a growing cotton, rail, and manufacturing center with four banks, not one. A few of the city's dirt roads were being paved, and new buildings were going up. Homes and business spaces were rented or bought almost as soon as material to build them touched the ground. The city's population would nearly triple in ten years.

M. T.'s lumber business was growing, too. Since settling in Terrell in 1875, he had opened lumberyards in other towns, acquired large tracts of east Texas timberland, and moved his family to Houston to be closer to his southerly holdings.[26] He wanted William to look after his northeast Texas interests. Once William got the family settled, he moved to Terrell to help run the M. T. Jones Lumber Company; meanwhile, Aunt Nancy enrolled the children in school in Dallas.

Dallas had four new four-room schoolhouses, two for whites and two for blacks.[27] Jesse attended the Third Ward School, where he formed an enduring bond with Blanche Aldehoff Babcock, his third grade teacher. "Miss Blanche" had been born in Tennessee and was related to John Sevier—the state's first governor and a comrade of Jesse's pioneer grandfather and great-uncle, Eli and Jesse. Miss Blanche was a link to home

24. Timmons, *Jones: Man and Statesman*, 17.
25. Jones, testimonial speech, Adolphus Hotel, Dallas, April 9, 1928, Jesse H. Jones Collection [HE].
26. *Houston Daily Post*, June 28, 1898.
27. McElhaney, "Childhood in Dallas."

and was a mother figure as well. Long after Jesse was grown, he and Miss Blanche corresponded frequently and at length.

From one of the many letters Jones wrote to her, it appears he still struggled at school. He called her "one of the strictest [teachers] that I ever had punish me. That's the only kind I ever had. Some threw books; others used the switch." He wrote her, "All you ever did was redden my hand with a ruler. I still love you for it, but would like a chance of bloodying the nose of one or two professors."[28] Jesse was rowdy, restless, bright, and bored. He excelled in arithmetic, the only subject that interested him. As a result he drifted toward the bottom of the class. In another letter to Miss Blanche, he recalled, "There was an examination of the third grade. They were divided about fifty-fifty. . . I was placed in the lower [half] and, being of such mature years, I knew I belonged in the upper half instead of the lower. It was probably the best thing that could have happened to me, but I never did learn easily at school, and was glad when I was permitted to quit and go to work."[29]

Summers let Jesse escape school. "One of the two summers when we lived in Dallas," he recalled, "I worked in cotton fields near town and got forty cents [$9.40] a day for chopping the weeds. However, in picking cotton we were paid by the pound, and I was able to make as much as a dollar [$24] a day." He continued, "During the next summer, when I was twelve, I herded and looked after a small bunch of cattle, between thirty and forty head, on a small ranch about thirty miles from Dallas. At the ranch, I lived alone in a one-room ranch house most of the time and did my own cooking, which was not much—meat, bread, and coffee. Aunt Nancy had taught me a little, but my enthusiasm for it was not very strong, and I have never cooked anything since."[30]

Jesse and his family stayed in Dallas for only two years. William missed his life as a farmer and when a 600-acre farm on the Tennessee-Kentucky border became available, he bought it with money he had made from investing in M. T. Jones Lumber Company stock. In 1886, when Jesse was twelve, William and Aunt Nancy took the family back to Robertson County.[31] The region's economy, like that of the Texas city they had just left, was growing vigorously. Springfield's second bank opened the year the Joneses returned, and the 30 or so blacksmiths in the area hustled to

---

28. June 9, 1947, Jesse H. Jones Collection [LOC].
29. Jesse Jones to Blanche Babcock, October 19, 1942, Jesse H. Jones Collection [LOC].
30. Timmons, *Jones: Man and Statesman*, 18.
31. Ibid., 19.

keep the horses, donkeys, and oxen shoed to meet the needs of the businesses and population.[32]

The Joneses' two-story brick home on a hilltop overlooking the farm and rolling countryside was said to be the finest house outside of Nashville.[33] The imposing house, with its ornate trim and grand columns, looked like the proverbial southern mansion on a hill. It was built in the 1860s by one of the largest distillers in the area. Jones recalled, "The house was modern, with the exception of plumbing and electricity. All the outbuildings, servant quarters, barns, stables, and the like were brick. It was one of the few homes that had an icehouse." He also remarked on his family's good fortune, noting, "Father unfailingly had a plentiful supply of meat in the smokehouse, from which less-thrifty neighbors would borrow a ham or a side of bacon during the summer months. There were always ample fruits, vegetables, and berries in season, and they were canned and preserved for the winter. We had a good table."[34]

Jesse may have lived in an affluent household, but poverty surrounded him. He saw it when he played with the impoverished sharecroppers' children, and he saw it in the farm kids who did not go to school. Even in booming Dallas, Jesse saw many families down on their luck. A report by the chief of police said, "The city is overrun with . . . little fellows ranging between the ages of seven and sixteen. Many of them have no parents and many others are allowed by their parents to run the streets at large . . . and engage in housebreaking, petty pilfering and gambling."[35] Buckner Orphanage was the only place in Dallas that took care of needy children, and it was always filled beyond capacity.[36]

In their grand new home in Tennessee, Jesse saw how William's open smokehouse doors helped struggling neighbors. He also saw Aunt Nancy keep track of who took what so she could make sure her brother's generosity was eventually repaid. Their charitable but frugal *pas de deux* showed Jesse that a loan often worked better than a handout and that, given sufficient time, most neighbors honored their obligations and helped others when they could.

Jesse learned life's lessons at home. One day Jesse's father told him and his brother, John, to choose any parcel for a tobacco crop of their own. Jesse chose almost three acres next to the house, knowing that the chick-

32. Reid and Gregory, *Robertson County, Tennessee*, 79.
33. Henderson, *Robertson County's Heritage of Homes*, 36–38.
34. Timmons, *Jones: Man and Statesman*, 20.
35. McElhaney, "Childhood in Dallas," 39.
36. Ibid., 38.

ens and turkeys would help keep the tobacco leaves free of worms. He proved creative in marshaling further help to "worm" his crop and prune out the suckers. As one early biographical sketch reported, "Jesse was a great favorite with the Negroes who worked with him and his brother, John, on his father's farm. About the time when he and John were big enough to take care of a plot of three acres of tobacco, Jesse bought an old-fashioned horse pistol. Firearms among Negroes at this time were almost unheard of, and Jesse often on Saturday afternoons, when the hands were having their half holiday, would get his three acres of tobacco 'wormed' and 'suckered' for a shot around among the Negro boys."[37]

Other efficiencies were less planned. On the day Jesse plowed his plot, William had to go to town, but before he left, he told Jesse to hitch up two mules and to begin breaking ground. When his father returned that afternoon, Jesse had almost finished a job that should have taken two days. Jones recalled, "I had been plowing in a semi-trot most of the time instead of a slow, steady walk, as is customary, and the mules were white with lather. Actually, I did not go in a trot because I wanted to get through in a hurry. The reason was that an old mule seems to know when a man is handling him and when a boy is handling him; consequently, I was fighting with the mules all the time, throwing gravel and clods of dirt at them, which would make them walk at double speed or even sometimes in a slow trot." William was not pleased. Jones continued, "As long as I lived on the farm, that was the last time I was allowed to plow . . . Father had good stock and did not allow it to be abused by anyone." He added, "While there were riding plows at that time, Father did not allow them on his farm. He did not want his mules to have to haul a lazy man, he said, in addition to pulling a plow."[38]

This first crop gave Jesse his first experience with credit. His father took him to the general store to open an account and said he could keep whatever he made on his crop after he had paid all of his expenses. Jesse made $120 ($2,800) and sent away for a mail order, double-barreled, breech-loading shotgun. He did not tell his father how he had spent his profits, but an acknowledgment of the order gave him away when it arrived. Jones remembered, "That night after supper, he handed me the postcard and said in a perfectly normal voice, with no indication of reprimand or question, 'If you will leave it in my top drawer, I will pay for it.' I was greatly relieved when he treated it that way, and the matter was

37. Wakefield, "Jesse Holman Jones."
38. Timmons, *Jones: Man and Statesman*, 21–22.

never mentioned between us again . . . Upon reflection, I have assumed that when my father gave me the use of the land to grow a crop of my own under the conditions he imposed, his purpose must have been to start me out thinking for myself and making my own decisions in my own way—to run my own affairs. There was perfect sympathy between my father and me, and I would not have offended him for anything. For some reason, he must have thought I needed special attention, for I do not recall that he ever scolded me or even corrected me, and certainly I was by no means a model boy."[39]

Jesse was still attending school, now about two miles from home, across the state line in Kentucky. He wrote, "We rode horseback to Adairville, carrying our lunches with us," then added, "I was frequently punished by my teachers, even after I was twelve and thirteen. Being kept in after school or part of the lunch hour was a common occurrence. I was always getting in scraps with boys my own age, and sometimes a little bigger. I seemed to think they were always teasing me or picking on me. Very likely it was my own fault."[40] Impatient as always with school, he quit after the eighth grade and went to work full-time for his father. William not only grew and processed his own tobacco, but also bought more tobacco from local sharecroppers and farmers, which he then sold and shipped to Europe. When William and two partners—both relatives—opened a second tobacco "factory" enterprise under the name Jones, Holman and Armstrong, they put fourteen-year-old Jesse in charge.[41]

Opening the new business account at the Springfield bank was another, more formidable rite of passage for the teenager. Jones wrote, "It was a proud day but a serious one for me when Father took me to the bank in town, where I left my signature and was told that my checks would be honored there, and that I had the sole responsibility of running this factory. When Father told me he was going to put me in charge of the factory, I asked him if he thought I could do it. He replied that I could do it as well as he could—that I knew tobacco, knew how to order and grade it, and how to put it up and ship it. I, of course, knew that I could not do the job as well as Father, but, when he told me I could do it, I felt I could."[42]

Still, it was a challenging job for a teenager. Jones recalled, "Tobacco can only be delivered in a rainy season, when there is moisture in the air,

39. Ibid., 22.
40. Ibid., 20.
41. Jesse Jones to J. Brown Bell, August 4, 1941, Jesse H. Jones Collection [HE].
42. Timmons, *Jones: Man and Statesman*, 23.

so as to make it pliable enough not to break and crumble. Sometimes, though, a farmer would bring his tobacco to the factory when it was 'too high,' that is, when it had too much moisture in it. Always, before unloading it, we would draw samples to see if it was in proper order. When it was found to contain too much moisture, the farmer would have to take it back home, dry it out, and deliver it in the next rainy spell, in proper shape."

This was not as easy as it sounded. He continued, "There were no hard-surfaced roads in those days, and most country roads were very bad in the rainy season. To require a farmer to take his tobacco back home, hang it up in the barn to dry, and deliver it the next rainy spell would of course make the farmer very mad. The farmers for the most part were men in their forties, fifties, and sixties. I had to take many a severe tongue-lashing when it was necessary for me to tell such a man to take his tobacco home and deliver it in proper order the next rainy season. Yet, if I accepted it damp, it would spoil and be a total loss, so I had no choice but to refuse it."

Jones admitted, "Sometimes, after one of these tongue-lashings, I would go out behind the factory and have a cry. My help was all Negroes and all of them were my good friends. I was ashamed to have these helpers see me cry, and I was too young to talk back to the men as I would have liked to do, but I was determined to do my job. I would not report these things to Father, for fear he might be bothered about it and maybe put some grown man in my place."[43]

Jesse revered his father. He once wrote to Miss Blanche, "I do not remember my mother, but my father was the best man I have ever known. He has always been my first ideal."[44] Indeed, William Jones was a pillar of the community, as well as a deacon at Hopewell Baptist Church, where he counseled members who swore in public or drank too much; he also donated a piano to the small congregation that gathered in the small, iconic white church building surrounded by fields and farmland.[45] His political views, however, especially on the Civil War, were less clear. Jones wrote in retrospect, "Being on the dividing line, so-called, in Tennessee, my father took no active part in the war."[46] But Jones's nephew had a different opinion, writing, "during the Civil War all of the Jones boys, or at least most of them who settled in Illinois, fought in the 115th Illinois Volunteer

43. Ibid.
44. Jesse Jones to Blanche Babcock, August 25, 1937, Jesse H. Jones Collection [LOC].
45. Pistole, "A History of Hopewell Church."
46. Jesse Jones to C. V. Jones, March 12, 1954, Jesse H. Jones Collection [HE].

Regiment, while their brother who stayed in Tennessee, William Hasque Jones, served in one of the Tennessee regiments."[47] A Houston business newspaper reported that William Jones was wounded "in the service of the Confederacy."[48] Jones wrote simply, "I do not know what, if any, interest Father took in politics, since it was never discussed at home. However, he must have taken a normal citizen's interest, since he was prominent in the community. Also, I never heard him mention the war. This was probably natural, since he was a Southerner and his brothers, all living in Illinois, were Unionists and Republicans. When I grew up, I assumed that Father was a Democrat, and I became one."[49]

Jesse also acquired his father's business skills. William was highly respected throughout the Tennessee-Kentucky border region. Jones declared, "I got my first business training and business principles from my father in the tobacco business, and his standards and principles have been my guiding influence in all my business and public life."[50] He cited in particular his responsibilities for the factory, saying, "While my uncle by marriage, Seph Armstrong, was supposed to be in charge of that business, I was in fact in complete charge of it and, incidentally, got some very valuable business experience early in life."[51]

Jesse did not spend all of his time working. He also played the mandolin with friends, attended church socials, and swam and fished in the river.[52] But after three years at the tobacco factory, he began to wonder if there were better ways to make a living. A move by the family back to Dallas when Jesse was seventeen gave him an opportunity to find out. The Joneses moved into a house on Washington Avenue, and Jesse enrolled in a four-month course at Hill's Business College, where within the first few weeks, his teachers realized he knew almost as much as they did and hired him as an instructor.[53]

He did not enjoy teaching, however, and soon set out to sell accounting services to shop owners and bookkeepers in small towns surrounding Dallas. After trying four towns without success, Jesse returned to Dallas, still uncertain what to do. He had ambition, but no direction. He clerked in a grocery store, then tried selling cigars, but quit that, too, after which

---

47. John T. Jones Jr. to Margaret Bailey, March 30, 1956, John T. Jones Jr. Collection [HE].
48. *Houston Business Journal*, September 10, 1984.
49. Timmons, *Jones: Man and Statesman*, 14.
50. Ibid., 24.
51. Jesse Jones to J. Brown Bell, February 4, 1941, Jesse H. Jones Collection [HE].
52. Ida Guller to Jesse Jones, February 22, 1915, Jesse H. Jones Collection [HE].
53. Jones, testimonial speech, Adolphus Hotel.

he happily smoked up his samples. About a year later, William returned to Tennessee, while Aunt Nancy stayed behind with the girls until they finished school. Jesse decided to work for his uncle M. T. Jones at his lumberyard in Hillsboro, Texas. With its many similarities to Springfield, Hillsboro must have felt familiar to him. A monumental courthouse recently had been completed in the center of the town's square, which was lined with busy stores, blacksmiths, and saloons.[54] But instead of tobacco and whiskey, cotton and the railroads fueled the economy. Even though its population was about the same as Springfield's, Hillsboro had three banks, which, according to the *Hillsboro Mirror,* were "solid as the rock of Gibraltar."[55] The paper reported on the town's rapid growth, writing, "Hillsboro is constantly on the upward growth. Improvements of a permanent character are constantly being made. New dwellings have been put up during the last year but not enough to supply the demand. More houses are needed to give the people homes who are coming here to live. Realty owners could materially assist their town and do a good turn for themselves by erecting houses to rent."[56] Seeds for Jesse's future as a builder may have been planted in his mind by the Hillsboro boom.

To be sure, Jesse was discovering new interests, including an interest in politics. He wrote Miss Blanche, "I voted for [Grover] Cleveland when I was eighteen. At that particular era, boys under twenty-one could not be served in bars, but [because I was] six-foot-two, the bartender never questioned my age, so I thought if I was old enough to drink at the bar, I was old enough to vote for Cleveland, and did at Hillsboro in 1892."[57] Jones also tried bare-fisted boxing, which he practiced at the lumberyard. He remembered, "I thought I could box and didn't think a man could knock me down. But one day my sparring partner knocked me cold and cured me of any further desire to be a boxer."[58]

Jesse discovered girls as well. Joe Didiot, a friend from Hillsboro, remembered, "He was then of [a] commanding appearance, tall, but somewhat thinner than we know him today; he was only eighteen and not yet grown. On his arrival among us, he soon came [to be] part of the business and social cosmos of the town. He was considered a good mixer of more than ordinary talent and ability, and also had some predilections

54. *Memorial and Biographical History of Johnson and Hill Counties,* 281.
55. *Hillsboro Mirror,* July 27, 1892.
56. *Hillsboro Mirror,* January 13, 1892.
57. Jesse Jones to Blanche Babcock, November 15, 1945, Jesse H. Jones Collection [LOC].
58. Jesse Jones, interview with publisher Bernarr Macfadden, February 6, 1941, Jesse H. Jones Collection [HE].

for the gentler sex. Those corn-fed prairie girls began to 'cast an eye to windward' to the newcomer as an escort to church, prayer meeting, and choir practice."[59] In response, Jesse acquired new clothes. Didiot recalled, "I remember that Sunday garb of his distinctly: a black Prince Albert with cream-colored pants of figurative design, a long, pointed, turn-down collar, the small and short black bowtie of that era suspended by a small rubber loop. He looked the part of the well-dressed man of that day." He also wore "from the bottom hole of his vest . . . a long, heavy, gold watch chain, and in the pocket was, if not the biggest gold watch in all Texas, [then] the second biggest."[60]

Life was not all fun and fine clothes, however. Jesse worked hard at the lumberyard. He stacked, sold, and loaded lumber, kept the books, collected debts, and referred to himself as a "general roustabout."[61] When asked years later if he had been the manager, he replied, "Practically so, but [I] did not have the title. The manager was away most of the time."[62] And despite his responsibilities, he was paid only a salesman's salary of $40 ($940) a month. He lived over the yard, saving money on rent, but he had to spend half his income on food, which left little for entertainment, courting, and new clothes. When he asked his uncle for a $20 ($470) raise—he was working at the yard all day and keeping the books at night—M. T. refused and said he could not understand what kept Jesse so busy. Seeing no future at the lumberyard, Jesse submitted his resignation, but when M. T. learned that the manager was away most of the time and the yard was being run improperly, he told Jesse it was his duty to stay.

Jones remembered, "This, of course, created an impossible situation; but, being an eighteen-year-old boy, I did not know any better than to try [to keep on at the yard]. However, the relationship between the manager and me soon became very strained, and I decided definitely to quit and go home." He continued, "I paid my bills, packed my valise, and bought my ticket home. It was Saturday, and I had not told the manager I was leaving. Having completed my arrangements, and with the books posted up-to-date, I went to the manager to tell him I was quitting, but he beat me to the draw by telling me he had been instructed to discharge me. I have never known whether he had actually been so instructed or whether he did it because I was in his way." He concluded his recollection, "My

59. Wakefield, "Jesse Holman Jones," 31–32.
60. Ibid., 32.
61. Jesse Jones, interview with publisher Bernarr Macfadden, 3.
62. Ibid.

father died on March 13, while I was en route home. I had not been told he was ill; in fact, neither the family nor the doctor had known how sick Father was."[63]

William Jones was laid to rest next to his wife, Laura, in the family cemetery. William had signed his will only thirteen days before he died. He appointed J. B. Farthing—Jesse's former teacher who had recently married Jesse's sister Lizzie—as one of two executors. Ida, Lizzie, and Carrie Jones each received two hundred acres, a home, and various out-buildings. Carrie, the youngest, also received the proceeds from their father's $5,000 ($118,000) life insurance policy. Jesse and John Jones inherited their father's remaining M. T. Jones Lumber Company stock and stock in the First National Bank of Waxahachie, which was worth about $4,000 ($94,300). The will directed trustees to manage the tobacco business until Jesse turned twenty-one, when he would take over. So whether he liked it or not, Jesse was back in the tobacco business.[64]

Still, his father's unexpected death did not keep Jesse from looking for adventures beyond Tennessee. A few years earlier, in 1890, President Benjamin Harrison had signed a bill that called "for celebrating the 400th anniversary of the discovery of America by Christopher Columbus by holding an international exhibition of arts, industries, manufactures, and the products of the soil, mine, and sea in the city of Chicago in the State of Illinois."[65] The president invited every nation to participate and established the Department of Publicity and Promotion of the Exposition, which sent out thousands of notices by mail each day, in every major language, promoting the fair as the greatest cultural and entertainment event in the history of the world. By the time it opened in May 1893, the fair had seized the nation's attention. Even though traveling to distant cities took days, one-quarter of everyone living in the United States attended the World's Columbian Exposition, including Jesse Jones.

Jesse's trip to Chicago became part of the myth surrounding the man. A 1934 article in *The New York Times Magazine* recounted, "At the age of nineteen, he was growing his own tobacco, but as tales of the Chicago World's Fair drifted across the countryside, it became apparent to him that the fair was the one thing in life which he must see. So he mortgaged his tobacco crop for $60 [$1,400], of which $10 [$235] went for a round-trip railroad ticket and $10 was sewed into the waistband of his breeches to

63. Timmons, *Jones: Man and Statesman*, 29.
64. William Hasque Jones's will, March 1, 1893, Jesse H. Jones Collection [HE].
65. Schulman, "Interactive Guide to World's Columbian Exposition."

be used for emergencies only." The article continued, "Then he got an old canvas valise, of the kind called telescope, and put into it a boiled ham, three baked chickens, several dozen biscuits, some light bread, dill pickles, and preserves. That was his food supply, and it lasted him for all the ten days he spent at the fair. When he got home, his valise was empty, his head was stored with the fruits of a post-graduate course in the civilization of the world, and his $10 was still sewed into his waistband."[66]

The story shows that Jesse was adventurous and frugal, but the fair had a considerable impact on him. It covered 633 acres and included more than 65,000 exhibitions. The scope was overwhelming, but the massive, white Beaux-Arts buildings that lined lagoons at the entrance managed to exemplify balance, harmony, and uniformity. The White City, graced with domes and Imperial Roman and Greek flourishes, was the genesis of the "City Beautiful" movement that influenced urban architecture and planning for decades.

The fair's cultural and educational purposes were not without commercial intentions. Exhibits in the eleven-acre Manufactures and Liberal Arts Building mingled price-tagged products from around the world with historic documents and artifacts. Fifty-two nations either built elaborate exhibition halls or purchased concessions for theaters, restaurants, and shops to depict their cultures. The eighty-acre Midway featured stereotypical glimpses of life from around the world, including replicas of Chinese, German, Japanese, and Turkish villages, an Indian bazaar, and a street in Cairo complete with tombs, huts, temples, and snake charmers.

The Midway was also home to the world's first Ferris wheel. It rose twenty-five stories into the air and could carry more than a thousand people at once. People strolling the Midway tasted Cracker Jacks, Juicy Fruit gum, carbonated sodas, and hamburgers for the first time. The World's Columbian Exposition embodied, and Jesse Jones personified, the national shift from rural to urban, from production to consumption, and from agriculture to industry and technology. Technology in 1893 meant electricity, and each day the fair used three times more than all of Chicago. Electric boats silently moved visitors through the waterways, overhead electric trains took them through the sky, and moving sidewalks transported them smoothly on the ground.[67]

Jesse saw everything his budget would allow. He marveled at the huge buildings, explored the exhibits, and spent one dollar ($23.50) to see

66. Adams, "The Man Who Lends Uncle Sam's Money."
67. Schulman, "Interactive Guide to World's Columbian Exposition."

Lillian Russell sing. He spent a dollar a day renting a six-by-eight-foot partitioned room in a converted warehouse and spent another dollar on a round-trip boat ride to Milwaukee and back that took him out onto Lake Michigan, where he had an unobstructed view of the fair and of the Chicago skyline.[68]

Jones recalled, "The things that impressed me most were the buildings in Chicago and the thousands of people on the street, apparently rushing pell-mell in every direction."[69] More than one and a half million people lived in Chicago, and after the catastrophic fire of 1873, the city had been rebuilt and became known as the "Cradle of the Skyscraper"; when the Masonic Temple Building opened in 1892 with its twenty-two floors, there was no taller occupied building in the world. He concluded, "Seeing Chicago, the tall buildings, so many people, and the World's Fair, gave me an ambition to get out into the big world."[70] The sight also may have inspired him later to build much of downtown Houston.

Jesse promised the black farmhands back home that he would share his adventure if they tended his tobacco while he was gone. When he returned, he told them all about the extraordinary sights, sounds, and technological inventions. To the semi-literate people who lived in isolated, rural shacks, the tales must have seemed like science fiction. Jesse knew they were real and he was determined to pursue that big city life. As soon as possible, he and his brother harvested and sold their tobacco crop, cashed in the stock their father left them, and used the proceeds to complete their sisters' homes. With family obligations met, Jesse headed for Texas again.

His first stop was Dallas. In the eleven years since he first moved there in 1883, the population had surged to 50,000. There were now fifty public and private schools, 150 factories, and ten banks.[71] His plan was to work at his uncle M. T.'s lumberyard at Main and St. Paul, his newest and largest.[72] However, the Hillsboro manager who had caused problems the year before now worked in the Dallas office. According to Jones, "I later learned that this man had poisoned my uncle's mind against me, telling him that I gambled and drank, that there were some irregularities in the cash account, and [that] he finally had to discharge me."

Jesse knew the cash shortfalls were the manager's doings. "There *were*

68. Timmons, *Jones: Man and Statesman*, 31.
69. Jesse Jones to J. B. Cranfill, February 22, 1930, Jesse H. Jones Collection [LOC].
70. Ibid.
71. *1898 Dallas City Directory*, 9, Dallas Public Library Collection.
72. *1896 Dallas City Directory*, 39, Dallas Public Library Collection.

some irregularities, but the shoe was on the other foot. It is true that I took an occasional drink, played a little penny-ante poker, and did most of the things an eighteen-year-old boy living away from home is likely to do, but nothing dishonorable or really to my discredit. I could not have been very bad on $40 a month, even if I did go into debt a little."[73]

Still, M. T. refused to give his nephew a job. C. T. Harris, the general manager of the lumber company, intervened. He knew Jesse was honest and capable, and asked him to keep the Dallas yard's books while he was out of town inspecting other operations. When Harris discovered that the troublesome manager had cooked the books in Hillsboro, he fired him and offered Jesse a permanent position as bookkeeper, which he accepted; it paid $15 ($370) a week. Within six months Harris had promoted the promising young man to manager of the new Dallas lumberyard, paying him $100 ($2,450) a month. Soon, "Jesse Jones, Manager," appeared in tall black letters on the side of the block-long yard wall, under "M. T. Jones Lumber Company."

M. T., who was skeptical of the move when Harris first told him he had given his nephew a job, was furious when Harris made Jesse manager. M. T. and Jesse had a tumultuous relationship similar to conflicts between a father and son; M. T. and his wife, Louise, essentially became Jesse's surrogate parents after his father's death. M. T. Jones was a strong-willed, self-made man who had arrived in Texas with very little to his name. Born in 1841, he was twelve years younger than Jesse's father, William, and took a different road, first moving to Illinois with members of the Jones clan, then fighting for the Union during the Civil War.[74]

Married to Louisa Woolard, an Illinois native, M. T. started out farming near the town of Pana in Christian County, Illinois, until the young couple moved with their two children, Augusta and Will, to seek a new livelihood just as the railroads began to make the rich timberlands of east Texas commercially accessible. Expansive stands of virgin pine blanketed 36,000 square miles of east Texas in the 1870s, covering all or part of forty-eight counties.[75] The trees had long been a burden to local farmers who struggled to clear patches of land for cultivation, and harvesting the timber was not feasible. Pulling enormous logs by ox-drawn wagon or floating them down rivers was both daunting and expensive.

The final spike of the east Texas section of the Texas and Pacific Rail-

---

73. Timmons, *Jones: Man and Statesman*, 36.
74. Bascom Timmons to Jesse Jones, September 29, 1953, Jesse H. Jones Collection [HE].
75. "Lumber Industry," 334.

road was hammered in on August 13, 1873, connecting Dallas and east Texas with each other and with the rest of the world. Speculators bought land, laid out towns, and gave property to railroads for depots. Immigrants from older states in the South, as well as from Europe arrived. Joining these other hopeful souls seeking a better life, M. T. Jones moved his family to Terrell, Texas, east of Dallas. Two businessmen had put the town together, spending just five dollars ($90) an acre.[76] M. T. opened a lumberyard in the growing town.

M. T. was ambitious. Not long after settling in Terrell, he opened yards in Ennis and Waxahachie.[77] His business quickly grew and eventually included vast tracts of southeast Texas timberland, a railroad, banks, and lumber mills in Orange, where east Texas timber was processed during the area's "Golden Age."[78] He also accumulated more than 6,000 acres along Buffalo Bayou near Houston, where he grew wheat and cotton.

With his commercial success came a rise in social standing. In 1882, M. T. moved his family to Houston and bought one of the city's grandest homes. The grounds included a tennis court where "several . . . young women and men meet every fair afternoon."[79] M. T. and Louisa helped build a community, becoming founding members of St. Paul's Methodist Church, the DePelchin Faith Home for orphans, and the Young Women's Cooperative Home for destitute pregnant women. M. T. also was founding president of the South Texas Commercial National Bank. By 1894, M. T. Jones was one of the pillars of Houston society and at the top of the state's number one industry.

M. T. and Louisa Jones were Jesse's role models. Even so, his uncle was a formidable figure. Twenty-year-old Jesse had to show his uncle that he was a responsible, honorable young man in the midst of a highly competitive environment. The Texas lumber industry was tough. The 1893 World's Columbian Exposition had proved that pine was perfect for building large structures, which accelerated the demand for east Texas timber and intensified competition throughout the industry.[80] M. T. ordered the managers of his yards to sell lumber at any price—profit or loss. He was a "double-ender," owning forests filled with timber and the mills to process trees into products, as well as stores throughout the state where he could

76. Stoltz, *Terrell, Texas*.
77. "Waxahachie, Texas," *The New Handbook of Texas*, 854.
78. "Orange, Texas," 1161.
79. "Fifty Years Ago—August 9, 1894," *Houston Post*, August 9, 1944.
80. "Angelina County," *The New Handbook of Texas*, 181.

Jesse Jones's uncle, Texas lumber titan Martin Tilford (M. T.) Jones, who was responsible for bringing his nephew to Texas and to Houston.

sell the processed wood. If he did not make money at one point, he would at another. M. T. was "vertically integrated."

Nine large yards competed for business in Dallas,[81] but Jesse turned a profit. Still preoccupied with what he believed were his nephew's deplorable personal habits, M. T. was unmoved by this success and continued to criticize the Dallas operation, never offering a word of praise. A few weeks after his twenty-first birthday, Jesse became convinced that he was, again, in a no-win situation. He sent a letter of resignation to his uncle and self-confidently warned that the yard's success depended on M. T.'s replacing him with a sharp, capable person who could handle the harsh competition. He wrote that he would help with the transition and stay at the yard for a few months until June 30, 1895.[82]

A complete accounting of the yard was made during Jesse's last day.

81. *1898 Dallas City Directory.*
82. Jesse Jones to M. T. Jones, April 1895, Jesse H. Jones Collection [HE].

Jesse Jones's aunt, Louisa
Jones, who was a mother
figure to her nephew.

Afterward, he went to Houston to report to his uncle and to spend time
with his aunt and cousins, including Will and his wife, Mary, who were
expecting their first child. For all his problems with M. T., Jesse enjoyed
his cousins and their families, and liked visiting with them whenever he
could. His relationship with his Aunt Louisa in later years grew closer
and warmer, and he would eventually call her "Mother." Mary also would
become more to Jesse than just his first cousin's wife. But at this point,
Jesse's relationship with his uncle M. T. concerned him the most.

While Jesse was visiting, M. T. checked the Dallas yard's books to verify
his nephew's reported profit. He discovered that the figures were right
and immediately regretted letting Jesse go. In fact, as Jones remembered,
"He insisted that I go back to Dallas and run the yard. At first I refused,
but . . . then it occurred to me that maybe I was making a mistake, since
during my first six months as a manager, I had been able to make a profit
against tough competition."

Jesse flexed his developing skills as a negotiator: "I decided to do a little trading with my uncle. I told him I would go back to Dallas and run the yard at a salary of $150 [$3,530] a month and six percent of the profits of the business. He stormed and stormed, and I left the office. The next morning at the breakfast table, he said to me, 'Go on back and have your way.' But he was still mad."[83]

Jesse went back to Dallas and made more money than ever. It showed. He wore patent leather shoes, a diamond in his tie, and parted his hair down the middle. When he went to court to collect a delinquent debt from a farmer, he lost the case when the tattered man's lawyer won the jury's sympathy by ridiculing Jesse's ostentatious appearance and calling him a "dude." Jones recalled, "It taught me a valuable lesson. I gave the diamond to my sister for a ring; began parting my hair on the side, where I should have parted it all the time; and quit wearing patent leather shoes and my best clothes, except on Sunday."[84]

Jesse was learning a lot of lessons, which paid off during the 1897 State Fair in Dallas. The World's Columbian Exposition had filled exposition operators with grand ideas, and organizers of the annual State Fair had visions far beyond their budget. Before filling orders to build the Fair that year, all the local lumber companies—except one—insisted on personal guarantees from the association's directors. Jesse was the exception, agreeing instead to accept the Fair's gate receipts until everything was repaid.

It looked like a risky loan. By opening day, the State Fair owed the lumber company more money than the entire Dallas yard was worth. M. T. went to Dallas as soon as he heard about the loan to quiz his nephew about the decision. It turned out his concern was also about his nephew's personal habits, based on reports about drinking and playing cards. Jesse was living at the Dallas Club, which, according to a newspaper report, "enjoyed an enviable reputation. All of its tenants—that is those who 'slept in,' as an old English phrase has it—were bachelors. It was a man's club, pure and simple." The article continued, "Young fellows just arrived at voting age regarded it as the pinnacle of ambitious citizenship. The privilege of entering its portals unchallenged was to be striven for and attained."[85] Jesse had arrived.

M. T.'s worry about the loan was allayed after he realized the State Fair was quickly repaying its obligation as promised. But it took a conversa-

83. Timmons, *Jones: Man and Statesman*, 40.
84. Ibid., 41–42; *Houston Chronicle*, September 20, 1984.
85. *Dallas Times Herald*, February 18, 1953.

Jesse Jones as a "dude" who, after losing a court case because of his flamboyant appearance, learned a lesson in humility, parted his hair on the side, and gave his diamond stickpin to his sister for a ring.

tion with an esteemed banker to dispel M. T.'s other worries enough that, after his trip to Dallas, he never criticized his nephew again. Jones remembered, "After his visit with me, he talked with Royal A. Ferris, the banker, about me. Mr. Ferris was in his late fifties, and certainly a good friend of mine. He knew my habits and how I lived; he also knew human nature better than my uncle. I recall one occasion when the vice president of his bank criticized a small loan that Mr. Ferris had made me. This gentleman made the criticism at a bank board meeting, stating that I was an inveterate poker player at the Dallas Club. Mr. Ferris replied, 'Yes, I know; and I understand he is a pretty good poker player.'" Jones continued, "After my uncle's visit with Mr. Ferris, his attitude toward me was entirely changed. This impressed me with the fact that two of the greatest assets anyone can have are a good record and friends willing to speak up for him when occasion requires."[86]

Ferris was, indeed, a valuable friend. His father had established Waxahachie's first bank in 1868, and Ferris was president of the Exchange National Bank in Dallas; among other endeavors, he helped establish the Texas State Fair in 1891 and the Dallas Club in 1895.[87] He merged Dallas's disorganized transit system into one unified line and, as president, oversaw the system's evolution from cars pulled by mules to cars powered by electricity.[88] Ferris's words and actions carried clout. They were the genesis of Jesse's future fortune.

Like Jesse's trip to Chicago, the story about his loan from Royal Ferris that got him into his own business was told so many times, it became part of the Jones legend. Jones himself recounted it in a letter: "I borrowed $500 [$12,700] from a bank of which Royal A. Ferris was the president . . . I had no capital or property, and it was necessary to establish credit if I was ever to get into business for myself. [So] I borrowed the $500 for the sole purpose of establishing credit. I took the money out of the bank but did not use it, and paid the note promptly when it came due six months later, losing the interest." He went on, "Some months later I borrowed $2,000 [$51,000] in the same manner and for the same purpose. When this note matured, I asked for the privilege of paying $1,300 [$33,000] and extending $700 [$18,000]. My request was granted, and I paid promptly when [that] note matured. I probably fibbed a little in both instances in explaining why I wanted the money, but do not recall what the story was. The purpose was honest, and I took no chances with the money, because it was not really mine."

He added, "A year or two later I had an opportunity to buy some pine timber land at what I thought was a bargain, and persuaded Mr. Ferris to lend me $17,000 [$433,000] with which to pay for it. It was not easy to get this loan, but I finally convinced him that I could and would work the loan out even if I should lose on the timber. I also, of course, tried to convince him that the timber was a good buy, and probably did." He concluded, "A few years later I sold the timber for several times what I paid for it, and that gave me a substantial start for going into business for my own account."[89]

86. Timmons, Jones: Man and Statesman, 45.

87. Dallas Newspaper Artists Association, Makers of Dallas, brochure, 1912, Jesse H. Jones Collection [HE].

88. Hill, History of Greater Dallas, 19.

89. Jesse Jones to Eugene Kelly, May 14, 1949, Jesse H. Jones Collection [LOC].

In a subsequent speech, Jones said, "I give Mr. Ferris credit for my start in a financial way. I believe he has helped more men in Texas than any other dozen bankers, and I would rather be a Royal A. Ferris in the banking world than any man that I know."[90]

By the time he was twenty-four, Jesse had two powerful people looking out for him: Royal Ferris and M. T. Jones, but just as M. T.'s confidence in his nephew had grown, his health began to fail. At the beginning of the year, he and his family left Houston for a trip west in the hope he would recover. He went with letters of introduction, including one from Houston's mayor H. Baldwin Rice that said, "The bearer, Mr. M. T. Jones of this city, is one of our most influential and respectable citizens and is traveling for his health. Any courtesies extended him will be appreciated not only by our good people but by yours respectfully, H. B. Rice."[91]

Enjoying the higher elevation of the Davis Mountains in west Texas, the dry climate in Arizona, and the sunshine in California, the Jones family was gone for months, yet all the while M. T. maintained a busy correspondence about business back home. He returned to Houston in May, while his wife and daughters remained out west. Around the first of June, he headed toward Dallas, making stops to inspect his timberlands, lumberyards, and sawmills. He checked into the Oriental Hotel when he arrived in Dallas and immediately fell ill; for the better part of two weeks, he was in bed. Then on June 21 he was taken to St. Paul's Sanitarium, where the next morning, at the age of fifty-six, he died from what the papers called "pernicious fever."[92] The *Houston Daily Post* reported, "The news of his death was a shock to the commercial community here with which Mr. Jones was largely and intimately connected." The article went on, "Mr. Jones was in every respect a valuable citizen. He was a member of the Methodist Church, a Mason, and a member of the Elks. He was a man generous in his charities but they were so unostentatious that few people knew their extent. He was a man of noble impulses, and by his thrift and energy he had amassed a considerable fortune."[93]

M. T. Jones was buried in Houston's historic Glenwood Cemetery. In his will, he had appointed five executors, one being Jesse Jones.[94] M. T. left a fortune worth more than $1 million dollars ($25 million) at a time when only a few citizens in the United States had wealth of that magnitude.

90. Jones, testimonial speech, Adolphus Hotel.
91. H. B. Rice, letter, January 4, 1897, Jesse H. Jones Collection [HE].
92. *Dallas Times Herald*, June 22, 1898.
93. *Houston Daily Post*, June 22, 1898.
94. M. T. Jones, will, December 15, 1897, Jesse H. Jones Collection [HE].

Jones remembered, "It may be that my uncle and I were too much of the same temperament to be entirely congenial, but after he found that I had energy and interest for business, as well as for play, we got on better, and I am glad to say were fast friends long before he died at St. Paul's Sanitarium in June 1898. In fact, he named me one of his executors and that took me to Houston, the headquarters of his business."[95]

95. Jones, testimonial speech, Adolphus Hotel.

1898–1914

◈

The Town Pump

HOUSTON WAS A MUDDY, buggy, swampy townsite with tents, some small wood houses, and around a thousand people when the city was incorporated in 1837, just one year after Texas won its independence from Mexico in 1836.[1] By the time Jesse Jones moved there in 1898, Texas was part of the United States, Houston's population had grown more than forty times, and the central streets were dense with businesses and turreted mansions that sat on lavishly landscaped, full block lots. Fancy horse-drawn carriages, wagons from the country, and mule-pulled streetcars passed along the dusty dirt streets, which turned to thick, gooey mud after the frequent Gulf Coast rains. Houston's development in its first fifty years was rapid and nonstop, and its future growth was almost palpable.

In 1898, the city had four banks, four train depots,[2] and a $50,000 ($1.3 million in current dollars) pledge from Andrew Carnegie for the city's first public library. Enterprises for repairing and maintaining railroad cars had created an industrial center just east of downtown and

1. Houghton, et al., *Houston's Forgotten Heritage*, 66.
2. McComb, *Houston: Bayou City*, 98.

Main Street and Texas Avenue when Jesse Jones came to Houston in the 1890s.
Courtesy Houston Metropolitan Research Center Photo Collection, MSS 114-686,
Litterst-Dixon Collection.

employed the majority of Houston's skilled workers.[3] Cotton flowed into
the city from the west, timber poured in from the east, and the spreading web of railroad tracks—along with Buffalo Bayou on the business
district's north border—provided routes to transport these in-demand
products to the rest of the world.

The city's new mayor, Samuel Brashear, who was elected the same year
Jones moved to town, began replacing the city's unreliable patchwork of
services with a coordinated water, sewage, and garbage system. General
Electric began building a plant to supply twenty-four-hour metered power
to homes and businesses, allowing customers for the first time to pay only
for the electricity that they used.[4] The corporate giant's participation in
the city's development and the transformation of electricity from a publicly owned service to a private commodity, sold at a profit exemplified
Houston's movement from an isolated settlement to a national commercial center.

Within twenty-four hours of his arrival, Jones opened an office in the

3. Platt, *City Building*, 83.
4. Ibid., 167.

city's most prestigious business building, the recently completed six-story Binz Building, which was the tallest in town and the crown of Houston's central business district at Main Street and Texas Avenue. Sightseers came to ride the building's elevator and enjoy the unobstructed view of lush coastal plains that surrounded and defined the town's borders in all directions.

The five-story Rice Hotel, which stood on the site of the former republic's capitol building across the street from the Binz Building, rented rooms at $2.25 ($57) a night and became Jones's first home in Houston.[5] He landed in a boomtown and was living and working at the city's most prominent commercial intersection. As an executor of the M. T. Jones estate, he also had a place in Houston's civic aristocracy and at the top of one of the state's largest lumber empires. His connections to Houston's leaders, the momentum of the city, along with his skills, vision, ambition, and audacity, combined to position him at the right place, at the right time to start a stupendous business career.

Although there were four other executors, Jones managed the entire M. T. Jones estate for his aunt and three cousins. He was now in charge of tens of thousands of acres of timberland spread over three east Texas counties and parts of Louisiana. The estate owned and operated sawmills and factories in Orange that had the daily capacity to turn hundreds of thousands of feet of raw timber into shingles, doors, window sashes, and two-by-fours. The logistics were equally huge: felled trees had to be moved to the plants, and finished products had to be delivered to lumberyards located throughout the state and beyond. With assistance and advice from the other trustees, Jones bought, sold, and managed the land, expanding the M. T. Jones Lumber Company even further.[6] His Aunt Louisa was becoming an exceptionally wealthy woman.

She remained at her large home on Polk and Main with her daughter Jeanette. The other daughter, Augusta, was married to the first of three husbands and cousin Will, who inherited 6,000 acres along Buffalo Bayou at Deepwater, settled there with his wife, Mary, and son, Tilford.[7] By now, Jones's siblings were all married too. John and Carrie lived with their spouses in Milford and worked for the M. T. Jones Lumber Company.

5. Rice Hotel receipt, January 22, 1902, Jesse H. Jones Collection [HE].

6. M. T. Jones estate, "Inventory and Appraisement," September 22, 1898; Angelina County tax receipts, January 22, 1900; Orange Lumber Company authorization to sell shares of stock, January 5, 1909; M. T. Jones estate authority over Louisiana property, August 28, 1899, all Jesse H. Jones Collection [HE].

7. Tilford Jones to Carl Barker, October 24, 1928, Jesse H. Jones Collection [HE].

Lizzie and Ida remained in Tennessee with their husbands, near the old family home. Jesse was on his own in Houston, but he had assumed a major role in his aunt's life, in the timber industry, and in Houston's business community. He was no longer on the outside looking in.

Three momentous events occurred around the start of the twentieth century that changed Houston forever: the 1900 Galveston hurricane, the discovery of oil at Spindletop, and Jesse Jones's move from Dallas to Houston.

The ferocious September hurricane still counts as the worst natural disaster in United States history and was the realization of Galveston's worst nightmare. The violent storm and its crushing tidal wave smashed through the barrier island, killing eight thousand people and destroying or damaging every structure in the city.[8] The storm decisively shifted development away from Galveston's port to Houston's Buffalo Bayou, a safer inland waterway.[9]

On January 10, 1901, four months after the hurricane demolished Galveston, oil surged from the ground at Spindletop near Beaumont. In one day, the gusher produced half as much oil as all other wells in the United States, combined.[10] During its first year of production, twenty percent of the nation's oil came from the Spindletop field[11] and even larger oil reservoirs were soon discovered in surrounding areas. The new oil companies that survived the fierce competition eventually established their headquarters in Houston. Spindletop marked the beginning of the city's evolution into the nation's oil and petrochemical capital.

Jones arrived just in time to accommodate and encourage the explosive growth that followed these developments. Back then, Houston encompassed a mere nine square miles, and the city government was vacillating between developing parks and neighborhoods or promoting growth through industrialization.[12] The cash-poor, still struggling post–Civil War South required money from northern banks to expand. In 1902, Houston's new mayor promised to bring a steady flow of capital from the north to promote the nascent oil and shipping industries.[13]

Jones needed northern capital, too. In the spring of 1902, he went to

8. McAshan, *Corner of Main and Texas*, 133.
9. Platt, *City Building*, 175.
10. McAshan, *Corner of Main and Texas*, 133.
11. Johnston, *Houston: Unknown City*, 124.
12. Betty Trapp Chapman, "A System of Government Where Business Ruled," *Houston History Magazine*, 4, no. 1 (Fall 2010): 30.
13. Platt, *City Building*, 183.

New York, stayed at the Waldorf-Astoria, dined at Del Monico's, and used his position and success as manager of the M. T. Jones estate to establish personal lines of credit with a number of banks and railroads. Since receiving his first loan from Royal Ferris, Jones had adopted the habit of borrowing more than he needed and leaving the unused portion on deposit so he had enough to cover his debt. He recalled, "As a policy, I usually borrowed two dollars when I needed only one, and kept the other dollar on deposit with the bank that I borrowed from. That made me a profitable customer for the bank. I never borrowed on collateral. My securities of whatever nature were always in my own safe."[14] For added protection, Jones also carried large amounts of life insurance.

While he was in New York, Aunt Louisa invited Jones to join her and his cousins on their annual trip to Europe. Jones toured Europe, riding in fine carriages with his cousins dressed in their elegant clothes; he saw the coronation of King Edward VII, but the most important moment of his trip occurred when he told his aunt that, in addition to managing her estate, he planned to go into business for himself.

Jones established the South Texas Lumber Company on September 16, 1902, with profits from a few Spindletop deals and proceeds from timberland he had bought with funds he borrowed from Ferris.[15] According to its charter, the company was established to purchase and sell "goods, wares, and merchandise, and especially lumber, shingles, cross ties, sashes, doors, blinds, and all other articles and material made and manufactured from logs and timber."[16] Jones began buying lumberyards in Houston and throughout Texas, New Mexico, and Oklahoma. His first purchase was the Reynolds Lumber Company for $1,600 ($39,000), which in addition to the lumberyard included "wagons, team, harness, buggy, and assorted merchandise."[17]

In 1902, Jones also was crowned King Nottoc of the Notsuoh Festival (i.e., King Cotton of the Houston Festival; spelling backwards was seen as trendy and fun in the early 1900s). The weeklong festival, held each November between 1899 and 1915, showcased the region's agricultural, industrial, and commercial might in an attempt to duplicate New Orleans's success with Mardi Gras. Notsuoh capped Houston's social season and

14. Jesse Jones to Eugene Kelly, May 14, 1949, Jesse H. Jones Collection [LOC].

15. Timmons, *Jones: Man and Statesman*, 63.

16. South Texas Lumber Company charter, September 16, 1902, Jesse H. Jones Collection [HE].

17. Reynolds Lumber Company proposal to Jesse Jones, October 8, 1902, Jesse H. Jones Collection [HE].

In Houston for only four years, Jesse Jones was elected King Nottoc during the 1902 Notsuoh Festival, indicating his quick embrace by the civic aristocracy.

included parades, carnivals, balls, and the coronation of King Nottoc, who reigned over the realm of Tekram (Market) in the domain of Saxet (Texas). King Nottoc was a position bestowed upon the city's most prominent civic leaders, and Jones's selection only four years after his arrival in town signified his quick embrace by Houston's business, civic, and social worlds. Tall, strapping, handsome, and on his way up, Jones was one of Houston's most eligible bachelors. But he was only interested in his cousin's wife, Mary Gibbs Jones.

Mary Gibbs, a doctor's daughter, was born on April 29, 1872, in Mexia, Texas, and grew up with nine brothers and sisters in a home filled with music and books. Her father died when she was just five, and his will declared, "If my children desire it, they are to be thoroughly educated."[18] So Mary attended Methodist College in Waco, Texas, when few women went to college, or even finished high school. She met M. T. Jones's son,

18. Jasper Gibbs, will, February 16, 1856, Jesse H. Jones Collection [HE].

Will, while he was working in Mexia at one of his father's lumberyards. They were married in 1893 and had one son named Tilford. Eventually they moved to the 6,000-acre ranch on Buffalo Bayou at Deepwater that M. T. had left to his son upon his death in 1898.

The rich estate allowed Will, his sisters and mother, Louisa, to enjoy a lavish lifestyle. They sailed to Europe each year for Archduke Ferdinand's balls and lived in their own Viennese schloss, where the men remained while the women went to Paris to have gowns made for the coming year.[19]

Despite their extraordinarily glamorous life, however, all was not well with Mary and Will. After arriving in Sicily from a cruise to Egypt and Israel, Mary wrote to Jesse, "Do you still intend to come over this summer? I have not heard from Will in quite a long time. I shall be glad to hear from you at *any* time." She signed it "Much love, Mary" and included a post-script about her son that read, "Tilford still speaks of you to other little boys as being the strongest man on Earth. He thinks you are a wonder."[20] So did Mary, evidently. Two months later she wrote from London, "I am very brave here. You know Will does not care for opera at all. I hope you will decide to come to Europe this summer. I know by August you will require a good rest, won't you?"[21]

In August, however, Jones was busy buying a lumberyard ten blocks down Main from Buffalo Bayou at Main Street and McKinney Avenue. He paid $29,320 ($690,000) for the yard and its contents, and leased the half-block for $500 ($12,000) a year.[22] He was also buying blocks of land farther south on Main and arranging with the city to pay half of the cost of grading and graveling the new streets.[23] He formed the Edgewood Realty Company and the Southern Loan and Investment Company to de-velop the land and to build and finance houses in what today is known as Midtown.[24] He had extended M. T.'s "double-ender" strategy by add-ing another business line—construction. Jones was preparing to turn his timber into homes as Houston's population grew and spread, just as he had seen others do years before in Hillsboro.

Jones supercharged his efforts with credit. The contract for each

19. Audrey Jones Beck, conversation with author.

20. April 3, 1903, Jesse H. Jones Collection [HE].

21. Mary Gibbs Jones to Jesse Jones, June 9, 1903, Jesse H. Jones Collection [HE].

22. Ed H. Harrell Lumber Company to Jesse Jones, August 10, 1903, Jesse H. Jones Col-lection [HE].

23. Jesse Jones to H. B. Rice, July 24, 1907, Jesse H. Jones Collection [HE].

24. R. M. Farrar to W. Flanagan, IRS, August 30, 1910, Jesse H. Jones Collection [HE].

house was different, with terms set to suit and encourage the buyer. One family, for example, bought a house for $600 ($13,600) down, with $10 ($227) monthly notes at eight percent interest and one $3,400 ($77,000) payment at the end of five years; for their $4,600 ($105,000), they got a two-bedroom, one-bath house with a "one-story out house to include servant's room, buggy shed, wood shed, and horse stall."[25]

Family came first for Jones. The first house he built in the Edgewood subdivision was for his Aunt Nancy.[26] When Jones wrote a will in 1902, he divided his $17,000 ($416,000) estate between Aunt Nancy and his sisters and brother, John, who was then president of Jesse Jones's new Dalhart Hardware Company and who had been elected Dalhart's first mayor.[27]

Jones's wealth grew dramatically in the next two years. In 1904 he bought the Campbell Lumber Company, which was heavily in debt. J. Lee Campbell remembered his family company's dire straits, testifying, "The 1900 storm blew down approximately 17,000 acres of virgin pine timber in East Texas belonging to the company. This blow was more than we could recover from."[28] The company struggled on for a few more years until Jones stepped in and bought Campbell's statewide chain of lumberyards and his mansion at 2908 Main Street. He moved his Aunt Louisa into the house and lived there with her and his cousins, including Will and Mary when they weren't at Deepwater. They called it the "Boarding House" because so many family members lived there; according to one relative, that was when the sparks between Jesse Jones and Mary first started to fly.[29] In his 1904 will, Jones listed $205,000 ($4.8 million) in cash gifts—and included a $25,000 ($590,000) bequest to his cousin Will's wife, Mary Gibbs Jones.[30]

In 1905, Jones became a director and stockholder of Union Bank and Trust, the first state-chartered bank in Texas and one of the first major banks in Houston organized almost entirely with local money.[31] The primary pieces of Jones's business life were now in place: he had access to

25. Southern Loan and Investment, contract with E. Reichardt, May 28, 1907, Jesse H. Jones Collection [HE].

26. Timmons, *Jones: Man and Statesman*, 66.

27. Jesse H. Jones, will, September 17, 1902, Jesse H. Jones Collection [HE].

28. J. Lee Campbell, notarized testimony, June 25, 1928, Jesse H. Jones Collection [HE].

29. Audrey Jones Beck, conversation with the author.

30. Jesse H. Jones, will, October 27, 1904, Jesse H. Jones Collection [HE].

31. Buenger and Pratt, *But Also Good Business*, 38.

Louisa Jones's "Boarding House," where much of the extended Jones family lived including Will, Mary, and Jesse.

capital, ability to multiply its power, and a vision of greater things to come.

Jones's Edgewood subdivision was growing and his lumber business was expanding. There were about eighty cars on Houston's roads, and new laws to accommodate them required a fifteen mile per hour speed limit, lights for night driving, and giving the right-of-way to horses.[32] Still, Houston still looked like a small village with few amenities. The city especially lacked a large hotel of distinction. Jones, who sensed and seized almost every opportunity to make his city and his fortune grow, bought the four-story Bristol Hotel at Travis and Capitol in June 1906 for $90,000 ($2.1 million) with plans to expand and improve it.[33] He wanted Houston to have a first-rate hotel like those he had enjoyed in New York and Europe.[34]

32. McComb, *Houston: Bayou City*, 104.
33. H. L. Stevens Co. contract with Jesse Jones, August 29, 1908, Jesse H. Jones Collection [HE].
34. Chapman, *Historic Photos of Houston*, 110.

Jesse Jones's construction of the Houston Chronicle Building in 1908 bought him a half interest in the growing newspaper. Jones bought the other half of the paper in 1926 from publisher M. E. Foster because of disputes over Foster's endorsement of "Ma" Ferguson for governor.

Two months later he bought a half interest in a piece of downtown land from *Houston Chronicle* publisher M. E. Foster, who had just purchased the parcel from the Shearn Methodist Episcopal Church for $115,000 ($2.7 million).[35] Foster wanted to expand the five-year-old newspaper he had started with Spindletop profits and needed a suitable building for one of Houston's major daily papers. Jones wanted to make money, enhance the city, and obtain a platform for influence.

Jones was increasingly visible, and older, more conservative colleagues had begun to worry that this brash newcomer was getting in way over his head. Watching him develop subdivisions, buy blocks of real estate, invest in rice mills, and operate an orchard and fig farm east of town (on land he hoped to subdivide and develop), they wondered how he could af-

35. Shearn Methodist Episcopal Church contract with M. E. Foster, August 26, 1906; Jesse Jones contract with M. E. Foster, August 30, 1906, both Jesse H. Jones Collection [HE].

ford to finance this flurry of activity. S. F. Carter, a colleague of M. T.'s and partner of Jones's in the new Lumberman's National Bank, went to Jesse's office and gravely said rumors were circulating that he had borrowed one million dollars ($23 million). Jones laughed and said not to worry—then told him he had borrowed three ($69 million).[36] The president of another Houston bank called in Jones's loans and added a bit of admonitory advice, writing, "I want to say to you frankly, Mr. Jones, that this bank does not care to loan money to any borrowing concern who keeps one or more other borrowing accounts locally. Candor compels me to say that I believe all institutions you are connected with are heavy borrowers and that sooner or later you may experience more or less difficulty in financing them unless your policy as regards borrowing is changed somewhat."[37]

It was true that Jones had amassed a lot of debt and a lot of assets, but apparently he knew what he was doing—his 1907 financial statement showed a net worth of $1,285,473 ($29,220,428).[38] His wealth had grown eight times in five years. Although he was doing well, Jones sensed that bad times were coming. In the fall of 1907, he told his employees to "crowd collections at our lumberyards" and "push sales for cash."[39] His instincts were right—the economy was going into a recession, and as it faltered, money for loans dried up, companies went bankrupt, nervous depositors demanded their money, banks failed, and the stock market crashed. Houston was slammed in 1907, particularly when T. W. House and Company, one of the largest private banks in town that had been established before the Civil War, failed. The founder's son, T. W. House Jr., was president of the bank and also an executor of the M. T. Jones estate. The lives and interests of Houston's small group of leading businessmen were closely intertwined, and what happened to one often affected the others. In this instance, Jones owed T. W. House and Company $500,000 ($11 million), which he knew needed to be repaid in order to liquidate the busted bank. Fortunately, he had unused lines of credit that he had established years before in New York, as well as a safe filled with interest-bearing, monthly paying mortgages. He began to sell the latter to investors who had more confidence in Jones's paper than they

36. Timmons, *Jones: Man and Statesman*, 72; Buenger, interview, in *Brother Can You Spare a Billion?*

37. W. B. Chew to Jesse Jones, September 20, 1907, Jesse H. Jones Collection [HE].

38. Jesse H. Jones financial statement, January 9, 1907, Jesse H. Jones Collection [UT].

39. Timmons, *Jones: Man and Statesman*, 67.

had in the nation's banks.[40] From his policy of keeping more assets than debt, Jones emerged unscathed from the economic panic of 1907.

The United States government and J. P. Morgan softened and abbreviated the panic by infusing the New York banks with cash, which in turn loaned it out nationwide.[41] The whole experience reinforced Jones's notion that national financial stability required better banking laws and protection for depositors. The panic also solidified New York's position as the nation's economic power center—which Jones would almost single-handedly move to Washington, D.C., one day. [42]

Jones's colleagues were amazed he survived. Many of them were barely standing and some, like T. W. House, went under. Then Jones stunned them all when he signed a contract in August 1908 to build a luxury addition to the Bristol Hotel for $90,000 ($2.1 million), followed soon by a $175,000 ($4.1 million) contract to build a ten-story fireproof office building for the *Houston Chronicle*.[43] Jaws dropped even further when he announced that he was adding two more floors to the Bristol Hotel plan and contracting a new ten-story office building for the Texas Company, seven blocks down Main Street from the bayou.

The new Bristol Hotel, with its roof garden for dining, dancing, and enjoying the view and the Gulf Coast breezes, elevated Houston's stature and enhanced Aunt Louisa's portfolio after she helped Jones with the financing. The Houston Chronicle Building, which Jones traded for a half interest in the paper, gave him clout in civic affairs. And by bringing the first important oil company to town with the Texas Company Building, which Jones leased to the fledgling company for $2,000 ($47,000) a month, he helped make Texaco and the petroleum industry a permanent part of the city's business community.[44] All three buildings stuck out above Houston's modest skyline, showing everyone that Houston and Jesse Jones were on the move.

Ever since Houston's founders, A. C. and J. K. Allen, sailed up Buffalo Bayou and landed at what became the foot of Main Street, people had dreamed of cargo-laden vessels going to and from the rest of the world via Buffalo Bayou and Galveston Bay. Buffalo Bayou starts just west of

40. Ibid., 70.

41. Buenger and Pratt, *But Also Good Business*, 45.

42. Ibid., 46.

43. Jesse Jones and Houston Chronicle Building Company contract with Selden-Breck Construction Company, September 1908, Jesse H. Jones Collection [HE].

44. Southern Loan and Investment Co. contract with The Texas Company, May 7, 1909, Jesse H. Jones Collection [HE].

Houston, meanders east along the northern edge of downtown, and continues about fifty more miles until it empties into Galveston Bay. At the beginning of the twentieth century, Jones and his contemporaries had the same dream as Houston's founders. They knew Houston's growth would be limited without ready access to the sea.

By 1909, federal funding was acquired to dredge Buffalo Bayou and build a turning basin and docks east of downtown through the diligent efforts of Congressman Tom Ball, Mayor H. B. Rice, and some of the city's leading businessmen.[45] The new large vessels, however, required a depth of at least twenty-five feet and sharp bends in the channel had to be straightened out so the long ships could turn. Some of the channel's advocates wanted to situate the port downtown, but that land near downtown—including land owned by Jones—had become too expensive for industrial use. But at this point, improvements to the channel were more important than the port's location.

More money was needed. Rather than asking Congress for the entire appropriation and risking rejection, Congressman Ball suggested that Houston pay half the cost of dredging the fifty-mile channel to twenty-five feet and straightening the bends. Congress duly adopted the "Houston Plan," and the Houston Ship Channel became one of the first, if not the first, major public projects to be funded by both local citizens and the U.S. government. As Congressman Ball reported, "Prior to Houston's offer, no substantial contribution had ever been made by local interests to secure the adoption of their projects, and no project has since been adopted by the national government without promise of local contributions."[46]

Congressman Ball and others lobbied the Texas state legislature to create a navigation district that could sell bonds to pay for Houston's share of the improvements. The bond issue required voter approval, and to generate excitement among the electorate, Captain James A. Baker (the former secretary of state's grandfather) inaugurated the 1909 Notsuoh extravaganza by sailing down the Buffalo Bayou channel as King Nottoc in his elaborate regalia and disembarking with his heavily costumed entourage at Main Street.[47] After a massive city-wide promotional campaign, the majority voted to establish the navigation district with $1.25 million ($29 million) in bonds to pay for the community's share of the Channel project—only many were not sure what navigation bonds

45. Sibley, *Port of Houston*, 132.
46. Ibid., 136.
47. Ibid., 133.

were and no one wanted to buy them.[48] Jones stepped in, lobbying his fellow bankers and persuading them to buy the bonds in proportion to their respective capital surpluses—and surplus funds were certainly on hand. The oil boom lifted Houston's bank deposits to well over the national average, and Jones knew the bankers could well afford the investment in Houston's future.[49] Within twenty-four hours, he had secured Houston's half of the funds needed to begin the construction of the Houston Ship Channel, a waterway longer than the Panama Canal.[50] Two years later a turnkey contract would be signed with Atlantic, Gulf, and Pacific Company to dredge and build the channel.[51]

Jones knew his success was directly tied to the condition of his community. If Houston prospered, he would thrive. He determinedly nurtured a reciprocal relationship with his community and began to devote nearly as much time to developing Houston as he did to developing his own businesses. Unlike most others during his time, Jones traveled widely and enjoyed opera, theater, symphonies, and lectures in the world's major cities; he wanted the same for Houston. To that end, Jones proposed to Mayor Rice and the City Council in 1910 that Houston build an auditorium that could seat thousands, a venue for performing arts events, hosting conventions and other gatherings. He was promptly appointed building chairman, and proceeded to oversee the design and construction of the City Auditorium.[52] When the Russian Symphony Orchestra visited town the following year and performed in the hall, Jones gave hundreds of schoolchildren tickets to hear the renowned ensemble; he received warm thank-you notes from many of them. The performances encouraged local citizens to establish a permanent ensemble of their own, which became the Houston Symphony Orchestra.[53]

Jones stirred up local politics with similar vigor. As finance chairman of Mayor Rice's 1911 race for reelection, he impatiently advised the campaign manager, "Hire a few brass bands and let's get some life into the campaign; it appears dead to a great many of our anxious friends, and I am of the opinion that we ought to move very strong and very rapidly from now on, having meetings and speakings every night."[54] Around

48. Ibid., 136.
49. Platt, *City Building*, 211.
50. Sibley, *Port of Houston*, 137.
51. Ibid., 140.
52. Timmons, *Jones: Man and Statesman*, 79.
53. *New Handbook of Texas*, 740.
54. Jesse Jones to T. H. Stone, February 21, 1911, Jesse H. Jones Collection [HE].

The City Auditorium, built in 1910, was Houston's center for cultural events, from operas and symphony performances to wrestling matches, until the Jesse H. Jones Hall for the Performing Arts opened on the same site in 1966. Jones Hall was built by Houston Endowment, the philanthropic foundation established by the Joneses in 1937, and was a gift to the City of Houston. Courtesy San Jacinto Museum of History.

that time, Jones changed his listed occupation on his poll tax receipt from lumberman to capitalist and, between his civic and commercial responsibilities, he complained that he was being worked "harder than the town pump."[55] But he strongly believed that simultaneously building both his business and his city was the way to succeed.

Mayor Rice won a third term in 1911. The population had almost doubled to more than eighty thousand during the past ten years and city government and civic leadership had successfully coupled Houston's rapid growth with strong industrial development.[56] The town now spread over more than sixteen square miles, and a thousand cars were on the roads.[57] Jones had a hand in almost anything of consequence happening

55. Timmons, *Jones: Man and Statesman*, 78.
56. Platt, *City Building*, 211.
57. *New Handbook of Texas*, 709.

in Houston. Envisioning a much larger city, he felt he had only started to build. Carter—the banker who years earlier had worried about Jones's borrowing—began building a sixteen-story downtown office building, effectively ending Jones's vision of a Parisian-styled skyline limited to ten floors. Following suit, Jones began planning Houston's most elegant hotel and its tallest building. After receiving a ninety-nine-year lease from Rice Institute for the block of land at the corner of Texas and Main where the five-story Rice Hotel stood, he incorporated the New Rice Hotel Company with capital stock of $1.25 million ($28 million)—seventy-five percent of which Jones assembled with a loan from Rice Institute. The balance of the capital investment was divided among thirty-nine other subscribers.[58]

At this point, Jones sold controlling interest in the South Texas Lumber Company to J. M. West and got out of the lumber business almost altogether.[59] Looking back over his time in the timber industry, he wrote, "I started with one lumber yard at Houston and increased my operations as fast as I could borrow the money with which to operate and to employ competent young fellows to manage the different yards. Many were boys I had grown up with. I soon bought a small sawmill, and later two more. On the two small mills, I lost and closed down, but the third was profitable." He continued, "I have forgotten the exact number of lumberyards I finally accumulated, but it was probably 20 or 25. At the end of nine years, I sold all of my lumber interests except one yard—at a profit of something over $1,000,000 [$23 million]."[60]

Demonstrating his allegiance to those who worked for him, he kept one yard so he could maintain jobs for its long-time employees, particularly Joe Didiot, whom he had known since he first worked for his uncle in the Hillsboro yard. Having sold his lumber interests, Jones then turned his attention to building and banking. He demolished the old Rice Hotel, his first home in Houston, and erected a full-scale model of the new first floor and a typical room so he could reconfigure and redesign them. In a letter to Blanche Babcock, he wrote, "I enjoy making the plans of the buildings over the drafting board in the evenings, trying to be a better architect, or at least a more practical one, than the professionals."[61]

58. New Rice Hotel Company Subscriptions, August 1911, Jesse H. Jones Collection [HE].

59. Memorandum of agreement between J. M. West and Jesse Jones, October 13, 1911, Jesse H. Jones Collection [HE].

60. Jesse Jones to Eugene Kelly, May 14, 1949, Jesse H. Jones Collection [HE].

61. Jesse Jones to Blanche Babcock, August 25, 1937, Jesse H. Jones Collection [LOC].

Under Baker's leadership as president of the board of trustees, Rice Institute specified that the school's funds were "to be applied toward the erection and construction of a steel-frame hotel building of not less than seventeen stories in height." The trustees were actively interested in this large investment, and Baker agreed to Jones's request that both men's signatures be on all work orders, changes, and contracts.[62] As the hotel took shape, Jones's ambition to build a landmark luxury hotel using the finest materials that met exacting standards became apparent. One contractor reported, "The mahogany used [is] to be the best quality of Honduras, Mexican, or African mahogany, pleasingly figured."[63] Meanwhile, the political world was about to request Jones's services—on the national stage.

On June, 29, 1912—after forty-six roll call votes at the Democratic national convention in Baltimore—Woodrow Wilson was finally chosen as the party's nominee for president of the United States.[64] Colonel Edward Mandell House—T. W. House's youngest brother who served as an advisor to Texas's governors and senators—secured Texas's forty votes, as well as William Jennings Bryan's endorsement.[65] He also brought Jones to Wilson's attention.[66] Wilson liked independent men who were not wed to Wall Street, who had ambitions for the under-developed South and West, and who saw government not as a Civil War agent of destruction and confiscation, but as a positive agent for progress. Jones was a new kind of southerner who appealed to Wilson.

An eloquent orator, Wilson spoke for those whose lives had not been improved by the Industrial Revolution, for those mired in poverty, and for those unable to participate in the American dream of acquiring affluence and material comfort. Wilson railed against monopolies, unregulated and rapacious utilities, and price-inflating tariffs. He argued for the direct election of United States senators, workmen's compensation laws, and banking regulations that would stabilize the nation's economic system and make credit more reliable and available so as to assure fair competition, just prices, and open markets. Wilson was against special

62. Jesse Jones to Mauran, Russell & Crowell, Architects, July 13, 1912, Jesse H. Jones Collection [HE].

63. Westlake Construction Co. to Union Trim & Lumber Co., April 13, 1912, Jesse H. Jones Collection [HE].

64. Heckscher, *Woodrow Wilson*, 251.

65. *New Handbook of Texas*, 711.

66. Timmons, *Jones: Man and Statesman*, 100.

interests, and he accepted no corporate donations. Although he formally segregated the White House and was almost hostile when it came to women's rights, he hoped to level the playing field so the "everyday man" had an opportunity to succeed in life. Jones was a step ahead of Wilson on equality issues: his *Houston Chronicle* began editorially advocating for women's right to vote in 1915.[67] Otherwise, the candidate's impassioned views ignited Jones's interest in national politics.

After winning the presidency, Wilson called on Colonel House for advice and counsel.[68] The powerful Texan immediately suggested to Wilson that he give Jones a position in his administration. Treasury Secretary William McAdoo asked Jones to be his undersecretary, and he declined. He was then offered ambassadorships to Argentina and Belgium, but declined both. Finally Wilson, through Colonel House, asked Jones to become Secretary of Commerce, giving him until February 1913 to decide, but he turned the job down.[69]

For all his admiration of Wilson, Jones could not be wooed away from Houston—there was too much happening for him to relinquish his commitments to the city and his growing businesses. The Houston Ship Channel was almost finished and Mayor Campbell appointed Jones as the Houston Harbor Board's first chairman, making him responsible for building all the required docks, wharves, and other public facilities in time for the opening.[70]

The grand opening of the Rice Hotel was only months away and Jones had three more ten-story Main Street buildings on the drawing board. On May 17, 1913, more than ten thousand people—ten percent of Houston's population—swarmed the Rice Hotel opening. The five-hundred-room hotel, with its opulent ballrooms and its popular restaurants and clubs, became Houston's social hub and remained so for decades. The Rice Hotel symbolized Houston's progress and Jones once again made it his home in Houston. But even as he settled downtown, ensconced in the midst of his sprouting empire that included more than twenty built or planned buildings in the surrounding five-square-block area, he still kept his room at Aunt Louisa's, which was only a little more than twenty blocks away.

67. Cox, *First Texas News Barons*, 59.
68. Heckscher, *Woodrow Wilson*, 239.
69. Timmons, *Jones: Man and Statesman*, 100.
70. Sibley, *Port of Houston*, 138.

Although it was a bold and risky venture in the then small city, Jesse Jones demolished the five-story Rice Hotel and replaced it in 1913 with an eighteen-story luxury hotel, just before the opening of the Houston Ship Channel. Jones's Houston Chronicle Building is seen on the left. Courtesy Library of Congress.

A year after the Rice Hotel opened, Houston's leaders honored Jesse with an elegant banquet there. On May 17, 1914, the Sunday after the celebration, Jones's *Houston Chronicle* ran a quarter-page picture of him on the front page with a headline that exclaimed, "The Master Builder!" The paper reported, "Close on to 200 men, whose names are linked indelibly, strongly, honourably in the up-building of Houston, . . . [t]he best and firmest of Houston's citizenry went gladly to the Rice last night to do him homage and to praise his name."[71] Not too long ago, many of "the best and firmest" had looked askance at Jones's sharp dealings, audacious speculations, and blatant manipulation of credit, but they appreciated him now, even those who got shaved by his tactics. Not only did they admire Jones's success, but their own businesses frequently profited from his devotion to the common good and to his personal benefit. As he would do in the future—to the benefit of the country as a whole—Jones had bucked convention and ideology to set his own path to success.

At the banquet, the men ate caviar, roasted giant squab, *paupiettes* of Gulf trout, asparagus points in cream, and tutti-frutti ice cream. The proper alcoholic beverage was served with each dish, while cigars, cigarettes, and Benedictine rounded out the seven-course meal. The Blitz Orchestra played selections by Georges Bizet, Felix Mendelssohn, Max Bruch, and Peter Tschaikowsky and, according to the *Houston Chronicle*, "The 16 Gwent Welsh singers appeared for a song in chorus and were encored. Other artists from the local vaudeville stage appeared in the course of the evening, lightening the program and making the evening pleasurable."[72] The event was more sophisticated and elegant than one might imagine occurring in Texas in 1914. Speeches honoring Jones comprised the main part of the evening. Jones sat at the head table with Mayor Campbell; Frank Andrews, the toastmaster and one of Jones's attorneys; *Houston Chronicle* publisher Foster; J. M. Rockwell, Jones's close friend and co-executor of the M. T. Jones estate; merchant Sam Taub; and Captain Baker. One by one they rose to acknowledge their competitor and colleague.

Toastmaster Andrews began, "About 17 years ago there came into this town unheralded, unknown, and unsung, a beardless boy. He brought with him judgment, determination, nerve, energy, and push. He looked upon [Houston] and saw that it would grow and said so. He startled the old-timers with the prices which he paid for real estate. With the energy

71. *Houston Chronicle*, May 17, 1914.
72. Ibid.

and push that had marked the success of his own business, he created an infectious spirit in the upbuilding of this city. His judgement was vindicated. He bet that Houston would grow and he has won every bet." Andrews then went on to perpetuate the fiction of Jones's humble beginnings, saying, "This man without money, influence, friends, a stranger in a strange land, has given us an illustration of what the young American can do." Otherwise, the evening's comments were mostly accurate.

Orson Wells, a local banker, recognized Jones's two hats and said he was "the one financier who stands alone in his community as a guardian of the public weal while working toward his private success."

Mayor Campbell declared, "Show me your citizenship and I will tell you what kind of a country you have." He went on, "Look about you [to] see what he has done in 15 years. A city depends upon what the people make of it. Mr. Jones has done more to loosen the purse strings of the tightwads than any 10 men in Houston. Some will say that the greatest thing that could happen to Houston would be to have paved streets, fine sewerage, general development, but I will say that the greatest thing that could happen to Houston would be to have 100 citizens like Jesse Jones."

Not all of the comments were quite so serious. Andrews observed that Jones was "pre-eminent among the men he knew in his capacity to borrow money." A colleague added, "But he is the only large operator whom I have ever known who guarded his obligations so zealously as never to let his paper go past due."

One friend mentioned Jones's apparently failed love life, saying, "It may be there are those who would charge our honoured guest, as regards love, with dalliance; or looking back across some score or more of years, during which the little god has shot a thousand bolts at him in vain." He concluded by hoping that God would send a woman to help Jones "proceed to the consummation of that high career for which nature has designed you."[73]

The coverage of the Rice Hotel anniversary banquet in Houston's other paper, the slightly less adulatory *Houston Daily Post*, was nearly as complete and just as expansive. The reporter mentioned that Jones, "probably more than any one individual in Houston, has given Houston a place in the world of music by his liberal contributions to the art." Jones had recently brought the Pavlova Ballet Company and the Canadian National Opera Company to Houston for a weeklong series of performances in the City Auditorium and in his Majestic Theater.

73. Ibid., all quoted speeches.

The *Post* reporter also wrote about the Rice Hotel, adding, "At a time when the building of such a structure was looked upon by many with wonderment, if not with a degree of fear and suspicion of its wisdom— when it was believed that Houston had not advanced to a stage where a hotel of such magnificence would be a profitable investment—Mr. Jones never hesitated but at the risk of fortune and reputation carried to completion the work. This one structure carried Houston forward over a stretch of 20 years and placed it far in the lead of any city of its size in the entire country."[74]

74. *Houston Post*, May 17, 1914.

The National Stage

◈

1914–1919

◈

Give Until It Hurts

ON JUNE 28, 1914, an agitator for Bosnian independence from Austria assassinated Archduke Francis Ferdinand in Sarajevo.[1] In retaliation, Austria declared war against Serbia. Intercontinental alliances and agreements kicked in, and a little more than a month after the Archduke's assassination, Europe was at war.

But Houston's citizens were focusing on an event closer to home—the opening of the Houston Ship Channel in November was arranged to merge with the annual Notsuoh extravaganza into one enormous five-day celebration. Committees were formed, assignments were made, and a professional artist and staff of six had been hired to help orchestrate the lavish citywide event.[2] In recognition of the Channel, the Notsuoh Festival was rechristened the Notsuoh Deep Water Jubilee, and a new king, King Retaw I (i.e., King Water I), replaced the old King Nottoc.

Houston had much to celebrate. The month before the channel was set to open, automobile dealers sold 105 new cars; bank deposits hit $22 million ($466 million in current dollars); the city led the state with $213,000

---

1. Gilbert, *First World War*, 16.
2. *Houston Chronicle*, November 8, 1914.

59

($4.5 million) in building permits,[3] and Houston continued to spread as more and more people moved into town. Some bought homes from Jesse Jones, whose Southern Loan and Investment Corporation ran newspaper ads that lured buyers in by declaring in bold letters, "Just the money that you have been paying for rent will enable you to have a home of your own. Our plan of home owning tells how to do it. Come and let us explain it." A lengthy narrative then explained how home owners make better citizens and advised that saving and caution can help create a secure life. The copy exhorted, "Even though you have neglected yourself in the past, you can immediately make amends by planning to own your home without delay. We will do all within our power to give you the correct start and know from past experiences that you can accomplish your purpose."[4]

"Accomplish" was the byword as well of the upcoming Notsuoh Deep Water Jubilee. Newspaper ads told readers that "Houston's Millions of Resources Have Guaranteed the Success" of the celebration and urged them to remember November 9 to 14 because "there will be something entertaining and instructive every minute," including dances, elaborate parades, football games, agriculture and horticulture exhibitions, and "thousands of electric lights."[5] No one would want to miss "the greatest of Houston's many successes—[the] Celebration of 40 years of loyal civic endeavor."[6]

On November 8, two days before the Ship Channel's official opening, articles and ads about Notsuoh and the port filled the city's papers. The *Houston Chronicle* reported, "Port Houston will be officially opened to the ships of all nations at 11 o'clock Tuesday morning, and at 8 o'clock Tuesday evening the commerce of the world will arrive in Houston typified by the Ships of All Nations Pageant, the most beautiful, original, and one of the most expensive pageants ever staged in the South." But first, two yachts traveling down Buffalo Bayou from the San Jacinto Battleground with an entourage of congressmen, the governor, Houston's mayor, and "50 duchesses and maidens from outlying counties" would dock at the foot of Main Street and reveal the identity of King Retaw.[7]

Cheering and waving people lined the banks of Buffalo Bayou as the two yachts, loaded with heavily costumed notables, passed by. According to the *Houston Chronicle*, when his excellency and his 225 attendants

3. *Houston Chronicle,* November 13, 1914.
4. *Houston Chronicle,* November 8, 1914.
5. Ibid.
6. *Houston Chronicle,* November 5, 1914.
7. Ibid.

arrived at the foot of Main Street, King Retaw's "costume from the tip of his crown to the soles of his pink satin slippers was alike in deference to water and cotton."[8] The article then revealed to all that Eugene A. Hudson, a local furniture magnate, had been crowned King. More than 20,000 people lined Main Street for ten blocks to watch the procession and to see him assume his throne.

The next day, thousands of citizens and hundreds of politicians and civic leaders gathered again, this time about eight miles from Main Street at the Houston Ship Channel's turning basin; the *Houston Chronicle* reported that "nearly all the visiting notables went in automobiles." Precisely at noon, President Woodrow Wilson interrupted a cabinet meeting in Washington, D.C., stepped into the Oval Office, and pressed a button that, through the coordinated efforts of the MacKay Telegraph-Cable Company and the Southern Pacific Railroad, fired the cannon resting on the banks of Buffalo Bayou. This officially signaled the opening of the Houston Ship Channel. As soon as the cannon boomed, the mayor's daughter approached the bank of the bayou, dropped a floral wreath into the water and said, "I christen thee Port Houston. Hither shall come the ships of all nations and find a hearty welcome." According to the paper, "As she did so . . . pandemonium broke loose. From a hundred throttles the shrill shriek of whistles rang out, cannon and salute guns were discharged, bells rang, men shouted, bands played patriotic airs, and joy reigned unrestrained."[9]

The revelry continued into the night. At eight that evening, twenty floats that took months to build began to move down Main Street, each representing a different nation and its culture. Norway had a Viking ship, Mexico had an Aztec theme, Greece had gladiators, and China boasted a huge eye that sensed all danger. The city of Houston was "represented by an ocean liner belching forth real smoke."[10] Torches illuminated the outlandish floats and some even had electric lights. Eleven bands played up and down the parade route. Dignitaries, police and firemen, Notsuoh royalty, soldiers, and politicians marched to welcome the world to Houston, where, as Chamber of Commerce stationery boasted, "seventeen railroads meet the sea."

The week finished with thrilling airplane stunts, the city's first "all-motor flower parade" that included "floats and decorated automobiles

8. *Houston Chronicle,* November 9, 1914.
9. *Houston Chronicle,* November 10, 1914.
10. Ibid.

owned by individuals and agencies," and elaborate balls.[11] The world beyond Houston remained in most people's imaginations as it was represented by the stereotypical floats, but the provincial city was on its way to becoming a part of the global community.

Jones had been in New York, but he returned in time to join the festivities and, as chairman of the Houston Harbor Board, began overseeing expenditure of the $3 million ($63 million) in bonds that Houston's citizens had overwhelmingly approved to construct modern port facilities. Houston's deepwater port and railroad network put the city in an enviable and opportune position. Newspapers around the country lauded local leaders' efforts and citizens' support and editorially wondered what about Houston made it lead others "in the matter of city building."[12] One reason, of course, was the presence of Jesse Jones and his determination to develop his community and businesses simultaneously.

Despite the hoopla and hope, six months passed before the first foreign oil arrived in Houston's port. Oceangoing captains were reluctant to navigate Houston's new and untested waters. Moreover, the festering European war had smothered international trade.[13] The day after the Houston Ship Channel opened, Jones warned, "A great European war is enough to disturb all business relations temporarily. The great business connections that the United States had built up with the old world could not be interrupted without things going wrong, for a while at least."[14]

As King Retaw took his throne in Houston, millions of soldiers were assembling overseas to fight in the "Great War." President Wilson may have fired a cannon on the banks of Buffalo Bayou to commemorate Houston's expanded port, but he was not about to shoot guns in Europe—he wanted instead to be a mediator among the warring nations and to maintain the United States' rights as a neutral nation under international law.[15]

Also hoping to stay clear of the conflict, Jones was busy developing the port, Houston's largest and most ambitious civic project to date, while still managing his growing business and taking care of family. He owned banks, finance and real estate development companies, large and popular hotels, a half interest in one of the city's three daily papers, the majority of first-class office space, and the best movie palaces and vaudeville houses in town.

11. *Houston Chronicle*, November 12, 1914.
12. *Houston Chronicle*, November 6, 1914.
13. Sibley, *Port of Houston*, 148.
14. *Houston Chronicle*, November 11, 1914.
15. Heckscher, *Woodrow Wilson*, 160.

A few years earlier, Jones acquired controlling interest in the National Bank of Commerce, putting a partner from his sawmill days—R. M. Farrar—in charge. As Jones said, "Our little bank, which was a runt pig that I took in out of the cold when it was about to go bust in 1912, has continually grown."[16] Historians Joe Pratt and Walter Buenger observed, "Although National Bank of Commerce was only one part of Jones's business empire, he understood how the various parts fit together and how the empire as a whole fit into the broader financial, political, and civic patterns of Houston."[17] Sheds, wharfs, hoists, cranes, and warehouses sprouted up along the bayou to accommodate the waiting ships. Jones anticipated that within a few years the Ship Channel would internationalize Houston, elevate the regional economy, further integrate the South with the rest of the country and—not coincidentally—help to fill Jones's office buildings, the consequence of consciously linking his success to the city's fortunes.

From the time he arrived in Houston some twenty years before, Jones had nurtured a reciprocal relationship with his community, intent on both building his business and improving his city. To Jones, they were connected—only if the city prospered, would he succeed. The nearly concurrent openings of the lavish Rice Hotel and the expansive Houston Ship Channel epitomized the best of Jones's diligent efforts to use capitalism to improve the common good and increase his personal wealth. Thousands found employment, the community flourished, and Jones's wealth grew. Seeing these positive outcomes, Jones would later use this same approach in public service to benefit people of the United States and other parts of the world. The only difference was that the tangible and intangible wealth that resulted from improving communities belonged to the nations' citizens.

For now, Jones, still a bachelor, who enjoyed playing poker, drinking good bourbon, and riding in his chauffeur-driven Pierce Arrow, was providing for a large family. His brother and two sisters had moved to Houston, so he had a raft of nieces and nephews to spoil and enjoy. Abiding by terms of the will, the M. T. Jones estate had been liquidated in 1913, and the proceeds distributed to his Aunt Louisa and three cousins, but they all still depended on Jones. Augusta asked him "to come to my rescue" before her divorce in 1915;[18] Jeanette and Augusta both gave him their powers

16. Jesse Jones to John Nance Garner, December 23, 1953, Jesse H. Jones Collection [UT].
17. Buenger and Pratt, *But Also Good Business*, 180.
18. November 18, 1914, Jesse H. Jones Collection [HE].

of attorney.[19] Most of the time, Mary lived with Louisa and Jeanette at the "Boarding House" on Main Street, while Will lived at the Deepwater ranch. Their son, Tilford, was away at preparatory school in Pennsylvania and would eventually enroll at Cornell to study engineering. Jones also continued to build for his extended family, including two small commercial buildings for his Aunt Louisa at Capitol and Travis, just one block over from Main and only six blocks down from Buffalo Bayou.[20]

Despite the sluggish international trade and the ongoing European war, which was approaching its third year, Houston thrived. In early 1917, as Harris County issued its 13,000th automobile license, the Houston Chronicle reported, "On the crest of a wave of prosperity, apparently Houston people are spending money lavishly on 'benzene buggies.'" It also noted that Houston's annual budget of $1.8 million ($30 million) included $590,000 ($9.8 million) for schools, $373,000 ($6.2 million) for police and fire protection, and $242,850 ($4 million) for streets and bridges.[21]

On the other hand, in the same newspaper, a headline read, "Waiters at Rice are ordered not to talk on war."[22] In Europe millions of soldiers from more than thirty nations were engaged in the first war fought on an industrial scale. Armored tanks, poison gas, hand grenades, machine guns, and deadly bombs disgorged from airplanes and zeppelins were all war innovations that had engulfed France and Belgium.[23] Men crouching behind machine guns had replaced men wielding bayonets on horses. Helmets to protect soldier's heads from gunfire and flying bomb debris replaced the soft, feathered caps of a more chivalrous past.[24]

Submarine warfare was another innovation, and when attacks on neutral ships began to kill Americans, President Wilson was pushed from neutrality to war. After almost three years of negotiating with the Germans, the United States intercepted telegrams indicating a possible Mexican-German alliance; that, and the sinking of one too many ships carrying U.S. passengers, pushed Wilson to cut off relations with Germany on March 3, 1917. Two days later, during his second inauguration, Wilson said, "We have been deeply wronged upon the seas, but we have

19. Jeanette Jones, document granting power of attorney to Jesse Jones, March 2, 1915, Jesse H. Jones Collection [HE].

20. The author's family's first store was located in the Wells Fargo Building from the 1940s to the early 1960s.

21. Houston Chronicle, March 4, 1917.

22. Ibid.

23. Gilbert, First World War, 305; In Flanders Fields Museum exhibition wall labels.

24. In Flanders Fields Museum exhibition wall labels.

not wished to wrong or injure in return . . . Although some of the injuries done us have become intolerable, we still have made it clear that we wished nothing for ourselves that we were not ready to demand for all mankind—fair dealing, justice, the freedom to live and be at ease against organized wrong."[25]

The president continued, "The part we wished to play was the part of those who mean to vindicate and fortify peace. We stand firm in armed neutrality, since it seems that in no other way can we demonstrate what it is we insist upon and cannot forego." This statement of armed neutrality was only one step away from a declaration of war. Wilson added, "We are provincials no longer. The tragical events of the 30 months of vital turmoil through which we have just passed have made us citizens of the world. There can be no turning back. Our own fortunes as a nation are involved, whether we would have it so or not."[26]

But Germany continued to sink ships and send U.S. citizens to their deaths in the icy Atlantic. On March 21, compelled to protect the rights of neutral nations and to work toward a world where the United States could prosper, he decided to call Congress into an extraordinary session to receive "a communication concerning grave matters of national policy."[27] As the Sixty-fifth Congress assembled on April 2, Colonel House, who came from New York to be with the president, was the only one allowed to review the upcoming speech before Wilson delivered it. In part, President Wilson said, "I advise that the Congress declare the recent course of the Imperial German Government to be in fact nothing less than war against the government and people of the U.S." Pausing for ovations and cheers, he continued, "We have no quarrel with the German people. We have no feeling towards them but one of sympathy and friendship." He went on, "We are glad . . . to fight thus for the ultimate peace of the world and for the liberation of its peoples, the German people included; for the rights of nations great and small, and for the privilege of men everywhere to choose their way of life and obedience. The world must be made safe for democracy."[28]

On April 4, 1917—Good Friday—the Senate approved by eighty-two to six the resolution to declare war against Germany and two days later the House approved the resolution 373 to fifty.[29] On April 6, one day after

25. *Houston Chronicle*, March 5, 1917.
26. Ibid.
27. Heckscher, *Woodrow Wilson*, 433, 437.
28. Ibid., 440.
29. Gilbert, *First World War*, 318.

Jones's forty-third birthday, the United States declared war on Germany. Life in Houston and in the United States was about to change.

War of a different kind was already raging in Houston. Instead of blood, Jones and his onetime ally Mayor Ben Campbell spilled gallons of newspaper ink over the $300,000 ($5 million) wharf that, two years ago the mayor had agreed to build for the Texas Portland Cement Company. The mayor wanted to build the Manchester wharf using part of the $3 million ($50 million) port bond fund. As chairman of the Houston Harbor Board, Jones vehemently opposed the move, arguing that the site was too far from the city, that the cement company had not kept its promise to send cargo through the channel, and that donating land and free facilities was no longer necessary to entice plant owners to the Ship Channel. As far as he was concerned, government had fulfilled its catalytic role.

In a letter published on the front page of Jones's *Houston Chronicle*, among headlines about submarine attacks, tens of thousands of young men marching off to war, and billions of dollars in war appropriations, the mayor said in part, "I feel that [members of] the harbor board, whether intentionally or not, have sought to make a goat of me." He also wrote that the Harbor Board's public actions—he meant Jones's actions—were "in exceeding bad taste on their part, and I can not give my consent to sit quietly by and have all of these things put upon me without a protest on my part."[30] Soon both the *Houston Chronicle* and the *Houston Daily Post*, which was on the mayor's side, were publishing all of the correspondence going back and forth between the two men.

In one letter to the mayor, Jones protested, "I am not mad about it nor am I at 'outs' with you or any other member of the harbor board or city council because of the fact that we entertain different views on the matter at issue." He instead questioned the promised tonnage from the cement factory and wrote that "the plant has been operating more than a year, and not a sack of cement has been exported. With the present disturbed and unsettled conditions of the world over, it is very problematical as to when there will be any exporting of any consequence from this plant, and there will never be enough to warrant our spending $300,000 for it."[31] Whether it was the public's or his own, Jones did not waste money, a trait that would manifest itself over and over again. Toward the end of the long letter, he wrote, "I am exceedingly sorry, Mr. Campbell, that you feel that there is a break between you and the harbor board, or that any

---

30. *Houston Chronicle*, April 4, 1917.
31. Ibid.

member of it expects you to forfeit your integrity or to do anything un-manly. I am unalterably opposed to this proposition because I do not feel that the city gets value received for the money it spends."[32]

On April 5, the day before President Wilson declared war on Germany, a special hearing was held to decide the matter.[33] It lasted more than four hours, and the courtroom was packed. Jones did not attend, but another Harbor Board member for the record read all of the sometimes caustic correspondence between the two leading citizens.[34] The City Council ended up approving the use of $300,000 ($5 million) from the port bond funds to build the wharf, and four of the five Harbor Board members, including Jones, immediately resigned. But the fight was far from over.

The incoming mayor, Joseph Pastoriza, opened the door to a referendum on the matter.[35] Within a week, more than 2,200 signatures were collected on petitions demanding that the city bring the matter to the citizens for a vote. A further twist in the controversy came when Mayor Pastoriza died after only two months in office.

In the election that followed, the public voted for the wharf ordinance and elected J. C. Hutcheson the next mayor of Houston. An annoyed editorial in the *Houston Chronicle* the day after the wharf was approved stated, "A very dangerous precedent has been established—a precedent by which future chief executives can divert large sums of money to the building of isolated docks and wharves for the benefit of private schemes, and because of which promoters of every kind will be justified in making goo-goo eyes at the city's treasury."[36]

Despite the European war and local political skirmishing, Houston's evolution into a city continued: a mix of shell and gravel was poured over 275 miles of new roads throughout Harris County; windows lit with electric lights allowed people on the street to see the displays at night at Sakowitz Brothers' new and expanded fine clothing store in the 300 block of Main Street.[37] Land was donated for the Museum of Fine Arts, Houston,[38] and the Houston Symphony Orchestra concluded its third successful season. Yet everyone was aware of the looming war. Soon after the acrimonious bond and mayoral election, city and county officials

32. Ibid.
33. Ibid.
34. *Houston Chronicle*, April 6, 1917.
35. *Houston Chronicle*, April 12, 1917.
36. *Houston Chronicle*, August 14, 1917.
37. *Houston Chronicle*, April 3, 1917.
38. *Houston Chronicle*, April 13, 1917.

called everyone in the area to a public meeting at the City Auditorium on Saturday evening, April 7, the day after the United States entered the war, so that "all citizens of Houston and Harris County, together with their families attending this meeting . . . may [be] in a better position to do their duty as American citizens."[39] For many, working for, or contributing to, the American Red Cross was part of that duty. To prevent duplication, President Wilson assigned responsibility for military medical aid and disaster relief in the United States and Europe to the American Red Cross. In a letter to its Washington headquarters, Wilson explained, "In order that the relief work which is undoubtedly ahead of us should be made thoroughly efficient, it is most desirable that it should be coordinated and concentrated under one organization. Having been made the official volunteer aid organization of the United States, the American Red Cross comes under the protection of the treaty of Geneva, and . . . has received due recognition from all foreign governments. Its status, both at home and abroad, is thus definitely determined and assured."[40] With war looming, American Red Cross membership soared.

In Houston, the wives of the city's civic and business elite held membership drives at all the hotels and stores. During the week of the tumultuous port hearing, 2,500 people signed up. Everyone was involved: Mary Gibbs Jones and her sister worked the sign-up table at Munn's Department Store; and Jesse Jones, at President Wilson's request, was put in charge of raising Houston's $250,000 ($4.1 million) portion of the American Red Cross $100 million ($1.7 billion) war fund campaign.

As the story goes, to start fundraising, Jones wrote a personal check for $5,000 ($83,000), showed it to his friends, and asked them to match it.[41] Sixteen of Jones's colleagues gave the requested $5,000.[42] Businessmen who had chided Jones ten years before for taking risks, abusing credit, and making hard-edged deals made donations. So did the recently bruised civic leaders who opposed Jones over the wharf. Everyone was encouraged to give—all donors who gave 50 cents ($8.30) to $15,000 ($249,000) were recognized and listed in the daily papers. Jones proudly pointed out that Houston raised more than its share, sent it to Washington before most other cities, and was the only major city in the state to meet its quota. In response, President Wilson again asked Jones to come

39. *Houston Chronicle*, April 6, 1917.
40. *Houston Chronicle*, April 15, 1917.
41. Timmons, *Jones: Man and Statesman*, 101.
42. *Houston Chronicle*, July 1, 1917.

to Washington. He wanted him to head one of two major branches of the American Red Cross—the Department of Military Relief (DMR)—which was responsible for providing medical aid and comfort to soldiers and sailors going to war-torn Europe.

Despite his devotion to his burgeoning businesses and city, and possibly stung by the arduous port campaign that had about run its course, this time Jones accepted Wilson's call to duty. He assigned his power of attorney to Fred Heyne, his closest business associate who started working for Jones after the 1907 closing of the T. W. House and Company bank, where he had been head cashier. Jones gave Heyne control over all his business interests, even calling him "his other self." In order to keep his business empire intact and to finance what would become an extended stay away from home, as one of its original investors, Jones sold his stock in the Humble Oil Company, saying he liked to have his assets above ground where he could see them. If he had lived long enough to see his investment grow into ExxonMobil, he might have thought differently.

Jones arrived in Washington, D.C., on a summer day in 1917 and immediately went to the American Red Cross's new headquarters across from the White House. President Wilson had recently formed the American Red Cross War Council to meet "the extraordinary demands which the present war will make upon the services of the Red Cross both in the field and in civilian relief."[43] He then appointed Henry P. Davison, a farm boy like Jones and now a top J. P. Morgan executive, as the War Council's chairman. Cleveland Dodge, a close Princeton classmate of Wilson's and head of Phelps-Dodge Copper Corporation, assured the president that Davison "could command the services of any businessman in the United States upon whom he might call to do any particular work."[44]

Jones vividly remembered meeting Davison: "Upon arriving at Red Cross headquarters in Washington," he wrote, "I was invited to lunch. There I met for the first time Henry P. Davison, but at the end of the luncheon, I felt not only that I had known him all of my life, but that he was a warm personal friend." Jones continued, "After luncheon, at which nothing but Red Cross [business] had been talked, he told me that I could be helpful in the great Red Cross undertaking; that he had an important post for me; and [that he] assumed I had come prepared to undertake it. I was assigned to [the] position of Director General of [the Department of] Military Relief and shown a desk. It was a busy beehive, and no one

---

43. Dulles, *American Red Cross*, 146.
44. Gaeddert, *History of the American National Red Cross*, 80.

seemed to have time to explain what it was all about." Jones recalled that Davison told him, "You are to see to it that the soldiers in the training camps, and travelling throughout the United States, and at the ports of embarkation, are furnished with any and everything that they need that the government has by any chance failed to supply, and particularly such attentions as will keep up their morale." Jones later ruefully noted that he went to Washington "with a suitcase and a few summer clothes, and was almost two years getting back home."[45]

Davison approached his mission with the "zeal of a convert," declaring, "I believe that every man, woman, and child in this country should realize that a contribution to the Red Cross is a contribution toward victory . . . I invite the American people to come in with me under President Wilson and make it a nationwide organization that is demanded by these times . . . Our job in the American Red Cross is to bind up the wounds of a bleeding world . . . Think Red Cross! Talk Red Cross! Be Red Cross!"[46] And the public responded. Cities competed to see who could sign up the most new Red Cross members. Ministers exclaimed from their pulpits that Red Cross work was among the highest expressions of religious life. Parades and evocative posters with glorified scenes and patriotic slogans boosted the fervor that swept the nation. In little more than a year, American Red Cross membership soared from 286,000 members in 250 chapters in 1916 to more than 31 million members in 3,800 chapters. More than one-quarter of the people in the United States answered the Red Cross plea to extend a hand to help the suffering and to care for soldiers and sailors after they left home.[47]

Explaining the role of Jones's Department of Military Relief, Davison said, "In all the formative stages of the soldier's development and, for that matter, at every step of his service, of all of the departments of the Red Cross, that of Military Relief was closest to him. The American boy—up to [age] forty-five—bumped into the Red Cross at the very moment almost of leaving his [front] door for the training camp. The last thing he saw from the train as the old town faded behind him was the Red Cross girl he had known from babyhood, waving goodbye. And at the first station [was] a group of Red Cross girls to let him know that the folks back home

45. Jesse Jones to George B. Case, response to June 5, 1923, request for biographical information about Henry P. Davison, Jesse H. Jones Collection [UT].

46. Gaeddert, *History of the American National Red Cross*, 106–7.

47. James L. Fieser, memo to staff at national headquarters and branch offices of American Red Cross, October 23, 1940, Jesse H. Jones Collection [HE].

were not the only ones who cared."[48] In the United States, more than 55,000 "Red Cross girls" voluntarily operated more than seven hundred canteens the DMR had established to provide soldiers with transportation, medical attention, a shower, a shoulder to lean on, and amusement. Davison said the canteens "not only made the soldier comfortable, but kept him from the station-saloon and other temptations of the night, and went further than most people know towards keeping him clean and straight and ready for his big job."[49]

Under Jones, the DMR shipped complete hospitals to England and France to care for the wounded and sick, and it recruited, trained, and dispatched 50,000 nurses who responded to the campaign call of "American nurses for American men." General John J. Pershing, commander-in-chief of the American Expeditionary Force, responded to the American Red Cross's offer of assistance: "If you really want to do something for me, for God's sake buck up the French. They have been fighting for three years and are getting ready for their fourth winter, and if they are not taken care of, nobody can tell what will happen to us." The DMR then implemented a giant program of military and civilian relief that brought aid to wounded soldiers, homeless citizens, and orphaned children in France who were left behind in the carnage.[50] It also distributed more than six and a half million sweaters, mufflers, socks, and comfort kits made by volunteers back home. As Davison remarked, "It was the age of wool; everybody was knitting."[51] The DMR also made sure soldiers had contact with their families, provided financial assistance to wives and parents whose primary earners went to war, and sometimes even helped with childcare.

The American Red Cross needed more money to continue this massive effort. A second $100 million fundraising campaign was scheduled for May 18, 1918. Houston was asked to raise $200,000 ($2.8 million). Before television and radio, people conveyed messages and inspired action in other ways. It was time for another parade. The *Houston Chronicle* duly announced, "On the opening day of the active campaign, a street parade, the like of which has never before been seen in Houston, will be held."[52] To promote the parade and raise funds, more than three hundred men

48. Davison, *American Red Cross in the Great War*, 38.
49. Ibid., 43.
50. Dulles, *American Red Cross*, 154.
51. Ibid., 155.
52. *Houston Chronicle*, May 5, 1918.

Jesse Jones as director general of the Department of Military Relief for the American Red Cross. Jones assigned his power of attorney to Fred Heyne, his closest business associate, and was away from Houston for two years because he was not willing to leave the important humanitarian work he was doing "for a money consideration" (Jesse Jones to N. E. Meador, February 18, 1919, Jesse H. Jones Collection [UT]).

and women boldly boarded streetcars "to present the cause of the Red Cross in a two or three minute speech." A *Houston Chronicle* article laid out the plan: "If he is able to get to the front of the car, he will face his audience. If he is compelled to occupy a place on the crowded rear end of the car, he will throw his voice in over the heads of the strap-hangers. Any way so he can be heard above the rattle of the wheels."[53] Volunteers also gave speeches in theaters before show time and in restaurants during lunch hour. As the *Houston Chronicle* reported, "All of the leading hotels and restaurants were invaded for the first time at the lunch hour Wednesday. The speakers consumed only five minutes in presenting the cause of the Red Cross. The proprietors have agreed to suspend operations, turn off fans so that speakers can be heard, and to co-operate in every possible way to make this feature of the campaign a success."[54]

Finally, Saturday, May 18 dawned, a perfect day for a parade—the

53. *Houston Chronicle*, May 10, 1918.
54. *Houston Chronicle*, May 15, 1918.

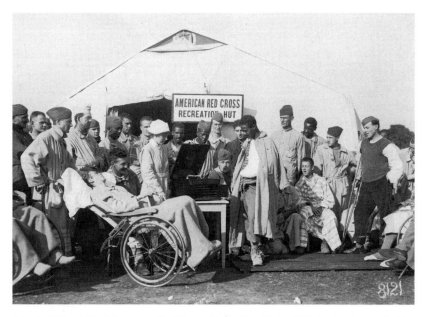

A typical World War I American Red Cross Recreation Hut established and operated by the Department of Military Relief. Courtesy American Red Cross.

skies were blue, the sun was shining, and it was not too hot. The *Houston Chronicle* called the parade "a sight that would have crushed the fighting spirit of the German Kaiser, had he been able to look on."[55] Thousands of people and every band in the county marched in the parade. Businesses and civic organizations carried half-block-sized flags parallel with the street to catch coins tossed by the hordes of cheering people on the sidewalks, eventually adding up to $2,000 ($28,000). Foley Bros., a leading Houston department store established in 1900, manned the largest flag.

Everyone participated. "Starting with an escort of soldiers, the column was headed by the army nurses and the Houston auxiliary of the American Red Cross," reported the *Houston Chronicle*. "Bringing up the rear were the colored auxiliaries of the city, the colored high school pupils, and other colored citizens, clinching the fact that the hearts of all the people of the community beat in unison on this great movement."[56]

Jones was in New York City with President Wilson on the day of the great Red Cross parades. With Jones working in Red Cross headquarters

55. *Houston Chronicle*, May 20, 1918.
56. Ibid.

just across the street from the White House, the two men had had a chance to get to know one another. In one of his letters to Blanche Babcock, Jones wrote that Wilson was one of his "ideals," adding, "he had the greatest command of the language I have ever heard or read."[57] Wilson's brother-in-law, Stockton Axson, a popular English professor at Rice Institute in Houston, admired Jones and had confirmed everything Colonel House had said about the tall, talented Texan.

Axson, who took a leave from Rice Institute to serve as the American Red Cross general secretary, observed about Jones, "Although allied in his interests with what was then known as the capitalist class, he came to subscribe in mind and spirit to the Wilsonian conceptions of enduring democracy, of untrammelled representative government, of lawfully selected leadership, of pitiless publicity for those whose self-interest prompted them to thwart the open processes of legislation, the end and object of which should be justice for all and private favors for none."[58]

To Wilson, Jones was a devoted Democrat who personified the promise of the underdeveloped South and West. And Jones was fun, letting the president drop his stiff and formal public persona and relax, tell stories, and share jokes. Jones soon enjoyed an open door to the White House and President Wilson.[59]

A week before the national Red Cross campaign took off, Davison asked Jones if he would ask the president to review the New York parade and speak that evening at Madison Square Garden. Preoccupied with the war, Wilson turned down Jones's request, but offered instead to shear the sheep grazing on the White House lawn and send packages of wool to each state's governor to auction for the Red Cross war fund. Jones returned to the White House the next day to thank the president for the wool and to ask him again about going to New York for the parade. Jones argued, "It seems to me that you should use the occasion to make a speech to the world, to the Allied Powers, to the Central Powers, and especially to the American troops in France. The occasion is a perfect setting for you."[60] President Wilson wrote Jones in reply, "I would if I could give you immediately my definite promise that I will be in New York on Saturday evening to speak for the Red Cross, but I dare not. I can only say that my present hope and intention are to be there, but I must frankly say that I

57. Jesse Jones to Blanche Babcock, February 25, 1937, Jesse H. Jones Collection [LOC].
58. Wakefield, "Jesse Holman Jones."
59. Timmons, *Jones: Man and Statesman*, 105.
60. Ibid., 106.

cannot speak at the Hippodrome. I know by many years experience my limitations in such matters, and I ought not undertake to speak in any auditorium larger than the Carnegie Institute or some one of the larger theatres." He added, "Confidentially, I would much prefer Mr. Cleveland Dodge as a presiding officer." He ended the letter, "In haste, sincerely yours, Woodrow Wilson."[61]

Jones immediately phoned Dodge and asked him to preside over the gathering, and to obtain a hall where Wilson could speak on Saturday evening after the parade if he should decide to. Jones continued to coax the president and by Friday, the day before the largest of all parades began, Jones was in a private railroad car headed to New York with President Wilson, First Lady Edith Wilson, and Admiral Cary T. Grayson, the president's private physician and confidant. Wilson agreed to march and speak for the American Red Cross: "Only," he told Jones, "I will not march with those Wall Street fellows."[62]

A limousine took the group to the reviewing stand, where the mayor and governor were surprised to see Mrs. Wilson leave the car and join them without the president. Jones then told the driver to go to the head of the parade, where a line of mounted police led over 100,000 marchers. President Wilson, Admiral Grayson, his secretary Joseph Tumulty, and Jones got out of the car, joined the parade, and began marching down Fifth Avenue among a sea of waving flags, falling confetti, and cheers and screams from throngs of citizens.

That evening, more than four thousand people packed the Metropolitan Opera House to hear President Wilson speak. Thousands more were in the streets trying to hear the first speech the president had given in New York since the United States had entered the war. Speaking without notes, Wilson began by asking for an unlimited draft. He rejected all of Germany's proposals for a settlement as "insincere" and shared his point of view of the war: "The story of this war, my fellow citizens, so far as we are concerned, is that it is perhaps for the first time in history an unselfish war. I could not be proud to fight for a selfish purpose, but I can be proud to fight for mankind."[63]

He then asked the packed crowd to "look at the picture. In the center of the scene, four nations engaged against the world, and at every point of vantage showing they are seeking selfish aggrandizement, and against

61. Woodrow Wilson to Jesse Jones, May 13, 1918, Jesse H. Jones Collection [LOC].
62. Timmons, *Jones: Man and Statesman*, 107.
63. *Houston Chronicle*, May 19, 1918.

(left to right) Jesse Jones, Admiral Cary T. Grayson, Joseph Tumulty, and President Woodrow Wilson marching down Fifth Avenue during the immense American Red Cross fundraising parade on May 18, 1918. Courtesy Campbell Photo Service.

them thirty-three governments representing the greater part of the population of the world, drawn together into a new sense of community of interest, a new sense of community of purpose, a new sense of unity of life." Praising the Red Cross, Wilson said, "Friendship is the only cement that will ever hold the world together, and this intimate contact of the great Red Cross with the people who are suffering the terrors and deprivations of this war is going to be one of the greatest instrumentalities of friendship that the world ever knew, and the center of the heart of it all, if we sustain it properly, will be this land that we so dearly love."[64]

To the "Wall Streeters," Wilson warned, "The duty that faces us all now is to serve one another, and no man can afford to make a fortune out of this war. There are men amongst us who have forgotten that, if they ever saw it. Some of you are old enough—I am old enough—to remember men who made fortunes out of the Civil War, and you know how they were regarded by their fellow citizens. That was a war to save one country—this is a war to save the world." At the end, he asked his audience, and the millions who would read his speech in papers across the world, to contribute to the work of the Red Cross. He urged, "I summon you to

64. Ibid.

the comradeship; I summon you in this next week to say how much and how sincerely and how unanimously you sustain the heart of the world." Wilson ended, "When you give absolutely all you can spare, do not consider yourself liberal in giving. If you give with self-adulation, you are not giving at all; you are giving to yourself. If you give until it hurts, then your heart blood goes into it."[65]

That night Jones wrote Wilson, "Permit me to express in a small, dignified way my appreciation. Your speech was the strongest and best utterance that could have been made, and the world needed just such a message from you at this time. Your marching in the parade and your letting the people see you as you did was just the big good man that you are."[66] The president responded, "It was generous of you to write me your note of May eighteenth. You may be sure that I enjoyed rendering such little service as I rendered the Red Cross in New York so much as more than to compensate me for the effort and inconvenience I was put to. I hope most sincerely that your hopes will be realized to the utmost in the present drive."[67]

Fifty million people donated $181 million ($2.5 billion) to the Red Cross campaign, exceeding its goal by $81 million.[68] This was the largest amount ever raised for a humanitarian purpose.[69] Houston even upped its goal to $300,000 ($4.2 million) after Jones reported "that President Wilson told him nothing short of $150 million [$2.1 billion] would meet Red Cross needs for the next 12 months."[70]

Demand for Red Cross assistance skyrocketed both in the United States and in Europe as the Spanish influenza epidemic, which began in Europe and spread worldwide, added to its burden. The DMR struggled to maintain sanitation, prevent spread of the flu and treat those who had caught it at the crowded military bases and hospitals. More than 500,000 people in the United States and nearly twenty-two million worldwide died from the disease.[71]

During the summer of 1918, the war began to turn. German forces withered as ten thousand soldiers a day poured in from the United States.[72]

65. Ibid.
66. Jesse Jones to Woodrow Wilson, May 18, 1918, Jesse H. Jones Collection [LOC].
67. Woodrow Wilson to Jesse Jones, May 22, 1918, Jesse H. Jones Collection [LOC].
68. Dulles, *American Red Cross*, 146; *American Red Cross Annual Report*.
69. Timmons, *Jones: Man and Statesman*, 108.
70. Dulles, *American Red Cross*, 150; *Houston Chronicle*, May 21, 1918.
71. "American Red Cross Nursing: A Tradition of Service."
72. Macmillan, *Paris 1919*, xxvi.

On November 11, 1918, Germany signed an armistice agreement, and the war was over. Jones wrote to Wilson that day, "Please accept my heartiest congratulations upon your remarkable achievement in banishing the Kaiser from power, and apparently from even decent society in his own country. It is most remarkable that your demands in respect to him and his kind should have been taken so literally by the people of the countries that have heretofore been ruled by kings, Kaisers, and autocrats. For this alone, you and your principles would live forever." He continued, "You have, without doubt, brought the war to a glorious conclusion, much earlier than if it had been left purely to military success, and while you perhaps now feel a more grave responsibility than that of making war, and have much to be seriously concerned about, you should, nevertheless, feel very great satisfaction in your wonderful accomplishments, which have so vitally affected the entire world, and take courage for the great task still before you."[73] The president quickly replied, "Thank you warmly for your letter of yesterday. It has done me a lot of good."[74]

Nine million soldiers and more than five million civilians were killed during the war and many millions more were crippled, homeless, abandoned, destitute, and hungry. Large parts of Europe were destroyed and in chaos, revealing a more urgent need for the Red Cross than ever.[75]

In the United States, the American Red Cross welcomed home more than three million returning soldiers. Upon their arrival, each one received discharge papers, a uniform, new shoes, a coat, and $60 ($850).[76] At this point, the DMR took over by helping soldiers contact their families and find their way back home. The DMR's Motor Corps' 12,000 volunteers—all women who maintained and drove their own cars—moved the sick and wounded to DMR convalescent homes and hospitals. Fifty-two convalescent homes had been built or were under construction in time for their return.[77] Davison remembered, "In lending a hand to the Army, cooperation between the Red Cross and the government was necessarily close, but, oddly enough, no phase of our work is less known than the almost Herculean labour undertaken on behalf of the soldier."[78]

Jones, who managed that "Herculean labour" for all but the first five months of World War I, was called "big brother to four million men in

73. Jesse Jones to Woodrow Wilson, November 11, 1918, Jesse H. Jones Collection [LOC].
74. Woodrow Wilson to Jesse Jones, November 12, 1918, Jesse H. Jones Collection [LOC].
75. Gilbert, *First World War*, xv.
76. Ibid., 519.
77. *American Red Cross Annual Report*.
78. Davison, *American Red Cross in the Great War*, 37.

khaki."[79] He was also a "big brother" to the Red Cross nurses, advocating for their improved status. Ahead of his revered president on women's issues, Jones wrote to Wilson two years before women won the right to vote, just before the end of the war, about "the question of military rank or relative rank for Army nurses." At the time, women could serve as nurses, but they had no military rank. Jones explained that, despite widespread opposition, giving them military rank would "attract the very best and most intelligent class of women." He continued, "It requires several years' study and severe training for a woman to equip herself for the exalted profession of trained nurse, and the duties and responsibilities and life's work of a trained nurse are such that everything that can properly be done to improve the standard of nursing, and the standing of the profession, should, it seems, be done."[80] He went on, "The Army nurse in the discharge of her duties and responsibilities, which in their very nature are of the gravest importance, needs military rank in order that her instructions to orderlies and enlisted personnel of the hospital will be properly obeyed." Jones then concluded, "The standing of the profession of trained nurse, and particularly of the Army nurse, should be so raised, socially and otherwise, as to attract the very best class of women who go in for professional careers, such as teaching, medicine, law, etc. I have heard of a number of Congressmen and Senators who would like to introduce the necessary legislation."[81] With additional endorsements from the American Legion and General Pershing, Wilson signed legislation after the war giving Army nurses military rank.[82]

Meanwhile, the responsibilities confronting the DMR were enormous, never-ending, and increasing. Jones, like everyone else, was busy all the time. He wrote Jeremiah Milbank, who had donated $50,000 ($706,000) to the DMR to build the first rehabilitation center for disabled veterans, "I am very sorry indeed not to be able to dine with you on Saturday and also that we could not have had lunch together. We opened our Convalescent House at Base Hospital #1 Saturday afternoon, and it involved my entire time until considerably after the dinner hour."[83]

Jones viewed his work with the Red Cross as an act of deep patriotism and morality. He wrote, "It taught the people to give and to sacrifice, and afforded them an opportunity to express their patriotism and loyalty, and

79. *American Red Cross Bulletin*, December 16, 1918, Jesse H. Jones Collection [HE].
80. Jesse Jones to Woodrow Wilson, November 4, 1918, Jesse H. Jones Collection [LOC].
81. Ibid.
82. Dock, *History of American Red Cross Nursing*, 1075.
83. April 1, 1918, Jesse H. Jones Collection [LOC].

to have a real part in the great struggle for world freedom. Only the fittest of our young men could join the actual fighting forces; but everyone could enlist in the great moral army of volunteers in the various relief organizations." Jones revealed, "I did not know there was so much patriotism in the hearts of human beings as was demonstrated through the activities of the Red Cross . . . I did not know that there was so much love for one's fellow man as was proven in those days by the desire and effort to do something somehow for the other fellow . . . To me the Red Cross is the Golden Rule, and I want no better religion."[84]

Although the war had come to an end, others were anxious to tap Jones's skills. Bernard Baruch, a prominent Democrat from South Carolina and an exceptionally successful financier, chaired the War Industries Board, which had militarized industry to manufacture and deliver everything needed for the war effort.[85] Baruch wrote to President Wilson after the war, "As Russia's greatest enemy, in my opinion, is going to be hunger and privation, might I suggest (and I do so most hesitatingly) that Mr. Hoover should head the mission. If anything at all has trickled into their minds from the outside world, the Russians will realize in sending him you are sending someone to help, not to conquer." Wilson had already put Herbert Hoover—an accomplished engineer and an emerging Republican—in charge of bringing food to millions of starving people in Europe. Baruch then continued, "May I ask if you have come to any decision regarding Mr. Jesse Jones whom I am very anxious to have placed on the Price Fixing Committee, which needs strengthening?"[86] But Wilson saw his resources as stretched too thin. "I agree with you in your estimate of Hoover," Wilson responded, "but I cannot, without dislocating some of the most important things we are handling, spare him from his present functions. I am sorry to say that I can't come to a definite conclusion about Jones yet, because my list in the other matter isn't made up, and I am not sure that I shall not need him."[87] The "other matter" Wilson referred to was Russia. Wilson considered sending Jones there to find out if the new government was going to cooperate at the Paris Peace Conference. Instead, on December 5, 1918, he appointed Jones to the American Red Cross War Council.[88] A few days before Wilson gave Jones the appointment, Axson and Davison went to see the president. Axson recalled,

84. *Red Cross Courier*, Jones, "Love for Fellow Men Was Proven in Those Days."
85. Heckscher, *Woodrow Wilson*, 465.
86. Bernard Baruch to Woodrow Wilson, July 13, 1918, Jesse H. Jones Collection [LOC].
87. Woodrow Wilson to Bernard Baruch, July 15, 1918, Jesse H. Jones Collection [LOC].
88. *Red Cross Bulletin*, December 16, 1918, Jesse H. Jones Collection [HE].

"We called one evening, by appointment, at dusk, after the electric lights had been turned on. When Mr. Wilson came into the room, the greetings between him and Mr. Davison were hearty, and the visit (lasting perhaps half an hour) was most amicable." He added, "I recall Mr. Davison in a characteristic attitude, leaning forward in his chair, his hands folded, and beginning to lay before the President, in his concise way, the object of the visit."[89]

Davison wanted the Red Cross to prevent disease and ease suffering around the globe, not just during war but also in peace. He wanted to coordinate "the efforts of all of the Red Cross societies of the world in the interest of mankind."[90] The president agreed, saying he did not want the American Red Cross to "contract" now that the war was over. He told Davison "to proceed to Geneva as quickly as possible and take counsel as to how the Red Cross organizations of the world can be brought together into a common understanding."[91] Davison asked Jones to go with him and joked, "I think two such distinguished linguists as you and I should go over and sell the plan." (Both country boys, they spoke only English.)[92] Before their departure, Davison announced that the Red Cross would "go forward on a great scale—not alone as heretofore, for purposes of relief in war, but as an agency of peace and permanent human service."[93]

Davison's vision for the Red Cross meshed with Jones's own sense of the importance of building up the larger community. Davison, Jones recalled, "saw the people in the fartherest corners of the earth being provided with the latest inventions of science and chemistry through the agency of the great Red Cross; he saw all countries brought closer together because of the agencies of the Red Cross; he had a vision that Russia could be brought around to a proper way of thinking, to a stabilized government, through the agencies of the Red Cross. So confident was he of this great possibility that he was willing, on behalf of the American Red Cross, to endow the League of Red Cross Societies with a fund of five million dollars [$48 million] to establish this in a neutral country, with headquarters at Geneva, the home of the International Red Cross."[94]

Jones, Davison, and almost every influential person in Washington appeared to be headed to Europe after the war. President Wilson announced

89. Stockton Axson to G. B. Case, October 8, 1923, Jesse H. Jones Collection [UT].
90. Ibid.
91. Reid and Gilbo, *Beyond Conflict*, 35.
92. Timmons, *Jones: Man and Statesman*, 108.
93. Reid and Gilbo, *Beyond Conflict*, 35.
94. Jesse Jones to G. B. Case, October 8, 1923, Jesse H. Jones Collection [UT].

he would go to France in December to work out peace settlements with the other world leaders. Not everyone thought he should go, especially those who thought it was inappropriate to take his lively, outgoing second wife, Edith. Jones, now clearly close with the president, wrote, "There has seemed no doubt in my mind but that you should go. Our fighting forces have done their full share, and it is now clearly your duty to finish the job. I feel sure that you need have no fear from the Congress during your absence. They are answerable for their acts, and time will prove the wisdom of your going. Bon voyage to both you and Mrs. Wilson."[95] Later, en route to Europe aboard the USS *George Washington*, Wilson, who was the first president to leave North America while in office, wrote to Jones, "It was certainly fine of you to send me such a cheering message of good bye as I was leaving, and I thank you for it from the bottom of my heart."[96]

Jones's Red Cross colleagues were pleased by his appointment to the War Council. One friend wrote, "I always realized that you were a big man, physically, mentally, and possibly morally, although of the last I have no direct evidence, and your appointment to the War Council confirms my opinion." He went on, "The great piece of constructive work which you have done as Director General of Military Affairs certainly entitles you to this new honor and all of us are delighted that it was accorded to you . . ." He added, "I understand that you have been considered the best [golf] player at National Headquarters."[97]

Jones and Davison set sail and arrived in London the day after Christmas. President Wilson, who had just been received with wild public jubilation and acclaim in France, arrived in London that same day.[98] "We were in London the last week of December 1918," Jones recalled. "President Wilson was at Buckingham Palace. Harry [Davison] and I were at the Barkley Hotel, he receiving during the day his many friends and associates. Late in the afternoon Harry asked if I would see President Wilson for him and explain that, realizing fully the great demand upon his time, he nevertheless felt it important that they should have a conference as early as the President's engagements would permit."[99]

Davison wanted to disband the American Red Cross War Council by March and include the League of Red Cross Societies as part of the peace treaty. Jones, who had never called first for an appointment with the presi-

95. Jesse Jones to Woodrow Wilson, December 3, 1918, Jesse H. Jones Collection [LOC].
96. Woodrow Wilson to Jesse Jones, December 9, 1918, Jesse H. Jones Collection [LOC].
97. C. Scott to Jesse Jones, December 24, 1918, Jesse H. Jones Collection [UT].
98. Timmons, *Jones: Man and Statesman*, 109.
99. Jesse Jones to G. Case, October 8, 1923, Jesse H. Jones Collection [UT].

dent at the White House, jumped in a cab and headed for Buckingham Palace. He remembered, "I immediately set out for Buckingham Palace, giving no thought to any difficulty in reaching the president, notwithstanding I had no credentials that would admit me."[100] A group of officials departing from the palace gates returned Jones's casual hand wave—he had only given them an automatic "Texas howdy"—so the guards evidently thought it was okay to let him in after he said he was there to see President Wilson on official business. The president and King George were at a meeting, and Jones was shown into a large ornate room with a crackling fire in the fireplace. He made himself comfortable, took off his shoes, and fell asleep. Some time later, the huge, heavy doors to the room swept open, and the king and queen of England, the president of the United States, and their entourages entered the room. One of many newspapers later reported, "Startled out of his slumber, our Texan friend stood at attention in his stocking feet and saluted! The procession passed. Afterward Admiral Grayson said to him, 'Why in the name of heaven did you take off your shoes before that fire?' The Texan, ignoring the question, said, 'Do you know, Grayson, that was the first time I got my feet warmed since I struck England!' "[101]

Grayson took great delight in circulating the story about Jones greeting the King of England in his stocking feet. He sometimes embellished the story by adding rolled up trousers and white socks.[102] Jones remembered, "In Paris a few days thereafter, H. P. Davison and Woodrow Wilson counselled and discussed, as two commanding generals, the future of the great American Red Cross and the organization of the League of Red Cross Societies."[103]

The Paris Peace Conference officially opened on January 18, 1919.[104] Hundreds of journalists from around the globe came to report on the private and public debates, world-changing decisions, and outsized personalities. Thirty nations swamped Paris with delegations that included top officials, their aides, their assistants, and countless hangers-on. All were there to have their say in the peace treaty, but the big decisions fell mostly to Georges Clemenceau, prime minister of France; Vittorio Orlando, prime minister of Italy; David Lloyd George, prime minister of Britain; and President Woodrow Wilson.

100. Ibid.
101. Unknown newspaper clipping, Jesse H. Jones Collection [HE].
102. Timmons, *Jones: Man and Statesman*, 110.
103. Jesse Jones to G. Case, October 8, 1923, Jesse H. Jones Collection [UT].
104. Macmillan, *Paris 1919*, 63.

Before he arrived in Paris Wilson had warned, "All of us have used the great words 'right' and 'justice,' and now we are to prove whether or not we understand these words and how they are to be applied to the particular settlements which must conclude this war."[105] Wilson came armed with his Fourteen Points, which he hoped would help guarantee "peace without victory."

The fighting and bloodshed had been worst in France and Belgium. One-quarter of France's men between the ages of eighteen and thirty had been killed; the French lost a higher proportion of its population than any of the other warring nations.[106] In northwest Belgium, "in Flanders' Fields," over 500,000 were slaughtered in the mud holding onto precious territory.[107] For these and many other reasons, the Europeans had a different understanding from Wilson of what was "right" and "just." They wanted revenge, along with territory and monetary reparations from Germany. Wilson, in the end, went along, hoping that his fourteenth point, the League of Nations, would fix all that he disliked about the proposed treaty.

Wilson proposed an association that would provide "mutual guarantees of political independence and territorial integrity to great and small States alike."[108] Establishing the League of Nations to sustain peace after the war was Wilson's highest ambition. On January 25, 1919, he presented his case to the Paris Peace Conference. Jones was there as part of the U.S. delegation. The president said, "We have assembled for two purposes, to make the present settlements, which have been rendered necessary by this war, and also to secure the peace of the world, not only by the present settlements but by arrangements we shall make at this conference for its maintenance. The League of Nations seems to me to be necessary for both of these purposes."[109]

Wilson noted, "In coming into this war, the United States never for a moment thought that she was intervening in the politics of Europe or the politics of Asia or the politics of any part of the world. Her thought was that all the world had now become conscious that there was a single cause which turned upon the issues of this war. That was the cause of justice

105. *Houston Chronicle*, December 28, 1918.

106. Macmillan, *Paris 1919*, 28.

107. In Flanders Fields Museum exhibition wall labels.

108. Woodrow Wilson, speech, joint session of Congress, January 8, 1918, Jesse H. Jones Collection [HE].

109. Woodrow Wilson, speech, Paris Peace Conference, January 25, 1919, Jesse H. Jones Collection [UT].

and of liberty for men of every kind and place." He went on, "Therefore, it seems to me that we must concert our best judgment in order to make this league of nations a vital thing. The fortunes of mankind are now in the hands of the plain people of the whole world. Satisfy them, and you have justified their confidence not only but established peace. Fail to satisfy them, and no arrangement that you can make will either set up or steady the peace of the world."[110]

The next day, Jones wrote the president, "I have never appreciated you in comparison with other men so much as since your coming on this mission. Your speeches everywhere, in England, France, and Italy, frequently on very similar occasions, coming one almost on top [of] another, have all been a great credit to you and to our country. I doubt if any true American can honestly say that he is not proud that you are our leader and our spokesman at this particular time." He continued, "Your speech at the Peace Conference on the principles of the League of Nations seems all and everything that it could have been—eloquent and classic, if I understand the meaning of the words, with great force and candor, based upon ideals not alone high and purposeful, but upon facts and conditions that must be acknowledged and reckoned with. It was a great speech on a great occasion by a great man." Jones concluded, "It is a rare privilege to see you, as you are, playing the part that you are playing in shaping the destinies of mankind. I am sure that you need no interpreter to tell you how eagerly the peoples of all nations are looking to you in the most critical hour in the history of the world. The knowledge of this fact will, I am sure, continue to give you added faith and courage to carry your plans and ideals to successful adoption."[111]

Grayson, who had already caught Jones with his shoes off in Buckingham Palace, recorded in his diary that Wilson's "speech was declared by many of those who had heard it to have been the best since his arrival in France. Only one of his hearers defied the rule of no demonstration of approval and applauded vigorously. This was Jesse H. Jones, a tall Texan who recognizes no foreign formalities."[112]

Within a few days, Jones was on his way to Cannes, France, with Davison to meet with British, French, Italian, and Japanese Red Cross officials to begin planning and organizing the League of Red Cross Societies. Davison wrote to Jones, "I believe the results of the conference may be far-reaching

110. Ibid.
111. Jesse Jones to Woodrow Wilson, January 26, 1919, Jesse H. Jones Collection [LOC].
112. Cary Grayson, diary entry, January 25, 1919, Jesse H. Jones Collection [LOC].

in the interest of mankind throughout the world."[113] President Wilson encouraged Davison, writing, "I cannot too strongly urge the importance of such a meeting, which should be held while recent experiences are fresh in our minds, and heartbeats throughout the world are in unison for the betterment of humanity."[114] The president then instructed Colonel House to send letters to the prime ministers of England, France, Italy, and Japan, endorsing the League of Red Cross Societies and requesting that representatives from their governments attend the conference.[115] When the meetings concluded on February 5, 1919, Jones cabled a report to Grayson, saying, "We have just had three days meeting here with British, French, Japanese, and Italian Red Cross associations . . . I would like the president to know that the societies represented at the Cannes meeting were all enthusiastically in favor of the suggestion that the Red Cross societies of the world should be brought together for the purpose of further developing the spirit and the activities of Red Cross throughout the world in the interest of suffering humanity." Jones added, "I have not thought that I would remain in Paris for any great length of time unless I can be of some service to the President or to the Peace Commission . . . [I] can perfectly well remain away from my business as long as there is anything for me to do at any and all events without the slightest expense of any kind or character to our government. I can return to Paris now and will gladly do so if you want to see me before you sail."[116] Grayson replied to Jones the same day, "I think it would be better for you to come here first."[117]

Once he was back in Paris, Jones wrote to Heyne in Houston, "I am very sorry not to be home during this opportune time for no doubt I could accomplish a good deal if I could bring myself to believe that my real duty did not lie here. The situation of the world is most alarming and chaotic, and I do not know how it is going to be adjusted. Surely there can be no peace unless people have the necessities of life—food and clothes; and it is just as essential that they be employed as it is that they should have food." He continued, "In addition to my Red Cross work, I am doing some very important things in connection with the Peace Conference, in an unofficial capacity . . . that seems to me quite worthwhile—in fact I cannot leave merely to look after my own private affairs . . . My responsibility

113. H. P. Davison to Jesse Jones, January 10, 1919, Jesse H. Jones Collection [UT].
114. Woodrow Wilson to H. P. Davison, January 23, 1919, Jesse H. Jones Collection [UT].
115. Colonel Edward Mandell House to Georges Clemenceau, draft, January 13, 1919, Jesse H. Jones Collection [UT]; the letter was sent out in February.
116. Jesse Jones to Cary Grayson, February 5, 1919, Jesse H. Jones Collection [UT].
117. Cary Grayson to Jesse Jones, February 5, 1919, Jesse H. Jones Collection [UT].

lies over here." He assured Heyne, "As soon as I can, in my own opinion, afford to leave, or as soon as it appears to me that the work I am doing is not important, to our own country and to the world, then I will immediately return . . . I haven't written before because I have not been thinking about matters at home. For one to know the conditions existing as I see them and be content to go about his own affairs is more than I can understand. I do not criticize anyone else and particularly the people in America, because they do not understand the seriousness of the world situation."[118]

Jones then recounted his journey, possibly to help Heyne understand why he was not eager to come home or perhaps to unload his thoughts and feelings after such an intense experience. He wrote, "I had a very interesting trip coming over with Mr. Davison. We had secretaries along and took advantage of the time to work out and formulate a plan of the things to be done. We landed in London while the President was there, and I had the pleasure of seeing him at Buckingham Palace." Jones did not mention greeting royalty in his stocking feet. "We were there only two or three days and then came on to Paris. I was present at the Peace Conference when the League of Nations was born, and I have never been so proud of President Wilson as I was on that occasion. I am convinced that he has scored the greatest accomplishment ever achieved by man in the creation of this League of Nations." Jones went on, "It is true that a great many people do not believe that we can have universal peace, and I can also understand that such aspirations are ambitious. But the greatest thing that the President has done on his trip over here has been to change the thoughts of the peoples of the world to peace rather than war, to reasonable and sensible adjustments of the present situation rather than a division of all the spoils that could possibly be exacted. I am as anxious as anyone that Germany should pay for every crime and every atrocity which she has committed; but I am also sensible to the fact that we must not undertake to get from her that which is impossible—in which event little would be gotten, because if so much is exacted as to completely discourage the German people, Bolshevism will prevail and there will be no organized society to meet what normally could and should be done."[119]

Jones ended his letter, "There is a great deal to do and a great many things to ascertain before it is possible for peace to be signed: I wish that you at home could feel justified in saying to me that I can stay away for

118. Jesse Jones to Fred Heyne, February 16, 1919, Jesse H. Jones Collection [UT].
119. Ibid.

the rest of this year if I care to do so. You must realize that I am depending on you . . . to look after things there and that I am giving no thought whatever to my affairs. If I could have a cable suggesting that I remain as long as I care to it would content me very much."[120] Jones sent another more direct communication in a cable a few days later to the home office: "Work engaged in is of great importance and if people there understood and appreciated conditions in the world, feel sure no one would care to hinder efforts of anybody to do everything possible to help . . . Am not willing to leave what I am doing here for a money consideration."[121]

But apparently something quite critical was happening at home. Jones was able to stay for another month, but then he was on his way back to Houston. A couple of days before he left, Baruch wrote Jones, "It is with extreme regret that I learn of the necessity for your departure because I was counting upon you for the continuance of your help and advice which has been so helpful. Hoping that you can return soon."[122] Jones sent a telegram to President Wilson, who was back in the United States for a short stay before returning to Paris to complete the peace treaty. Jones wrote, "My work with the Red Cross is completed and I am sailing for home March first by the *Adriatic*. If you have not sailed from America [for France] prior to my arrival, I would like a short interview. If you have sailed, I hope you will call on me to do anything that you think I can do to help now or later. I believe I have some conception of the very critical world situation and very naturally want to do anything that I can to help in the adjustment. My own affairs should have my attention for a little while, after which I will be glad to do anything for you anywhere on a voluntary basis."[123]

The wheels kept turning after Jones left Paris. Leaders of the International Red Cross, which provided services during war, were skeptical of the League of Red Cross Societies and possibly felt threatened by the suggested expansion of its mission. Jones observed, "The Swiss, who were in charge of the International Red Cross, could not understand the generosity—the magnitude—the spirit which Harry Davison carried to them, and the League of Red Cross Societies was never properly launched, in my opinion because of the failure on the part of the International to grasp and to understand just what Davison proposed and was offering."[124]

120. Ibid.
121. Jesse Jones to N. E. Meador, February 18, 1919, Jesse H. Jones Collection [UT].
122. Bernard Baruch to Jesse Jones, February 27, 1919, Jesse H. Jones Collection [UT].
123. Jesse Jones to Woodrow Wilson, February 28, 1919, Jesse H. Jones Collection [UT].
124. Jesse Jones to G. Case, October 8, 1923, Jesse H. Jones Collection [UT].

Instead, on May 5, 1919, came the simple announcement that "there was organized in Paris today a League of Red Cross Societies."[125] Jones recalled, "And so the League of Red Cross Societies, instead of being set up at Geneva and instead of becoming a part of the International Red Cross, was launched with headquarters at Paris."[126] Eventually the League did move to Geneva and its peacetime mission was adopted by the International Red Cross.

On June 28, 1919, the fifth anniversary of Archduke Ferdinand's assassination, the Treaty of Versailles was signed. Germany, although defeated, was still the largest European nation west of Russia. The inconsistently enforced treaty, resentment over lost territory, forced reparations and disarmament fueled nationalism and helped set the stage for the next world war.[127]

More than 100,000 people greeted Woodrow Wilson when he returned to Washington on July 8. Two days later, he presented the Treaty of Versailles to Congress for its approval. Some thought Wilson looked terribly tired and that he had deteriorated mentally and physically while he was away.[128]

Meanwhile, Jesse Jones had quickly become involved with his life in Houston again and was about to embark on the most ambitious phase of his building career. He was also about to get married.

125. Reid and Gilbo, *Beyond Conflict*, 41.
126. Jesse Jones to G. Case, October 8, 1923, Jesse H. Jones Collection [UT].
127. Macmillan, *Paris 1919*, 482.
128. Ibid., 489.

1919–1924

◈

The Family Won't Discuss It

JESSE JONES WAS A TOWERING FIGURE by his mid-forties, physically and publicly. People were shorter then, and his imposing six-foot-
three frame, large square face, direct blue eyes, and head of thick, wavy,
dark hair made him stand out in a crowd. So did his personality and reputation. No matter what else anyone thought, because of his contributions during the war and because of his close relationship with Woodrow
Wilson, Jones's stature was at new heights when he returned to Houston.

Some people at the time called him "Mr. Houston" for all that he had
done to help the city grow. A few called him "Ten-percent Jones" for the
amounts they mistakenly thought he charged for loans and mortgages, or
from the popular notion that he owned only ten percent of his holdings
and the rest was on credit. They were wrong, of course. The loans on the
Rice Hotel, for example, were almost paid off, and from the time Jones
returned to Houston, he was offering to buy back the hotel stock from
those who had originally supported the risky venture. From 1917 to 1919, the
hotel made more than $1 million ($12 million in current dollars) after taxes.[1]
Jones also entertained offers on the hotel from interested buyers. He
wrote to one inquiring agent, "If you have a purchaser for the Rice Hotel,

1. Financial statement, March 28, 1919, Jesse H. Jones Collection [UT].

I will be glad to see him and go into the details. You must understand that I would not hawk such a property as the Rice or offer it promiscuously. It is a very valuable property and earning good money."[2]

All kinds of things were happening when Jones returned home from Europe. Besides the buzz around the Rice Hotel, someone had offered to buy Jones's Bankers Trust Company, a successful mortgage and loan operation. Someone else was competing with him for a big piece of land.[3] The Harbor Board and mayor were moving toward buying land and building wharfs south of the Turning Basin, away from downtown. And Mary and Will Jones were about to divorce.

In 1919, divorce was rare, usually scandalous, and often ruinous. In June, Will borrowed $150,000 ($1.8 million) against his 6,000-acre Deepwater farm, gave $50,000 ($600,000) to Mary "in contemplation of final separation," used another $50,000 to pay "sundry items of indebtedness," and took another $50,000 to live on. In August, he gave his power of attorney to Jesse Jones, turned over care of the rice farm and cattle ranch at Deepwater to his son, Tilford, and moved to San Francisco, where he soon began living with a woman named Mertz.[4] Mary moved into the Rice Hotel and Will's mother, and sister, Augusta—divorced herself three times—went to the Battle Creek Sanitarium in Michigan for most of the summer and into the fall as the divorce proceeded.

Jones had resumed his family duties. In early August he reported to his Aunt Louisa, "I forwarded your letter to Will, who has gone to California . . . I had a wire from [him] yesterday, stating that they had a delightful trip." He then reported on the weather and explained why he was not staying at the "Boarding House" on Main Street but at the Rice Hotel, where nothing to date blocked the tall building from the prevailing breezes. He wrote, "Saturday night was so hot that I slept at the Hotel, and found it so much cooler that I decided to stay down [here] most of the time . . . Ike comes down mornings and brings my clothes and takes care of the rooms for me. I will go out to the house often enough to look after everything." He continued, "Aunt Nancy is getting along as well as usual, considering the weather. She goes to the picture show almost every day, and takes a little ride." He then added information about some investments he was making on Louisa's behalf in the Bristol Hotel block

2. Jesse Jones to L. L. Thomas, June 28, 1919, Jesse H. Jones Collection [UT].

3. Jesse Jones to Fred Heyne, February 16, 1919, Jesse H. Jones Collection [HE].

4. Will E. Jones, contract with Bankers Trust Company, August 1, 1919, Jesse H. Jones Collection [HE].

and suggested that she accept an offer on some old family property back in Pana, Illinois.[5]

For all of Jesse's easy sense of business as usual in his letter to his aunt, cousin Will presented a problem. Will and his son, Tilford, shared an undivided interest in the Deepwater farm. Although the farm fronted the Houston Ship Channel, it was far from downtown and the developments around the Turning Basin. Will and Tilford grew rice and raised cattle on the land, waiting until, as everything indicated, the land would be more valuable. However, Will evidently was so broke when he left Houston that he had had to pledge the Deepwater farm as collateral to obtain his $150,000 loan. He needed Tilford's half of the farm to do so. Tilford conveyed his interest in the farm to his father on the condition that it was to be returned as soon as the loan had been arranged. But Will reneged on this agreement.

After an exchange of many heated and pointed letters between Jones and his cousin, by the end of the year things settled down. Will returned Tilford's half-interest in Deepwater and stayed in San Francisco with Mertz in their apartment at the top of Nob Hill overlooking the bay.[6] Tilford announced his engagement to Audrey Thompson. Oil companies began buying small tracts of the Deepwater farm for refineries and storage. And Mary got her divorce from Will.

At the same time that he was refereeing family matters, Jones had not forgotten his friend in Washington. President Wilson was facing tough opposition from the Republican-dominated Congress over the League of Nations and the Versailles Peace Treaty. When Jones heard in the summer of 1919 that Wilson might delay a trip across the country to promote his cause, he wired Joseph Tumulty, the president's secretary, saying, "I believe it greatly to the interest of our country, if not imperative, that he make an extended speaking trip. I believe that it will do more to settle the unrest than anything that can happen, and that the only thing to be considered is his physical ability to stand the trip . . . I just want to say that I will personally be glad to defray any part of the expense that there are not appropriations to meet, and will consider it a privilege to do so."[7] He received an immediately reply of thanks from Tumulty, but no commitment.

A few days later, Jones pressed the issue again, writing, "I hope you

5. Jesse Jones to Louisa Jones, August 4, 1919, Jesse H. Jones Collection [HE].
6. Will E. Jones to B. Davison, January 28, 1920, Jesse H. Jones Collection [HE].
7. Jesse Jones to Joseph Tumulty, June 26, 1919, Jesse H. Jones Collection [LOC].

will include Houston as one of the places that the President will visit. We have an auditorium here that seats about seven thousand people, and I would be glad to make all arrangements for the President's comfort while here. There is no spot in the country as cool as the seventeenth floor of the Rice Hotel; or I would be glad to vacate my own residence and put it at the President's disposal if he should be here for a day or two. [Houston] is Dr. Axson's home and Dr. Edgar Odell Lovett, President of the Rice Institute, was made such at the suggestion of the President; it is the birthplace of Col. House, and while none of these little sentimentalisms should influence in the matter, they are nevertheless facts. We are on the direct route from California to Washington."[8]

At the same time Jones wrote to President Wilson directly, "You have rendered a service to the world and to humanity that is perhaps impossible to fully appreciate. It seems a travesty that men occupying public positions of responsibility should trifle with the welfare of the world as certain of our public men have been doing in their efforts to thwart your purpose. I am perfectly sure that you have accomplished all the good that could have been accomplished, and I am equally sure that without your towering strength and personality at Paris during these past few months, that the settlement would not have been a dignified one, or enduring. I feel that you have done all that mortal man could have done, and take pleasure in telling you so." He then advised, "In making your speaking trip through the country, I believe you should go as far as your strength will permit, and let as many people as possible see you, and talk to as many people as possible. I believe that this trip will do a great deal to settle the unrest in the country, but as much as I believe that, I hope you will not undertake such a program as to overtax yourself. The world is going to need you as much during the next few years as those just passed."[9]

Wilson openly replied, "Your generous letter of the fifth gave me a great deal of pleasure, and I thank you for it with all my heart. I know how to value your judgment because I know your own disinterested and devoted spirit in public service, and I want you to know that I feel, and shall always feel, that my warmest thanks are due to you for all you have done, and you have won my very warm admiration by the way in which you have done it. I hope it will not be long before we have a personal glimpse of you."[10]

8. Jesse Jones to Joseph Tumulty, July 5, 1919, Jesse H. Jones Collection [LOC].

9. Jesse Jones to Woodrow Wilson, July 5, 1919, Jesse H. Jones Collection [LOC].

10. Woodrow Wilson to Jesse Jones, July 15, 1919, Jesse H. Jones Collection [LOC].

Jones responded in kind, "Your good opinion . . . is the greatest possible compensation to me for anything that I have done for you as President and leader of our country, or as President and head of the American Red Cross. I have always been in such complete sympathy with you and such thorough accord with your ideas and principles, and the things that you have been doing since your entrance into public life, that I have felt peculiarly close to you . . ." With no reluctance to share deep feelings or to express his emotions, Jones continued, "The sight of you, or a word with you, is the greatest imaginable inspiration to me. You came at a time in the world's history when a great man was necessary—greater perhaps than at any other period. You have been equal to the occasion at every turn, and will be. It is a very great privilege to know you, and have your confidence."[11]

Wilson's brother-in-law, Stockton Axson, reported to Jones, "The President is extraordinarily well considering the burden that is upon him. At times he seems a little tired, but his recuperative capacity is enormous and a good night's sleep or a game of golf seems to rest him completely . . . Congress is doing all it can to block him, but I am satisfied that the Treaty will be ratified, particularly if he is able to get away from Washington soon and make his appeal to the country. Everybody I see, and no matter from what part of the country, tells me the same thing, that the people are with him."[12]

President Wilson began a cross-country speaking tour on September 2, 1919, to sell the League of Nations and the Versailles Peace Treaty to the nation's citizens.[13] Twenty-three days later, delivering a speech in Pueblo, Colorado, he said, "There is one thing that the American people always rise to and extend their hand to, and that is the truth of justice and of liberty and of peace. We have accepted that truth and we are going to be led by it, and it is going to lead us, and through us the world, out into pastures of quietness and peace such as the world never dreamed of before." Those were the last words Wilson delivered to a public audience. That evening he had a transient ischemic attack, a brief impairment of the brain that can be a precursor to a catastrophic stroke. Edith Wilson, Cary Grayson, the president's physician, and Tumulty agreed to end the tour and rush the president back to Washington.[14]

11. Jesse Jones to Woodrow Wilson, July 26, 1919, Jesse H. Jones Collection [LOC].
12. Stockton Axson to Jesse Jones, August 13, 1919, Jesse H. Jones Collection [UT].
13. Heckscher, *Woodrow Wilson*, 595.
14. Ibid., 609–10.

On October 2, less than a week after the episode in Colorado, Edith Wilson found her husband unconscious on the floor in his White House bedroom. His head was bloody and his left side was paralyzed. He had had a massive stroke.[15] From then on, Mrs. Wilson and Dr. Grayson determined who saw the president and what issues he considered, virtually controlling the executive branch of government for the last seventeen months of Wilson's second term in office.

Jones remained a staunch friend of the president after he left office. When the Democratic Party's 1920 presidential candidate, James Cox, and his running mate, Franklin Roosevelt, lost in a landslide to Republicans Warren G. Harding and Calvin Coolidge—an expression of the nation's yearning for "normalcy" after the war and its rejection of almost anything international—Jones reassuringly wrote President Wilson, "I do not believe that the overwhelming Republican vote meant in any sense a repudiation of the League of Nations. I am firmly of the opinion that the people in this country want the League of Nations, but the thing dearest to the great majority of people is their pocketbook, and they thought the Republicans would, in some way, manage to reduce taxes, and possibly bring about a return of the prosperity to which all had become accustomed and liked." On a more personal note, he added, "What I hope most is that you are not permitting this apparent change of sentiment to depress you. I feel certain that you are sage enough to understand the reasons, and that it was the inevitable [result] when conditions and men are taken into account . . . You must necessarily be an onlooker after March 4th, but you will be thinking and observing as the representative of silent millions."[16]

Wilson remained incapacitated, so may not have directly written the response Jones received in just a few days, which said, "My dear Jones, I have read your letter of December fourth with greatest interest and appreciation. I have no doubt that your diagnosis of the election results is substantially correct; at any rate, I assure you I have not been in the least discouraged by the results and, I think and hope, I have not been misled by them."[17]

Other than his devotion to Wilson, Jones had largely turned his attention away from the national political scene. Financially speaking, 1919 had been a good year for Jones: from rents, interest, and dividends, he

15. Ibid., 611.
16. Jesse Jones to Woodrow Wilson, December 4, 1920, Jesse H. Jones Collection [LOC].
17. Woodrow Wilson to Jesse Jones, December 9, 1920, Jesse H. Jones Collection [LOC].

reported $204,494 ($2.5 million) in gross income to the IRS. In addition to the Red Cross, he contributed to at least forty-two local charitable organizations, including a $100 ($1,230) donation to the Dickson Colored Orphanage, $2,500 ($31,000) to the Salvation Army, and a $550 ($6,800) donation to his church, St. Paul's Methodist.[18]

The DePelchin Faith Home, a Houston orphanage, had especially pressing needs. It was housed in a dilapidated building that needed new plumbing and heating, as well as quarters to separate sick children from the rest. When the director asked Jones for help, he threw himself into the cause, perhaps recalling the hordes of desperate orphaned children he had seen in France. At Jones's urging, Abe and Haskell Levy agreed to contribute land valued at $7,500 ($92,000) once $50,000 ($615,000) was raised for a new building.[19] Jones then sent requests to his friends and colleagues to raise the targeted amount. Houston's civic and business leaders enjoyed an interlocking, familiar relationship with each other, like an extended family bound by allegiance to the city. They served on each other's corporate boards, helped with their business and charitable causes when they agreed with their purpose, and fought to the bitter end when they did not. Accordingly, Jones did not hesitate to return a donation and ask for more if someone failed to give the requested amount. "Let me have that Faith Home check," he wrote to Howard Hughes, who was born and raised in Houston. "I asked you for a thousand dollars, but you might send five hundred at this time and I will try to get by with that amount."[20] On that same day, after returning their $100 ($1,060) check, he wrote to some close colleagues, "You pinched your Faith Home donation a little strong. Suppose you send in $400 more, making a total of $500. I feel sure that you can afford to do this, and certainly there is no worthier cause."[21] And Jones was even tarter with another prospect: "You have not sent me your check for the Faith Home. For all I know, you are responsible for some of those unfortunate children, and whether you are or not, you have got to kick in just the same; so come on across for $2,000. I asked you for $1,000 the first time, but you did not hear me."[22] The joking suggestion that the foot-dragging contributor had fathered some of the orphans in question was typical of the casual, clubby interac-

18. Jesse Jones 1919 tax returns, Jesse H. Jones Collection [HE].
19. Jesse Jones to Abe Levy, August 9, 1919, Jesse H. Jones Collection [HE].
20. Jesse Jones to Howard Hughes, June 10, 1920, Jesse H. Jones Collection [HE].
21. Jesse Jones to Sakowitz brothers, June 10, 1920, Jesse H. Jones Collection [HE].
22. Jesse Jones to Bassett Blakely, June 10, 1920, Jesse H. Jones Collection [HE].

tions among Houston's elite—and of Jones's aggressive fundraising techniques and his standing with his colleagues.

One constant source of disagreement among them remained the Houston Ship Channel and port, primarily disputes over the location and funding of its wharves and warehouses. The recently reconstituted Houston Harbor Board and the mayor recommended that voters approve $2.5 million ($27 million) in bonds to build wharves and "purchase additional channel frontage, both above and below the turning basin."[23] Jones and his *Houston Chronicle* vehemently opposed the bond issue and the purchase of "the Manchester tract, lying below Harrisburg on the south side of the channel," the same land that was too far away and that had been a point of acrimonious contention before the war.[24] Newspapers once more blared with arguments, declarations, and accusations that continued right up to the 1920 November election.

The *Houston Chronicle* gave Jones a unique and powerful platform from which to express his opinions, persuade voters, and promote improvements to the city. Advising against financial overreaching, a *Chronicle* editorial declared that "Houston's debt is larger than that of any city of similar size in the whole United States," and worried about obtaining funds for paving, drainage, water supplies, parks, schools, and libraries. The port's proximity to Houston was another concern. The editorial warned, "If we make our final bet on Manchester, the chances are that we shall have done no more than establish our principal terminal several miles below the Turning Basin. If, on the other hand, we make it at the Turning Basin, we may be able to hold our principal terminal that much nearer to the city."[25]

No matter where the wharves were located, Jones and his family would benefit since he or a family member owned land below Manchester, above Manchester, on the south side of the channel, on the north side of the channel, downtown, in outlying areas, and in surrounding counties. Although his opponents viciously attacked him for supposedly having a special interest in the outcome of the election and questioned his motives, Jones sincerely felt that the city could not afford the debt, that the port was better off with facilities closer to town and concentrated in one spot, and that private industry could be trusted to eventually fill

23. *Houston Chronicle*, September 23, 1920.
24. Ibid.
25. *Houston Chronicle*, September 28, 1920.

the channel with plants that would "do more to the commodities passing through than to merely transfer such commodities from ship to train.
Crude oil needs to be reduced to refined products, wheat to flour, cotton
to cloth, iron to hardware."[26] He even offered to give to the city thousands
of acres north of the Turning Basin as evidence of his lack of personal financial motive, but his opponents were not assuaged. They accused Jones
of holding a grudge against those involved in the last vote, of building
useless facilities when he was Harbor Board chairman, and of seeking
enormous personal profit, despite evidence to the contrary.

To Jones, it was more a question of government's role in commerce.
He expressed his philosophy, which would inform his actions for years to
come, in a *Chronicle* editorial by writing, "The only license this city has for
the ownership and control of terminals on the Ship Channel is to guide
and regulate trade in favor of public interests . . . It had a natural right to
employ a reasonable part of its credit and resources to get the Ship Channel going, and to do enough by way of terminal construction to prove the
port's practicality. It had a right to start developments in such a way as
promised to hold channel trade to the head of navigation. The rest should
be left to personal initiative."[27] Jones wanted government to provide the
catalyst for development, then step back and let the private sector sink
or swim.

To make his case, Jones paid for ads in the *Houston Post* and the *Press*,
and published a letter to the citizens of Houston in the city's three papers.
He explained, "I have given the development of the channel and our port,
as well as the all round welfare of Houston, probably as much thought
and consideration as the mayor, or the editors of these papers who are
impugning my motives, or even [any] member of the Harbor Board. Practically my entire business life has been spent in studying Houston and
in contributing to the building of Houston. I am entirely willing for my
constructive activities in Houston to be considered in comparison with all
that every member of the Harbor Board and city government combined
has done, and this I say with such apology as may be considered by the
reader as appropriate." He recalled, "I piled bricks upon top of bricks by
the hundreds of thousands, at times when returns from the investments
were not sufficient to pay interest on the money. Personally, I have asked
no favors of my city and have been granted none. No better properties are
to be found anywhere in the country, the larger cities not excepted, than

26. *Houston Chronicle*, October 11, 1920.
27. *Houston Chronicle*, October 2, 1920.

those that are the result of my individual efforts. These structures are located in the heart of the city, and their value does not fluctuate except as the welfare of Houston may fluctuate . . ." Summing up his overarching approach to business and public service, he added, "Every good to Houston necessarily is beneficial to me, and Houston can't be hurt without hurting me."[28]

Jones's argument prevailed. In November, Houstonians approved $850,000 ($9 million) in bonds for paving streets, building bridges, erecting schools, and laying sewer lines. Despite endorsements by the city's two other leading newspapers and most of the civic leadership, the voters turned down the two propositions that would have provided $2 million ($21 million) to buy the Manchester land far from downtown and build wharves and warehouses on the Ship Channel. In Jones's mind, government had done its job and it was time for private enterprise to make or break the Houston Ship Channel.

Meanwhile, Jones was buying land up and down Main Street, but usually no farther than ten blocks south of Buffalo Bayou. He planned a six-story cold storage warehouse on the land north of the bayou that he had tried to give to the city. He also bought a block of land at Elm and Harwood in downtown Dallas and began to acquire parcels in Fort Worth. He went in—and out—of what he had hoped would be a statewide automobile and tractor business before realizing that the supply of cars would soon exceed demand.[29]

Despite Wilson's veto, the eighteenth amendment went into effect on January 16, 1920, prohibiting the production, sale, and distribution of alcohol, but not its consumption or possession. Jones took the challenge in stride, inquiring in a report to the head of a bank that had a large mortgage on one of his buildings, "I wonder if you have a good supply of 'spirits,' and if I am able to get some in Saint Louis?" He then complained, "The Prohibition laws and tax laws have made liars and thieves out of ordinary good people."[30]

Jones's family continued to take a lot of his time and attention. He had set up the automobile and tractor business, the South Texas Truck Company, partially to provide good jobs for the son of his sister Elizabeth (Lizzie) and for Will's son, Tilford.[31] Jones managed the sale of Aunt

28. *Houston Chronicle*, October 11, 1920, Jesse H. Jones Collection [UT].
29. Jesse Jones to W. J. Farthing, October 17, 1920, Jesse H. Jones Collection [HE].
30. Jesse Jones to E. J. Russell, April 2, 1920, Jesse H. Jones Collection [UT].
31. Jesse Jones to W. J. Farthing, September 17, 1920, Jesse H. Jones Collection [HE].

Louisa's remaining Angelina County timberland and helped his cousin Gussie with her acreage in Newton County.[32] Jones also received letters from his cousin Will, who badgered him about "oil propositions" and, on one occasion, wondered if Fred Heyne had filled out his tax returns, all without a single mention of Mary, from whom he had been divorced close to a year.[33]

To the surprise of some and the horror of a few, on December 15, 1920—after years of waiting—Jesse Jones and Mary Gibbs Jones were married. The unannounced ceremony took place in Tilford and Audrey's apartment. Jones's *Houston Chronicle* was the most discreet in its reporting of the event and published only one column of ten lines with a tiny headline.[34] The *Houston Post* article, on the other hand, was less restrained, printing a story that was three times longer and contained two distinct headlines, one exclaiming, "Members of Family Won't Discuss It." The *Post* article reported that the wedding "was a surprise to their closest friends" and that "between 40 and 50 persons were present." It closed by saying that the news had "spread rapidly over the city."[35] In fact, the news spread all over the country. Former president William Howard Taft, who had served as vice president of the American Red Cross and lived with Jones in Washington during World War I, wrote him the following spring, "I congratulate you on being married. I thought you were hopeless, but I am delighted to know that you have finally had a lucid interval and made a happy woman and a happy man."[36]

Within hours of the wedding, the newlyweds boarded a train and left town. They stopped for a few days in Jones's hometown of Springfield, Tennessee, where they arrived just in time to see his mother's brother before he died on December 18. Two days later, the Joneses were leaving Springfield and the past behind as they headed for New York and the future.[37]

Only one of Mary Gibbs Jones's daily journals from the 1920s exists today. It begins on the day she married Jones and stops at the end of 1921. To designate the days of the week, seven horizontal lines cross each slightly perfumed page of the black, leather-bound book with 1921 embossed in

32. W. O. Huggins to Augusta Jones, March 18, 1920, Jesse H. Jones Collection [HE].
33. Will Jones to Jesse Jones, November 17, 1919, Jesse H. Jones Collection [HE].
34. *Houston Chronicle*, December 16, 1920.
35. *Houston Post*, December 16, 1920.
36. William Taft to Jesse Jones, May 30, 1921, Jesse H. Jones Collection [HE].
37. *Houston Chronicle*, December 17, 1920.

Jesse H. and Mary Gibbs Jones

gold numbers on the front cover. Many of the daily spaces reveal Mary's mostly factual handwritten accounts of her day's activities.[38]

Living in New York for two months, the Joneses stayed at the St. Regis, had lunch with financier August Belmont Jr. and his wife, Eleanor, at the

38. Quotes in this chapter attributed to Mary Gibbs Jones are from this 1921 journal, Jesse H. Jones Collection [HE]. Ten other journals from the 1930s and '40s were recently discovered and donated to Houston Endowment by George E. Skelton. He found them in the attic of his father's house after his death. His father, Howard Skelton, managed Jones's Metropolitan Theater next to the Lamar Hotel, the Joneses' home. Soon after Mary Gibbs Jones's death in 1962, Howard Skelton found a box meant for the trash, set out on the street and blocking one of the theater exits. He looked inside, saw the diaries, took the box home, and stored it in his attic. His son George found it in 2009 and donated the diaries to Houston Endowment in memory of his parents, Howard and Natalie Skelton.

Ritz-Carlton, went to the theater and played bridge with banker William Averell Harriman and his wife, Kitty, took long walks, and received "lots of telegrams" and "flowers from President and Mrs. Wilson" on Christmas Eve. Similar socializing, along with critiques of plays and a record of gains and losses at bridge, filled the calendar's pages until the couple arrived in Washington on February 20, 1921. On that day, Mary wrote they were "stopping at the Shoreham," that "Dr. and Mrs. Grayson" had called on them in the afternoon, and that they were "early to bed." The next day she reported, "Awoke at 9 am. I rode for an hour with Jasper and Mary Anne [her brother and sister-in-law, who lived in the area]. Jess made some business calls." Then, in the most enthusiastic language and heaviest handwriting in the entire volume, she wrote and underlined, "Xtra event. Lunched at the White House. Truly a red letter day."

Only twice in the book did Mary expand an entry onto the back of the page: the day she married Jesse Jones and the day she went to the White House. In describing the latter event, she wrote, "Monday, February twenty-first. Lunched at the *White House* with President and Mrs. Wilson, Mrs. McAdoo, Miss Margaret Wilson, and Miss Bones. Mrs. Wilson took me over the main rooms and upstairs through the bedrooms." Mary also observed, "The President is very feeble."

President Wilson was at the end of his term, preparing to leave office in early March. In one of the most remarkable cover-ups in United States history, his wife had collaborated with his physician and his personal secretary to keep the public, the press, the Congress, and the cabinet from knowing about his partial paralysis, his blindness, and, even more essential, his inability to write and think clearly. The incapacitated president had spent most of his time in bed or in a wheelchair with his infirmities concealed under a full black cape.[39] On the day Jones saw his broken hero, he wrote to the president, "You and Mrs. Wilson gave my wife and me a pleasure today that we greatly appreciate—and will never forget." He went on, "The sight of you or the sound of your voice, especially if speaking to me, has always been the greatest inspiration to me. You came at a time when you and the qualities you possess were especially needed, [and] you gave more to mankind & the world than is now realized or appreciated except by the unbiased thinking people. You fell in the great battle—wounded—but not until you had carried the flag to Victory." He added, "The principles that you have paid so dearly for—and with

39. Levin, *Edith and Woodrow*, 351.

such poor assistance and understanding in many instances . . .—must ultimately survive." Jones ended his letter, "I salute you, The Commander in Chief of a great cause as well as of our great country."[40] Congress had rejected Wilson's "great cause," the League of Nations, primarily because of the president's refusal, or possibly because of his inability, to compromise with Republican Senate leader Henry Cabot Lodge over the provision that would force participating nations to come to the aid of another if attacked. Wilson was for it; Lodge was opposed.

On February 22, the day after their momentous lunch, Mary wrote in her calendar, "Flowers from the White House yesterday—roses, hyacinths and carnations." On February 23, the Joneses boarded a train for Houston; Tilford and Audrey met the couple at the Houston train station and drove them home to the Rice Hotel. Mary reported that "Jess's rooms on the 17th floor were newly done over" and that "flowers were in each room." The next evening, the family had a dinner party to welcome home the newlyweds and to celebrate their marriage.

Shortly after the Joneses returned to Houston, Mary received a letter from Edith Wilson, who, after President Harding's inauguration, had moved with her husband into their new home on S Street in Washington. The letter reveals the Wilsons' feelings about Jones and signals the start of a deep friendship between the two women that lasted the rest of their lives. Edith wrote: "My dear Mrs. Jones, I am addressing this to you, but it is meant for you both, to tell you how warmly we both value yours and Mr. Jones's letters and to thank you for your thought of us on March fourth and the message of welcome you sent to greet us when we came into our own house." She went on, "We do not feel you are a stranger, for being so fond of your husband and counting him as one of our *real* and valued friends, we could not feel his wife was less. And so it gave us both very genuine pleasure to have you with us when you were here in Washington." She added, "I am sure you can say for me better than I could to your husband of how touched I was by the beautiful little note he sent on the day you were leaving. I have kept it and shall always value it among my treasures." She then concluded, "We will look forward to welcoming you under our own roof when you are next here and until that time we will anticipate your happy messages."[41]

After welcoming Jones back to Houston, Stockton Axson reported to

40. Jesse Jones to Woodrow Wilson, February 21, 1921, Jesse H. Jones Collection [LOC].
41. Edith Wilson to Mary Gibbs Jones, February 1921, Jesse H. Jones Collection [HE].

Edith Wilson, "You made them both very happy, and *he* will never forget that the President greeted him with 'Hello, Jess!'"[42]

At Bernard Baruch's request, Jones had been one of ten who gladly donated $10,000 ($119,000) toward the Wilsons' new home on S Street.[43] He could well afford it: his January 1921 financial statement showed a net worth of $8,571,000 ($102 million).[44] Despite his long absences, his buildings, banks, and newspaper were all well managed, returning healthy profits and increasing in value as Houston continued to expand. During the 1920s, the city's population would more than double from 138,000 to 292,000, and surrounding Harris County would grow from 187,000 to 359,000.

For years Jones had been accumulating land up and down Main Street, intent on making it Houston's primary commercial thoroughfare by placing most of his office buildings, hotels, and movie theaters there. By 1921, Jones had just about succeeded. A real estate agent breathlessly explained to a prospective New York client that Main and Capitol was a "wonderful corner, being in the block with Woolworth's and directly opposite Kress, and practically across the street from the leading department store, and only one block removed from the Rice Hotel, and right in line with the progress of the city." He explained, "You will understand that Houston is a one street town, which accounts for somewhat higher rentals than some other Texas cities."[45] Jones's commercial structures on Main Street extended seven blocks south of Buffalo Bayou. As Houston's population surged and the decade progressed, though, he moved even farther south down Main. He also purchased properties and put up buildings in Fort Worth, Dallas, and New York.

During the summer of 1921, Jones continued to put his stamp on downtown Houston by demolishing a few of the one- and two-story buildings that were prevalent and replacing them with much larger and, in most cases, more ornate structures. At the aforementioned corner of Main and Capitol, he tripled the size of one of his early ten-story skyscrapers, originally built for the Texas Company, by horizontally extending it. This building, at one of the most prominent commercial corners, was renamed the Bankers Mortgage Building and became Jones's business headquar-

42. Stockton Axson to Edith Wilson, February 26, 1921, Jesse H. Jones Collection [Rice].

43. Cleveland Dodge to Cary Grayson, February 14, 1921, Jesse H. Jones Collection [Rice].

44. Financial statement, January 1921, Jesse H. Jones Collection [HE].

45. F. F. McNeny to Mr. Sabine, November 8, 1920, Jesse H. Jones Collection [HE].

Jesse Jones with his principal architect, A. C. Finn. Jones once said, "I am happiest when building and planning" (*Houston Chronicle*, May 13, 1923). Courtesy San Jacinto Museum of History.

ters. He planned a ten-story office building next to the Houston Chronicle Building and another ten-story building for the local electric company, this one nine blocks south of the bayou and one block east of Main.

Jones actively participated in every aspect of the construction process, from negotiating prices for materials, equipment, and furnishings to haggling over the speeds of the elevators, which he liked to run fast. Alfred C. Finn was Jones's principal architect. They had first worked together on the Rice Hotel and on the ten-story Main Street buildings Jones built during the Houston Ship Channel's opening in 1914. Finn, who would play a major role in the next extension of Houston's skyline, received almost daily telegrams from Jones with suggestions about where to place columns, windows, toilets, and corridors. Jones's energy was boundless; even as he was busy reworking downtown Houston, he began building the Melba Theater in downtown Dallas and pursued an aggressive building program in New York.

The Joneses returned to New York in September, pausing for a stay at the luxurious Greenbrier hotel and resort in White Sulphur Springs,

West Virginia. From New York Jones "telecommuted" with his colleagues back home by phone, mail, and telegram. He stayed in constant touch with Finn about the buildings, with Heyne about the bank and the mortgage businesses, and with his brother, John, about the lumber company. He kept up the same active participation in each business, warning John to "quit doing a careless credit business" and, although known for his steadfast loyalty to good employees, recommending that he fire one man "without delay." He told John to remind his employees that they "must all understand that they have got to work—not for one day or for one week, but for every day and for every week."[46] He expected almost as much from his employees as he did from himself.

Jones also corresponded on an almost daily basis with M. E. Foster, the publisher of, and Jones's partner in, the *Houston Chronicle*. Jesse's correspondence with Foster in 1921 on the subject of the Ku Klux Klan provides insight into how he handled the people who ran his businesses and how he combined commercial success and civic responsibility. The Ku Klux Klan was established in 1866 to promote white supremacy during Reconstruction. Its name came from the Greek word *kuklos*, meaning "circle" or "band." As the nation became more insular after World War I, the movement targeted Catholics, Jews, and "other foreign elements," in addition to blacks. The Klan grew rapidly in Texas and by the end of 1921, its membership exceeded 100,000. Angry, hooded mobs frequently marched through towns and cities and terrorized citizens with burning crosses.

After the Klan won majority power in the city governments of Dallas, Fort Worth, and Wichita Falls, Foster wanted to prevent local violence and a possible takeover of Houston's government.[47] In September 1921 he purchased from the *New York World* a twenty-part series about the Ku Klux Klan and told Jones about the articles in a telegram: "They are red hot with inside secrets. Will make a sensation but self respecting law upholding newspapers should print the facts about this insidious organization despite threats of violence or libel. Do you agree?"[48] Jones wired back the next day, "The *Chronicle*'s position is thoroughly understood, and I am in accord with the way you have handled it. However, I cannot pass upon the articles referred to without seeing them, but am entirely willing to abide by your judgment."[49] Foster responded that he was not asking for Jones's

46. Jesse Jones to John T. Jones Sr., September 7, 1921, Jesse H. Jones Collection [HE].
47. *New Handbook of Texas*, 1165.
48. M. E. Foster to Jesse Jones, September 5, 1921, Jesse H. Jones Collection [HE].
49. Jesse Jones to M. E. Foster, September 6, 1921, Jesse H. Jones Collection [HE].

approval—he simply wanted to warn Jones that he and his business interests might be threatened. Jones did not back down from the danger or take offence at Foster's independence. Instead, he wrote a long, friendly letter and said, "I have heard some slight rumblings about it being an ill-advised policy for the *Chronicle*, but that does not influence me in the slightest. The *Chronicle* should stand for the right, without fear, financial or otherwise." Always including a note of personal inquiry and interest in his correspondence, Jones went on to ask Foster about his daughter's cold, told him Aunt Nancy was feeling better, and said that he wanted to stay in New York for the theater season.[50]

The *Chronicle* was only one of three major daily papers in Texas that published the series.[51] Afterward, Foster enthusiastically wrote Jones in September, "I think it is the biggest thing that the *Chronicle* ever undertook and it has been our greatest victory. It is especially big in that there is not one taint of commercialism in our part of it. Our Manchester victory was nothing in comparison to the one just accomplished in making the people of this City and State realize the dangers that were confronting them."[52] Two days later Foster pointed out that W. C. Munn & Co. was the only department store to withhold advertising because of the series. In the two-page, single-spaced letter, Foster reported, "So far this month our department store advertising excess has been more than double that of *The Post*. The Munn firm is simply imbued with the Klan spirit of hate and animosity and is losing business in an effort to hurt us."[53]

Jones was ahead of his time on racial issues, but not by leaps and bounds. There is no available record that indicates a person of color served on any of Jones's boards, ran any of his companies, or played cards with him in any of his many games. Houston was segregated, and it appears that Jones did little to upset the status quo. However, he felt all people deserved to be treated with dignity and to succeed in life, as evidenced by his personal, commercial, and philanthropic actions.

The Joneses went from New York to Washington, D.C., for a short visit during which they lunched with Axson, enjoyed the horse races with the Graysons, and briefly called on President Harding at the White House before seeing the Wilsons on S Street. Jones had lived next door to Harding in Washington during the war, and they had had adjoining

---

50. Jesse Jones to M. E. Foster, September 14, 1921, Jesse H. Jones Collection [HE].
51. Cox, *First Texas News Barons*, 143.
52. M. E. Foster to Jesse Jones, September 26, 1921, Jesse H. Jones Collection [HE].
53. M. E. Foster to Jesse Jones, September 28, 1921, Jesse H. Jones Collection [HE].

lockers at their country club. Jones once observed that Harding "was a delightful personality but either didn't understand men or couldn't say no." Dr. Grayson, Wilson's doctor, confidant, and gatekeeper, was an admiral in the Navy and, thus, subject to transfer; Jones went to the White House to get Harding's pledge that he would not transfer Grayson as long as Wilson was alive.[54]

Mary recorded in her daily calendar on October 4 that they had "a delightful evening" with the Wilsons. The former president, still physically impaired and devastated by the League's defeat and the country's political turn to an isolationist conservatism, needed affirmation and solace. Jones wrote, "It was a privilege that I fully appreciate, seeing you on yesterday, and I was pleased to see the decided progress that you have made since we were here in February. I realize that your disappointment at the turns things have taken must be more of a tragedy to you than anything that could happen to you personally. You lifted the ideals of the people of the world to a high level, but were stricken before you could get the props all set." He went on, "The people are getting impatient with the present administration, but they have got a lot of disappointment coming to them. I do not believe that there is another man in the world that could have accomplished the things that you accomplished, and if you had kept your health, you could have rendered a further service to the world, greater, perhaps, than can be imagined." Jones then concluded, "My esteem, affection, and profound admiration grow, as I more fully realize your greatness, and the power and influence for good throughout the world that you and your administration were. Mrs. Jones shares my sentiments, and we wish for you every comfort, and a complete restoration of health."[55]

The Joneses returned to New York, and as they had during their first two months of marriage, the couple had fun. During those earlier months, Mary recorded in her calendar that in between luncheons, bridge games, and car rides, they had attended thirty-two plays, five operas, and two concerts, and now they were back for more.[56] Jones wrote Foster, "I am having a very good time, playing golf about three days a week and bridge the other three days. The nights are all filled, either with bridge or theaters, and both of us will soon be in need of a rest cure."[57]

54. Jesse Jones to Blanche Babcock, August 25, 1937, Jesse H. Jones Collection [LOC].
55. Jesse Jones to Woodrow Wilson, October 5, 1921, Jesse H. Jones Collection [LOC].
56. Mary Gibbs Jones, 1921 diary, Jesse H. Jones Collection [HE].
57. Jesse Jones to M. E. Foster, October 18, 1921, Jesse H. Jones Collection [HE].

By the first of November, Jesse's colleagues in Houston were beginning to wonder when he would come back. Jones wrote Foster that he "would like to play a while," but also encouraged Foster to "write me as often as you feel like it. I am always glad to have your letters."[58] On another occasion, Jones wrote "I hate like to smoke to hurry this trip." Alluding to local controversies mentioned in Foster's letter and revealing a bit of personal growth, he continued, "At all events, I have quit worrying about matters of that kind. A certain amount of dollars are a good thing to have, but as long as one has the requisite number to provide the essentials and some of the pleasures of this life, it is hardly worth while worrying about more, though we all seem to do it more or less."[59]

Evidently approving of this change in attitude, Foster wrote back, "Your letter of November 15th indicates to me very clearly that an occasional trip to New York is as good for you as it is for me . . . Just before you left Houston, every little thing worried you, and the meanness and the contemptibility of your enemies caused you to want to get even whenever and wherever you could. Now, you realize just how small your enemies are, how little they have really accomplished, and how well you can afford to ignore them."[60]

While taking a breather from his demanding life, Jones in turn advised Foster to "keep your mind free of annoying things. I realize more and more every day the character and strength of the *Chronicle*. It stands for the right fearlessly, and all must respect it, even those that hate certain of us who are interested in it. So get your pleasure and satisfaction from that, and from your lovely family and home-life."[61]

"Home-life" helped bring the Joneses back to Houston. Mary's son, Tilford, and his wife, Audrey, had their first and only child on March 27, 1922. They named her Audrey Louise Jones in honor of her mother and great-grandmother, Louisa. Audrey was Mary's first and only grandchild, but also Jones's first cousin twice removed. Despite the complicated ancestry, the three became so close that Audrey frequently said she had two sets of parents—her own and Jesse and Mary. By the time she was eighteen months old, they all had nicknames for each other, which they used throughout their lives. While still learning to talk, Audrey started

58. Jesse Jones to M. E. Foster, November 1, 1921, Jesse H. Jones Collection [HE].
59. Jesse Jones to M. E. Foster, November 15, 1921, Jesse H. Jones Collection [HE].
60. M. E. Foster to Jesse Jones, November 21, 1921, Jesse H. Jones Collection [HE].
61. Jesse Jones to M. E. Foster, November 23, 1921, Jesse H. Jones Collection [HE].

calling Jones "Bods" and Mary "Muna." For better or worse, the Joneses called her "The Baby."

Jones also had lots of nieces and nephews. His brother, John, had five children (the one boy, John T. Jones Jr., would play an important role in his uncle's life in later years), his sister Ida also had five children, while his sister Lizzie's two children were a little older than the rest. Still, Audrey was like the child they never had, and they loved her immensely. She would eventually live with the Joneses as much as she did with her own parents, and she claimed not to know that Will Jones was her real grandfather until the day she got married.[62]

Jones's life was full. Buildings were going up all over downtown Houston, in Fort Worth, and in New York. Deposits flowed into Jones's National Bank of Commerce. His backing of Gus Wortham's fledgling American General Life Insurance Company exemplified Jones's ability to identify and finance young promising business talent who, once successful, were certain to be lucrative National Bank of Commerce customers.[63]

The community recognized Jones's singular value. He was Houston's preeminent developer during the first half of the twentieth century, and only nine years after the first dinner, it was almost necessary to have another banquet to honor Jones's remarkable contribution to the city's development and verve—no matter how sharp a dealer some thought him to be. More than 550 people gathered at the Rice Hotel on May 12, 1923, at a banquet sponsored by the Red Roosters to celebrate the city's most accomplished citizen. The Red Roosters, formed as part of the Notsuoh Festival in 1913, recognized individuals who had made great contributions to the city; its motto was "First for Houston, one for all and all for one." They could not have selected a more appropriate recipient for that honor than Jesse Jones.

Giant pictures of Jones's twenty-two downtown buildings bordered the grand ballroom. The evening's beautifully bound, multi-page program was entitled "Fellowship Dinner to honor Mr. Jesse H. Jones, City Builder," and included a two-page spread of the same pictures decorating the ballroom. The Finlay Orchestra played "America," thirty-eight children from the DePelchin Faith Home presented a "Musical Revue and Tableau," prayers were offered, the mayor spoke, and Miss Mary Carson sang selections from *La Traviata*. The *Houston Chronicle* reporter and photographer had arrived early enough in the evening to take a picture

62. Audrey Jones Beck, conversation with the author.
63. Buenger and Pratt, *But Also Good Business*, 88.

and "let the room clear of smoke from the flashlight before the banquet began."[64]

Stockton Axson, who had spoken last at the banquet nine years before, was, as he had been then, the last to speak. A highly regarded Rice Institute English professor who had served closely with Jones in the American Red Cross during World War I, Axson was on fairly intimate terms with the honoree and he identified three traits that characterized Jones—a "shrewd knowledge of human nature;" his "ability as a business organizer," including a "most casual and nonchalant way of impressing people into service;" and "the directness of his approach to each problem, a ruthless cutting of red tape." Axson said, "He seemed leisurely in manner, but in reality he was swift in his decisions and execution." He took delight in telling the crowd how "Jones would saunter into an office, sit down, prop his feet upon a desk, exchange a few seemingly casual remarks, and then saunter out as if he had all eternity at his disposal. It seemed as if nothing in particular had happened, just a sort of lazy Southern social call. But in a few hours, it developed that everything had happened. A big piece of machinery had been set in motion."[65]

Finally, the Red Roosters presented Jones with a huge Reed & Barton loving cup engraved with his buildings, decorated with two enameled Red Roosters, and inscribed, "Presented to Jesse H. Jones (City Builder) by his fellow Houstonians, May 12, 1923."

Newspapers throughout Texas and across the nation published stories about the event. The paper in Cisco, Texas, said, "Jones couldn't say much when the cup was presented. He's afflicted or endowed with a painful modesty. Speechmaking is not one of his accomplishments. But he can build buildings and build them well."[66]

Jones's words printed in the *Chronicle* on the day after the banquet revealed more about himself than the few words he said after receiving the cup. He explained that the rent check was the least rewarding part of building and that as far as banking went, "there was no fun . . . in lending money." He went on to say that "there is a great deal of fun and satisfaction in planning and building—indeed, it is fascinating, and I am happiest when planning and building." Jones then reminisced about one of his first skyscrapers, the Houston Chronicle Building, and offered, "We have

64. *Houston Chronicle*, May 13, 1923.
65. Ibid.
66. Newspaper clipping datelined Cisco, Texas, May 15, 1923, Jesse H. Jones Collection [HE].

seen Houston grow and develop for the past dozen years, but I wonder if we can visualize the city that is to be here a generation hence." Chicago, the booming metropolis he had visited as a Tennessee farm boy when he was just seventeen, had been his model. He said that, like Houston, Chicago had no "unusual natural advantages," but that its "lines of travel and progress by land and water" made it the "Midwestern clearinghouse" for "trade, commerce, manufacture, and agriculture." Chicago at this time had more than three million inhabitants and was one of the nation's major ports.[67] Even though only 200,000 people lived in Houston and the port was still largely a work in progress, Jones optimistically declared, "The situation here is very similar."[68]

He remarked on the region's evolution, saying, "Twenty years ago, the south and southwest were not commercially important. It was looked upon by the people of the North chiefly as a land of old romance. Now it is a land of immense commercial potentialities. Capital has begun to flow in, and population has begun to flow in, both seeking new opportunities. Our Ship Channel and the great transcontinental railway systems meeting deep water here make Houston the inevitable gateway through which the products of this growing southern and western empire can best reach the markets of the world."[69] In fact, Jones was betting on it. The buildings he had on the drawing board would dwarf those that had been celebrated the night before.

The laudatory editorial in the next day's *Houston Post*, a newspaper usually hostile to Jones, was his biggest surprise. It began, "Mr. Jones is not only Houston's greatest builder, but no other citizen of the state has to his credit a career of such constructional distinction in the manner of city building." Encapsulating Jones's holistic approach, it went on, "In extending Houston's business district, he has stimulated growth in all the city's activities. He has supplied room for commercial expansion as rapidly as demanded; he has given labor opportunity in the sum of many, many millions; he has added many millions to the taxable values of city and state; and in all respects his business acumen and genius have contributed to the common welfare."[70]

Jones admitted shock at this positive editorial in a letter to Wilson, who

67. *Houston Chronicle*, May 13, 1923.

68. Ibid. In 2010, the Port of Houston ranked first in the United States in foreign tonnage. The port directly and indirectly employs more than 785,000 people (*Houston Business Journal*, December 17–23: 24).

69. Ibid.

70. *Houston Post*, May 12, 1923.

had sent him a congratulatory letter the day after the banquet: "I hope you read the *Houston Post* editorial. That paper is extremely unfriendly to me and frequently stoops very low in its attack, so that editorial was more a shock to me than a surprise." He explained, "I have had many fights in the development of our little city, and have made my full share of enemies. At times I am vilified, and then again applauded. I have never stood for office, but usually take a stand in matters affecting the public welfare, and having gained some degree of prominence in a business way, am frequently singled out for attack." He closed by saying that he and his wife "expect to spend a day or two in Washington en route East, sometime during July or August, and hope that it may be our good fortune to see you and Mrs. Wilson at least for a handshake."[71] The Joneses spent almost as much time in New York as they did in Houston, not only because Jones was about to break ground on the first of his many Manhattan skyscrapers, but also because they enjoyed a wide circle of friends and the city's many cultural offerings.

Wilson immediately responded, "Mrs. Wilson and I both hope that we shall have the pleasure of seeing you both. The conditions of my present convalescence are somewhat exacting, and in order to be sure that I may be able to find a space in them to see you, I beg that you will let me know a few days in advance of your coming, and where a message will reach you in Washington."[72]

Jones replied that they would be happy to see them. He also reported that "Axson has been considerably below par during the past few months" and that he was thinking about returning to Princeton from Rice. Jones thought that was a mistake and went on to say, "He is popular in Texas with every class of people. I have been trying ever since the conclusion of the war to persuade him to enter politics. I would like to see him in the United States Senate. He does not take these suggestions seriously, but I have every confidence that he could be elected to any office in Texas that he would stand for, and make a campaign."[73]

Jones and Axson, along with Wilson's friend and Princeton classmate Cleveland Dodge, had begun to confer about the Wilsons' financial situation. There were no pensions for ex-presidents then, and Wilson had made and saved little during his career as an academician and as a politician. That summer Axson wrote from a sanitarium in upstate New

71. Jesse Jones to Woodrow Wilson, May 31, 1923, Jesse H. Jones Collection [LOC].
72. Woodrow Wilson to Jesse Jones, June 4, 1923, Jesse H. Jones Collection [LOC].
73. Jesse Jones to Woodrow Wilson, June 12, 1923, Jesse H. Jones Collection [LOC].

York where he was being treated for persistent and hereditary depression about "Mr. W's sore need of a new car," adding that Edith's brother, Randolph Bolling, had been speaking with Rolls-Royce agents about special car bodies that could accommodate the crippled ex-president. The Pierce-Arrow that Wilson bought from the government when he left the White House was worn out and, because of his increasing disabilities, was now "impossible for him to get in and out of." Axson felt awkward about the request—the Rolls-Royce, less the Pierce Arrow trade-in value, would cost $15,500 ($193,000)—and wrote Jones, "I know you will be quite candid. Of course this suggestion is wholly and solely my doing—and as my mental condition is now only two degrees removed from imbecility, you can just set this down to my idiocy."[74] Jones also received a letter from Dodge, who had talked with the Wilsons' daughter, Margaret, about both the car and her parents' financial position. After offering 500 shares of New York Central stock toward the cause, Dodge suggested, "I think, whatever we do, we ought to confine it to just as few people as possible, and have it come from those who are so close and near to Mr. Wilson that he would be willing to accept it."[75] Jones soon wired Grayson and asked him to order the Rolls-Royce for the Wilsons.[76]

Arranging a pension for the ex-president was a more delicate matter. Dodge and Jones exchanged several more letters about funding an annual cash gift and how the president should be informed. Dodge wrote Jones, "Unless you think otherwise, I will write to Mrs. Wilson on the first of October and send her a check for $2,500 [$31,000], as a quarterly amount, telling her that I understand she will explain to Mr. Wilson that three or four of his friends are helping them out on their finances."[77] Jones, writing to Dodge with a copy to Axson, agreed that a $10,000 ($125,000) annual pension was the best course of action and offered to pay any portion that was not picked up by the two other possible benefactors, Cyrus McCormick Jr. and Thomas Jones (no relation to Jesse), who were, like Dodge, both Princeton classmates of Wilson's.[78] A grateful Axson wrote Jones, who was in New York inspecting his newest buildings, "It will be a wonderful thing for our friend to have this release from anxiety . . . I should think that Mr. Jones and Mr. McCormick would certainly want to join you and Mr. Dodge in this generous provision for their old classmate,

74. Stockton Axson to Jesse Jones, August 14, 1923, Jesse H. Jones Collection [LOC].
75. Cleveland Dodge to Jesse Jones, September 4, 1923, Jesse H. Jones Collection [LOC].
76. Jesse Jones to Cary Grayson, September 20, 1923, Jesse H. Jones Collection [LOC].
77. Cleveland Dodge to Jesse Jones, September 25, 1923, Jesse H. Jones Collection [LOC].
78. Jesse Jones to Cleveland Dodge, September 26, 1923, Jesse H. Jones Collection [LOC].

but I cannot forget that the man who started the machinery going this summer was not a classmate, but a much younger man whose friendship dates much less far back than that of the others. In short, you have been *wonderful* about this whole business."[79]

Edith Wilson was grateful as well, writing Jones, "Our dear friend, the Dr. [Grayson], has told me of all the wonderful things you have planned, and thought of, as evidences of your affection and friendship for my dear husband—and I just can't deny myself the pleasure of thanking you." She continued, "It is all so consistent with what we know you to be, and when he knows of your thought, it will mean everything to know the affection and appreciation it represents." She went on, "I wish I knew how to give you a fuller evidence of gratitude, but know you understand." She closed the letter, "Please give my love to Mrs. Jones and tell her I am having such pleasure in my tapestry work." She added, "We hope it will not be long before you are both again in Washington and then I can say some of the things I have tried to write."[80]

Jones, Axson, and Dodge continued to correspond about the best way to present the gift to the proud ex-president, conferring with Grayson and exchanging multiple drafts among themselves. Jones suggested to Axson that they send Wilson "a letter explaining to him just who—and only who—knows about it, and [that] our reasons for doing it is not because he needs any money, but purely as a slight token, or reward, for services well and generously rendered." Axson was still recuperating in the Catskills and Jones added, "You must not permit yourself to let go, or to despair, and let me know when you will be here, and we would love the best in the world to have you dine with us, go to the theater, ride in the country, go motoring, or anything in fact you can think of. I myself need a little recreation. I am all out of sorts, ill-tempered, nervous, and probably should be ducked in the Hudson River until I learn how to try not to do everything."[81]

Dodge and Jones decided to present the pension directly to Wilson instead of through Edith, and on October 1, 1923, the two men mailed a letter to Wilson that said in part, "We have created a trust that will provide an income to you, throughout the remainder of your life, of ten thousand dollars a year, and though we are prompted by our love and admiration for you, the trust is in fact intended as a slight material reward for your

79. Stockton Axson to Jesse Jones, September 27, 1923, Jesse H. Jones Collection [LOC].
80. Edith Wilson to Jesse Jones, September 28, 1923, Jesse H. Jones Collection [LOC].
81. Jesse Jones to Stockton Axson, September 28, 1923, Jesse H. Jones Collection [LOC].

great service to the world."[82] Jones and Dodge also sent individual letters. In his, Jones reassured Wilson, "It is not our intention or desire that there be any publicity or public record regarding it, and unless advised to the contrary, payments will be sent to you at your Washington address quarterly by Mr. Dodge."[83] Jones also sent a telegram to Grayson and asked him to "drop by S Street Wednesday morning after the mail has been delivered" and to wire him after his visit as to Wilson's reaction.[84]

Wilson wrote Jones, "My dear Friend, I must admit that I am quite overwhelmed by the wonderful kindness and generosity of which the letter signed by you and Dodge informs me." He continued, "I cannot for a moment consider myself worthy of such friendship or of such benefits. I can only hope that they will inspire me for the services that lie ahead of us in the redemption of the country from the ignoble position into which it has been drawn by ignorant and unprincipled partisans." He closed, "I will not attempt to express my gratitude to you and those with whom you are associated in an ideal act of confidence and friendship. I know of no words that would be adequate but let me say at least that I am deeply proud that such men should think me worthy of such benefits."[85]

In the end, Dodge agreed to give $5,000 ($62,500) toward the annual $10,000 ($125,000) fund. Jones donated $2,500 ($31,250), and Thomas Jones and Cyrus McCormick each put in $1,250 ($15,625). The four-paragraph, one-page memorandum they all signed said, "We are doing in part only what we think Congress should do for all retiring presidents, and are prompted by our sense of fairness and justice to this great man for his patriotic and unselfish life, and also by the possibility that in devoting his life to education, statesmanship, and politics, he may not have laid aside sufficient savings to provide himself properly with the reasonable necessities and comfort which he so richly deserves."[86]

Wilson enjoyed long car rides and took almost daily excursions through the mountains of Virginia and Maryland, earlier for relief from the pressure of office while president, and now from the tedium of retirement and incapacitation. When he asked for his car on December 28—his sixty-seventh birthday—a new Rolls-Royce pulled up to his front door.

82. Jesse Jones and Cleveland Dodge to Woodrow Wilson, October 1, 1923, Jesse H. Jones Collection [LOC].

83. Jesse Jones to Woodrow Wilson, October 2, 1923, Jesse H. Jones Collection [LOC].

84. Jesse Jones to Cary Grayson, October 2, 1923, Jesse H. Jones Collection [LOC].

85. Woodrow Wilson to Jesse Jones, October 4, 1923, Jesse H. Jones Collection [LOC].

86. Memorandum signed by Cleveland Dodge, Jesse Jones, Thomas D. Jones, and Cyrus McCormick Jr., October 1, 1923, Jesse H. Jones Collection [HE].

Newspaper reports said that "Mrs. Wilson had been in on the secret" and that the car "had been purchased by anonymous donors through a third party."[87] The third party, of course, was Grayson, and the anonymous donors were the same four gentlemen who provided Wilson with his pension. On the day Wilson received his Rolls-Royce, Dodge wrote Jones, "Our little trust, therefore, is finally completed, and we all owe a great debt of gratitude to you for your initiative in this delightful arrangement."[88]

Wilson later wrote Jones, "The check which I have just received from Cleve Dodge again makes me vividly conscious of the extraordinary privilege I enjoy in having such friends as you and he and the others of the little group who have so generously and so thoughtfully relieved Mrs. Wilson and me of pecuniary anxieties. He also writes me that you have joined with the others in the gift of the beautiful car which I received on my birthday." Wilson continued, "There are no adequate words in which I can express my feeling in this matter. I can only trust that as the years go by I may have many opportunities of making you conscious of my deep affection, trust and gratitude."[89]

Jones replied, "I have never done anything that gives me the enjoyment and satisfaction I get and shall always have from my participation in the 'Woodrow Wilson Personal Trust.' It is a rare privilege you have given me and the other three gentlemen with whom I have the honor to be associated in this matter, and I am perfectly sure that neither of us will ever again have an opportunity to do a thing that will afford us as much pleasure, or that we will take as much pride in doing."[90]

Three and a half weeks later, on February 3, 1924, Wilson died at home on S Street with Grayson and Edith Wilson at his side. On the day Wilson died, Jones wired heartfelt condolences to Axson, Grayson, and Edith Wilson. He also wired President Coolidge and suggested that Wilson "be laid to rest in Arlington by the side of his comrade at arms, the Unknown Soldier."[91] Edith arranged a short service at her home before the service at the Washington National Cathedral, where Jones had agreed to be one of the pallbearers. The Coolidges accepted the invitations to both, but Edith stiffly "disinvited" Lodge who had opposed and defeated the League of Nations after Wilson refused to accept his compromises to its charter. She wrote to the senator, "I note in the papers that you have been

87. Unknown newspaper clipping, December 28, 1923, Jesse H. Jones Collection [LOC].
88. Cleveland Dodge to Jesse Jones, December 28, 1923, Jesse H. Jones Collection [LOC].
89. Woodrow Wilson to Jesse Jones, January 4, 1924, Jesse H. Jones Collection [LOC].
90. Jesse Jones to Woodrow Wilson, January 9, 1924, Jesse H. Jones Collection [LOC].
91. Jesse Jones to Calvin Coolidge, February 3, 1924, Jesse H. Jones Collection [LOC].

designated by the Senate of the United States as one of those to attend the funeral service of Mr. Wilson." She continued, "As the funeral is a private and not an official one, and realizing that your presence there would be embarrassing to you and unwelcome to me, I write to request that you do not attend."[92] The president, at the family's request, was laid to rest in the Washington National Cathedral.

The four benefactors agreed to make the April and June payments of the Woodrow Wilson Trust to Edith, thinking that her interest in a family jewelry business and a pending pension from Congress would sustain her. Although their generosity benefited the president for only a matter of months, the four benefactors had no regrets. Dodge wrote Jones, "I can never cease rejoicing that we arranged our trust when we did and made the last few months of the dear man's life so much happier, although it was a costly gift. I am especially glad that we gave him that fine Rolls-Royce."[93] The newspaper photographs taken just six weeks before of Wilson riding in his new car on his birthday were the last ever taken of the president.[94]

Jones wrote Dodge and assured him that he would be glad to assist Edith "from time to time, or at any time there might be a pinch." He said, "I had such reverence for Mr. Wilson, and have such pride in his memory, that I would like to assist in his absence, if assistance is needed, those dependent upon him." Jones also told Dodge that he had advised Grayson and Edith not to make any kind of request to Congress for a pension. Rather, he said, "Congress should, without a dissenting voice, vote a pension to every ex-president's widow, just as it should vote a pension to every ex-president, but Congress does not always do what it should."[95]

92. Edith Wilson to Henry Cabot Lodge, February 4, 1924, Jesse H. Jones Collection [Rice].

93. Cleveland Dodge to Jesse Jones, February 17, 1924, Jesse H. Jones Collection [LOC].

94. *Rolls-Royce Quarterly* (Winter 1924), Jesse H. Jones Collection [LOC].

95. Jesse Jones to Cleveland Dodge, March 1, 1924, Jesse H. Jones Collection [LOC].

1924-1928

◈

Draped and Drowned in Decorations

IN THE 1920 ELECTION, voters repudiated the Democrats' and Woodrow Wilson's internationalism and moral fervor. Warren G. Harding and Calvin Coolidge trounced James Cox and Franklin Roosevelt. The Republicans also won a twenty-two-seat majority in the Senate and a 167-seat majority in the House.[1] In the midterm election, the Republican majority in the House shrank to twenty, and in the Senate to ten.[2] As the 1924 national election approached, the Democrats figured they would ride the Teapot Dome scandal to victory. Albert Fall, Harding's Secretary of the Interior and card-playing crony, had taken bribes in exchange for drilling rights to federal oil reserves at Elk Hills in California and Teapot Dome in Wyoming. Before the full force of the scandal became apparent and understood, however, Harding died in office on August 2, 1923.

Coolidge was now president, taking the oath of office on his mother's Bible in a room lit by an oil lamp at his farm in Vermont. Known as "Silent Cal," Coolidge said as little as possible; he thought campaigning for votes was undignified and inappropriate. His morally upright persona and the preceding two years of prosperity promised to trump the Teapot Dome

---

1. Shields-West, *Almanac of Presidential Campaigns,* 214.
2. Timmons, *Jones: Man and Statesman,* 128.

scandal, and at the 1924 Republican National Convention in Cleveland, Ohio, Coolidge was nominated for president on the first vote.[3] The convention was so uneventful, humorist Will Rogers said the city should "open up the churches to liven things up a bit."[4]

But it was exactly the opposite for the Democrats: their 1924 Convention took place at New York's Madison Square Garden during a heat wave. The party split between Woodrow Wilson's son-in-law—former Secretary of Treasury, William G. McAdoo—and New York Governor Alfred E. Smith. Smith appealed to the anti-prohibition ("wet") and anti-Klan contingent of the party, who lived primarily in the East and North. To appeal to voters from the South and West, McAdoo skirted the Ku Klux Klan issue and ran as a "dry" candidate.

Jones's front-row box at the convention signified his stature in the Democratic Party. It seated nine, cost $2,500 ($31,000 in current dollars) and was almost directly in front of the podium. Bernard Baruch's box was off to one side and Roosevelt's was down the way.[5] Jones invited Edith Wilson "to our box, if you care to look on."[6]

The Convention lasted from June 24 to July 9 and broke all records for speeches, votes cast, demonstrations, fistfights, and committee meetings. Neither McAdoo nor Smith could garner the votes needed to become the party's candidate for president and neither would bow to the other. Finally, on the 103rd ballot, John W. Davis was selected as the compromise candidate. Democrats would always refer to the debacle with words like "the disastrous convention of 1924." Disgusted with the Democratic choice, labor, farmers, and socialists resurrected the Progressive Party and chose Robert M. LaFollette as their candidate.[7]

Two days after the exhausting convention, the Joneses were ready to sail to Europe aboard the *Leviathan*. Their bags were headed for the ship, but before they left their hotel, Clem Shaver, whom Davis had selected to run his campaign, phoned to ask Jones to serve as finance chairman of the Democratic National Committee. Jones politely declined and explained he was about to board a ship for Europe.[8] Then Davis got on the phone.

Davis had helped draft the Versailles Treaty, served in the House of Representatives and as Solicitor General and, most recently, as ambassa-

3. Shields-West, *Almanac of Presidential Campaigns*, 162–63.
4. Ibid., 219.
5. A. B. Jones to Jesse Jones, June 5, 1924, Jesse H. Jones Collection [LOC].
6. Jesse Jones to Edith Wilson, June 13, 1924, Jesse H. Jones Collection [LOC].
7. Shields-West, *Almanac of Presidential Campaigns*, 220.
8. Timmons, *Jones: Man and Statesman*, 135.

dor to Great Britain.[9] He was impossible to turn down. Jones knew the party was divided, deep in debt, and had little chance of winning the election, which was only five months away. After Davis promised Jones that Bernard Baruch would contribute at least $120,000 ($1.5 million) to get the campaign started, Jones canceled the trip, got his bags off the ship, and set up office in the Democratic Party's headquarters at the Belmont Hotel in New York.

Jones recalled, "I raised money with difficulty for there was a general feeling that we were in a losing fight, that the Democratic Party had assured the election of Calvin Coolidge by its bad convention behavior."[10] Jones solicited contributions from his friends in Wilson's administration. He and financier Thomas Fortune Ryan, each contributed $50,000 ($622,000). Baruch's unexpectedly small contribution—and criticism of the campaign after he returned from a summer hunt in Scotland— provoked an uncharacteristically harsh letter from Jones. Out of exhaustion, frustration, or anger, Jones pointed out "the power and prominence throughout the world" Baruch enjoyed was because of his selection by Wilson as chairman of the War Industries Board during World War I. He wrote, "Baruch, chairman of the War Industries Board, the man of power during those critical days, got a place which makes it possible for him to go far afield in any direction he wants to go. That you should be willing to withhold your means from the Committee, which is exerting every possible effort at its command to elect . . . John W. Davis, is impossible for me to comprehend." Jones confided, "I confess that your attitude greatly depressed me . . . God knows I did not want this thankless task and reluctantly accepted it . . . To have refused would have been a refusal to serve my party and my country in what I regard a critical situation, for if our Government is to endure, we must meet present-day conditions with so-called liberal policies in our national Government."[11]

Baruch sent a long response ten days later. Instead of "My dear Jones" from days gone by, he started with "Dear Sir" and continued, "I am amazed and hurt at the intemperateness of tone and recklessness of statement contained in your letter . . ." He told Jones that he had promised Davis $120,000, with the open-ended provision that "the money be spent wisely and not foolishly." So far, he had donated only $25,000 ($311,000) of his original pledge. He closed, "Further correspondence with you on this

9. Shields-West, *Almanac of Presidential Campaigns*, 159.
10. Timmons, *Jones: Man and Statesman*, 138.
11. Jesse Jones to Bernard Baruch, October 1, 1924, Jesse H. Jones Collection [LOC].

subject would be fruitless and irritating."[12] This would not be the last time the two men butted heads.

During the election, internationalism, Prohibition, immigration, the Klan, economic prosperity, and the role of government were all issues. Davis summed up positions on government's role and the age-old divide between the major parties when he said, "The democratic party stands for the position that law and government policy should encourage the distribution of wealth with all proper regard for the toil of the men who produce it; the republican party, for the doctrine that if we turn the major portion of that wealth to a competent few, they will themselves distribute it for the benefit of the many."[13] For the second time in a row, the Democrats lost: Coolidge received fifty-four percent of the popular vote, Davis received twenty-nine percent, and LaFollette got seventeen percent. The day after the election, within the first fifteen minutes of the opening bell, the stock market enjoyed a "sharp upturn" on heavy trading of more than 100,000 shares.[14] Roosevelt, who had nominated Smith at the convention, said at the Belmont Hotel, "On the basis of returns we have received, I believe the party is defeated. But there are men in this room tonight who will live to see the Democratic Party in power again."[15]

Jones was left to pay the bills. The campaign cost the Democratic National Committee $1.1 million ($13.7 million)—and it was $300,000 ($3.7 million) in the hole. Jones sent letters to the Committee's leading members and detailed the party's income, expenses, and prospects. He said that the Party "has had many vicissitudes in its more than 130 years of existence, but always comes back to serve and save our country. The call will come again and we must be ready." He also helped initiate a sea change by adding, "The custom of waiting until after the nomination of our presidential candidates to start organizing places the party at too great disadvantage."[16]

Unaccustomed to defeat, Jones wrote Davis, "I regret having done so poorly the task assigned to me in your campaign for the presidency; hindrances and obstacles are no excuse for failure in an undertaking no more complex than mine was." Nonetheless, he said he would look back on the experience "with satisfaction and pleasure" and he was determined

12. Bernard Baruch to Jesse Jones, October 10, 1924, Jesse H. Jones Collection [LOC].
13. *Houston Chronicle,* October 28, 1924.
14. *Houston Chronicle,* November 5, 1924.
15. Timmons, *Jones: Man and Statesman,* 139.
16. Jesse Jones to William A. Comstock, November 18, 1924, Jesse H. Jones Collection [LOC].

to fix the "hindrances and obstacles" and to push the party forward.[17] In another solicitation, Jones insisted that instead of shutting down until the next election, the Democratic National Committee needed to raise $30,000 ($370,000) to "maintain its organization and headquarters at Washington during the next twelve months." As yet unaware that fundraising and campaigning would become year-round, non-stop operations, he reiterated, "The custom of waiting until after our presidential nomination to start organizing for the campaign places our party at too great disadvantage, and if we are to succeed at the polls, we must perfect our organization and keep it fully alive." True to form, he added, "I regard it necessary that Democrats perfect and maintain party organization on a sound business basis."[18]

Roosevelt agreed with Jones and sent letters to every convention delegate asking for suggestions of how the national party could be improved. After adapting to paralysis from polio in 1921, Roosevelt was once again on the ascent in the Party. He had served as undersecretary of the Navy during World War I, had been the party's candidate for vice president in 1920, and had recently grabbed everyone's attention and admiration at the chaotic 1924 convention when, with the help of his son James and a crutch, he made his way to the podium to nominate Smith, the "Happy Warrior," for president.[19]

Roosevelt wrote that he assumed everyone agreed "on certain fundamental truths" about the needs and direction of the Party. The first "fundamental truth" he declared was, "The national committee or its executive machinery should function every day in every year and not merely in presidential election years." He also argued for cooperation between state and national organizations, operating on a businesslike basis, increasing publicity, and meeting more frequently. Roosevelt continued, "We [need to] stop wasting time in booming or opposing this man or that for a nomination four years away . . ." If instead the party devotes itself to "presenting our own logical and progressive program, we shall gain the confidence of the country and find it far easier to choose a representative and successful ticket when the time comes."[20] Jones and Roosevelt were changing the nature and length of political campaigns—and beginning an important relationship.

17. Jesse Jones to John W. Davis, November 19, 1924, Jesse H. Jones Collection [LOC].
18. Jesse Jones to the Democratic National Committee, December 4, 1924, Jesse H. Jones Collection [LOC].
19. Alter, *Defining Moment*, 58.
20. Franklin Roosevelt to W. B. Ross, December 5, 1924, Jesse H. Jones Collection [LOC].

But other close relationships were ending for Jones. Among the many personal bonds in his life, his relationship with Aunt Nancy was one of the deepest and dearest. Hardly a letter passed between Jones and a relative that did not include something about her. For instance, his brother-in-law, Congressman Daniel Garrett, wrote to Jones about some big political figures in Washington, then closed by saying Jones's sister Ida "reported Aunt Nancy's condition was much improved for the past week."[21] And in the last sentence in a long telegram about leases and land deals, his brother, John, included a report on Aunt Nancy's health and activities.[22]

Jones's aunt had earlier moved from her bungalow in the Edgewood subdivision to an apartment in the Rice Hotel. This caring woman, born twenty-five years before the Civil War in rural Tennessee, had lived to see the nephew she raised as her own child since he was six, build a city and walk with presidents. Jones visited her every day when he was in town and was at her side, holding her hand, when she passed away on April 23, 1925.[23]

M. E. Foster, publisher of the *Houston Chronicle*, would soon leave Jones's immediate orbit, too, over editorial differences. Miriam Amanda ("Ma") Ferguson was elected governor of Texas in 1924. Her husband had been impeached in 1917 during his second term as governor. Miriam was a housewife with two daughters and since her initials spelled "Ma," handlers decided it was perfect for an aspiring Texas governor. Fifteen days after Nellie Ross was inaugurated as Wisconsin's governor, "Ma" Ferguson became the second woman in the United States to hold a state's top office.

It was understood that "Ma" would do as her husband advised, and she also opposed new liquor regulations and condemned the Klan, pushing for legislation to ban masks that hid Klan members' faces at rallies. "Ma" and "Pa" Ferguson were eventually accused of taking bribes for highway contracts and favoring relatives and friends with government business.[24] For this reason, the *Houston Chronicle* editorial board and Jones opposed the Ferguson administration, but Foster continued to support "Ma" because of her opposition to the Klan. Judge W. O. Huggins, the *Houston*

---

21. Daniel Garrett to Jesse Jones, November 21, 1923, Jesse H. Jones Collection [LOC].
22. John T. Jones Sr. to Jesse Jones, February 14, 1921, Jesse H. Jones Collection [HE].
23. *Robertson County Times*, April 23, 1925.
24. *New Handbook of Texas*, 981.

Chronicle's chief legal counsel, corresponded with Jones via coded telegrams about the situation at the paper.

After Jones and Huggins pleaded unsuccessfully with Foster to change the paper's position, Jones wrote him a long letter, revealing a bit of his political and personal philosophy: "I wish you could have been an advocate of the public's interest rather than one of Ferguson['s] political fortunes . . . When people run amok with the social, criminal, and civil laws of the land, public opinion rises up to stop them, and public opinion is a stronger law than any written in the statute books." He qualified his criticism, "It is our first trial with a woman governor and woman suffrage has found ready acceptance in Texas . . . I am just as anxious to see the Fergusons succeed in their administration as you can possibly be. I entertain no ill will for either of them. For that matter, I entertain ill will for very few people, if any at all. Hatred is a great destroyer and has no reward."[25]

Jones went on, "With regard to the policies of the *Chronicle*, I believe that I have interfered as little with your management as would be possible for any man owning the controlling shares . . . But when it comes to the point of your defending rather than condemning such flagrant wrongdoings, and . . . when I have asked . . . that you adopt a different policy, and you send me word that regardless of the consequences . . . you will proceed in the matter in your own way, such an attitude . . . is neither friendly nor fair . . ." Jones then demanded that Foster hold monthly meetings with the board of directors and "submit for discussion all important matters affecting the paper, its business as well as editorial policy."[26]

Even as Jones was grieving over Aunt Nancy, arguing with Foster, and helping to reform the Democratic Party, his buildings were opening in New York, Houston, and Fort Worth. His first New York building was a co-op apartment building at Fifth Avenue and 79th, where units sold quickly for between $9,000 ($109,000) and $37,000 ($450,000).[27]

Jones never did anything halfway. After completing the Mayfair House at Park Avenue and 65th, he advertised its apartments in a heavily illustrated, beautifully bound booklet that addressed itself "To people who are living in luxury and dying of responsibility." The hotel was promoted as the "sort of house that will look after you when you are in town and

25. Jesse Jones to M. E. Foster, November 17, 1925, Jesse H. Jones Collection [HE].
26. Ibid.
27. Sales contracts for 1158 Fifth Avenue, June 15, 1924, and May 28, 1926, Jesse H. Jones Collection [HE].

In 1925 Jesse Jones built the full-service Mayfair House apartment and hotel on Park Avenue and 65th Street in New York City to serve "people who are living in luxury and dying of responsibility" (Mayfair House marketing brochure, Jesse H. Jones Collection).

look after itself when you are not," and promised to be "a harmonious addition to the architectural splendors of Park Avenue apartments and private homes." The one- to six-room suites would be rented at rates that would be "consistent with advantages."[28] The Mayfair's land, construction, decoration, and furnishings cost $3,444,000 ($42 million).

As soon as Jones had a building up and running, he mortgaged it and used the proceeds to build another. His next New York building sat across from J. Pierpont Morgan's home in the Murray Hill section. The Morgans had opposed the intrusion of "business buildings" in their neighborhood of four-story brick houses, but Jones persisted. After he purchased the block at 36th and Madison Avenue from Lord Astor's estate and submitted plans for Morgan's approval, he proceeded to build New York's third tallest building, a twenty-nine-story wedding-cake

28. Mayfair House marketing brochure, Jesse H. Jones Collection [HE].

structure at 200 Madison Avenue.[29] Marshall Field's first store outside of Chicago was located on the first four floors, and offices occupied the rest. The block-long lobby featured a vaulted ceiling with gold-leaf medallions in relief plaster, and deep blue, red, and yellow terrazzo and marble on the walls and floors.[30] The $11 million ($136 million) building also was home to Houston Properties Corporation, which Jones created to manage his New York operations.

Growth of the same intensity was happening in Houston. The Houston Ship Channel had been dredged from twenty-five to thirty feet, allowing larger ships carrying more cargo to use the channel, which further increased business throughout town.[31] Just as Jones had predicted, enormous cotton warehouses, compresses, and terminals sprang up on the channel. Houston was becoming the largest exporter of ginned cotton in the world.[32] Meanwhile, gushers erupted and new record-breaking oil fields continued to produce around the city. Public spending also increased: ten new schools were under construction—seven for white children and three for blacks[33]—and the City Auditorium, built in 1910, was about to undergo a $300,000 ($3.7 million) facelift. More and more people moved to Houston, got jobs, and spent money. There would soon be twenty-one banks in town instead of the four Jones found when he arrived almost thirty years before.[34] For his own part, Jones added a third wing to the Rice Hotel, built a ten-story addition to the Electric Building, and started the sixteen-story Kirby Lumber Company Building and Kirby Theater on the ninth block of Main.

Fort Worth was another Jones target for major construction. The $2 million ($24 million) eighteen-story Medical Arts Building included a then-novel "private passage for ambulance service leading direct to elevators" and an agreement with the tenants to allow only those approved by the local medical and dental associations.[35] Jones also broke ground on the twenty-two-story Worth Hotel and Worth Theater. As he explained to a representative from the Publix Theatre chain, "The Worth Hotel was prominent in Fort Worth for a generation until it was torn down for The Texas, and we thought, [with Fort Worth] being more a western or frontier

29. *Houston Chronicle*, December 18, 1924.
30. *Architecture and Buildings* (July 1926): plates 136–42 [HE].
31. *Houston Chronicle*, July 21, 1923.
32. Buenger and Pratt, *But Also Good Business*, 65.
33. *Houston Chronicle*, October 26, 1924.
34. Buenger and Pratt, *But Also Good Business*, 8.
35. *Houston Chronicle*, June 10, 1926.

town, at least more so than Dallas or Houston, that we would revive this old name."[36] John Jones oversaw the Fort Worth building programs for his brother.

Jones had clearly established himself as a preeminent businessman, "city builder," civic leader, and public servant. Philanthropy, with a tilt toward education, now began to emerge as a larger part of an already full life. From the beginning of their marriage, Jesse and Mary had made generous donations to charities that helped improve and enhance life in their community. These values showed in the thirty-odd organizations they supported in one year: $5,000 ($62,000) to the Houston Community Chest; $5,000 ($62,000) to the fledgling Museum of Fine Arts, Houston; $2,500 ($36,000) to the Methodist Hospital; $750 ($9,300) to the Dickson Colored Orphanage; and $100 ($1,240) to the Texas League of Women Voters, among others.[37] Jones also sent many $50 ($620) and $100 ($1,240) gifts throughout the year to assist friends and family back in Tennessee.

The Joneses' largest donations went to education. When he was asked for a contribution toward a new stadium at the University of Texas at Austin, Jones responded with a $1,000 ($12,400) check and a typically long letter to the two students who had made the request. He wrote, "Our great educational institutions must have their tracks, courts, gymnasiums, stadiums, and other facilities for developing the physical and combative ambitions of our young people." Jones revealed, "My own educational training was decidedly limited, and I have keenly felt it a great handicap, and when I can do so, [I] am glad to assist other ambitious young men and women in equipping themselves for life's problems with a college training." He said that he felt the university and the state's educational institutions in general "have been threatened with political invasion" and wanted to "add what influence I may have . . . to remove . . . the possibility of political interference or dominance." Sounding very Wilsonian, Jones closed, "I commend . . . your efforts to build a stadium, but wish to impress upon you that your greater responsibility is in preserving the integrity of the University, and in keeping the faculty free from political dominance and encouraged to perform their duties and responsibilities uninfluenced by fear or favor."[38]

Jones was more interested in scholastics and students than stadiums.

36. Jesse Jones to Harold B. Franklin, November 6, 1926, Jesse H. Jones Collection [HE].

37. Jesse Jones 1924 tax return, Jesse H. Jones Collection [HE].

38. Jesse Jones to M. Hogg and R. Dickson, June 13, 1924, Jesse H. Jones Collection [HE].

When he was approached to help an endowment fund for Southwestern University—a small, private college in Georgetown, Texas—Jones pledged $25,000 ($312,000). In a telegram to lumber magnate John Kirby, he declared, "I have heretofore promised twenty-five thousand, and am willing to double the amount, making a total of fifty thousand, if you and Jim West will join for an equal amount." He said, "I do not believe that we can do any more good with the same amount of money than to help perpetuate Southwestern University."[39]

Two years later, Southwestern bestowed upon Jones his first honorary degree, citing his "distinguished service to the nation and the State of Texas in the world of business and politics" and his "great interest in humanity." Up to now, Jones had offered only brief, sometimes awkward remarks at banquets attended by his business colleagues and other civic leaders. For the graduation ceremony, however, he delivered his first major public address titled "Elements of Success" and detailed for the class of 1925 what he thought it took to succeed in life.

The first requirement was "high moral character." Jones explained, "It can be truthfully said that the whole fabric of our society depends upon the moral strength of our citizenship. Wealth, political power, knowledge, learning—all come to ultimate ruin and disgrace unless supported by true moral stamina." He said, ". . . never to compromise with truth and honor." The second element was "positiveness," as Jones declared, "You will never succeed by don'ts and can'ts . . . It takes vision, faith, and courage to say, 'Yes.'" He added, "The word 'can't' should be abolished." He listed "industry" as the third "great element of success" and suggested that "you will be happiest when are you are busiest" because "We do best and succeed most in doing those things we love to do."[40]

Jones encouraged the graduates to profit by their mistakes and to "recognize and grasp opportunity." He acknowledged that "in times past . . . opportunities were given to the men only, and women by law and custom were not allowed to share in them. All of this is changed now . . . Women are succeeding today as lawyers, doctors, lecturers, authors, and in a thousand ways in the industrial world."[41]

Jones concluded with, "I want especially to emphasize humility, charity, and service as essential to greatness. No person can be a really great person who has not charity in his heart in the greatest abundance and

39. Jesse Jones to John Kirby, September 26, 1923, Jesse H. Jones Collection [HE].
40. Timmons, *Jones: Man and Statesman*, 140.
41. Ibid.

who is not truly humble. Humility is a rare gift, and if it is not ours by nature, we should cultivate it. And it is in service that you will grow the greatest . . . Service to our country in time of war is easy to render . . . It nevertheless remains that the responsibilities of citizenship are as great in time of peace as in time of war."[42]

Back in Houston, Jones's charity toward Foster, however, had run out. "Ma" Ferguson had announced for reelection and Foster endorsed her candidacy. Jones finally had had enough and offered to buy Foster's half of the paper. On June 25, 1926, the front-page *Chronicle* headline read, "Changes in Management of Chronicle Announced, Jesse H. Jones Buys Stock of M. E. Foster." Foster received $162,500 ($1.95 million) in cash, $500,000 ($6 million) in Chronicle Building Company bonds, and an annual salary of $20,000 ($240,000) to serve as president of the paper and write columns for "so long as he and Jones agree for him to continue in the *Chronicle*'s employment."[43] That last part of the arrangement did not last long.

Franklin Roosevelt sent Jones a letter of congratulations that rhetorically asked, "Will you let me tell you of my pleasure at the announcement of your purchase of the '*Houston Chronicle*'?" His real intention, however, was to clear up something. He wrote, "I heard in a round about way the other day that you had given out some kind of a statement about democratic finances in which you took me to task for something." Jones had been reported as saying that, unlike Roosevelt, he thought it was okay to rely on large donors to clean up old debt. Roosevelt continued that he was "opposed to public dissensions among individual democrats at a time like this when people of the same political faith should work together."[44] The Democratic Party was widely seen as "flat on its back," and after Shaver, chairman of the National Committee, Jones was in charge.[45] Roosevelt now made his intended point: "I have been opposed in principle to the collection of democratic funds . . . from a mere handful of very rich or moderately rich gentlemen, and, as you know, I think that other means should at least be tried . . ." He conceded, "In spite of all this . . . you are to be most heartily congratulated in actually raising the full amount of the debt of the National Committee, so that from now on we can start with a clean sheet."[46]

42. Ibid.
43. *Houston Chronicle*, June 25, 1926.
44. Franklin Roosevelt to Jesse Jones, July 7, 1926, Jesse H. Jones Collection [LOC].
45. *Houston Chronicle*, December 27, 1924.
46. Franklin Roosevelt to Jesse Jones, July 7, 1926, Jesse H. Jones Collection [LOC].

Jones thanked Roosevelt for his good wishes and, perpetuating the public version, explained that Foster "wanted to retire . . ." He said that the *Chronicle* "is a really fine paper and successful on its own. It has had many fights about men and measures, losing some and winning some, but getting stronger all the time. Its most serious and determined fight was on the Klan, and all of our lives were threatened at intervals during that period."[47]

Getting down to business, Jones told Roosevelt that he had said nothing "in any sense critical or derogatory" about him and that "somebody has been inspiring stories . . . about our party finances, its deficit, Shaver, my methods of meeting the deficit, etc." With foresight into Roosevelt's political future, he continued, "I certainly am not finding any fault whatever with you, my good friend. As a matter of fact, I regard you [as] one of the best assets of our party . . . and it is my sincere wish . . . that your health would so improve that you could take a much more active part in our national party affairs." He argued, "I can see no possible harm to come from patriotic democrats giving substantial amounts to pay for stale water long since over the dam . . . We have yet quite a considerable amount to raise to clear the slate before 1928." Jones wanted to start the 1928 campaign debt free and, if possible, with money in the bank. He said he was "considering putting on a campaign to raise the money in small amounts," but was skeptical about the success of that method.[48]

Jones had no doubts, however, about Houston's success. At the end of August 1926, the Texas boomtown led all southern cities in building contracts; Atlanta was second, and New Orleans was third. There was still an insufficient supply of money in local banks to fund the more than $36 million ($432 million) in construction contracts, so developers like Jones still relied on northern and eastern bankers to finance major projects.

Industrial development along the Ship Channel accounted for most of Houston's construction, but Jones had made a mighty contribution, too. Before demolishing them, he first tested the structural integrity of the two-story buildings that remained on the seventh block of Main, next to his new Bankers Mortgage Building, to see if floors could be added to them. He also demolished his Main Street lumberyard in the tenth block, moved its operations to the east side of town, and tore down the remaining small buildings next to where the lumberyard had stood. Jones swept

47. Jesse Jones to Franklin Roosevelt, July 8, 1926, Jesse H. Jones Collection [LOC].
48. Ibid.

the block clean and started over with plans to erect two huge hotels and Houston's most elaborate movie theaters in their place.

On Christmas Day 1926, Jones's Metropolitan Theater, "a vision of ancient Egypt . . . transplanted to the heart of Houston," opened where the lumberyard once stood.[49] The 2,500-seat theater looked like the inside of an Egyptian tomb. Enormous murals of kings, queens, sphinxes, and chariot races covered the walls. Colorful mosaic tiles resplendently wrapped drinking fountains, doorways, and massive carved columns. Over the stage, a mythical bird with outstretched wings the width of the movie screen watched over the audience. After a trumpet fanfare, "followed by deep notes from the mighty-voice Wurlitzer organ," mobs poured into the Metropolitan Theater.[50] Before the feature film, *Stranded in Paris*, starring Bebe Daniels—who coincidentally was born in Texas— wowed Houstonians hooted at stand-up comedians and a violinist who fiddled while dancing the Charleston.[51]

Jones leased the Metropolitan to the Publix Theatre Corporation, a division of Famous Players-Lasky, which was founded by Adolph Zukor. Marcus Loew, Samuel Goldwyn, and Cecil B. DeMille were Zukor's partners. They produced movies through Paramount Studios and owned, leased, and operated theaters through Publix. Stage shows from New York were sent out to tour all theaters in the chain, so a new show arrived in Houston each week with music, dancing, and lavish sets. Large theaters no longer needed to employ local talent.

In Fort Worth, Jones opened the eighteen-story, 300-room Worth Hotel and adjoining 2,500-seat Worth Theater, which were also operated by Publix. According to the *Houston Chronicle*, "Every room in the hotel has a bath, a large ceiling fan, and circulating ice water."[52] John Jones reported, "Opened the Worth Saturday and it is up to our expectation in every way."[53] The theater and hotel were expected to generate $536,000 ($6.6 million) each year and return $265,000 ($3.2 million) after taxes.[54]

Amon Carter, one Fort Worth's most influential and powerful citizens, owned and published the Fort Worth *Star-Telegram*, established WBAP—the city's first radio station—and was part owner of the fledgling

49. *Houston Chronicle*, December 24, 1926.
50. *Houston Chronicle*, December 26, 1926.
51. *Houston Chronicle*, December 25, 1926.
52. *Houston Chronicle*, November 27, 1927.
53. John T. Jones Sr. to Jesse Jones, September 27, 1927, Jesse H. Jones Collection [HE].
54. Undated financial statement, Worth Hotel and Theatre, Jesse H. Jones Collection [HE].

Jesse Jones built many of Fort Worth's tallest buildings in the 1920s, including the Texas Electric Building and the Hollywood Theatre. Courtesy Houston Public Library.

American Airlines. Carter actively promoted Jones's building ventures in Fort Worth, which may be why Jones concentrated more on Fort Worth than on Dallas. Carter beseeched the president of the local electric company, "I figure that you will be the means of Fort Worth acquiring another large office building and theater," then listed all the reasons why he should "trade" with Jones. Carter wrote, "Personally, I feel that the city owes a debt of gratitude to Jesse Jones for his activity in this community. It is the first instance where we have had an outsider come in and do some actual development."[55] Carter was convincing. Eight months later,

55. Amon Carter to A. J. Duncan, March 17, 1927, Jesse H. Jones Collection [HE].

the front page of the Fort Worth *Star-Telegram* announced construction of "an 18-story office building on the northeast corner of West Seventh and Lamar Streets" for the Fort Worth Power & Light Corporation.[56] Jones relied on Carter to turn up potential tenants, writing, "If it comes easy for you to do a little scotching in that direction, will be much obliged."[57]

In Houston, Jones continued his huge hotel and theater project on Main and opened the Loew's State Theater next to the Metropolitan. The new theater equaled the Metropolitan in splendor, only the brocade wallpaper, classical statuary, and enormous crystal chandeliers gushed French Provincial instead of Egyptian tomb. The $18,500 ($227,000) pipe organ accompanied the silent films and filled the 2,500-seat theater with the rich sounds of tubas, drums, piccolos, castanets, Chinese gongs, sleigh bells, car horns, and "aeroplanes."[58] For generations, going to the Main Street theaters was an anticipated weekly event for many white Houstonians, particularly teenagers who would travel by bus to see the Saturday matinee and then go afterwards to D'Arcy's for ice cream or to James Coney Island for a hot dog and chili.

Jones filled up the block with two hotels and an office building, pushing the city's action farther south and away from the first four blocks of the central business district. A group formed to protest the lack of development there and promote construction, but the absence of tall buildings in the area today indicates that they failed.

On the other side of the Metropolitan Theater, Jones opened the Lamar Hotel, named for the second president of Texas when it was an independent nation. The Lamar offered accommodations for overnight guests and three- to nine-room apartments for long-term living. The Joneses never owned a conventional house and had spent their first six years of marriage at the Rice Hotel; now, the entire top floor of the Lamar became their new home. Renowned local architect John Staub remembered when Jones "called me on the phone and said, '[Alfred] Finn's doing the Lamar Hotel, but the whole top of the thing is just a concrete slab, and I want you to design me a house up there.'"[59] Their bedrooms, a small gymnasium, and a forty-by-forty-foot, pine-paneled living room faced Main. Granddaughter Audrey had her own room, next to Mary's. Screened terraces on both ends of the expanse across Main Street caught the damp Gulf Coast

56. Fort Worth *Star-Telegram*, November 12, 1927.
57. Jesse Jones to Amon Carter, December 1, 1927, Jesse H. Jones Collection [HE].
58. Contract, Houston Property Corporation and Robert Morton Organ Co., May 4, 1927, Jesse H. Jones Collection [HE].
59. Barnstone, *Architecture of John F. Staub*, 114.

Jesse Jones filled the entire tenth block of Main Street with the Lamar Hotel, the McKinney Hotel, the Metropolitan and Loew's Theaters, and Levy Brothers department store. Foley's, now Macy's, was built on the block to the left in the late 1940s. Courtesy Houston Public Library.

breeze and helped ventilate the spacious apartment. Staub remembered Jones once saying he built the beautiful new home so he could "properly entertain Mrs. Woodrow Wilson" if she came to town.[60] One could stand at the floor-to-ceiling windows and look out in every direction at Jones's empire of big buildings and at the growing city.[61]

60. Ibid., 116.
61. Timmons, *Jones: Man and Statesman,* 117.

In the spring of 1927, rumors, comments buried in newspaper articles, and feelers began to emerge about locations for the 1928 Republican and Democratic national political conventions. In May the *New York Herald* reported that Atlanta, Memphis, and Detroit were preparing to make bids. The article quoted Jones about Al Smith's lack of popularity in the South, primarily because he was wet and Catholic. Even so, according to Jones, the southern leadership felt "Smith would have a better chance of election than any other candidate." Toward the end of the article, the reporter casually noted, "Mr. Jones said Houston would make a bid for the national convention for that city."[62] Houston was hardly ever mentioned as a prospect again.

On January 12, 1928, the Democratic National Committee met at the Mayflower Hotel in Washington, D.C., to select the site for the June convention. Back then conventions were planned from start to finish within a matter of months. Detroit and San Francisco were the frontrunners, and each had a delegation that lobbied for days before the decision was to be made. Detroit eliminated itself by outraging Prohibitionists with a promotional booklet that promised orators with "dry" throats could find "relief" across the border. Dry Democrats knowingly objected, saying they refused to hold the convention in Canada.[63] Representatives of other interested cities, however, jostled for their allotted 15 minutes to make their case to the committee. No group was there to "boom" for Houston.

The din created by hundreds of delegates milling around made it almost impossible to hear, and shouts of "louder, louder" permeated the room. Then Jones rose to speak. "With his appearance," it was reported, "applause and then cheers rang out, and the committee rose as one to honor the huge Texan who had been a wheel horse of the democratic national organization ever since Colonel House first brought him into the circle of party leaders 15 years ago."[64]

Either Jones decided only the night before the meeting to make a bid,[65] or his strategy all along had been to remain silent and swoop in at the last minute. He personally offered $200,000 ($2.4 million) and, supposedly without their knowledge, declared, "On behalf of the Mayor and City Council, all of the civic bodies and all of the people of Houston, I respectfully extend a most cordial invitation to the Democratic National committee to

62. *New York Herald*, May 4, 1927.
63. *Houston Chronicle*, January 29, 1928.
64. *Houston, Chronicle*, January 13, 1928.
65. *New York Evening Post*, January 27, 1928.

hold its 1928 convention in Houston." He bragged about the 1,000-room Rice Hotel and the city's other hotels, attractions, and convention facilities.[66] He went on to reassure listeners, "Houston's temperature in June is very comfortable. It ranges from the 80s to the low 90s." According to a newspaper reporter, "Jones grinned and the delegates roared."[67]

When San Francisco upped its bid to $250,000 ($3.1 million), Jones reportedly tore up his first check, put a blank one on the table, signed it, and told party chairman Shaver to "fill it in for whatever it takes."[68] That did not actually happen, and Jones unsuccessfully tried to stop the story from spreading, telling reporters, "It was not a blank check. It was for $200,000. My phrase was that Houston's hospitality is a blank check and that it could be filled in for what the committee desired."[69]

To almost everyone's great surprise, after four ballots it was announced that Houston had been selected for the Democratic Party's convention, the first national convention held in the South since before the Civil War. The other cities had offered larger convention halls, better climates, and similar amounts of money, but more than anything else, Jones's stature in the Democratic Party snagged the convention for Houston. Jones modestly said the next day, "There was no log rolling, no trading, and no precampaign whatever. I didn't solicit a vote. The delegates just wanted to go there."[70]

All of a sudden, Houston was expecting 25,000 people to come to town. So far, the largest convention Houston had hosted was back in 1920 when the United Confederate Veterans brought in 10,000 ex-Civil War soldiers. The Democratic National Committee officially gave Jones full authority to do everything necessary to stage the convention.[71] Mayor Oscar Holcombe, City Council members, the "hotel men," and everyone else eagerly waited for Jones's return. They all grasped the importance of this unique opportunity for Houston to be seen by the nation and the world. Their city became front-page news and filled the radio waves.

Jones was flooded with congratulatory telegrams. One of the first said, "Congratulations. No one else could have done this. Much Love,

66. Jesse Jones, speech, Democratic National Committee, January 12, 1928, Jesse H. Jones Collection [LOC].

67. *Houston Chronicle,* January 29, 1928.

68. *Austin American-Statesman,* January 14, 1928.

69. Clipping from unknown newspaper, January 13, 1928, Jesse H. Jones Collection [HE].

70. *Houston Chronicle,* January 14, 1928.

71. Democratic National Committee minutes, January 12, 1928, Jesse H. Jones Collection [HE].

Mary."[72] Global cotton merchant Will Clayton wrote, "It seems too good to be true. Heartiest congratulations."[73] Attorney and local judge James Elkins declared, "You have caused the south and Texas to receive greater recognition than any other individual in the history of this country."[74] A civic group wrote, "In appreciation of your successful efforts in putting Houston, 'Our City,' on the map of the world, the members of the Women's City Club of Houston today endorsed you for the democratic nominee for president."[75] It would not be his only endorsement. Mayor Holcombe wired Jones, "All that we need is the suggestion of what should be done to insure success and it will be promptly undertaken by the citizens of Houston."[76] With only five months to go, there was much to do.

Jones's triumphant homecoming exemplified the convention's importance to Houston, Texas, and the South. As soon as his train crossed the Texas border, crowds began to gather at train depots in the east Texas piney woods to wave at, or catch a glimpse of, Jones as he headed south. In Marshall, two hundred people greeted Jones at the station for an official welcome home. W. N. (Bill) Blanton, head of the East Texas Chamber of Commerce, warned Jones to expect a band at Longview. When pressed to give a speech from the back of the train, Jones humbly and characteristically said, "Of course, I am happy to be here, but it ought to be enough to do a thing without having to talk about it afterwards."[77] In Conroe, a sea of "Jones for President" signs greeted him as the train inched toward Houston.[78]

Airplanes released bombs that exploded in midair, factories throughout the city blasted their whistles, and drivers honked their horns as Jones's train pulled into Houston's Union Station. Fifty thousand people packed the streets and cheered with abandon as Jones disembarked, kissed his Aunt Louisa, and headed down a police-lined path through the crowd to the temporary platform in front of the columned station. When the band finished playing "Hail, Hail, the Gang's All Here," Jones was introduced by Mayor Holcombe and said, in part, "The fact that the convention is coming here is a tribute to the south and to Texas, not only

72. Mary Gibbs Jones to Jesse Jones, January 12, 1928, Jesse H. Jones Collection [LOC].

73. Will Clayton to Jesse Jones, January 12, 1928, Jesse H. Jones Collection [LOC].

74. James Elkins to Jesse Jones, January 13, 1928, Jesse H. Jones Collection [LOC].

75. Women's City Club of Houston to Jesse Jones, January 13, 1928, Jesse H. Jones Collection [LOC].

76. Oscar Holcombe to Jesse Jones, January 12, 1928, Jesse H. Jones Collection [LOC].

77. *Houston Chronicle*, January 31, 1928.

78. *Houston Chronicle*, February 1, 1928.

to Houston." Jones explained, "It wasn't hard to bring the convention here . . . I assured the delegates that Houston would open its heart as well as its doors. Now we have a responsibility and an obligation. We must extend our most cordial hospitality." In this moment of glory, he spoke to the idea of nationhood, saying, "We must forget there is a North, or South, or East, or West, but seek to remember that we are all one nation, seeking the right and standing for what we think is just."[79] With that, Jesse and Mary Gibbs Jones were led to a line of cars waiting to parade them down Main Street to their home at the Lamar Hotel. Red, white, and blue bunting, five bands, and tens of thousands of celebrating citizens waving ribbons, banners, and placards lined the riotous ten-block route, with airplanes screaming overhead.

Houston was big news. Respected columnist Walter Lippmann wrote, "Although your reporter is no political expert, he can safely predict right now that Houston, Texas, will win the nomination. It won't be the presidential nomination, of course. Houston before next June will be nominated as the one and only point of interest in these United States."[80]

The *New York Evening Sun* reported, "Houston is now happier than ever because it hustled around in Washington the other day and grabbed this year's convention while other cities were fighting among themselves to see which would have to take it." The paper told how Houston, although miles away from the Gulf of Mexico, wanted the sea at its back door and "now brags of its thirty or more regular steamship lines." The glowing article described the city's can-do spirit by presciently adding, "If Houston takes a notion some day to annex the moon, it will be a dreadful time for the astronomers who, once set in their ways, dislike to be disturbed."[81]

Like most papers, the *Philadelphia Morning Public Ledger* said that the site "comes as a surprise, for it had not been mentioned in recent convention-city gossip." It went on to speculate about the effect "bone-dry" Texas would have on "the fortunes of the wet forces and the presidential aspirations of Governor Smith."[82]

A *Houston Chronicle* editorial stated that the location will give the region "a new voice in party affairs" and that southerners will finally be considered and consulted, not taken for granted or, worse, ignored.[83] Jones, resenting the power held by the east coast financial community,

79. *Houston Chronicle*, February 1, 1928.
80. *New York World*, January 14, 1928.
81. *New York Evening Sun*, January 13, 1928.
82. *Philadelphia Morning Public Ledger*, January 13, 1928.
83. *Houston Chronicle*, January 13, 1928.

liked to point out that most of the country was west of the Mississippi and none of it was east of the Atlantic seaboard. He was very happy to open a door that let the South and the West in from the cold.

Houston and Jones's personality, appearance, and life story made great copy. The *Seattle Times* said, "In the little more than twenty years that he has been here, Jesse Jones has shown Houston what he can do. His latest achievement in landing the convention is but another step in a record that shows no failure." The reporter estimated Jones's wealth at more than $50 million ($600 million) and said the figure was "conservative."[84] The *New York Times* said he was worth more than $100 million ($1.2 billion).[85] The *Literary Digest*, although accurate in its description, made Jesse sound as if he came from central casting: "Mr. Jones is six feet three inches tall, and not as slim as he used to be, quite a chunk of a man even for the Southwest, where they grow them big . . . It is when he speaks that his personality counts most. He has one of those easy, gentle, never-in-a-hurry voices that soothes listeners and drugs them into acquiescence, and he has a nice choice of words to go with the voice."[86]

With those easygoing words, Jones kicked Houston into high gear. Mayor Holcombe went to New York right after the announcement to confer. They had five months to prepare for 25,000 visitors, bringing with them national and international attention. They quickly decided to build a new convention hall that would accommodate the entire convention crowd, and the mayor secured a $100,000 ($1.2 million) appropriation from the Houston City Council for the structure.

Quashing insulting rumors about Houston's holding the convention in a Ringling Brothers circus tent, Associated Press dispatches from New York described the planned building and claimed that the "immense temporary auditorium . . . will be practically heatproof."[87] The Democratic National Committee's publicity department boasted, "The roof on this coliseum, which has a total floor space of about six and one-half acres, is the greatest span of roofing in the world without column supports." It added, "Immense typhoon fans . . . will supply fresh air constantly to the interior of the auditorium."[88] Construction of the Sam Houston Hall began just four months before the convention, and only after the city agreed to pay

84. *Seattle Times,* January 15, 1928.

85. *New York Times,* January 18, 1928.

86. "Where Will the Next President Be Named?"

87. *Houston Chronicle,* January 27, 1928.

88. W. W. Sherrill Jr., statement from publicity committee, Democratic National Committee, June 1928, Jesse H. Jones Collection [HE].

$5,000 ($60,000) to demolish the small houses occupying the land bordering Buffalo Bayou selected for the site; an additional $7,500 ($90,000) was set aside for landscaping the area.[89] Explaining the decision to erect a new building for the convention, Jones said, "The City Auditorium could easily seat all delegates and alternates, but the temporary structure will be built so that spectators, many of them Houstonians, may attend. Houston would not be livable for me if they did not get to go."[90]

New York architect Kenneth Franzheim and Houston architect, Finn, designed the hall. It required more than one million feet of east Texas pine, was longer than three football fields and "33 per cent larger than Madison Square Garden."[91] The massive building would seat all of the conventioneers and thousands of spectators, accommodate the press, have its own post office and include a "colored section," fenced off by chicken wire. Large openings between the roof and walls helped ventilate the hall and allowed spectators who could not get inside to stand on ramps and see what was going on.

The effort to dress up the city in its "best clothes" was widespread. Houston's park superintendent launched a campaign urging everyone to "trim their hedges and beautify their homes in every way possible." He declared, "We want visitors to see a city here in keeping with what they expect to find—the most beautiful City in the South." He said $100,000 ($1.2 million) would be needed to do the job right and received appropriations to plant flowers and shrubs in all thirty-two parks, around city hall, and at the central library.[92] County commissioners rushed to finish road projects, including the highway that connected Houston and Galveston. Merchants prepared for a boom. A furniture storeowner, who had just completed a cross-country buying trip, exclaimed, "Few people can realize what the Democratic National Convention means to the city of Houston from an advertising viewpoint."[93]

It also brought "year-round" radio to town. Radio was fairly new, and Houston had only recently hooked up with the National Broadcasting Corporation (NBC), which began putting programs on the air from New York just a year and a half before. NBC's "red" network broadcast entertainment and news; its "blue" network offered non-sponsored news and cultural programs. Houston's KPRC radio, an affiliate of the *Houston Post*,

89. *Houston Chronicle,* January 26, 1928.
90. *Seattle Times,* January 15, 1928.
91. Sam Houston Hall souvenir booklet, Jesse H. Jones Collection [HE].
92. *Houston Chronicle,* January 16, 1928.
93. *Houston Chronicle,* January 24, 1928.

went on the air in 1925, broadcasting area church programs, impromptu speeches, and reports about local news and events. It had joined NBC's blue network in 1928, so programming was wired from New York to a Houston transmitter, allowing almost static-free, year-round reception. What with Houston's first link to a national network and the upcoming national convention, retailers made "plans for an unprecedented sale of [radio] apparatus to Houstonians and Texans."[94]

The 1924 conventions had been broadcast, but most people back then did not have radios. Now more than three-quarters of all homes in the United States had radios, and broadcasts from both national conventions would be widely received. News of national and international importance—this time originating from Houston—would be not only read in newspapers, but also heard by millions over the radio. Understanding the power of this revolutionary technology and remembering the disastrous 1924 convention, Shaver said, "I think our experience at Madison Square Garden will keep anybody from doing anything nasty or vituperative that would go out over the radio to the country."[95]

Accommodating the huge onslaught of people remained the city's biggest challenge. There were, at most, 5,000 hotel rooms to house the expected 25,000 to 30,000 visitors. Within two days of the site selection, Houston hotels received more than 4,000 requests for rooms and thousands more poured in as the weeks passed. Jones was swamped with requests from almost every notable Democrat, including Edith Wilson, Bernard Baruch, and Franklin Roosevelt, who asked for a room at the Rice Hotel. A central committee was formed to arrange accommodations for everyone. The hotels were reserved for those who had official business at the convention, including almost a thousand members of the press, who had to share rooms. The committee went into action, converting schools into dormitories, commandeering sleeping cars from trains, establishing "tourist camps" to accommodate thousands of campers and their cars in Memorial and Hermann Parks and accepting, after inspection, invitations from Houstonians offering to rent their homes to convention guests. Several hotels under construction were also rushed to completion.[96]

As Houston prepared for its moment in the sun, Jones kept one eye on the effort and the other on the party's finances. He had sent out a raft of to-the-point fundraising letters to the party faithful and by the end of

94. *Houston Chronicle*, January 15, 1928.
95. *Houston Chronicle*, June 12, 1928.
96. Ibid.

February, was able to report that the "entire indebtedness of the National Committee has been paid." Jones was particularly pleased to tell Shaver that there was also about $250,000 ($3 million) to start the next campaign.[97] Jesse had pulled three rabbits out of his hat: landing the convention for Houston, erasing the party's persistent debt, and ending up with an unheard-of surplus.

Letters of congratulations poured in from party members and grateful politicians, including one from Tennessee Congressman Cordell Hull, who wrote, "This great accomplishment could only be the result of the most tremendous exertions on your part. I doubt if any other person would have been nearly so successful. The Democratic Party is vastly indebted to you for this outstanding service. As one democrat and member of the Committee, let me thank you in unmeasured terms."[98] In response to Senator Carter Glass's thanks, Jones reported, "We are making good progress in our preparations for the convention: our money has all been raised, the convention hall well under way."[99]

The *Washington Post* reported, "The miracle man of the occasion is Jesse Jones of Houston. The finance chairman of the Democratic national committee has accomplished in three months more than even the most optimistic friends thought was possible . . . The selection of Houston as the meeting place for the Democratic national convention was considered a good stroke of politics. The discovery of Mr. Jones appears to have been even more fortunate."[100]

Syndicated political cartoonists began to feature Jones. One cartoon's headline proclaimed, "Democrats' Paul Revere," and showed Jones riding a donkey while waving a bundle of money in front of the mascot's face and saying, "Wake up, Mule, Wake up!" He was identified in the cartoon as "Millionaire Jesse H. Jones, the good natured 'angel' of Houston."[101] Mentions of Jones as a candidate for vice president and president followed the publicity. Mayor Holcombe of Houston was one of the first to offer an endorsement when he responded to a question about potential candidates for vice president by saying, "Personally, I am for one J. Jones, and you will find that a great many people in Texas feel the same way about it. I have had letters from prominent people in all parts of the state

97. Jesse Jones to Clem Shaver, February 29, 1928, Jesse H. Jones Collection [LOC].
98. Cordell Hull to Jesse Jones, March 12, 1928, Jesse H. Jones Collection [LOC].
99. Jesse Jones to Carter Glass, March 13, 1928, Jesse H. Jones Collection [LOC].
100. *Washington Post*, March 9, 1928.
101. Cartoon by S. Shafer, Washington, D.C., 1928, Jesse H. Jones Collection [LOC].

strongly advocating his nomination. There is no question that he would make an ideal candidate."[102]

Woodrow Wilson's brother-in-law and Jones's friend, Stockton Axson, wrote Jones, "The eyes of the nation are fixed upon you, and the nation is going to have you, as either its vice president or president . . . Before Woodrow Wilson had any serious thought that he would ever be nominated for the Presidency, he used to say frequently that the country could never be safely directed until free men, new men, men with no political debts to pay, should be at the head of the government. You stand very much as he stood in 1910, and ever since I knew you (that is to say, since 1914), you have stood for the things for which he stood. If he were alive, I am sure he would rejoice in the prospect of you as his successor in the great office."[103]

The idea was not far-fetched, nor was it confined to Jones's immediate circle. After repeat presidential candidate McAdoo bowed out, it was clear that New York Governor Smith would most likely be the Democrats' candidate for president. Smith was wet, from the east coast, and (worst, for some) Catholic. Jones, who was (publicly at least) dry, southern, and Protestant, could balance the ticket as the candidate for vice president. *The Literary Digest* noted that Jones's candidacy also "would appeal strongly to the Wilson old guard."[104]

Jones's popularity was widespread. On April 5, 1928—as he turned fifty-four—South Dakota Governor W. J. Bulow asked Jones if he would consent to "letting us place your name on the primary ballot as the choice of the Democrats of South Dakota for vice president."[105] Jones declined by telegram, saying that he was not a candidate and that his principal concern was the June convention in Houston, after which he would devote his "time and efforts toward helping to win a Democratic victory in the November election."[106]

Texas Democrats, however, were not to be denied. At the party's state convention in May, a resolution was passed instructing the delegation "to cast the vote of Texas for The Honorable Jesse H. Jones for the democratic nomination for President of the United States."[107] His long-ago patron,

102. *Houston Chronicle*, January 24, 1928.
103. Stockton Axson to Jesse Jones, January 31, 1928, Jesse H. Jones Collection [LOC].
104. "Where Will the Next President Be Named?"
105. W. J. Bulow to Jesse Jones, April 5, 1928, Jesse H. Jones Collection [LOC].
106. Jesse Jones to D. C. Lewis, April 6, 1928, Jesse H. Jones Collection [LOC].
107. Resolution of the Texas State Democratic Party convention, May 2, 1928, Jesse H. Jones Collection [LOC].

Royal Ferris, wrote Jones, "You were certainly very popular at the state democratic convention held in Beaumont . . . and this is to congratulate you and hope you may receive the nomination for President."[108] In response to the state party resolution, Jones released a statement—in which he never quite declined the honor. He said, "While I appreciate the esteem and confidence of my friends in Texas, who are suggesting that the Texas delegation be instructed to cast its vote for me at the Houston convention for the presidency, and while such a vote would be the greatest compliment that the people of Texas could pay me—and I would be insincere if I should say or infer that such a procedure would not make me very happy—nevertheless . . . I would greatly prefer that there be no contest whether or not the instruction should be for me." He added, "I have never held political office, nor have I . . . any political aspirations, but to be considered or thought qualified for the presidency by the people of Texas is compensation enough for any service that I may ever be able to render."[109]

Not everyone in Texas liked Jones. W. C. Hogg, whose father was the state's first Texas-born governor, had gained prominence as a developer and oilman and, like many of Jones's business competitors, was leery of a man who so determinedly played to win in business, politics, and poker. When Hogg realized Governor Dan Moody planned to lead the Texas delegation in voting for Jones for president at the convention, he wrote, "As the leader of Texas democracy and as Dan Moody, you owe it to your State and to yourself to scrutinize the record of this man . . . If you are not acquainted with Jesse Jones' local history, we ask that you investigate a few things that are a matter of record and of common knowledge in this community." Hogg then listed three settled lawsuits involving Jones and wrote that there was additional evidence of "Jesse Jones's stalwart avarice and piratical trading spirit." He said, "Mr. Jones is fairly not to be trusted in ordinary matters, much less in high places of State." He concluded, "So, please don't proffer as President this ill-fitted pseudo-statesman who is now a talented gambler with buildings and banks as he formerly was with pitch and poker."[110]

Other competitors of Jones's, however, knew where business ended and community service began. Ross Sterling, along with Jones, was a

108. Royal Ferris to Jesse Jones, May 25, 1928, Jesse H. Jones Collection [LOC].

109. Jesse Jones, statement on resolution of the Texas State Democratic Party convention, May 2, 1928, Jesse H. Jones Collection [LOC].

110. W. C. Hogg to Dan Moody, June 10, 1928, Jesse H. Jones Collection [HE].

founding partner of Humble Oil Company and the local chairman of the Convention's Finance Committee. That Sterling also owned Jones's rival newspaper, the *Houston Post*, did not matter. Both supported the Convention for their own good and for the benefit of their community. Sterling was a primary participant in one lawsuit mentioned by Hogg and he came quickly to Jones's defense, pointing out that Jones had exchanged bonds secured with speculative real estate for something safer—at the buyer's request. Although criticized and resented, Jones could hardly be faulted for quickly selling the returned land at a substantial profit.[111] As the movement urging Jones for president escalated, so did Hogg's campaign to discredit him. It did not work.

At the end of March, citizens of Fort Worth made Jones an honorary citizen at a banquet held in his honor by the Exchange Club. Not to be outdone, a week later the citizens of Dallas hosted an equally lavish affair at the Adolphus Hotel "in testimony of their esteem for Mr. Jesse Holman Jones."[112] Jones delivered an unusually long speech at the event. He recounted his childhood years in Dallas and described his revered teacher Blanche Babcock. He said, "I shall never forget her gentleness and her kindness to one timid country boy who had great difficulty in keeping up with his classes." And he told how Dallas banker Royal Ferris had given him a "start in a financial way." But most of his speech was devoted to the Convention, politics, and his positions on policies affecting the upcoming presidential campaign. Although Jones and many others personally ignored the Prohibition laws, he toed the party line in public and so declared in Dallas, "Texas is overwhelmingly dry in sentiment." But he also asked, "Why fuss among ourselves as to who of us are the best prohibitionists or whose motives are the purest?" He pointed out that the eighteenth amendment was now part of the Constitution, "as if it had been written in there by Thomas Jefferson," and could only be repealed "by an orderly process," which was not likely to happen. He explained that the laws had not "been given a fair trial under the maladministration of the Republican party." Jones left the subject with, "Prohibition enforcement is an issue in Texas and will be an issue in the national campaign. But by no means is it the paramount issue."[113] Jones continued, "Honesty in government, my friends, and legislation that will stabilize the farming

111. R. S. Sterling, undated signed statement, Jesse H. Jones Collection [HE].
112. Banquet program, Adolphus Hotel, Dallas, April 9, 1928, Jesse H. Jones Collection [HE].
113. Jesse Jones, speech, Adolphus Hotel, Dallas, March 1928, Jesse H. Jones Collection [HE].

industry are the outstanding issues of the national campaign. They are the real issues." He explained, "By farm legislation, I do not mean farm relief . . . It sounds too much like begging or patronizing, and the American farmer, the backbone of American civilization, does not beg." He explained his priorities: "Manufacturing, transportation, banking, merchandising, and public utilities of all kinds are operated on a basis that yields a fair profit one year to another, and there is no reason why agriculture, livestock, and other rural pursuits cannot be put on the same businesslike basis and operated at a fair profit." He declared, "With a democratic government we can have equal opportunities for all classes of people, and all kinds of businesses, if we will but unite for that purpose." Jones asked for "equal opportunity and legislation that will make it possible for the farming business to be operated on as safe a basis as any other kind of business."[114]

Jones agreed with the provisions of the pending McNary-Haugen bill that would create a farm board to buy and sell surplus domestic crops on the world market and establish guaranteed prices in the United States to help farmers survive. U.S. farmers had prevented mass starvation in Europe during and after World War I. When fertile fields were destroyed on the war-torn continent, U.S. farmers increased their production, which meant acquiring debt to buy more land so they could meet the soaring overseas demand for grain and produce. Once Europe stabilized after the war, and as other countries jumped into the grain market, demand for U.S. crops plunged—farm income fell almost by half between 1919 and 1921.[115] For the first time more people lived in cities than on farms, but agriculture still contributed more to the nation's economy than any other sector.[116] The health of the U.S. economy hinged in great part on agriculture's vitality, but President Coolidge vetoed the McNary-Haugen bill.

The effects of vanishing farm income reverberated throughout the economy. Farmers had less to spend and more were losing their farms and homes to foreclosure as their demand for manufactured goods evaporated. In a front page, above-the-fold *Houston Chronicle* op-ed, Jones asserted, "The farm question will be the paramount issue of the coming presidential campaign . . . [and] problems confronting the farmer must be placed foremost."[117] Party stalwart William Church Osborn had written

114. Ibid.
115. Schlesinger Jr., *Crisis of the Old Order*, 103.
116. Schwarz, *New Dealers*, 36.
117. *Houston Chronicle*, January 18, 1928.

Jones a year earlier, "There is a movement on foot here to see whether we can't take the Democratic campaign out of a discussion of prohibition and Catholicism and put it on the basis of an attack upon the commercial, short-sighted, and hesitating character of the Coolidge administration."[118] Jones immediately responded, "I concur heartily in the idea of lifting our . . . campaign to a higher level and entirely above religious or other factional issues."[119] Jones knew more daunting challenges faced the nation than issues of personal morality and religion.

Roosevelt also acknowledged the party's challenges and wrote Jones a letter filled with suggestions about "a great many important matters relating to the campaign . . . which should be attended to before the convention." Preparing lists of "leading Democrats in every part of the United States," along with "Independents" and "foreign language citizens" was Roosevelt's first proposal. He wrote, "I doubt whether any one has this information in proper shape at the present time." He recommended sending out "some one of great capacity to make arrangements with the various radio stations, especially the smaller stations," adding, "The Republicans have already started to do this." Roosevelt brought up something he and Jones had discussed before—expanding the impossibly short campaign season. He wrote, "Every campaign in the past has been delayed . . . until the end of August, and I am very strongly of the belief that July and the first part of August should be made use of." He continued, "Unless the preliminary work is done beforehand, it is almost impossible to get things going until at least six weeks after the convention."[120] Roosevelt asked Jones to speak with Shaver about his proposals, indicating that Jones, not the DNC chairman, was the go-to guy, as far as Roosevelt was concerned.

Jones waited two weeks to reply, "Your . . . suggestions are very sound. In fact, they are exactly what I have been working to for the last three years." To counter Roosevelt's concerns about radio access—and perhaps to answer the condescension, intended or not, in his letter—Jones reported that he had been in touch with Owen Young, founder of RCA and chairman of General Electric, and with "Mr. Aylesworth, President of the National Broadcasting Company, for definite information as to how we should proceed in this respect." Jones assured Roosevelt that "we

118. William Church Osborn to Jesse Jones, February 1, 1927, Jesse H. Jones Collection [LOC].

119. Jesse Jones to William Church Osborn, February 2, 1927, Jesse H. Jones Collection [LOC].

120. Franklin Roosevelt to Jesse Jones, March 13, 1928, Jesse H. Jones Collection [LOC].

will have an equal apportionment of time with the Republican campaign committee."[121]

The Republican convention was held in Kansas City, Missouri, on June 12, 1928. Herbert Hoover was selected on the first vote and Kansas Senator Charles Curtis was chosen as his running mate, the first vice presidential candidate with Native American ancestors.[122] Hoover had been raised on a farm in Iowa, became a successful and wealthy engineer, and at age forty began to devote himself to public service. As U.S. food administrator under Wilson during World War I, he personified the home front war effort. Hoover was acclaimed for the relief he brought to the starving people of Belgium during the war and for the distribution of food throughout Europe after the last shots were fired. He orchestrated a voluntary effort in the United States that encouraged people to refrain from eating certain foods on specific days of the week so everyone could make sure the armed forces and citizens of Europe had enough to eat.[123] Hoover admired Wilson and was a principal economic advisor during the Paris Peace Conference. He then served as Secretary of Commerce under Presidents Harding and Coolidge before becoming the Republican nominee for president in 1928 at the age of fifty-three.

Except for the farmers, most people felt prosperous, and some were drawn into the "speculative craze" sweeping the stock market. On opening day of the Republican convention, all records were broken when 5,109,700 shares were traded on the New York Stock Exchange. The ticker took almost two hours after the close of business to compute and report the last transaction.[124] Accepting the nomination, Hoover said, "We in America today are nearer to the final triumph over poverty than ever before in the history of the land." He called Prohibition "a great social and economic experiment, noble in motive and far-reaching in purpose." The Republicans also promised that tax cuts and high tariffs would put "a chicken in every pot and two cars in every garage."[125]

While the Republicans met in Kansas City, Houstonians scurried to complete final preparations for the coming throngs. Synchronized traffic lights were installed throughout downtown.[126] The Hospitality House, which offered "numerous electric fans, plenteous supplies of ice water,"

121. Jesse Jones to Franklin Roosevelt, March 26, 1928, Jesse H. Jones Collection [LOC].

122. Shields-West, *Almanac of Presidential Campaigns,* 223.

123. Heckscher, *Woodrow Wilson,* 466.

124. *Houston Chronicle,* July 1, 1928.

125. Shields-West, *Almanac of Presidential Campaigns,* 225.

126. *Houston Chronicle,* June 14, 1928.

restrooms, first-aid stations, and information booths, sat across from the nearly completed convention hall. Banks installed burglar alarms and hired extra guards to prevent holdups "during the convention rush."[127] But no one was prepared for the horrifying event that dampened everyone's enthusiasm and besmirched Houston.

On June 20, six days before the convention was set to open—and just as the press began to arrive—a gang of unmasked white men forced its way into Jefferson Davis Hospital, seized a black man from his bed at gunpoint, took him six miles from downtown and hung him from a bridge on Post Oak Road. The man, Robert Powell, who was recovering in the hospital from a bullet wound, had been accused of murdering popular city detective A. W. Davis during an arrest attempt. The gang, some of whose members were nicknamed "Slim," "Spec," "Shuck," "Clyde," and "Tack," took justice into their own hands. It was the first lynching in Houston in more than fifty years, and black and white leaders alike were appalled.

With some trepidation, local black leaders and members of the black press publicly voiced their outrage and, as much as was safely possible, joined with the white leadership to save Houston's damaged reputation. Mayor Holcombe immediately appointed a committee to investigate the lynching and received a $10,000 ($120,000) appropriation from the City Council to conduct the probe. Governor Moody offered a reward for the arrest and conviction of the perpetrators. Jones declared on the front page of the *Houston Chronicle*, "Certainly we deplore the death of Detective Davis, but that does not justify the bitter revenge of men for taking the law into their own hands. The South, and especially Texas, has been comparatively free of lynchings for the last few years, and we all deeply deplore this one. The local authorities are being aided by the governor in the assignment of Texas rangers and state officers to run down those guilty of the crime."[128] Within two days, five of the seven men had been arrested and put in jail. Nevertheless, Houston's ambitious effort to put itself forward as a progressive, thriving industrial center was tarnished.

The importance of the 1928 Democratic national convention to the South and to Houston was clear. Weeks before the convention, as Jones was still making the rounds of testimonial banquets in his honor throughout the state, he seized each opportunity to expand the audience's worldview and spell out the significance of the upcoming Convention. At a rooftop garden gathering at the Raleigh Hotel in Waco, Jones

127. *Houston Chronicle*, June 17, 1928.
128. *Houston Chronicle*, June 20, 1928.

said, "I feel we should have no East and no West in national politics and no North or South. Things that affect one part of the country affect the other; that is, there are reflections everywhere." Jones hoped the convention would "wipe out sectional lines" and advised his rapt listeners to be "world-minded in our thoughts about matters economic."[129] Then he got down to the nuts and bolts: "I believe we have been on the front pages of a thousand papers a day since we got the convention . . . We can not imagine, we can not conceive, the benefit in advertising we have obtained from securing this convention." He explained that thousands of people were coming, not just for the convention, but to see Texas. Jones always encouraged his eager audiences to decorate their cities and towns, especially railroad stations, roads, and highways, and in Waco he suggested, "It would not hurt if we had reception committees, some young girls to give a smile, give a flower, a watermelon, a cup of coffee, or something with a touch of personal hospitality. There will be men and women here in Texas, in Houston, from almost every county of every state in the Union."[130]

One of those headed to Texas was the acclaimed cowboy-philosopher Will Rogers, star of the Ziegfeld Follies and movies and a popular commentator. As a nationally syndicated newspaper columnist, Rogers reported from Fort Worth five days before the convention: "Was met at the [air] field by the champion host of the world, Amon Carter; also by H. L. Mencken. Mencken says, after seeing the South, he is going to start picking on the North." He continued, "Texas starts entertaining you when you hit the State line. I thought the convention was held here, the way they act. It ain't just Houston, it's Texas that will show you something."[131] Arriving in Houston the next day, Rogers reported, "Great trip in here by air from Fort Worth on the Texas Transport Mail Line. See Houston from the air. Jessie [sic] Jones has a sky line."[132]

When Jones asked the time of his Houston arrival, Rogers suggested some tentative dates and added, "You can call on me for any devilment that you may want put over."[133] Rogers arrived on Friday, June 21, as other attendees also began to trickle in.

On Saturday, more dignitaries, delegates, and thousands of spectators swarmed into Houston from every direction, where they found the

---

129. *Houston Chronicle,* June 10, 1928.
130. Ibid.
131. Rogers, syndicated column no. 594, Will Rogers Museum.
132. Rogers, syndicated column no. 595, Will Rogers Museum.
133. Will Rogers to Jesse Jones, June 12, 1928, Jesse H. Jones Collection [LOC].

town "draped and drowned in decorations."[134] By Saturday night, when Roosevelt arrived from Warm Springs, Georgia, more than 15,000 conventioneers had already been greeted by noisy bands, bunting, banners and fluttering flags, crammed hotel lobbies, and packed elevators. Roosevelt told reporters that Smith's prospects looked "mighty good" and, referencing the 1924 disaster without mentioning it directly, added that he hoped this convention would begin and end in the same week.[135]

On Sunday, when Edith Wilson's private train car pulled into the station, a band played "Auld Lang Syne" and thousands cheered as she disembarked. She was whisked away to the Joneses' Lamar Hotel penthouse, where she would be their houseguest for the convention's duration. After lunch and a short rest, the Joneses and Mrs. Wilson were driven six blocks to the Sam Houston Hall for the huge building's dedication ceremony. Texas rangers and local police turned away thousands before the 3:00 p.m. ceremony began. Mrs. Wilson, accompanied by Jones, came to the stage seconds before the program started and was cheered and applauded as she took her seat.

Nearly 17,000 people made it into the enormous yellow and green building that was lavishly festooned in all things red, white, and blue. The cavernous hall looked as if it housed an endless field of butterflies once everyone sat down and began flapping their paper fans. Mayor Holcombe declared the Convention Hall open and explained that his gavel was made from a cedar tree planted by General Sam Houston at his farm in Huntsville, Texas. Then the praying, singing, and speaking began—one wag said it felt more like a revival than a political convention. After six prayers, three hymns, and two Kiwanis Glee Club performances, the Reverend William States Jacobs of Houston's First Presbyterian Church introduced Jones. But before he brought Jones to the podium, the reverend lambasted politicians for rejecting the League of Nations and President Wilson and declared that if Texas were a republic, Jones would be its president. The crowd went wild as Jones approached the podium. The *New York Times* reported, "The man who has given Houston a skyline like Manhattan's and who won the convention for his city seemed nervous as he faced the audience after its demonstration."[136]

Jones began, "All stations in life, all religious faiths and creeds have assembled here this afternoon to dedicate this hall to a great purpose, de-

134. *Houston Chronicle*, June 24, 1928.
135. *Houston Post*, June 24, 1928.
136. *New York Times*, June 25, 1928.

In a practice typical for the time, the site for the 1928 National Democratic Convention was selected only five months before it began. As Jesse Jones promised, the hall was built and ready to receive the 25,000 delegates and onlookers who came to town. The Hobby Center for the Performing Arts now stands at this site.

mocracy, and to give it in the name of that great soldier, statesman, and patriot, General Sam Houston." He repeated his standard message and his hope for the nation when he declared, "The convention in Texas, I believe, will further erase the sectional lines."[137] Then he introduced former first lady Edith Wilson, saying, "In the spirit of the greatest of them all, in the name of the man who held the torch for the world during the dark days of 1918, a man who lifted the ideals of the whole world by the force of his own mind, Woodrow Wilson." He was drowned out by raucous acclamation. Like a wave, the sea of people before him rose out of their chairs and a military band burst into song. When able, he continued, "And I wish to introduce to you the right-hand of that great man, his wife, Mrs. Woodrow Wilson."

As Jones escorted her to the podium, the crowd shouted, cheered,

137. Ibid.

(left to right) Edith Wilson, Mary Gibbs Jones, and Jesse Jones. Mary Gibbs Jones and Edith Wilson studied languages and played bridge together; they remained close friends throughout their lives and corresponded until their deaths in 1962. Courtesy Northmore-*Detroit Times*.

whistled, and waved flags to honor the president's widow. After thanking Jones for his kind words and for the reception she had just received, with a wise and cautioning smile on her face, she said, "I know herein will be held the most harmonious and the greatest Democratic National convention the country has ever known."[138] The War Mothers of Houston then presented Edith Wilson with a bouquet of flowers. After she sat down, Rabbi Henry Barnston of Temple Beth Israel delivered the closing prayer.

So far, the six-acre convention hall that Jones had built in just sixty-four days appeared to be a success. A reporter who had just covered the Republican convention wrote, "Wider seats and more air will be found here than at Kansas City, and the general arrangement for delegates and the scheme of decoration is better."[139] While bemoaning the lack of shade on the streets leading from the hotels to the hall, another reporter observed that the two huge ceiling fans "and the open-work design of the building kept its interior well below the blazing temperature outside."[140]

138. *Houston Chronicle,* June 25, 1928.
139. *New York Times,* June 24, 1928.
140. *New York Times,* June 25, 1928.

Things were less sanguine in the downtown hotels, particularly the Rice, where almost everything of importance was happening. The candidates' headquarters on the mezzanine buzzed with activity; every major political organization—including the relatively new League of Women Voters—and political potentate had rooms at the Rice. The hotel's five small elevators could not accommodate the crowd. A reporter observed, "Dismally certain that they would never get elevators . . . [guests] were plodding and puffing upward to their rooms on the tenth, seventeenth, and nineteenth floors in some cases." He added, "Down at the railroad station it was even worse. Although a steady breeze blew through the streets, it stopped at the portals of hotels or stations, and one entering stepped into [a] sweltering atmosphere."[141]

Will Rogers added his impressions: "The Rice Hotel lobby is so packed I have reached up and mopped three other perspiring brows before I could find my own." About the behind-the-scenes drinking, he exclaimed, "The whole talk down here is wet and dry; the delegates just can't wait till the next bottle is opened to discuss it . . . The South say they are dry, and by golly if the bootleggers don't rush on some more mighty quick, they will be."[142]

Despite the heat, crowds, and inconvenient Prohibition laws, everything seemed to be going smoothly and everyone appeared to be having a good time. By now the sixth of the seven men accused of lynching Powell had been arrested, and the horrifying story slipped further and further from the news and public awareness as the Convention commenced. On Monday the Joneses had lunch at home with Edith Wilson and Will Rogers. From the top floor of the Lamar, they could watch the throngs crowding the almost impassable streets. Special trains unloading conventioneers came and went all day long at the city's three stations, while thousands lined the streets to watch the delegates arrive and to enjoy the endless parade of jubilant bands and political fervor. Presidential candidates did not appear at national conventions, so Governor Smith's wife left her husband behind in Albany and arrived in Houston late Monday afternoon with her children.

That evening, most state delegations met to strategize. The Texas delegation gathered on the mezzanine of the Lamar. After voting to make Governor Moody chairman, Colonel Thomas Ball, who had led the effort years before to develop the Houston Ship Channel, made a motion

141. *New York Times,* June 26, 1928.
142. *New York Times,* June 25, 1928.

Jesse Jones and Will Rogers enjoyed a close friendship until the actor's death in 1935. Jones assisted the family with funeral arrangements and finances, helped establish the Will Rogers Memorial Commission, and went to Paris to advise sculptor Jo Davidson about the statues that now grace Statuary Hall in the nation's Capitol Building and at the Will Rogers Memorial at Claremore, Oklahoma (Timmons, *Jones: Man and Statesman*, 273).

to nominate Jones for president and for the delegation to cast all of its forty votes for him. According to the *Houston Chronicle*, "The motion carried by acclamation with only two or three voicing [in opposition]."[143] Even before the Convention officially opened the next day, however, it was almost certain that New York Governor Smith and Arkansas Senator Joseph P. Robinson would head the Democratic ticket in 1928. Jones's name continued to circulate for president and vice president, but any attempt to recruit him at this point was honorary.

Tuesday began with a breakfast in honor of Edith Wilson, hosted by the Daughters of the American Revolution, at the River Oaks Country Club. The *New York Times* reported, "Mrs. Wilson, in purple chiffon and a small purple hat, received an ovation, all other guests rising when she entered

143. *Houston Chronicle,* June 26, 1928.

with Mrs. Jesse Jones."[144] The Convention officially opened right after noon. Will Rogers said, "It took Clem Shaver twenty minutes of steady hammering to get enough order for them to listen to a prayer. They didn't want to listen to a prayer. It was an argument that they wanted to listen to."[145] After announcements and minor official business were tended to, however, the convention was suddenly adjourned. The national leaders had decided to delay the keynote speech until 7:00 p.m. so people at home could hear it after work over the radio.

At the GOP convention in Kansas City, NBC announcer Guy McNamee and his colleagues had used newspaper reporters to gather and write on-the-spot news and information for them to broadcast. The experiment worked, so they carried it over to the Democratic convention, where eleven million listeners throughout the nation would receive instant accounts of events in Houston via "the colourful noise picture that radio alone can transmit to far away places."[146]

Instead, listeners heard thunder around 6:00 P.M. An hour before the evening session was set to open, a torrential downpour pummeled Houston, soaked the outdoor decorations, and leaked into Sam Houston Hall through its giant rooftop fans. The rain lasted for less than an hour and dampened hardly anyone's spirit. Conventioneers clearly were determined to have fun and to get along. The floors were mopped, as jokes were made about dry states getting the "worst of the enforced wetness." While the crowds were still thin, Edith Wilson took her place on the front row with her friend, Mary Gibbs Jones.

That night the Eveready Hour was cut short on the Columbia Broadcasting Company network so those sitting by their radios could hear popular journalist and author Claude G. Bowers deliver the convention's keynote address. For almost an hour, he eulogized Woodrow Wilson and savaged Republicans while the enormous crowd fanned, cheered, and jabbed their states' signs in the air. Will Rogers reported, "Well, brother, I don't have to tell you. You had a radio. You must have heard it. If you didn't, you missed the treat of a lifetime . . . It wasn't a keynote speech. It was a 'lock and key' speech, and after he had finished, why, the whole Republican Party should have been put under lock and key. It must be true, or they could sue him. Course, him just being an editorial writer, he hasn't got anything. But Barney Baruch and Jesse Jones . . . have got a little left

144. *New York Times*, June 26, 1928.
145. *New York Times*, June 27, 1928.
146. *Houston Chronicle*, June 23, 1928.

over from the Democratic Administration and they put this fellow up to saying it."[147]

Baruch, who was meeting with Party powers in his room at the Rice Hotel, may have still been nursing wounds from Jones's tirade of four years before. He initially declined Jones's invitation to buy a box for $5,000 ($60,000), but not long before the convention he relented, sent a wire agreeing to take one for not more than $2,000 ($24,000), and offered to help however else he could.[148]

The day after the Convention speeches, decorations were soggy and cars got stuck in the mud, but spirits were high. Bellhops rushed up and down hotel hallways with trays of seltzer water, ice cubes, and corkscrews as Wednesday morning's *Houston Post* was delivered. The paper featured a large picture of Mary Gibbs Jones, identifying her as the "Democratic Hostess." That morning the Joneses accompanied Edith Wilson to a ceremony on Buffalo Bayou where they planted a tree in memory of President Wilson in front of the new Women's Club building. Jones made a speech while Mary held a parasol over Mrs. Wilson's head; six-year-old Audrey Louise, the Joneses' granddaughter, handed the former first lady the ceremonial shovel and later pulled a cord that released a small American flag and revealed a bronze plaque that read, "To the Memory of Woodrow Wilson."[149]

Immediately afterward, Edith Wilson and Mary Gibbs Jones went to the Rice Hotel for a breakfast in honor of retiring Democratic National Committee vice chairwoman Emily Newell Blair. They reached the roof in a freight elevator, arriving while Will Rogers, the only man in attendance, was making a speech. He later reported, "Us women sure had some fun . . . I had the surest fire finish in the world. I introduced Mrs. Woodrow Wilson, who made an awful nice and appropriate speech . . . The breakfast was billed for 9 o'clock on the roof of the Rice Hotel, and on account of the elevators we all arrived for a lovely luncheon. Everybody talks about 'what the country needs.' What this country needs is more elevators."[150]

No one seemed to mind the crowds or the heat. When Senator Robinson gave the keynote that afternoon, the listless crowd perked up when he mentioned the vehement attacks made on Smith's Catholicism.

147. *New York Times,* June 27, 1928.
148. Bernard Baruch to Jesse Jones, June 16, 1928, Jesse H. Jones Collection [LOC].
149. *Houston Chronicle,* June 28, 1928.
150. *New York Times,* June 28, 1928.

Robinson, permanent chairman of the Convention and the presumptive vice presidential candidate, declared, "Jefferson rejoiced in the provision of the Constitution that declares no religious test shall ever be required as a qualification for office or trust in the United States."[151] With that, people jumped to their feet, grabbed their states' signs, and converged for a mass demonstration. During the chaos, some of the North Carolina delegates who opposed Smith's candidacy and religion punched at other delegates to prevent their state's sign from being included. The fighting spread to the Alabama and Tennessee delegations and police rushed in and broke up the brawls. After everyone sat down, Robinson finished his speech and closed the session.

The conventioneers returned that evening in a more conciliatory mood, eager to nominate a candidate for president. The roll call vote had barely begun when Arizona yielded to New York. Roosevelt—ubiquitous nominator and himself a candidate for New York governor—once again submitted "Happy Warrior" Smith for president of the United States. Will Rogers wrote, "Franklin Roosevelt, a fine and wonderful man, who has devoted his life to nominating Al Smith, did his act from memory. Franklin Roosevelt could have gotten far in the Democratic Party himself, but he has this act all perfected and don't like to go to the trouble of learning something else. So he just seems satisfied going through life nominating Al Smith. It was a fine speech. It always has been. But it's always been ahead of its time. Now he has 'em believing it."[152]

After Roosevelt placed Smith's name in nomination, most of the 17,000 people in attendance took to the aisles, waved signs and flags, and sang "On the Sidewalks of New York." Extra police posted along the procession quickly stopped the pushing and shoving among the Mississippi delegation, but not before several ended up wrestling on the floor to stop their sign from making it into the celebration for Smith. Radio audiences heard nothing but pandemonium for twenty-seven minutes. Finally, Nellie Taylor Ross, former governor of Wyoming, made the seconding speech. After a few other speeches and announcements, convention chair Robinson adjourned the meeting.

On Thursday, the roll call continued. Ohio put Smith over the top and made him the first Catholic candidate for president. Although the Democrats had selected their candidate before the first ballot ended, the vote continued. When Texas was called, Colonel Ball placed Jesse Jones's name

151. Ibid.
152. *New York Times*, June 29, 1928.

in nomination "as Texas's choice for president of the United States." His nomination was seconded by newspaperwoman Lee J. Rountree and by Governor Moody.[153] A crush of people, banners, and signs surged toward the aisles while three bands playing "The Eyes of Texas" pushed their way into the hall from three different directions. Thousands of green balloons emblazoned with "Jesse Jones for President" only multiplied the clamor. The jubilation over Jones's nomination lasted almost twenty minutes. Jesse and Mary Gibbs Jones and Edith Wilson witnessed the spectacle from the speakers' stand. A reporter wrote, "Mrs. Wilson was smiling out over the crowd. Mrs. Jones, slender and quiet, sat by Mrs. Wilson. Her head was up, and there was a fire of pride in her eyes."[154] Eventually, the police had to shove people back toward their seats to restore order.

Jones received Texas's forty votes, plus two from Alabama. Smith received 849 votes, more than enough required to win the nomination. After behind-the-scenes, all-night arguing between wets and drys, the Resolution Committee finally submitted the "Houston Platform," which was adopted without contention. Instead of a "bone-dry" plank or a call for repeal of the eighteenth amendment, the "harmony seekers" won the debate with more general, less inflammatory language that called for enforcing the eighteenth amendment and all other provisions and laws of the Constitution.

Another plank called for a farm board, and for financial and marketing mechanisms to handle surplus crops and tariffs for agriculture similar to those that benefited and protected other industries.[155]

Jones occasionally composed editorials for his *Houston Chronicle* and usually reviewed and approved them. Friday's lead editorial said, "In endorsing the principles of the McNary-Haugen farm relief bill, the democrats of the nation have done a courageous thing—and a thing of vision. They have shown they have a mind to see the plight of agriculture, a heart to sympathize with those who are suffering because of its plight, and a will to remedy the obvious evils."[156]

The presidential candidate had been selected and the platform had been approved. By the last day of the Convention, only two-thirds of the hall was filled. Some spectators had already left, but delegates and die-

153. *Houston Post*, June 29, 1928.
154. *Houston Chronicle*, June 29, 1928.
155. *Houston Chronicle*, June 28, 1928.
156. *Houston Chronicle*, June 29, 1928.

hards remained. They had come to nominate a candidate for vice president and to finish up the party's business. As expected, Arkansas Senator Joseph Robinson, a dry Protestant, won the party's nomination and was the first southerner since the Civil War to have a place on a major party's ticket. Before the convention adjourned, Mississippi Senator Pat Harrison asked for silence and said, "I know I am going to carry out your wishes [by giving] you an opportunity to show that we appreciate what has been done for us and for the Party by . . . asking to speak, Mr. Jones of Houston." Thousands cheered and carried on. Jones said, "We have worked hard. We have been a united citizenship working together to prepare for this Convention . . . Naturally, there have been some disappointments and mistakes, but they were not of the heart. We have done the best we could. I want to congratulate this convention on its deliberations."[157]

By 1:45 P.M., the 1928 Democratic national convention was over. Smith sent the Democratic National Committee a telegram accepting the nomination and stating that the Prohibition laws should be changed: "Common honesty compels admission that corruption of law enforcement officials, bootlegging, and lawlessness are prevalent throughout the country." He said the change could only be brought about through legislation and continued, "I feel it to be the duty of the chosen leader of the people to point the way which . . . leads to a sane, sensible solution of a condition which I am convinced is entirely unsatisfactory to the great mass of our people."[158] Against the wishes of most southern Democrats—including Jones—Smith placed Prohibition front and center. Will Rogers summed it up, "Democracy has found a candidate. Now they are looking for a drink."[159]

By most accounts, the Houston convention was a huge success. One reporter gushed, "The Democratic National Committee never entered upon a convention so elaborately and lavishly provided for as this one."[160] The hall, built in just a matter of months, was a standout. A *New York Times* columnist reported, "Sam Houston Hall, where the delegates met, was unanimously voted one of the best meeting places the party had encountered."[161] One representative for a group of Washington correspondents said, "The arrangements for the press here were the best

---

157. Ibid.
158. Ibid.
159. Ibid.
160. *Sunday Citizen* (Asheville, N.C.), June 24, 1928.
161. *New York Times,* June 30, 1928.

at any national convention ever held. Houston has the good will of the hundreds of newspapermen who came here."[162] Will Rogers chimed in, "Sam Blythe, who sits by me in the convention, and [is] the best political writer that ever lied for a candidate, told me that out of fifty years going to conventions, this was the prettiest and best hall he ever saw."[163] Another *Times* reporter observed, "One feature of the convention hall that made an impression on the delegates of the North, but [that] custom had robbed of novelty for the Southerners, was the segregation of Negroes in Sam Houston Hall. They had their own section, a small one, in a corner. Few of the colored population appeared at the meetings, perhaps because they were rather busy filling the many new jobs offered by the rush of trade to town. The colored section was the same as the other sections, as far as construction went."[164]

Except for the occasional fistfights, the convention was—comparatively—harmonious. In Madison Square Garden four years before, one policeman patrolled every two delegates. In Houston, 150 police controlled the entire convention. For the first time in forty-six years, there were no minority reports protesting the platform. For the first time in ninety years, no parliamentarian was required. Instead of breaking records for ballots, speeches, and fistfights, the Houston convention broke records for the number of bands that performed. Instead of taking 103 ballots to select a candidate as in 1924, the conventioneers chose Smith on the first try; instead of eighteen days, the Houston convention lasted four. A *New York Times* reporter wrote, "Bitterness is buried politically today beneath the multicolored carnival spirit of the happy-go-luckiest democratic convention in history."[165] Although the sectional lines Jones hoped to erase were still there, if a bit more blurred, it was clear that Houston had come of age and Jones was a prominent national figure.

Not quite two weeks after the convention, Democratic Party leaders met at their Belmont Hotel headquarters in New York. Jones delivered a report saying, "I shall to the longest day I live be under obligation to you for having given us the convention. That is the principal point that I want to leave with this committee. I want also to say that I have really enjoyed the work of Director of Finance of this Committee. It has been hard work,

162. *Houston Chronicle,* June 30, 1928.
163. *New York Times,* June 28, 1928.
164. *New York Times,* June 30, 1928.
165. *Houston Chronicle,* June 28, 1928.

arduous and discouraging at times, but it has brought me in contact with you men and women and with others from all parts of the country." After sharing a bit more, Jones reminded the group, "Mr. Chairman, I omitted to say that our debts are all paid and we have approximately two hundred thousand dollars [$2.5 million]."[166] Since 1925, Jesse Jones had raised more than $700,000 ($8.7 million)—enough to pay all the 1924 convention debt, operate the Washington, D.C., headquarters, stage the 1928 convention in Houston, and leave $200,000 ($2.5 million) left over to start the campaign.[167]

Over many objections, Smith picked John J. Raskob to replace Shaver as chairman of the Democratic National Committee. Raskob was Catholic, wet, vice president of General Motors, and a Republican. Herbert Lehman, whose father and two uncles founded Lehman Brothers, was named to Jones's position as director of finance of the Democratic National Committee.

Newspapers ran a story by a Scripps-Howard reporter who claimed Jones was ousted because of "his attempt to have himself nominated as the candidate for president." It ended, "The national committee is being reorganized today, and in all the key places men are being appointed whose loyalty to Governor Smith throughout has not been questioned."[168] The *Houston Press*, an afternoon paper operated by Foster in violation of his non-compete contract with Jones, ran the story on its front page.

Huggins at the *Houston Chronicle* immediately telegraphed the entire story to Jones in New York and suggested an attorney be sent to ask the reporter and papers "if they wish it to stand that way before the public."[169] All evidence suggests, however, that Jones voluntarily retired from the position. He shared with a colleague in Dallas, "Under no circumstances would I have continued as Director of Finance of the Democratic National Committee. Four years of that kind of work is enough for any man to contribute, aside from the fact that the nominee naturally wants the prominent places filled by immediate personal friends."[170] No one in the Party's highest ranks appeared to be mad at Jones. For example, Robinson, the candidate for vice president, sent him an admission that he derived

166. T. J. Ahearn Jr., telegram to *Houston Chronicle*, text of article in *New York World*, July 12, 1928, Jesse H. Jones Collection [HE].
167. Jesse Jones to Clem Shaver, July 11, 1928, Jesse H. Jones Collection [LOC].
168. *Houston Press*, July 11, 1928.
169. W. O. Huggins to Jesse Jones, July 12, 1928, Jesse H. Jones Collection [HE].
170. Jesse Jones to J. B. Cranfill, August 28, 1928, Jesse H. Jones Collection [LOC].

"great pleasure" from their association, and an invitation to come and see him whenever he was nearby.[171]

The day after he resigned and Lehman was appointed to his position, Jones wrote, "You probably have not formulated plans for financing the campaign, but I shall be more than happy to render any assistance that I can and to personally contribute all or part of $25,000 [$310,000] to the campaign payable as needed."[172] Lehman thanked him in person, then sent a gracious letter. A few days later, he sent another letter, this time asking Jones to serve as vice chairman of the national Finance Committee, but he declined because he and Mary just wanted to rest.

The Joneses spent the month of August "fishing and loafing" on the Saint Lawrence River, but by September, Jones was back in the saddle.[173] He accepted a position on the party's national Advisory Finance Committee and asked cotton mogul Will Clayton to join. Although Smith's position on Prohibition contradicted the intention of the Houston Platform and offended much of the South, Jones was more concerned about preserving two-party politics. In a *Houston Chronicle* editorial he concluded, "The two-party system, with one group always in opposition to the other, and seeking to take over control of the government from it, [is] the best safeguard of honest and able government." Identifying the key to progress, he said, "Under our system there must be sacrifices for the greater good. Those who refuse to make the sacrifices simply help [to] drag us away from party government, from the orderly expression of the popular will, to the utterly chaotic conditions which would prevail."[174]

In defense of Smith, Jones tempered his own inner conflict about Prohibition by stating in editorials, correspondence, and speeches that the Democratic candidate knew, first and foremost, he was a "law-enforcer, not a law-maker"—even when he disagreed with the law and wanted it changed. Jones said Smith "makes it clear that the final responsibility for any change will be with Congress and the people themselves. That is democratic and should not be objectionable to fair-minded people who disagree with him on this question."[175] Smith still complied with the Houston Platform, which stipulated that all provisions of the Constitution should be enforced.

171. Joseph Robinson to Jesse Jones, July 23, 1928, Jesse H. Jones Collection [LOC].

172. Jesse Jones to Herbert Lehman, July 12, 1928, Jesse H. Jones Collection [LOC].

173. Jesse Jones to William Church Osborn, July 24, 1928, Jesse H. Jones Collection [LOC].

174. *Houston Chronicle*, July 27, 1928.

175. Jesse Jones to Everett Lloyd, October 4, 1928, Jesse H. Jones Collection [LOC].

Jones thought the "farm issue" was more urgent and more potentially dangerous than Prohibition. He wrote to Clayton, "All thinking people must realize that the prosperity of the entire country is threatened because of the chaotic conditions in the farming industry. Governor Smith's way of meeting it is business-like and sound."[176]

Things heated up as the November election drew near. Jones urged Al Smith's 1924 Democratic opponent, McAdoo, to endorse the ticket, writing, "It is my profound belief that if the Republican Party continues in power, the whole country will come to grief."[177] Because of his vociferous anti-Smith and bone-dry public positions, McAdoo confided, "[The endorsement] presents a problem to me which I have found more difficult to solve than any that has ever faced me throughout my long career."[178]

On November 3, McAdoo released a statement that made front-page news, saying, "I am absolutely opposed to Governor Smith's position on Prohibition and the eighteenth amendment, but I shall preserve my party allegiance."[179] Former 1920 presidential candidate Cox had made news a day earlier when he declared, "Stand patism is the bedevilling disorder of the Republican Party."[180] Edith Wilson said to the Woman's National Democratic Club in Washington, D.C., "No one can speak for Woodrow Wilson, but I feel sure his sentiment would be for Governor Smith."[181] Congressman John Nance Garner from Uvalde, Texas, was more direct when he spoke in San Antonio before the election. He pointed out that Wilson, Cox, and 1924 candidate Davis were all wet. "Why?" he asked. "If you ever believed in the Democratic Party any time in 1912, 1916, 1920, or 1924, why can't you believe in it now, in 1928?"[182]

In the end, it did not matter. The voters rejected Smith and elected Hoover, who received fifty-eight percent of the vote. Smith lost in almost all states, including New York—where he was governor—and Texas. Some blamed it on Prohibition; others said it was Smith's religion. It could even have been the radio: Smith's pronouncing words like "radde-o" for *radio*, "foist" for *first*, and "horspital" for *hospital* did not sit well

176. Jesse Jones to Will Clayton, September 6, 1928, Jesse H. Jones Collection [LOC].

177. Jesse Jones to William Gibbs McAdoo, October 4, 1928, Jesse H. Jones Collection [LOC].

178. William Gibbs McAdoo to Jesse Jones, September 26, 1928, Jesse H. Jones Collection [LOC].

179. *Houston Chronicle*, November 3, 1928.

180. *Houston Chronicle*, November 2, 1928.

181. *Houston Chronicle*, November 3, 1928.

182. *Houston Chronicle*, November 4, 1928.

with many, particularly those from the South.[183] Still, Hoover probably got it right when he said, "General prosperity was on my side."[184] Or, as Will Rogers put it: "You can't lick this prosperity thing. Even the fellow that hasn't got any is all excited over the idea."[185]

183. Shields-West, *Almanac of Presidential Campaigns*, 168.
184. Ibid., 227.
185. Ibid., 166.

The Great Depression

1928–1932

◈

Never Rope a Steer Going Downhill

JESSE JONES JUGGLED A LOT OF BALLS. Even as he obtained and hosted the 1928 Democratic national convention, he had major buildings under construction in New York, Fort Worth, and Houston. His new projects in New York included the sixteen-story LeRoy Sanitarium, a medical professional building at E. 61st Street. In Fort Worth the eighteen-story Fair Building would soon house the Fair Department Store in its lower levels. In Houston, down toward his theaters and the Lamar Hotel, Jesse was now building an ornate four-story shoe store for Krupp and Tuffly and an eight-story building for Levy Brothers department store; Jones put a foundation under the smaller buildings that would allow him to add floors in the future. Up toward Buffalo Bayou, on the seventh block of Main, the 1928 conventioneers saw the start of Houston's tallest building, the thirty-five-story Gulf Oil Company Building, whose steel skeleton stuck out above the lower-lying skyline.

Returning to Houston from New York just before Thanksgiving, Jones declared in an interview, "Houston never looked better to me than it does today. Its prospects and possibilities are brighter than they have ever been." He continued, "If we can have some stabilizing legislation in the interest of the farming class, the prosperity about which we have heard so much in recent weeks and months will be better distributed." He added

The 1929 Gulf Building (now the JPMorgan Chase Building) remained Houston's tallest skyscraper until the forty-four-story Humble Oil Company (now ExxonMobil) Building opened in 1963. In the photograph, Jesse Jones's Bankers Mortgage Building is to the right of the Gulf Building; the top of the Rice Hotel, now with three wings, is on the far right; the top of the Bristol Hotel is in the center; and Jones's first National Bank of Commerce Building is in the bottom right corner.

concerns about "mass production of every kind and the ability of the country to continue to absorb the many things . . . that can now be produced so rapidly."[1]

Financially, publicly, and personally, it had been a great year for Jones. His buildings produced more than $5 million ($62 million in current dollars) in rent and netted $2.5 million ($31 million) after expenses.[2] The Democratic National Convention made "Houston as well advertised as any city in America"[3] and shone a glowing spotlight on Jones. During the 1928 holiday season, he sent sixty-eight crates of Texas Rio Grande valley grapefruits. Newly-elected New York Governor Franklin Roosevelt received a box and wrote, "Ever so many thanks for the delicious grapefruit. We all enjoyed them so much. I wish you could have been here for the Inauguration; it was a great day."[4]

Jones began 1929 by purchasing a bankrupt sixteen-story hotel in Houston which he furnished and opened, changing its name to the Texas State Hotel. It was his fourth major downtown Houston hotel. In April, the Gulf Building's impending completion was signaled by the opening of Sakowitz Brothers' men's and boy's clothing store. More than 40,000 Houstonians mobbed the greatly expanded and elegant store on its first day. To the delight of ladies, Sakowitz introduced fine clothing and accessories for women.[5] That same month, also with great fanfare, Krupp and Tuffly opened its four-story Art Deco shoe store.

In May, Jones completed a forty-four-story office tower at 10 East 40th Street in New York. Interviewed about the building and allowed to edit the final copy, the revisions reveal a bit about him and his ideas about building. The first line of the interview was originally written to say, "New York's ever-changing skyline has a new contribution of importance, and it comes from Texas." Jones redirected attention by changing the line to, "New York's ever-changing skyline has a new contributor of importance, and he comes from Texas." He also added that, after the Woolworth Building, his new building was the tallest in New York. He pointedly did not change the statement that read, "It is said his real estate holdings approach the $100,000,000 [$1.2 billion] mark."[6]

1. *Houston Chronicle*, November 21, 1928.
2. Financial statements, 1928, Jesse H. Jones Collection [HE].
3. *Houston Chronicle*, November 21, 1928.
4. Franklin Roosevelt to Jesse Jones, January 7, 1929, Jesse H. Jones Collection [HE].
5. *Houston Chronicle*, April 16, 1929.
6. Interview manuscript with handwritten notes by Jesse Jones, Jesse H. Jones Collection [HE].

Jesse Jones's forty-four-story 10 East 40th Street Building in New York City was completed just months before the 1929 Wall Street crash. Courtesy Library of Congress.

Jones explained toward the end of the interview, "I build in New York because, in my opinion, there is no safer investment than New York real estate." He said he liked the "tower building . . . because it provides better and more perfect light and ventilation, [and] it minimizes street noise. An executive or a clerk can do much more work in a quiet, well lighted, well ventilated office, and that justifies the tall building. Furthermore, there is more beauty to a tower building, and people like to occupy good looking buildings." Jones also appreciated access to convenient transportation and said, "The commuter who can walk from the train to his place of business without the added thirty or forty minutes a day on the subway is rapidly coming to appreciate this advantage."[7]

Jones cajoled reluctant bankers who would not make real estate loans to credit-worthy customers by saying, "Bankers and investors could contribute to the general welfare or what we are pleased to call prosperity if they would encourage and favor real estate financing, because of the tremendous effect that building and building operations have upon general economic conditions."[8] Jones thought too many banks had too much tied up in risky stocks and safe government securities.

The interviewer observed at the end, "While this Texan deals with his projects on a strict business basis, he cannot conceal the fact that he puts a good deal of love and pride into his building operations." When the writer picked up a picture of the partially finished Gulf Building, Jones said, "I played and worked with the plans and design of that building for three years trying to build the best business building that has ever been built. In my opinion, it is the most perfectly planned and designed business building, all things considered, that has yet been built." The interviewer noted, "He said this with a feeling not unlike that which a lover of art puts into his words about a great painting."[9]

To Jones, the Gulf Building was a monument to Houston, to Texas, to the South, and to himself. On June 28, 1929, the *Houston Chronicle* published a forty-eight-page supplement extolling the features and eminence of this newest addition to Houston's growing skyline. In the editorial that day, Jones explained, "The Gulf Building symbolizes my conception of the Houston of Today. Both are essentially modern. Yet, in developing this building, which I dedicate to the memory of my parents, I have had in mind the strong hearts who pushed civilization westward a hundred

7. Ibid.
8. Ibid.
9. Ibid.

years ago and opened up this marvelous country for those who were to follow."[10] When Jones first arrived in Houston in 1898, the city encompassed nine square miles; now it covered more than forty square miles. From 40,000 residents, the city had grown to almost 300,000, making it the largest city in the state. The unique building epitomized the new South and Jones's role in its progress.

The Gulf Building was not only Houston's tallest building to date, but its most dramatic. Three Gothic-like brick setbacks rose, wedding-cake style, from a six-story base. According to the illustrated bound book commemorating the opening of the building, the "three setbacks convey the impression that the entire mass was hewn from a solid block of stone growing out of the pavement on which it rests." Everything about the building reportedly broke records: the elevators were supposedly the "fastest in the world," traveling at nine hundred feet a minute, or one and a half floors a second; the building was the "tallest south of Chicago;" the mail chutes were the "largest in all the south, capable of each holding 10,000 letters."[11] Even Gulf Oil Company's move from its Jones-owned headquarters across the street was, according to Ben Hurwitz, president of Westheimer Moving and Storage, "the largest thing of its kind that has ever been done south and west of St. Louis."[12] Indeed, Main at Rusk was roped off for ten days between 7:00 p.m. and 11:00 p.m. while movers trundled equipment, desks, and cabinets across the street to the oil company's new, spacious headquarters.

The new hall for Jones's National Bank of Commerce was the most spectacular part of the Gulf Building. Murals depicting moments in Texas history, painted on wet plaster by Vincent Maragliotti, decorated its entrance. The hall's soaring ceiling, covered in ornate, backlit gold medallions, extended five stories up from the ground level. Green and red terrazzo, separated by bright aluminum strips, radiated from the center of the long rectangular floor. Art Deco designs in Benedict nickel lavishly embellished doors, archways, radiator grills, tellers' cages, and stairways.

Authorized by the U.S. Department of Commerce, the Jesse H. Jones Aeronautical Beacon atop the skyscraper served as a guide to the Houston Airport, which had opened only the year before. One beam of bright white light shot straight up into the air while another beam threw a horizontal

10. *Houston Chronicle*, July 28, 1929.
11. Gulf Building commemorative book, 1929, Jesse H. Jones Collection [HE].
12. *Houston Chronicle*, July 28, 1929.

shaft toward the airport. At night, the building was bathed in light from 232 "projectors" which, along with the two aeronautical beams, made the awesome glowing tower visible from as far away as Sugar Land, about twenty miles southwest of downtown.

The commemorative book explained, "The Gulf Building is more than an office structure . . . it is, in intent and fact, a monument. A towering pillar of inspired architecture which expresses the true importance of the new south." In a possible reference to Jones's critics, the book said the building was "a monument to every Texan who with unsurpassed courage has met the work and trial of pioneering and, overcoming the handicaps of ignorance and prejudice, has risen to an undisputed position of distinction." The book summed up Jones's vision and intention: "Today the enterprise and progress of Texas is unchallenged. It is to visualize and enhance this rise to dominant power in trade, finance, industry, agriculture, art, and education that the Gulf Building has been erected. It is a monument to a glorious past and the promise of a broader future."[13] During the official opening of the new headquarters on Saturday evening, September 21, 1929, Jones and all the officers and staff of the National Bank of Commerce greeted thousands of people pouring in to gawk and marvel at the dazzling hall.[14] The "promise of a broader future" seemed assured.

One month later, on October 29, 1929, Wall Street crashed. The day after the record-breaking stock market drop, the *New York Times* reported on the front page, "Billions of dollars in open market values were wiped out . . . From every point of view, in total extent of losses sustained, in total turnover, in the number of speculators wiped out, the day was the most disastrous in Wall Street's history."[15] An astonishing 16,410,030 shares traded hands, a figure not to be exceeded for thirty-nine years.[16] The enormous volume clogged the exchange's machinery. The stock market closed at 3:00 P.M., but according to the *New York Times*, "The Exchange ticker did not tap out the final quotation on stock prices until 5:32 P.M." The paper also reported that all records for telephone, cable, and telegraph traffic had been broken and that "transatlantic telephone messages . . . showed a more than 100 percent increase over the normal average for this season."[17] Jones wired Will Rogers on the day of the crash,

13. Gulf Building commemorative book, 1929, Jesse H. Jones Collection [HE].
14. *Houston Chronicle*, September 29, 1929.
15. *New York Times*, October 30, 1929.
16. Ellis, *Nation in Torment*, 88.
17. *New York Times*, October 30, 1929.

"Apropos stock market . . . old cow friend says never rope a steer going down hill. You will get hurt every time."[18]

The New York Stock Exchange reached its peak in September. During October, the value of the stocks listed on the exchange plunged seventeen percent. In the same *New York Times* article on the front page the day after the crash, the reporter wrote, "The liquidation has been so violent, as well as widespread, that many bankers, brokers, and industrial leaders expressed the belief last night that it now has run its course."[19] They were wrong.

The Great Depression did not begin exactly on October 29, 1929. The stock market crash was only one of many simmering pots that finally boiled over. As Jones had warned, farmers and the banks that supported them had been in trouble for years. Annual per capita income for farmers in 1929 was $273 ($3,387), while for all U.S. citizens it averaged $750 ($9,307).[20] Between 1921 and 1929, more than five thousand small-town banks that served rural communities had failed.[21]

Simultaneously, automated industrial production had expanded and output per person had soared sixty-three percent.[22] New consumer products—radios, washing machines, electric irons, and refrigerators—flooded the market, along with advertisements promoting them as the way to improve life. But eighty percent of the nation's families had no savings. The cash-strapped farmers constituted one-quarter of the employed. Since someone had to buy these "must-have" products, installment credit became the rage. Saving for a rainy day and thinking that a penny saved was a penny earned had vanished with the horse and buggy. By 1929, 23 million automobiles were rolling on United States roadways, up from 7 million ten years before.[23]

The prosperity of the 1920s was shared by many, but not equally. Productivity increased faster than wages; workers were denied raises, despite the enormous increase in their output. The number of hours worked per person actually fell seven percent from 1920 to 1929. More sales and higher productivity brought huge profits for manufacturers and corporations, which provided only very small increases to workers' wages. Two hun-

---

18. September 29, 1929, Jesse H. Jones Collection [LOC].
19. *New York Times*, October 30, 1929.
20. McElvaine, *Great Depression*, 21.
21. Olson, *Saving Capitalism*, 3.
22. McElvaine, *Great Depression*, 17.
23. Ibid., 18.

dred corporations controlled nearly half of all industry, and more wealth and income was concentrated at the top of the economic scale than ever before.[24] In short, there simply were not enough people earning enough money to buy everything being produced. Income distribution so heavily skewed toward the top dragged down the economy and consequently hurt everyone.[25] But people who relied on wages, who rented their homes or paid mortgages, and who were deep in debt were the most vulnerable. These ominous events and trends were at first unnoticed, misunderstood or denied by most, consciously or unconsciously. But they were gathering into a vicious storm.

In response to the crash, a *Houston Chronicle* editorial offered sympathy to the small investor, expressed concern about almost everyone's diminished power to buy, and hoped that "people generally are led to restrain some of their speculative urges and are led to invest their funds in sounder enterprises." During the decade, investment funds had moved from bonds to stocks, making credit for major building projects and municipal undertakings hard to obtain. The editorial concluded, "If a better market for bonds, and for sound securities in general, results from the present deflation . . . then much development work which heretofore has been slowed up should soon be under full speed."[26]

In December, Charles Schwab, president of Bethlehem Steel, came to Houston to discuss business with Colonel R. C. Kuldell—general manager and vice president of Hughes Tools and president of the Houston Chamber of Commerce—and to deliver the keynote speech at the annual Chamber of Commerce dinner. Adding to the assignment of "most," "first," and "largest" by practically everyone to anything happening in town, Colonel Kuldell said that the evening's banquet "was expected to be the largest affair of its kind in the history of Houston."[27] But in the adolescent city, these constant claims were usually true. More than 1,500 enjoyed a seated dinner in the City Auditorium, while five hundred more filed into the balconies after the meal to hear Schwab speak. A noted

---

24. Ibid., 39.

25. Coincidentally, after the top 1 percent of the population earned 23 percent of all income in 1928, their share of the nation's total income began to drop until it hit a low of 9 percent in the 1970s. Since then, income has again steadily accumulated at the top, reaching the 1928 peak of 23 percent once more in 2007, right before the onset of the Great Recession. Reich, *Aftershock*, 20–21.

26. *Houston Chronicle*, October 30, 1929.

27. *Houston Chronicle*, December 18, 1929.

storyteller and a highly respected captain of industry, Schwab lived in a seventy-five-room mansion that occupied an entire square block in New York, but he called his farm in Pennsylvania home.[28]

With a hand on Schwab's shoulder, Jones introduced him and told the rapt audience how "Charley" had built twenty-five submarines and headed the emergency fleet during World War I. He called Schwab a "world figure" and a "loved friend."[29] Schwab told a series of warm, funny stories and shared his view of the crash with the grid of people seated at eighty-eight long tables stretched across the City Auditorium's floor and with those in the packed balcony. He told the eager listeners desperate for reassurance what they had come to hear when he said, "These stock market crashes will have no permanent effect on American business . . . The stock market hasn't crippled my industry. Most of the losers are speculators who knew nothing about what they were buying." He continued, "If I can bring a note of optimism to this assemblage I will feel that my trip is justified."[30]

In addition to introducing Schwab, Jones also welcomed W. N. (Bill) Blanton as the new general manager and vice president of the Houston Chamber of Commerce, saying, "The chamber has exchanged inertia for energy and avoirdupois for ambition." He also said the chamber needed better quarters and a bigger budget, then concluded, "To preserve the prosperity of our city, we must keep alive the community spirit that has been such an important factor in the growth of Houston. We must strive for that unity of action, the force that makes great achievements easy."[31] His words evoked his own role in developing the Houston Ship Channel, DePelchin Faith Home, and the American Red Cross during World War I; almost everyone there knew what he meant because they had all, for the most part, participated in those same efforts.

Efforts to build a community and their businesses had paid off. In 1929, $36 million ($447 million) in building permits had been issued, breaking all records. On average, Bell Telephone every hour installed nine new automatic dial telephones in homes and businesses throughout the city.[32] Houston ranked seventh in the nation for cities with buildings over twenty stories, surpassing Boston, Baltimore, and St. Louis. In 1922 there were 35,000 automobiles in Harris County, but by 1929 the num-

28. Ellis, *Nation in Torment*, 152.
29. *Houston Chronicle*, December 19, 1929.
30. Ibid.
31. *Houston Chronicle*, December 19, 1929.
32. *Houston Chronicle*, October 27, 1929.

ber had climbed to 97,000.[33] More than five hundred lawyers practiced law in Houston,[34] and twenty-one banks served the area. Jones's National Bank of Commerce had grown the fastest during the 1920s.

That the production of oil rather than financial speculation lay behind this rapid growth, for the moment, buffered Houston's economy. Jones and his National Bank of Commerce were among the first to recognize the safety of making loans to recognized and respected businessmen venturing into the oil business. Houston banks, however, were still too small to offer the large amounts needed to expand exploration and production, build refineries, and construct pipelines.[35] And just as Jones depended on east coast banks to finance his larger building projects, the oil companies also went east to get what they needed beyond what Jones and a few other bankers would and could supply locally.

Schwab concluded, "My idea of democracy is the desire of one man to do something for his fellow man. There is no socialism in that."[36] Jones's and Schwab's admonitions to serve others for the good of all would gain more relevance with time.

The economy and people's confidence rattled from all sides. People quit buying, borrowing, and investing. Personal consumption in the United States dropped from $77 billion ($956 billion) in 1929 to $60 billion ($764 billion) in 1930. Inventories piled up, merchants slashed orders, and manufacturers laid off workers.[37] Railroads especially felt the pinch. Throughout the 1920s, more and more freight had been shipped on trucks and airplanes instead of by rail. Railroad securities, once blue chip investments, were now poison.[38] Banks found that their loans were secured by assets that nobody wanted, especially railroad bonds and deflated stocks. They then had to sell these assets at give-away prices to pay depositors when they demanded their cash. Eventually, some banks simply ran out of money. Empty-handed, desperate depositors were left to stare at closed doors and realize they had no way to pay the mortgage or buy food. In 1930, 1,350 banks closed, including large ones in big cities.[39]

President Hoover mounted a "confidence campaign" soon after the crash and got businessmen to pledge not to reduce wages—instead, they

33. McComb, *Houston: Bayou City*, 102.
34. *Houston Chronicle*, October 24, 1926.
35. Buenger and Pratt, *But Also Good Business*, 79, 121.
36. Ibid.
37. Olson, *Saving Capitalism*, 9.
38. Ibid., 8.
39. Ibid., 9; Ellis, *Nation in Torment*, 109.

stopped hiring altogether and cut production. Investment by United States businesses fell thirty-five percent from 1929 to 1930. Hoover hoped the voluntary action that proved so successful in feeding European nations during and after World War I would prevail again.[40] He urged citizens to spend to reverse the "depression"—a word he coined because he thought "panic" and "crisis" sounded too severe. Unfortunately, too few had money to spend, or hoarded what they had. Hoover also pledged to cut taxes, balance the budget, and reduce his $4.1 billion ($52 billion) budget for 1930 by $150 million ($1.9 billion).[41] On December 2, 1930, in his annual message to Congress, President Hoover said, "The fundamental strength of the nation's economy is unimpaired."[42] Eight days later the United States Bank in New York defaulted. That bank, with fifty-seven branches and 500,000 depositors, was the first in New York to close since the stock market crashed fourteen months before, and it was the largest bank in the nation's history ever to do so.[43]

Cracks were beginning to appear in Houston's banking structure, too. Texas produced more oil than any other state in the nation, and its physical and financial flow through Houston had helped protect the city from the unfolding crisis. But by 1931, dwindling national demand had resulted in enormous gluts of cotton and oil, as well as diminished shipping from Houston. This turned into layoffs, depressed prices, little shopping, high loan losses, and too many banks with depleted resources.[44] The largest older banks, including Jones's, had the most secure loans on their books. The smaller, newer banks had taken what was left, assuming much greater risk.[45]

Although Jones carried mortgages on most of his buildings, he was still secure. From the time he sewed ten dollars into his waistband for the 1893 trip to the Chicago World's Fair, Jones always kept something back for emergencies, opportunity, and safety. He owned very little publicly traded stock and invested primarily in buildings and real estate. Jones scrambled a little more for mortgage money, refinanced some loans, and negotiated harder than usual with the east coast bankers, but he lost no buildings during the Great Depression and reportedly laid off

40. McElvaine, *Great Depression*, 59.
41. *Houston Chronicle*, December 4, 1929.
42. Ellis, *Nation in Torment*, 110.
43. Ibid., 112.
44. Buenger and Pratt, *But Also Good Business*, 90.
45. Ibid.

no employees. Frequent rent reduction requests from struggling tenants were almost always granted.[46]

After the stock market crash, Jones proceeded with projects already under way. He put KTRH radio on the air in March 1930 after W. O. Huggins, who ran the *Houston Chronicle*, complained about the *Houston Post*'s advertising advantage because of its affiliation with KPRC. As new products flooded the market during the 1920s, the advertising industry had flourished, and the common practice of briefly identifying a radio program's sponsor at the beginning of a show was changing fast. Huggins wrote to Jones, "All of the radio entertainments, which we receive here, are interspersed with extended advertising speeches . . . It looks like the time has come when we can no longer ignore the radio."[47] Accordingly, in December 1929, just two months after the crash, the *Houston Chronicle* announced on the front page, "Rice Hotel Is To Have Big Radio Station." The station's call letters—KTRH—corresponded to the Rice Hotel, its headquarters. The article said, "The new station . . . will broadcast the popular programs of the Columbia broadcasting system, giving that important national network its first entrance into South Texas."[48] At the start of 1930, Houston finally had two radio stations linked with national systems.

By 1931 Will Rogers, who had three weeks off between movies, was performing at benefits in Texas, Oklahoma, and Arkansas to raise money for the unemployed. He underwrote the entire tour. On his way to Houston, he wired: "Jesse, this is confidential and not for Democratic consumption. I am coming to Texas to make a one-week charity tour. Everything to go to your unemployed, Red Cross, or Community Chest. I been talking to Amon [Carter in Fort Worth] and I sure want to include your town and jip your rich birds for some dough. I am letting the women's club handle it, but the receipts to go where you think the best. Everything must be donated. It will be the only charity with not a nickle [sic] of expense."[49]

Rogers's help was needed. In 1931, instead of amazing new skyscrapers and nationally linked radio stations, the city saw a commissary open to feed the hungry. Thousands of citizens contributed to the Community Chest drive to help the unemployed. At the same time, two tottering banks

46. Bankers Mortgage Company documents, Jesse H. Jones Collection [HE].
47. October 4, 1928, Jesse H. Jones Collection [HE].
48. *Houston Chronicle*, December 11, 1929.
49. Will Rogers to Jesse Jones, January 9, 1931, Jesse H. Jones Collection [LOC].

were threatening to bring down all the others. Public National Bank was owned by W. L. Moody III and Odie Seagraves, who had invested heavily in natural gas wells and pipelines.[50] As commodity prices dropped and rumors spread, Public National Bank depositors began withdrawing their money. Houston National Bank, owned by Governor Ross Sterling, had more than $1 million ($14 million) in problem loans.[51] Jones heard Public National Bank had only enough money to get through Saturday, October 24, and if it did not reopen on Monday, Houston National Bank would probably follow—and from there, it would get worse. As Jones later wrote to a colleague, "The Public could not have gone through another day, and the officers of the Houston National told us, quite frankly, that if the Public closed, they would be forced to, and those two closings would have affected a great many small banks in this section."[52] Rural banks often kept their reserves in larger banks in bigger cities.

On the afternoon of October 25, Jones called all of Houston's bankers to his office at the top of the Gulf Building. He told them what he thought was about to happen and suggested that each lend to a pool large enough to keep both banks in business. The group of men deciding Houston's fate at this moment had, for the most part, known each other for years. With rancor, debate, and compromise, they had decided the city's future before.

R. M. Farrar, president of Union Bank and Trust, was probably the most conservative banker among the bunch. Farrar went to work for Jones in 1902 at the South Texas Lumber Company. He advanced in Jones's organization and served as president of the National Bank of Commerce until he left in 1920, over the seemingly endless dispute with Jones about where to locate the heart of the Houston Ship Channel. Now Farrar argued that mismanaged banks that took irresponsible risks should go out of business. The city's bankers and leading businessmen dickered until five on Monday morning and only managed to supply enough money to keep the two banks open that day. They agreed to reconvene at five that afternoon.

Bookkeepers cranked noisy mechanical calculators into the night while the men debated, pounded the table, and threatened each other. The two banks needed $1.25 million ($17.4 million) to stay open. Finally, at two in the morning, Jones phoned Captain James Baker, a major stock-

50. Buenger and Pratt, But Also Good Business, 96.
51. Ibid., 102.
52. Jesse Jones to W. T. Kemper, November 14, 1931, Jesse H. Jones Collection [LOC].

holder in one of Houston's largest banks, for backup. From his vacation in Massachusetts, Baker's support for Jones shoved the holdouts to come together on a rescue plan. By Tuesday morning Jones's National Bank of Commerce owned Public National Bank and the Joseph Meyer Interests owned the Houston National Bank. Twelve local banks, the electric, gas, and telephone companies, and Anderson Clayton & Company put together $1.25 million in guaranteed funds to pay depositors, support the transition, and save Houston's banks. When customers arrived at Public National Bank on Tuesday, they were directed to the National Bank of Commerce where Jones, who had had no sleep, welcomed them to his (and now their) bank.[53]

Revealing raw emotion and his innermost values, Jones wrote Farrar later that day, "You have been very, very, very helpful in this trying situation, and I want you to know that from the bottom of my heart I appreciate it, not so much for myself, but I believe that all we have done, are doing, and must continue doing, is necessary for the general welfare, and we cannot escape being our brother's keeper."[54]

A couple of days later Jones wrote to Captain Baker, "My telephone talk with you the other night gave us real courage after several days and nights of a very harrowing experience. I felt that none of us had a right not to stop the tragedy that would have followed our failing to do that which we did."[55]

In a letter asking the chairman of the Southern Pacific Line for a contribution to the rescue fund, Jones wrote, "If the Houston National and the Public National had closed, any number of country banks would have been forced to close because of having their reserves in these banks, in addition to the uneasiness that would have resulted. I am convinced also that the trouble would have reached as far as New Orleans, Shreveport, Dallas, Fort Worth, San Antonio, and, in fact, covered all of this section."[56] Jones did not need to mention that Southern Pacific's deposits would have been frozen if those banks had closed. Nonetheless, the railroad and all other national concerns approached for contributions to the rescue fund declined to participate. With Jones's leadership, it was the local businessmen, despite their differences, who came together for the good of their community and rescued their banks on their own.

53. Jesse Jones to Hale Holden, November 30, 1931, Jesse H. Jones Collection [LOC]; *Houston Chronicle*, October 27, 1931.

54. Jesse Jones to R. M. Farrar, October 27, 1931, Jesse H. Jones Collection [LOC].

55. Jesse Jones to James A. Baker Sr., October 29, 1931, Jesse H. Jones Collection [LOC].

56. Jesse Jones to Hale Holden, November 30, 1931, Jesse H. Jones Collection [LOC].

Houston's civic and business leaders enjoyed something like a brotherhood. For the most part, they all had their community's best interests at heart, and they knew each other well. One banker wrote another about their contributions to the fund, "Malone and I both expected to raise a little at the last minute if we were compelled to do so in getting up the amount of guaranty necessary, both of us knowing Jones so well that we knew, when all thought the trade was closed, he would begin to ask for a little additional protection, just as he did."[57] When Jones wrote Farrar about the possibility of another bank rescue, Farrar spared no words, "I would like to suggest that you get a pair of cheap cutters and cut that telephone wire. Do not constitute yourself as a guardian or a Santa Claus for the community—none of us are in any way qualified to look after anything or anybody beyond our own affairs, and not so well for that even. If you are unconvinced, I refer [you] to the files of your own newspaper for conclusive evidence as to the one, and your own Note and Asset files as to the other. And the same observations apply to all of the rest of us, bud, and put that in your pipe and smoke it."[58]

Jones was undeterred. He felt everyone's best interests were served when capitalists protected and promoted the common good. He wrote to a colleague, "Other communities are having plenty of bank troubles and all of them will pay dearly for not stopping the fire before it starts."[59] By now Jones was less concerned about Houston than about the country as a whole.

In 1931, eighty-two breadlines in New York served more than 85,000 meals a day to thousands of hungry and destitute citizens.[60] Thirty states were reeling from effects of the worst drought in the country's history.[61] When winter came, people began burning their furniture to stay warm, and they ate grass and rummaged through garbage cans to ward off hunger. Some committed suicide in the hope that their life insurance would help save their families after they were gone.

President Hoover was still relying on voluntary humanitarian action to rescue the national economy, willing to use the government only to encourage people to cooperate, share, spend, and help their neighbors.[62] He thought business cycles were "natural" processes that could not

57. Buenger and Pratt, *But Also Good Business*, 104.
58. R. M. Farrar to Jesse Jones, December 18, 1931, Jesse H. Jones Collection [LOC].
59. Jesse Jones to A. D. McDonald, October 29, 1931, Jesse H. Jones Collection [LOC].
60. Ellis, *Nation in Torment*, 129.
61. Ibid., 144.
62. McElvaine, *Great Depression*, 58.

and should not be influenced by legislative action.[63] He once said using government to solve the depression was like believing one could "exorcise a Caribbean hurricane by statutory law."[64] As the situation worsened, he resisted suggestions for more vigorous government action beyond simply encouraging volunteerism to stop the economic slide. He continued to announce "the depression is over" and somehow hoped that would solve the problem.[65] The facts said differently.

Investment by United States businesses fell another thirty-five percent in 1931, and the next year dropped to practically nothing.[66] Another 2,300 banks failed.[67] Anyone who still had money did not trust the banks, and citizens hoarded and hid billions of their precious banknotes in shoeboxes, under mattresses, or underground. Bankers called in loans and refused to make new ones.[68] Businesses went under and unemployment escalated.[69] Thousands of shantytowns and squatters' camps developed, one right across the street from Schwab's magnificent mansion in New York.[70] The precipitous drop in consumer spending, miserly bank loans, virtually no business investment, and less and less money in circulation brought the United States economy to a grinding halt. Millions upon millions of citizens suffered, and everyone was scared.

As things grew even worse, Federal Reserve chairman Eugene Meyer suggested that President Hoover establish an agency similar to the War Finance Corporation (WFC), which helped businesses and banks mobilize and manufacture material for World War I by providing government credit beyond what was privately available.[71] Meyer thought that loans to banks, railroads, and businesses on the brink of bankruptcy might stabilize them and help get the wheels of the economy turning again.[72] Still loath to mingle government and business, Hoover reluctantly accepted the idea in hopes such an organization would restore confidence and halt the unfolding disaster.[73] Private initiative had had more than two years to correct the calamity, and it was becoming apparent that

63. Ibid., 65.
64. Ibid., 67.
65. Ibid., 62.
66. Ibid., 73.
67. Ellis, *Nation in Torment*, 187.
68. Ibid.
69. McElvaine, *Great Depression*, 75.
70. Ellis, *Nation in Torment*, 152.
71. Ibid., 186.
72. Ibid., 187.
73. Ibid., 188.

government might be the only institution powerful enough to reverse course. In contrast to the year before, when he declared that the fundamental economy was "unimpaired," President Hoover announced on December 8, 1931, in his annual message to Congress, "In order that the public may be absolutely assured and that the Government may be in position to meet any public necessity, I recommend that an emergency Reconstruction [Finance] Corporation of the nature of the former War Finance Corporation should be established. It may not be necessary to use such an instrumentality very extensively. The very existence of such a bulwark will strengthen confidence."[74]

Rumors quickly surfaced about who would be on the board of the Reconstruction Finance Corporation (RFC) which, according to the act, would include four Republicans and three Democrats. Hoover had selected Meyer as chairman and Chicago banker Charles Dawes as president. Dawes had served as Calvin Coolidge's vice president and ambassador to Great Britain. One month after Hoover's announcement, a front page *Houston Chronicle* article revealed, "Jesse H. Jones, Houston financier, businessman, and publisher, was today being widely discussed among Democratic leaders here as a probable member of the board of directors of the emergency $2 billion [$31 billion] Reconstruction Finance Corporation, approved last night by the senate and to be approved by the house of representatives later this week."[75]

Arkansas Senator Joe Robinson, Virginia Senator Carter Glass, and Speaker of the House John Nance Garner, all of whom conferred with Hoover about the Democratic appointees,[76] knew Jones to varying degrees. Robinson, who was Senate minority leader (and had been Al Smith's 1928 running mate), liked Jones. Glass, who had served in Congress since 1902 and was drafting and promoting legislation to institute federal deposit insurance—something Jones long had felt was fundamental to the nation's financial stability—also admired Jones, particularly for his Democratic party accomplishments. Garner, a Texas banker who had also served in Congress since 1902, was acquainted with Jones, but the two men were not yet particularly close. They both aligned themselves with Woodrow Wilson and attended the 1924 Democratic convention as Texas delegates, but at the time were on different career paths: Garner in government and Jones in business. By 1932, however, both men were

74. Jones, *Fifty Billion Dollars*, ix.
75. *Houston Chronicle*, January 12, 1932.
76. *Houston Chronicle*, January 23, 1932.

in government and on the same page when it came to the need for federal deposit insurance, for separating speculative investments and dubious business practices from banking, and for government action to address the economic catastrophe.[77] When Hoover asked Garner for a list of RFC nominees, Garner handed him a piece of paper with one name: Jesse Jones.

As for the RFC board, Jones said those considered for it "should be men of broad experience who realize that most of our country lies west of the Hudson River and none of it east of the Atlantic Ocean."[78] He made it clear that if appointed, he intended to push progress, growth, and power toward the South and West, and away from the east coast—particularly away from Wall Street.

On January 22, 1932, Hoover signed the bill creating the RFC and said, "It brings into being a powerful organization with adequate resources, able to strengthen weaknesses that may develop in our credit, banking, and railway structure, in order to permit business and industry to carry on normal activities free from the fear of unexpected shocks and retarding influences." He clarified: "It is not created for the aid of big industries or big banks. Such institutions can take care of themselves. It is created for the support of the smaller banks and financial institutions, and through rendering their resources liquid, to give renewed support to business, industry, and agriculture. It should give opportunity to mobilize the gigantic strength of our country for recovery."[79]

Two days later, President Hoover identified the three Democrats he was appointing to the board: Arkansas banker Harvey Couch, Utah banker Wilson McCarthy, whose father had ridden for the Pony Express, and Jesse Jones.[80] Will Rogers reported in his daily column, "What's this I hear about my two best Democratic friends, Jesse Jones and Harvey Couch, going to be allowed to distribute some government money? This can go on record as being my application for some."[81]

Jones was in Washington to attend the annual National Press Club dinner, where the *Houston Chronicle*'s Washington correspondent, Bascom Timmons, was being installed as president. At the dinner, Garner presented Timmons with a gavel made from the horn of a Texas longhorn

77. Timmons, *Jones: Man and Statesman*, 134, 162, 177.
78. *Saturday Evening Post*, June 12, 1937.
79. Jones, *Fifty Billion Dollars*, ix–x.
80. Olson, *Saving Capitalism*, 14.
81. Rogers, syndicated column no. 1719, Will Rogers Museum.

Jesse Jones (front row, second from left) and President Herbert Hoover (center), 1932.
Courtesy Library of Congress.

that had been raised on a ranch where Timmons had worked as a young boy.[82]

The RFC board was sworn in on February 2, 1932. After the ceremony, Meyer abruptly told photographers to "make it snappy because we have a lot of work to do." Dawes complained about the bright lights, "I haven't got but one pair of eyes, and I don't want them put out by these lights now." Jones tossed his scrolled commission in the air like a college diploma, tried to catch it, and missed.[83] Like their demeanor during the photo op, their ideas and positions would differ, but they were all there to save the country. Jones remembered, "In accepting the appointment, I was influenced by the thought that every man should respond to his country's call in emergencies, and I was convinced that conditions were rapidly approaching such a precarious state that only the federal government through unusual methods could deal with them effectively."[84]

Hoover said the RFC was created "for the support of smaller banks

82. *Houston Chronicle*, January 21, 1932.
83. *Houston Chronicle*, February 2, 1932.
84. *Saturday Evening Post*, June 12, 1937.

and financial institutions," but A. P. Giannini, president of the huge and struggling Bank of America, was at the RFC's door almost before it opened. Giannini's Transamerica Corporation operated four hundred banks throughout California and needed a quick infusion of cash to stay open and pay depositors. The RFC loaned Bank of America $65 million ($1 billion), all of which was repaid with interest within two years.[85] Indicating that Jones was the driving force, Giannini sent a telegram the day after receiving the loan, "You're a brick, Jesse. May I on behalf of my associates and myself thank you sincerely for your very prompt action."[86]

While Gianinni was in conference with the RFC board, Oris and Mantis Van Swearingen were out in the RFC lobby waiting their turn. The bachelor twin brothers owned the largest railway system in the United States and were deep in debt. They had just borrowed $1.5 million ($23.3 million) from a large east coast bank to keep their Missouri Pacific line from going under, which was made with the understanding that the brothers would get an RFC loan and return the money within a matter of weeks.[87] The brothers, though, needed much more than $1.5 million, asking the RFC for ten times that amount—$15 million ($233 million). The request ignited the first of many disputes among the RFC board. Jones felt the bank was intentionally unloading bad debt onto taxpayers. He recalled, "I didn't think the government should bail out private banking houses that for years had been profiting from railroad financing, especially when the bankers were amply able to take care of themselves, as was true in this case." Jones continued, "I could see ahead of the RFC a long and ugly road along which we should need the confidence of the Congress if we were to revive the depressed state of our entire economy."[88] Jones asked his fellow board members for a day to convince them not to make the loan and if he could not change their minds, he would vote for the loan to maintain the appearance of a united front for Hoover's new confidence-building organization. Jones was unable to persuade them, however, and the RFC loaned the Missouri Pacific $23 million ($358 million). One year later the railroad was bankrupt.[89]

The RFC was much more than seven men sitting around a table debating the merits of huge government loans. Their staff set up offices in thirty-two Federal Reserve banks and branches all across the nation to

---

85. Jones, *Fifty Billion Dollars*, 19.
86. A. P. Giannini to Jesse Jones, March 9, 1933, Jesse H. Jones Collection [HE].
87. Ellis, *Nation in Torment*, 192.
88. Jones, *Fifty Billion Dollars*, 123.
89. Ibid., 129.

accept applications, examine books, and counsel tens of thousands of desperate businessmen seeking loans. The RFC headquarters originally took up two floors of the old Department of Commerce building at Nineteenth Street and Pennsylvania Avenue, but quickly spread over the entire building. More than 30,000 people applied for three hundred jobs when the RFC opened.[90]

The RFC attracted eager, bright people, including Thomas Corcoran, who became assistant general counsel and immediately began to recruit Harvard law school graduates recommended by his former professor, Felix Frankfurter. The press called them the "Corcoran gallery of lawyers," in mock comparison with the nearby Corcoran Gallery of Art. By including Jews, Catholics, and women among his recruits, Corcoran clearly diversified the RFC.[91] RFC attorney and Columbia law school graduate Ida Klaus remembered the time, saying, "It was like a mission; we were dedicated day and night to resolving the economic problems of the depression and putting America back on its feet. The very bright ones were sent to the RFC to work with Jesse Jones. That was considered the great salvation area, and the area where probably the most important subjects were going to be handled. We got there as young people out to save the country, and there was nothing else we talked about."[92]

Despite its good intentions, the RFC was soon lambasted for making loans only to large institutions. Given that 210 of the largest banks controlled forty percent of the nation's financial assets, large loans to large banks made sense, but they were still misunderstood and unpopular. In seven months, the RFC made loans to more than one-quarter of the nation's banks, seventy percent of them in towns with less than 5,000 people.[93] The RFC also disbursed more than $300 million ($4.6 billion) to prop up sixty-two railroads.[94] But criticism continued. No matter the size of its loans, the RFC offended many who thought it brought too much government into private life. Some critics complained it was not doing enough for small businessmen, especially after the RFC made a $90 million ($1.4 billion) loan to its recently departed president, Charles Dawes.

Dawes abruptly resigned from the RFC in June, just four months after he had been sworn in as its president. Only the Republican members of the board knew he was leaving for Chicago to resume control of his

90. *Houston Chronicle*, February 5, 1932.
91. McKean, *Tommy the Cork*, 48.
92. Klaus interview, in *Brother Can You Spare a Billion?*
93. Jones, *Fifty Billion Dollars*, 19.
94. Ibid., 109.

very troubled Central Republic Bank, which he stopped actively managing when he became Coolidge's vice president. Jones wryly remembered, "Neither Eugene Meyer, our chairman, nor Ogden Mills, who as Secretary of the Treasury was an ex-officio member of our board, had yet learned the desirability of taking us three country-boy Democratic members into their confidence and counsel."[95] The three Democrats found out why Dawes was leaving only a few minutes before he boarded the train to Chicago.

Ten days after Dawes's departure, Jones went to Chicago as a delegate to the 1932 Democratic National Convention. Many of the nation's most respected journalists, including Walter Lippmann, H. L. Mencken, Heywood Broun, and Arthur Krock, opposed Roosevelt as the Democratic candidate for president.[96] Jones was no different, and his *Houston Chronicle* endorsed Garner's candidacy, as did newspaper magnate William Randolph Hearst and powerful Senator William Gibbs McAdoo of California. The *Houston Chronicle* editorial endorsing Garner said its second choice was Chicago banker Melvin Traylor, who was coincidentally one of Jones's largest lenders. The editorial never once mentioned Roosevelt.[97] Will Rogers was more prescient, having pegged Roosevelt as the candidate in 1930, after Roosevelt won the New York governor's race by a landslide. The day after the 1930 election, Rogers wrote, "The Democrats nominated their 1932 candidate yesterday."[98]

Instead of attending the convention, potential presidential candidate Traylor stood in the packed lobby of his First National Bank and tried to convince frantic customers that their money was safe. Thirty-five smaller banks in the area had recently fallen like a row of dominoes, and Chicago's large downtown banks had disgorged more than $100 million ($1.53 billion) in one week. Half of all the money in Dawes's bank had been removed by leery depositors during the past year, and it was now going out at $2 million ($31 million) a day. On June 26, the day before the Democratic National Convention began, Traylor picked up Jones at his hotel for an emergency meeting of leading Chicago bankers and businessmen. There Dawes announced he would not open his bank in the morning and everyone knew if the Central Republic Bank did not open, a frenzy of withdrawals would force all of Chicago's banks—possibly all of

95. Ibid., 73.
96. McElvaine, *Great Depression*, 81.
97. *Houston Chronicle*, March 12, 1932.
98. Alter, *Defining Moment*, 84.

the nation's banks—to close. Traylor asked Jones to call President Hoover about a loan to keep the Central Republic Bank in business.

Jones and the local RFC staff examined what they could of the bank's books in the little time they had and concluded the bank needed $95 million ($1.45 billion) to pay depositors and stay open. As he had in Houston, Jones tried to get the bankers and businessmen to create a pool, but $5 million ($78 million) was all the beleaguered men could muster. Jones, however, figured if the bank was liquidated, an RFC loan would eventually be repaid. He called Hoover and told him if the loan was not made, the bank would not open. At the very least, all the banks in the area would then collapse and hundreds of thousands of people and businesses would have no access to their money. With only a few hours to spare before opening time Monday morning, the RFC loan was arranged, Central Republic Bank opened, and catastrophe was averted for a little while longer.[99]

Back at the convention, no candidate had been selected after three ballots. A disastrous deadlock like 1924 was on everyone's minds. Some worried that Newton D. Baker, Wilson's secretary of war and a known "internationalist," was about to win the nomination as a compromise candidate. Using both possibilities as arguments, James Farley, Roosevelt's campaign manager, convinced Garner to withdraw and switch his Texas delegates to Roosevelt. He also asked McAdoo to switch California's support from Garner to Roosevelt. Both agreed, and Roosevelt won on the fourth ballot.

Roosevelt flew from Albany to Chicago and became the first presidential candidate to accept the nomination at the convention, as well as the first candidate to fly in an airplane. The flight from Albany to Chicago took nine hours and required two refueling stops along the way.[100] Garner reluctantly became Roosevelt's running mate. Weeks before, the Republicans, on the first ballot, had selected Hoover and Charles Curtis as their party's candidates.[101]

News about the "Dawes Loan," as it became known, exploded. The government had loaned $90 million ($1.4 billion) to a huge bank, but offered nothing to the 700,000 unemployed people in Chicago or to the city's 14,000 teachers who were owed $20 million ($310 million) in back pay.[102] The same scene was enacted throughout the nation: government

99. Timmons, *Jones: Man and Statesman*, 169–72.
100. Alter, *Defining Moment*, 116.
101. Shields-West, *Almanac of Presidential Campaigns*, 169.
102. Ellis, *Nation in Torment*, 202.

made huge loans to big banks and businessmen, but offered nothing to the millions of desperate, hopeless individuals who had absolutely nowhere to turn.

In response, Senate Minority Leader Robinson proposed allowing the RFC to provide direct federal relief. Hoover refused, declaring, "Responsibility for relief to distress belongs to private organizations, local communities, and the states. That fundamental policy is not to be changed."[103] Democratic Senator Robert Wagner, speaking on the Senate floor, pointed out the discrepancy in lawmakers' attitude toward desperate citizens and toward the big businesses who had received RFC loans, saying sarcastically about those businessmen, "We did not preach to them rugged individualism. We did not sanctimoniously roll out sentences rich with synonyms of self-reliance. We were not carried away with apprehension over what would happen to their independence if we extended them a helping hand."[104] Will Rogers, maybe with Jones's encouragement, joined the fray and wrote, "The Reconstruction loaned the railroads money, medium and small banks money, and all they did with it was pay off what they owed to New York banks. So the money went uphill instead of down."[105]

In short, the RFC was resented. It was not increasing employment, wages, or available credit. It enabled banks to return deposits, but otherwise it was not putting food on people's plates or roofs over their heads. Railroads, even as they cut back on employment and maintenance, used RFC proceeds to pay back east coast bankers. Smaller banks often used RFC proceeds to pay back loans to larger banks. Most banks made no new loans with the government money, instead using it to build and hoard reserves. More credit, not less, was urgently needed. Jones said, "There has been too much reluctance on the part of banks . . . to borrow [from the RFC] for the purpose of relending . . . Most banks have been endeavoring to get as liquid as possible . . . too much [so] for the public good."[106] Clearly, if the RFC were going to restore confidence and turn the economy around, loans to banks would not be enough.

Bowing to public pressure, Hoover finally introduced legislation that allowed the RFC to make relief loans to states and cities. Speaker of the House and vice presidential candidate Garner wanted to go further; he

103. Ibid., 197.
104. Ibid., 193.
105. Ibid., 194.
106. Olson, *Saving Capitalism*, 17.

introduced amendments that would allow the RFC to finance national public works; to make loans to states, cities, and towns for local public works; to make loans to individuals, businesses, and farmers; and to disclose details about all RFC loans. Up until then, the RFC had operated in secrecy. Meyer and Republicans on the RFC board avoided the press out of fear that depositors would rush in to remove their money once they discovered a bank had received an RFC loan. Jones, however, agreed with Garner, who said, "I have contended consistently that there has been too much secrecy about what has been going on . . . If the truth scares people, let it come. Let the people know all about everything the government does."[107] Jones echoed his fellow Texan, "Yes, the truth can hurt, but not as badly as uncertainty and fear."[108]

Hoover promptly vetoed Garner's legislation and said it was the most "dangerous suggestion ever seriously made to the country . . . Never has such power for evil been placed at the unlimited discretion of the seven individuals" who sit on the RFC board.[109] Senator Wagner submitted a substitute bill that raised the RFC's lending capacity by $1.5 billion ($23 billion), allowed it to make loans for public works, permitted it to make loans to cities and states for relief purposes, and established twelve regional agricultural credit corporations to make loans to farmers.[110] The act, however, did not permit loans to individuals or demand disclosure about RFC activities. Hoover signed the Emergency Relief and Construction Act on July 21, 1932, increasing the RFC's power. Indirectly through RFC loans to cities and states, the federal government for the first time gave assistance during an economic emergency to the unemployed. As Senator Wagner explained, "Modern unemployment is a consequence of national developments which must be dealt with, not as a purely local concern, but as a national problem."[111] Lippmann later wrote that the New Deal really started with the RFC and Hoover, not with the inauguration of Roosevelt.[112]

This new power was not taken lightly. Jones knew how to use the latest technology to reach and influence a mass audience. Speaking over national radio, he said the RFC board appreciated "that in their hands has been placed the lending of more than three and a half billion dollars

107. Jones, *Fifty Billion Dollars*, 83.
108. Ibid., 87.
109. *International Herald Tribune,* July 12, 1932.
110. Olson, *Saving Capitalism*, 19.
111. Ellis, *Nation in Torment*, 200.
112. McKean, *Tommy the Cork*, 32.

Jesse Jones became a familiar and reassuring voice over national radio during the Great Depression and World War II.

[$54 billion]—the largest governmental peacetime undertaking in the history of the world . . . It is my firm belief that by judicious handling of this vast amount of money and credit placed at the disposal of the Reconstruction Finance Corporation—taken in connection with the rehabilitation program of both governmental and private initiative—business can be got under way, employment started, and an exceedingly tragic era ended."[113]

The RFC Chairman Meyer, who had opposed revealing loan recipients' identities and lending for relief and public works, left the board. Hoover appointed Democrat Atlee Pomerene in his place, giving the Democrats a majority. As it turned out, the policy changes did not make enough difference. Large RFC-funded public works projects, like the San Francisco Bay Bridge, required months of planning and engineering, and could not immediately generate many jobs because they were not "shovel ready." The $300 million ($4.6 billion) provided to states for emergency relief proved entirely inadequate. In one day, five states together asked the RFC for $200 million ($3.1 billion), two-thirds of all the government money

113. Jesse Jones, radio speech, NBC, August 29, 1932, Jesse H. Jones Collection [UT].

available to the entire country to provide food and shelter for millions of frantic, jobless people. To avoid competing with rural banks, RFC set higher interest rates at the agriculture credit corporations, and farmers refused to borrow.[114] Hoover's policies of balancing the budget and raising taxes did not "boost confidence" as planned, nor did it ease the financial implosion.

In October 1932, stock prices began to slide again and 102 banks failed. Applications for RFC loans were soaring.[115] When one of the twenty banks in Nevada threatened to close, the governor shut down all of them.[116] In a Detroit campaign speech, Hoover declared, "The gigantic forces of depression are in retreat," but by the 1932 election, almost one-quarter of all able workers in the United States were without jobs[117] and over a third of those with jobs had only part-time work. Suicides tripled, and calls for revolution were common and sometimes violent.[118] The RFC had loaned more than $1.5 billion ($23 billion) to thousands of banks, railroads, and insurance companies, but the economy and the people were no better off.[119] The United States was veering toward chaos and collapse.

When Roosevelt accepted the Democratic nomination, he said, "Let it be from now on the task of our party to break foolish traditions." He spoke both to those at the convention and to the millions glued to their radios when he said, "I pledge you, I pledge myself, to a new deal for the American people. Let us all here assembled constitute ourselves prophets of a new order of competence and courage. This is more than a political campaign; it is a call to arms. Give me your help, not to win votes alone, but to win in this crusade to restore America to its people."[120]

Roosevelt may not have formulated specific policies or articulated them on the stump, but people hungered for his words of change and hope. He talked about plans "that build from the bottom up and not the top down, that put their faith once more in the forgotten man at the bottom of the economic pyramid."[121] In a speech at Oglethorpe University, he said, "The country needs, and unless I mistake its temper, the country demands bold, persistent experimentation. It is common sense to take a

114. Olson, *Saving Capitalism*, 20–23.
115. Ibid., 23.
116. Jones, *Fifty Billion Dollars*, 17.
117. *Houston Chronicle*, October 23, 1932.
118. Alter, *Defining Moment*, 75.
119. Olson, *Saving Capitalism*, 23.
120. Alter, *Defining Moment*, 119.
121. Ibid., 90.

Jesse Jones confers with President-elect Franklin Roosevelt and Senator Cordell Hull of Tennessee, future Secretary of State, in 1933 one month before Roosevelt's first inauguration. In a rare instance, Roosevelt's leg braces are visible in the picture. Courtesy Corbis.

method and try it. If it fails, admit it frankly and try another. But above all, try something."[122]

No one was quite sure what to do during these perilous and unprecedented times, except to vote. Sixty-two percent of eligible voters participated in the 1932 election. Three million more voted than four years before and overwhelmingly elected Roosevelt and Garner as president and vice president. The two men received 57.4 percent of the popular vote, the highest Democratic percentage since Andrew Jackson in 1832. They received 472 electoral votes versus fifty-nine for Hoover and Curtis, the highest total since Lincoln was elected during the Civil War.[123] Republicans lost twelve seats in the Senate, along with their majority, and 101 seats in the House.[124] Democrats held 306 of the 414 House seats and

122. McElvaine, *Great Depression*, 117.
123. Simon Michelet, handout prepared for National Get-Out-The-Vote Club, October 23, 1933, Jesse H. Jones Collection [HE].
124. Alter, *Defining Moment*, 134.

fifty-nine of ninety-six Senate seats. The *Houston Chronicle* crowed, "As a result of their party's smashing victory at the polls, Southern Democrats will dominate virtually every important committee in both House and Senate."[125]

Like everyone else in the country, both parties had less to spend in 1932 than they did in 1928. Hoover's national campaign had cost about $2.9 million ($44 million), while Roosevelt's spent $2.3 million ($36 million). The largest expenditure for both was buying time on the radio, where Roosevelt was especially effective—most listeners thought Roosevelt was talking to them when he said, "My friends."[126]

125. *Houston Chronicle*, November 10, 1932.
126. Shields-West, *Almanac of Presidential Campaigns*, 173.

1933

At the End
of Our String

THE COLD WINTRY MONTHS between Franklin Roosevelt's November 1932 election and his March 1933 inauguration were among the most painful and harsh of the Great Depression. From 1929 to the start of 1933, national income had shrunk by half and stock prices had fallen seventy-five percent.[1] Wheat sold for thirty cents ($4.92 in current dollars) a bushel, down from its high of three dollars ($49.20).[2] Home foreclosures surged from a normal 78,000 annually to 273,000 by the end of 1932.[3] Twenty percent of the nation's children did not have enough to eat.[4] During 1932, more than three times as many people left the United States as immigrated to it.[5] As people's confidence disappeared and their anxiety escalated, runs on banks spread. After a Davenport bank failed on January 20, 1933, Iowa's governor closed all the banks to prevent a statewide chain reaction.[6] On February 14, Michigan Governor William A. Comstock closed the state's banks after Jones and President Hoover failed to convince

1. Alter, *Defining Moment*, 148.
2. McElvaine, *Great Depression*, 135.
3. Ellis, *Nation in Torment*, 231.
4. Ibid., 240.
5. Ibid., 232.
6. Olson, *Saving Capitalism*, 26.

Henry Ford and Senator Jim Couzens to create a pool to support Detroit's two weakest banks, similar to what Jones had done in Houston—although this time the U.S. government, through the RFC, was a willing participant. Jones proposed lending $65 million ($1.06 billion) in RFC funds to the Union Guardian Trust Company if Ford agreed to contribute to a rescue fund and allow smaller depositors and investors to have first claim on the bank's resources before he collected his $20 million ($328 million) in deposits. Instead, according to Jones, "Mr. Ford refused to put his chips into the kitty and said, 'Let the crash come. There isn't any reason why I, the largest individual taxpayer in the country, should bail the government out of its loans to banks.'"[7] Jones recalled, "The closing of all banks in the motor capital . . . was the principal prelude to the collapse, during the next three weeks, of the nation's entire financial system."[8]

After Michigan's banks closed, Maryland's governor quickly followed suit. On March 1, Alabama, Louisiana, and Oklahoma closed their banks. The next day, seven more states, including Texas, shut theirs. On March 3, the only U.S. banks still open were in New York and Chicago, but they and the New York Stock Exchange shut down that day. When Hoover heard the New York banks had closed, he said, "We are at the end of our string."[9] Still, he took time on the day he left office to write a note to Jones that said, "Before I leave Washington, I want to express to you my deep appreciation for the cooperation which you have shown to me in these difficult times. I trust that the future will bring you prosperity and contentment."[10] When Roosevelt was inaugurated on March 4, the nation's financial system had completely collapsed.

Roosevelt took the oath of office with his hand on his family's centuries-old Dutch Bible, which was opened to the First Epistle of Paul. The passage said, "And now abideth faith, hope, charity, these three; but the greatest of these is charity."[11] Roosevelt declared to the gathered dignitaries, to the mass of people assembled in front of the White House, and to the millions of anxious Americans gathered around their radios, "This is a day of national consecration." He delivered what would become timeless watchwords: "This great nation will endure as it has endured, will revive and will prosper. So, first of all, let me assert my firm belief that the only thing we have to fear is fear itself." He then laid his cards on

7. Jones, *Fifty Billion Dollars*, 62–63.
8. Ibid., 54.
9. Ellis, *Nation in Torment*, 267.
10. Herbert Hoover to Jesse Jones, March 3, 1933, Jesse H. Jones Collection [HE].
11. Ellis, *Nation in Torment*, 271.

the table, saying, "I shall ask the Congress for the one remaining instrument to meet the crisis—broad executive power to wage a war against the emergency as great as the power that would be given to me if we were in fact invaded by a foreign foe."[12]

Two days after Roosevelt's inauguration, the *Houston Chronicle* summed up the nation's shift toward accepting federal government help: "Most of us do not see clearly what is ahead. We are in the midst of an economic crisis such as we have not known before. Federal action in the situation now supersedes state action. We must look to Washington for our major solutions."[13] Jones knew the days of gathering local leaders to solve major problems were over. The bank rescue in Houston may have been the last of its kind.[14]

The four busiest men in Washington after the inauguration were, reportedly, President Roosevelt, Secretary of the Treasury William Woodin, Director of the Budget Lewis Douglas, and RFC board member Jones.[15] They were known as the "16-hour-a-day men."[16] The day after his inauguration, the new president declared a nationwide bank "holiday," as opposed to Hoover's less festive and unimplemented "moratorium." He reassured the panicked public by saying only sound banks would be permitted to reopen. On Thursday, March 9, a special session of Congress passed the Emergency Banking Act only seven hours after it was introduced. The first three of the act's five titles contained its substance. The first title legalized the bank holiday Roosevelt had already declared (and Hoover had considered, but resisted). The second title permitted the controller of the currency to reorganize insolvent banks for the benefit of depositors with frozen assets. The third title authorized the RFC to purchase preferred stock in banks and trust companies.[17] A *New York Times* headline blared, "Roosevelt Gets Power of Dictator," the important distinction being that he did not seize those powers. Congress unanimously granted them to Roosevelt.[18]

The Emergency Banking Act had its beginnings in Hoover's administration, only Hoover could not bring himself to place that much power in government hands despite the precipice on which the nation found

12. Roosevelt, "Inaugural Address."
13. *Houston Chronicle*, March 6, 1933.
14. Jones, *Fifty Billion Dollars*, 23–25.
15. *Houston Post*, May 6, 1933,
16. *Houston Chronicle*, May 5, 1933.
17. Olson, *Saving Capitalism*, 30.
18. Alter, *Defining Moment*, 251.

itself. As historian John Morton Blum explained, "When the Reconstruction Finance Corporation bought preferred stock, it was owning that portion of the bank that the preferred stock represented. And that was a venture of government into the private sector beyond anything that Hoover, the Republicans, or most conservative Democrats would previously have tolerated."[19]

Hoover's reluctance to employ the RFC's full potential had made Jones squirm. Jones said, "The conception of the RFC, for which credit must be accorded President Hoover, had been good, but it was a year too late. Even when it started, its board, for a time, was entirely too timid and slow to save the country from the disasters of 1932 and 1933. And the funds available to it were far too small." He followed with a stunning statement: "A few billion dollars boldly but judiciously lent and invested by such a government agency as the RFC in 1931 and 1932 would have prevented the failure of thousands of banks and averted the complete breakdown in business, agriculture, and industry."[20]

Title III of the Emergency Banking Act gave the RFC the power not simply to lend, but also to invest. Instead of just making loans to banks, which put them deeper in debt, the RFC could now strengthen banks by enlarging their capital structures and increasing their lending limits: the amounts banks could lend rose as their capital structure grew. *Fortune* magazine said, "The stampede of fear came to its awesome, abrupt end on the Saturday of Mr. Roosevelt's inauguration. And then came enthralling action. Within five days Congress changed the direction of [the] RFC from one of prevention to one of reconstruction."[21]

Thousands of inspectors from the Federal Reserve, the Treasury Department, and the RFC fanned out across the nation to inspect banks and determine which could reopen and which would stay closed. It was a massive undertaking, and precisely what the public needed to see to realize that something was being done. Regaining the public's confidence in the nation's banks required fast action. It also required leadership.

Banks that received licenses were scheduled to reopen between March 13 and March 15, only one week after Roosevelt declared the bank holiday. On March 12, the night before the banks were set to reopen, Roosevelt delivered his first "Fireside Chat" over the radio, the newest way to reach many people at once. He explained the new banking law to

19. Blum interview, in *Brother Can You Spare a Billion?*
20. Jones, *Fifty Billion Dollars*, 46.
21. "RFC: The House of Jesse."

sixty million frightened listeners, all about how things would work and what depositors should do. Roosevelt reassured them with facts, not ideology. Will Rogers reported, "He made everyone understand it, even the bankers."[22]

People flooded the reopened banks the day after Roosevelt's address and began to redeposit their hoarded cash. A. D. Simpson, vice president of Jones's National Bank of Commerce, wrote to his boss in Washington and described the scene: "When we opened our doors Tuesday [March 14], the building lobby and out on the street was jammed and, as quickly as possible after the doors were opened, our lobby was completely filled and yet . . . I did not find one case of impatience or discourtesy from the people who went through our doors that day, or subsequently. It seemed to me that the people were so happy to have a bank into which they could put their money that that was all that mattered."[23] By March 15, with RFC and Treasury Department approval, seventy percent of the nation's banks had reopened.[24] At the same time, Roosevelt asked for legislation to legalize beer and wine. The stock market surged and commodity prices climbed.

But more than 2,000 banks were still unable to open. The burden of resurrecting and then qualifying them for insurance through new Federal Deposit Insurance Corporation (FDIC) membership by January 1, 1934, fell to Jones and the RFC. Getting all banks in the deposit insurance program was crucial to the FDIC's success. An immediate challenge was Detroit's two largest banks—the ones Jones tried to save in June—which still did not have enough money to reopen and pay depositors. More than a month had passed since the banks' 800,000 desperate individuals and businesses had had access to their accounts, so Jones went to Detroit to reorganize the two huge banks.

He and General Motors (GM) President Alfred P. Sloan began working to form a new bank to service both banks' debts and deposits. Walter P. Chrysler bought a few shares to support the effort, but no one else was willing or able to pony up except the federal government through Jones and the RFC. The RFC loaned more than $230 million ($3.77 billion) to pay both banks' depositors, and matched GM's $12.5 million ($205 million) in common stock by buying an equal amount of preferred stock in the new bank. Of the 800,000 depositors who finally had access to their money,

22. Alter, *Defining Moment*, 269.
23. March 22, 1933, Jesse H. Jones Collection [HE].
24. Olson, *Saving Capitalism*, 66.

more than 600,000 had balances of $300 ($4,900) or less. The "forgotten man" had finally been remembered by his government, the only institution large enough to offer assistance of this magnitude. Within months the new National Bank of Detroit's deposits increased from $29 million ($475 million) to $163 million ($2.7 billion), and the number of accounts climbed from 4,386 to more than 90,000.[25]

Although Ford had organized his own bank in Detroit without government assistance, Roosevelt and Jones wanted all banks in the nation to participate in the RFC's preferred stock program, so the strong banks could lead the weak ones, by example, to the one program that provided stability, liquidity, and economic survival. Appeals from some New Dealers to nationalize the banks outright were resisted, but the RFC's preferred stock came with an ownership position, voting rights, and what Jones called a "look-in" on management, hence some federal control. Jones expected institutions using government funds to conduct business responsibly and did not hesitate to apply pressure to replace management and directors when necessary. RFC loans, investments, and oversight thus nudged economic power from Wall Street to Washington, and Jones shoved the power shift along whenever possible. To lead the new Detroit bank, for example, Jones insisted on a midwestern banker with regional knowledge instead of automatically installing a New York financier. Nationalizing the banks was never Roosevelt's nor Jones's intention; they used the RFC to rescue and stabilize the banking system, to provide credit, to help citizens and businesses, and ultimately, to preserve capitalism.[26]

The RFC relied on Congress to increase its capital and expand its authority, but it was largely self-sustaining. Its independence grew from interest payments on its loans, dividends on its preferred stock, and sales of its bonds. The RFC required no Congressional approval for its activities and decisions, and it became politicians' favorite source of funds for their constituents and Roosevelt's agency of choice for funding programs and experiments.

Even Eleanor Roosevelt turned to Jones and the RFC. She wrote to him only a month after her husband took office about acquiring funds for a low-income housing project. The RFC had recently made a loan for one, but Mrs. Roosevelt thought the project she liked, which had been ignored, was better because it would employ more people. She was concerned that "the people interested in it are going to say that the scheme which

25. Jones, *Fifty Billion Dollars*, 68.
26. Olson, *Saving Capitalism*, 42, 59, 116–17.

was granted the money was granted it on account of politics." She asked Jones to give her project "absolutely careful and impartial consideration."[27] Jones responded, "The almost insurmountable trouble with all of these housing loans is the absence of sufficient equity money to fully and adequately secure them." He detailed RFC's security requirements, pointed out the loan she was asking about was five times larger than the one the RFC had recently made, and added, "There has been great pressure to have these housing loans granted, and while their soundness is open to question, in times like these it may be necessary to disregard sound business principles in the interest of the public welfare, if we can put enough safeguards around the Government funds so used."[28] Jones closed with, "You will pardon such a long letter, but your interest in all public questions is so great that I feel justified in giving you these facts. In closing, I was especially pleased to have a White House letter from you dated April 5th, because that was my birthday."[29]

Putting "safeguards around the Government funds" meant that Jones would not "disregard sound business principles." He was as careful with taxpayers' money as with his own. David Ginsburg, an RFC attorney, remembered, "Jones . . . took great pride in his role as a banker. His [RFC] reports [were] always calculated to the very single penny. He took pride in the fact that every penny that he loaned was, in fact, repaid."[30] Some criticized Jones for being too stingy and careful during dire economic times; others feared the RFC was bringing the country close to socialism. Jones thought what he was doing was simply good business and sound public policy.

A month after Jones's birthday, President Roosevelt officially made him RFC chairman. Rumors of this appointment had surfaced a month before Roosevelt's inauguration, when an Associated Press news release claimed, "Jesse H. Jones of Texas appears destined to head the Reconstruction Finance Corporation under the Roosevelt administration. Through this giant agency and its billions of credit, Mr. Roosevelt is looking for a strong hand in his plans for assisting the nation on the upward swing which he believes will result from his 'new deal.'"[31]

A Main Street banker hailing from Texas with an eighth-grade education at the financial heart of the New Deal thoroughly disrupted the

27. Eleanor Roosevelt to Jesse Jones, April 5, 1933, Jesse H. Jones Collection [HE].
28. Jesse Jones to Eleanor Roosevelt, April 6, 1933, Jesse H. Jones Collection [HE].
29. Ibid.
30. Ginsburg interview, in *Brother Can You Spare a Billion?*
31. *Houston Chronicle*, February 7, 1933.

stereotype of liberal eastern elites at the helm of government, and Jones was both extolled and opposed almost daily. One newswire story stated, "Mr. Jones played the dominant part in reweaving the financial fabric of both Detroit and Cleveland."[32] Another observed, "It is thought that he will be needed simply because he can say yes and no at top speed and intelligence 20 hours a day."[33] Other articles reported that the "New York banking interests" opposed Jones's selection because he refused to lower interest rates on self-liquidating loans.[34] A more detailed article revealed, "The Texan's efforts to keep some of the larger banks from 'freezing up' on RFC funds which went into their vaults after being advanced by the RFC . . . has been a large factor in the opposition."[35] The New York financiers also feared—accurately—that Jones would draw power away from them. Nonetheless, Roosevelt wanted a credible and respected bridge to the business community "west of the Hudson," and Jesse Jones was his man. He had known the Texan for years and knew what he could do. It also helped that Jones was from the South and had a reputation for being comparatively conservative.

In the midst of a packed schedule, Jones received reports about his business interests in Houston. After reading a particularly positive statement, Jones wrote R. P. Doherty, president of the National Bank of Commerce, "From the figures for June '33, I judge you must be operating a still or a crap game. I feel that we all are to be congratulated upon the good showing that the bank has made. I certainly appreciate the loyalty and devotion that all the officers and employees have displayed."[36] Jones relied on his staff back home to take care of things while he was away. They cheered him on and reveled in his acclaim. Simpson, the bank's vice president, in a frankly personal, handwritten letter to Jones, exclaimed, "Everywhere I go . . . I hear the same thing—that there is not a major decision made in Washington until after you have been consulted."[37] For the most part, that was true. Bankers, farmers, industrialists, railroad tycoons, homeowners, politicians, and the president all turned to Jones and the RFC for economic sustenance.

While Jones initiated, financed, and managed many New Deal programs, he was not a typical "New Dealer." Neither a theorist, an ideologue,

32. *Houston Chronicle*, April 16, 1933.
33. *Houston Chronicle*, April 19, 1933.
34. *Houston Chronicle*, April 16, 1933.
35. Ibid.
36. Jesse Jones to R. P. Doherty, July 6, 1933, Jesse H. Jones Collection [HE].
37. A. D. Simpson to Jesse Jones, July 4, 1933, Jesse H. Jones Collection [HE].

or an intellectual, Jones could read and analyze a balance sheet or a financial statement like a high-speed computer. He was a common-sense capitalist who believed in the power of public service and the importance of the common good. He was called the "conservative force" of the New Deal because he assiduously protected the bottom line and taxpayers' money in all programs under his jurisdiction. He was attacked from the left for his frugality and from the right for his supposed socialism. Still, almost everyone respected and trusted Jones though more than a few in the New Deal amalgam totally disagreed with his tactics and priorities.

Jones and Secretary of Agriculture Henry Wallace personified two divergent New Deal directions but both of their approaches were used to solve the same problem. Farmers made up almost half of the U.S. workforce; for the past twenty years they had suffered from collapsing commodity prices, more costly consumer goods, and insurmountable debt on their land and equipment. In 1933, they could not get credit, were selling their crops in already heavily saturated markets, and the year promised a bumper harvest. The solution was "controlled inflation"—by slowly raising depressed prices, bankers, businessmen, and farmers would eventually have more money to repay debts, to spend, and to invest. Theoretically, as more money began to flow, demand for goods would increase, new jobs would begin to appear, and wages would start to rise. Some called it "re-flation."[38]

On May 12, 1933, Roosevelt signed the Agricultural Adjustment Act (AAA) to help "adjust" farm production, relative to national consumption, and to inflate prices to what they had been before World War I. Through the AAA, Wallace, a brilliant and renowned agriculturist, paid farmers to destroy every third row of the cotton currently planted in their fields and to refrain from planting crops in the future. Not surprisingly, paying farmers to create scarcity when so many people were starving, was at the very least controversial. *Time* magazine called the AAA the "most radical experiment so far in the New Deal."[39] But Roosevelt, as he declared at Oglethorpe University, was willing to try anything to whip the depression.

Twenty-two thousand AAA agents swarmed the sixteen-state cotton belt to recruit the region's two million farmers, and more than half agreed to destroy part of their crop. The Department of Agriculture paid them $112 million ($1.83 billion), and ten million acres of cotton were plowed

---

38. *Houston Chronicle*, October 12, 1933, September 15, 1933, and April 20, 1933.
39. Ellis, *Nation in Torment*, 312.

under in August 1933.[40] It did not help—the cotton crop was still larger than the one from the year before. The pig surplus was as bad as the cotton glut. In 1933, a 400-pound sow sold for less than four dollars ($66). To keep the next "crop" of pigs off the market, Wallace announced the Department of Agriculture would purchase and kill five million full-grown hogs. Piglets were also destroyed. Unfortunately, piglets did not fit in the machinery made for butchering adult pigs, and Wallace and the program were vilified for cruelty as well as communism and waste. Some of the meat from the slaughter reached the hungry, but most was thrown away. The program only slightly elevated the price for hogs, barely reduced the overabundance and, along with crop destruction, was not tried again.[41]

While launching these agricultural experiments, Roosevelt simultaneously turned to the RFC. He asked Jones to lend ten cents on the pound for cotton that currently sold for nine cents. After Jones conferred with RFC general counsel Stanley Reed, the Commodity Credit Corporation (CCC) was created to lend farmers money on their crops. Roosevelt signed an executive order creating the CCC as an RFC subsidiary on October 16, 1933, right after Wallace's program to destroy crops and kill pigs had ended.[42]

The CCC concept was simple. A farmer warehoused his cotton and received a loan on it from his local bank at ten cents a pound. The RFC reimbursed the bank and held onto the cotton until prices climbed. Farmers would immediately have money to buy food and pay bills, the vulnerable rural banks would be revitalized through the new fee-based activity, and the government would eventually make money on the sale of the cotton. In 1934, 4.5 million bales were removed from the market, and 1.2 million loans were made, mostly to small farmers, for less than $250 ($4,098). The program worked so well, the CCC soon made loans on other commodities, including wheat, wool, figs, mohair, and turpentine.[43] In 1939, at Wallace's insistence, the CCC was transferred to the Department of Agriculture. Under the RFC, the CCC lost a bit of money, but later as war raged in Europe, the crops the CCC had stored were sold at a profit.[44]

The RFC also helped farmers by lending them a total of $1.16 billion ($19 billion) to redeem foreclosed property and refinance their debt. The loans saved thousands of small farms and rural banks from bankruptcy

40. Ibid., 318.
41. Ibid., 327.
42. Olson, *Saving Capitalism*, 144.
43. Ibid., 93.
44. Jones, *Fifty Billion Dollars*, 98.

at next-to-no cost to the government because almost all of the loans were eventually repaid with interest.

Jones even made loans to other nations so they could buy surplus crops from the United States. He negotiated a $50 million ($820 million) loan with the Chinese to buy U.S. wheat and corn.[45] His loans to Russia led to front-page speculation, wondering if "the Roosevelt administration's first attempt to tap the great Soviet Russian market . . . might lead to American recognition of the land of communism."[46] (The U.S. had not yet officially recognized the U.S.S.R.)

Some months into his administration, Roosevelt turned to Jones and the RFC to help raise the price of gold. Responding to pleas from assorted "inflationists" and acting on advice from assorted economists, Roosevelt hoped raising the price of gold might devalue the dollar and inflate the price other commodities.[47] He instructed the RFC to buy and sell gold in the United States and from around the world. The president also asked Jones and soon-to-be Treasury Secretary Henry Morgenthau and others to help him set the price of gold each day. Starting October 23, 1933, Morgenthau and Jones would meet with the president in his bedroom, while he was having breakfast in bed and reading official papers, to decide what the price of gold should be that day. Jones recalled, "At that first meeting, I suggested to the President that to keep speculators from figuring what we were doing, we should not raise the price of gold on a formula, but should jump it around from day to day until the ultimate price was determined at which the dollar would be reestablished on a gold basis."[48] Roosevelt agreed, and the three men came up with "lucky numbers" and joked around with the figures to hide even from themselves the gravity of their mission. Economist John Kenneth Galbraith later observed, "That must have been one of the most wonderful meetings in the world. I think it's fair to say that not one of them knew quite what they were doing, but there was the theory that if you changed the price of gold that this might have a recovery effect. Obviously, this was something that couldn't be done just by issuing a memorandum, so these somber, sober men had to meet in the morning to decide what to do."[49]

At first, the experiment appeared to work. On October 26, a Dow Jones

---

45. *Houston Post*, June 5, 1933.
46. *Houston Chronicle*, July 3, 1933.
47. Olson, *Saving Capitalism*, 105.
48. Jones, *Fifty Billion Dollars*, 249.
49. John Kenneth Galbraith to Steven Fenberg, November 22, 1996, Oral History Project [HE].

summary said, "The RFC's quotation of $31.36 ($514) an ounce for gold was somewhat lower than Wall Street optimists had forecast, but did not put a quietus on securities prices. The market opened higher and successive waves of heavy trading in the morning session swept all groups to new highs on this latest movement. Copper, rubber, utilities, and rail stocks were in front of the advance."[50] During a White House press conference a few days later, someone asked if the program's "mechanics had started to work." Roosevelt replied, "You would have to ask Mr. Jones of the RFC."[51] That same day Jones reported that the city of San Francisco had purchased RFC notes and paid for them with 66,231.151 ounces of "newly mined domestic gold."[52] By then the men had nudged the price up to $32.12 ($527) an ounce at their morning meetings in the president's bedroom. Unfortunately, commodity prices went back down, and Roosevelt suspended the experiment in January. True to his word at Oglethorpe University, Roosevelt was willing to experiment, admit failure, and move on to something else. But as he ended the experiment within the first months of its implementation, he showed an unusual side of himself by writing a poem that immortalized the gold program, Jones's legendary negotiating tactics, and outgoing Secretary of the Treasury Woodin. With nautical flair, the president wrote:

> Shiver me timbers
> Over the stones,
> I, too, have a tale
> 'Bout Jesse Jones.
>
> One morning drear
> I had a cold,
> And all I needed
> Was just more gold.
>
> 'O, Jones, O, Jones,
> Give me some gold,'
> And all I got
> Was just more cold.
>
> Just then Bill Woodin
> Came along,

50. *Wall Street Journal*, October 26, 1933.
51. Norman Baxter, press release, November 1, 1933, Jesse H. Jones Collection [LOC].
52. November 1, 1933, Jesse H. Jones Collection [LOC].

And joined to mine
His beauteous song.

'O, Jones, O, Jones
Give us some gold,
Or else we'll give you
Back your cold.'

As one we sneezed
At Jesse Jones—
He handed out his gold
With groans.

So now we hold
This lovely gold
We got with groans
From Jesse Jones.[53]

The gold-buying program basically did little good. If anything, the higher gold price devalued the dollar and made U.S. exports less expensive, and so more attractive, on world markets. Although hardly acknowledged when the program is discussed today, it was because of Jones's negotiating skills and "groans" that the U.S. government made $143 million ($2.3 billion) on the more than four million ounces of gold it bought and sold. On January 31, 1934, Roosevelt permanently set the price of gold at $35 ($574) an ounce, where for the most part it stayed until 1971.[54]

As the RFC's reach into the national and global economy grew, its main focus still remained on U.S. banks. Unless banks made credit available for agriculture, business, and industry to deploy, Roosevelt and Jones feared all recovery attempts would fail. Bankers were still not lending, and most resisted selling stock to the RFC. Some were afraid the government was trying to take over the banks, while others thought they would look weak if they participated in what Jones called the "bank repair program." Jones had the monumental task of converting feelings about government involvement from abhorrence to acceptance.

At Roosevelt's request, Jones spoke to the nation about the RFC over the radio. He warned, "There can be no sustained prosperity, no return to normal conditions, without actual, available bank credit for all legitimate

53. Jones, *Fifty Billion Dollars*, 246.
54. Olson, *Saving Capitalism*, 110.

purposes." He urged banks with frozen assets to "avail themselves of RFC aid . . . in order that they might do their part in pumping needed credit into the channels of trade and industry." Jones said banks "are amply supplied with cash, [so] none should hold back or hesitate to extend needed credit." He put the ball in the bankers' court when he said "the manufacturer, the processor, the merchant, the employer, must all have additional capital and additional credit if they are to be able to carry on in the recovery program . . . Banks must exert themselves to meet the situation by lending . . . upon a going country instead of a busted one."[55]

To those afraid of government involvement, he said, "For the government to be willing to buy stock in a bank and advertise to the world that it is a partner in that bank is the greatest compliment and source of strength that could come to any bank." Jones summed it up with, "Credit is the bloodstream of all business, and banking is the heart . . . Banks that accept deposits [but] do not extend credit in a reasonable way will not contribute to the general economic welfare nor to business recovery."[56]

But Jones was not done. He asked to speak at the American Bankers Association's annual convention, where he beseeched the financiers to "be smart, for once. Take the government into partnership with you and then go partners with the President in the recovery program without stint."[57] They did not like his remarks. As Jones wryly recalled, "I was followed on the program by Eugene R. Black Sr.," chairman of the Federal Reserve Board of Governors. "A good part of his time was devoted to apologizing for my speech."[58] That evening, the American Bankers Association hosted a dinner, a floorshow, and another speech by Black. When he finished, he unexpectedly called upon Jones to offer a few impromptu remarks. Jones declined, but Black insisted. Jones remembered, "I said I had addressed them once that day, and that they had not liked my speech. I added that all I had to say on this second appearance was that more than half the banks represented . . . in front of me were insolvent, and no one knew it as well as the men in our banqueting room. I then sat down."[59]

The following day, a *Houston Chronicle* editorial warned, "Credit, as Mr. Jones states, is the life blood of business. It must be provided. Unless the banks provide it, we can be sure that the next session of Congress will

55. *Houston Chronicle*, August 2, 1933.
56. Ibid.
57. *New York Times*, February 4, 1934.
58. Jones, *Fifty Billion Dollars*, 26–27.
59. Ibid., 27.

put the government directly into the banking business. We don't want that if we can avoid it, but we must accept it in preference to the stifling of credit." It said sale of preferred stock by banks to the RFC "was a symbol of honor and patriotism."[60]

Quoted in another *Chronicle* editorial, Jones said, as one banker to another, "We must go out and find our chance to help some merchant whose business can be put into sound condition by a loan . . . When we make a customer more prosperous, we put him in a position to make others more prosperous. Study the needs of your businessmen; find a way to help them. Sound policy and patriotism alike direct this course. Build up morale among your customers."[61]

In the end, Jones's exhortations and the FDIC's impending implementation turned the tide. Whereas in August, the RFC had bought only $2.8 million ($46 million) of preferred stock in U.S. banks, by the end of October, after national haranguing by both Roosevelt and Jones, the first New York bank stepped up and sold $25 million ($410 million) of its preferred stock to the RFC. An Associated Press news release reported, "This was the first of the large New York banks which Jones had been endeavoring to induce to enter the administration's . . . program."[62] As a further inducement, Jones reduced the preferred stock dividend banks paid to the RFC from six percent to four and slightly eased collateral requirements.[63] When another New York bank sold $50 million in preferred stock ($820 million) to the RFC at the first of December, Jones wrote Roosevelt, "This new capital should multiply itself many times in credit for agriculture, business and industry."[64] Once the strong, stable New York banks began to sell their stock to the government, others quickly followed. *Fortune* magazine observed, "That the banks were finally jolted out of their mixed position of stubborn conservatism and distrust was due to two factors: the equal mulishness of Jesse Jones and the fact that an FDIC guarantee of deposits could be given only to banks found to be solvent by the government."[65] In December 1933, the RFC infused banks with more than $310 million ($5 billion) by purchasing their preferred stock. It was not a minute too soon.

January 1 was the deadline for banks to prove their solvency so their

60. *Houston Chronicle*, September 7, 1933.
61. *Houston Chronicle*, October 20, 1933.
62. *Houston Chronicle*, October 28, 1933.
63. Olson, *Saving Capitalism*, 79.
64. Ibid., 80.
65. "RFC: The House of Jesse."

deposits could be covered by the FDIC. Thousands of banks still did not qualify and needed RFC assistance to improve their capital structures in order to receive a license for admission from the Treasury Department. If too many banks were left out, no one would have faith in the insurance system. Despite Roosevelt's initial opposition to the FDIC, it had been included in the Banking Act of 1933, also known as the Glass-Steagall Act. Favored and promoted by Jones, the bill separated banks engaged in commercial banking from those involved in securities investment and insurance underwriting; it also created the FDIC to insure individual bank deposits up to $2,500 ($41,000). Only banks whose assets exceeded their liabilities could participate.[66]

Toward the end of December, Jones pledged to Treasury Secretary Morgenthau that within six months he and the RFC would restructure the more than 2,000 banks that did not then qualify for participation in the FDIC if Morgenthau would agree to let those banks join on January first, just days away. Both men knew the spectacle of customers lining up to withdraw their funds from banks that were all of a sudden singled out as ineligible for government guarantees could ruin the entire plan to restore confidence in U.S. banks. Morgenthau agreed and issued the licenses. On January 1, 1934, the comptroller of the currency announced that the FDIC had enrolled 13,423 banks as members and had rejected only 141.[67] As promised, Jones and the RFC stabilized the weak banks and, by the time they were through, the U.S. government owned $1.1 billion ($18 billion) in stock in more than half of the nation's banks. If the "bank repair program" had not succeeded, the entire system most likely would have collapsed. Through the RFC, Roosevelt's New Deal revived, stabilized, and saved the U.S. financial system, and made a profit on the vital program.

66. Olson, *Saving Capitalism*, 72.
67. Ibid., 81.

1934

◈

Go Directly to the RFC

JESSE JONES MADE THE COVER OF *TIME* MAGAZINE on January 22, 1934. The caption under his picture said, "BIG JESSE JONES: He had to have more in a hurry." The cover story described the RFC's gargantuan allocation of more than $6 billion ($95 billion in current dollars) to 8,541 institutions since its 1932 inception and explained that more than $1 billion ($15.8 billion) had already been repaid. The article reported that Jones had recently testified before the Senate and House Banking and Currency Committees about extending the RFC for another year, giving it more capital, and expanding the scope of its activities.[1]

Jones was a prodigious "visitor" on Capitol Hill, where he used Vice President John Nance Garner's office to meet and persuade politicians to create the legislation he needed, all while he played cards, had drinks, and shared dirty jokes with them. He would sometimes corner a reluctant politician and wrap his long arm around him so he could get closer; looking down, Jones would let his intense blue eyes and his big square face help push his point across. His looming presence and the billions of government funds at his disposal made Jones impossible to ignore and extremely difficult to turn down.

1. "Texas Titan," 16–17.

Jesse Jones goes eye-to-eye with Senator George Morris of Nebraska (left), wrapping his arm around him, while Senator Guy M. Gillette of Iowa (center) looks on. Courtesy Corbis.

The *Time* article reported that Jones's "legislative gardening bore handsome and unprecedented fruit in the form of identical House and Senate bills extending RFC's activities until Feb. 12, 1935." It also said Jones "called most of the members by their first names [and] told a joke on an associate who had inadvertently related a dirty story in front of his stenographer." The cover story further pointed out that the RFC "was well on its way to becoming not only the largest single investor in U.S. finance and industry, but also the biggest business organization in the land," and added, "As is the case of all governmental authority under the New Deal, RFC's new potency naturally fell into President Roosevelt's strong grip. But everyone believed that the President would continue to delegate RFC's power of life and death over U.S. finance and industry to one man and one man alone."[2] That one man was Jesse Jones.

Jones wrote *Time* editor Henry Luce a letter of thanks for the article, asked if the cover picture original was available, and requested "one or two hundred extra copies" of the magazine if there were overruns. He also congratulated Luce on the growth of *Time* and *Fortune*, confiding, "It has

2. Ibid.

not been advisable or even possible to be frank about the banking situation. With few exceptions no bank has sold the [Reconstruction Finance] Corporation preferred stock or capital notes that did not need to do so, and incidentally the job is by no means completed. We will not have any more bank troubles, but there is much work yet to be done by this Corporation in building up the capital structure of banks. This information, of course, is, as you will understand, not for publication."[3]

The RFC had strengthened and enlarged banks' capital structures by buying their preferred stock, and the Federal Deposit Insurance Corporation, for the most part, had restored people's confidence that their deposits were safe. Since most banks could lend, Jones never missed an opportunity to push bankers to do so. The New York State Bankers Association meeting on February 5, 1934, was just such an opportunity. He told the financiers that they had the "power to extend or withhold credit," but that they had "greater responsibility in the recovery program and in maintaining that recovery than any, save President [Franklin] Roosevelt himself." He knew they were "shell-shocked" and reluctant to lend, but added, "If we continue waiting on the sidelines for complete recovery and assured values . . . naturally, there can be no recovery." Then he warned, "If the banker fails to grasp his opportunity and to meet his responsibility, there can be but one alternative—government lending. The question therefore follows—will our banking be continued in private hands or, of necessity, be supplanted by the government? The answer is with you—the banker."[4] Jones would always give the private sector first shot. He was not advocating "loose credit" or "unsound banking," but he said to the shaken bankers, "No one must be allowed to suffer for a lack of food or clothing or shelter, or become mendicants, for the lack of credit for agriculture, business, and industry, small as well as large." Jones hoped to further the U.S. recovery through the nation's bankers: "Banking should be conducted more in a spirit of public service than purely for profit. It should be more a profession than a business involved with speculation."[5]

Evoking Roosevelt, Jones added, "I would be less than frank, however, if I did not say that the president [will] be greatly disappointed if the banks do not assume their full share in the recovery program by performing all

3. Jesse Jones to Henry Luce, January 1, 1934, Jesse H. Jones Collection [LOC].
4. Jesse Jones, speech, New York State Bankers Association meeting, February 5, 1934, Jesse H. Jones Collection [UT].
5. Ibid.

of the functions that banks are intended to perform." He warned again, "The common cry almost everywhere is that the banks are not lending . . . and there is a persistent demand . . . to authorize the RFC to make direct loans. Unless deserving borrowers can get credit at the banks, we need not be surprised if Congress yields to this pressure." He advised them to "go back to [the] first principles of banking, where every banker takes care of his own customers and his own locality, lending at home, supporting and helping the farmers, merchants, and industries of his own neighborhood." If bankers do that, he said, then "the credit situation will, to a very large extent, be relieved, and employment provided for millions of people."[6]

The speech made news. Will Rogers reported, "Say, did you read what Jesse Jones, head of the Reconstruction Finance, told the New York Bankers' Convention? Jesse told 'em, 'You boys will either start in loaning business and industry some money to operate on or the government will do it.'"[7]

Just as he seized every chance to berate bankers, Jones never missed an opportunity to praise Roosevelt. He said in his speech to the New York bankers, "Let us not forget as we go about our daily lives, the debt of gratitude that we owe to the man in the White House—to his wisdom, his courage, and his determination to end human suffering and give us in fact a New Deal." He added, "We are living in a new world this February, as compared with last February, and if we support the President as we should, and follow his leadership, there need never be a repetition of the distressing conditions through which we have just passed."[8]

Jones had a long-standing relationship with Roosevelt. On a Florida fishing trip before his inauguration, Roosevelt told a reporter, "Don't ask me what I have done on matters of business. I haven't even opened the briefcase . . . The only person I am going to see within the next 36 hours is Jesse Jones."[9] During the race for the presidency, Jones had met with Roosevelt in Albany to explain the RFC's potential and to ask him not to criticize the agency during the campaign. Roosevelt complied. After his inauguration, instead of abolishing the RFC as he had once thought he would do, Roosevelt made it the New Deal's bank and put Jones in charge. He also appointed Jones to his "super-cabinet," comprised of Roosevelt's

6. Ibid.
7. *New York Times*, February 8, 1934.
8. Jesse Jones, speech, New York State Bankers Association meeting, February 5, 1934, Jesse H. Jones Collection [UT].
9. *Houston Post*, July 16, 1933.

cabinet officers and a few other select officials who met weekly at the White House to strategize and exchange ideas.[10]

Jones and Roosevelt's relationship was not just professional. They both liked to play cards, tell jokes, and exchange gossip. On occasion, Jones even addressed the president as "Frank." Once Jones wrote, "Dear Frank: This is purely a personal letter, and I am indulging myself in the privilege of a friend in calling you by your first name." He thanked the president for sending him two autographed pictures with inscriptions and said, "I shall always hold [them] as sacred and dear." He noted the photographer was "a marvel" because he had succeeded in making Louis Howe, the president's assistant, "handsome." In a more serious vein, Jones continued, "Allow me to take this opportunity, please, to say to you how wonderful you have been in getting things going, and how I am sure we all appreciate the support that you give those of us who are privileged to have a part in the great responsibility which has come to you." Reflecting the tenor of the time, he went on, "I venture it has never before been accorded any man to hold the confidence and have the wholehearted support and good will of so nearly all of the people of our country as has come to you in the short period that you have been at the head of our Government. It is your own character, your frankness, and your determination to serve and save that has won for you this extraordinary place in the confidence and affection of the American people."[11]

Popular columnists Drew Pearson and Robert Allen quipped, "Wagers are being laid that before President Roosevelt returns from Warm Springs that Jesse Jones will have visited him. The ambitious R.F.C. Chairman makes it a point to keep close to FDR's coat-tails."[12] Pearson and Allen were among the very few who dared take shots at Jones. They reported in one column that RFC loans had been made to one of Jones's Houston companies and revealed in another that Jones was disappointed he had not been appointed Secretary of the Treasury when William Woodin retired; Roosevelt instead had appointed his friend and neighbor, Henry Morgenthau. Pearson and Allen reported that the choice "was a bitter shock to the big, ambitious chairman of the RFC. Next to being President, Jesse would rather be boss of the Treasury than anything else."[13] They frequently called Jones "big," as well as "bulky," "hulking," and "conservative."

10. *Houston Chronicle*, July 11, 1933.

11. Jesse Jones to Franklin Roosevelt, July 31, 1933, Jesse H. Jones Collection [LOC].

12. Pearson and Allen, "Washington Merry-Go-Round," November 25, 1933.

13. Pearson and Allen, "Washington Merry-Go-Round," November 22, 1933.

Today, it would be hard to classify Jones as "conservative," but compared to some New Dealers he was. In one column where Pearson and Allen reported that Jones's "persistence" had removed the "bank repair" programs from the Treasury Department to the RFC, the columnists described how Woodin, ailing and sidelined, was "urged by friends to keep the conservative Jones out of the plan." The reporters ended, "When the plan was announced, it was Jones who was in, Woodin who was out." Still, they claimed, "If some of the Brain Trusters have their way, Jesse Jones . . . will be replaced."[14] Pearson and Allen would continue to predict Jones's ouster for many years to come, even though Roosevelt almost always sided with the so-called conservative in disputes over turf and policy. It was thought that Roosevelt liked Jones because he was more Democrat than New Dealer. Jones claimed Roosevelt "frequently indicated to me that he thought my course a good antidote for the extreme liberals, a sort of balance, as it were. He allowed me to run my job my own way."[15] In return, Roosevelt received RFC funds for his programs and maintained credibility with constituents who, without Jones's presence and sagacity, would have turned their backs on the president.

Pearson and Allen kept up their irreverent digs, even making fun of Jones's bridge game. "Mrs. Jones is an expert, but Chairman Jesse hadn't played for more than a year," they wrote about a Washington bridge party. They then reported, "His cards were terrible. At the end of the evening he owed $2." They delightedly added that Jones had to borrow the money from his wife.[16] In another column they wrote, "Mrs. Jesse Jones, wife of the RFC chief, is probably the most expert bridge player of official Washington. And husband Jesse is probably the worst."[17] They also revealed that "RFC's Chairman Jesse H. Jones has decorated the walls of his office with cartoonists' caricatures of Jesse H. Jones."[18] Referring to his indisputable power, they called him "Emperor Jones."[19]

But Pearson and Allen were part of a tiny minority—even Republicans praised Jones. Representative Robert Luce, ranking Republican on the committee that had extended the RFC for another year, said, "I am grateful to the Democratic party for having produced such an honest, upright, capable man to conduct this huge enterprise . . . This is the one

14. Pearson and Allen, "Washington Merry-Go-Round," October 24, 1933.
15. Jones, *Fifty Billion Dollars*, 262.
16. Pearson and Allen, "Washington Merry-Go-Round," March 27, 1934.
17. Pearson and Allen, "Washington Merry-Go-Round," October 6, 1934.
18. Pearson and Allen, "Washington Merry-Go-Round," October 3, 1934.
19. Pearson and Allen, "Washington Merry-Go-Round," November 4, 1933.

undertaking of the government that has fully stood the test, and that has already made good."[20] Historian Jordan Schwartz concluded, "Aside from the President, [Jones] was the single most powerful man in the New Deal, deriving his power from the billions of Reconstruction Finance Corporation dollars he controlled, the financial policies he influenced, the esteem politicians and the press bestowed upon him, and the reluctance of putative enemies to cross swords with him."[21]

Jones cultivated the press and was in the news almost every day. *Today* magazine named him "The Dough Doctor" and said "he has out-traded and out-smarted the traders and smart boys so often it has become a habit." The reporter then described how Jones munched on a sack of popcorn as he held "three conference meetings in three adjoining rooms, moving from one to another, carrying the precious sack along." He wrote that Jones's "vast experience . . . enables him to find out with two or three pointed questions what shape a business is in," and observed, "It does not take him long to decide whether he will trust you or not."[22]

As he did after the *Time* cover story, Jones wrote a letter of thanks to *Today* editor Raymond Moley—a defector from the Brain Trust and New Deal—remarking how the RFC had "grown from an appointed Board of Directors to an organization of more than 1,500 in Washington and as many more scattered among our 32 agencies." He shared, "The responsibility of it all is a little short of appalling, which is one reason that I must stick constantly at the job" and told Moley what he told Luce: "It has not been possible to be entirely frank about the banking situation. We have talked patriotism, the President's program of recovery, etcetera, when in many instances we should have said to the banker, 'You are without capital, or your capital is impaired, and you know it as well as we.'" He concluded, "banking is yet one of the big unsolved problems."[23]

By 1934, the RFC had stabilized and strengthened more than six thousand banks and positioned them to lend, but Jones was still waiting for them to make loans that would turn the wheels of the economy again. Unfortunately, most of the nation's six thousand other banks that had not participated in bank repair needed help, too.[24] Toward the end of April, with Roosevelt's approval, Jones asked Senator Duncan Fletcher, chairman of the Senate Banking and Currency Committee, to allow the RFC and

20. *Houston Chronicle*, January 16, 1934.
21. Schwarz, *New Dealers*, 59.
22. Mallon, "The Dough Doctor," 9.
23. April 14, 1934, Jesse H. Jones Collection [LOC].
24. Jesse Jones to J. C. Hutchinson Jr., January 29, 1934, Jesse H. Jones Collection [LOC].

Federal Reserve banks to make direct loans to industry and businesses. Jones explained, "Unless . . . credit . . . for small and medium-sized industries can be provided, our relief problems will continue to multiply . . . While not generally favoring direct Governmental loans to industry, I am convinced that in our present situation this character of credit is essential to recovery and the public welfare." He continued, "There are crippled industries of the smaller and medium-sized type that will need nursing for several years . . . Many of them deserve a chance to reestablish themselves, and society generally will be better for it . . . We are not ready for the 'survival of the fittest' . . . or to scrap all except the most efficient and, let us say, the more fortunate." In conclusion, Jones wrote, "The President authorizes me to say that he favors the bill," and Roosevelt added a handwritten notation: "especially [so] that the smaller industries be given full chance to survive in approximately equal terms as the larger industrial properties."[25]

To Jones and Roosevelt, loans to small businesses required common sense, not legislation. A banker from Poughkeepsie, New York, wrote Jones that his bank had many borrowers of "sterling character . . . who are confronting great difficulty in discharging their obligation, and yet are dominated by a feeling of conscientiousness, which is so plain as to be unmistakable." But those patrons, who pay as much as they can and always at least pay the interest on their loans, were "classified by the Comptroller of the Currency as either Loss or Doubtful." "Loss" and "Doubtful" designations prevented banks from extending them loans. The banker asked if "less pressure might be brought against" the borrowers so he could fulfill his civic duty and make loans to deserving clients, as the administration had requested. Jones forwarded the letter to Roosevelt, who returned it with a handwritten note: "Jesse, Won't you discuss this whole thing with JFTOC [Jeffery T. O'Connor, Comptroller of the Currency]? I *personally* know of so many cases in other banks, where the examiners have not used *common sense*, that we *must* do something!"[26]

After months of pressuring reluctant bankers to lend, on June 21, 1934, Roosevelt signed legislation authorizing the RFC and the Federal Reserve banks to make direct loans to businesses and industry. Thus the government—through the RFC—became the bank of last resort. The legislation was largely initiated by Jones and written by Tom ("Tommy the Cork") Corcoran, RFC lawyer and Roosevelt speechwriter and adviser who, with

25. April 30, 1934, National Archives.
26. E. K. Satterlee to Jesse Jones, May 2, 1934, Jesse H. Jones Collection [LOC].

Ben Cohen, drafted some of the New Deal's most influential legislation.[27] Corcoran played the accordion at Washington parties and knew almost everyone of influence because he got so many of them their jobs. His standing with the left, talent in drafting and driving legislation, and allegiance to Jones and Roosevelt were enormously helpful in promoting and expanding the RFC's mission to expedite recovery.

Days after Roosevelt signed the bill, Jones gave a nationwide speech on the radio. "Until credit is actually being extended to deserving borrowers," he said, "the resources of the Reconstruction Finance Corporation will be available to all those to whom we are authorized to lend." Still hopeful the banks would loosen up and credit would wash through and renew the economic system, Jones instructed his listeners to deal locally first, saying, "It would be helpful . . . if prospective borrowers would approach the RFC and Federal Reserve banks through their local banks and, wherever possible, with an agreement on the part of the local bank to participate in the loan." Otherwise, desperate businessmen could go directly to the RFC.[28]

The legislation brought more government into private life, enlarged the RFC's reach and power, and put Jones in a delicate spot, between those who wanted more intervention and planning and those who wanted less or none at all. Historian James Olson summed it up in his authoritative book about the RFC and the New Deal, "Jones walked [a] tightrope between a government agency and a commercial bank."[29] The urgent need for a restoration of the nation's economy overcame Jones's reluctance to rely on government intervention, but did not stifle his determination to keep banks and businesses in private hands and to protect the people's trust and their tax dollars. To qualify for a government loan, the borrower had to be solvent, have adequate security, and prove that he had been rejected by a bank. Loans were limited to $500,000 ($7.9 million) and could last up to five years, considered a long-term loan back then. These loans were not nearly large or long enough for Jones, who wanted ten-year loans up to $1 million ($15.8 million). Nonetheless, he was satisfied for now and said loans would be made "when deemed to offer reasonable assurance of continued or increased employment."[30]

27. Olson, *Saving Capitalism*, 58–59.
28. Jesse Jones, speech, National Radio Forum, June 26, 1934, Jesse H. Jones Collection [UT].
29. Olson, *Saving Capitalism*, 212.
30. Jesse Jones, speech, National Radio Forum, June 26, 1934, Jesse H. Jones Collection [UT].

Jesse Jones offers RFC assistance to "distressed" small businessmen after reluctant bankers refuse to lend and Roosevelt signs legislation authorizing government loans to business. Jones appeared frequently in political cartoons, and he framed and hung the autographed copies sent to him by the artists. Courtesy Jesse Holman Jones Papers, Dolph Briscoe Center for American History, University of Texas at Austin.

Despite glimmers of economic improvement, unemployment remained intractable. Millions of destitute people still could not find work, food, or shelter. At the same time, some citizens prospered: automobile production and sales were up, and so was national income. The number of individuals with a net income of a million dollars or more had more than doubled between 1932 and 1933, and the number would, along with executives' salaries, climb again in 1934. Aware of this trend, and concerned about the inappropriate use of RFC funds, Jones said during his radio address about direct government loans, "The Corporation . . . feels that borrowers having to come to the Government for credit should not pay or draw excessive salaries, and that corporations borrowing from the Government should forego dividends to their stockholders [while borrowing during the term of the loan]."[31]

Distinguishing between lending and spending and between relief and loans, he explained to a skeptical public, which included industrialists anxious for investment and the unemployed desperate for work, "We are furnishing Government credit to so many classes of our citizenship, it is entirely consistent to assist crippled industry with credit, not in the interest of the industry alone, but to keep people at work. Money loaned that will provide work in private enterprise is much better than money given in relief." He continued, "While the Government cannot go on indefinitely acting as banker for all of its citizens, loans to struggling industry are constructive, fit . . . into the whole recovery program, and can be justified by the most conservative. As a matter of fact, most of these loans can be made with little or no ultimate loss."[32]

Jones's *Houston Chronicle* was more direct about the role of government in business: "Probably not one member of the RFC board believes in direct banking activities by the government except as a depression relief measure . . . Banking and credit business by the government would mean business and industrial control, and eventually operation, by the government, or certain and complete socialism. The . . . present government credit agency, however . . . [puts] capital where it is obviously needed to bolster business institutions, [and] to maintain and expand employment."[33]

Government loans to industry got off to a disappointing start, mainly because many applicants were not creditworthy, no matter how much RFC examiners bent the rules. By August—two months after the legislation had been signed into law—the Federal Reserve, which was never on board with the plan in the first place, had loaned only $5,000 ($79,000). In the same period, the RFC had loaned $4 million ($63 million) and had conditional agreements for an additional $1.3 million ($21 million). But that still was much less than Roosevelt, Jones, and the RFC board had

31. Ibid.
32. Ibid.
33. *Houston Chronicle*, June 23, 1934.

anticipated.[34] By October the situation had slightly improved. According to a news release, the RFC's "loans to industry passed the $30,000,000 mark in the administration's drive to spur private business through government funds."[35] The loans helped, but they were not enough to significantly increase employment or bring relief to the millions who could not find work or pay their bills.

New Deal and RFC programs multiplied in response to mass unemployment. Some succeeded, others did not, and a few were declared unconstitutional. Like Roosevelt, Jones was willing to admit mistakes. As he said in a speech at the George Peabody College for Teachers, "No one claims that the Roosevelt administration has proceeded without error. The president himself does not claim that, but the mistakes have been far outweighed by the successful steps. Of greater importance is the fact that everything that has been done has been actuated by one motive—the welfare of the people as a whole."[36]

The Electric Home and Farm Authority (EHFA) was one of the RFC's most "successful steps." Originally under the Tennessee Valley Authority (TVA), the EHFA was transferred to the RFC in 1934 and, unlike some of the other lending programs, took off like a rocket. Electric power was slowly making its way into rural areas, where only two out of ten farm families enjoyed the luxury of electricity.[37] Once power was brought to their homes, however, strapped farmers could not afford to buy the refrigerators, stoves, radios, and washing machines that would allow them to plug into the modern age. To address this problem, the EHFA helped hundreds of thousands of "tenants and homeowners" by financing their appliance purchases. The EHFA reimbursed appliance dealers after a consumer made a purchase, then the local utility company included a small monthly charge for the appliances in each customer's bill. Once the customer paid the charge, the utility company sent the payment, with a little interest, to the EHFA. Jones explained, "The main trouble with small loans is the proportionately heavy cost of making and collecting them. The EHFA went around that hurdle by arranging with the utility companies supplying [the] electricity and gas to do the collecting. Along with the bill for their services, they would send the consumer the

34. *Houston Chronicle*, August 4, 1934.

35. *Houston Chronicle*, October 6, 1934.

36. Jesse Jones, speech, George Peabody College for Teachers, Nashville, June 18, 1934, Jesse H. Jones Collection [LOC].

37. Kennedy, *Freedom from Fear*, 252.

monthly . . . installment due on the equipment whose purchase we had underwritten."[38]

The benefits were multiple. The program increased demand for durable goods. It helped hundreds of thousands of citizens to have modern conveniences otherwise unavailable to them. It brought business to Main Street stores and utility companies. And it increased employment. In 1934 the EHFA collaborated with forty-one utility companies, seventy appliance manufacturers, and 409 retail outlets in ten states, making thousands of loans that averaged $150 ($2,375). The program eventually included thirty-seven states, 428 manufacturers, and 3,824 retailers. More than one million appliances would be sold through the program.[39] In addition to all of its economic benefits, the EHFA made money. Upon its liquidation in 1943, the agency returned all of its original capital to the U.S. Treasury with, according to Jones, "a tidy profit of $175,000 [$2.8 million]."[40]

The RFC began buying municipal bonds in 1934 to help cities increase their borrowing power for public works projects. Jones even intervened in negotiations on a bond issue floated by New York. He wrote Vice President John Nance Garner after a few days of much needed rest on two different yachts at Watch Hill and Newport, Rhode Island, that he and Mary had stopped for "refreshments and a little mix-up in New York City between Mayor LaGuardia and Wall Street." New York had recently put $72 million ($1.14 billion) in bonds on the market and had received only one offer from "a syndicate of 70 banks," which proposed to charge a little more than four percent in interest. Jones said Mayor LaGuardia had come to his hotel on a "social call and incidentally to discuss the bond matter." LaGuardia made sure his visit was noticed by barreling through town with a "siren-blowing motorcycle squad."[41] Jones explained, "After two or three days of back-and-forth from bankers to City Hall, the bankers agreed to take the bonds at an average of about 3.75%, or a saving . . . on this particular issue of $3,500,000 [$55 million]." He concluded, "The mere fact that a government representative acted as mediator and brought the bankers and the City officials together, after they had been calling each other names and had gotten so far apart, would naturally be accepted by the public as at least an Administration influence."[42] Jones also wrote

38. Jones, *Fifty Billion Dollars*, 204.
39. Olson, *Saving Capitalism*, 142.
40. Jones, *Fifty Billion Dollars*, 203.
41. Lubell, "New Deal's J. P. Morgan," 10.
42. July 21, 1934, Jesse H. Jones Collection [LOC].

tongue-in-cheek to Garner, "I shall expect you to keep it a profound secret that I ever went to Newport. As a matter of fact, when [it was] necessary to call the office, I went to some nearby village to place the call."[43]

Jones's friendship with his fellow Texan was closer than the one with President Roosevelt. Garner had served fifteen terms in Congress before he was elected vice president, a position which he famously said was "not worth a pitcher of warm piss." (He called reporters "pantywaists" when they changed the descriptive word to "spit.") He smoked cigars throughout the day and once claimed, "I'm living a good Christian life. I don't get drunk but once a day."[44] Jones's frequent use of Garner's Senate office to woo and entertain recalcitrant Congressmen caused the vice president to say, "I guess it's our office. Jones uses it as much as I do."[45]

Jones wrote Garner during another vacation that, "Mrs. Jones, Mrs. Wilson, and I had a very enjoyable twelve days with Mr. and Mrs. Fred Fisher on their yacht in Lake Huron and Lake Superior. We caught a few fish, but that was merely incidental to a pleasant outing." Working sixteen- to twenty-hour days, seven days a week, for more than a year, Jones needed a summer break. But he was a pioneer in "telecommuting" while he was away. He explained to Garner, "I was in constant communication with the office by wireless, which fact made it possible for me to enjoy my vacation." As during the Newport trip, Jones went ashore when required. On this occasion, it was to spend "two days in Chicago making a loan to pay teachers' back salaries."[46] Newspapers soon reported, "Uncle Sam Monday granted a $22,500,000 [$355 million] loan for the payment of back salaries to Chicago teachers. Shortly after 5 p.m., Jesse H. Jones, chairman of the Reconstruction Finance Corporation, emerged beaming from a seven-hour conference with Mayor [Edward Joseph] Kelly and other public officials to announce that the happy day had arrived for the teachers—whose pay had been irregular for the last four years." Like most RFC loans, the Chicago loan was collateralized, this time with "130 pieces of property . . . valued at more than $35,000,000 [$555 million] by RFC appraisers," including one block in the "Loop district . . . bounded by State, Madison, Monroe, and Dearborn streets." After the loan received approval from the other RFC board members through a long-distance "hookup conference," Jones went to an adjoining room reserved for the

43. Ibid.
44. Dingus, "Last Page."
45. Timmons, *Jones: Man and Statesman*, 264.
46. August 24, 1934, Jesse H. Jones Collection [LOC].

press and distributed a release. "After a single glance," one newspaper said, "the reporters made a concentrated rush from the room to commandeer all the telephones on the eighth floor of the hotel." Meanwhile, Mayor Kelly announced, "It looks now as if the finances of the school board will be in good shape in the future and Chicago's most worrying problem has been solved in an intelligent fashion."[47]

Jones's working vacation was not over. The next day, he went to Detroit to finalize liquidation of the two huge banks that he had been dealing with since 1932. He agreed to lend First National $91 million ($1.44 billion) to pay back depositors, but only if those with the largest amounts in the bank agreed temporarily to take only a portion of their deposits so the 567,000 depositors with $300 ($4,750) or less in the bank could be paid in full. To Garner, Jones optimistically wrote, "The plan is not yet fully completed, but is well on its way."[48] Two months later it still had not been settled.

The problem was rivalry among the automakers. Pearson and Allen reported, "Three of the biggest producers in the auto industry are waging a hammer and tongs war behind the scenes. The controversy—not directly connected with the motor vehicle business—is a continuation of a long-standing commercial feud." They explained, "The dispute revolves about RFC Chairman Jesse Jones's plan for a partial payoff to depositors of the First National Bank of Detroit, the largest closed bank in the world." They continued, "Three of the biggest depositors are Henry Ford, General Motors, and Chrysler Motor Co. Ford, with $25,000,000 frozen in the bank, is willing to accept the Jones proposal. But General Motors and Chrysler—his bitter competitors—are yet to agree."[49]

The federal government could have paid all of the depositors instead of making loans to closed banks against their remaining assets. However, no matter where people saved, stored, or invested their money, most everyone had lost some or all of it during the Great Depression. In an earlier radio broadcast, Jones had addressed the government's unwillingness to replace frozen deposits in closed banks not covered by the FDIC, saying, "Those who had their savings and investments in real estate, stocks, bonds, mortgages, or in business, industry, or farming have suffered a much larger percentage of loss than have depositors in closed banks, and it is not possible to justify paying this character of losses [the lost

47. *Houston Chronicle*, August 7, 1934.
48. August 24, 1934, Jesse H. Jones Collection [LOC].
49. Pearson and Allen, "Washington Merry-Go-Round," October 2, 1934.

deposits] with taxpayers' money . . . more than other losses." He elaborated, "I estimate that depositors in banks closed during the past three years will receive, on the average, approximately sixty-five percent of their deposits."[50] Even so, Jones did his best to make sure small depositors received all of their money.

Jones and the RFC offered credit to banks, businesses, railroads, consumers, municipalities, and farmers. RFC credit was even extended to other nations and it was controversial, but U.S. exports had dropped by one-third between 1929 and 1932. If bankers were unwilling to make domestic loans, they were even less enthused about funding international commerce, so the RFC stepped in. Others like Cordell Hull, now Secretary of State, thought increasing international trade could help end the depression.[51] The success of the EHFA loans to consumers and the CCC's loans to farmers, along with steady repayments on all RFC loans in general, convinced Jones that there were good loans to be made and that plentiful credit, both domestic and international, was an essential part of the solution.

On February 2, 1934, President Roosevelt established the Export-Import Bank (EIB) of Washington to make loans to the U.S.S.R. Secretary of State Hull, Secretary of Commerce Daniel Roper, and RFC Chairman Jones comprised the board. The RFC financed the operation by purchasing $10 million ($158 million) of the bank's preferred stock. There was just one snag. The government, by law, could not lend money to any nation which still owed World War I debts to the United States. After the Bolsheviks formed the Soviet Union in 1917, they repudiated Russia's more than $200 million ($3.2 billion) U.S. war debt. Roosevelt, the first U.S. president to recognize the Soviet Union, agreed to let the U.S.S.R. repay part of the disclaimed debt through an additional interest payment on EIB loans. However, negotiations collapsed and the bank never disbursed one dime to the Soviet Union.

But other countries wanted loans, too. One month after he had created the first EIB, Roosevelt formed the second EIB to make loans to "all countries except Russia." As with all RFC organizations, Jones controlled the bank. He intended to provide medium- and long-term loans to other nations "to encourage exports of durable goods or the construction or im-

50. Jesse Jones, speech, National Radio Forum, June 26, 1934, Jesse H. Jones Collection [UT].
51. Olson, *Saving Capitalism*, 148.

provement of heavy industrial installations in distant climes," with a top priority being the United States worker. He recalled, "The bank's first aid went to the American manufacturer and the American workman whose job often depended upon whether a plant's front office was successful in bidding for overseas orders."[52] The EIB loaned $7 million ($111 million) in 1934.[53] Cuba, among the first applicants, received an RFC loan to buy U.S. silver and have it made into Cuban coins.[54] The EIB's Central and South American loans were used to buy equipment and material made in the United States to build parts of the Inter-American Highway in Mexico, Costa Rica, Colombia, Paraguay, and Bolivia. The EIB also helped sell domestic surplus grain by lending other nations the funds to buy it. The EIB got off to a slower start than Jones would have liked, but it would become indispensable within a few years.

At the end of October, it was time for another American Bankers Association annual meeting. The year before, Jones's bold remarks had been unpopular with the assembled bankers and this year would be no different. The group would have preferred to hear from Roosevelt, whom it initially invited, but the president declined and asked Jones to go instead. After an introduction by Francis M. Law, president of the American Bankers Association, a Houstonian, and another influential Texan, Jones opened in a conciliatory manner, "September a year ago, I spoke in Chicago and am glad to play a return engagement. We are better acquainted now, and I hope have a somewhat better understanding." He continued, "I shall try to be less blunt than I appeared to be in Chicago." But he was not.

Bankers continued to sit on piles of cash that they would not lend. Jones pleaded with them to "show leniency . . . toward deserving and honest debtors until conditions improve." He explained to those who were calling in "slow loans" or not lending, "A continuation of forced liquidation will put the government further into the lending business. You cannot sacrifice people's savings or their investments . . . by forced sale, or continually harass them about their debts, without creating a bad state of mind and causing ultimate repudiation." He suggested they instead "encourage borrowing by people who have demonstrated their ability to use borrowed money profitably, under normal conditions." Jones stated,

52. Ibid., 220.
53. Olson, *Saving Capitalism*, 165.
54. Jones, *Fifty Billion Dollars*, 216.

"It is the money borrower, individual and corporate, who buys and hires and makes for business, so let's stake him again—hold him in check, yes—but let's rebuild his morale and start him working."[55]

Jones always included RFC figures in speeches and interviews, in particular: how much the RFC had loaned, how much had been paid back, and how much the RFC had passed through to other New Deal agencies. He now reported that of the RFC's $8 billion ($127 billion) authorization, $4.6 billion ($73 billion) had been disbursed, $2.1 billion ($33 billion) had been repaid, and $850 million ($1.3 billion) had been "allocated by congress to other government agencies." Jones, as always, praised President Roosevelt and closed his talk with these words: "I would remind you—lest we forget—that the entire banking situation was saved by the constructive policies of the Roosevelt administration. If it had not been for those policies, made effective largely through the RFC, with the co-operation of the treasury, the comptroller of the currency, and the state banking authorities, many banks that are now strong and sound would have been in the discard [pile], and the others would have had a hard time maintaining their existence."[56]

The midterm elections showed that many voters felt Roosevelt was doing something right or, at the very least, doing something. Historically, the party in power lost seats in midterms, but this time the Republicans lost thirteen seats in the House and ten in the Senate, reducing their standing to only 103 House members and twenty-five Senators.[57] The *Houston Chronicle* declared, "For the first time since the Republican Party was established just before the Civil War, the Democrats today obtained more than a two-thirds majority of the Senate."[58] Harry S. Truman from Missouri was one of the new Democratic senators. Now that the Democrats had unparalleled power, and the Great Depression continued to grind on, the question became, which way would the government go?

The Joneses, who had been away from Houston for almost two years, decided to go home for Christmas. The excitement of the city's movers and shakers at this news could not be contained. Insurance magnate and Houston Chamber of Commerce President Gus Wortham said, "Our fellow townsman has attained national and international status as the individual who, next to the president, sways the policies of the United States

55. Jesse Jones, speech, American Bankers Association meeting, October 24, 1934, Jesse H. Jones Collection [HE].
56. Ibid.
57. Leuchtenburg, *Roosevelt and the New Deal*, 116–17.
58. *Houston Chronicle*, November 7, 1934.

where finance is an issue." He continued, "Because our estimate of Mr. Jones has been vindicated in such sweeping fashion, Houstonians have been anxious to express their sentiments in some official way."[59]

The Chamber of Commerce delayed its annual meeting so Jones could speak and be recognized at the gathering. Four thousand people were expected to attend the affair on December 21, at the City Auditorium.[60] Dinner was catered by Jones's Rice Hotel and included turkey, dressing, cranberry sauce, yams, string beans, and pumpkin pie. The Bach Singers sang eight ballads. Just after the Joneses were seated, an all-girl pep squad, "dressed in snappy uniforms of black and yellow, marched in and played 'The Eyes of Texas.'"[61] Many speeches were delivered, including orations by Wortham and Jones's longtime colleague, R. M. Farrar. But everyone came to hear what Jones had to say.

He began, "I would be unusually happy coming home this Christmas if it were not for the faces that are absent. Some had been close to me through the years."[62] He talked first about J. B. Farthing, his grade school teacher who had married his sister Elizabeth and who had worked for Jones Interests in Dalhart and Houston. Most of all, Jones was referring to his beloved Aunt Louisa, who had passed away at the age of eighty-five just days before.

Louisa and M. T. Jones had been responsible for bringing Jesse to Texas and to Houston. When they had arrived in Houston in 1882, according to a *Houston Post* memorial, "it was little more than an overgrown village with mud streets."[63] Louisa became a founding member of St. Paul's Methodist Church, the Women's Co-Operative Home for unwed mothers, and the DePelchin Faith Home for orphaned children. The "Boarding House," her home at Main and Anita, was the Jones family center during the first twenty years of Jesse Jones's life in Houston. Jones concluded his remembrance with, "I am consoled that they are here in spirit."[64] Then he got down to business.

He congratulated the Chamber for "having missed the many tragedies visited on many other sections of the country."[65] Houston had, indeed, dodged the worst of the Great Depression. It had avoided the pernicious

59. *Houston Chronicle*, October 31, 1934.
60. *Houston Chronicle*, December 21, 1934.
61. *Houston Chronicle*, December 22, 1934.
62. Ibid.
63. *Houston Post*, January 18, 1935.
64. *Houston Chronicle*, December 22, 1934.
65. Ibid.

bank problems because of Jones's intervention in 1931, and oil had cushioned the decline. By 1934 the city's major banks had more deposits than they had in 1929.[66] And the city's 1,500 street lights, which had been extinguished for two years to save money, were back on.[67]

Jones then talked about the RFC: "No one had the slightest idea the extent to which the depression would reach, the distress and tragedy we would meet." He said it would take all night to tell everything the RFC had done, but he tried to sum it up, "We have made more than 20,000 different loans ranging from $1,000 to $140 million [$15,800 to $2.22 billion], and the same principles apply to the $1,000 loan, and the same care is taken, as for the $140 million loan." He shared, "You cannot appreciate the tragedy that passed our door every day from every section of the United States. Strong men, leaders in communities, honorable, fine people, hysterical."[68]

Now, Jones observed, the banks are strong, and he called the FDIC "a blessing." He said, "We loaned this year and last to re-establish the price of cotton, corn, and tobacco, and those commodities are selling at living prices." But, "With 15 million people on relief, the job is not finished . . . There must be a fair distribution of available work so that all who want to work can work and make an honest living." Jones then adopted a more intimate tone, saying, "My wife tries to get me to come home nights when I work too late, but I cannot go home when men are waiting in distress. Sometimes I wonder at the endurance, physical and mental, [by which] we have been able to go on, but I have a fairly light heart now as far as the affairs of our country are concerned, compared to two years ago." He optimistically said, "There is now no distress that cannot be relieved."[69]

While he was in town, he was asked for speeches and interviews, and to deliver the Sunday morning sermon at a local church. When Mayor Holcombe declared December 26, 1934, "Jesse H. Jones Day," the civic leadership gathered once more. A ceremony was held at the Scottish Rite Cathedral, where the Joneses' granddaughter, Audrey, unveiled a bronze bust of Jones by Enrico Cerrachio. Fifty men had each contributed $100 ($1,580) toward the sculpture, which would be prominently displayed in Houston's public library. Mayor Holcombe said he hoped "children visit-

66. Buenger and Pratt, *But Also Good Business*, 109–10.
67. *Houston Chronicle*, January 5, 1934.
68. *Houston Chronicle*, December 22, 1934.
69. Ibid.

On December 26, 1934, sculptor Enrico Cerrachio and Jesse Jones's granddaughter, Audrey, unveil the bronze bust of Jones commissioned and paid for by fifty of Jones's closest friends and colleagues in Houston.

ing the Public Library and gazing on the likeness of the eminent Houstonian would say, 'I'm going to try to be a second Jesse Jones.'"[70]

The Joneses savored their time in Houston, especially when they joined with their family to remember Aunt Louisa, celebrate Christmas, and bring in the New Year. Despite Jones's declarations about the promising future, twenty percent of the nation's workforce remained unemployed, and he faced an uncertain political agenda when he returned to Washington. He wrote Vice President Garner that putting real estate and railroads "on some sound basis" would be important to "ultimate recovery" and that they were the two major problems "remaining for the RFC."[71] But first, the RFC had to be authorized for another year.

70. *Houston Chronicle*, December 28, 1934.
71. Jesse Jones to John Nance Garner, November 6, 1934, Jesse H. Jones Collection [LOC].

1935

$$\diamondsuit$$

Friendly, Industrious, Intelligent Dollars

BY 1935, THE RECONSTRUCTION FINANCE CORPORATION (RFC) and other New Deal agencies had pumped billions of dollars into the national economy. Most banks were back in business and were stable, for the most part, though they were still not lending. Jones felt the "bank repair program" was just about complete. Commodity prices, stocks, industrial output, and income were going up. In some homes it appeared that the depression was over, or at least, coming to an end. But it did not feel that way for one-fifth of the nation's workforce who could not find jobs and for the millions who continued to receive federal relief.

The cotton belt, where one-third of the farming families lived, was especially hard hit. Most of the farmers were tenants or sharecroppers. They owned no land and earned at most $350 ($5,400 in current dollars) a year; only sixteen percent of farmers earned more than the national median annual income of $1,500 ($23,200). Only one in ten enjoyed indoor plumbing, and only one in five had electricity.[1] On top of their arduous lives, endless drought and overproduction had turned the farm belt from Texas to the Dakotas into the Dust Bowl. Life was just as daunting in many cities, where tenements and shantytowns teemed with Dust Bowl survi-

---

1. Kennedy, *Freedom from Fear*, 192.

vors who struggled with the filth, disease, and violence of those crowded living conditions, as well as their own despair. Prospects for low-skilled, older workers were nil. In South Dakota, for example, one-third of the people were "on the dole."[2] The nation obviously needed more jobs.

In his message to Congress on January 4, 1935, President Franklin Roosevelt asked lawmakers to appropriate $4 billion ($62 billion) to create jobs for those already receiving monetary relief from the Federal Emergency Relief Administration (FERA). The proposed Public Works Administration (PWA) would replace the FERA by giving people jobs instead of handouts. Harry Hopkins would run the PWA, and part of the RFC's unspent $2 billion ($31 billion) authorization would be used to start it. After Roosevelt's address, newspapers reported, "The administration reached Saturday toward the coffers of the RFC for the funds to finance its next major effort—the transition from dole to work relief."[3] The PWA allocation would greatly enlarge the pass-through figure in the RFC numbers that Jones frequently recited.

Meanwhile, Jones had his own request. On January 19, 1935, he submitted a report to Congress and President Roosevelt that listed hundreds of RFC allocations and many pages of explanatory notes. The report concluded, "It is probably a safe assertion that everyone in the United States has been directly or indirectly benefited by the operations of the RFC."[4] Columnist Arthur Krock wrote about the report in the *New York Times*: "With such a record, it is not surprising to discover in Congress only negligible opposition to the proposed extension of powers."[5] Tom Corcoran and Ben Cohen drafted the RFC reauthorization bill: Jones wanted authority to operate for at least two more years, to extend loans from five to ten years, to increase loan amounts, and to assist the real estate markets and the railroads.

The Senate approved the bill four days after it was submitted.[6] A week later, Jones was present while the House approved the bill.[7] Drew Pearson and Robert Allen reported on the House hearings, writing, "RFC Chairman Jesse Jones is noted for his easy-going imperturbability. But on occasion the big, drawling Texan can be definitely vitriolic." They described how "Jesse was subjected to some barbed interrogation by Massachusetts

2. Leuchtenburg, *Roosevelt and the New Deal,* 124.
3. *Houston Chronicle,* January 6, 1935.
4. *Houston Chronicle,* January 20, 1935.
5. *New York Times,* January 17, 1935.
6. *Houston Chronicle,* January 23, 1935.
7. *Houston Chronicle,* January 30, 1935.

Republican Representative Charles L. Gifford" about failing to save the textile industry and for having a "glass-eye," or insincere sympathy, for it. The reporters recounted that "Jesse's smile dropped like a plummet, and he sat up stiffly in his chair. 'That's ridiculous,' he snapped back. 'Ours is a very real sympathy. If you will see to it that the law is changed so that we can do something for the industry, our glass eye will cease shedding crocodile tears. Just like yours,' he added."[8]

Most of Congress, however, had only good things to say about Jones and the RFC. Bertrand Snell, Republican leader of the House, said, "For once I am pleased to know that the American Congress seems to be practically unanimous in its praise and general approval of the work that has been done by Mr. Jones . . . and the RFC."[9] Jones remarked later, "The only criticism that congress had of the RFC in extending its life was for not making loans rather than for making them."[10]

Some members of Roosevelt's famous "Brain Trust" wanted the RFC to do more than make loans, liquefy credit markets, and save industries. In particular, they wanted it to control the flow of capital, determine dividend rates, and hire and fire corporate management. Corcoran wanted it to control Wall Street, and Secretary of Commerce Daniel Roper thought the RFC should supervise insurance companies' investments. On the other hand, Secretary of the Treasury Henry Morgenthau wanted the RFC abolished so he could use its authorized, but unspent, billions to balance the budget—Morgenthau most likely also resented Jones's power and close relationship with Roosevelt. Federal Reserve Chairman Eugene Black, who had introduced Jones at the 1933 American Bankers Association meeting, thought Jones had too much power and that the Federal Reserve board should have the most decisive role in national economics. Comptroller of the Currency J. F. T. O'Connor also thought the RFC had too much power. Leo Crowley, head of the Federal Deposit Insurance Corporation (FDIC), had clashed with Jones over purchasing banks' preferred stock and wanted it brought to an end. In response to Crowley's public position, Jones wrote every bank in the nation, urging them to let the RFC keep their stock until it was certain the financial markets were stable.[11]

Jones, who had worked closely with and debated all of these men, had Roosevelt's support as he successfully maneuvered between those who

8. Pearson and Allen, "Washington Merry-Go-Round," January 28, 1935.
9. *Houston Chronicle*, January 31, 1935.
10. *Houston Chronicle*, February 3, 1935.
11. Olson, *Saving Capitalism*, 113–14.

wanted the RFC to manage, plan, and control the economy permanently and those who wanted a balanced budget and small government. More than anything, Jones wanted to build a solid, safe financial foundation that would allow capitalism to serve the best interests of the most people at the least risk. His concepts of government "were more democratic than New Dealish."[12] At the very least, as he frequently pointed out, "The control of credit has been transferred from New York City to Washington."[13]

Finally, on January 31, 1935, only hours before the RFC was due to expire, President Roosevelt—with Jones watching over his shoulder—signed the legislation that extended RFC operations two more years and expanded its powers. According to newspapers, while Roosevelt was signing, "Jones said he understood the president to say something about how he would like to have it a five-year sentence instead of two."[14]

With the RFC's new authorization in hand, Jones turned his attention toward real estate. Mortgage debt had dropped by half from 1929 to 1934.[15] Foreclosures had forced hundreds of thousands out of their homes, and abandoned, unfinished commercial structures scarred urban thoroughfares. Billions in decaying mortgages threatened banks, insurance companies, savings and loans, and public institutions. Roosevelt had established the Home Owners Loan Corporation to help people refinance and keep their homes, and the Federal Housing Administration to encourage people to buy new homes with longer-term mortgages. The RFC supported both organizations with loans and pass-through appropriations, but neither agency was under the corporation's—or Jones's—control. At least for now.

Two days after receiving RFC reauthorization, Jones delivered a speech to the Real Estate Board of New York and said the Corporation would provide loans to owners of urban properties ineligible for assistance through existing agencies. Speaking from experience, he declared, "Real estate is the basis of all wealth. It supports our schools, pays for our fire and police protection, and to a very large extent supports state, county, city, and town governments." Grabbing another opportunity to castigate Wall Street bankers, he said once they had overcome their prejudices and "craze" for liquidity, then "real estate will again have a fair chance." In the meantime, the RFC would "do everything within our power to assist in unfreezing

12. Jones, *Fifty Billion Dollars,* 290.
13. Jesse Jones, speech, George Peabody College for Teachers, Nashville, June 18, 1934, Jesse H. Jones Collection [LOC].
14. *Houston Chronicle,* February 1, 1935.
15. Olson, *Saving Capitalism,* 172.

the mortgage situation." He added, "Construction will prove the greatest contribution at this period in getting people back to work."[16] In another *New York Times Magazine* feature, Jones nudged Wall Street again by pointing out that many mortgages "are worth more than they are selling for and are a legitimate field for RFC assistance . . . The ownership of homes is beyond all value to us as a nation, and what the RFC can do must be done."[17]

Jones established the RFC Mortgage Company in March. He observed later that although the "farmer and small home-owner had . . . been taken under the government umbrella, there was still no provision for federal refinancing of such income-producing properties as apartment houses, hotels, and office buildings." He added, "In that neglected field, the RFC Mortgage Company began its financing of real estate."[18] Announcing the formation of the RFC Mortgage Company, Jones said, "We will be able to make loans directly to individuals if we choose, but we are most interested in accelerating loans by private companies."[19]

Jones also turned the force of the RFC toward the railroads. Rail ticket sales had plunged from $876 million ($14 billion) in 1929 to $306 million ($4.7 billion) in just four years. Jobs and freight revenue dropped by half during the same period. At the same time, debt and interest payments escalated, along with increasing competition from airplanes, cars, and trucks. President Hoover had realized the railroads were in trouble, but only offered six-month RFC loans to service their debt because he thought recovery was right around the corner.[20] He also wanted to prevent defaults on railroad bonds held by banks, insurance companies, and public institutions. While Jones agreed that stability and liquidity depended on the health of the railroad bond market, he did not want taxpayer dollars used to pay large salaries, dividends to stockholders, or excessive interest to Wall Street financiers. He preferred to see long-term RFC loans go toward maintenance, employment, innovation, and restructuring.

Although he was exasperated with their unwillingness to lend, Jones did not criticize bankers as a whole. After all, Jones himself was an extremely successful banker. But he did resent the control east coast financiers had over the flow of capital to the rest of the nation and their

16. *Houston Chronicle*, February 3, 1935.
17. *New York Times Magazine*, February 17, 1935.
18. Jones, *Fifty Billion Dollars*, 149.
19. *Houston Chronicle*, March 15, 1935.
20. Olson, *Saving Capitalism*, 99.

A cartoon by the *Akron Beacon Journal*'s Web Brown shows Jones preventing railroad executives from using federal funds to pay back "big bankers" and railroad "bond holders." Courtesy Jesse Holman Jones Papers, Dolph Briscoe Center for American History, University of Texas at Austin.

tendency to place personal gain before national recovery. He certainly had no sympathy for "the private banking institutions that distributed [railroad] securities." He said they were not so much bankers, as "brokers and promoters."[21]

After the RFC's reauthorization, Jones gave a raft of speeches to promote the corporation's mission and jurisdiction. On February 22 at the Commodore Hotel, Jones explained to the Traffic Club of New York that the RFC's new authority allowed it to lend to railroads to purchase new equipment, maintain tracks, and reorganize their debt. "We should like to assist railroads in getting cheaper interest rates and to make them more independent of bankers," said Jones. Referring to interlocking railroad board memberships, he said, "The primary interest of a banker in serving as a director of a railroad, when stripped naked, is to make money out of the banking or financing of the road." He added, "Many of our railroad

21. Jones, *Fifty Billion Dollars*, 106.

executives . . . are required to spend entirely too much of their time traveling to and from New York to get orders from their bankers."[22]

Jones and the RFC intervened more with the railroads than with other businesses, possibly because Jones took a personal interest in the industry's reform; in fact, by his own account, he "assumed personal charge of practically all of the RFC's negotiations in the railroad field."[23] Using his novel clout as a government official, Jones required railroad executives seeking RFC loans to live near their lines and to accept salaries of no more than $60,000 ($928,000). President Roosevelt suggested a salary cap of $25,000 ($387,000), but Jones felt that cut was too severe for those accustomed to earning as much as $150,000 ($2.3 million) per year. If they balked, he did not hesitate to let them know "the President's views."[24]

Slashing interest rates was another tactic. Jones knew banks would capitulate and take less in interest if they knew someone else was competing for the loans. Jones and the RFC frequently assumed the "low-ball" role. Time and again, lending institutions dropped their rates after the RFC offered to buy a distressed railroad's bonds. But if the government participated with taxpayers' money, Jones imposed restrictions and requirements on those taking RFC loans, straddling the line between those who called for nationalization and consolidation of the railroads, and those who preferred the free market's survival of the fittest.

Trains had to compete with airplanes, automobiles, and trucks. In his speech to the Traffic Club, Jones noted a conundrum: "We develop an excellent system of railroads, serving every nook and corner of the nation, built with private capital and by enterprising initiative. We then proceed to parallel these railroads with competing highways, built and maintained at public expense." Jones admitted that abandoning some lines would be inevitable, but countered, "[R]ailroads can regain some of their lost ground by improved equipment, air-conditioned trains, faster schedules . . . [and] store-door service for freight." He added, "this recovery may be offset in part by the continued development of highway and motor services." He did not spare railroad management, accusing it of not being "as far-sighted and as energetic as it might have been in meeting the growing highway competition by improving their service . . . [and] by instituting economies in operation."[25]

22. *Houston Chronicle*, February 22, 1935.
23. Jones, *Fifty Billion Dollars*, 106.
24. Jesse Jones to G. Humphrey, April 26, 1954, Jesse H. Jones Collection [LOC].
25. *Houston Chronicle*, February 22, 1935.

Bolstered by Congressional authorization, public approval, adoration of most of the press, and presidential support, the RFC's reach into the nation's economy and life continued to expand, primarily because of Jones. Still slow to cover rural areas, electric power in 1935 had reached only two farms in ten.[26] When Senator George Norris of Nebraska went to see President Roosevelt about the situation, FDR turned him over to Jones. Aware of Jones's bargaining power and his priorities, Norris protested and said Jones would want too much interest and too much security for the enormous undertaking. Roosevelt told Jones and Norris to figure it out. As the story goes, Jones asked Norris how much he needed. Norris said $40 million ($619 million) a year for ten years and insisted he would not pay more than four percent in interest. Jones said, "Then how about three percent?" Norris quickly agreed and negotiations for the Rural Electrification Administration (REA), according to Jones, were concluded in less than ten minutes.[27] Jones was willing to accept less interest because of the REA's likely impact on the overall economy and because small cooperatives, municipalities, and businesses would be paying interest to the government, not to New York banks and brokerage houses.

On May 11, 1935, President Roosevelt authorized the REA by executive order. It ultimately loaned more than a billion dollars to cooperatives, cities, and private utilities to build and operate power plants. Within ten years, the REA helped bring electricity to ninety percent of the nation's farms.[28] It was a task private industry had been unwilling and unable to undertake; only the federal government was large enough to accomplish the large-scale, transformational project. The Electric Home and Farm Authority (EHFA), established earlier to help low-income home owners and tenants acquire appliances, dovetailed perfectly with the REA.

The RFC was everywhere. It helped fund schools and pay teachers. It made loans to towns, cities, and individuals whose property had been destroyed by natural disasters. One of the smallest loans was for $20 ($309) to a barber in Kentucky to replace his combs, soaps, razors, and scissors that were washed away in a flood. Its largest loans were to huge "self-liquidating" public works started in Hoover's administration, which were nearing completion, and to new ones recently initiated by the Works Progress Administration (WPA), which were still underway. At a speech in July at the dedication of the Frontier Bridges that cross

26. Kennedy, *Freedom from Fear*, 252.
27. Jones, *Fifty Billion Dollars*, 200–201.
28. Kennedy, *Freedom from Fear*, 252.

Niagara Falls, Jones said, "Whenever it is necessary for the Government, national or local, to provide its citizens with work, this character of projects—these bridges that pay for themselves—things that will be useful to, and used by, all people—should be given first consideration." Jones added, "I am here because it is my privilege to work with President Roosevelt as head of the government agency that loaned the money with which these bridges were built—the RFC."[29]

Wellington Brink, writing about Jones and the RFC, said, "Every nook and cranny of the nation is being revitalized. The billions of dollars are tonic dollars . . . friendly, industrious, intelligent dollars . . . Jesse Jones dollars."[30] And in a radio broadcast less than three months before he was killed in an airplane crash, Will Rogers claimed, "I get all my money information from Jesse Jones, head of Reconstruction Finance."[31]

Will Rogers's death deeply saddened Jones, who counted the humorist as one of his closest friends. Rogers and famous pilot Wiley Post had set out on a trip to explore and fish in Siberia. Soon after they left Fairbanks, Alaska, on August 15, 1935, dense fog rolled in, and Post landed their pontoon plane on Harding Lake. Once it was clear to go, they took off and climbed fifty feet, then the engine sputtered. The plane plunged to the ground. Upon impact, the airplane's right wing was sliced off, and the engine smashed into the cockpit. Both men were killed. Washington correspondent Bascom Timmons reported, "Two of Rogers' closest friends, Vice President [John Nance] Garner and Chairman Jesse H. Jones of the RFC, waited in vain for reports correcting . . . rumors that the two men had been killed. Then came definite confirmation of the reports."[32]

A stunned nation grieved for its celebrated spokesman. President Roosevelt and Vice President Garner each released official statements. A newspaper story two days after the crash reported that the funeral service would be in Los Angeles and that Rogers would be buried in Oklahoma, his birthplace. The second paragraph of the article said, "The widow, Mrs. Rogers, announced through Jesse Jones, chairman of the Reconstruction Finance Corporation in Washington, a family friend, that his body would be placed temporarily in a vault at Forestlawn Cemetery." The article continued,

29. Jesse Jones, speech, Frontier Bridges, Niagara Falls, July 15, 1935, Jesse H. Jones Collection [UT].

30. Brink, "Jesse Jones," 7.

31. "Good Gulf Show," radio broadcast, May 26, 1935.

32. *Houston Chronicle*, August 16, 1935.

"Jones, who hurried to New York today to meet Mrs. Rogers on her arrival here from Maine en route to California, said the family would leave New York by train tomorrow afternoon for the coast."[33]

Jesse Jones and Will Rogers were devoted friends. When Rogers was in Washington, it was known that "a meal at the White House was usually part of [his] . . . visits,"[34] but what was not known is that in the mornings Rogers frequently joined Jones at his home to have coffee and read the papers. Jones's granddaughter, Audrey, remembered those visits and said she always enjoyed serving Rogers a cup of coffee and kidding him for leaving the full cup behind because he had talked the whole time he was there. The nation's number-one box office star would promise the teenage girl that he would drink it the next time.[35]

Jim Rogers, Will's son, said about Jones, "Of all dad's political friends . . . he is the only one that I know who went out of his way to help my mother, and I will be very grateful to him forever for that."[36] Front page newspaper stories told how Jones "took over the task of arranging details for Mrs. Rogers."[37] One report claimed, "The RFC chairman, an old friend, talked with her daily by telephone since Rogers was killed in an Alaskan plane crash."[38] Jim also remembered what happened after his father's large income suddenly ceased. He said they still had "all the obligations based on projected income" and suddenly found themselves "in a really very tough financial situation." Rogers added that Jones "was very helpful" and was "very wonderful with advice."[39]

If the low point of Jones's year was Will Rogers's death, the high point may have come in the fall when a life-size portrait of the RFC chairman was dedicated and hung in the senate chamber of the Texas state capitol. According to Lieutenant Governor Walter Frank Woodul, Rogers had suggested the portrait and promised to attend the ceremony if his idea were adopted.[40] The Joneses left Washington by train on Friday, October 4, and arrived in Austin on Sunday, October 6, for the unveiling on Monday. At the press conference upon his arrival, reportedly the largest

---

33. *Houston Chronicle,* August 18, 1935.
34. *Houston Chronicle,* August 16, 1935.
35. Audrey Jones Beck, conversation with the author.
36. Jim Rogers to Steven Fenberg, April 15, 1996, Oral History Project [HE].
37. *Houston Chronicle,* August 18, 1935.
38. *Houston Chronicle,* August 30, 1935.
39. Jim Rogers to Steven Fenberg, April 15, 1996, Oral History Project [HE].
40. *Houston Chronicle,* October 8, 1935.

ever in Austin, two dozen men and three women reporters lined up to interview him.[41]

Hundreds of Jones's Houston friends arrived by special train and many more came by car. Senator Alben Barkley of Kentucky represented the U.S. Senate and was the principal speaker at the Monday afternoon ceremony. After the University of Texas band played the seemingly ubiquitous "The Eyes of Texas," Jones's portrait by Edmond Pizzella was unveiled in the capitol's more spacious house chamber, where "crowds jammed . . . and stood in the corridors."[42] The portrait was later hung in the senate chamber, where other distinguished state dignitaries and citizens had been immortalized.

Six former governors, the current governor, Jones's family and friends, assorted local, state, and national political figures, and thousands more capped the day with a reception at the University of Texas's Gregory Gym, the only building large enough to accommodate the more than four thousand people who came to honor Jones. The University of Texas and Rice Institute bands suspended their rivalry long enough to perform together, and once again everyone heard "The Eyes of Texas," this time to start the evening's revelry.

All of official Washington knew about the portrait because Jones had invited them to the unveiling—the president, his cabinet, his assistants, congressmen, senators, and dozens of his colleagues, from Bernard Baruch to Charles Schwab, were notified by formal invitation. Letters of acknowledgment and praise—all sincere—poured in. Many touted Jones for president. Conservative Democratic Senator Josiah Bailey from North Carolina, who openly criticized Roosevelt and called for lower taxes and less spending, wrote Jones that the RFC "has been recognized throughout the country as the most efficient of all the agencies of the government in coping with the depression. Maybe in 1940 we will be looking to you to lead our party to victory."[43]

Bank of America Chairman A. P. Giannini declared at the ceremony, "When the full record is written of our recovery from the greatest depression ever experienced, the name of Jesse Holman Jones will be most prominent."[44] A cousin in Nashville who received an invitation and later saw Jones's picture in the local papers, wrote to Jones that "Mrs. Jones

41. Ibid.
42. Ibid.
43. Josiah Bailey to Jesse Jones, September 1, 1935, Jesse H. Jones Collection [HE].
44. A. P. Giannini, speech, Texas State Senate, Austin, October 3, 1935, Jesse H. Jones Collection [HE].

supplied the good looks" and then promised to "scour the woods" for "a bottle of pre-war Tennessee whiskey."[45]

The Joneses went to Houston the day after the portrait was unveiled to rest and relax before Jones hit the road again to give more speeches about the RFC. In only a few days, he attended a dinner in San Antonio, luncheon in Dallas, dinner in Oklahoma City, and dinner in Fort Worth, with a small party afterward at Amon Carter's farm. The day after Carter's party, a Fort Worth business colleague wrote Jones, "When I arrived at the office this morning about 9:15, I found your 'howdy' note on my desk, which I understand you left about 8:20 a.m. You must be a brute for punishment to survive Amon's party last night and then come up smiling . . . by 8:20."[46] Jones could hold his own and always had a more than full schedule. By the time his colleague had read his note, Jones was on his way back to Houston to tend to matters regarding the upcoming Texas Centennial celebration, check on his many businesses, and prepare for his return to Washington.

The Joneses reached Washington on the first of November. The next day Jones greeted the Rice Owls football team, in town to play the George Washington Colonials. He delivered a speech to the National Paint, Varnish, and Lacquer Association and, that evening, gave a radio address over the National Broadcasting Corporation and Columbia Broadcasting System to promote, on behalf of President Roosevelt and Vice President Garner, the Will Rogers Memorial Commission. Later in the month, Jones flew to New Orleans to deliver, again, the principal speech at the American Bankers Association annual meeting.

Standing before the less than friendly gathering, Jones began, "It is a pleasure to meet with you again. But you are entitled to new faces at your annual meetings, and funnier speeches, so I promise not to accept an invitation to address you next year should I be so fortunate as to receive one." This year he wanted to talk about railroads, not banks, but the bankers were not off the hook. Within ten seconds of his soft opening, Jones said, "Entirely too many railroads are dominated by bankers who sit on their boards, or dominate them in other ways, and who make money out of their financing." He accused bankers who sat on railroad boards of charging too much for their services, charging too much for loans, and promoting their own interests at the expense of the railroad they were supposed to serve and protect. He said, "The perpetuation of

45. Joseph W. Holman to Jesse Jones, October 26, 1935, Jesse H. Jones Collection [HE].
46. W. T. Dinkins to Jesse Jones, October 19, 1935, Jesse H. Jones Collection [HE].

poor management through small cliques who may be in control of a property should be made impossible."[47]

Jones proposed an alternative. He encouraged the bankers to finance "better tracks, new and better equipment, maintenance, and better service," all of which required "more labor." He also talked about the competitive pressure from automobile and air travel and said "sound reasoning cannot defend the continued operation of railroad mileage that does not directly or indirectly pay its cost." Jones again gave the bankers options, but unsheathed his power by adding, "Of one thing I am convinced, railroads are a common problem to us all and will require the attention of our leaders both in and out of Congress if we are to avoid Government ownership."[48]

At the beginning of 1935, Jones had announced that railroads and real estate were the two remaining problems for the RFC to address. On that November evening, having finished talking about the railroads, Jones started in on real estate. He told the bankers, "Since real estate is the basis of all wealth, and industry the most essential factor in employment, these should have, to a reasonable and safe extent, favored treatment by banks in making loans." He urged them to "change their attitude of frowning upon and condemning real estate loans. They . . . can be made upon a perfectly sound basis." Even as Jones tried to paint a hopeful and realistic economic picture, he admitted, "We still have the problem of unemployment, and I am afraid we will have [it] much too long . . . We simply are able to produce more of everything than we consume, and our foreign markets . . . absorb very little of our surplus." He talked to the bankers as if they were community leaders, saying, "Unemployment is your problem, as it is the problem of every class of our citizenship. No one is without responsibility in finding the answer. The Government cannot do it all."[49]

Jones included his usual recitation of RFC activity, with more detail than usual—either he thought the bankers appreciated numbers more than others, or he wanted to make a point. After reeling off a mind-numbing list of programs and the amounts authorized, disbursed, and loaned to each, he summed up the RFC grand totals since its February 1932 inception, saying that, to date, the RFC had been authorized to disburse $10.3 billion ($159 billion). Of that amount, $2.7 billion ($42 billion) had

47. Jesse Jones, speech, American Bankers Association, November 12, 1935, Jesse H. Jones Collection [UT].
48. Ibid.
49. Ibid.

been passed through to other government agencies; and of the remaining $7.6 billion ($117 billion) authorized, $5.7 billion ($88 billion) had been disbursed. Jones took great delight in reporting that $3.1 billion ($48 billion) of the $5.7 billion ($88 billion) disbursed had already been repaid. He said, "When it is considered that these loans were all made during the depression, and on security that you gentlemen . . . could not accept, the more remarkable is the fact that repayments have been so rapid and so large. This could not have happened if our country was not sound. I offer this record in support of my statement that the depression, as such, is over."[50]

At the end of his speech, Jones relaxed and said, "Now, a little off-the-record word to you bankers. I think you are a swell lot of guys. Some of you are afraid of your shadows and wouldn't lend more than ten dollars on a twenty dollar bill. Some of you are worried about where we are going. I don't know what's ahead of us, but I know what's behind us. I [also] know, whatever is ahead of us, that there is meat in the smoke house and flour in the barrel, and that whatever it is, we can lick it."[51]

Despite a packed schedule, Jones for the second year in a row was able to return to Houston with Mary for the holidays. They arrived just in time for Jones to speak to the Salesmanship Club where, as he had done the year before, he remembered those who had passed away. This time he talked about Will Rogers and Stockton Axson, Woodrow Wilson's brother-in-law, Rice Institute professor, and Jones's friend of twenty years.[52]

Right after Christmas, the Joneses and their granddaughter, Audrey, boarded the Alamo, a private railcar, and headed for Los Angeles to be the houseguests of Betty Rogers and her family at their 400-acre ranch just outside of Beverly Hills. Mrs. Rogers wrote Jones, "Just drop us a line, or a wire, stating when you will arrive, and we will meet you at the station."[53] Little did they know, a huge crush of California's biggest businessmen and politicians, and hordes of press would also meet the Joneses at the station. A private memo from the RFC's California manager to Jones's chief assistant, William Costello, confided, "It was remarked by several . . . that never before had a reception committee in Los Angeles been composed of such outstanding financial and business men . . . It was overheard that Mr. Harry Chandler, publisher of the *Los Angeles Times*, very seldom came

50. Ibid.
51. Ibid.
52. *Houston Chronicle*, December 22, 1935.
53. September 24, 1935, Jesse H. Jones Collection [HE].

in person to welcome visitors to the city." It continued, "Mr. Chandler . . . furnished a car and chauffeur and a car for the baggage. The Mayor of Los Angeles provided a motorcycle escort for the Jones car and offered to provide such an escort for any of Mr. Jones's movements in southern California."[54]

On New Year's Day, the Joneses enjoyed the Rose Bowl football game played between the Southern Methodist University Mustangs of Dallas and the Stanford University Indians (now Cardinals). The next day Jones attended a celebration of the opening of the Coachella Tunnel, part of the 244-mile aqueduct that would eventually bring water from the Colorado River in Arizona to Los Angeles and southern California. Funded by a $208 million ($3.2 billion) loan from the RFC, the aqueduct was the largest of the RFC's "self-liquidating" projects and another of its transformational efforts. From Los Angeles, Jones went to San Francisco to inspect progress on the San Francisco-Oakland Bay Bridge, an RFC-funded project that paid for itself through small tolls. He was met in San Francisco with the same acclaim and adulation he received wherever he went.

Public service, friends, and family meant more to Jones than the clamor and excitement that surrounded him. On his way back to Washington, he wrote Betty Rogers, "Have had a very pleasant day in San Francisco but shall never forget the very beautiful days with you and the boys on the ranch. Worlds of love, Jesse Jones."[55] Then he wrote Mary, who was returning directly to Washington, "Having a delightful day through the snow covered mountains of Nevada and wish you were with me."[56]

54. Thomas L. Scroggins to William Costello, January 9, 1936, Jesse H. Jones Collection [HE].

55. Jesse Jones to Betty Rogers, January 4, 1936, Jesse H. Jones Collection [HE].

56. Jesse Jones to Mary Gibbs Jones, January 5, 1936, Jesse H. Jones Collection [HE].

1936

No Actual
Ultimate Cost

JESSE JONES WAS NOT A ONE-MAN BAND. He conducted the Reconstruction Finance Corporation (RFC) like a finely tuned orchestra that responded and followed his lead. Bill Costello, his closest assistant, was an essential player, filtering out demanding politicians, mail, and phone calls before they reached Jones. Costello organized most of Jones's appointments and made sure names in important newspaper clippings were underlined, times of important radio broadcasts were listed, and passages from the Congressional Record were waiting at his desk when he arrived in the morning. Before he got there, Jones had already read the *New York Times* and the Washington newspapers, and had dictated letters over the phone to a secretary. About the latter habit, Jones recalled, "I think best in the morning. Also, by the time I get down [to the office], I have a draft of what I dictated."[1]

Jones accomplished an enormous amount over the phone. One wag claimed Jones was responsible for AT&T's $4 ($61 in current dollars) dividend. A reporter wrote that he "averages 80 to 90 phone calls a day . . . Three telephones are on his desk, one an unlisted private number. All calls over the office wires are monitored by a special operator who follows

---

1. Lubell, "New Deal's J. P. Morgan," 92.

up each call." While listening to the conversation with Jones, the operator would record the caller's name and request, then forward information from the conversation to the appropriate RFC department. The department would later send Jones a report about the loan and the caller. The caller's name stayed on the operator's books until she had been notified that Jones or an RFC representative had responded. Operators also lined up callers waiting to speak with the RFC chief so he could go from one call to the next without interruption.[2] Jones sometimes spoke on two or three phones at the same time.

The RFC operated efficiently and fast. Men and women, loaded with papers and talking a mile a minute, raced down hallways and took stairs rather than stop for the elevator. They were on a mission—to serve Jones and save the economy. One reporter suggested to President Roosevelt that he send some of the New Dealers "for a few years of schooling at the RFC." The writer explained, "The office and field forces of this gigantic agency, for example, number only 3,200 people, and the overhead is one-half of one percent as compared with the ten and fifteen percent of other New Deal bodies." He added, "Not one cent of upkeep comes from the tax revenues of government, for the corporation takes care of its own operating expenses."[3]

If Jones was the orchestra conductor, then the seven RFC board members were the first chairs. Jones had approved each member, and they were all a bit in awe of the unusually powerful man. Each was a distinguished expert who was devoted to public service. Emil Schram, future president of the New York Stock Exchange, was an Indiana farmer who, as head of the National Drainage Association, first became acquainted with the RFC in 1932 while seeking a loan for his organization. He was invited to join the RFC staff to manage the drainage, levee, and irrigation division. It refinanced bonds that counties had sold during boom times at high interest rates to finance and build infrastructure. The new bonds, with lower interest rates and longer maturities, saved farmers and rural communities millions of dollars in taxes and made money for the government. Carroll B. Merriam from Topeka, Kansas, president of a large bank and director of a railroad, knew Jones from the American Red Cross during World War I. He joined the RFC board in 1933 and oversaw loans to closed banks.

The board was a mix of businessmen, politicians, and farmers, Re-

2. Ibid.
3. Creel, "Hard-Boiled Jesse," 42.

publicans and Democrats, conservatives and liberals. Former Wisconsin governor and Progressive Senator John J. Blaine joined the board in 1933. He had been a delegate for Robert M. La Follette at the 1912 Democratic convention, became a Republican supporter of Woodrow Wilson, and authored the U.S. Constitution's twenty-first amendment, repealing Prohibition.[4] Blaine's Progressive credentials broadened the RFC's and Jones's point of view. Referring to the diversity, Jones recalled, "Senator Blaine had the universal respect of his associates in the corporation and the genuine affection of many of us, certainly my own . . . Working together night and day, Sundays included, in emergency-relief work soon brings men close together and makes for strong ties of friendship."[5] Republican Charles T. Fisher, head of the RFC's Detroit loan agency since its 1932 inception, replaced Blaine after his death in 1934.[6] In addition to Jones, Merriam, Schram, and Fisher, Republican Frederic H. Taber and Democrats Charles B. Henderson and Hubert Stephens rounded out the group.[7]

RFC attorney Tom Corcoran—also one of Roosevelt's closest advisers—was Jones's liaison to the more ardent New Dealers and to Treasury Secretary Henry Morgenthau, who relentlessly lobbied the president to abolish the RFC and use its resources to balance the budget.[8] As the economy improved in 1936, Morgenthau's arguments began to carry more weight. He pressed Roosevelt to order Jones to stop making loans, redeem the preferred stock the RFC held in more than six thousand banks, and sell its government bonds. The flood of cash would reduce the deficit and avoid a tax hike.[9] Roosevelt, however, thought the RFC had bigger fish to fry.

The RFC effectively allowed the president to skirt Congress and its power of the purse. To sidestep Congressional wrangling, Roosevelt often turned to the RFC for resources to fund projects, agencies, and new programs, and to satisfy individual requests from members of Congress. Not surprisingly, this was not always to Jones's liking. The more than $2 billion ($31 billion) passed through to the Works Progress Administration (WPA), the Public Works Administration (PWA), and other agencies concerned him, and he accounted for the billions as separate entries on the RFC balance sheets. It was not so much the programs that bothered him,

---

4. *Wisconsin State Journal*, April 17, 1934.
5. Jones, "Billions Out and Billions Back."
6. Olson, *Saving Capitalism*, 53.
7. Jones, *Fifty Billion Dollars*, 597.
8. Olson, *Saving Capitalism*, 58.
9. Ibid., 180.

but that he had no control over them. Still, the RFC was Roosevelt's bank for the New Deal, and Jones was his bridge to the often hostile business community and skeptical public. No matter how much the economy improved, Roosevelt was not ready to disband the RFC or to lose Jones.

New Deal programs, plus the $2 billion ($31 billion) "bonus" payment made to World War I veterans in 1936, helped move the economy forward. Industrial output doubled during Roosevelt's four years in office, and farm income almost quadrupled. In 1936 Detroit churned out more cars than at any time since 1929. Six million of the thirteen million unemployed were back at work, dropping national unemployment from twenty-five percent to around seventeen percent.[10]

By 1936 most of the RFC's agencies were up and running, some since 1932. Their efforts to stabilize the banking system were largely complete. At the beginning of the year in Baltimore, Jones reminded his audience, "Probably the billion dollars capital stock invested by the RFC in 6,000 banks did more good than any government activity. It gave us a strong banking system. Our banks are now stronger in deposits, [in] excess reserves, and in capital than they have ever been." He explained, "Rebuilding the banks was like putting a new foundation under the house. It was absolutely necessary to prevent the house from falling down."[11] In a speech in May, Jones was more direct: "This bank repair work, through putting capital in banks, saved our entire banking system, which I am glad to say is now stronger than ever in the history of our country."[12]

The RFC, unfortunately, had had less success with the railroads—no matter what was spent on railroads, it would never be enough. In 1936 more than half the railroads still operated at a loss: of the $500 million ($7.6 billion) in RFC loans, almost thirty percent were in default and half were outstanding.[13] Railroad debt climbed while revenue dropped due to relentless competition from cars, trucks, and airplanes.

The RFC tried to help by offering the railroads lower rates for their bonds and loans when bank interest rates went too high. As Jones said in a speech, "Some of my banker friends, and others in that environment, including some of our financial writers, are all hot and bothered about our efforts to reduce interest rates. We are not only trying to help the average

10. Leuchtenburg, *Roosevelt and the New Deal*, 194.
11. Jesse Jones, speech, Jackson Day dinner, January 11, 1936, Jesse H. Jones Collection [UT].
12. Jesse Jones, speech, Princeton-Harvard-Yale Conference of Public Affairs, May 9, 1936, Jesse H. Jones Collection [UT].
13. Olson, *Saving Capitalism*, 120.

man—the small borrower—but we would like to help the railroads in getting lower interest rates. This is one way the government can help the railroads, without loss to the government." Then he said, "I should like to repeat here, with emphasis, statements . . . to the effect that too many of our railroads are dominated by bankers whose principal interest . . . is to make money out of their financing. This is within the law, but should not be."[14] He gave as an example the Great Northern railroad that had been paying seven percent interest on bonds it sold fifteen years ago, even though prevailing rates were now much lower. Bankers had offered to renew the maturing debt at five percent interest with a $1 million ($15.2 million) underwriting charge, rejecting Jones's suggestion to charge four and a half percent and a $500,000 ($7.6 million) underwriting fee. Using its power to set interest rates, the RFC came in with a loan offer at four percent and no fee. Jones said, "We will save the Great Northern more than $11 million [$168 million] on this one issue . . . and that . . . will give many a man a job, and incidentally improve the railroad."[15]

On the railroad issue as on others, Jones was attacked from all directions while he forged his own path. A loud, powerful contingent wanted to consolidate the railroads; others wanted them nationalized. But Jones wanted to stabilize the railroads by reducing their debt and interest, and by making them more efficient, modern, and competitive. Toward that end, the loans for equipment that Jones had implemented in 1934 were beginning to show results. On March 25, 1936, Illinois Central's Green Diamond train left on a one-month "exhibition trip" before it was officially put into service between Chicago and St. Louis. The shiny silver, green, and red train looked as if it had landed from outer space. Instead of a hulking black locomotive, the front of the engine car slanted back from its bottom to its top, had curved, rounded edges, and was covered in aluminum. The conductor's narrow horizontal windows wrapped around the top like aviator goggles. No visible break interrupted the engine and the four cars it pulled, making the train look as if it were in a permanent wind tunnel even as it stood still. According to Illinois Central's national advertising campaign, the Green Diamond was "America's first standard-size, Diesel electric, streamlined train."[16]

Thousands of people swamped local train stations to see the modern

14. Jesse Jones, speech, Jackson Day dinner, January 11, 1936, Jesse H. Jones Collection [UT].
15. Ibid.
16. *Houston Chronicle*, April 13, 1936.

Illinois Central billed the RFC-funded Green Diamond as "America's first standard-size, diesel electric, streamlined train" (*Houston Chronicle*, April 13, 1936). It was inaugurated on March 25, 1936, by Jones's granddaughter, Audrey.

marvel as it passed through their towns. Schools closed in some places so children could see it.[17] More than 18,000 gawked at the train in San Antonio, and nearly 20,000 crowded the train station to see it in Shreveport, Louisiana. Newspapers alerted farmers in rural areas and people in small towns to the train's schedule so they could gather at remote tracks in the countryside and catch a glimpse of the modern vehicle as it whizzed by. The Illinois Central president claimed that the Green Diamond was "a rolling laboratory of experimentation for ideas that may be of service in the general plan of modernization in which the Illinois Central System is engaged."[18] The train also included an "up-to-the-minute air-conditioning system, which washes the air and constantly changes it."[19] Government was helping industry fund progress.

17. "Green Diamond Creates Good Will on Tour."
18. Ibid.
19. *Houston Chronicle*, April 13, 1936.

During the train's visit to Houston, Illinois Central officials invited Jones's granddaughter, Audrey, to christen the Green Diamond in Chicago on May 17, 1936, the day it would officially go into service. While her parents, grandparents, and thousands of others eagerly watched, fourteen-year-old Audrey Louise Jones smashed a bottle of champagne across the nose of the most modern train in the United States and sent it on its first regular run to St. Louis. The inaugural ceremony and nearly five-hour trip to St. Louis were broadcast over the radio. Right before Audrey christened the train, her grandfather made a short speech. Jones explained to the gathered throng and to the millions listening over the radio that the "Green Diamond is a direct result of the federal government cooperating with the Illinois Central to provide work for men . . . The government provided equipment loans on favorable terms," which will be paid back "from the earnings of the train. This Green Diamond pays for itself while at the same time evidencing progress and a determination by Illinois Central management to keep pace with the times." Jones went on to congratulate the line's officers, including his friend Averill Harriman, and added, "The Reconstruction Finance Corporation is prepared to finance other Green Diamonds and railroad equipment of all kinds, for all railroads, to provide work for more men and improve railroad service."[20]

Audrey, a perfectly poised young lady, rode the train with her parents to St. Louis and took part in the national broadcast. She wrote her grandmother that she was "having so much fun" and had just had her picture taken again "with the conductor's hat on." She also told "Muna" that she was in the last car and "getting all the turns and twists."[21] Jones was delighted with his granddaughter's role in the important event and wrote, "Your letter written on the Green Diamond when you were traveling at the rate of 110 miles an hour indicates that you were enjoying your trip . . . You acquitted yourself creditably in the part you had to play and made all of us quite proud of you." He then reminded her, if she had not done so already, to send thank you letters to all who had "extended courtesies" to her and her family.[22] Jones was also pleased that wherever Audrey went during her excursion, she always reminded people, whether over the radio or on an observation platform, to "come to the Centennial!"[23]

The Texas Centennial, celebrating the anniversary of the state's inde-

20. Jesse Jones, speech, Green Diamond christening, Chicago, May 17, 1936, Jesse H. Jones Collection [LOC].

21. May 17, 1936, Jesse H. Jones Collection [HE].

22. May 25, 1936, Jesse H. Jones Collection [HE].

23. *New Orleans Item*, May 15, 1936.

pendence from Mexico in 1836, was drawing closer. The idea had its origins in Corsicana, Texas, when on November 6, 1923, the keynote speaker at the Advertising Clubs of America meeting suggested a celebration that through "patriotism and commercialism" would sell Texas to the rest of the nation. The idea caught on. A group was formed, and as the search for a leader began, the board set its sights on Jones.[24] While flattered, Jones rejected the first few invitations, but he was intrigued by the prospect of organizing the largest statewide event ever presented to the nation and finally accepted on April 14, 1926. After that, he did very little to further the cause.[25]

Bascom Timmons, Jones's *Houston Chronicle* Washington correspondent and 1956 biographer, wrote, "On at least four occasions [Jones] was called to tasks that he . . . expected would require his attention only at policy-making board meetings. These were the development of the Houston port, his Red Cross services under President Wilson, the Texas Centennial, and . . . the RFC."[26] Yet in 1926 Jones did not throw himself into the Centennial as he had with his other appointments because he felt "five or six years seemed . . . enough to prepare for a Centennial," and he was in no rush to get started ten years before the fact.[27] Others were concerned at this leisurely approach, but Jones delivered a speech to the executive committee in 1928, two years after his appointment as Centennial chairman, and assured them that he had not been "derelict" in his duties and had given "the matter much consideration."[28]

Jones may have been inactive, but he was still imaginative and influential. The Centennial originators wanted a national marketing campaign, capped by an extravagant exposition to draw people and business to Texas. But Jones thought the occasion called instead for permanent shrines throughout the state that would inspire and educate people about Texas history and culture. He said in his 1928 speech, "It seems to me that the day of the world's fair is passed. The hootchy-kootchy and Midway Plaisance were great drawing cards in 1893 in Chicago," but the recent Sesquicentennial celebration at Philadelphia "was a complete failure in point of attendance" and a "great financial loss." He went on to say the Centennial "can be made as comprehensive and as magnificent and as fascinating as we are willing to back our imaginations with money and

24. Ragsdale, *Year America Discovered Texas*, 12.
25. Ibid., 13.
26. Timmons, *Jones: Man and Statesman*, 394.
27. Ragsdale, *Year America Discovered Texas*, 18.
28. *Houston Chronicle*, April 1, 1928.

effort. It will involve the employment of the best historians and the best artists, the best sculptors and the best scenario writers, as well as the very earnest attention of leaders in all lines of enterprise and business, industrial, live stock, and agriculture."[29]

Jones frequently tried to broaden his fellow Texans' worldviews. In the case of the Centennial, he wanted to include other nations in the festivities and instructed, "We would ask them in a proper way, by sending the right sort of invitations, by the best available messengers, or through such diplomatic channels as might be adopted." He said, "Out of this Centennial would come a better and a more friendly understanding between the nations of the world." Thinking globally rather than locally about building a community, Jones followed, "It is impossible to know your fellowman in a neighborly way and to hate him." Then he concluded, "I should like to add that I am ready and anxious to pass the leadership of this movement to other hands at the very first opportunity."[30] The coming 1928 Democratic National Convention in Houston was breathing down his neck. The economic calamity that followed a few years later caused him to officially resign on December 28, 1931, right before his appointment to the RFC.[31]

The Texas Centennial that opened in Dallas on June 6, 1936, combined both Jones's and the committee's ideas and visions. The $25 million ($383 million) exposition center, built on a "Texianic" scale, included elegant and energetic Art Deco halls showcasing everything good and new about Texas. Statues and monuments planned for other parts of the state included the restoration of the Alamo in San Antonio and the erection of the San Jacinto Monument at the San Jacinto Battleground near Houston, which Jones said should be memorialized in perpetuity. More than six million people visited the Centennial Exposition in Dallas within the first months of its grand opening. Many came from outside the state, including President Roosevelt, whose first stop was Houston.

William Howard Taft had been the last sitting president to visit Houston back in 1909. When President Roosevelt arrived by train on the morning on June 11, 1936, during one of Houston's hot, sweltering summer days, people crammed up to fifteen deep on both sides of Main Street to see him. Stores, schools, and factories had been closed. People stood on cars and hung out of every skyscraper window that opened on Main Street.

29. Ibid.
30. Ibid.
31. Ragsdale, *Year America Discovered Texas*, 22.

Jesse Jones, President Franklin Roosevelt, Eleanor Roosevelt, and Houston Mayor Oscar Holcombe. Courtesy *Houston Chronicle*.

The *Houston Chronicle* reported, "Most of Houston's 350,000 citizens jammed the downtown streets or assembled on the San Jacinto Battle ground 20 miles east of here."[32] Mayor Oscar Holcombe suspended the recently imposed noise ordinance for the day.

Music began on Main Street at 8:00 in the morning when a local band started playing "Dixie" and "The Eyes of Texas." After the president arrived at around 10:00 a.m., he, Jones, and other officials rode down Main Street toward Buffalo Bayou, showered with unadulterated acclaim and, there, boarded a private yacht that took them to the San Jacinto battleground. During the parade down Main, Mayor Holcombe told Roosevelt that crippled children from a local hospital would be at a certain place along the way. When they approached the spot, Holcombe reported, "The president gave orders for his car to slow up and swing over near the children. This was done and the president waved and called out, 'How are you?' But the children were so overawed they couldn't speak."[33]

32. *Houston Chronicle*, June 11, 1936.
33. *Houston Chronicle*, June 12, 1936.

Jesse Jones with Sam Houston's son, Andrew Jackson Houston, at the San Jacinto battleground site. When recognizing Houston during a battleground site ceremony, President Franklin Roosevelt exclaimed, "What a splendid combination of names" (*Houston Chronicle*, June 11, 1936). Courtesy San Jacinto Museum of History.

More than 28,000 people awaited them at the battleground to see and hear Roosevelt. After Jones introduced him, the president recognized Sam Houston's son, Andrew Jackson Houston, and commented, "What a splendid combination of names!" The president told the crowd how his own father as a young man had delivered legal papers to Sam Houston in his Washington, D.C., hotel bedroom. Roosevelt then lauded the pioneer Texans who fought and died for independence and called San Jacinto a "historic shrine." By 12:30 p.m., about three hours after his arrival in Houston, the president was on his way to San Antonio, and from there to Dallas and the Centennial Exposition.[34]

The day after Roosevelt's visit to Houston, Jones went to Dallas to deliver a speech, after which he, his secretary Joe Toomey, former Texas governor William P. Hobby and his wife, Oveta, left Dallas for Houston in a private plane. About twenty minutes into the flight when the plane was at an altitude of about 7,000 feet, a leaking gasoline line burst into

34. *Houston Chronicle*, June 11, 1936.

flames and engulfed the cockpit. Eugene Schacher, one of the two pilots, rushed into the cabin, warned his passengers about the fire, and slammed the door shut to separate them from the leaping flames. While Ed Hefley, the other pilot, put the plane into a nosedive to get to the ground as fast as possible, Schacher fought the flames. Hefley recalled, "We hit flat on the belly of the ship. The impact tore the motor loose from the frame. The plane slithered and bumped to a stop, with flames eating at the forward compartment." The four passengers escaped. From his hospital bed, where he was being treated for severe burns, Hefley said, "Mr. Jones met me at the door of the pilot's compartment and pulled me through. He helped Eugene out, too. The ship was burning fiercely by that time." Jones said, "If the [pilots] had not stuck to their posts, we all would have been killed."[35]

President Roosevelt insisted on direct word from Jones that he was OK. The passengers were a little bruised, and Hefley would eventually recover. However, Schacher passed away two days after the accident from smoke inhalation and burns. Jones composed and published a hero's eulogy on the front page of the Houston Chronicle where he prayed to "God for the knowledge to understand for what purpose he saved my life by sacrificing yours."[36] Jones also established a trust for Schacher's children. The day after the accident, Jones and the Hobbys returned to Houston in a private Missouri Pacific railroad car. They were met with great relief and joy at the station by their family and friends. Jones went directly to his Lamar Hotel apartment, where he soon announced that "he felt recovered from his harrowing experience."[37]

Jones had almost no choice. It was an election year, and the Republicans had just concluded their convention in Cleveland, where on the first ballot they selected Kansas Governor "Alf" Landon, the only Republican governor reelected in 1934.[38] Chicago newspaper publisher and former Rough Rider Frank Knox was selected as his running mate. Papers announced on the day of Jones's airplane crash, "The Republican ticket against the New Deal is Landon and Knox."[39] Not quite two weeks later, Jones spoke at the Democratic National Convention in Philadelphia and delivered a line only believable because it came from him, "Speaking from the point of view of business . . . I say to you that the Roosevelt Ad-

35. Houston Chronicle, June 13, 1936.
36. Houston Chronicle, June 14, 1936.
37. Ibid.
38. Shields-West, Almanac of Presidential Campaigns, 177.
39. Houston Chronicle, June 12, 1936; Leuchtenburg, Roosevelt and the New Deal, 175.

ministration has been a blessing to every man, woman, and child in the United States. And, admitting some mistakes here and there, I proclaim its accomplishments." Jones listed the five New Deal lending agencies— the RFC, the Home Owners' Loan Corporation, the Farm Credit Administration, the Public Works Administration, and the Federal Housing Administration—and said that without them, "I shudder to think where we would be today." Combined, he said, those "agencies have provided credit to farmers, home owners, our banks, insurance companies, railroads, [and] financial and industrial institutions of all character, to the extent of $15 billion [$230 billion], and there will be little or no actual ultimate cost to the taxpayer."[40]

He revealed his limits. "I am not one who favors government in business," he said, "but when business runs amuck, and private credit is no longer available, the government must step in." Jones also shared, "I have seen so much distress, so much tragedy, so many broken men in the four years that I have been doing relief work for the business of our country, that I want no more of it." He concluded his speech before the mass of Democrats, "Lifting a hundred [and] twenty-five million people out of the depths of despair and degradation in which they found themselves by March 1933, and bringing them to a state of comparative comfort and happiness in the short period of three years, is an accomplishment that none of us thought possible, and one for which the entire nation owes a lasting debt of gratitude to the Congress of the United States, and our President, Franklin Delano Roosevelt."[41]

Roosevelt and John Nance Garner were nominated by acclamation on the first ballot. The president accepted his nomination at Franklin Field, where more than 100,000 people heard him say, "Better the occasional faults of a government that lives in a spirit of charity than the consistent omissions of a government frozen in the ice of its own indifference. There is a mysterious cycle in human events. To some generations much is given. Of other generations much is expected. This generation of Americans has a rendezvous with destiny."[42]

Instead of focusing on Landon, Roosevelt went after Herbert Hoover's record, big business interests, "economic royalists," and "privileged princes"—in other words, New Deal opponents who had been repulsed

40. Jesse Jones, speech, Democratic National Convention, June 25, 1936, Jesse H. Jones Collection [UT].

41. Ibid.

42. Kennedy, *Freedom from Fear,* 281.

by his policies and his intention to make capitalism stable and safe for everyone. Exceptionally wealthy individuals, particularly those who owned large businesses, detested Roosevelt the most and thought he was a traitor to his class. Some referred to him only as "that man."[43] William Randolph Hearst endorsed Landon through his fifteen newspapers, as did almost two-thirds of all papers in the country.[44] Less than one-third of the elite U.S. citizens listed in *Who's Who* favored Roosevelt's reelection.[45] One month before the national conventions, the United States Chamber of Commerce had denounced Roosevelt and his New Deal.[46]

During his nomination acceptance speech, President Roosevelt reminded his supporters and opponents, "It was this administration which saved the system of private and free enterprise after it had been dragged to the brink of ruin."[47] In a later campaign speech, Roosevelt identified his "enemies" as "business and financial monopoly, speculation, reckless banking, class antagonism, war profiteering," and "organized money." He declared, "They are unanimous of their hatred of me, and I welcome their hatred."[48] But Roosevelt had an ace up his sleeve when it came to deflecting their animosity: Jones and the RFC.

Economist John Kenneth Galbraith, who dealt with Jones during the Great Depression and World War II, observed that he was a potent counter to Republican criticism in that he "was regarded—inaccurately or ambiguously—as a conservative. Second, he was a Texan, and you did not expect a Texan to go all out for the New Deal in those days. And third, he gave the impression of somebody who was accustomed to handling . . . tens of millions of dollars, and liberal New Dealers could not project that impression. He was a financier."[49] The business community, for the most part, trusted and respected Jones much more than Roosevelt, and the president frequently sent Jones in his stead.

That fall Jones presented his first campaign speech for the president over national radio. He began, "My time is short tonight, and I will go

43. Leuchtenburg, *Roosevelt and the New Deal,* 176.

44. Shields-West, *Almanac of Presidential Campaigns,* 178.

45. Kennedy, *Freedom from Fear,* 283.

46. Leuchtenburg, *Roosevelt and the New Deal,* 147.

47. Franklin Roosevelt's acceptance speech at the Democratic National Convention, June 27, 1936.

48. Shields-West, *Almanac of Presidential Campaigns,* 178; Kennedy, *Freedom from Fear,* 282.

49. John Kenneth Galbraith to Steven Fenberg, November 22, 1996, Oral History Project [HE].

immediately into my subject, the Roosevelt administration [and] its effect upon and relationship to business." He said he spoke as someone "who has worked all his life." He said he spoke to them as "an employer . . . and also as head of the Reconstruction Finance Corporation, the biggest and most varied business and banking enterprise in the history of the world." He told his listeners that Roosevelt "is not and never has been against business. To make any such charge is ridiculous. As much has been done for business as for those out of work." He explained, "A democratic government cannot be against business. Its revenue comes from the profits of business. But that does not mean that we can play the game without an umpire." Jones reminded his millions of listeners, "The big and the little, the powerful and the weak, were hot footing it to Washington, appealing to President Roosevelt to do something—anything. He did—and on all fronts." He added, "Old and deliberate methods, dear to many, were necessarily brushed aside in order that people might have food, clothing, and shelter, and that their homes and savings might not be taken from them." To give perspective, he said, "Fighting a depression is no different from fighting a war. In either case, the entire resources of the nation must be used if necessary."[50] Jones continued, "Private charity can cope with ordinary situations, but when things get out of control, taxes must be resorted to, and naturally the man or woman who has the greatest income, whether from business or investments, must necessarily contribute the most. This is as it should be." He added, "To meet the responsibilities of citizenship, each must be willing to share the burden in proportion to his ability . . . Certainly it is fair for those who profit most to pay most." He also said the 1936 Revenue Act should be modified so that tax structures "encourage expenditures for modernization of all character; for replacement of plant, machinery, and equipment; for rebuilding; and . . . [for efforts to] make some further provision for institutions laboring under debt."[51]

Then he emphasized, "Let's not forget that business and banking failed miserably under Republican rule, and that government—government under the Roosevelt administration—had to come to the rescue not only of business and banking, but also of industry and agriculture, and of people thrown out of work by reason of this failure." He wrapped up, "What we need most now, as always, is a fairness of attitude toward

---

50. Jesse Jones, NBC radio address, October 13, 1936, Jesse H. Jones Collection [HE].
51. Ibid.

one another, a willingness to work together for the good of all . . . All are inter-dependent, and the well-being of all is the aim and the accomplishment of the Roosevelt administration."[52]

The race was on. Roosevelt's victory was not certain: some slammed the New Deal as the "Raw Deal," and others feared "creeping socialism" and "confiscatory taxes."[53] Al Smith, whom Roosevelt had nominated for president at the 1924 and 1928 national conventions, and who had preceded Roosevelt as governor of New York, had since then joined the Liberty League, a New Deal opposition organization. Referring to the Roosevelt administration, Smith proclaimed at one of Liberty League's many sold-out banquets, "It is all right with me if they want to disguise themselves as Norman Thomas, or Karl Marx, or Lenin, or any of the rest of that bunch, but what I won't stand for is allowing them to march under the banner of Jefferson, Jackson, and Cleveland." Smith said he would "take a walk" in the upcoming election.[54] So did John Davis, the 1920 Democratic candidate for president. The *Literary Digest*, which had accurately called the last three elections, predicted that Landon would win with 370 electoral votes to Roosevelt's 161.[55]

Jones gave his second campaign speech in Detroit, and according to flattering newspaper reports, "Persons who have heard him for many years told him it was the greatest speech he has ever made." According to one reporter, Jones's speech was broadcast "over a four-state radio hookup to an invisible audience in Michigan, Ohio, Indiana, and Illinois. It was in this region that the depression hit hardest and the RFC, which Mr. Jones heads, had its biggest recovery tasks."[56]

Jones reminisced, "We have but to look back to conditions in 1930, '31, and '32 and take stock today. The very great improvement in the well-being of everyone . . . did not just happen . . . It is the result of government taking a constructive, determined stand for the welfare of its people under a leadership that combined vision, courage, and action." He then declared, "I represent the original alphabetical relief agency, the RFC," and pointed out, as he had in the past, "The idea of the RFC was good, but it was a year late, and under Republican leadership . . . was entirely too timid and too slow to save us from disaster. Five to seven billion dollars judiciously lent in 1931 and '32 would have prevented . . . the complete

52. Ibid.
53. Shields-West, *Almanac of Presidential Campaigns*, 177.
54. Ibid.
55. Ibid., 174.
56. *Houston Chronicle*, October 24, 1936.

breakdown in business, agriculture, and industry—and in private charity . . . The Roosevelt administration did not junk the RFC because it was
created under a Republican administration. It overhauled it, [and] gave
it gas and acceleration."[57]

Jones recounted RFC successes, including the bank repair program,
and explained, "While we have invested in many of the larger banks of the
country, in four-fifths of all the banks in which we put capital, our investment was $100,000 [$1.52 million] or less." He described the $2.8 billion
($43 billion) in loans to agriculture that raised crop prices and rescued
distressed farmers. He referred to the other lending agencies besides the
RFC and explained how the Home Owners' Loan Corporation had "saved
a million American homes from foreclosure" and how the "Farm Credit
Administration saved more than a half million farms." He talked about
how the Public Works Administration (PWA) had built "self-liquidating"
projects throughout the country, including tunnels, highways, and roads.
Jones explained that the RFC had helped finance the PWA by buying half
of its bonds, adding that the RFC had made a $9.3 million ($142 million)
profit when they were sold. About the government lending agencies and
their accomplishments, Jones declared, "There will not be enough loss
from the entire operation to appreciably affect the taxes of anyone."[58]

He followed, "I should like to ask the farmer, the home owner, the business man, the banker, the industrialist, the investor, and the wage-earner,
what would have been his situation without this government credit? And
I should like to ask who will condemn this emergency government relief
to its people, this help in starting the wheels of industry?" He continued,
"Let's not forget that the lives of human beings are involved, and none
must be allowed to suffer for want of food, clothing, or shelter. No one is
willing to allow this." Jones concluded, "Because of what he has accomplished for all of us, I regard the reelection of President Roosevelt to be
in the best interests of everyone." He then added something new, saying
that the president "is especially well qualified to handle our international
affairs, and while there may be little likelihood of another World War any
time soon, the skies are none too clear even now."[59]

Jones next took the campaign to Texas. On Thursday, October 29, the
Joneses arrived in Dallas, where the RFC chairman held a press conference

57. Jesse Jones, speech, campaign rally, Detroit, October 23, 1936, Jesse H. Jones Collection [UT].
58. Ibid.
59. Ibid.

at the Adolphus Hotel. He gave the reporters encouraging news about Roosevelt's reelection, the state of the economy, and the RFC's prospects for Congressional renewal in 1937. When Jones asked the reporters if they had any questions for E. J. Kiest, publisher of the *Dallas Times Herald*, Kiest, who was standing off to the side, said, "They don't want to ask me any questions. They want to talk to you. You're going to be president four years from now."[60]

By Governor James Allred's proclamation, the next day was declared Jesse H. Jones Day at the Texas Centennial and throughout the state. Jones began the day with a commemorative ceremony at the Centennial Exposition in honor of the two pilots who had saved his life. Both the Joneses and the Hobbys were there to pay tribute to the two heroic aviators, as were Schacher's widow and children, who came from South Dakota for the ceremony. Afterward, a luncheon was held in Jones's honor at the Adolphus Hotel. That evening, one thousand attended another elaborate banquet at the Baker Hotel. Speaking over national radio at the banquet, Vice President Garner introduced Jones. Garner declared, "He has allocated and loaned more money to various institutions and enterprises than any other man in the history of the world." Garner added, "Now, to have done the biggest job, and to have done it well, is some accomplishment, and that is what your Texas man, Jesse Jones, has done."[61]

Jones gave his customary campaign speech about the role of government, Republican failings, the accomplishments of the Roosevelt administration, and the practically tax-free contributions the RFC and the four other government lending agencies had made to recovery. He also included usual reassurances, saying, "Business certainly has nothing to fear from government as long as it avoids oppressive and monopolistic methods, and as long as it is willing to share its fair proportion of the cost of government. We all know people who are always complaining, and usually they are the best off." In a response to Smith and the Liberty League, Jones testified, "I yield to no man in my allegiance to the principles of Jeffersonian democracy, nor in my admiration of democracy as interpreted and administered by Andrew Jackson, Grover Cleveland, and Woodrow Wilson."[62]

Jones received hundreds of telegrams and messages congratulating

60. *Houston Chronicle*, October 24, 1936.
61. *Houston Chronicle*, October 31, 1936.
62. Ibid.

him about Jesse H. Jones Day and his speech. Secretary of State Hull, Secretary of Agriculture Wallace, Secretary of Commerce Roper, and President Roosevelt sent messages. Jones replied to them all. He wrote to Roosevelt, "Your telegram[s] to the Texas Centennial Commission and to me at Dallas were the high spots of a very happy day for Mrs. Jones and me . . . It has been a privilege to work with and under you during this present trying period in our history, and your confidence and whole hearted support will ever be outstanding among the sweetest and most satisfying memories of my life."[63] The Joneses went to Houston the next day. Upon his arrival he told the reporters, "I'm happy to be back home. Mrs. Jones and I will remain over to vote and will return to Washington soon after the general election."[64]

The Republicans spent almost $9 million ($137 million) to defeat the Democrats, and the Democrats spent $5 million ($77 million) to win. On and off through the evening of November 3 at Hyde Park, Tommy Corcoran played his accordion while Roosevelt, his family, and friends enjoyed the music and the banter, and waited for the returns. Jones wired an encouraging report, "First count Harris County, the home of many royalists, Democratic 6,898, Republican 882."[65] When all votes were in, the Democrats had won in a landside not seen since the 1820 victory of James Monroe against John Quincy Adams. In the end, Roosevelt received nearly sixty-one percent of the popular vote and 523 electoral votes. Landon received thirty-six percent of the popular vote and eight electoral votes from Maine and Vermont.[66] Roosevelt won in 104 cities with populations of 100,000 or more; Landon won in two.[67] For the first time since the Civil War, the Democrats won the black vote. In Congress the Democrats took 331 seats in the House, leaving the Republicans with eighty-nine. In the Senate, the Democrats held seventy-six seats, an overflow that forced many Democratic freshmen to sit on the Republican side.[68]

On November 4, Jones sent Roosevelt another telegram, "As more complete returns come in, I am deeply impressed, as I am sure you are, of your increased responsibility. Never in the history of our country have the people turned to a leader with such implicit faith as they have to you.

---

63. Jesse Jones to Franklin Roosevelt, November 1, 1936, Jesse H. Jones Collection [LOC].

64. *Houston Chronicle*, October 31, 1936.

65. November 3, 1936, Jesse H. Jones Collection [LOC].

66. Shields-West, *Almanac of Presidential Campaigns*, 176.

67. Leuchtenburg, *Roosevelt and the New Deal*, 185.

68. Kennedy, *Freedom from Fear*, 286.

Never has there been a greater vote of confidence."[69] Roosevelt felt the weight of this faith. In his response to Landon's concession telegram, Roosevelt wrote to his opponent, "All of us Americans will now pull together for the common good."[70]

In Houston, people were more interested in celebrating Jones's work than that of the reelected president. The giant Democratic convention hall where Smith had been nominated eight years before was to be torn down and replaced with a $1.3 million ($20 million) "exposition center" that could accommodate 17,000 spectators in one large auditorium and 2,250 in a smaller performance hall. The new center was being funded by the PWA. On the afternoon of November 4, Jones was given the honor of breaking ground for the steel and concrete building designed by his own architect, Alfred C. Finn. The complex was originally named in honor of Jones but was later called the Sam Houston Coliseum.[71]

The public spotlight on Jones continued when Texas A&M University awarded him the second honorary degree in its sixty-one-year history. The first had been given to F. M. Law, president of the University's board of trustees and previous president of the American Bankers Association—who had introduced Jones the year before at its annual convention. A band played while Texas A&M President T. O. Walton and Jones led the formal processional of four hundred people dressed in "academic regalia" from a luncheon on campus to the college auditorium, where the official ceremony took place. Rice Institute President Lovett, Rice Institute Chairman Baker, former Governor Hobby, and Senator Connally were seated at the front, right behind Jones. According to the *Houston Chronicle*, "The ceremony lasted 50 minutes and was broadcast by radio station KTRH of Houston."[72]

Jones gave a short speech that offered words of wisdom to the thousands of students who came to see and hear one of the most powerful men in the nation. He told them, "I'd be more comfortable in the audience than up here," then went on to say, "The best way to learn to give orders is to learn first to take them. If we expect to lead men, we must first learn to do the things we tell them to do." He also advised, "It is important that you learn to concentrate, to think out and through any problems

---

69. Jesse Jones to Franklin Roosevelt, November 4, 1936, Jesse H. Jones Collection [LOC].

70. *Houston Chronicle*, November 4, 1936.

71. Ibid.

72. *Houston Chronicle*, November 6, 1936.

that confront you." Jones also reassured them, "This land still abounds in opportunity."[73] The ceremony continued outdoors where four thousand cadets and a band of 175 paraded by to honor Jones.

In a matter of days, Jones had been recognized at the Texas Centennial, at the Sam Houston Coliseum groundbreaking, and at Texas A&M University. As the *Houston Chronicle* noted about his honorary law degree, "Thursday's honor was the third bestowed on the towering figure of finance since his return to Texas from Washington a week ago."[74] The Joneses' return to Washington, however, was not nearly as triumphant. Columnists Drew Pearson and Robert Allen predicted, "It is curtains for the Reconstruction Finance Corporation as the world's biggest lending agency. Its power to lend money to banks, railroads, and insurance companies expires January 30, 1937, and a plan to allow this authority to lapse is on the presidential list of things-to-be-done." They told how the Treasury Department—meaning Morgenthau—and the Federal Reserve board wanted the RFC stripped of lending powers, writing, "The accelerating tempo of economic recovery, the increasing availability of private credit, plus the Administration's desire to balance the budget, make curtailment of RFC operations desirable . . . The move will have the warm approval of banking interests." They concluded, "The deflation of the RFC presages the exit of its big gun, Chairman Jesse Jones."[75]

Despite the gloating prediction, Jones's removal remained to be seen. Five days after Pearson and Allen's column, Jones gave a national radio address that was more philosophical than usual. Instead of the numbing list of RFC figures he frequently presented in his talks, he spoke as Roosevelt's indispensable bridge to the business community and showed his distinct sides of capitalist and public servant. Jones began, "There is something to be learned from the great vote [Roosevelt] received—the controlling influence in our country is neither reactionary nor radical, but democratic and socially minded." He reminded the president's opponents "that the profits of business have been multiplied many times under his administration, and largely through his policies." He then asked, "Will business support the president?" and replied, "The answer is, it will. Its leaders, particularly in big business, are much too smart not to. That is, they are too smart, money- and business-wise; that is why they are at the

<hr/>

73. Ibid.
74. Ibid.
75. Pearson and Allen, "Washington Merry-Go-Round," November 18, 1936.

top. However, they have been none too wise politically, or with respect to our social problems."[76]

Jones continued, "The president is not and never has been against business. In the campaign he said, in effect, that he wanted to preserve it, but for all the people instead of for a select few. He spoke of preserving economic democracy as well as political democracy. Both are essential to the welfare of our country . . . In his view, private enterprise is the backbone of the economic well-being of America." Jones identified the real enemy when he said, "Half of the industrial corporate wealth of our country has come under the control of less than 200 huge corporations . . . and many of these . . . have interlocking influences . . . It is certainly not to the best interest of our country that control of the wealth, industry, and credit be concentrated in a few hands. This is so fundamental as not to be open to argument." With emphasis he added, "The continued struggle for corporate expansion is dangerous; it not only puts too much power in a few hands, but too many people in the employee class. If we ever have serious social disturbance, it will be due to this. The distance between the palace and the hovel is too great—the mountain too high to climb."[77]

Describing how to keep government out of business, Jones used Winthrop Aldrich, president of Chase National Bank and Roosevelt opponent, to make his point. He explained, "Mr. Winthrop Aldrich, outspoken against the President's reelection, said the other day in a public speech that if business is to avoid the danger of prescriptive government regulations, it must guide its activities for the public good." Indeed, Aldrich had told a group of powerful businessmen that they could not do as they pleased, "irrespective of outside consequences," and warned, "If we wish to avoid the dangers inherent in centralized authority, everyone in responsible positions must guide his actions with a view to the public good."[78]

Jones mentioned a dollar amount only once in his speech—the $15 billion ($230 billion) disbursed by the five government lending agencies. He said their enormous contribution to recovery would cost the taxpayers next to nothing. He followed with an uncommon, but substantiated and informed opinion, "Our government can operate efficiently in business when necessary."[79]

Jones next addressed the swirling rumors about the RFC's demise,

76. Jesse Jones, NBC radio address, "Business and the Future," November 23, 1936, Jesse H. Jones Collection [UT].
77. Ibid.
78. Ibid.
79. Ibid.

saying, "Most government credit agencies are curtailing their activities and operating expenses, but I doubt if the country is ready for them to withdraw entirely. High interest rates and severe credit requirements would cause another setback. They would retard building and expenditures for capital goods in general, and would take away from the country, particularly users of credit, a feeling of security they now have in the knowledge that such agencies as the RFC, Federal Housing, Farm Credit, and Public Works can, if necessary, provide credit." Jones recognized the dramatic change these programs had brought when he said, "This is the first time government has fought a depression as determinedly as it wages war, and since we have more panics and depressions than wars, economic preparedness could well be a part of our national policy." He qualified his words with, "By this I do not mean to indicate that I favor government in business one day longer than necessary, but would counsel against abruptly discontinuing all government lending."[80]

He then switched gears: "But enough about economics and business—Thanksgiving is upon us again . . . We have much to be thankful for this year—greatly improved conditions and a better morale generally. The wheels of industry are speeding up, unemployment is receding, initiative is again on the upswing, and confidence has replaced fear. So when we grace our Thanksgiving boards Thursday, let us thank God for the blessings He has brought into our lives." As always, he remembered those without: "There are still several millions of our citizens who are not able to provide for themselves. Those who should be most thankful are the ones who are able and willing to divide with these, and see to it that none suffer for lack of food, clothing, and shelter." He concluded, "We are thankful that our domestic problems are rapidly being solved and that we are at peace with the world."[81]

80. Ibid.
81. Ibid.

1937

We Are Not
Going Haywire

THE JONESES WENT TO HOUSTON for Christmas, but did not linger long after the holiday. Jones was eager to return to Washington so he could, as much as possible, influence events and decisions that would determine the future of the Reconstruction Finance Corporation and the state of the nation. Times had changed since his last official RFC New Year's statement when he talked about the improving economy, the RFC's accomplishments, and, as always, the need for bankers to lend.[1] This year Jones found himself urgently defending the RFC. In his 1937 statement, he said, "While the principal emergency is past, there are certain situations in which the corporation can continue to be helpful, and if the President and Congress wish it, the life of the RFC can be extended without any strain upon the federal treasury or the taxpayer."[2]

The next day Jones was interviewed on a prominent radio program that featured world leaders and top journalists—Jones was the first guest of the year. The interview was heard "over a world-wide network through the facilities of the Columbia Broadcasting System." The interviewer

---

1. Jesse Jones, speech, RFC New Year's statement, January 1, 1937, Jesse H. Jones Collection [LOC].
2. *Houston Chronicle*, January 1, 1937.

greeted his guest with the frequently used description of his role at the RFC: "Mr. Jones, as Chairman of the greatest lending agency in the world, there has passed through your hands more money than ever passed through the hands of a single individual in history." Then the interviewer asked, "On the basis of that experience and your general knowledge . . . what do you see ahead for 1937?"[3]

Jones talked about world affairs and domestic economics, explaining about World War I, "The further we get from the upset economic conditions resulting from the World War, the more we have a right to expect world-wide economic recovery. That terrible catastrophe so thoroughly and completely disarranged world economics, as well as our thinking processes, that it made difficult the establishment of order in the ordinary relations between countries." He said resolution would take more time and there would always be struggles "between governments, and among people, but these struggles," he counseled, "should be confined to [the] betterment of economic conditions and living standards." Jones had already broadened his concept of reciprocity—that he would prosper if his community thrived—from Houston to the nation. Now he applied it internationally as he said, "We would all do well to keep constantly in mind the thought that the people of one country cannot long be prosperous and happy if those in other countries are miserable and unhappy. This applies as well to the people within a country, and especially our own country."[4]

He explained that the vast and expanding gap in U.S. incomes during the 1920s meant too few had enough to buy everything produced. He said the disparity had helped bring on the Great Depression and declared, "There should not be too wide a difference between living conditions in the various strata of society." At the end of the broadcast, Jones finally answered the interviewer's first question: "I would say that we have every reason to look forward to continued improvement in conditions at home," and that unemployment—the lack of work "at fair wages"—was the remaining problem to solve. He said, "[E]mployment will be largely provided when we get really at the job of needful building and rebuilding that has been neglected during the depression." Jones concluded, "We may properly consider that the depression is over, and with care and cooperation between business and government, there need be no setback."[5]

3. Jesse Jones, CBS radio interview, January 2, 1937, Jesse H. Jones Collection [UT].
4. Ibid.
5. Ibid.

The RFC was set to expire at the end of January. Despite Treasury Secretary Henry Morgenthau, reporters Pearson and Allen, and other Jones opponents, Franklin Roosevelt sent a bill to Congress for a three-year extension. During House debates, Republicans and Democrats had a rare bipartisan love fest and praised Jones and the RFC. Winning points by disparaging Jones would have been a losing proposition, regardless of party affiliation and allegiance. Republican Representative Jesse P. Wolcott from Michigan, where Jones and the RFC had earlier been most active, said that even though the RFC had not made every loan requested, "In the quiet of our offices and our homes, we felt safe in the fact that . . . [the RFC] had established and was maintaining safe and sound policies." He stated that the RFC's gargantuan efforts "have resulted now in a net profit to the government of the United States of $160 million [$2.4 billion in current dollars]." Hamilton Fish, a Republican congressman from New York, even said, "I have the greatest respect and admiration for the Honorable Jesse Jones, and if you Democrats decide to make him your candidate for the presidency in 1940, it would suit me."[6]

Time magazine reported on the Senate hearings, stating that the RFC was "easily the public's favorite New Deal agency" and that Jones was "perhaps Washington's favorite administrator." Indeed, the senators debated only about the length of the RFC's extension, not its abolition. Virginia's junior senator, Democrat Harry Byrd, claimed consolidation of the government's lending agencies would save $30 million ($444 million) a year. He wanted to extend the RFC for only one year, then transfer it to another agency. Virginia's senior senator and Jones's close colleague, Carter Glass, said he would also agree to one year if "it would save one single dollar," but countered that such a limited extension would not; he wanted the RFC extended for three years, almost solely "because Jesse Jones was RFC's chairman." Byrd's one-year amendment was voted down and the RFC was extended for three years by a vote of seventy-four to one. *Time* reported, "The smashing result of 74–1 was less a rebuke to Senator Byrd, everyone agreed, than it was a rare tribute to Jesse Jones from 74 of his admiring friends."[7]

The following month, for the first time in more than a year, the RFC established a new agency. Congress passed a special act to allow the RFC to make "disaster loans;" they were typically very small, some for only $20 ($296), and usually went to individuals and families who needed

6. *Houston Chronicle*, January 24, 1937.
7. "National Affairs: Jesse Jones's Friends"; *Houston Chronicle*, January 27, 1937.

(left to right) Senator Carter Glass of Virginia, Secretary of Interior Harold Ickes, Jesse Jones, and Senator William Gibbs McAdoo of California confer before hearings to extend RFC's lending powers during the Great Depression. Courtesy Corbis.

help restoring homes, businesses, and lives damaged by floods, fires, and storms. The RFC loaned $12 million ($177 million) between 1934 and 1936 to help out. Then on January 24, 1937, "Black Monday" came, as the Ohio and Mississippi Rivers gushed over their banks in eleven states and broke all regional flood records. Unusually heavy snowmelt and eighteen days of rain, hail, and sleet had filled the rivers beyond their capacity, from Illinois to Louisiana and on to the Gulf of Mexico. Towns, homes, and farms on both sides of the two rivers were awash in water and covered with debris. Cairo, Illinois, where the Ohio meets the Mississippi, was completely submerged. Secretary of War Harry Woodring issued evacuation orders for everyone living within fifty miles of the Mississippi River and said the floods were "America's greatest emergency since the world war."[8] Thirty-five thousand trucks descended on the region and moved more than 500,000 people out of harm's way, leaving waterlogged, smelly, dangerous devastation behind. Hundreds died, more than a million were homeless, and property damage was in the hundreds of millions of

8. *Evansville [Indiana] Courier Press*, March 16, 2008.

dollars. The Red Cross served more than 1.5 million people and reported two-thirds of them were "completely dependent on the agency for every primary necessity of life."[9] President Roosevelt promised help and turned to the RFC.

On February 11, Congress approved the Disaster Loan Corporation (DLC), a new RFC entity that helped disaster victims systematically by lending them money to restore their lives. The DLC allowed Jones to separate business loans from disaster loans, which he knew the RFC would lose money on. But he was still cautious.[10] Drew Pearson and Robert Allen reported, "If RFC Chairman Jesse Jones doesn't show more generosity in granting flood relief loans from the recently voted appropriation to his agency, the big Texan is in for some caustic buffeting on Capitol Hill." They wrote that Jones was "one of the smoothest lobbyists and glad-handers in the business" and that he had been "beautifully successful in smothering congressional criticism. But this time he is on the spot."[11]

A few days after Pearson and Allen first criticized Jones for his "tight-fisted policy on flood relief loans," they reported, "The towering RFC chairman has quietly ordered his subordinates to loosen up and be more lenient to needy flood victims . . . But Jesse's critics warned that they would keep an eye on him."[12] Setting up the complex DLC program probably caused the supposedly slow start. The fact was, RFC board members Emil Schram and C. B. Henderson went immediately to the flooded region and spent three weeks setting up the lending machinery to help people repair and restart their lives. Jones remembered, "We . . . set up field offices and [sent] examiners and attorneys into the afflicted areas to expedite the making of loans." He described how "citizens of each stricken community set up a committee whose members could appraise the real needs of their neighbors and recommend to us the size of each individual loan . . . Almost invariably we followed their recommendations."[13] A loan was typically made within one day of application. When asked why he did not take $50 ($740) from the Red Cross, but accepted it from the RFC, one applicant said, "I don't want it given to me. I'll borrow the money and pay it back."[14]

The DLC's $350,000 ($5.2 million) loan to help move the small town of Shawneetown, Illinois, "out of the river valley onto safe, high ground" was

9. Ibid.
10. Jones, *Fifty Billion Dollars*, 195.
11. Pearson and Allen, "Washington Merry-Go-Round," March 14, 1937.
12. Pearson and Allen, "Washington Merry-Go-Round," March 18, 1937.
13. Jones, *Fifty Billion Dollars*, 193.
14. *Houston Chronicle*, March 16, 1937.

one of its largest, whereas a Tennessee blacksmith borrowed $20 ($296) to replace his anvil, leading Jones to remark, "Some flood, that washed away an anvil!"[15] In communities where "the overflow had invaded almost every house and place of business," people typically received around $500 ($7,400), mainly for furniture and clothing. In the end, the DLC fielded 375 examiners and forty attorneys among thirty-six offices that were located from West Virginia to Louisiana, along the Ohio and Mississippi Rivers. The RFC made approximately 7,500 loans totaling $7 million ($103 million). The loans were interest-free for the first three months, with three percent charged thereafter. Most loans were "character loans" made with no security. The RFC Mortgage Company joined in and offered eighty percent loans at four percent interest to those who wanted to build new homes on higher ground.

The DLC assisted with other calamities as they occurred. By the time the corporation was liquidated in 1945, it had loaned $55 million ($813 million) and had to write off only $2.1 million ($31 million) of that. As if he were standing by the smokehouse at his childhood home in Tennessee with Aunt Nancy and his father, Jones observed how "the scrupulous manner in which those hard-hit citizens stinted to repay our loans . . . testified touchingly to the fact that most 'little' people, when treated fairly by a lender, will do their best to fulfill their obligations."[16]

While millions of people in the Mississippi and Ohio River valleys were struggling for their survival, Roosevelt was struggling with Congress over the Supreme Court. Emboldened by his smashing reelection victory, the President had decided to strike back at the Supreme Court for invalidating New Deal programs, threatening his agenda for recovery, and standing in the way of his turning over to the next president "a nation intact, a nation at peace, a nation prosperous, a nation clear in its knowledge of what powers it has to serve its own citizens."[17] On February 5, 1937, Roosevelt asked Congress to allow him to appoint one justice to the Supreme Court for every current justice who was seventy or older; he also asked permission to appoint forty-four new judges to lower federal courts. At the time, six of the nine current Supreme Court justices were over seventy, and their longevity—and refusal to resign—meant Roosevelt had not yet appointed a member to the court during his presidency.[18] He noted

---

15. Jones, *Fifty Billion Dollars*, 193.
16. Jones, *Fifty Billion Dollars*, 196–97.
17. *Houston Chronicle*, March 5, 1937.
18. Kennedy, *Freedom from Fear*, 325.

that the dockets were crowded and as justices aged, they could not keep up; he argued that more judges would speed up justice, but most everyone knew Roosevelt had a different agenda.

Congress, not the Constitution, determines the number of justices serving on the Supreme Court. Earlier Congresses had approved requests from John Adams, Thomas Jefferson, Andrew Jackson, Abraham Lincoln, and Ulysses S. Grant to change the size of the court, so Roosevelt's action was not without precedent.[19] His unstated intention to "pack" a court with judges sympathetic to his policies, however, was seen as devious, and the strong-arm tactics offended many, including Jones.

Roosevelt had not mentioned expanding the Supreme Court during his 1936 campaign. And outside of his 1937 State of the Union message, when he called for interpreting the Constitution "as an instrument of progress, and not as a device for prevention of action," he did not lobby Congress or lay any groundwork for his surprise proposal.[20] Instead, he sent Tommy Corcoran to pressure lawmakers. Armed with an engaging personality, close association with presidential power, and a position at the RFC, Corcoran knew how "to turn the heat up" for the president.[21] But legislators were not buying it. Roosevelt's blatantly political proposal and aggressive method for getting it gave many wavering politicians the push they needed to oppose him.[22] Even Vice President John Nance Garner packed his bags and went home to Uvalde in disgust, taking with him a source of Democratic support in the Senate. One Texas hill country politician campaigning for a House seat during a special election, however, stood by Roosevelt and vigorously promoted the president's cause. The special election had been called when Congressman James P. Buchanan, who had held the seat for twenty-four years, passed away while in office. Lyndon Baines Johnson won the race and, at age twenty-nine, was elected to the House of Representatives, capturing Roosevelt's notice because of his loyalty.[23]

"Tommy the Cork," as Corcoran was sometimes called, lobbied almost everyone he knew who could help push Roosevelt's legislation, which meant he naturally visited his nominal boss, Jesse Jones. Jones, who could get Congress to do just about whatever he wanted, recalled, "When it be-

19. *New York Times*, July 26, 2007.

20. Roosevelt, "1937 State of the Union Message"; Leuchtenburg, *Roosevelt and the New Deal*, 233.

21. McKean, *Tommy the Cork*, 91.

22. Leuchtenburg, *Roosevelt and the New Deal*, 234.

23. McKean, *Tommy the Cork*, 95; *Houston Chronicle*, April 11, 1937.

gan to appear that he would not get his way, the President sent . . . Tommy the Cork to ask me if I would sound out some of my friends in the Senate as to whether it would be possible to increase the Court by two members." Jones added, "I had no sympathy with the plan to pack the Court, but went up the Hill and saw some of my friends. They made it clear to me that had the President in the beginning asked for only two additional members for the Supreme Court, he probably could have got them, but as the score then stood, with everyone embittered, the Senate would not authorize any increase."[24] Roosevelt gathered only twenty votes in the Senate, the plan was discarded, and the Democrats were divided. Worse, the public and Congress were not nearly as enchanted with the president as when they reelected him in November.

Meanwhile, the Joneses had a party to plan. On April 5, 1937, Jesse would turn sixty-three and they decided to celebrate with a reception "in the Chinese Room at the Mayflower Hotel." One reporter effused, "The reception was, with the exception of the state functions held at the White House, the largest of the official Washington season."[25] Just about everyone who was anyone in Washington was invited and attended. More than 1,500 guests mingled in the flower-filled ballroom to enjoy a sumptuous buffet and music provided by an orchestra playing popular tunes that were all selected by Mary. The Joneses and Edith Wilson stood together in the receiving line to greet the guests, who included "members of the cabinet, most of the diplomatic corps, senate and house congressional leaders, both Democrats and Republicans, heads of the big independent agencies of government, artists, writers, and men and women prominent in private life."[26] The *Washington Post* reported the day after, "Most of Washington was there, and appropriately enough, just as the orchestra struck up 'The Eyes of Texas Are Upon You,' into the party strode Vice President John Nance Garner, accompanied by Mrs. Garner—two people who rarely go to parties, [but] they would not miss celebrating the birthday of a fellow Texan."[27]

Texas was never far from Jones's mind, and lately he had been able to spend more time there. The RFC was operating smoothly, had been extended for another three years, and as the economy improved, it was making fewer loans. As with his businesses, Jones had assembled an efficient

---

24. Jones, *Fifty Billion Dollars*, 263.
25. *Washington Post*, April 5, 1937.
26. *Houston Chronicle*, April 5, 1937.
27. *Washington Post*, April 5, 1937.

(left to right) Mariette Garner, Vice President John Nance Garner, the Joneses, and Edith Wilson celebrate Jesse Jones's sixty-third birthday in 1937 at the Mayflower Hotel in Washington, D.C. According to a reporter, "Most of Washington was there" (*Washington Post*, April 5, 1937).

and devoted team at the RFC who gave him freedom to pursue what he needed and wanted to do. Two weeks before his big birthday party, Jones went to Texas to check on the progress of the San Jacinto Monument, monitor local flood control legislation pending in the Texas senate, and encourage Houstonians to approve $4.1 million ($61 million) in municipal improvement bonds in an upcoming election. Jones said to a reporter during his trip, "I am not certain that Houston is keeping up with its growth. In fact, I'm of the opinion that we're not."[28] Based on the number of new telephones in the city, Houston's population had hit 400,000 at the first of March.[29] Hugh Potter, chairman of the City Planning Board, said in a speech to promote the bond issue, "Houston simply has to spend some real money on itself or suffer the bitter consequences of social and physical

28. *Houston Chronicle*, March 16, 1937.
29. *Houston Chronicle*, March 4, 1937.

deterioration."[30] Jones agreed and while he was in Houston, gave a speech that was broadcast over the city's three major radio stations—all of which he happened to own.

He said he wanted to talk "neighbor to neighbor." Jones first confessed, "I am always glad to be at home, even for a short while. I am happiest in Houston," then continued, "I am told that we are now a city of 400,000 people, and it is obvious on all sides that the city proper is not keeping pace with our rapid growth." Jones noted that streets needed paving, widening, and straightening, and that "flood control is of paramount importance." He said, "All of this growth means increased municipal expense of all kinds; for fire protection, for water service, for police service, and [for] all of the many things that cities must supply and furnish to its citizens." Then Jones commented, "We are especially and particularly backward in our airport." The runways were obsolete and "now many ships have a wing spread of 120 feet and weigh from seven to 11 tons. They require hard-surfaced runways at least 150 feet wide and 4,500 feet long. Ships of this type are unable to come to Houston now because of our inadequate airport."[31] Jones knew Houston's growth required up-to-date transportation facilities and shipping services, just as when the Houston Ship Channel was developed twenty-five years before. On April 3, the voters of Houston approved the bonds.

This speech was typical of Jones's efforts to keep in touch with what was happening in Houston and answered his need to nurture the city's development and his businesses. A Washington reporter revealed, "Almost every day he talks for at least an hour to Houston. He gives the long distance operator a list of people to get. As soon as one conversation is finished, she says, 'Your next party is waiting.'" The reporter also wrote that Jones had shared some of his "maxims for comfortable living." He first advised, "Say yes or no! Don't hedge. You will have to give a direct answer anyhow before you finish. Better do it at the beginning. It keeps things from getting confused." He also offered, "Don't get mad. You only upset the other fellow and don't help yourself." And finally he suggested people "stay out of other people's affairs" and not "give advice where it hasn't been asked."[32]

Jones went to Texas again a couple of weeks after his birthday party, this

---

30. *Houston Chronicle*, April 2, 1937.
31. Jesse Jones, radio address, Houston, March 21, 1937, Jesse H. Jones Collection [HE].
32. Unknown newspaper clipping, March 14, 1937, Jesse H. Jones Collection [HE].

time to lay the cornerstone and deliver the dedication speech at the San Jacinto Monument. On April 21, 1937—the 101st anniversary of Texas's independence from Mexico—thousands gathered at the San Jacinto battleground to honor those who had died fighting for freedom and dedicate the monument that enshrined their valor. Many attending the solemn ceremony were descendants of the San Jacinto soldiers. Thousands of voices filled the heavy Gulf Coast air with their singing of "America" and the San Jacinto soldiers' battle song, "Will You Come to the Bower?" Then Jones rose to speak. He had been born in Tennessee, but in his heart, his persona, and reputation, Jones was a Texan. He solemnly declared, "Few battles of the world have been more decisive or had a greater influence over civilization than the Battle of San Jacinto. It changed the map of the North American continent and opened the way for the United States to extend its boundary to the Rio Grande and the Pacific. It sealed the destiny of the Texas Republic and confirmed its Declaration of Independence. It established liberty where tyranny sought to enthrone itself."[33]

He explained how Stephen F. Austin's settlers had been "subjugated" by the Mexican government, and how fighting for independence and becoming a nation in 1836 gave Texas "a history peculiarly and distinctly its own." Jones recalled the three most notable battles of that war and said, "Braver men or greater heroes never died for the cause of liberty than those who died at the Alamo. And without the tradition of the Alamo, America would lack one of the noblest symbols of its spirit."[34] Colonel William Barrett Travis and all 183 men were killed while defending themselves at the small San Antonio mission against the invading Mexican Army. They heroically chose "victory or death."

Jones described Goliad, saying, "History does not record a more inhuman act than the massacre of Colonel James W. Fannin and his 400 stout-hearted, ragged young Americans, who were shot down by a firing squad of Mexican soldiers at Goliad after having been promised honorable treatment as prisoners of war as a condition of their surrender . . . It was this unspeakable act, following the fall of the Alamo . . . three weeks before, that aroused the Texans and fired them with a determination to avenge these deaths and to make Texas freedom secure." He then spoke about the decisive fight at San Jacinto and how General Sam Houston inspired his men to victory with the battle cry, "Remember the Alamo! Remember Goliad!" Jones said, "Far more was accomplished at San Jacinto

33. *Houston Chronicle*, April 21, 1937.
34. Ibid.

than the mere winning of a battle and the creation of another state . . . San Jacinto opened another gateway for the westward sweep of the American people, across the plains and mountains, to the Pacific."[35]

Texas was an independent nation for nine years. The U.S. Congress voted in 1845 to annex the nation, and sent troops under Zachary Taylor to the Rio Grande to secure its borders with Mexico. Mexico and the United States declared war and after two years of fighting, the United States entered and took Mexico City in August 1847. The Mexican government surrendered, signed the Treaty of Guadalupe Hidalgo in February 1848 and, consequently, lost more than half of its territory to the United States. The Rio Grande was established as the border between the two nations, and the United States acquired what would become Arizona, California, New Mexico, and parts of Colorado, Nevada, and Utah.[36] Jones said, "There would be no United States as we know it today had it not been for San Jacinto," and concluded, "It is with a sense of deep reverence and humble veneration that I level this cornerstone in this lasting monument to the heroes of the Battle of San Jacinto and of the Texas revolution and to the mighty deeds they wrought."[37]

Jones stayed in Houston for almost four weeks, where he took care of personal and public business. On the first of May, President Roosevelt arrived in Galveston for ten days of tarpon fishing, turning a suite of rooms at the Galvez Hotel into the temporary White House. The president's secretary, Marvin McIntyre, described it as "the bottle-neck through which all official communications must pass before being forwarded to the president aboard the fishing yacht Potomac, out in the Gulf."[38] Between Jones and Roosevelt, the strings of government were pulled for a while from southeast Texas.

According to reports, Roosevelt "caught two tarpon and acquired a healthy coat of tan" after ten days of fishing. On his way back to Washington, his train stopped for ten minutes in Houston, where he, Jones, Governor James Allred, and Roosevelt's son Elliot greeted thousands from the rear platform of the presidential car.[39] New congressman Johnson, elected only the month before, stopped by; grateful for Johnson's support with his Supreme Court fight, Roosevelt gave him a scrap of paper with Corcoran's phone number and told Johnson to call him for whatever he

---

35. Ibid.
36. "The Treaty of Guadalupe Hidalgo."
37. *Houston Chronicle*, April 21, 1937.
38. *Houston Chronicle*, May 2, 1937,
39. *Houston Chronicle*, May 11, 1937.

needed when he returned to Washington.[40] That transaction marked the beginning of an important relationship between Corcoran, and Johnson and his wife, Lady Bird.

Soon after he returned to Washington with Mary, Jones left for Philadelphia to receive another honorary degree and deliver the commencement address at Temple University on June 10. The head of the RFC's Philadelphia loan agency warned Jones about his accommodations at the Bellevue-Stratford, "The double bed . . . is the longest the hotel has. It looks to me, however, that you will probably have to lie in it diagonally for it to hold you."[41] This was not an uncommon problem—once when Jones was traveling to St. Louis, he wrote his host, "I hope to spend at least part of Friday night in bed and wish you would see to it that the bed is wide enough." Always self-deprecating and folksy, he continued, "Modern twin beds are entirely too narrow for a horse, and I take about as much room as a horse."[42]

At the Temple University commencement, Jones, an eighth grade dropout, spoke about the value of education. He said, "I have always thought that one of the advantages of college is that you learn how to learn." He spoke about poverty and, arguing from recent experience, said, "Try as hard as we may to improve social conditions, to equalize opportunities, and to make it possible for everyone to earn more than the bare necessities of life, we will always have a degree of poverty . . . The Bible tells us so. These, society must care for, and it can without undue burden to the rest."[43] The RFC was Jones's evidence of this.

Then he talked about economics, the Depression, and government. Jones said, "Try as hard as we may to prevent panics and booms, we will probably always have them. The best way to avoid panics is to prevent booms—inflated values." After summing up the cause of the Great Depression: "We gave the machine too much gas and the wreck was inevitable," he noted, "Except for occasional disasters . . . the federal government has never before been called upon to aid its citizens from the Federal Treasury. But this depression hit every phase of business, industry, agriculture, and finance so hard that there was practically no market for anything, and employment was reduced to a minimum." Then he said, "Recovery has been achieved, but we still have unemployment, and the government is

40. McKean, *Tommy the Cork*, 96.
41. Robert J. Kiesling to Jesse Jones, June 9, 1937, Jesse H. Jones Collection [LOC].
42. Jesse Jones to Thomas N. Dysart, March 1, 1936, Jesse H. Jones Collection [LOC].
43. Jesse Jones, speech, Temple University commencement, Philadelphia, June 10, 1937, Jesse H. Jones Collection [UT].

still being called upon to do many things that should be done by private enterprise."[44]

Jones listed the government's achievements, informing the students, faculty, and dignitaries that the RFC and other credit agencies had "been the principal factor in recovery." He said they had saved "banks, building and loan associations, insurance companies, railroads, and industry." He described how they had helped build schools, bridges, dams, and aqueducts, and "saved a million urban homes and half a million farm homes from foreclosure." He said the lending agencies had "built several hundred thousand new homes, and repaired and modernized a million and half other homes in cities and towns." Jones remarked, "Most of it was accomplished through loans that are being [re]paid from earnings on the projects themselves." He emphasized that the government was using sound credit—not taxes—to enhance the common good.[45]

Acknowledging the changing relationship between citizens and government, Jones said, "It is a resourceful country that can meet emergencies . . . But however rich, there is a limit to what a government can do, or what it should be required to do." Anticipating John F. Kennedy's unforgettable admonition, Jones declared, "No one should be allowed to suffer from want, but people must support their government and not expect the government to support them." He told the students, "Just how we are to get back to self-reliance and quit demanding so much of the government will test the wits and ingenuity of all of us . . . You who are graduating today will help in these readjustments." With evolving awareness, he added, "It may be truthfully said that we are in a new social order and cannot or should not go back to the old." He advised the students to "take a keen interest in who represents you in government" and knowing the country would prosper if everyone had the opportunity to thrive, told them the "cost of providing work and subsistence for those unable to make their own way must be borne by everyone."[46]

To lend perspective, Jones said, "Thirty years ago, which seems a long time to you but not to your speaker, our greatest industries were the railroads, coal, lumber, steel, and iron. Since then we have had the great development in oil, the motor industry and good highways, moving pictures, the radio, and travel by air . . . Other things that the imagination has not yet conceived will be discovered and developed. Progress

44. Ibid.
45. Ibid.
46. Ibid.

will go on ad infinitum." He told the students that the privilege of their education "carries responsibilities" and that their "leadership should be directed toward peace and good citizenship." Jones, one of the wealthiest and reputedly the most powerful man in the nation next to the president, showed his first priority when he concluded, "I would remind you that success is not measured by the accumulation of property, but much more by accomplishments and service."[47]

Toward the end of July, the Joneses decided to join the Fred Fishers on a trip out west. Jones continued to correspond with Blanche Babcock, his beloved third-grade teacher from Dallas. While on the Fishers' yacht, Jones wrote what he claimed "was the longest letter" he had ever written. He said, "I am making it in the nature of a report to you as I would to my mother or father." The letter was filled with reminiscences about his childhood, the presidents he had known, his business career, his public service, and thoughts about himself. Jones confided, "I have always been restless and in a hurry, for what I do not know, because I have been fortunate and reasonably happy. I long since realized that I was my own biggest problem and believe we all are." He then wrote that his success had come from "work and energy guided . . . by a fair amount of common understanding and reasoning," and recalled a time he played school with his two little nieces. "I was the teacher and finally asked a question that neither of the little girls . . . could answer . . . One of them . . . said, 'Are you going to keep us in until we think it out?' I have profited a great deal from that child's question . . . It is the simple, direct means that are most effective."[48]

In contrast to his image as a solid rock, Jones showed he was not impervious to pain and shared that during the first two years of the Great Depression, "I saw more broken men than it seemed I could endure . . . For a period of eighteen months, I had the feeling of continuous sadness, akin only to that which comes to us when we suffer the loss of those most dear to us." As conditions slowly improved, Jones said, "This feeling of sadness passed."[49]

Returning to the enjoyable present, Jones told Babcock that he, his wife, and the Fishers had enjoyed San Francisco, Seattle, and Vancouver, and that he and Fred Fisher had traveled "about 175 miles" to the Campbell River where he "landed a 42 pound salmon after an hour and a quar-

47. Ibid.
48. Jesse Jones to Blanche Babcock, August 25, 1937, Jesse H. Jones Collection [LOC].
49. Ibid.

ter tussle." The two men rejoined their wives and "boarded Mr. Fisher's beautiful yacht, the *Nakhoda*, at Duluth," cruised the Great Lakes, and fished for bass in the Georgian Bay for a week. He closed, "I am still on Lake Huron in most comfortable surroundings, and send you a heart full of love."[50]

Action replaced rest and reflection as soon as the Joneses returned to Washington in September. Secretary Morgenthau continued to pound Roosevelt about closing the RFC and using the proceeds to balance the budget.[51] The Treasury Secretary had already convinced Roosevelt to prohibit banks from counting newly acquired gold as capital from which to make new loans, insisting that the new gold be "sterilized." Concurrently, the Federal Reserve doubled the amount of cash banks had to keep on hand to back their loans. As the opposite of the government's efforts to fight deflation, both policies were meant to prevent inflation.[52] Unfortunately, they were shortsighted: sterilizing gold, increasing reserve requirements, and slashing spending to balance the budget would unintentionally reverse almost all of Roosevelt's successes in restoring the U.S. economy and counteract Jones's efforts to expand the economy with sound credit.

Unaware of the coming crisis, Houston in 1937 was growing by leaps and bounds. In April Humble Oil and Refining Company, The Texas Company, Gulf Oil Company, Shell Company, and many other smaller oil concerns all announced ten percent pay hikes, affecting nearly 100,000 workers in the region.[53] In August the Works Progress Administration added $150,000 ($2.2 million) to the city's recently approved bonds to help make Houston's airport the "major air terminal of the South."[54] In September the Public Works Administration matched $1.6 million ($24 million) of the city's bond money to help build Houston's new city hall, improve the city's sewage system, build new facilities at the DePelchin Faith Home orphanage, and build schools in Pasadena and Goose Creek.[55] Building permits for the first eight months of 1937 topped $14 million ($207 million), exceeding those of Dallas, San Antonio, and Fort Worth combined.[56] Jones was responsible for $750,000 ($11 million) because,

50. Ibid.
51. Leuchtenburg, *Roosevelt and the New Deal*, 244.
52. Olson, *Saving Capitalism*, 185.
53. *Houston Chronicle*, April 9, 1937.
54. *Houston Chronicle*, August 28, 1937.
55. *Houston Chronicle*, August 24, 1937.
56. *Houston Chronicle*, September 3, 1937.

for the first time in a long while, he was building again in Houston. The *Houston Chronicle* had become the largest paper in Texas, with a circulation of more than 100,000, and it needed more space and better equipment.[57] A four-story addition to house the new gigantic printing presses was under construction next to the original building Jones had built in 1908. At the same time, air-conditioning systems were being installed in Jones's Lamar, Rice, and Texas State Hotels,[58] and KXYZ, one of his three radio stations, had hooked up with the National Broadcasting Corporation (NBC). Before the end of the year, it would begin to broadcast twenty-four hours a day, only the second radio station in the nation to do so.[59]

Not everything was perfect in Houston. There were still large pockets of poverty, despair, neglect, and decay, as Jones had pointed out during the spring bond election. Results from a $10,000, ($148,000) "43-day" study commissioned by the city, the county, the Community Chest, and the Council of Social Agencies were released in August. Noted social workers from across the nation had examined Houston's problems and its responding relief agencies, and, according to a full-page story in the *Houston Chronicle*, their report presented "a rather dark picture, shot through with critical observations."[60]

The paper quoted the lead author, Pierce Atwater of St. Paul, Minnesota, as saying, "Houston is an American city in a class by itself . . . [It] is increasing at the unbelievable rate of 30,000 persons a year." The problem was, the city could not keep up with its growth. The report noted that if someone builds a home "in a newly-opened section, there is little chance to connect with the sewer." It claimed the city had only "one day's reserve water supply" and, tongue-in-cheek, observed that "trains and planes must dodge the oil derricks which surround the city like sentinels. Figuratively the smell of oil is in the air . . . A child could see that Houston is destined to have an important future—that even today it is a great city having real economic and industrial strength." Yet the report warned, "It is clear that Houston's problems of human welfare have grown just as rapidly as its commerce."[61]

The report said services for "dependent children" were completely inadequate, that too many people were hungry, and that "dietary deficiency," bad health, and dirty clothes were seen too often in too many children,

57. *Houston Chronicle*, February 7, 1936.
58. *Houston Chronicle*, May 9, 1937.
59. *Houston Chronicle*, July 1, 1937; *Houston Chronicle*, December 30, 1937.
60. *Houston Chronicle*, August 21, 1937.
61. Ibid.

especially in those who did not go to school. The report counted 4,500 Houstonians employed through WPA programs, 2,000 on other forms of relief, and multitudes who received no help at all. Entire families lived in their trucks or under bridges. The city's health department had only three nurses to treat Houston's entire indigent population. The study identified bad management, bad policies, and no coordination between agencies as the culprits in this failure to provide adequate services and in the disastrous results that had followed. The authors recommended establishing one central agency to take care of all relief, health, and welfare needs. And instead of twenty-four cents ($3.55) per capita for the city's public health clinic, the report suggested $2 to $2.50 ($29 to $37).[62]

The study's authors also boldly told Houstonians that they needed to change their attitude. Reflecting a cultural shift, they concluded, "Houston must understand and appreciate the fact that the United States has committed itself to the principle of some minimum of social and economic security for that section of the population which heretofore has been least protected." They continued, "The public welfare program now in the making all over the United States has as its objective the establishment of certain minimum standards of living, lower than which it seeks to keep people from falling."[63]

By now most everyone agreed that something needed to be done to help those who could not help themselves, but opinions about what was to be done, or who should be responsible, were as numerous as those discussing the problem. In the midst of the debate about government assistance, private action, and personal responsibility, and in the midst of very real poverty and deprivation, with no fanfare, Jesse and Mary Gibbs Jones established a philanthropic foundation to formalize their charitable giving and to support the community they called home. They had already donated more than $1 million ($14.6 million) during their seventeen-year marriage to help organizations that improved Houston. Jones had made profound contributions through his businesses and public service, but now he was formally adding philanthropy as another way to use capitalism and his consequential wealth to support his community and to help those who were in need. Instead of naming the foundation for themselves, the Joneses called it Houston Endowment.

Jones had already dissolved and transferred most of his many corporations—including one of the first, the Edgewood Realty Company—into

62. Ibid.
63. Ibid.

one entity called Commerce Company. Out of 30,000 Commerce Company shares, the Joneses kept 18,000; they donated 10,500 to establish Houston Endowment; and created trusts for their brothers, sisters, nieces, and nephews with the remaining 1,500 shares.[64] Houston Endowment operated out of the Bankers Mortgage Building, and Fred Heyne—Jones's "other self"—W. W. Moore, and Milton Backlund were the original three trustees.[65] Between 1937 and 1944, Houston Endowment quietly donated $218,000 ($3.2 million), mostly to "schools and colleges." Although Jones would eventually give much of his attention to Houston Endowment, for now his main focus was on the nation and its economy.

In October, bowing to Treasury Secretary Morgenthau's insistence, President Roosevelt instructed Jones and the RFC to stop lending. Soon afterward Jones spoke at the Waldorf-Astoria to a group of bank regulators. He took the opportunity not only to describe what the RFC had done for the banks, but also to announce this move by the president.

Jones began by saying that, of the $1.1 billion ($16.2 billion) in stock the RFC owned in 6,103 banks, half had been retired. Yet the U.S. government, through the RFC, still owned stock in 5,087 banks. Jones explained that the amount owned in most banks had never been more than $100,000 ($1.48 million) per institution and added, "Our prepondering [sic] service to banks has been to those in the smaller cities and towns." As with the RFC's industrial loans, if banks paid promptly, Jones reduced the dividend they paid to the RFC from three and a half percent to three percent. This prompted criticism that this policy failed to help slow-paying banks that appeared to need the lower rate more. But he explained, "The reduction was meant to induce banks to replace . . . some part of their RFC capital with private capital . . . Amortizing one's debts, paying a little each month or each year, is good house-keeping . . . There are . . . entirely too many banks that are not making effort enough to replace RFC capital with private capital." Making his intentions clear, he said, "We all want the government to get out of banking as soon as it can without loss or inconvenience to those it has helped."[66]

Jones then summarized all of the RFC's financial activities to date. Its total authorization had climbed to $12 billion ($177 billion). Of that, $2.8 billion ($41 billion) had been passed through to other agencies "by

64. H. Creekmore to F. Liddell, November 26, 1949, Jesse H. Jones Collection [HE].

65. Houston Endowment corporate charter, September 25, 1937, Jesse H. Jones Collection [HE].

66. Jesse Jones, speech, National Association of Supervisors of State Banks, New York, October 9, 1937, Jesse H. Jones Collection [UT].

the direction of Congress." Of the remaining $9.2 billion ($136 billion), $6.6 billion ($98 billion) had been loaned and invested and of that total, $4.8 billion ($71 billion), or seventy-three percent, had been paid back. After reeling off these numbers, Jones said, "This record of repayments is significant. It demonstrates that a sound, slow loan with provision for a proper amortization is frequently better and more easily collected than some that are technically liquid." He said such loans should not be categorized as "slow loans," but should be compared to "long-time bonds."[67] Jones wanted to change the perception of a sound, long-term loan from "slow paying" to profitable and beneficial. He had seen their value long ago when he built small homes in Houston and sold them with long-term installment plans.

Jones acknowledged, "The RFC has been making comparatively few loans for the past year, and it is our purpose to discontinue general lending for the very good reason that there is enough available private credit to meet legitimate demands for all purposes. Our agency managers have been instructed to accept no more applications unless a real emergency can be shown." Jones quickly reassured his audience, "Our country has seldom been more prosperous," yet his listeners had reason to be skeptical: from August to October, when he delivered his speech, the stock market had dropped forty percent, from 190 to 115. Still, Jones attributed the "falling securities market" to "fear" and concluded, "The country needs a lot of things, things that will give people work, but it needs nothing as badly as it needs confidence. We are not going haywire."[68]

Pearson and Allen gave the news their own spin and reported on the "long-sought triumph by Secretary Henry Morgenthau over RFC chairman Jesse Jones." They went on, "Knowing Jesse's power in Congress, Young Henry laid off his drive last session. But once Congress was out of the way, he resumed his pressure on the President." Pearson and Allen almost gleefully concluded, "This means *finis* for the RFC. Henceforth it will be merely a collecting agency for its outstanding loans. How Jesse will take his thumping remains to be seen. Some of his intimates predict an early resignation."[69]

One such "intimate," John E. Davies, had a different take on Jones's situation. Davies had been chair of the Federal Trade Commission during the Woodrow Wilson administration and been one of Wilson's advisors at

67. Ibid.
68. Ibid.
69. Pearson and Allen, "Washington Merry-Go-Round," October 26, 1937.

the Paris Peace Conference. He was now ambassador to the Soviet Union. The distinguished statesman wrote Jones from Moscow after reading the speech he had made to the bankers, "The outstanding fact . . . which history will record with reference to the RFC is not only that it served such a tremendously useful function in the greatest war against depression, but [also] that it was done with practically no financial losses to the State." Even from afar, Jones's power was apparent. Davies declared with conviction, "When Jesse Jones tells the country, 'we are not going haywire,' it goes a tremendous way to the restoration of confidence."[70]

And confidence is what the country needed. In 1936 the federal government had pumped more than four billion extra dollars ($59 billion) into the economy. In 1937, in an effort to balance the budget, prevent inflation, and—according to Secretary Morgenthau—see what private business could do on its own, the infusion dropped to $800 million ($12 billion).[71] The WPA under Harry Hopkins had built 2,500 hospitals, 5,900 schools, and 13,000 playgrounds, and improved 1,000 airports. The PWA under Interior Secretary Harold Ickes had built sixty-five percent of the nation's new courthouses, city halls, and sewage infrastructure, and thirty-five percent of its new hospitals and public health facilities.[72] Now in 1937, Roosevelt abruptly cut WPA and PWA spending and told the RFC to quit lending. In addition, the Federal Reserve doubled the amount banks were required to keep on hand to back up loans; and as noted earlier, "sterilized" gold could not be counted toward those reserves. As well, for the first time, $2 billion ($29.6 billion) in new social security taxes was extracted from paychecks and the economy. The impact of these new policies was almost immediate.

After the stock market dropped forty percent in three months, Ickes wrote in his diary, "The year 1929 isn't so far back in history but that people can be shaken when the stock market reaches the lowest point in two years as it has done recently."[73] Their worries had foundation. Within those same few months, industrial production dropped by one-third, business profit declined by three-quarters, and national income plunged thirteen percent.[74] The escalating threat of war in Europe added to the unease.

Jones went back to Houston for the eighth annual meeting of the Independent Petroleum Association of America and to attend the Oil World

70. October 27, 1937, Jesse H. Jones Collection [LOC].
71. Olson, *Saving Capitalism*, 187.
72. Leuchtenburg, *Roosevelt and the New Deal*, 125, 133.
73. Ickes, *Secret Diary*, entry for October 9, 1937.
74. Olson, *Saving Capitalism*, 187–88.

Exposition at the new Sam Houston Coliseum. More than 100,000 people visited the exhibition during its four-day run. Scientists and technicians presented papers, and manufacturers displayed the latest drilling and refining equipment. Dances and parties were festive, bands played, and Jones gave a short speech before the exposition's wrestling match held at 8:30 on Thursday evening at the City Auditorium.[75]

Introducing Jones, W. N. (Bill) Blanton, president of the Houston Chamber of Commerce, declared, "He has been acclaimed throughout the nation as the moving force, the great moderator, the wise counselor in America's great reconstruction program."[76] Jones praised the producers, chemists, and engineers, talking to them "as one citizen to another." He said, "It is from the background of more than five years in government that I venture to comment on national problems." He assured the independent oilmen that the administration did not intend to appear "unfriendly to business," but the cost of bringing "about greater security for those who must work for a living, and against poverty and old age," must be financed by everyone, including "business and industry." To be sure, Jones had clearly stated on many occasions that he wanted government out of business and banking as soon as possible, but he also knew government had a role to play. He summarized, "It is government's responsibility to protect the weak from the strong." He was as direct with the oilmen as with the bankers, saying, "Human beings still have the spirit of dominance. You have it in the oil business. One trouble with the strong and powerful is that they don't appreciate how hard they hit or how ruthless they sometimes are without necessarily intending to be. To the fleetest goes the race, but we all have to eat."[77]

Jones softened his tone by adding, "All too often we forget our early struggles when we reach a position of security, and are inclined to drive on with not enough concern about how the other fellow gets along." Recent years had intensified his compassion and he said, "I have seen so many broken, distressed, and humiliated men in the last five years that my sympathies go out to every insecure person. Social security within reason, and by proper effort on the part of those secured, is right, and we will be remiss in our duty if we do not try to achieve it."[78] The social security to which Jones referred was not just the new old-age program and tax,

75. *Houston Chronicle*, October 14, 1937.

76. *Houston Chronicle*, October 15, 1937.

77. Jesse Jones, speech, Oil World Exposition, Houston, October 14, 1937, Jesse H. Jones Collection [UT].

78. Ibid.

but the overall ideal that citizens, government, and business in a wealthy nation should work together to create and maintain a minimum standard of living, so no one goes without "food, clothing, or shelter," thereby fostering economic and national security. In other words, to create a community where all can thrive.

Jones turned to the tumbling stock market, telling the oilmen, "The present quoted prices seem low from an investment standpoint, that is, if we still believe in our country, and of course we do." He warned, "Whatever the cause, we should all realize that it is better to make money by working for it than by betting on the rising and falling figures of the ticker tape or which horse can run the fastest." And about taxes, Jones said that the Treasury Department was studying the "entire situation" and would soon make recommendations for adjustments. He admitted, "I have no check of taxes in other countries, but we know they are very high and are being largely expended for military purposes rather than civil, as with us. Our government expenditures are to build people, not to destroy them."[79] At the time, the U.S. military ranked behind even Poland, Sweden, and Switzerland in terms of machinery and men.

According to Pearson and Allen, Jones made speeches to stay noticed. And as far as they were concerned, with the RFC going out of business, Jones was on the defensive. They wrote, "RFC Chairman Jesse Jones, quietly being shelved by the White House, is making a desperate last-ditch fight to keep himself in the public eye." They claimed, "Jesse has a burning ambition to be Democratic vice presidential candidate in 1940." They also accused him of jumping "the gun on important government news releases in order to grab personal publicity for himself."[80] Those premature announcements had been about cotton and corn loans.

Jones may well have been on the defensive. In the past, he and the president exchanged brief notes after either of them gave a speech. A typical note from Roosevelt said, "Just a brief note to tell you how kind I think it was of you to send me that telegram concerning the address. I am delighted to know of your approval. Affectionate regards."[81] Jones wrote Roosevelt after the president spoke in October, "I have been thinking and hoping you would say what you said today at Chicago. Heartiest congratulations."[82] But suddenly Roosevelt's response to Jones's speeches were not so nice.

79. Ibid.
80. Pearson and Allen, "Washington Merry-Go-Round," November 12, 1937.
81. September 8, 1936, Jesse H. Jones Collection [LOC].
82. October 5, 1937, Jesse H. Jones Collection [LOC].

In December Jones gave a speech at the annual dinner of the New York Southern Society, an organization of professional men who had moved to New York from the South during and after Reconstruction. The society held events to "perpetuate the memories and traditions of the Southern People" and provided scholarships and financial assistance to southerners in need who lived in New York.[83] At the banquet, Jones briefly mentioned his Tennessee and Texas background, but he was not there to talk about the South. He wanted to talk about government and business. Jones said, "For more than four years now, we have experienced marked and generally steady economic improvement . . . but in recent weeks there has come a definite and marked recession in almost all lines. A feeling of uneasiness prevails." He went on, "It would be a sorry commentary if, with the greatest abundance of everything imaginable for a comfortable and pleasant existence, the American people were unable to compose their differences and avoid another depression."[84]

Jones said the "slowing up of business" was due to "fear of Washington—fear of government, but that is not a good reason. Our government is what we make it." He suggested, "We probably got out too soon after our recent illness. Maybe we overtaxed our strength, or put the machine in high when we should have tried it a little while in second speed. We were very low in '31 and '32; the country had been almost liquidated." Jones continued, "[But] 1936 was a fairly good year as business goes, and we started clamoring for a balanced budget. You can balance the budget all right, personal or government, but you will get hungry when there is no meat in the smoke house or meal in the barrel." Jones offered, "In my opinion, the key to the situation confronting us today is intelligent, cordial, friendly, determined cooperation between government and business—government and all the people. It cannot be sectional; it cannot be class [driven]; it cannot be political. It cannot be achieved if we let ourselves believe that our government is our enemy."[85]

Jones counseled, "Government must be the friend of business, but business must learn . . . that government is the umpire—the senior partner— and that it is the government's responsibility to see . . . that business plays the game squarely." Good government, Jones thought, depended more on good administrators than on good laws. He said, "Congress passes the

83. Flora and MacKethan, *Companion to Southern Literature*.
84. Jesse Jones, speech, New York Southern Society, New York, December 3, 1937, Jesse H. Jones Collection [UT].
85. Ibid.

laws, but the Bureaus administer them, and from my observation the interpretation and administration of the law is of equal, if not greater, importance than the law itself." Jones then warned the southern gentlemen, "One thing is certain; we all either go up together or we go down together. I prefer to believe we will go up." He half-jokingly concluded, "If we can't manage to get along, we should give the country back to the Indians."[86]

None of these statements upset Roosevelt. But he jumped all over Jones's remarks about taxes. Switching from community leader to capitalist, Jones had suggested that any tax relief enacted by Congress be extended to cover the previous year. He also noted that "the undistributed surplus tax, in so far as preventing unnecessary accumulation, is a good public policy. But as now written, it works a hardship on the great majority of corporations, those that need their earnings for expansion and for debt payment. Relief to these taxpayers is imperative." Jones said that any new tax law should provide sufficient revenue "without stifling business and industry."[87]

The president sent Jones a curt, three-page memo without the usual warm salutation. Instead, in large block letters, the correspondence began, "MEMORANDUM FOR HON. JESSE JONES." The president got straight to the point, writing, "I am a good deal troubled by the last paragraph on page 9 of your speech of December third in New York." Referring to the consequences of his Supreme Court defeat, Roosevelt said he and Jones both knew that "tax changes were and are physically impossible at this session of the Congress." Additionally, applying tax relief retroactively would result in a loss of "two or three hundred million dollars of revenue." Roosevelt wrote, "That makes the suggestion silly." He said that current and pending tax laws present no hardship to business because "the great majority of corporations made so little in the way of profits that they were not affected . . . at all." Finally, he advised Jones, "I think we must all be very careful not to make general assertions but to separate the sheep from the goats and talk in terms of actual facts."[88]

As the economy continued to falter, most everyone was feeling testy. One December morning, after Jones testified before a Senate Banking Committee, newspapers reported the following exchange:

86. Ibid.
87. Ibid.
88. Franklin Roosevelt to Jesse Jones, December 14, 1937, Jesse H. Jones Collection [LOC].

Jones, explaining the work of the RFC, outlined its accomplishments "during the depression."

Republican senator Townsend from Delaware inquired, "Which depression, the other one or this one?"

"This isn't a depression," Jones shot back. "Your face isn't pale."

"Some of us have been led to believe it is a depression," insisted Townsend. "What would you call it?"

"Recession is the new word for it," Jones replied.[89]

89. *Houston Chronicle*, December 3, 1937.

1938

Spenders and Lenders

THE ECONOMY CONTINUED TO DETERIORATE and, as always, Franklin Roosevelt sought a wide variety of opinions about what to do. Treasury Secretary Henry Morgenthau, Democratic bigwig Jim Farley, and others continued to hound the president to balance the budget, slash federal spending, prevent inflation, and reduce fear among businessmen about government intentions. Tommy Corcoran, Harry Hopkins, and Harold Ickes blamed the recession on "monopolists," with Ickes publicly accusing "America's Sixty Families" of controlling the economy, while they continued "the old struggle between the power of money and the power of democratic instinct."[1] Then there were those who thought after four years of growth, the ordinary cycle of business dictated a bit of cooldown time and that no action was needed. Others, like Federal Reserve Chairman Marriner Eccles, believed that the government had to spend until the economy had improved and stabilized. "The government," Eccles said, "must be the compensatory agent in this economy."[2]

Prominent British economist John Maynard Keynes had recently

---

1. Leuchtenburg, *Roosevelt and the New Deal,* 247.
2. Ibid., 245.

published *The General Theory of Employment, Interest, and Money* (London: Macmillan, 1936). Keynes advocated government spending to reverse unemployment, and instead of viewing deficit spending as something to be avoided and disparaged, he transformed the notion into a powerful, beneficial, and sometimes necessary remedy. At the beginning of Roosevelt's presidency, Keynes wrote the president and called him "the trustee for those in every country who seek to mend the evils of our condition by reasoned experiment within the framework of the existing social system." He warned, "If you fail, rational change will be gravely prejudiced throughout the world, leaving orthodoxy and revolution to fight it out."[3] Now he wrote that he was "terrified" that everything the president and his New Deal had accomplished during the past four years might go down the drain. Keynes said that renewed spending on railroads, utilities, and housing would increase employment and revitalize the economy. He said that housing was "by far the best aid to recovery" and advised the president to put "most of your eggs in this basket."[4]

Roosevelt was unsure what to do and when Morgenthau accused him of "treading water," Roosevelt agreed and said that he was—"absolutely." Banks were stable, commodity prices and farmers had support, many in need had received aid, credit was available, and the stock exchanges were supervised. Yet in a matter of months, four million people lost their jobs and unemployment shot back up to nineteen percent from fourteen percent. Widespread hunger became common again. Between the fall of 1937 and the spring of 1938, the number of people on relief in Toledo doubled; in Detroit it quadrupled. Around 50,000 more destitute citizens joined the 75,000 already on Chicago's relief rolls.[5] Roosevelt had received credit for the recovery, now he was blamed for the downturn. The president, who had enjoyed an outstanding victory just one year before, was now tagged with the "Roosevelt Depression." Ickes observed that the president was "punch drunk from the punishment that he has suffered recently."[6]

As administrator of a bipartisan government agency, Jones found that publicly stating his opinions about policy could be challenging; such statements were prohibited for Reconstruction Finance Corporation employees, especially during an election year.[7] So while Jones did not publicly

3. Kennedy, *Freedom from Fear,* 357.
4. Ibid.
5. Leuchtenburg, *Roosevelt and the New Deal,* 249.
6. Ibid, 250.
7. *Houston Chronicle,* August 21, 1938.

endorse one solution over another, he stood ready to reopen the RFC lending spigot as soon as he got a green light. He saw no reason for the government to slam on the brakes, at least when it came to making productive loans that would probably be repaid.

The Joneses returned to Washington immediately after New Year's Day, but Jones was soon back in Texas to deliver the keynote at the annual Jackson Day Dinner in Dallas.[8] In his speech, he blamed part of the economic downturn on "quicker communication." He explained, "A falling off of business in one part of the country is immediately communicated to all other parts, and the more we talk about it, the more widely it spreads. Sometimes we talk ourselves into believing that conditions are much worse than they really are. And, if I may venture the assertion, that is the situation with us today." He warned against depending on what would years later become known as "sound bites" and said, "Instead of a quiet, deliberative people—a people of poise—we seem to be continually looking for something unusual. We grab newspapers as fast as they are published and keep the radio going, always looking for something to happen. We are headline readers."[9]

In January, President Roosevelt finally began to make his moves. He did not turn to Hopkins and the Public Works Administration (PWA) or to Ickes and the Works Progress Administration (WPA). Instead, he wrote to Jones, "I desire that you give consideration to new construction loans which would tend to maintain or increase employment where there is an economic need . . . and, in this connection, that you discuss with me these requirements, the needs of the general situation, and conditions prevailing in individual fields of credit."[10] With Jones's counsel, Roosevelt officially instructed the RFC on February 7, 1938, to "organize a national mortgage association in Washington . . . and provide it with management."[11] Banks and other lending institutions shunned construction and home loans because it was difficult to resell the mortgages.[12] Though the National Housing Act of 1934 had authorized the creation of private associations to purchase mortgages from lenders, and the RFC had offered to back them, there had been no takers. So Jones established the Federal National Mortgage Association (FNMA), noting later, "We again

8. *Houston Chronicle,* January 9, 1938.
9. Jesse Jones, speech, Jackson Day Dinner, Dallas, January 8, 1938, Jesse H. Jones Collection [UT].
10. Franklin Roosevelt to Jesse Jones, January 10, 1938, Jesse H. Jones Collection [HE].
11. Franklin Roosevelt to RFC, February 7, 1938, Jesse H. Jones Collection [HE].
12. Olson, *Saving Capitalism,* 195.

entered the mortgage field only after our offers to become partners with private capital had fallen on deaf ears . . . In the jargon of the government's alphabetical agencies, it quickly came to be called Fannie Mae."[13]

Roosevelt explained his rationale to Jones, "It is my hope that builders, material and supply people, working men, prospective home owners, and those who may desire to build private or multiple dwellings for rent or sale will cooperate in taking advantage of this new law. The obvious effect of such whole-hearted cooperation will stimulate business and provide employment for hundreds of thousands." He continued laying out the advantages, noting that the mortgages bought and held by the FNMA "are backed indirectly, but nevertheless effectively, by the credit of the United States Government."[14] Bascom Timmons wrote a front-page story for the *Houston Chronicle* four days after Roosevelt asked Jones to establish the FNMA. He explained that the Association was "designed to give new liquidity to real estate mortgages" and that it had more than $200 million ($3 billion in current dollars) at its disposal. He reported, "It is intended, Chairman Jones explained . . . as a pattern or demonstration project of the part which such financial agencies can play in a healthy recovery in housing construction, especially on a large scale basis."[15]

The FNMA board was composed of RFC board and staff, including Emil Schram, C. B. Henderson, and Bill Costello. As with every other RFC agency, the board was devoted to Jones and he called the shots. He announced at an early press conference, "This association will invest in first mortgages insured by the Federal Housing Administration and sell its debentures against them." In other words, FNMA intended to buy government-insured mortgages from lenders, who would in turn use the proceeds of the sales to make more new loans. Jones declared, "A real building program will increase employment and stimulate business more perhaps than any other one thing that can be done." The board and Roosevelt hoped it would attract builders of large-scale housing projects who had previously been unable to obtain credit for such enormous ventures. Jones concluded by saying, if the president thought it wise to do so, in addition to launching the FNMA, the RFC could resume lending as it had before.[16]

A week later, Roosevelt ordered just that. Four months after shutting

13. Jones, *Fifty Billion Dollars*, 151.
14. Franklin Roosevelt to Jesse Jones, February 7, 1938, Jesse H. Jones Collection [LOC].
15. *Houston Chronicle*, February 11, 1938.
16. Ibid.

RFC board member Emil Schram with Jesse Jones. Schram expanded the Electric Home and Farm Authority to thirty-seven states, and later served as RFC chairman and deputy federal loan administrator before he became president of the New York Stock Exchange in 1941. Courtesy Underwood and Underwood.

down RFC lending, Roosevelt reversed course, writing to Jones, "It is my wish that you make credit available to all deserving borrowers to which you are authorized to lend, especially loans that will maintain or increase employment."[17] Jones wasted no time and immediately released a statement that said, "In connection with the president's letter to me of today, we are instructing the managers of our 32 loan agencies to accept applications for loans that qualify under our act, and especially loans that will maintain or increase employment. This includes all types of business, little and big."[18] Much to Secretary Morgenthau's chagrin and counter to many predictions, Jones and the RFC were back in business. Wielding his power, Jones agreed to start lending again only if the more than $2 billion ($30 billion) that Congress and the president had passed through to

17. Franklin Roosevelt to Jesse Jones, February 18, 1938, Jesse H. Jones Collection [HE].
18. *Houston Chronicle,* February 19, 1938.

other agencies was removed from the RFC's books. Jones also reduced the RFC board from seven to five and removed the Treasury Secretary as an ex-officio member.[19]

The next day, Stewart McDonald—one of the Joneses' favorite bridge partners and the federal housing administrator—signed the charter that authorized the FNMA. McDonald was quoted, "This not only offers a means of maintaining a constant flow of money from one end of the country to the other for residential purposes, but, in turn, gives the individual investor an opportunity to place his savings in a tax-free investment, backed by insured mortgages."[20] Within its first year, Fannie Mae bought 26,276 new mortgages and foreclosed on only twenty-five of them (back then, anything resembling a "sub-prime" mortgage was unacceptable). The more than $100 million ($1.5 billion) it paid for the mortgages was used by lenders to fund more new mortgages. The RFC Mortgage Company, which had been established in 1935 to finance commercial building, now began servicing and refinancing existing mortgages on older homes.[21]

In addition to increasing employment and helping the economy by investing in construction—something Jones knew well from his days in Houston—the renewed RFC turned its attention to small business. From the start of the New Deal, small businessmen had complained about banks and the RFC rejecting their loan requests, and the last thing many wanted was for the RFC to remain in charge of those loans. Rumors about plans for small businesses swirled around the nation's capital. Drew Pearson and Robert Allen wrote, "One of the big plans being discussed behind the scenes for the extension of easier credit to business is the creation of regional government banks . . . These . . . would attempt to do for smaller industry what Jesse Jones and his Reconstruction Finance Corporation have so miserably failed to do. Among other things, they would take much more speculative risks than the RFC or the average bank."[22]

Senator Carter Glass had just introduced a bill to allow the RFC to finally make longer-term loans, to buy stock in private companies, and to "meet all legitimate demands of business that for any reason are not being supplied from private sources."[23] In other words, the RFC could do just about whatever Jones wanted it to do. Far from revoking Jones's

19. Olson, *Saving Capitalism*, 192–93.
20. *Houston Chronicle*, February 20, 1938.
21. Jones, *Fifty Billion Dollars*, 151.
22. Pearson and Allen, "Washington Merry-Go-Round," March 29, 1938.
23. *Houston Chronicle*, March 27, 1938.

power, which some lawmakers had advocated in the fall, the Glass bill increased it.

Jones testified before the Senate Banking Committee that the "RFC had approximately $1.5 billion [$22.5 billion] in unused funds available for all types of loans." He wanted the legislation to "tell anybody, anywhere, if you've got a legitimate right to borrow money for 5, 10, or 15 years, come and get it."[24] The U.S. Senate passed the Glass bill on April 1, 1938. Four days later, on Jones's sixty-fourth birthday, newspapers reported, "A more direct attack on the recession as far as the average business man was concerned . . . was foreshadowed by house passage of the senate bill to give the Reconstruction Finance Corporation almost unlimited discretion in making loans to aid commercial and industrial enterprises."[25] President Roosevelt signed it into law on April 13, 1938. Jones said in an interview that he did not intend to buy stock in companies, but planned only to make loans. He advised businessmen to go first to their "home town bank. If the bank doesn't want to make the loan . . . the RFC might underwrite it, or if the bank will grant only part of the loan, the RFC may loan the balance." He continued, "But if the bank won't do anything about the loan, the next place to go is to the nearest of the 32 RFC branch offices." Jones explained, "There's no need to come to Washington. If a businessman makes out an acceptable application, he can get his money in a few weeks without any trouble."[26]

Pearson and Allen complained, "Since 1934 the RFC has had the power to lend up to $300 million [$4.5 billion] to industry on easy terms. But under Jones' tight-fisted, banker-minded rule, only $107 million [$1.6 billion] has been disbursed . . . This is a trifle more than $25 million [$375 million] a year, an insignificant drop in the economic bucket." They claimed, "Jones was so tight-fisted about helping small business men and distributing money appropriated for flood relief that, after last spring's disastrous floods, a determined move was made to take the new relief money out of his hands. But he is one of the most effective wire pullers in Washington and the attack got nowhere." They referred to the proposed regional banks and said the Treasury Department and the president favored them. "But Jones was hostile," Pearson and Allen wrote. "He would not have been boss of the new regional banks. So he hastily evolved his $1.5 billion [$22.5 billion] scheme and with the aid of his potent allies rushed it

24. *Houston Chronicle*, March 29, 1938.
25. *Houston Chronicle*, April 5, 1938.
26. *Houston Chronicle*, April 7, 1938.

Jesse Jones announces that the RFC is back in business after President Roosevelt renews lending and spending programs to reverse the resurging economic meltdown. New legislation allowed the RFC to make longer-term loans, to buy stock in private enterprises, and to "meet all legitimate demands of business that for any reason are not being supplied from private sources" (*Houston Chronicle*, March 27, 1938). Courtesy Jesse Holman Jones Papers, Dolph Briscoe Center for American History, University of Texas at Austin.

through Congress."[27] Spotlighting the RFC chairman's unique clout, days later the columnists continued, "How shrewd Jesse Jones is at monopolizing the government purse-strings was illustrated by his cornering of the $1.5 billion loans-to-industry authorization. In this he triumphed completely over the Inner-Circle."[28]

In addition to RFC lending, Roosevelt went on to request billions of dollars for new spending to renew the PWA, the WPA, the National Youth

27. Pearson and Allen, "Washington Merry-Go-Round," April 14, 1938.
28. Pearson and Allen, "Washington Merry-Go-Round," April 22, 1938.

Authority, the Civilian Conservation Corps, and other New Deal agencies. Pearson and Allen preferred this more open-handed spirit and voiced their approval as the president rejected the budget balancers and sided with the "spenders and the lenders" to turn the economy back around.[29]

Jones spoke over national radio soon after Roosevelt put the RFC back into business, saying that he wanted to talk about "business and credit." But he really wanted to respond to critics who accused him of being "tight-fisted." Along with the RFC's loans to railroads, those to small businesses had been the worst performers. Since 1934, more than twenty-five percent of small business borrowers had defaulted on their RFC loans and ten of the fifteen largest railroads that had received RFC loans went bankrupt.[30] By comparison, payments on eighty-eight percent of the Disaster Loan Corporation's payments were up-to-date.[31] Furthermore, several independent studies had showed that banks were fulfilling most legitimate requests for credit by qualified borrowers, reducing the need for government intervention.[32] Basically, Jones was tight-fisted about loaning to small businessmen who were not creditworthy because he refused to throw taxpayer money away on bad loans.

He began the address by giving the RFC a place in history and declaring, "The March 9, 1933, law was the most important of all. It made it possible for us to save the banks by buying their preferred stock, capital notes, or debentures." Jones recounted that the RFC had made more than "3 million separate loans" to agriculture, averaging "less than $500 [$7,500] to each borrower," and that "probably 20 million depositors in closed banks were aided through RFC loans." He said, "Almost every line of business has been helped by the RFC and we were getting along fine until last autumn."[33] That was when Roosevelt closed down RFC lending.

Jones said that the newly passed Glass bill allowed the RFC to "lend to public bodies . . . for the construction of useful public works projects" and explained that the longer payback times "will be particularly helpful in industrial loans for plant construction and new equipment." Staring down his critics, Jones stated in no uncertain terms, "We will not feel authorized to make such loans unless in our opinion the borrower will be able to pay the money back. Too much debt and inflation of values were the principal causes of the 1929 collapse, and prudent borrowing is just

29. Pearson and Allen, "Washington Merry-Go-Round," April 20, 1938.
30. Olson, *Saving Capitalism*, 196.
31. *Houston Chronicle*, February 19, 1938.
32. Olson, *Saving Capitalism*, 201.
33. Jesse Jones, national radio address, April 18, 1938, Jesse H. Jones Collection [UT].

as essential as prudent lending." He explained, "It does no good to lend a man or a business money which he will lose. It merely postpones the inevitable re-adjustment of his affairs." Nevertheless, "We try to find a way to authorize every such loan for which we have an application." The RFC could even make loans on inventory, which was now piling up in stores and warehouses as demand evaporated. Jones said, "We will bring to the manufacturer the same assistance and same assurance . . . that we give to the producers of farm commodities through commodity loans." Almost reflexively, he added, "Loans on inventories, like loans on commodities, will necessarily require the inventories to be warehoused or so segregated as to permit an enforceable lien."[34]

For almost six years, Jones had nagged, begged, and bullied bankers to lend, and this address was no exception. Only now he moderated his appeal, having discovered from recent experience that there were fewer worthy loans to make than expected. He gave the private sector a chance and said, "We would like for every bank in the United States . . . to make its lending facilities available to those of its customer-depositors who feel they are being deprived of credit." He asked bankers who, after due diligence, declined a loan to forward the rejected application to the nearest RFC agency. Jones said, "I am convinced . . . that if the banks would go into the problems of more of their potential borrowers, they would be able to work out many good loans, loans that would be profitable to them and to the borrower—loans that would create employment and stimulate business."[35]

Jones tried again to challenge the received knowledge on "slow loans." He had pushed the financial capital from New York to Washington, and altered public attitudes about government assistance, but he was still trying to change the common perception of long-term loans, insisting that they were good, not bad. He proffered, "The fact that a borrower needs money which he cannot pay back except over a period of five or ten years" should not be classified as a slow loan by either banks or the four federal agencies charged with examining and supervising the financial industry. Jones compared long-term loans to bonds and asked, "Why should they discriminate against a well-secured, amortized industrial or a real estate loan that is a sound legal bank investment?" He summed up, "With our very liberal banking laws and the fact that deposits are insured, making

34. Ibid.
35. Ibid.

extreme liquidity unnecessary, there should be ample credit for every legitimate purpose. Banks are bulging with loanable funds."[36]

Nevertheless, Jones put the RFC into high gear. Among other actions, it delivered, in conjunction with the American Red Cross, aid to flood victims in California.[37] To maintain prices on once-again saturated markets, the Commodity Credit Corporation loaned $50 million ($750 million) to producers against their 250 million pounds of warehoused wool.[38] Jones also was willing to help utilities expand and offered "to supply that money, either through loans or through purchases of bonds."[39] Even the problematic railroads got more help, including loans for new equipment, to rehire laid-off workers, and to maintain track and facilities. While warning that he would refuse any loan to a railroad that paid dividends to stockholders before it repaid the government, Jones said the loans would "not only bring about reemployment, but would preserve a national resource by keeping the railroads in good physical condition," an effort that would prove to be invaluable within the next couple of years.[40]

Everyone was so desperate to see improvement in unemployment that Jones was prepared to bend RFC rules. He wrote President Roosevelt, "As you know, it has never been the policy of the RFC to lend for the manufacture of automobiles and tires, the distilling of whiskey and brewing of beer, the production and refining of petroleum, or the publication of newspapers and magazines" because, he explained, "capital and credit are usually available for these industries. As for lending to newspapers and magazines, it has been our thought that the Government should not be in a position to . . . influence on the editorial policy of any publication." Now, Jones told the president, he had been receiving quite a few inquiries and some applications "from the smaller units" in U.S. industry; he said that the RFC had tried to meet the demand by offering to fund half of a loan if a bank would take on the rest, but, "The borrowers have difficulty in getting banks to make the loans even on this basis. In each instance, it is represented that unless the applicant can secure a loan from the RFC, the enterprise will be forced to greatly reduce employment [or] suspend operations." He therefore wondered "whether we should forego our policy for a time and aid those in need of credit where the loans can be properly secured and prevent further unemployment." Jones finished,

36. Ibid.
37. *Houston Chronicle,* March 8, 1938.
38. *Houston Chronicle,* March 13, 1938.
39. *Houston Chronicle,* April 21, 1938.
40. *Houston Chronicle,* May 5, 1938.

"I am aware that the administration of the RFC rests with its directors, but we try to keep you advised as to our operations, and I am bringing this situation to your attention for such suggestions as you may wish to make."[41] The following day, Roosevelt endorsed Jones's plan with a hand-written addendum: "especially in the case of small enterprises."[42]

With this in hand, Jones went on national radio to garner support for creating employment through Roosevelt's "lending-spending campaign." He put the pressure on, saying, "We are asking banks throughout the country, every bank in the United States in fact, to cooperate with the RFC or to allow the RFC to cooperate with them in making an extra effort to provide whatever credit that can be properly used in stimulating business and creating work." Jones advised, "Every business, however small, that is being honestly conducted is entitled to some line of credit. Most banks maintain small loan departments, and every bank should. A $500 [$7,500] or a $5,000 [$75,000] loan is relatively as important to the whole economic structure as is the big loan." Jones told his listeners that RFC applications had been "revised and shortened," and that he had sent "a letter to every bank in the United States asking their cooperation in an effort to meet the meritorious credit needs of their communities."[43]

On May 4, 1938, Jones spoke at the annual meeting of the U.S. Chamber of Commerce. He told the crowd that he had sent out a second letter to the nation's banks, "outlining conditions upon which we would participate with them in making loans." He was coaxing loans from the banks the same way he once wheedled donations to the DePelchin Faith Home. At the end of his talk, Jones answered a question from the audience, "You ask if in my opinion the RFC or some similar government lending agency will be necessary after the expiration of our present lending authority, which is June 30, 1939. My reply to that is that I am afraid so."[44]

The RFC's resurgence was immediately apparent. Pearson and Allen commented that "Jesse has galvanized into action," although they said the less than altruistic reason "was to keep the RFC, and himself, in the forefront as a potent agency . . . and to keep a tight grip on the tap of government spending." They also made their usual mention of Jones's supposed ambition for elected office, writing, "With his eye on the White House in 1940, Jesse has been quietly booming himself in big business and banking

41. Jesse Jones to Franklin Roosevelt, April 20, 1938, Jesse H. Jones Collection [LOC].

42. Franklin Roosevelt to Jesse Jones, April 21, 1938, Jesse H. Jones Collection [LOC].

43. Jesse Jones, radio address, April 30, 1938, Jesse H. Jones Collection [UT].

44. Jesse Jones, speech, U.S. Chamber of Commerce annual meeting, May 4, 1938, Jesse H. Jones Collection [UT].

circles as an economizer and 'Jeffersonian' Democrat." They once more accused him of being "tight-fisted" with RFC loans, writing, "Jesse is getting himself very badly in Dutch on his presidential ambitions. Little businessmen, unable to get the government credit so glibly promised them, are bombarding their Congressmen with hot denunciations of Jesse and demanding his scalp."[45] Whether it was his own or taxpayers' money, Jones had risk limits, and the record shows he knew when to stop.

Even so, Jones said that since the RFC had resumed lending, more applications had been received than anticipated and that they were being "approved at the rate of from 25 to 40 per day . . . a faster rate than at any time since the RFC began to make industrial loans several years ago." In addition, new five-year, two percent FNMA notes were immediately oversubscribed by more than a billion dollars, the largest oversubscription "on any bonds of the government or a government agency in history." Jones said the offering was oversubscribed because the FNMA was "a good bond and there is a big demand for good bonds," and also that he was optimistic about "the future business outlook and expected a substantial pickup in the late summer and autumn when people begin to harvest and sell their crops."[46]

Roosevelt had put the "lending" portion of his solution to the economic crisis into action when he asked Jones to resume RFC business, then goosed it when he signed the Glass bill. Now in mid-June, Roosevelt launched the "spending" portion of his recovery program, supplying $3.75 billion ($57 billion) to the WPA, PWA, Civilian Conservation Corps, and other agencies. After months of acrimony and furious debates, Roosevelt also signed the Fair Labor Standards Act that established a forty-cent ($6.00) minimum hourly pay rate and a maximum forty-hour workweek, and that prohibited child labor in interstate commerce. So many exceptions and amendments had been tacked onto the original bill, that it wasn't clear if anyone was subject to the legislation. However, Roosevelt signed the bill on June 25, 1938. Whether from exhaustion after the bitter fight, or whether he was running out of options, after Roosevelt signed the Fair Labor Standards Act, he sighed and said, "That's that."[47]

People were frightened about their drained pocketbooks, their economic survival, and world affairs, but they were happy to be distracted by what was happening up in the sky. On July 14, Howard Hughes broke all

45. Pearson and Allen, "Washington Merry-Go-Round," May 12, 1938.
46. *Houston Chronicle*, May 24, 1938.
47. Leuchtenburg, *Roosevelt and the New Deal*, 257–63.

records by flying around the world in three days, nineteen hours, and seventeen minutes. The fastest previous flight had taken more than six days. The day after he landed, millions of people packed the streets in New York, or waved and cheered as they hung out of skyscraper windows and tossed almost two thousand tons of confetti and ticker tape at the handsome aviator passing by in the celebratory parade.[48] Hughes received the same reception in Washington, D.C., where he was honored at the annual Press Club luncheon with a speech given by Jones.

Jones revealed, "I have known Howard, a Houston boy, all his life, and his father before him. We were friends. Naturally, I have pride in Howard's achievements." He explained that Hughes's trip "was not a stunt . . . but the accomplishment of a worthwhile purpose, the testing of equipment and devices designed to perfect flying as a useful enterprise." He mentioned Hughes's other achievements, saying, "he established and still holds the speed record for a coast to coast flight, averaging 327 miles per hour for the 7 hours and 28 minutes required." Jones continued, "This plane and Howard's accomplishments have contributed to the sum of knowledge which has kept our country in the forefront in the construction of aircraft." Turning to Hughes's film career, he said, "Howard . . . could have been a play boy, with more money to spend than he could spend," but "wanted to make good on his own," so it was "rather natural that [he] undertake the production of motion pictures, probably the most fascinating of our newer industries a dozen years ago." Jones stated, "He produced some of the best pictures of those years. These included particularly 'Hell's Angels,' a war picture showing something of the part aviation played in the world war and picturing vividly what we may expect in the next."[49]

Jones now consistently alluded to war and world events in his speeches, topics that were unavoidable. Adolf Hitler had assumed power in Germany in 1933, had made the Nazi Party the country's sole legitimate political force, and had withdrawn Germany from the League of Nations. Through the Nuremberg Decrees, Hitler took away Jews' rights and citizenship, prohibited them from working in professional positions, and forbade them from marrying "Aryans." He tried to create a nation where "racially pure" Germans could flourish and rule. In 1935 Hitler renounced the Versailles Peace Treaty, revealed he was developing an air

48. *Houston Business Journal*, March 14, 1997.
49. Jesse Jones, speech, Press Club luncheon, Washington, D.C., July 21, 1938, Jesse H. Jones Collection [UT].

Howard Hughes and
Jesse Jones leave the State
Department building on July 21,
1938, after Hughes met with
Secretary of State Cordell
Hull to thank him for the State
Department's assistance with
his record-breaking around-the-
world flight. Courtesy Corbis.

force, and said he intended to build a half-million man army. (At the time, the United States had a standing force of approximately 140,000 men.) In 1936 Hitler sent 35,000 of his soldiers into the Rhineland, a zone between France and Germany that, according the Versailles Peace Treaty, was to remain a demilitarized buffer in perpetuity. Soon after Hitler took over the Rhineland, he entered into protective alliances with Italy and Japan and then on March 14, 1938, he marched into Vienna and took Austria.

Despite the turbulence, European travel evidently was still safe for Americans in the summer of 1938. The Joneses' sixteen-year-old grand-daughter, Audrey Louise, was headed to England and France with friends and a chaperone after school let out. Her grandparents decided to follow wherever they went. Jones wrote John Nance Garner in August, "After planning a little vacation in the west, Mrs. Jones and I finally decided, or rather she decided, that since Audrey Louise was with a party of girls her age in England, we would go to England. So here we are aboard one of the biggest ships afloat, the *Normandy*."[50]

Jones said Stewart McDonald was along to "study housing in other countries." He gave Garner some facts and figures about the RFC, complained about bankers not lending, and mentioned the virtues of long-term loans. Then, "But that's work, and I left work behind." Jones said he was looking forward to "eating, drinking, sleeping, and playing a little bridge, a truly lazy life." He told Garner, "We land at Southampton tomorrow, will have two or three days in London, and then go to Scotland at the invitation of Mr. B. M. Baruch to shoot grouse. I have never seen a grouse, let alone shot at one, but look forward to the experience."[51]

Audrey's European vacation profoundly influenced her life, leading her to eventually amass and donate to the Museum of Fine Arts, Houston, a renowned collection of Impressionist and Post-Impressionist paintings. As an adult she recalled, "My romance with Impressionism began when I first visited Europe at the age of sixteen as a student tourist, complete with camera to record my trip. I paid homage to the *Mona Lisa* and the *Venus de Milo*, but the imaginative and colorful Impressionist paintings came as a total surprise." She continued, "Works by these avant-garde artists, who had rebelled against the academic tradition of the day, were scarce in American museums at that time. For me, they were not only the epitome of artistic freedom, but also a visual delight. I returned home with many . . . museum reproductions."[52]

Audrey, her friends, and the Joneses safely returned home, but before Jones went, he wrote Bernard Baruch a letter of thanks for his hospitality in Scotland; evidently their row over Party politics during the 1920s was water under the bridge. Jones began, "Dear Bernie," and said, "I want to see you in New York and Washington and have the benefit of your counsel and advice from time to time. World conditions are in an uncertain state and we will all need to make our contributions."[53]

In fact, Baruch was in Europe to do more than hunt grouse. According to newspaper reports, he was on a "three-month confidential mission in Europe." Upon his return to the United States, a reporter revealed, "The distinguished financier and authority on world affairs told the president the only way the United States can prevent a German onslaught on the

50. Jesse Jones to John Nance Garner, August 7, 1938, Jesse H. Jones Collection [LOC].
51. Ibid.
52. Beck, *Collection of John A. and Audrey Jones Beck*, 9.
53. Jesse Jones to Bernard Baruch, September 6, 1938, Jesse H. Jones Collection [LOC].

New World is to build immediately an army, navy, and air force second to none, and mobilize the nation's industry on virtually a war footing." Baruch spoke from experience, having militarized U.S. industry during World War I as head of the War Industries Board. He told the reporter, "The United States' defense forces are in a desperate situation and woefully lacking." He continued, "The president knows it too and has been trying to do everything possible to remedy this condition, but he can go only so far; the people of the nation must decide the rest." At various times, Roosevelt had proposed legislation to "upgrade" the military, but Baruch said the United States should "launch immediately a vast scale rearmament program." He exclaimed, "Why, we haven't a powder factory, or a munitions factory in the country . . . Our immediate needs include shells and guns that we don't even know how to make." He also said the United States "should have an army of a minimum of 400,000 men, and not a few hundred, but thousands of airplanes." Baruch instructed, "We should have both government and private plants turning out guns, tanks, planes, and shells," noting that a "rearmament program would go a long way toward solving the nation's unemployment problem."[54]

Two days after Baruch's interview, reports of a possible $5 billion ($75 billion) spending program showed up in the papers. A group of "business leaders" and "executives" who asked not to be identified were quoted, "The rearmament program, viewed economically . . . marks a basic change in the government's recovery program, a switch of emphasis—which many business leaders have long sought—from consumer goods to heavy industry." According to the article, the "broad plans now being worked out in conferences" included "public utility expansion . . . railroad rehabilitation . . . and industrial plant rehabilitation, chiefly in chemical, automobile, airplane, and heavy industry machine-making plants." The article said that whatever could not be financed privately "would be financed by the government . . . through the Reconstruction Finance Corporation."[55]

The public, though, wanted nothing to do with the European conflict. They had endured the seemingly fruitless savagery of a European war just twenty years before and were currently preoccupied with basic survival, the midterm elections, and the economy, which once again was showing signs of improvement. Stock prices and industrial production had

54. *Houston Chronicle,* October 14, 1938.
55. *Houston Chronicle,* October 16, 1938.

Jesse Jones shown wearing his lucky rabbit's foot from a belt loop. Courtesy Library of Congress.

begun to move up.[56] General Motors announced it was rehiring tens of thousands of employees and removing some pay cuts. Relief rolls in many cities were going down.[57]

Jones traveled and campaigned throughout the election season. The midterms did not bode well for Roosevelt or the New Deal. Many were still sore about his scheme to pack the Supreme Court and after that failed, his attempt to purge Congress of conservative Democrats. Moreover, ten million people were still without jobs. Jones wasn't taking chances. He gave a speech in Chicago and afterward wired the Stevens Hotel, "I left a small, silver tipped rabbit's foot on the speaker's stand at the Bankers meeting this morning. Will greatly appreciate your finding it and sending it to me at Washington. It is most important."[58]

As treasurer of the Will Rogers Memorial Commission, Jones went to

56. Olson, *Saving Capitalism*, 214.
57. *Houston Chronicle*, October 19, 1938.
58. Jesse Jones to Stevens Hotel, October 15, 1938, Jesse H. Jones Collection [LOC].

Claremore, Oklahoma, to help dedicate the Will Rogers Memorial Museum that had been built on land where Rogers had planned to retire. Oklahoma Governor E. W. Marland and Jones gave speeches on-site, while President Roosevelt delivered his from Hyde Park over "the wire." Jones, as usual, wrote the president afterward, "Your speech was most appropriate and came over perfectly. Mrs. Rogers and the entire family were very appreciative. It was a nice occasion."[59]

Jones made moving remarks about his dear friend and reported on the fundraising efforts on his behalf. For the past three years, thousands of movie theaters across the nation had staged an annual Will Rogers Memorial Week, and more than ten million moviegoers, with their nickels and dimes, had contributed $1.1 million ($16 million) dollars to the commission. It used the contributions and other donations to support sick and struggling stage actors at the Will Rogers Memorial Hospital in Saranac, New York, and to fund scholarship programs at the "state universities of Oklahoma, California, and Texas . . . in aiding handicapped boys and girls to get an education or in helping students who might wish to equip themselves for devoting their lives to handicapped children." Jones explained in his speech, "State universities were selected to carry out the trust because they are non-sectarian, they are representative of all the people, and they should have continuous existence." Jones concluded, "Will Rogers was a friend alike to the mighty and the weak . . . He was strong and brave and true. He rode straight and hard, and played the game square. His wit was keen but never barbed. Within the shell of humor was the kernel of great wisdom. He brought the precious gift of laughter to a somber world."[60]

From Oklahoma the Joneses went to Texas to vote. The anticipated midterm backlash occurred, and Republicans gained eight seats in the Senate, eighty-one seats in the House, and thirteen governorships.[61] Many said Roosevelt was finished and hardly anyone mentioned a third term.[62] And yet he was the first president since James Monroe to hold both houses of Congress midway through his second term.[63] The Democrats still had majorities in both the House and Senate.

Jones remained in Houston after the election to speak at the American

59. Jesse Jones to Franklin Roosevelt, November 4, 1938, Jesse H. Jones Collection [LOC].

60. Jesse Jones, speech, dedication of Will Rogers Memorial Museum, Claremore, Oklahoma, November 4, 1938, Jesse H. Jones Collection [UT].

61. McElvaine, *Great Depression*, 305.

62. Leuchtenburg, *Roosevelt and the New Deal*, 272.

63. McElvaine, *Great Depression*, 305.

Legion's Armistice Day Exercises at the City Auditorium, commemorating when the Allies and Germany signed a ceasefire, stopped hostilities, and ended World War I. The day before he gave his speech to celebrate world peace, Nazi-backed mobs in cities across Germany, Italy, and Austria rioted, burning down stores and businesses owned by Jews and destroying the synagogues where they prayed. The violence erupted after a Polish Jew shot and killed a German diplomat, but was part of a larger anti-Semitic campaign. This became evident when German Propaganda Minister Paul Joseph Goebbels announced, "New restrictive laws are being prepared and will be issued during the next few days." These new laws would ban Jews from concert halls and movie theaters, cancel their insurance policies, and force them to pay for restoring their destroyed property. Goebbels disingenuously claimed, "The anti-Jewish outburst which vented itself in the burning and dynamiting of synagogues and destruction of Jewish shops was spontaneous."[64] The night of terror became known as "Kristallnacht," or night of broken glass. In Austria, all twenty-one synagogues in Vienna were partly or completely destroyed. Newspapers reported, "A trainload of about 800 Jewish prisoners left Vienna last night for an undisclosed destination." Italy passed emergency legislation banning Jews from government jobs, restricting their business activities, and forbidding them to marry Italian "Aryans."[65]

While this horror unfolded, Jones said in his Armistice Day speech in Houston, "We are living in a disturbed era, an era in which countries are at war." Jones coaxed his local audience to turn its attention overseas. He said, "We must remember . . . that if a democracy is to function effectively, its citizens must take an active interest in its vital problems and keep themselves informed about them. It is important that the American public continue its interest in world affairs and keep strong."[66] The fight for the hearts and minds of the American public was on.

In his speech, Jones recognized President Woodrow Wilson, talked about World War I, and honored the millions of soldiers who "went over there" and those who "did not come back." He warned of the dangers of isolationism, saying, "We hope and pray the time will never again come when we have to take up arms. But if we are to realize that hope, we must not become impotent. In some countries and with some people, only

64. *Houston Chronicle,* November 11, 1938.
65. *Houston Chronicle,* November 10, 1938.
66. Jesse Jones, speech, Armistice Day, Houston, November 11, 1938, Jesse H. Jones Collection [UT].

strength commands respect." Jones candidly admitted, "Foreign affairs are not my province, nor yours, but as simple Americans—and I speak from my own heart—we have a stake in them." With foresight, he said, "We must not have on this continent a situation in which every airplane that flies across our borders is a cause of fear lest it drop a bomb on our families. We do not want our borders to become endless miles of fortresses."[67]

Jones, a primary player in the war effort during World War I and one of Wilson's closest friends, eloquently explained, "Fundamentally, our entry into the world war occurred because the people of the United States felt forces were loose in the world which, if they succeeded, would outrage every moral law. If force was to take the place of right, if truth and honor were dead, if the pledged word meant nothing, if the common human rights of endless races were to be freely violated, then the world would cease to be civilized." Jones concluded, "In a belligerent world, it is no small task to keep the peace." He added, "It is the greatest task in the world today. It is peculiarly an American task, calling for American leadership. It is to that task that we must dedicate ourselves on Armistice Day."[68]

Though he promised not to return after his address in 1935, Jones had given the keynote speech at the American Bankers Association annual meeting for four of the past five years. Each time he lambasted his audience with little restraint, and each time they welcomed him back. In November of 1938 the bankers were in his backyard. Jones welcomed them to Houston and admitted, "I do not like making speeches, and I like writing them less." He added, "Maybe it is because I have never learned the art of using language to conceal my thoughts rather than to express them." Jones went on, "I have talked to you a number of times, and write occasionally, never because I want to talk or write, but in the interests of improving conditions generally, and banking in particular." [69]

Jones openly complained that only one percent of the 14,000 banks he had written to about lending had acknowledged his letters. He impatiently warned, "Congress will meet this demand if banks do not, and I know that most of you do not like government lending—unless it is to some borrower to take up one of your frozen loans." Jones added a twist:

67. Ibid.
68. Ibid.
69. Jesse Jones, speech, American Bankers Association, Houston, November 15, 1938, Jesse H. Jones Collection [UT].

"Our economy is geared to produce vast quantities of industrial and agricultural products for world markets. We require large importation of
raw materials and tropical products. American investments are in every
continent." Jones was suddenly no longer talking about domestic economics. Using practically the same words as in his Armistice Day speech,
Jones followed, "We must remember, therefore, that if our democracy is
to function effectively, its citizens must take an active interest in all its
vital problems and keep themselves fully informed. It is of the greatest
importance that the American public continue its interest in world affairs." He added, "And bankers have their full share of responsibility."[70]

The Joneses went to Washington right after he had had his way with
the bankers. For the first time in years, they were not able to spend the
holidays in Houston. On Christmas Day, Jones published a message on
the front page of the *Houston Chronicle* that said, "Circumstances prevent
my being at home this Christmas where Mrs. Jones and I would most like
to be . . . I love Houston the more for my continued enforced absence
and wish everyone a happy Christmas." Then he finished, "Frankly, I am
homesick."[71]

70. Ibid.
71. *Houston Chronicle*, December 25, 1938.

World War II

1939

◈

An Avalanche of Orders

ON JANUARY 4, 1939, President Franklin Roosevelt delivered his annual message to Congress and focused on international affairs. The president began, "In reporting on the state of the nation, I have felt it necessary on previous occasions to advise the Congress of disturbance abroad and of the need of putting our own house in order in the face of storm signals from across the seas. As this Seventy-sixth Congress opens, there is need for further warning."[1] Roosevelt devoted barely twenty percent of his speech to domestic economics.

The president said, "We want to get enough capital and labor at work to give us . . . a total national income of at least eighty billion dollars a year." The economy was still struggling to return to its peak from the year before. He said, "That figure can be attained working within . . . our traditional profit system," and added that reaching this goal would require maintaining and refining current domestic programs, and embracing new "world conditions and technological improvements." Roosevelt explained, "By our common sense action of resuming government activities last spring, we have reversed a recession and started the new rising tide of prosperity and national income which we are now just beginning

---

1. Roosevelt, "1939 State of the Union Message."

to enjoy."[2] Indeed, national income and employment had already started to go up, showing improvement even before the coming military buildup began.

Near the end of his speech, Roosevelt said, "Events abroad have made it increasingly clear to the American people that dangers within are less to be feared than dangers from without." He concluded, "Once I prophesied that this generation of Americans had a rendezvous with destiny. That prophecy comes true. To us much is given; more is expected. This generation will 'nobly save or meanly lose the last best hope of earth' . . . The way is plain, peaceful, generous, just—a way which, if followed, the world will forever applaud and God must forever bless."[3]

Although he proposed none of them in his message, Roosevelt urgently wanted three bills passed as soon as possible: extend the life of the RFC, expand the military, and reorganize the executive branch of government. All three involved Jesse Jones.

Without a reauthorization, the RFC would expire on June 30, 1939. Jones asked that the RFC be extended until February 15, 1941, a date "suggested by President Roosevelt." He explained, "A new presidential term and a new congressional session begins in January 1941, and there might be a desire then to change or discontinue these functions." One House Banking Committee member asked about the persistent small business loan problem. Jones succinctly described the dilemma: "The RFC is sometimes criticized for lending to a business that is not profitable and is in competition with one that is profitable . . . [thus] subsidizing a business that is improperly run and injuring one that is operated prudently." Someone else grilled Jones about his opposition to insuring all government loans. He pointed out, "We could insure all the loans, but that would put the government really in the banking business."[4]

The RFC's extension did not occur automatically. It and other New Deal programs were under fire. On February 21, newspapers reported, "Unsuccessful in their first efforts to curtail emergency federal agencies, house Republicans endeavored today to prevent a new lease on life for . . . the Export-Import Bank." They were concerned the bank "might involve the United States in foreign entanglements." Secretary of State Cordell Hull tried to reassure them that Export-Import Bank loans would be used primarily to increase trade with South America. Representative Hamilton

2. Ibid.
3. Ibid.
4. *Houston Chronicle*, February 7, 1939.

Fish from New York responded, "If the bank is to support legitimate trade, particularly with South America, I'm for it; if it is to finance wars, I'm against it." Amendments to abolish the Electric Home and Farm Authority and the Commodity Credit Corporation were also proposed, but they failed, too. Before the final vote on the RFC, Representative Robert Luce from Massachusetts testified, "I would vote for the continuance of the RFC as long as [it] is headed by Jesse Jones, who has been the outstanding man in the present administration for his efficiency, for his judgment, for his prudence, and for his usefulness."[5]

By the end of February, the RFC had been renewed by a unanimous vote. Its record was impressive, if not historic. Jones's annual report covered the Corporation's operations since its inception in February 1932. The report stated that the RFC had received authorizations of $13 billion ($199 billion in current dollars) and that $3 billion ($46 billion) had been distributed "by direction of congress in which our directors had no discretion." The RFC itself had disbursed $7.2 billion ($110 billion), and of that amount, $5.3 billion ($81 billion), or seventy-four percent, had been repaid.

The detailed list of RFC beneficiaries appeared to cover almost everyone in the United States and some beyond. For starters, the RFC had rescued the United States financial system by boldly buying stock in the nation's banks and enabling them to lend money and qualify for FDIC membership. Countless bankers, depositors, farmers, tenants, schoolteachers, consumers, businessmen, disaster victims, and home owners had all been helped through RFC loans and activities. The creation and repair of the nation's infrastructure—its railroads, utilities, dams, bridges, tunnels, and levees—had been financed by the RFC. Jones concluded with surprising information: "Our operating expenses have been slightly less than 1 percent," followed by the most astonishing fact of all, "We have accumulated operating reserves sufficient, in the opinion of our board, to cover any and all probable losses. So that the vast amount of credit which has been made available through the RFC and the services it has rendered throughout the country have been without any net loss to the government."[6]

After the RFC received its extension, in March the president achieved his second goal: Congress passed and Roosevelt signed a bill that added $358 million ($5.5 billion) to the U.S. Army's $499 million ($7.6 billion)

---

5. *Houston Chronicle*, February 26, 1939.
6. Ibid.

annual budget. Most of the new appropriation went toward airplanes and about $36 million ($550 billion) went toward a Navy shipbuilding program that had been authorized the year before. After signing the new military spending bill, Roosevelt, claiming discretionary power, instructed Admiral William Leahy to commission two 45,000-ton battleships, soon to be the largest ships in the Navy's fleet.[7] The stated purpose was to defend the United States only in case of an attack. Roosevelt knew the public had no desire to participate in, or contribute to, the European war, which was escalating—Germany had just seized Czechoslovakia.

Roosevelt's third desired piece of legislation gained ground the same day he made his request for the battleships. The Senate approved the bill to reorganize the government and sent it to the House for its approval.[8] In presenting his plan, Roosevelt said, "It is our responsibility to make sure that the people's government is in [a] condition to carry out the people's will promptly, effectively, without waste or lost motion." The plan "was concerned with . . . reducing the number of agencies which report directly to the president and . . . giving the president assistance . . . by modern means of administrative management." Roosevelt proposed consolidating the multitude of public works, welfare, and lending agencies into three organizations: the Federal Works Agency, Federal Security Agency, and Federal Loan Administration (FLA). According to a news release, "the plan represented two years of study and conformed to methods of executive administration used by large private enterprises."[9]

Drew Pearson and Robert Allen jumped on the plan, writing, "Government brass hats were in a high state of jitters all last week, but it wasn't for fear of war in Europe. What had the boys talking to themselves was government reorganization." The reporters claimed, "Most agitated was RFC Chairman Jesse Jones." Rumors swirled that the RFC and the FLA would be transferred to the Commerce Department under Harry Hopkins. Pearson and Allen predicted Jones's departure once more, "Friends of Jesse . . . hinted that if he was subordinated, he would quit."[10] Three days later, the columnists hinted, "It is not supposed to be known, but the principal obstacle facing Roosevelt on reorganization is personality and prima donna stuff. He can't shift bureaus away from chiefs who are powerful with Congress and who don't want them shifted." They had heard

---

7. *Houston Chronicle*, March 28, 1939.
8. Ibid.
9. *Houston Chronicle*, April 25, 1939.
10. Pearson and Allen, "Washington Merry-Go-Round," April 24, 1939.

that Roosevelt wanted to put Jones at Commerce and replace the current Navy secretary, an elderly man, with Hopkins "to give the Navy Department, at this crucial time, an active executive as its chief."[11]

While Roosevelt's reorganization plan wound its way through Congress, the Joneses finally were able to head home at the end of May. They met Betty Rogers in Norman, Oklahoma, where they presented $125,000 ($1.9 million) to the University of Oklahoma to endow a scholarship. The scholarship, according to school officials, would "aid handicapped students enrolled in the university."[12] From there, the three went to Houston, to celebrate Audrey Louise's graduation from the Kinkaid School. School trustee James A. Baker Jr. delivered the commencement address to the class of twelve and their families. Events around the world and at home were on everyone's mind. Baker said, "In these days of international strife, there is too much hate in the world. Dislike and distrust hinder us from attaining the ideals for which we strive." He told the graduating seniors, "Unfortunately, wherever you go now, you find criticism of Catholics, Jews, Protestants, Germans, and of our government itself. Such censure does not solve our problems . . . We need to build and not to tear down."[13] The twelve young people were graduating into a world shaken by economic distress and violence. The day after Audrey's graduation, Jones was inducted into the Alabama-Coushatta Indian tribe. He was given the name Chief Cue-ye-la-na, or Chief Yellow Pine, a name the tribe selected because the yellow pine was the tallest and largest living thing on their reservation, a giant tree that served both poor and rich alike. The tribe's chief laid his tomahawk on Jones's shoulder to help him fight "the battles of the future."[14]

Jones then went to Austin to present a second Will Rogers Memorial Commission check to the University of Texas. While there, he delivered a short speech before the Texas legislature. Former Governor Hobby introduced Jones and declared, "The Reconstruction Finance Corporation has done more in the fight against depression than any other agency of government. The banking structure of the country was rescued from wreckage. Because of . . . that body, money necessary for the conduct of business was provided. Today money flows as easily as the ebb and flow of the tides of an ocean." He then touted Jones for president in 1940, to which

11. Pearson and Allen, "Washington Merry-Go-Round," April 27, 1939.
12. *Houston Chronicle*, May 21, 1939.
13. *Houston Chronicle*, May 27, 1939.
14. *Houston Chronicle*, May 28, 1939.

Jesse Jones is inducted into the Alabama-Coushatta Indian tribe.

he responded, "I would say to you, Governor Hobby, and to others, that I have no political ambitions, no expectations, no hopes. I am part of the present administration. I am in favor of the purposes of this administration. While I realize everything that has been attempted has not worked as admirably as it might, I am convinced that, given time, the many laws put on the statute books at Washington during the last six years will function—and will function for the welfare of all the people."[15]

Despite his repeated demurrals, talk of Jones for president in 1940 was widespread. Harold Ickes and President Roosevelt had mentioned the possibility back in 1936. Pearson and Allen mentioned it all the time. At the start of the year, Elliott Roosevelt, the president's son, promoted Jones and predicted, "The time will soon come for a Texan to be elected to the presidency of the United States."[16] Postmaster Jim Farley—a lead-

15. *Houston Chronicle*, May 30, 1939.
16. *Houston Chronicle*, January 17, 1939.

Jesse Jones with his close friend former Texas Governor William P. Hobby. Jones took over ownership of the *Houston Post* from Governor Ross Sterling as collateral for a loan and helped finance the sale of the newspaper to the Hobbys in 1939.

ing Democrat who had managed Roosevelt's campaigns in 1932 and 1936, had been head of the Democratic National Committee, and had supported Roosevelt's New Deal policies and programs—favored the idea. He did not think the president should stand for a third term and neither did Vice President Garner.

Farley sent Jones a June 3 editorial from the *Memphis Tribune*. It said that Roosevelt's decision to run again would be influenced by his estimation of the public's reaction and whether or not a "strong candidate can be found who is generally acceptable to the Democratic party . . . and whom he trusts and respects." It said, "It is strange that in all the speculative discussion bearing on Democratic presidential possibilities, so little attention has been given to the one man who . . . could reconcile the party's grievous differences and who today enjoys the confidence of almost every element within it." It continued, "While the discussions run . . . to such potential candidates as Garner and Farley, the name of Jesse H. Jones is

Jesse Jones and Harry Hopkins, who served as head of the Civil Works Administration and the Works Progress Administration, and who preceded Jones as Secretary of Commerce. Hopkins lived in the White House for a time and was one of Franklin Roosevelt's closest advisors. Jones frequently enjoyed card games at the White House with Hopkins. Courtesy Briscoe Center for American History, University of Texas at Austin.

much less often mentioned. This is surprising because Mr. Jones is . . . the ideal compromise candidate and, in . . . sheer competence, stands head and shoulders over most of the others mentioned."[17]

The editorial then identified Jones as a "stalwart Texas Democrat . . . who now numbers among his closest friends and confidantes such diverse representatives of the Democratic Party as Farley, Garner, and Harry Hopkins." Jones once kidded Hopkins for not knowing the difference between a loan and a handout, but liked him very much; they frequently played cards at White House poker games and on at least one occasion Jones had invited him to be his guest at the Kentucky Derby. The editorial claimed Jones had "a keen understanding of the problems of government finance and a broad social outlook." It concluded, "If President Roosevelt is casting about for a Democrat worthy of the 1940 nomination, he must surely account among the eligibles the competent and loyal Mr. Jones."[18]

17. "A Democratic Dark Horse," *Memphis Tribune,* June 3, 1939.
18. Ibid.

Word had leaked out that Roosevelt planned to appoint Jones as head of the Federal Loan Administration, which included the gargantuan RFC and all of its agencies, plus the Federal Home Loan Bank Board, Home Owners' Loan Corporation, Federal Savings and Loan Insurance Corporation, and Federal Housing Administration. Pearson and Allen reported, "Some figured it was a good idea to kick Jesse upstairs, where he would no longer have his fingers immediately on the Reconstruction Finance Corporation."[19] That was not to be the case. After appointing him federal loan administrator, Roosevelt agreed to appoint RFC board member Emil Schram to replace Jones as chair of the Corporation, essentially leaving the RFC in Jones's hands while adding all of the nation's other lending agencies to his portfolio. The Senate unanimously approved his appointment.[20] Jones worked at the same desk in the same office, and his government pay was increased from $10,000 ($153,000) a year to $12,000 ($183,000) a year, but his power and reach had once again dramatically multiplied.

Twenty baskets of flowers and many notes of congratulations poured into Jones's office. Henry Morgenthau swallowed his pride to congratulate Jones "very heartily" upon his appointment and to wish him luck.[21] Senator Claude Pepper of Florida wrote, "You were the unanimous choice of the country, and we all know that you are going to continue in this larger field the same splendid service that you have rendered to the country through the RFC. All rejoice in the just recognition which constantly comes to your great ability and your splendid personal qualities."[22] Jones clearly had broad appeal. One journalist observed, "Jones has been able to work in harmony with men of . . . opposing viewpoints." As evidence, he wrote, "Among those loudest in their praises are the financially orthodox Carter Glass and brain-trusting Tommy Corcoran."[23]

Back home, Dee Simpson, vice president of Jones's Houston bank, reported, "Much excitement on the streets this afternoon with Chronicle newsboys yelling all about Jesse Jones."[24] Lyndon Johnson, elected to the House two years before, wrote Jones, "As a native Texan, I am proud of your outstanding accomplishments for our country and wish you much

19. Pearson and Allen, "Washington Merry-Go-Round," July 9, 1939.
20. *Houston Chronicle*, June 23, 1939.
21. Henry Morganthau to Jesse Jones, June 23, 1939, Jesse H. Jones Collection [LOC].
22. Claude Pepper to Jesse Jones, June 24, 1939, Jesse H. Jones Collection [LOC].
23. Lubell, "New Deal's J. P. Morgan," 89.
24. A. D. Simpson to Jesse Jones, June 24, 1939, Jesse H. Jones Collection [LOC].

success and happiness."[25] Johnson received a polite and standard response which indicated at this point little familiarity in their relationship.[26]

Pearson and Allen devoted an entire "Washington Merry-Go-Round" column to Jones. Usually caustic critics, the columnists this time were almost reverential. They called Jones a "unique character" and described him as "six feet three, soft-spoken and as benign as a doting grandfather." They also said, "He is a combination of hard-boiled, tight-fisted banker, daring big-time gambler, and grandstanding, nimble-footed wire-pulling politician." They noted, "No one has ever heard Jesse raise his voice in anger. He is the gentlest and mellowest of companions." They said he had "great wealth," lived "quietly and simply," had "little to do with the giddy social whirl," and enjoyed "motoring with his wife and an occasional game of bridge with a few intimates." They even repeated the old story: "Once he took off his shoes while nobody was looking in Buckingham Palace."[27]

The two reporters enjoyed writing about the high and the mighty and told how Jones had brought the Democratic convention to Houston, how he wanted to be Secretary of the Treasury back in 1933, and how his bank was "loaded with cash and bonds" while he begged other bankers to be "open-handed." They also described Jones's close-to-the-vest politicking style and claimed, "Throughout all the historic legislative battles of 1936, '37, and '38, nobody knew where Jesse stood on any of the great issues . . . He never dropped a word in public by which they could call him." Toward the end of the article, they said, "Real inside is that Jesse has ambitions of his own. There was a time when he dreamed of the White House, but that dream is over. He does, however, fancy himself as a vice presidential dark horse." They finished, "For a gangling Tennessee farm boy who got his start as a day laborer in an uncle's lumber yard in Dallas, Jesse has come a long way by speaking softly and at the right time. He is hoping to do that again in 1940. Sixty-five years old, it will be his last chance to realize a carefully nurtured ambition."[28]

Jones had two letters to write before his appointment as federal loan administrator was official. The first was to the RFC board of directors, tendering his resignation. To establish a final account of his record at the RFC, he wrote, "The RFC has rendered a great service to the American

25. Lyndon Johnson to Jesse Jones, June 24, 1939, Jesse H. Jones Collection [LOC].
26. Jesse Jones to Lyndon Johnson, June 26, 1939, Jesse H. Jones Collection [LOC].
27. Pearson and Allen, "Washington Merry-Go-Round," July 8, 1939.
28. Ibid.

people, far greater than can be generally known. It has averted ruin and disaster for millions of our citizens." He provided details: "It has saved millions of depositors and shareholders in banks and building and loan associations; it has strengthened . . . more than 10,000 banks; it has aided millions of farmers and stockmen through loans and advances . . . and . . . [it] has enabled a great many farmers and landowners to reduce by two-thirds the water and debt charges on their lands." He continued, "[The RFC] has helped thousands of home owners save their homes . . . it has created work for millions . . . through loans to business enterprises and for useful public works; it has extended aid to thousands of victims of disasters; and in many other ways [it] has contributed to the economic stability of our country." Saving the best for last, he stated, "All this has been accomplished without any net loss or cost to the Government." Then Jones opened his heart, "If I were leaving the RFC entirely, I would be unhappy beyond expression. I love the organization and have a deep affection for every member of it. I appreciate the service and loyalty they have given it, and like to believe that everyone connected with the Corporation has the same pride in its achievements that I have. I love the very name, RFC. It represents seven and a half years of my life and is a part of me."[29]

Next was Jones's official resignation letter to President Roosevelt. He said that when he "came to the RFC [in], February 2, 1932, it was assumed that the conditions which caused the creation of the Corporation by Congress would soon pass." He said, "The breakdown in our financial and economic affairs has been repaired, but the readjustment is taking much longer than any of us expected." Jones told the president, "My greatest compensation in my RFC work has been the continued confidence and support which you have given me, and the confidence of Congress, my associates in the Corporation, and the business world generally. Whatever success I may have had in furnishing leadership to the organization has been due to that confidence and support." Jones reported, "The Corporation is solvent. It has sound assets sufficient to pay all of its debts and return to the Treasury the entire capital stock invested in it, with something in addition."[30] Jones later claimed the "something in addition" amounted to approximately $500 million ($7.6 billion). Jones and the RFC showed that the government can help people and make money at the same time.

29. Jesse Jones to the RFC Board of Directors, July 15, 1939, Jesse H. Jones Collection [LOC].
30. Jesse Jones to Franklin Roosevelt, July 15, 1935, Jesse H. Jones Collection [LOC].

President Roosevelt accepted Jones's resignation "only because of your undertaking the work of Federal Loan Administrator." He wrote, "The Reconstruction Finance Corporation under your chairmanship has made an amazing record of financial efficiency, while at the same time assisting many banks, corporations, and individuals to continue solvent and to do their part in giving employment and keeping the wheels of industry turning." Roosevelt acknowledged the RFC's profit and remembered those who predicted "the government would not get back more than fifty cents on the dollar." He wrote, "These people were in some cases honest in their belief, but in many cases were making these ghoulish statements with the hope that their own type of partisanship would thereby be served . . . Their gloomy predictions proved false." The president concluded, "You, the fellow members of your board, and all of us who have some confidence in the good sense of the American people, and confidence in the ability of honest government to cope with difficult situations which have not been solved by wholly private efforts, have a right to some measure of pride in the Reconstruction Finance Corporation."[31]

One month after his appointment as federal loan administrator, Jones set his record straight with the rest of the nation through a radio address. He listed ten major agencies under his supervision and, alluding to what was coming, said, "These are all seasoned agencies, with good organizations, managed by capable men, prepared to meet whatever demands that may be put upon them."[32] He explained how these agencies put a solid foundation under the wobbly economy.

He began with how the Federal Housing Administration had enabled "families of moderate means . . . to build, buy, or repair homes on the most favorable terms ever known in our history" and reported that "more than 10,000 banks and other lending institutions throughout the country are cooperating in the movement." Jones declared, "More than 600 new homes have been started every day this year under the FHA Mortgage Insurance Plan, and this number should be doubled. New homes not only improve living standards, but [also] create work and employ capital."

Jones talked about the Home Loan Bank System, the Federal Savings and Loan Insurance Corporation, Fannie Mae, and the RFC Mortgage Company, and said, "With all these facilities for financing homes on easy payments, every family in the United States should own its own home.

---

31. Franklin Roosevelt to Jesse Jones, July 18, 1939, Jesse H. Jones Collection [LOC].
32. Jesse Jones, CBS radio address, August 30, 1939, Jesse H. Jones Collection [UT].

It can do so as cheaply as paying rent. We should be a country of home owners."[33]

Jones also spoke about aid to business, "The RFC is especially interested in lending for construction purposes of all character, for plant modernization and the replacement of uneconomical and antiquated equipment, and for self-liquidating projects to public bodies . . . The RFC is prepared to lend for these purposes on favorable terms, either directly or in cooperation with banks and other lending institutions." Recognizing one of the Great Depression's hardest-hit sectors, Jones explained, "Our greatest sympathies in lending . . . are with the smaller units—so called small business . . . Over a third of our loans . . . have been for $5,000 [$76,500] or less, and over one-half for $10,000 [$153,000] or less." Still pushing reluctant lenders, he said, "Each of the 15,000 banks in the country should be willing to aid any prospective borrower in preparing his application to the RFC . . . Our banks . . . and industrial institutions have a great deal of unused capacity, and our government is prepared to meet any reasonable condition that may arise."[34]

Two days later, on September 1, 1939, Germany invaded Poland. Adolf Hitler rejected ultimatums from Great Britain and France to withdraw, and on September 3 the two nations declared war against Germany. President Roosevelt delivered a "Fireside Chat" that evening, saying to his anxious audience, "For four long years, a succession of actual wars and constant crises have shaken the entire world and have threatened in each case to bring on the gigantic conflict which is today unhappily a fact." The president told his listeners that they were "the most enlightened and the best informed people in all the world" and that it was "of the utmost importance" that they "think things through." He explained, "It is easy for you and for me to shrug our shoulders and to say that conflicts taking place thousands of miles from the continental United States . . . do not seriously affect the Americas—and that all the United States has to do is to ignore them and go about its own business." But, he countered, "We are forced to realize that every word that comes through the air, every ship that sails the sea, [and] every battle that is fought does affect the American future." Roosevelt could only go so far and he said, "This nation will remain a neutral nation, but I cannot ask that every American remain neutral in thought as well . . . Even a neutral nation cannot be asked

33. Ibid.
34. Ibid.

to close his mind or close his conscience." He added, "The United States will keep out of this war . . . Let no man or woman thoughtlessly or falsely talk of America sending its armies to European fields."[35]

Roosevelt told his cabinet, "We need only think of defending this hemisphere," but Germany, Italy, and Japan threatened the world.[36] Hitler had seized Austria in 1936, conquered Czechoslovakia in March 1939, and captured Poland six months later. Dependent on other nations for natural resources, Japan was intent on expansion and self-sufficiency, and had increased its military spending six hundred percent between 1936 and 1939. It seized Manchuria in 1931, and launched a vicious war against China in 1937. In 1939 it captured the Spratly Islands, only four hundred miles from the Philippines. Western interests, most notably owners of natural rubber plantations, were at risk, and many feared Japan would transform the Pacific into a "Nipponese lake."[37] Italy also intended to expand its borders, conquer territory, and settle old scores. It had invaded Ethiopia in 1936 and Albania in 1939.[38]

These three aggressors joined in a series of pacts. In 1936 Germany and Japan had signed the Anti-Comintern Pact to protect each other from the Soviet Union; Italy joined in 1937. Italy and Germany also signed a treaty in 1936 whereupon Benito Mussolini predicted the two nations would form an "axis" around which all other nations would revolve. With the Pact of Steel, Germany and Italy enlarged their official friendship with additional declarations of trust and cooperation, and promises of military aid in the event of war. The pact prohibited either nation from declaring peace during war without the approval of the other. Both nations sent airplanes, pilots, and infantrymen to help Francisco Franco take over Spain's Republican government. Fascist forces achieved their goal in 1939, a pivotal year when events congealed and pointed toward world war.

Meanwhile, Roosevelt's hands were tied. The public staunchly opposed intervention, even as worldwide tensions escalated. Starting in 1935, Congress passed and subsequently renewed a series of Neutrality Acts that prohibited arms sales and loans to warring nations. Less than five percent of United States citizens were amenable to raising immigration quotas to

35. Kennedy, *Freedom from Fear*, 427.
36. Ibid.
37. Leuchtenburg, *Roosevelt and the New Deal*, 290; National World War II Museum exhibition notes.
38. Kennedy, *Freedom from Fear*, 425.

provide a haven for vulnerable refugees.[39] Eighty percent were willing to declare war against Germany or Japan only if the United States itself was attacked.[40] The situation was complicated by the fact the United States was essentially unarmed. In 1939 seventeen nations had armies larger than the United States, which now had about 175,000 men in its armed forces. Even though the U.S. 1940 defense budget had been upped to $1.3 billion ($20 billion), Germany's military budget was still twenty times larger.[41] By 1939 Japan had 7,700 airplanes and Germany had 8,295, while the United States had only 2,500, and most of them were obsolete.[42]

Roosevelt wanted to prepare the United States to help its allies, but public opinion—and the law—prevented him from doing so. Repealing, or at least revising, the Neutrality Act, therefore, became the president's top priority. To that end he called for a special session of Congress on September 21, 1939. It would be an uphill battle. Between Germany's invasion of Poland and the special session of Congress three weeks later, millions of letters and telegrams flooded congressional offices opposing revisions to the law. Prominent isolationists, notably Charles Lindbergh and Father Charles Coughlin, employed radio, newspapers, and speakers' platforms to vehemently denounce intervention of any kind. It was only with strong support from southern conservative Democrats that a revised Neutrality Act was passed and signed by Roosevelt on November 4, 1939. The act allowed belligerent nations to buy armaments from the United States for cash, not credit, and they had to be shipped on foreign vessels.[43] As newspapers reported, "An avalanche of orders for American war planes and engines followed." The article predicted "current and prospective orders will require 100,000 workers by next summer." It also reported that one "prominent manufacturer" estimated that "top warplane speeds" would increase from 350 to 450 miles an hour.[44] The War Department had already announced its intention to expand the army to its peacetime limit of 280,000 men.[45] But the United States had to race to catch up—in addition to its antiquated planes, the military had at most 350 old tanks and no antiaircraft ammunition.[46]

39. Ibid., 415.
40. Fleming, *New Dealers' War*, 5.
41. Schwarz, *New Dealers*, 311.
42. National World War II Museum exhibition notes.
43. Kennedy, *Freedom from Fear*, 433–44.
44. *Houston Chronicle*, December 3, 1939.
45. *Houston Chronicle*, October 7, 1939.
46. Leuchtenburg, *Roosevelt and the New Deal*, 303.

With the surge in production, unemployment dropped. Since March 1938 more than ten million jobless people had found work.[47] Per capita wealth went up.[48] Higher farm prices, larger dividends, and growing paychecks added $2 billion ($31 billion) to the national income during 1939.[49] At the same time, German warplanes began scouting missions over France and the Netherlands. Jones, who had been attending cabinet meetings since September, was asked to continue "for the duration of the emergency."[50]

He and Mary went home to Houston in November. As was customary in those days, a large crowd of friends and family gathered at the station to greet the them as they stepped off the train. Fred Heyne, Mary's son, Tilford, and the couple's close friend Sam Taub were there, along with Jones's architect, Alfred C. Finn, and George Butler, his attorney and nephew by marriage. Dee Simpson and R. P. Doherty were there from the bank and reporters were there, too. One asked if the European war had anything to do with improving business. Jones replied, "We had a good start before the war started," and insisted the economic improvement was not a "boom."[51]

In Houston, Jones wrote to his pal Vice President Garner, "I had two days duck hunting with John Scott and was able to get the limit each day with little difficulty." He also wrote, "We will go to College Station tonight, [to] attend the ceremonies dedicating the new A&M dormitories and in the afternoon witness the championship football game between Texas and A&M." What Jones did not say was that the RFC had loaned the school $2 million ($31 million) for the twelve new dormitories and a dining hall that seated three thousand. He also did not brag that the wildly popular Thanksgiving Day game would be dedicated to him. After the game he was catching a train for Washington, where "I will make up some of my recent neglect of Mrs. Jones by going with her and our granddaughter to the Army-Navy Game at Philadelphia . . . And, I promised to go on with Mrs. Jones to New York . . . and witness the Giants-Redskins game there Sunday afternoon. So, Thursday, Saturday, and Sunday, I should have a good fill of football, all by crack teams."[52]

Back in Washington the following week, Jones began arranging loans

47. *Houston Chronicle*, December 3, 1939.

48. *Houston Chronicle*, October 7, 1939.

49. *Houston Chronicle*, October 27, 1939.

50. *Houston Chronicle*, September 8, 1939.

51. *Houston Chronicle*, November 20, 1939.

52. Jesse Jones to John Nance Garner, November 29, 1939, Jesse H. Jones Collection [LOC].

for Finland and Norway. The Soviet Union had attacked Finland on November 30, hoping to build a buffer around Leningrad and to gain control of Finnish ports. The Soviets outnumbered the Finns in manpower
and equipment, but the Soviet soldiers were untrained, unable to fight
effectively in winter, and they underestimated Finnish determination
and prowess. Eight days after the attack, Jones wrote Roosevelt that the
RFC would lend Finland $10 million ($153 million) to buy surplus crops
and industrial products from the U.S. for "civilian purposes." Jones reported that Norwegian representatives were seeking a similar loan. He
wrote, "The directors of the RFC are prepared to authorize either or both
of these credits if in line with your policies." The president scribbled "JHJ
OK FDR" at the bottom of the letter and returned it the following day.[53] By
law the United States could not send desperately needed military equipment or sell weapons without cash in hand, but it could make loans for
"non-military" purposes, which Jones was careful to stipulate.[54]

Jones returned to Houston in mid-December with his friend Fred
Fisher, a member of the RFC board and co-founder of Fisher Body Works,
and with General Motors President William Knudsen, whom Jones would
introduce as the keynote speaker at the annual Chamber of Commerce
dinner. Rising to speak, Jones began by talking about Houston's "very
healthy growth." Direct as always, he pointed out problems that needed
to be fixed and said, "I do not mean to sound a sour note, but this is a
business meeting. For one thing, our streets seem to be in bad shape, and
traffic regulation is plainly inadequate." He said development required
expanded water and sewage facilities and that the city limits should be
enlarged to "include everyone who makes his living here and who enjoys
the advantages of Houston." Jones also encouraged port improvements
"to accommodate passenger ships." Then he turned to the war, saying,
"We are fortunate in being removed from the wars that are destroying
life and property in many countries. But advanced methods in transportation and communication make distances much shorter, and we will
need to watch our step during the next year or two. We must not become
involved in these wars." Jones then recognized Fisher with the remark,
"It is to Fred Fisher that we are indebted for the closed car," before he
introduced Knudsen.[55]

Knudsen had come to the United States from Denmark in 1900, work-

53. Jesse Jones to Franklin Roosevelt, December 9, 1939, Jesse H. Jones Collection [LOC].
54. Leuchtenburg, *Roosevelt and the New Deal,* 297.
55. *Houston Chronicle,* December 13, 1939.

ing as a bicycle mechanic until the firm where he was employed merged with Ford Motor Company. At Ford Knudsen helped to develop the concept of mass production and perfect the assembly line. He went to General Motors in 1922, was appointed president of Chevrolet in 1924, and in 1937 became president of GM.[56] Unsurprisingly, Knudsen talked about cars. He said, "We have something we do not have to sell the public [on]. It is simple. There are always people who want to get from point A to point B—sitting down." He added, "Safety is all important. After that come comfort and economy. The United States is far ahead of other countries in skill. Also this country spends million for research, which pays." But Knudsen also addressed the war, saying, "The United States has no place in the war in Europe. We want to stay busy here, and we will give to the fellow in need. But the United States should not fight unless it is on these shores." Reporting that General Motors' plants in Europe had been closed since the start of war, he defensively declared, "We won't make munitions. It's a damn outrage that some think all we want is to make money," then admitted, "We do make airplane motors at one of our factories, but our only customer is the United States government."[57] For all their denials of involvement in the war, and whether they knew it or not, within months Knudsen and Jones would be working together to militarize the nation's industrial base.

Jones returned to Washington immediately after the banquet, but returned to Houston once more to celebrate the Christmas holidays with his family. The Joneses arrived on December 22 and were met at the station by the usual enthusiastic crush of relatives, business associates, and reporters. Jones said to the eager newsmen, "We just came home for Christmas. We will stay here through the holidays and take in the Sugar Bowl game at New Orleans on the way back to Washington."[58]

56. *Houston Chronicle*, December 12, 1939.
57. *Houston Chronicle*, December 13, 1939.
58. *Houston Chronicle*, December 22, 1939.

1940

◆

Just Another Loan

THE JONESES GOT BACK TO WASHINGTON in time for President Franklin Roosevelt's State of the Union message. On January 3, 1940, the president explained his focus on the war by saying, "The impact of war abroad makes it natural to approach 'the state of the union' through a discussion of foreign affairs." He reassured Congress and the public that "American youth" would not be asked "to fight on the soil of Europe," but he also said that the United States could not live "inside a high wall of isolation while, outside, the rest of civilization and the commerce and culture of mankind are shattered." Roosevelt said, "There is a vast difference between keeping out of war and pretending that this war is none of our business."[1]

Roosevelt talked briefly about "our continued progress in the social and economic field," then warned, "We have not yet found a way to employ the surplus of our labor," although the war was rapidly changing that situation. He asked Congress to renew legislation that allowed him to negotiate and implement trade and tariff agreements with other nations because he had only trade enabled by the revised Neutrality Act and the Export-Import Bank in his international quiver, with little else to offer the

1. Roosevelt, "1940 State of the Union Message."

343

beleaguered Europeans. He could, however, strive to prepare the nation for what was coming. The president said, "The only important increase in any part of the budget is the estimate for national defense. Practically all other important items show a reduction." Unwilling to defer responsibility, he explained, "But you know, you can't eat your cake and have it, too . . . I am asking the Congress to levy sufficient additional taxes to meet the emergency spending for national defense." Roosevelt also asked for "national unity." He said, "These words—'national unity'—must not be allowed to become merely a high-sounding phrase, a vague generality, a pious hope to which everyone can give lip-service. They must be made to have real meaning in terms of the daily thoughts and acts of every man, woman, and child in our land during the coming year and during the years that lie ahead. For national unity is, in a very real and a very deep sense, the fundamental safeguard of all democracy."[2]

Jones wrote Roosevelt that evening, "Your message under all the circumstances I believe to be the best and the best delivered I have ever heard. It will rank among the great state papers of all our presidents."[3] Roosevelt responded, "I want you to know how deeply I appreciate your telegram. What you say about the message to the Congress is indeed generous, and I am grateful for your kind approval."[4]

Jones and the RFC were as essential as ever in helping Roosevelt fulfill his newest mission. The president needed Jones's power and influence, and the RFC's resources, to push forward the industrial infrastructure required to produce everything needed to wage a world war. The RFC's Export-Import Bank had already made loans to Finland and Norway, and Jones was currently arranging one with Sweden. As newspapers reported, "The loans, it was widely believed, were for strengthening the nations against Russia."[5] Further extensions of credit to countries under threat were needed, and just days after the State of the Union message, Roosevelt asked Congress to increase the Export-Import Bank's lending authority by $100 million ($1.5 billion in current dollars).[6] A $20 million ($300 million) loan to China soon followed. The Chinese bought U.S. trucks and road building equipment, paying back with tin, an essential metal that was not yet being produced in the United States.[7] Referring to the loans, the *Wall*

2. Ibid.
3. Jesse Jones to Franklin Roosevelt, January 3, 1940, Jesse H. Jones Collection [LOC].
4. Franklin Roosevelt to Jesse Jones, January 5, 1940, Jesse H. Jones Collection [LOC].
5. *Houston Chronicle*, January 12, 1940.
6. *Wall Street Journal*, January 17, 1940.
7. *Wall Street Journal*, March 8, 1940.

Street Journal wrote in support: "If the millions of Europe's dispossessed, knowing that help cannot reach all of them, still know that somewhere in the civilized world there are those who care about their wretchedness and stir themselves to mitigate it, something will have been done to keep the flame of western civilization burning."[8]

Drew Pearson and Robert Allen pointed out, "Unlike the case in the last war, American bankers are ardent rooters for peace. This time not they but Uncle Sam, through Jesse Jones, is lending the money."[9] Bankers and industrialists had funded most of the last world war, and many found themselves left holding the bag once hostilities ceased and their factories and products were no longer needed. For now, they were on the sidelines.

Meanwhile, the situation in Europe was deteriorating further. On March 12, Finland signed the Moscow Peace Treaty, which ceded ten percent of its territory, including an important industrial district and its second largest city, to the Soviet Union. In return, the Soviet Union promised to end its quest for complete annexation.

Jones still focused publicly on domestic issues like housing. When he spoke at the annual meeting of the Federal Home Loan Bank in March, he said, "I am a great believer in people owning their own homes. It is an incentive to good citizenship." He talked about the value of good mortgages and long-term loans, and told his audience, "I am pleased to have had my work broadened . . . to permit me to have an interest in the affairs of the Home Loan Bank System and its affiliated institutions." Jones shared, "I have always liked real estate, farm land, pasture land, timber land, and city property. I have had experience with all of them. I guess I just naturally like 'the good earth,' the foundation of all our wealth." Jones gave his usual positive accounting of the RFC, saying, "We have made more than $10 billion [$150 billion] credit available, and for every imaginable purpose . . . We have loaned where private capital was unable to lend or could not afford to take the risk." Noting that the RFC had operated at a profit and had supplied "credit necessary for the business life of our country," Jones immodestly pointed out, "There is no line of business that we have not aided, and probably every man, woman, and child in the United States has benefited from RFC operations."[10]

8. *Wall Street Journal*, March 16, 1940.
9. Pearson and Allen, "Washington Merry-Go-Round," March 14, 1940.
10. Jesse Jones, speech, Federal Home Loan Bank meeting, March 27, 1940, Jesse H. Jones Collection [UT].

At the end, gingerly dipping a toe into "national defense" (the official and publicly acceptable reason for militarizing the economy), Jones mentioned the European and Pacific wars, concluding, "I would like to be able to say something encouraging about the situation . . . of the world at this time, but I am no Prophet. It is clear, however, that while we are not directly involved in the war, we will be affected by the results of the war." He suggested, "If I were asked to name the most pressing problem that confronts us, I would say . . . preparation for peace is the most important, and . . . add that that involves adequate preparation for national defense . . . We must not allow the disorders of Europe to undermine the integrity and national character of our great country and our form of government."[11]

Jones had to be cautious. He was still the face of the RFC, and his personal charm was needed to protect the corporation from those skeptical of its ascent to power. The May 1940 issue of *Fortune* magazine used Jones and the RFC as a prime example of a troubling "fourth branch of government." The article included dozens of black and white pictures, several large graphs, and a full-page, full-color reproduction of Jones's portrait that had been painted for the issue by P. R. Neilson.

The first paragraph of the editorial in the multipart feature referred to a recent *Fortune* article by Republican Wendell Wilkie, who had cautioned that "the power of the central government, and especially of the Executive, has enormously increased" and that no less than the "principles of American liberty upon which private enterprise is founded" were at stake. The editorial then said the RFC might seem a strange way to illustrate government's greater reach since "it was not started under the New Deal, but under Mr. Hoover; it is not a commission . . . but a corporation; it is not concerned with law, but with finance; and . . . in the handling of its vast power it has given the citizen little cause for complaint." Nevertheless, the magazine argued, it represented drift "from certain elementary concepts of government," namely the "division of power among three branches—Legislative, Executive, and Judicial."[12]

The magazine said that this "fourth branch" was getting out of hand, stating, "The vast power at [the RFC's] disposal . . . is illustrative of the dangers inherent in this governmental form." Noting that the RFC is "one of the biggest banking operations in the land" and had more power than

11. Ibid.
12. "Business and Government," editorial, 2.

Chase because "behind it stands the President and Congress," the editorial warned, "The two conditions that are essential to its proper functioning—business judgment and self-denial—are not conditions that can be created by legislation." It then admitted, "Now it so happens that in Jesse Jones, who has run the RFC since 1933, the American people have found the perfect man."[13] For now, Jones's almost universal popularity buffered the RFC from harsher critique.

The main article, which opened with Jones's full-color portrait, took a comprehensive look at the RFC. Ten pictures illustrating the broad range of RFC loans and collateral included New York's Essex House hotel, a mule, a mortuary, and a reindeer farm. It said the RFC "has so extended its influence in the U.S. economic life that its disbursements add up to $10.5 billion [$158 billion]," while "the underwritings of J. P. Morgan & Co. and its syndicates from 1919 through 1933 aggregated but $6 billion [$90 billion]." With fresh perspective on Roosevelt's New Deal, the authors also pointed out that the RFC could "pay back the $500 million [$7.5 billion] that the Treasury paid out for its capital stock and show a minimum profit of $160 million [$2.4 billion] . . . a remarkable operation considering it included some of the leanest years and most desperate business situations in U.S. history." In light of this, "It is easy to understand why almost everyone in Washington, Republican or Democrat, New Deal or anti-new Deal, readily states that [the] RFC is a splendid demonstration that government in business can be competent."[14]

Their conclusion? "Jesse Jones, more than anyone or anything else, is principally responsible for RFC's competency." Jones's success and nonpartisan, non-ideological approach to power both endeared him to and frustrated the right, the center, and the left. "Trying to scalp Jesse has been a favorite sport with New Dealers," they wrote, while also observing, "He has given them an omnipresent laboratory of government in business; and he has made it into a yardstick that has popular appeal, not only because it has established itself as a standard of competency, but also because it has experimented in a new field without costing the taxpayers a cent." Whether accurate or not, the writers said Jones was the only one in the administration "who knows in his guts what it feels like for a businessman to lay a million dollars on the line. That is the quality that sets Jesse Jones apart from the rest of those around Franklin Roosevelt." They

13. Ibid., 3.
14. "RFC: The House of Jesse," 5.

suggested that "Jones's cooniness and knack for command" was partially responsible for the widespread admiration he enjoyed.[15]

The article offered a lengthy history of the RFC's origins, activities, and accomplishments, but devoted most of the coverage to the banks. It concluded, "Jones's judiciously aggressive leadership not only revitalized the weaker elements of the banking system, but also established the fact that New Deal participation in the banking business was not necessarily inimical." They added, "Thanks to Jesse Jones's policy of publicity on all loans and to guarantees such as those offered by the Federal Deposit Insurance Corporation, the psychological reaction to government assistance has changed materially." As a result, "RFC's big job in the banking field is done." Turning next to farming, the writers said, "Aid to agriculture has been one of RFC's biggest lines." They explained how the Commodity Credit Corporation had enabled "farmers to hold crops for a better market," noting it had "put a bottom under farm prices" and that "all of the RFC's advances have been repaid." They also recounted how the Commodity Credit Corporation was moved from the RFC to the Department of Agriculture during Roosevelt's government reorganization in 1939. In the first inklings of the brewing battle between Jones and the Agriculture Secretary, the authors reported, "Jesse doesn't think that Henry Wallace knows how to lend money."[16]

The article explored Jones's management style, showing how he "minds the politicians" and frees the other directors from politics. "The leitmotiv of government efficiency at a profit so pervades the RFC that it is known by almost everyone who works for it . . . as 'The Corporation,' and not by its initials as are most agencies in Washington," explained the authors. As evidence of Jones's priorities, they described the RFC's "dilapidated building," washed walls, plain furniture, and hat racks that seemed "out of keeping with the spirit of 'The Corporation's' bigness. The place is in keeping with the air of informality, with the complete lack of the side that too many big executives love."[17]

The authors declared, "[The] RFC has been a tantalizing compromise between the forces of further government intervention in business and those who would follow a laissez faire policy." Jones "has no . . . highfalutin notions, and he is no intellectual . . . Jesse feels that [the] RFC is great precisely because it is needed by capitalism and yet has not jim-

15. Ibid., 16.
16. Ibid., 12–13.
17. Ibid., 15.

mied the system." Quoting Jones at his folksiest, "[The] RFC should be a permanent thing, all right, but on a temporary basis." The exposé ended with an afterword titled "Mr. Jesse Jones's RFC." Piling on more glowing press, the authors stated, "RFC today is certainly the happiest possible example that business and government can peacefully and profitably collaborate when the proper circumstances are provided. With the RFC, the 'proper circumstances' are very largely Mr. Jesse Jones."[18]

The last paragraphs described how Jones had invited the reporters to sit in his office and observe so they could see how the RFC worked, noting, "The team had the priceless experience of watching Mr. Jones conduct his business with every manner of congressman, businessman, banker, foreign delegation." They revealed that the Swedish trade delegation was put off by their presence and stammered before timidly asking Jones for an official contract for the $15 million ($225 million) loan they had just received. When Jones said his signed letter of intent was sufficient, they insisted on a contract, and he finally agreed—but characteristically demanded, "Make it short." In contrast, Chinese banker K. P. Chen "paid no attention whatever to *Fortune*, went right to the point, and in two minutes by the clock settled with Jones [the] details for a $20 million [$300 million] loan for China." The reporters wrote, "It takes a good deal of healthy self-confidence to let members of the untrammeled U.S. press sit in on your life and watch every move in your business day. Mr. Jones has it." They concluded, "It is the editorial's contention that such governmental operations as the RFC are safe for a democracy only when they are conducted in a goldfish bowl. And that is just where Mr. Jones conducts them."[19]

A timely observation about the RFC's efficiency, buried in the body of the main article, said, "One very good reason why [the] RFC has broadened so extensively is the fact that [it] is, to a very large extent outside the budget and possesses a revolving fund of its own . . . Thus [it] is a convenient device for getting things done, within its elastic limitations, without the necessity of getting a budgetary appropriation through Congress."[20] In other words, the RFC—meaning Jesse Jones—had the power of the purse. The RFC's unique ability would soon be used to begin militarizing industry—eighteen months before the United States officially joined the world war and while the nation and Congress dithered over intervention.

With no further overt aggression since Germany's invasion of Poland

18. Ibid., 16.
19. Ibid., 20.
20. Ibid., 13.

in September 1939 and Russia had gone into Finland two months later, accusations of a "phony war" had begun to surface. Some accused New Dealers of hyping the threat to increase employment through unnecessary military spending. But belief in a "phony war" ended in April when Germany invaded both Denmark and Norway. Doubts about Adolf Hitler's intentions vanished for good after he launched "blitzkriegs" against Belgium, Luxembourg, the Netherlands, and France on May 10. Hitler softened his targets by bombing them first from the air before he unleashed his motorized troops, wielding modern weapons. Luxembourg was occupied by the end of the first day. The Netherlands, which had not been invaded in 175 years, fought back with weapons from World War I, but finally surrendered on May 17 after the Germans demolished Rotterdam and Middleburg from the air.

The day before the Dutch surrendered, President Roosevelt called a special session of Congress to request emergency appropriations for national defense. He said to the solemn conclave, "These are ominous days—days whose swift and shocking developments force every neutral nation to look to its defense in the light of new factors. The brutal force of modern offensive war has been loosed in all its horror . . . The American people must recast their thinking about national protection . . . [which] calls for ready-at-hand weapons capable of great mobility because of the potential speed of modern attack." The president explained that the Pacific and Atlantic Oceans were "reasonably adequate defensive barriers when . . . fleets and convoys propelled by steam could sail the oceans at fifteen or twenty miles an hour [at most]." But now, he warned, "air navigation steps up the speed of possible attack to two hundred, to three hundred miles an hour."[21]

Roosevelt wanted the country to drastically increase production of warplanes and other equipment. Of Germany, he said, "One belligerent power not only has many more planes than all its opponents combined, but also appears to have a weekly production capacity at the moment that is far greater than that of all its opponents." He noted, "During the past year, American production capacity for war planes, including engines, has risen from approximately 6,000 planes a year to more than double that number, due . . . to the placing of foreign orders here." Then the president said, "I should like to see this nation geared up to . . . turn out at least 50,000 planes a year." He also said the Army must "procure more equipment of all kinds, including motor transport and artillery, tanks,

21. Roosevelt, "Address to Special Session of Congress, May 16, 1940."

anti-aircraft guns, and full ammunition supplies." Roosevelt requested $1.2 billion ($18 billion), almost doubling the current military budget, saying, "Our defense as it was yesterday, or even as it is today, does not provide security against potential developments and dangers of the future."[22]

Jones immediately conferred with the president and announced two days later, "We can loan to aircraft plants which want to expand or to any other business which wants to expand to promote the national defense programs . . . It will be just another loan to business of the type we have been making for a long time." Newspapers covering his announcement noted that the RFC had just loaned $5 million ($75 million) to Boeing Aircraft Company to enlarge its plant.[23] Soon forty aircraft manufacturers were on their way to Washington to see Jones. He also began meeting with metal manufacturers and raw material importers to figure out how to build up large quantities of strategic materials. The vast amounts of tin, rubber, aluminum, magnesium, and steel essential to creating Roosevelt's hoped for air armada were currently not available to U.S. industry.

Within a week, the Senate had approved more for national defense than the president had requested. Funds were allocated for tanks, battleships, aircraft carriers, submarines, and hundreds of new military bases, along with armor, weapons, and ammunition for the nation's rapidly expanding armed forces. One-quarter of the current $3.2 billion ($48 billion) military budget was devoted to building 50,000 airplanes.

President Roosevelt delivered a "Fireside Chat" on May 26 to talk "about a number of subjects that directly affect the future of the United States." He painted a harrowing picture: "Tonight over the once peaceful roads of Belgium and France, millions are now moving, running from their homes to escape bombs and shells and fire and machine gunning, without shelter, and almost wholly without food." He said, "The past two weeks have meant the shattering of many illusions," and suggested that listeners "calmly consider what we have done and what we must do." The president talked in detail about the military buildup and said planes "cost money—a lot of it." He spelled it out, "One modern interceptor pursuit plane costs $133,000 [$2 million]; one medium bomber costs $160,000 [$2.4 million]." He continued, "I know that private business cannot be expected to make all of the capital investment required for [the] expansions of plants and factories and personnel which this program calls for at once . . . Therefore, the government of the United States stands ready

22. Ibid.
23. *Houston Chronicle*, May 18, 1940.

to advance the necessary money to help provide for the enlargement of factories, the establishment of new plants, the employment of thousands of necessary workers, the development of new sources of supply for the hundreds of raw materials required, the development of quick mass transportation of supplies." He said, "The details of all of this are now being worked out in Washington, day and night."[24] "All of this" would essentially fall to Jones and the RFC.

On May 28 Belgium fell to the Germans. Roosevelt promptly asked Congress for $1 billion ($15 billion) more in military spending. Jones also asked Congress for additional "powers to make defense loans for plant construction and expansion" and further "to extend the RFC's life five more years and to increase its lending power another $1.5 billion [$22.5 billion]."[25] Pearson and Allen reported, "Jesse Jones, Federal Loan Administrator, is playing a much greater part in the national defense picture than most people realize."[26] On June 22, Germany conquered France, two weeks after Norway capitulated. From his invasion of Poland in September 1939 to occupying France, Hitler had mowed down Europe in nine months' time. Great Britain was the only nation left standing between Hitler and the rest of the world.[27]

Congress gave Jones the power he requested. He recalled, "The Act of June 25, 1940—which gave us the dictionary—authorized us to purchase plants, lease plants, build plants, whatever we wished, and in any way we might find feasible." He continued, "It empowered the RFC to manufacture arms, to train aviators, to do almost anything else that would strengthen the nation's armed might. We could buy or build anything the President defined as strategic or critical."[28] Jones and the RFC almost immediately formed the Rubber Reserve Company and the Metals Reserve Company to begin accumulating and stockpiling strategic materials from around the world. Those were the first of seven major RFC corporations established to respond to the global emergency. Before Congress acted, the RFC could make loans only if they were sound and backed by proper collateral; now it could lend for national defense without restriction.[29] Jones's role would dwarf what he had done during the Great Depression.

Over the years people had pushed Jones to run for president or vice

24. Roosevelt, "Fireside Chat radio address, May 26, 1940."
25. Jones, *Fifty Billion Dollars*, 341.
26. Pearson and Allen, "Washington Merry-Go-Round," June 18, 1940.
27. Leuchtenburg, *Roosevelt and the New Deal*, 299.
28. Jones, *Fifty Billion Dollars*, 341.
29. White, *Billions for Defense*, 17.

president. As the 1940 Democratic national convention approached, the political pace picked up. The Republicans had selected Wendell Wilkie, who had recently switched parties, as its presidential candidate. Head of a public utility company, Commonwealth and Southern Corporation, Wilkie had never held an elective office. Oregon Senator Charles McNary, who had authored the McNary-Haugen bill in the 1920s to support agriculture and farmers, was Wilkie's running mate. Interior Secretary Harold Ickes wrote in his diary, "It was the general opinion that the Republicans had nominated their strongest possible ticket."[30] On the Democratic side, Roosevelt would not declare his intention to run for a third term, so the position was wide open.

Jones, among many others, was "boomed" for president. The Detroit papers were particularly enthusiastic. General Motors President Bill Knudsen sent Jones an editorial from one of the papers that said, "The quest of the Democratic party for a distinguished member of its own organization qualified to be president . . . must very logically lead to serious consideration of Chairman Jesse H. Jones of the Reconstruction Finance Corporation."[31] Charles "Chick" Fisher sent Jones a *Detroit Times* editorial, which said, "Mr. Jones refutes the erroneous impression the New Deal has been entirely barren of good and sound American leadership. He most certainly refutes the mistaken assumption that the Democratic Party has no leader worthy and capable of succeeding Mr. Roosevelt."[32] And William Randolph Hearst titled an editorial, "Jesse Jones—Fitted for Presidency," sending a copy to Jones.[33]

Roosevelt did not want to appear to be seeking a third term, something George Washington and Thomas Jefferson had refused to do, and instead hoped for his spontaneous draft by the convention.[34] The convention began in Chicago on July 15, with no leader to unify and excite the party. Commerce Secretary Harry Hopkins, Interior Secretary Ickes, and Labor Secretary Frances Perkins begged Roosevelt to attend, but he refused. He wanted the convention to come to him and arranged to send Eleanor instead.[35] On Tuesday night, Senator Alben Barkley read Roosevelt's state-

---

30. Ickes, *Secret Diary*, 223 (entry for June 30, 1940).

31. Bill Knudsen to Jesse Jones, May 20, 1940, Jesse H. Jones Collection [LOC].

32. *Detroit Times*, July 6, 1940; Charles Fisher to Jesse Jones, July 12, 1940, Jesse H. Jones Collection [LOC].

33. William Randolph Hearst to Jesse Jones, May 22, 1940, Jesse H. Jones Collection [LOC].

34. Goodwin, *No Ordinary Time*, 113.

35. Ibid., 125.

ment where he said he had "no wish to be a candidate" and that "all the delegates to this convention are free to vote for any candidate." But he did not refuse to run if nominated. After Barkley finished, from out of no-where—like a match lighting gas—a voice filled the auditorium, "We want Roosevelt!" The invisible prompt ignited the crowd and delegates poured into the aisles to demonstrate for Roosevelt. It was discovered later that Chicago Mayor Edward Kelly had placed the superintendent of sewers in front of a microphone in the auditorium basement with instructions to begin the chant as soon as Senator Barkley ended. The next day Roosevelt won the nomination on the first vote.[36]

Jockeying began among the viable candidates for vice president. Many, including the American Federation of Labor, Democratic National Committee Chairman and Postmaster James Farley, and Roosevelt's son, Elliot, wanted Jones on the ticket. The *Houston Chronicle* reported, "Some of his close friends think that [Jones] would accept the nomination if it were tendered to him."[37] Jones said later that he had been prepared to accept the nomination if Roosevelt offered it to him, but only if he could select his successor as federal loan administrator.[38] Elliot Roosevelt visited Jones at his hotel and said, "Farley is going to place you in nomination, and I am going to second it."[39] But by then, Roosevelt had selected Agriculture Secretary Henry A. Wallace as his running mate and would accept no one else. When Farley met Eleanor Roosevelt at the Chicago airport, and they were on their way to her hotel, she said she thought it "was a mistake to nominate Wallace." She soon phoned her husband and said, "I've been talking with Jim Farley and I agree with him, Henry Wallace won't do."[40] She echoed Farley's opinion, saying, "Jesse Jones would bolster the ticket, win it business support, and get the party contributions."[41] Determined to get his way, however, Roosevelt drafted a speech refusing the nomination unless Wallace was selected as his running mate.

Hopkins told Jones the president wanted Wallace.[42] Jones then informed the Texas delegation that he did not want to have his name placed in nomination except "after suggestion by President Roosevelt." When a member of the Maryland delegation unexpectedly nominated Jones

36. Ibid., 128.
37. *Houston Chronicle*, July 17, 1940.
38. Jones, *Fifty Billion Dollars*, 278.
39. Ibid.
40. Roosevelt, *Autobiography of Eleanor Roosevelt*, 216–17.
41. Jones, *Fifty Billion Dollars*, 279.
42. Timmons, *Jones: Man and Statesman*, 278.

anyway, he left his seat next to Mary and their guest Edith Wilson and made his way to the podium to deliver a statement to the convention. He said in part, "Since coming to Chicago, I have had many voluntary offers of support for the Vice Presidency by delegates from almost every state in the Union, and this I keenly appreciate, but at no time have I been a candidate, and [I] have requested that my name be not presented to the Convention."[43] Cheers and applause rang out as Jones began to speak, followed by cries of "no" when he declined the nomination.

Wallace's idealism, liberalism, and reputed mysticism put off many in the party. Boos, hisses, and catcalls filled the arena when his name was placed before the convention. But his policies, the geographic advantages he brought as an Iowan, and his experience as Agriculture Secretary, publisher, and a hybrid seed developer appealed to Roosevelt, and Wallace offered a clear alternative to the Republican's candidate, McNary.

Eleanor Roosevelt spoke after the nominating speeches and before the balloting for vice president—the first time a first lady had ever addressed a national convention. Her words transformed the disgruntled room. She began by thanking Farley, the retiring Democratic National Committee chairman, saying, "Nobody could appreciate more what he has done for the party, what he has given in work and loyalty." The first lady continued, "This is no ordinary time, no time for weighing anything except what we can best do for the country as a whole." She asked the delegates to respect the president's judgment and to give him what he asked for. The voting commenced after Eleanor's rousing speech, and Wallace won on the first ballot.[44] When Wallace thanked Roosevelt, the president advised him to seek out the other leading candidates, including Jones, and to thank them for their "sportsmanship."[45] Speaking from Hyde Park, his words amplified for the convention, Roosevelt informed the gathered delegates and the nation that he accepted the nomination and was running for a third term.

Jones's power most likely would have shrunk had he been nominated and elected vice president. He reported to Roosevelt in early August that "under RFC authority to aid in the national defense," the Corporation had so far committed $70 million ($1 billion) to buy and stockpile rubber, and $105 million ($1.6 billion) for tin. The RFC had loaned $92 million ($1.4 billion) to the Wright Aeronautical Corporation to construct a plant for the

43. Jesse Jones, statement to Democratic National Convention, July 18, 1940, Jesse H. Jones Collection [LOC].

44. Goodwin, *No Ordinary Time*, 133.

45. Pearson and Allen, "Washington Merry-Go-Round," July 25, 1940.

manufacture of airplane engines. It had also made a $16 million ($240 million) loan to Reynolds Metal Company to manufacture aluminum—a loan that effectively destroyed Alcoa's monopoly on the metal. In all, Jones detailed $608 million ($9.2 billion) in ongoing or proposed projects, mostly for rubber and airplanes.[46]

Jones then informed the president that Congress was trying to block additional RFC borrowing authority for defense and instead wanted to direct the appropriations to the War and Navy Departments. The problem was, while the War and Navy Departments had appropriations to acquire airplanes, ships, tanks, weapons, and ammunition, most of their orders could not be filled until manufacturing capacity was expanded or built. That was the RFC's job. Jones continued, "It appears that we will need some additional borrowing authority, and I should like to know your pleasure about our asking for it." Roosevelt wrote on the letter, "OK—Why not $1,000,000,000?" and sent it back.[47] After testifying before Congress, Jones got $1 billion ($15 billion) more for the RFC and $500 million ($7.5 billion) more for the Export-Import Bank.

Within days he set up two new corporations. The Defense Supplies Corporation (DSC) was established to "produce, acquire, and carry critical and strategic materials, including particularly 100-octane gasoline."[48] Only 30,000 barrels of 100-octane gasoline were currently being produced each year; Roosevelt's 50,000 airplanes would require billions more.[49] And on August 22, two days before Germany dropped its first bombs on London, the Defense Plant Corporation (DPC) was established to supply the almost limitless capital needed to expand the nation's industrial base. The DPC was possibly the most important RFC wartime agency.

To coordinate the massive military buildup, Roosevelt formed the National Defense Advisory Council (NDAC) with seven commissioners, each with a different responsibility and a separate division. One appointee was Knudsen who was responsible for plant expansion. He immediately turned to the RFC, knowing it had the resources, the infrastructure, and the ability to act fast. Jones and Knudsen had a direct telephone line installed between their offices and for a while spoke many times each day.

The NDAC devised the Emergency Plant Facilities Contract (EPFC), which enabled manufacturers to borrow from banks and the RFC to build

46. Jesse Jones to Franklin Roosevelt, August 3, 1940, Jesse H. Jones Collection [LOC].
47. Ibid.
48. Jesse Jones to Emil Schram, August 16, 1940, Jesse H. Jones Collection [LOC].
49. Jones, *Fifty Billion Dollars*, 354.

or expand their plants, while using the proceeds from guaranteed sales to the armed services to pay back their loans. As an added incentive, they could write off twenty percent of their investment each year. Essentially manufacturers were invited to join in a no-risk deal with no money down and get a free plant after the war.[50] RFC attorneys Clifford J. Durr and Hans Klagsbrunn, infused with the Corporation's ethos of protecting taxpayers' money, had other ideas. They thought the better deal was to have the government build or expand the plants, retain title to them, lease the facilities to operators, and then give the operators options to purchase the plants after the war.[51] Jones agreed with his attorneys, despite the angst among many about government ownership and control.

As clouds of destruction shrouded Europe and the Pacific, and desperate appeals began coming from England for assistance, public debate about the military buildup escalated. By now the U.S. government was doing everything possible "short of war." Meanwhile, Hopkins resigned as Secretary of Commerce because of health. Hopkins had headed the Federal Emergency Relief Administration, the Civil Works Administration, and the Works Progress Administration during the Great Depression. He was extremely close to the president, had lived at the White House, and even stood in for Roosevelt at the national convention.[52] Either to diminish Jones's power, to keep a closer eye on him, or to give him something in return for his lost chance at the vice presidency, President Roosevelt asked Jones to take Hopkins's place in his cabinet. Jones took "the offer under advisement"[53] and soon made it clear he would not accept the cabinet post unless he could retain his position as federal loan administrator. If Roosevelt and others were hoping to rein in Jones's power by moving him away from the RFC, then they miscalculated. Once the invitation was made and Jones offered his conditions, popular opinion forced Roosevelt to acquiesce.

Holding two government jobs at once was against the law, so Jones's cabinet appointment required a joint resolution from Congress. As if there were no question about accommodating Jones's demand, Steve Early, Roosevelt's press secretary, promptly wrote to Jones's chief assistant, Bill Costello, that the attorney general had drafted, and the president had approved, the joint resolution for Congress. Knowing that Jones could get

50. White, *Billions for Defense*, 9.
51. Ibid., 15.
52. *Houston Chronicle*, August 24, 1940.
53. *Houston Chronicle*, August 25, 1940.

Congress unanimously exempted Jesse Jones from federal laws prohibiting one person from holding two government jobs. When Jones became secretary of commerce and federal loan administrator, conservative Republican Senator Robert A. Taft remarked, "I have no great objection to giving Mr. Jones the additional power to act also as secretary of commerce, but I think it is an extraordinary precedent, which is justified only by the character of the man and which I hope may not be repeated" (*Houston Chronicle*, September 8, 1940).

Congressional approval more quickly than anyone else, Early wrote, "As I told Mr. Jones on the telephone today, we are leaving to him the task of having this joint resolution introduced into the Congress and passed by the Congress as expeditiously as possible."[54]

54. Steve Early to Bill Costello, August 26, 1940, Jesse H. Jones Collection [LOC].

Pearson and Allen wasted no time weighing in. They reported, "Reason for Roosevelt's request to Congress for special legislation permitting Jesse Jones to be both Loan Administrator and Secretary of Commerce was that this was the only condition on which the wily Texan would accept the cabinet post." They elaborated, "It was also the reason for that unusual White House announcement that Jones had been offered Harry Hopkins' job but still was undecided about taking it . . . Jesse wasn't so eager for the title of Secretary to be willing to swap it for the vast power he wields as Federal Loan Administrator." They said Jones suspected "a secret scheme to kick him upstairs" and that he "refused to budge." The columnists concluded, "Reason Roosevelt was forced to give in is that Jones is the most powerful one-man lobby on Capitol Hill. He can get anything he wants out of Congress." They gave Jones a little and added that he "has been doing a magnificent job for Roosevelt in getting certain key appropriations passed."[55]

Jones explained his reluctance to leave his position as federal loan administrator to Vice President Garner, writing, "I feel that I should continue the supervision particularly of the RFC since much of its authority has been given to it by Congress upon my advice and testimony, and in the belief that I would look after it. I feel this responsibility keenly and would not like to be taken away from it for any cause."[56]

On September 11 the U.S. Senate unanimously exempted Jones from federal laws prohibiting one person from holding two government jobs.[57] New Deal opponent, anti-interventionist, and perennial Republican presidential hopeful Senator Robert A. Taft from Ohio did not oppose the resolution, but said during the debate, "I merely wish to call attention to the fact that Mr. Jones already probably has more power than any other man in the government, with the single exception of the president. He has unlimited power to lend money to anyone, to any industry in the United States, or refuse to lend . . . I do not think that, with the exception noted, any man in the United States ever has enjoyed so much power." The conservative senator concluded, "I have no great objection to giving Mr. Jones the additional power to act also as secretary of commerce, but I think it is an extraordinary precedent, which is justified only by the character of the man and which I hope may not be repeated."[58] Supreme Court Justice

55. Pearson and Allen, "Washington Merry-Go-Round," August 30, 1940.
56. Jesse Jones to John Nance Garner, August 30, 1940, Jesse H. Jones Collection [LOC].
57. *Houston Chronicle*, September 11, 1940.
58. *Houston Chronicle*, September 8, 1940.

Jesse Jones is sworn in as Secretary of Commerce on September 19, 1940, by Associate Supreme Court Justice Stanley Reed, who was formerly the RFC's general counsel. Courtesy Corbis.

Stanley Reed, who had previously served as RFC general counsel, administered the oath of office to his former boss in President Roosevelt's office. President Roosevelt, Mary, Jones's sister Elizabeth, his secretary Gladys Mikell, and his assistant Costello attended. Afterward Roosevelt said, "I'm giving you a lot more work to do now, Jesse."[59]

The need for war production was great. The British were desperate for arms, and they were running out of cash. Public opinion was split: many in the United States wanted new military equipment kept in the country for its own defense, while others wanted weapons sent overseas to keep the war "over there." Meanwhile, plane production was still stymied. At present there were only three companies manufacturing high-horsepower aircraft engines and only thirteen airframe plants operating in the United States. Supplies of steel, aluminum, magnesium, tin, rubber, and hundreds of other mandatory materials were completely inadequate

59. *Houston Chronicle*, September 19, 1940.

to meet the urgent demand.[60] To break the bottleneck, the DPC signed the first contract using its pioneering lease agreement in September. Upon request from Knudsen and the NDAC, the DPC bought $8 million ($120 million) in machinery and equipment, and leased it to the Packard Motor Car Company so Packard could produce eight hundred aircraft engines every month. To cover rent on the equipment, Packard paid the DPC $1,500 ($22,500) for each engine it sold to the U.S. government. Packard had an open option to purchase all of the equipment at cost, plus four percent annual interest on the loan, and less ten percent annual depreciation on the equipment.[61] The efficient, standardized DPC lease agreement quickly became preferred over the NDAC's EPF contract, which depended on banks and often exceeded their lending limits because of the size of the investments required. The NDAC contract was also complicated. Throughout the war, less than $350 million ($5.3 billion) was invested in industrial plants through the EPF contract.[62] The DPC, however, quietly signed contracts under its own lease agreement for almost that amount during the last months of 1940, more than a year before the U.S. officially entered the war.

Rubber was front and center, along with airplanes. Jones reported to Roosevelt, "I am prepared to recommend that the RFC finance the construction of [a] synthetic rubber manufacturing plant, or plants, preferably to be built and operated by one or more of the companies that have been experimenting with synthetic rubber." He noted that the U.S. stockpile of raw rubber was approaching 415,000 tons "if the raw rubber supply is not cut off or seriously interrupted," which was not quite enough to last one year. He also wrote that the British and Dutch cartels were "extremely anxious to sell . . . rubber and are not enthusiastic about our building synthetic plants." Jones asked for the president's approval and concluded, "We will pursue the matter with a view to building one, two, or three small plants at a total cost of not more than ____." Jones left a blank, which Roosevelt filled in with "$25,000,000 [$375 million]."[63]

Rubber industry executives and the NDAC had hoped for a lot more, but at that point, according to Jones, synthesizing rubber was speculative and had not yet "emerged from the test-tube stage." Rubber, oil, and

---

60. White, *Billions for Defense*, 19.
61. Ibid., 25
62. Ibid., 33, 30.
63. Jesse Jones to Franklin Roosevelt, September 16, 1940, Jesse H. Jones Collection [LOC].

chemical companies had all been experimenting with the process, and each had different formulas and theories. Goodrich had just introduced the revolutionary half-synthetic rubber "Ameripol" tire. Plantations in Indonesia, Singapore, and Malaysia continued to supply most of the rubber consumed in the United States, and the Japanese were closing in.

Rubber was essential to the war effort. It was required for tires, tubes, belts, and hoses. Airplanes required massive rubber tires. A single armored tank contained one-half ton of rubber. Jeeps needed tires. Battleships had 20,000 rubber parts. Rubber covered electric wire. Without rubber, the United States and the rest of the world would be—literally— stuck in place and left in the dark.

The emerging military and domestic economies also needed a lot of metal. During those same pivotal months, the *New York Times* reported on a $25 million ($375 million) RFC loan to China: "[To] secur[e] the loan, Jesse Jones, Federal Loan Administrator, announced that the United States would obtain from China $30 million [$450 million] worth of tungsten to build up its reserve stocks of this essential material not produced in quantity in this country." The article pointed out, "It was regarded as significant that the announcement of the loan to China tonight was made by Mr. Jones rather than by the State Department or the White House." The reporter explained, "A direct loan to China by this country would constitute an unfriendly act," and noted that "Japan today encircles Hong Kong." Jones made an official statement, reporting that earlier loans to China were being repaid with tin and wood oil essential to paint, both urgently needed for national defense; sounding as if he were referring to a domestic farm program or a struggling bank, he closed, "Of all loans heretofore authorized to China, both by the RFC and the Export-Import Bank, $43,824,528 [$657 million] has been disbursed and $13,160,253 [$198 million] repaid, with nothing past due."[64]

The day after the Chinese deal was announced, word came about a $20 million ($300 million) loan the Export-Import Bank had just arranged with Brazil to help "set up her own steel industry." The report said, "The . . . agreement makes accessible Brazil's vast iron resources that have been dormant for centuries," and that the deal "is a blow to the non-American nations that have been coveting the rich Brazilian iron deposits."[65] Of course, the deal had strings—Brazil had to put up $25 million ($375 million). In his committal letter to the president of the Brazilian Steel Plan Jones explained, "The management of the enterprise should include man-

64. *New York Times*, September 26, 1940.
65. *New York Times*, September 27, 1940.

agerial officers and engineers experienced in the manufacture of steel in the United States until successful operation has been assured to the mutual satisfaction of the Export-Import Bank and Brazilian investors."[66]

In the fall, the RFC established the Defense Homes Corporation, its fifth wartime organization, to build housing for defense workers as they poured into areas where factories were all of the sudden humming twenty-four hours a day. The president of each RFC wartime agency also served on the RFC board. Emil Schram was president of the Defense Plant Corporation, Howard Klossner served as president of the Rubber Reserve Company, Sam Husbands ran the Defense Supplies Corporation, and Charles B. Henderson was president of Metals Reserve Company. They coordinated their far-flung and complex activities at RFC board meetings. As the RFC evolved from domestic economics to global defense, its efficiency never faltered.

The *Wall Street Journal* reported in September, "The multi-billion dollar Reconstruction Finance Corp. is one of the more important units in the Government's program to develop, in private industry, facilities for speeding up national defense production." The report recounted, "The world's largest lending agency has already loaned or committed more than a half billion dollars for industry plant expansion and other defense objectives, including the storing of essential defense materials such as rubber, metals, and high-test aviation gasoline . . . The man behind the RFC funds is Texan Jesse Jones." After describing the RFC's growing trade with Latin America, the article concluded, "It appears that on the one hand the Government's No.1 banker is participating in the national defense program to meet any industrial demands for capital, and on the other he is planning a long-range post-war trade program for American industry."[67] Cultivating Latin American markets was at Roosevelt's behest, who wrote Jones, "Because markets for forty percent of the normal exports of Latin America have been lost due to the war, there is grave danger that in some of these countries economic and political deterioration may proceed to a point where defense of the western hemisphere would be rendered much more difficult and costly." The president asked Jones to "give sympathetic consideration to Latin American products in the procurement of strategic and critical materials for the defense program." Possibly reminding Jones who was boss, he concluded with

66. Jesse Jones to Dr. Guilherme Guinle, September 26, 1940, Jesse H. Jones Collection [LOC].

67. *Wall Street Journal*, September 16, 1940.

emphasis, "When buying in foreign markets for defense needs, it is my earnest desire that priority of consideration be given to Latin American products and I so request."[68]

In response, Jones appointed Houstonian Will Clayton as deputy federal loan administrator, saying, "We expect to expand our whole study of the South American situation and want as much talent as possible."[69] Clayton knew how to trade commodities and how to negotiate. He had formed Anderson, Clayton, and Company in 1904 with several relatives, turning it into the largest cotton brokerage in the world.[70] He had just served a six-month stint as Nelson Rockefeller's deputy coordinator of inter-American affairs at the State Department and was on his way back to Houston when Jones made his request. At first Clayton refused, so Jones asked Roosevelt to give him a call.[71]

Jones and Clayton had a lot in common. Their ancestors landed in Virginia in the 1600s. Both left school after the eighth grade and went on to obtain great success. They were interested in, and contributed to, Houston's commercial and civic growth, and as young businessmen they had depended on and resented the east coast's financial power and dominance. They participated in Democratic Party politics and both men were tall, commanding, and talented. The Joneses and the Claytons were constant bridge partners and enjoyed many evenings together throughout the war years.

Clayton was particularly skilled in foreign trade and diplomacy, which enabled him as deputy federal loan administrator to wage and win the "Warehouse War." Through the various RFC agencies under his control Clayton bought and "warehoused" essential metals and materials from around the globe. His efforts provided a constant flow of resources to domestic manufacturers gearing up for war, helped align North and South America in a common purpose, and deprived the enemy of precious commodities, forcing the Axis powers to pay much more and even change weapon designs.[72] With Clayton on board and the "Warehouse War" under way, Jones reassured Roosevelt, "We are buying and will continue to buy every exportable commodity in Latin America."[73]

68. Franklin Roosevelt to Jesse Jones, September 27, 1940, Jesse H. Jones Collection [LOC].
69. *Houston Chronicle*, October 18, 1940.
70. Fossedal, *Our Finest Hour*, 26.
71. Ibid., 72.
72. Ibid., 75.
73. Ibid., 76.

As the November election grew near, Jones gave a speech over national radio on "Business and Government." In discussing the RFC, Jones also sought to prove that Roosevelt was the best-qualified candidate, that he supported business, and that national defense was under control. He began by saying it was "the time of year when politics inspires many misleading statements about business for partisan purposes." Now a familiar figure to those listening, Jones could credibly say, "I have been a businessman, as most of you know, all of my life." After he detailed the RFC's accomplishments and contributions over the past eight and a half years, Jones said, "It is the principal vehicle through which this Administration has served and saved business." He explained, "The RFC has been used by the President and Congress through the various stages of recovery, as it is now being used to strengthen [our] defense in a situation which . . . aggressor nations have forced on us." Jones continued, "We are now engaged in lending for the accumulation of reserve supplies of rubber, tin, manganese, and many other critical and strategic materials, which will be necessary in case of an emergency. We are building and financing plants for the manufacture of airplanes and other supplies for national defense." Knowing industrial mobilization was beyond private banks' capacity, he let them off the hook with, "Most of these are loans and investments that private capital cannot take the risk of making. It is clearly a government responsibility and the risk should be taken by the government—it is for all the people."[74]

Jones pointed to the RFC's exemplary record, saying that through its actions and "the other manifold activities of the Roosevelt Administration, the annual national income has been raised from $40 billion [$600 billion] in 1932 to $70 billion [$1 trillion] in 1939, with a further estimated increase for 1940. This increase in national income has brought about better living, better housing, more work for people . . . and a better chance of security in old age." Jones then endorsed Roosevelt, declaring, "The President had the vision and furnished the leadership." He summed up the Roosevelt administration's attitude toward business by saying, "Government makes it possible for business to operate, and business must support government through its earnings. The government must be the umpire. It represents all the people." Stating the obvious, he added, "If everyone followed the Ten Commandments and the Golden rule, we would have no need for laws . . . But they don't."[75]

74. Jesse Jones, NBC radio address, October 7, 1940, Jesse H. Jones Collection [UT].
75. Ibid.

Concluding by comparing Republican Wilkie's lack of experience as a public servant, Jones said, "Franklin D. Roosevelt . . . started as a very young man in local politics and has successively occupied important positions of trust in his county, his state, and his nation. He is well known to you, and the experience he has gained over this long period in dealing with public questions is an invaluable asset at this particular time when the world is on fire and dictators are on the march."[76]

Jones received many letters about his speech, including one from his longtime friend, Captain Baker. The two men had known each other since Jones first arrived in Houston. Jones wrote back, "I enjoy work. I enjoy building—men and institutions. Whatever I have accumulated has been in making values." He continued, "My work in the Government has been along the same constructive lines. I like to believe that I have built many billions of values for the American people, and I also like to believe that I have rebuilt many shattered men, and believe I have." Contradicting popular opinion of his politics, Jones admitted, "I suppose I am a liberal politically, and have always been."[77]

Jones gave another radio speech on the Saturday before the national election. First he scoffed at "the dire predictions as to what may happen to us if President Roosevelt is reelected." He explained, "The strong, the successful, and the well-to-do can look after themselves, but the great majority of the American people . . . do not have any too easy a time making ends meet. Many are actually dependent upon the justice of government, the benefits of our social laws, or the generosity of those who are able and willing to help them." Jones declared, "It is the great majority of our citizenship which President Roosevelt has tried so hard to help. And if reelected, he will continue to help them, not by taking away from the well-to-do, but by continuing to increase the national income, and bringing about a better distribution of that income, so that everyone can have a better chance to make their own way. To be independent."[78]

Jones reminded listeners, "Certainly no man ever came to the Presidency when our country was in a worse economic state than President Roosevelt." Today, "Our industrial institutions are busy, employment is steadily on the increase, and several million more people are now working in private industry, at good wages, than at any time in the last ten years." Jones also pointed out, "Many of the bigwigs in business and finance were

76. Ibid.
77. Jesse Jones to James A. Baker Sr., October 14, 1940, Jesse H. Jones Collection [LOC].
78. Jesse Jones, NBC radio address, November 2, 1940, Jesse H. Jones Collection [UT].

rushing to the government to be saved in 1932 and '33 . . . They were the first to holler in 1931 and '32 when their values were melting and their positions were in jeopardy . . . By no means have all relief recipients been in the WPA. Many were people in high places."[79]

Jones discounted other Republican fears, saying, "We hear a good deal about the disappearance of free enterprise in this country . . . [S]uch talk is pure bunk. Private enterprise in the United States is much freer than in any other country in the world." He cautioned, "I hope we will never risk a return to the conditions of the late twenties, when unbridled speculation got us all in trouble . . . In my opinion, business—big business and little business—does not realize, or is unwilling to admit, just how much the Roosevelt administration has actually done to help business." He recited the RFC's long list of contributions to the nation's recovery and followed, "We must now devote our energies toward national defense, and we are doing that in a big way. And we are perfectly able to do it."[80]

Jones addressed one final point of public concern, "In closing, I want to say just a word about the third term. I realize that some people are concerned over that question. But in making the decisions in life . . . I have never felt it necessary to rely on precedent. I have never felt that I should do something because someone else did." Jones explained, "I try to make my decisions [based] on what I believe to be right under the circumstances at the time. If our forefathers had not broken precedent, we would still be a colony. And fear of breaking the third term precedent should not prevent your voting for the reelection of President Roosevelt."[81]

Roosevelt won the election with 54.8 percent of the vote, his narrowest win so far.[82] The economic recovery may have played a small role. Unemployment had shrunk to 14.6 percent, mostly because the British were buying weapons manufactured in the United States. But it was the fear of war, not the improving economy, that pushed voters to Roosevelt and away from Wilkie.[83]

After not being invited back on the ticket, Vice President Garner had tried to mount a run against Roosevelt. He was opposed to the president's third term, uncomfortable with parts of the New Deal, offended by Roosevelt's attempt to pack the Supreme Court, and worried by the lack of a balanced budget. After the national conventions, he essentially moved

79. Ibid.
80. Ibid.
81. Ibid.
82. Shields-West, *Almanac of Presidential Campaigns*, 181.
83. Kennedy, *Freedom from Fear*, 464.

back to Uvalde and ignored the election. Jones candidly wrote him after Roosevelt's win, "A good deal was said about your not voting, but that was to be expected."[84] Garner responded, "No, I didn't vote, but you can imagine the reason. I never was much of a hand to profess one thing and do another. I prefer to say nothing rather than say something I don't mean."[85] Jones also heard from Miss Blanche, his third-grade teacher, who wondered about the election's impact on her former pupil. Jones informed her, "I will do what I can to assist the President as long as he feels that I can be of assistance. There is much about his Administration that I do not like but a great deal about it that I do like . . . At all events it is over and we will try to make it a success—all of us."[86]

During the Great Depression, Jones enjoyed almost unanimous approval and acclaim from the press, the public, and Congress. As war loomed, that changed. Samuel Lubell's intimate two-part story about Jones in the *Saturday Evening Post* marked the beginning of a turn. In the first installment on November 30, Lubell, an up-and-coming journalist and Bernard Baruch protégé, wrote that "Uncle Jesse . . . homespins himself as a 'country boy from Texas,'" but he quickly exploded that myth, saying, "No New Deal administrator stands higher in the public confidence." He stated, "Next to the President, no man in the Government and probably in the United States wields greater powers." Lubell explained, "Today, Jesse—as he is known to everyone in Washington—could write Government checks up to $2.5 billion [$37.5 billion] before one would bounce . . . Whenever there is a financial chore to be done, he gets the job." As a result, "Almost everyone is nice to Jesse," and members of Congress "stand in awe of him." He said, "When Jesse arrives in town, mayors generally take the day off to pay their respects. Jones is a mighty handy man to have around for a city which wants to build bridges, tunnels, markets, schools and other things."[87]

The reporter expressed qualms about Jones's financial autonomy. He wrote, "So vast are Jesse's powers, so tricky the techniques of financial control, that it is virtually impossible for anyone short of a congressional investigating committee to check the RFC's operations . . . Where RFC power begins and ends, no one can say." Lubell added, "Jones, who

84. Jesse Jones to John Nance Garner, November 13, 1940, Jesse H. Jones Collection [LOC].

85. John Nance Garner to Jesse Jones, November 19, 1940, Jesse H. Jones Collection [LOC].

86. Jesse Jones to Blanche Babcock, November 13, 1940, Jesse H. Jones Collection [LOC].

87. Lubell, "New Deal's J. P. Morgan," 9–10.

handles more of Uncle Sam's coin than any other one person, submits no accounting to the President." He continued, "The ceiling on Jesse's lending power is so high as to be meaningless. Jones, not Congress, decides how much of the billions entrusted to him is or is not to be loaned." Lubell said Jones could "stimulate competition in any field" and he used the loan to Reynolds Metal Company and its effect on Alcoa as an example. Lubell then listed Jones's thirteen RFC corporations, eight Commerce Department bureaus, and seventeen advisory and honorary jobs, observing, "To say that Jones holds more jobs than any Government official before him is an understatement." He said that Jesse is not "a figurehead. Over all RFC subsidiaries, he is absolute lord and master." Lubell described how Jones goes "visiting" on Capitol Hill, embraces doubtful members in a "fatherly fashion," and invites them to "come on in and have a drink of the Vice President's whisky" (a custom that would end after Wallace was inaugurated and banned alcohol from his Senate chambers). Lubell also revealed, "Jesse is known as Washington's leading off-color storyteller," a presumed boon in Congressional hallways. Other observations—that he was "shy and timid socially" and that he had read only one book in the last ten years—were off the mark, though part of the popular image. Hitting closer to home, Lubell said Jones was "thin-skinned" and "likes flattery, delights in having his photograph taken, and often will print up his speeches in little booklets and distribute them."[88]

It was less about Jones's personal foibles, however, than his power and influence that concerned the reporter. Lubell wrote, "The President . . . facing defeat or an embarrassing fight on a measure, can get his blank check if he will agree to let Jones endorse it." He elaborated, "Through the last eight years, Jesse has remained in the middle between crusading New Dealers and becrusaded [sic] businessmen; between spenders and budget balancers, Democrats and Republicans, Congress and the President. In the amazing bargain that Jesse has struck between these conflicting elements lies the explanation of the unique one-man Government role he is playing." Lubell declared, "In all American history there is no parallel for it."[89] And that was only the first, relatively mild, part of the article.

The second part, published one week later, was accompanied by an editorial that compared Jones to "Aladdin with the wonderful lamp in his lap," adding, "New Deal finance required magic, and he was the master magician." The editorial described the RFC as the "Government's alter

88. Ibid., 11, 92.
89. Ibid., 88.

ego," noting that "it might embarrass the Government diplomatically to make direct loans to China as a belligerent; therefore . . . let the RFC do it."[90] The editorial argued that the RFC as the fourth branch of government had gone too far.

Lubell's second installment had a sharper tone than the first. He said Jones "handles Congress as if it were composed of overeager children, at times acts as a parental brake on the President, and also likes to play the role of father confessor and Lord Bountiful to friends and employees." All of that may have been true, but Jones did not want it publicized. Lubell accused Jones of being "fussy," "demanding," and "crafty," which was also true, and that he "dreaded meeting people and never had a real pal," both of which were false. Lubell paid homage to Jones's father and Aunt Nancy and repeated the story about the hungry Tennessee neighbors who borrowed hams, adding, "Jones' handling of the RFC smokehouse reveals evidences of both his father's paternalistic generosity and Aunt Nancy's collecting efficiency." As Lubell speculated about Jones's life story, he observed that Jones was "always extending himself to prove that the uneducated country boy can beat the best of them."[91]

Lubell recounted the RFC's great success during the Great Depression, "To Jones, the profit is the line of credit on which the House of Jesse rests. Without it, he knows he would be unable to maintain the bargain he has struck between Congress and the President." Lubell ended the exposé by suggesting that "RFC lending in different fields could be separated, some powers scrapped, others given to the President, others kept by Congress. That would mean the end of the RFC as a fourth branch of Government and would restore to elected representatives the responsibility for the far-reaching economic decisions now made by Jones." Lubell accurately predicted, "Failing some such solution, it would seem only a matter of time . . . for the house that Jesse built to become the prize of a crucial struggle for control."[92]

Jones was not amused. In a speech to life insurance executives, he said, "I want to deny entire responsibility for the *Saturday Evening Post* article. I did not like the article in any sense. I am not powerful, not even at home. I am a public servant who takes his responsibilities seriously and does the best he can with the things that are given him to do."[93] Jones responded

90. "Billions Wild," editorial, 28.

91. Lubell, "New Deal's J. P. Morgan," 29, 107.

92. Ibid., 116.

93. Jesse Jones, speech, 34th Annual Convention of the Association of Life Insurance Presidents, New York, December 5, 1940, Jesse H. Jones Collection [UT].

to an acquaintance about the articles, "I was glad to have your letter but, frankly, I did not appreciate much of the stories."[94]

Jones had had the privilege of reviewing and revising the *Fortune* magazine article from six months ago, which basically said the same things as the *Saturday Evening Post* article, but arrived at a different conclusion, saying the RFC's power was not a threat as long as Jones was in charge and operated it, as he did, in a transparent "goldfish bowl." Jones had reproduced the *Fortune* article and sent it to everyone he knew, including directors of the RFC's thirty-two branches. This was not the case with Lubell's articles. After receiving an inquiry from the *Saturday Evening Post* about copies, Jones's assistant wrote back, "Mr. Jones has decided that he does not want any reprints of the article."[95]

Despite growing concerns about national defense and the mind-boggling raft of responsibilities Jones had to manage, he still found time to relax. When he wasn't working in the evening, Jones frequently played cards with Mary, Edith Wilson, the Claytons, Stewart McDonald, and other friends and colleagues. Pearson and Allen once reported, "There's never a dull moment when Jesse Jones, Secretary of Commerce and Federal Loan Administrator, plays cards with his good friend Defense Commissioner William Knudsen. The two men carry on a running fire of ribbing." One night, the reporters disclosed, Jones chided Knudsen for his one-dollar bet and said he was risking "a whole year's pay on one card. That's downright reckless." The reporters revealed that "Knudsen resigned a $300,000 [$4.5 million] job to come to Washington, [and] now gets $1 a year. He insisted all night that he was 'just learning the game,' but wound up winner of $60."[96] Jones also enjoyed the occasional party. These ranged from an off-the-record National Press Club roast where ten possible candidates explained why they were not qualified to be President[97] to a dinner honoring the Brazilian delegation.[98]

For her part, Mary attended events with Jesse and played bridge, studied French and Spanish, and had weekly luncheons with Edith Wilson. Although they were not close, Mary occasionally socialized with Eleanor Roosevelt. At the beginning of the year, the first lady invited Mary to be

94. Jesse Jones to Joseph Stephenson, December 10, 1940, Jesse H. Jones Collection [UT].

95. William Costello to Martin Sommers, December 11, 1940, Jesse H. Jones Collection [UT].

96. Pearson and Allen, "Washington Merry-Go-Round," October 4, 1940.

97. *New York Times*, March 2, 1940.

98. *New York Times*, August 7, 1940.

her guest in the presidential box at a morning musicale held at the May-flower Hotel. Lotte Lehmann and Lauritz Melchior from the Metropolitan Opera performed for hundreds of Washington dignitaries before a beautiful luncheon.[99] Soon after the November election, Mary began planning a luncheon in honor of the first lady. Reciprocating in early 1941, Mrs. Roosevelt wrote Mary, "My daughter and her husband will be here for the Inauguration, and they have expressed a desire to see you and Mr. Jones while they are here. Will you and the Secretary dine with us on January 20th at eight o'clock informally? We hope very much to see you."[100] Mary accepted. Jones felt comfortable enough to approach the first lady on behalf of his friends, the Claytons (Clayton's wife was reputedly one of President Roosevelt's biggest financial donors). He first explained, "Mr. and Mrs. W. L. Clayton, of Houston, are living in Washington" and that "the President and the Administration have no greater friend or advocate than Mrs. Clayton." He then requested, "Mrs. Jones and I would appreciate it if you could include the Claytons sometimes in your White House social functions."[101]

Jones revealed his soft side and his feelings toward his wife in a simple poem he composed for Mary on December 15, their twentieth wedding anniversary. He wrote:

TO MY WIFE

If you gaze into this crystal clear,
All past pleasures will there appear,
These years so full of interesting things
We must admit have gone on wings.

And so they go, these pesky old years,
But not one shall carry tears.
It's on and on, up and about,
We'll do it together, we'll work it out.

Since 1920, what do you see?
From a Houston roof-top to RFC,
(And because you were ever beside me, dear)
A Cabinet chair is reflected clear.

99. *New York Times*, January 9, 1941.
100. Eleanor Roosevelt to Mary Gibbs Jones, January 8, 1941, Jesse H. Jones Collection [HE].
101. February 14, 1941, Jesse H. Jones Collection [LOC].

Your love, your courage, your patient ways,
Have filled with graciousness all our days.
Oh! They've never been dull, but the greatest fun—
These twenty years that seem like one!

So here's to you, my love, my dear,
Yours is the voice I want ever to hear,
May you always be like you are today,
Without a change, no other way.

The Joneses went to Houston on December 21 to enjoy the holidays with family and to celebrate the hundredth anniversary of the Houston Chamber of Commerce, at which Jones was the speaker. The Chamber had been chartered in 1840 by Texas President Mirabeau B. Lamar, the same year when 240 Houstonians—ten percent of the city's population—died from yellow fever. One hundred years later, 400,000 people lived in Houston. At the sold-out banquet, the Houston Symphony performed, the San Jacinto Monument Museum provided a display of historical artifacts, the manager of radio station KPRC presented a dramatization of the chamber's history, Mary lit a ceremonial candle, and sixteen living past presidents of the Chamber of Commerce were honored.[102] Then Jones delivered a rousing speech.

Just as he had pushed bankers to lend, he jumped on the civic leaders once more and told them to fix up the city. He said, "We must not fail to provide essential facilities . . . if we are to be a city of opportunity, a desirable city in which to live." Jones complained about streets, drainage, sanitation, the water supply, and the police, then admonished, "Houston has many natural advantages and is destined to be a much greater cultural and industrial center. It is the responsibility of our generation to see that it is not retarded in its march to that destiny."[103]

From local concerns Jones moved straight to the war. He had known many in the banquet hall since he arrived in Houston as a young man. Now he was speaking in his own hotel to some of the first men to be his business associates and to his family and his friends. Jones told them, "We are pledged to maintain on this hemisphere a form of government which madmen in Europe seek to destroy . . . It has already been necessary for Government to underwrite plant expansion, set up reserves of

102. *Houston Chronicle*, December 19, 1940, and December 22, 1940.
103. Jesse Jones, speech, Houston Chamber of Commerce, December 21, 1940, Jesse H. Jones Collection [HE].

strategic and critical materials, aid in the financing of preparedness contracts, and to do many things to prime the productive pump for our national defense." He added, "The output must be multiplied many times before we can feel that we are entirely safe . . . We may soon be forced to devote all of our energies to what is now only a part-time undertaking . . . It has been hard to realize that war can come to us . . . I appeal to all of you to give the most serious consideration to the possibilities that confront us."[104]

Jones noted the start of U.S. militarization, "We find ourselves forced into changing from a nation which desires peace to one which must prepare to defend itself, and I am afraid it is too much to hope that we can survive the outcome of the conflicts which now inflame the world unless we create those implements and measures of defense which will make it impossible for an aggressor to land on the shores of the Western Hemisphere, or to dominate the seas and destroy trade between people and countries." He continued, "We can prepare for our defense only by making sacrifices, all of us, not just a few." Jones spelled it out, "The Congress has already authorized more than $17 billion [$255 billion] for preparedness and more will be needed," compared to a *total* annual budget in 1939, including military appropriations, of only $10 billion ($150 billion). Always the realist, he explained, "These vast sums must come from higher taxes and from borrowing against the future incomes of the American people. Everyone will be called upon to pay his share and should do it willingly, for it is the welfare of all for which we are preparing: the defense of our form of government, our homes, our liberty. We must be a united people."[105]

104. Ibid.
105. Ibid.

1941

———— ◈ ————

You'd Better See Jesse

EN ROUTE TO WASHINGTON on January 1, 1941, Jones telegrammed Franklin Roosevelt with a "wish for you today and throughout the year, and that wish is for health and strength to give courageous leadership to our own people and to the rest of the world that wants peace on Earth."[1] In his State of the Union message five days later, the president noted that "at no previous time has American security been as seriously threatened from without as it is today." He said, "The need of the moment is that our actions and our policy should be devoted primarily—almost exclusively—to meeting this foreign peril . . . The immediate need is a swift and driving increase in our armament production." Roosevelt said he would ask Congress "for authority and for funds sufficient to manufacture additional munitions and war supplies . . . to be turned over to those nations which are now in actual war with aggressor nations. Our most useful and immediate role is to act as an arsenal for them as well as for ourselves."

The British were almost out of cash, so Roosevelt proposed an alternative, "What we send abroad, we shall be repaid, within a reasonable time

———

1. Jesse Jones to Franklin Roosevelt, January 1, 1941, Jesse H. Jones Collection [LOC].

following the close of hostilities, in similar materials or, at our option, in other goods of many kinds." These arrangements circumvented the cash-only part of the Neutrality Act—what became known as the "Lend-Lease" policy. He pledged to send "ever-increasing numbers of ships, planes, tanks, and guns."[2] Days later the president submitted a $17.4 billion ($251 billion in current dollars) annual budget, $10.8 billion ($156 billion) of which was devoted to national defense.[3]

At the same time, Jones reported in a press release that, since the legislation to expand the Reconstruction Finance Corporation, its various subsidiaries had loaned more than $1 billion ($14.4 billion) for national defense. Half went to building plants, forty percent to purchasing strategic materials, and the rest to "providing working capital or other funds necessary for a manufacturer to carry out defense contracts."[4] The opening of several synthetic rubber plants and a tin smelter was promised within the year.

Seven years after Jones's first appearance in *Time*, he was featured on the magazine's cover again. The caption under his imposing picture said, "If jobs were wives, he would be the patriarch of polygamists." The positive story began, "Jesse Jones is Biblically big. One day last week the U.S. had a reminder of his size." The magazine reported that Jones had neutralized some proposed Federal Reserve legislation to contain inflation by simply saying that there was at present no danger of inflation. "There was no need of higher authority," stated the article. "Not J. P. Morgan, not even Franklin Roosevelt could be of as much comfort to the public. To many a U.S. citizen, great or small, if Jesse Jones says O.K., O.K."[5]

The article told the familiar story of Jones's ascent to power and admitted, "Nearly all appraisals of Jesse Jones sound like the baldest kind of hokum success stories, 1929 model." Describing his earlier Houston life, the article said that Jones was so adept at delegation "that he had only to expand his horizons to include the nation." As Samuel Lubell had done in the *Saturday Evening Post*, the writer called Jones "tough, shrewd, [and] tricky as ever." But the article cut him some slack: "If he drives a hard bargain . . . it's in the interest of the Government—which is supposedly all the people." Presenting Jones as the consummate businessman, the article concluded: "He tests every problem with his same old rabbit's foot

2. Roosevelt, "1941 State of the Union Message."
3. *Houston Chronicle*, January 8, 1941.
4. *Houston Chronicle*, January 9, 1941.
5. "National Affairs: The Cabinet—Emperor Jones," 10–12.

touchstone. The million questions he has faced are always the same question: Is it a good risk?"[6]

Time confirmed, "In all the U.S. today there is only one man whose power is greater: Franklin Roosevelt." It described Jones as "huge—6 ft. 3 in. high, with great pale hands, small, blue-greenish eyes . . . His face can be kind, as he can be." But, the writer added, "sometimes he looks like the Ten Commandments." The story also reported that Jones "plays superb poker and bridge," that "he stopped smoking years ago" and "when he stopped, he stopped," and that "he likes whiskey, but not to the point of risk. Man for man, he gets along better than anyone else with everyone in Washington." The article described Jones as "part-author and part-organizer of the national defense program." Attesting to his unequaled power, "He works as a team-member with the Defense Commission, with the State Department, the other Cabinet offices. Primarily he works with Franklin Roosevelt." It continued, "The President knows Congress will give more to Jones without debate than he can get after a fight," and explained, "Jones's knack of making profits while lending money to people and countries who can't borrow anywhere else suits Congress—and the whole situation suits Jones." Restating the obvious, the article declared, "Emperor Jones is the greatest lender of all time." *Time* was not alarmed by Jones's power, seeing his efforts as always directed to the public good. The article said, "He was banker to the world—on his terms, but for reasons that concerned every person now alive," and concluded that people should take comfort "in grain or large dose" knowing that Jones thinks "Democracy is a good risk."[7]

Roosevelt was inaugurated for a third term on January 20, 1941. More than 250,000 people flooded Washington to witness the historic event, and those who could get tickets paid up to $10 ($144) for one of the 40,000 seats at the Capitol and along the parade route.[8] The Texas delegation included the Hardin-Simmons College Cowboy Band and "six of its famous white horses." The day before, the band had visited outgoing Vice President John Nance Garner in his Senate office, where they played "The Eyes of Texas," then played it again for Speaker of the House Sam Rayburn. After the band finished at the Capitol, it headed for the Commerce Department lobby and once more played "The Eyes of Texas" for Jones.[9]

6. Ibid.
7. Ibid.
8. *Houston Chronicle*, January 18, 1941.
9. *Houston Chronicle*, January 19, 1941.

The inaugural parade included the Civilian Conservation Corps, the National Youth Administration, and a Works Progress Administration (WPA) delegation in work clothes. Otherwise, the parade was mostly military. Cadets from West Point and Annapolis, infantrymen carrying rifles, and Marines in full-dress uniform marched in formation and displayed the growing strength of the nation's armed forces. Army Chief of Staff George C. Marshall served as Grand Marshal.[10] In his inaugural address, President Roosevelt spoke about preserving the nation, saying, "Prophets of the downfall of American democracy have seen their dire predictions come to naught. No, democracy is not dying. We know it because we have seen it revive and grow." Roosevelt quoted George Washington from his first inaugural address, "The preservation of the sacred fire of liberty and the destiny of the republican model of government are . . . deeply [and] finally staked on the experiment entrusted to the hands of the American people," then added, "If you and I in this later day lose that sacred fire . . . then we shall reject the destiny which Washington strove so valiantly and so triumphantly to establish. The preservation of the spirit and faith of the nation does, and will, furnish the highest justification for every sacrifice that we may make in the cause of national defense."[11]

Planes, tanks, guns, and ammunition were slowly beginning to roll off U.S. assembly lines, while new cargo ships were being launched from shipyards across the nation. Jones's granddaughter, Audrey, a sophomore at the University of Texas at Austin, stepped in and christened the *Cape Lookout* in a ceremony at the Pennsylvania Shipyards in Beaumont, Texas. The 410-foot cargo ship slid down the ways into the Neches River on more than 7,000 pounds of peeled and sliced bananas (bananas cost about one-third less and worked better than grease). Jones wrote his granddaughter, "Muna and I wish with all our hearts that we could be with you at the reception this morning in your honor and at the shipyard when you are to sponsor the launching of the *Cape Lookout*. Be careful of those bananas. Worlds of love, Bods."[12] According to a reporter at the nationally publicized event, the *Cape Lookout* was the "largest ever launched on ways greased with ripe bananas" and was the largest ship "ever built in this part of the United States."[13]

Militarization brought development to all regions, most noticeably

10. *Houston Chronicle*, January 18, 1941.
11. Roosevelt, "Third Inaugural Address, January 20, 1941."
12. Jesse Jones to Audrey Jones, January 25, 1941, Jesse H. Jones Collection [LOC].
13. *Houston Chronicle*, January 25, 1941.

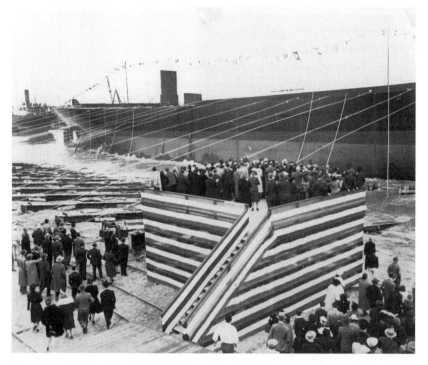

The cargo ship *Cape Lookout* at the Pennsylvania Shipyards in Beaumont, Texas, is christened in 1941 by Jones's granddaughter, Audrey, then launched on banana peels. *Cape Lookout* carried men and supplies to Guadalcanal and Tulagi during the war in the Pacific.

to the relatively underdeveloped South and West. Industrialist Henry J. Kaiser adroitly used government financing to bring shipbuilding, steel, aluminum, and magnesium enterprises to his businesses based in the West. During the war, more than half of all U.S. warships would come from the new Pacific coast shipyards.[14] The Midwest also prospered: the Defense Plant Corporation built more plants in Ohio, Michigan, and Pennsylvania than anywhere else because the existing steel and automobile industries converted easily into building tanks, jeeps, and planes.[15] By policy and for reasons of security, government-financed industries were geographically spread out. Also, Jones explained at a press conference, "If

14. Schwarz, *New Dealers*, 312.
15. Ibid., 321.

overbuilding of a particular type of defense plant occurs in any one city, acute labor shortages immediately follow."[16]

Where California and the West had Kaiser, Texas had Jones, Will Clayton, Garner, Rayburn, and the powerful Congressmen Lyndon Johnson and Wright Pattman. The Gulf Coast also had oil and safer shipping ports than the more vulnerable Atlantic and Pacific coasts.[17] In early February construction of a $17 million ($245 million) steel plant along the Houston Ship Channel was announced. The Houston Chamber of Commerce president called the enormous American Rolling Mill plant, "[a] milestone in the industrial development of Houston." A *Houston Chronicle* reporter wrote that the "new plant . . . involves the coming of an entirely new and permanent industry to Texas."[18] Ten days later Shell announced that it was building a plant in Deer Park, southeast of Houston, to produce butadiene, a major component of synthetic rubber.[19] And at the end of the month, Jones reported that the RFC had entered into an agreement with N.V. Billiton-Maatschapij in the Netherlands to build a tin smelter in the United States. Jones said the smelter "would belong to the RFC but would be built and operated by the Dutch company to process 18,000 tons of Bolivian tin a year."[20] The plant was placed in Texas City, another town on Houston's outskirts near the Ship Channel. Jones also announced that the RFC had given Kaiser's Todd Shipbuilding Corporation a loan for a plant to extract between 12,000 and 15,000 tons of magnesium a year from Nevada ore. In addition to steel and aluminum, magnesium was crucial for the production of tanks, jeeps, airplanes, ships, and bombs, and Kaiser's new plant more than doubled U.S. magnesium production.

The demands were endless, and Jones was the go-to guy. Writing about wool, Roosevelt declared, "The matter is urgent."[21] The president followed with another letter that formally requested action, writing, "This is to advise you that I have determined wool to be essential to the national defense, and you are, therefore, authorized to provide for the establishment of an adequate reserve of this material."[22] The RFC's Defense Supplies Corporation immediately bought 250 million pounds of Australian wool that had already been pledged to the British. Because the British needed

16. *Houston Chronicle*, September 25, 1941.

17. Jones, *Fifty Billion Dollars*, 345.

18. *Houston Chronicle*, February 9, 1941.

19. *Houston Chronicle*, February 20, 1941.

20. Ibid.

21. Franklin Roosevelt to Jesse Jones, October 3, 1940, Jesse H. Jones Collection [LOC].

22. Franklin Roosevelt to Jesse Jones, October 4, 1940, Jesse H. Jones Collection [LOC].

money more than wool, and the U.S. needed wool since it was not able to replace all that it consumed, the DSC purchased the commitments from the British and had the wool shipped to the United States.[23] Once a material was deemed "strategic," RFC companies swept in and scooped up as much as it could from all over the world. In this way the RFC acquired, manufactured, and accumulated everything from quinine, opium, and penicillin to hemp, raw silk, and radio equipment.

Roosevelt also turned to Jones to establish and equip remote bases. Instead of requesting an appropriation from Congress, the president wrote Jones as if to his own banker, "I wish you would arrange with one of the lending agencies under your supervision to advance to Commander Foster up to $30,000 [$432,000] to enable him to proceed to the [Galapagos] Islands and there establish himself."[24] Eight months later, the RFC would loan an additional $500,000 ($7.2 million) to develop a trading mission there.[25] Operating in his "goldfish bowl" as usual, Jones innocently announced the loan to the press and, unknowingly, revealed the Navy's top-secret plan to use the mission as a military base.

Other nations relied on Jones, too. England was broke and desperately needed more weapons to resist the German onslaught, but they could not buy on credit from the United States by law. The *New York Times* explained, "The British [say] they must liquidate quickly every potential dollar resource in this country to fulfill their immediate need for cash."[26] Jones, through the DPC, bought a number of British-owned plants that were located in the U.S. for $46 million ($663 million). Jones still looked out for the bottom line even as he aided the beleaguered British, saying, "To the extent that any of these plants continues to manufacture for the account of Great Britain, the Defense Plant Corporation will receive a rental or a charge at a rate sufficient to amortize the cost of the plant over a period of five years."[27]

Jones supplied more than cash. He also provided crucial information about new commercial and industrial developments to other government agencies, to industrial leaders, and to the public, through the Bureau of Foreign and Domestic Commerce, to help everyone know who was doing what, and where, and when. Jones transformed the languishing bureau into a clearinghouse "to concentrate the flow of essential business facts

23. *New York Times*, January 4, 1941.
24. Franklin Roosevelt to Jesse Jones, November 13, 1940, Jesse H. Jones Collection [LOC].
25. *New York Times*, July 20, 1941.
26. *New York Times*, February 8, 1941.
27. *New York Times*, March 16, 1941.

from foreign and domestic fields, thresh out the significant data for defense decisions, and make [that data] readily available to government and business."[28] The information was useful, but RFC cash was more urgently needed to transform and build up industry.

All this government spending had varying effects on the U.S. economy. The billions that the government spent on militarization dwarfed New Deal expenditures and solved the unemployment problem. Ironically, however, escalating taxes, uncertainty about the economic future, and the liquidation of British assets prevented the stock market from rising in tandem with mass industrialization and increasing employment. Trading volume on the New York Stock Exchange in 1930 was four times higher than it was at the end of 1941. A seat on the exchange now cost only $30,000 ($432,000), down from $600,000 ($8.6 million). A *New York Times* editorial about Jones's dominance observed, "Companies that want to raise capital outside the high-grade bond market are likely to find that all roads lead to Jesse Jones's locker."[29] Economist John Kenneth Galbraith, who was in charge of price controls during the war, affirmed, "When any money was needed for any wartime purpose . . . Jesse was the man you went to . . . There were many [points] in the rapid dynamic of the war where money was immediately needed, and this Jesse could provide." Galbraith explained that Jones controlled an "unlicensed flow of money where you could borrow and spend . . . for all the war purposes." He said, "It was an authority, a power I suppose in practical terms, second only to the president . . . He was the conduit, the great canal, between the financial world and the war needs."[30]

The public tolerated the militarizing of U.S. industry as long as it was "short of war" and under the guise of "national defense." But those in Washington had to be careful with their words. While promoting a bill before a House Currency and Banking Committee that would allow Federal Housing Administration (FHA) loans to home builders who wanted to rent new houses to defense workers, Jones made the mistake of saying ten months before Pearl Harbor, "We're in the war." He immediately tried to backtrack, "At least we're nearly in the war; we're preparing for it; when you do that, you've got to throw money away."[31] Realizing he had said, "We're in the war," Jones asked for his remarks to be removed from

28. *Houston Chronicle*, January 23, 1941.

29. *New York Times*, February 1, 1941.

30. John Kenneth Galbraith to Steven Fenberg, November 22, 1996, Oral History Project [HE].

31. *New York Times*, February 19, 1941.

the official record, but it was too late. The cat was out of the bag. Isolationists flew into high dudgeon. Two days after Jones's appearance, the American First Committee and the Keep America Out of War Congress held a rally in New York. Senator Burton K. Wheeler said to the indignant crowd of more than three thousand, "Do the American people want war? Mr. Jesse Jones, Secretary of Commerce and RFC Administrator, stated we are already in war." The Senator continued, "Mr. Jones himself qualified this blunt statement with the ominous declaration of 'we are nearly in it.' What this Roosevelt Cabinet officer probably meant was that the United States would be at war when the lend-lease-give bill is finally enacted."[32]

The pending "lend-lease-give" bill that the Senator fulminated against would authorize the United States to supply the Allies with war material in exchange for services, like free rent for air bases. Despite isolationist fervor, "Lend-Lease" passed by substantial majorities in both houses of Congress. More than 900,000 feet of fire hose was part of the first shipment to England under the new plan that allowed Britain to buy on credit.[33] Concurrently, Roosevelt requested and received an additional $7 billion ($100 billion) for more military equipment. The demand for capacity to manufacture the additional armaments pushed the RFC's investments in plants and materials from $1 billion ($14.4 billion) in January to $3 billion ($43 billion) by July.

The RFC's shift from repairing the economy to funding global defense gave Drew Pearson and Robert Allen all new material. Whether it was accumulating strategic materials, building a tin smelter, or developing synthetic rubber, they thought, as always, that Jones was too slow. They called him "the most sought after" man in government, noting that everyone had "to mark time waiting for a chance to see Jesse Jones." Concerning negotiations with the Dutch, they wrote, "The plan to set up a tin smelter in the United States using Bolivian ore . . . still is clutched in the large hand of Jesse Jones," and blamed his packed schedule. They added that the "tin situation" was "even more difficult" because Jones "wants to know all the details." They went on, "Meanwhile the threatened Japanese conquest of Asiatic tin supplies proceeds. Meanwhile also the United States lacks enough tin actually on hand to last a full year."[34] They also wrote about delays in synthetic rubber production and blamed Jones for favoring small experimental plants instead of moving full speed with

---

32. *New York Times*, February 21, 1941.
33. Kennedy, *Freedom from Fear*, 475.
34. Pearson and Allen, "Washington Merry-Go-Round," September 29, 1940.

four or five large installations. They said that "the acquisition of emergency stocks of natural rubber is moving all too slowly" and reported that projected supplies were insufficient to meet "U.S. consumption of 600,000 tons a year."[35] The reporters insisted that Jones "has entirely too much to do."[36]

Challenges to Jones's authority over the RFC's supposed sluggishness may have erupted from inside the organization itself. Emil Schram, RFC chairman and president of the DPC, was the most independent of the RFC's corporate presidents. Schram preferred to use the standardized DPC contract for fairness and speed, while Jones's first instinct was to negotiate and bargain for the best deal, particularly when transactions involved hundreds of millions of dollars or when they concerned "scrambled facilities," where existing privately owned plants were being expanded at government expense. People who had never criticized Jones before were beginning to wonder if his need to bargain was slowing the process.

Schram left to become the president of the New York Stock Exchange, only the second to hold the job since it became a paid position. The *Wall Street Journal* reported that Schram's appointment "will answer the contention of many members who have felt that the Exchange, now subject to federal regulation, should seek out someone who knows his way around in Washington." Alluding to a possible breach with Jones, the report also indicated that Schram had been suggested for the position by an unnamed "non-member," that as chairman of the RFC "he has been largely in the shadow of Mr. Jones, his sponsor," and that he was "regarded by some in Washington as more New Dealish than Mr. Jones." The article then incorrectly predicted, "Will Clayton . . . is slated to be the new RFC chairman."[37] Whether or not Jones arranged Schram's appointment to ease a source of RFC discord, he was surely glad to have one of his own managing Wall Street. Jones appointed Charles B. Henderson, who had been with the RFC since 1934, as the Corporation's new chairman, putting RFC operations more firmly in Jones's hands than ever before.[38] And so was Wall Street, through Schram.

That summer Jones went to Congress for more power. He wanted it clarified just how far the RFC could go for national defense. Referring to the materials used to manufacture weapons, an RFC lawyer explained

35. Pearson and Allen, "Washington Merry-Go-Round," December 8, 1940.
36. Pearson and Allen, "Washington Merry-Go-Round," February 11, 1941.
37. *Wall Street Journal*, May 7, 1941.
38. *New York Times*, June 29, 1941.

that the original 1940 legislation laying out the RFC's expansion into militarization matters did not make it "certain how far removed from the final process materials may be and still be properly included with the terms of the Act." The new act would allow the RFC to manufacture all implements of war and do anything else the president and the federal loan administrator deemed essential to national defense. It would bypass the Johnson Act prohibiting loans to nations in default on World War I debts, and allow the RFC to lend to them against their U.S. assets. The act also would allow the RFC to produce and own railroad equipment and commercial aircraft, and to set up facilities to train aviators. The new act essentially gave Roosevelt and Jones unlimited power. Erecting its only barrier, Congress meekly forbade the RFC from engaging in projects that Congress had defeated within the last fifteen years. The amended act passed on June 10, 1941, and in addition to clarifying (or, more to the point, removing) the Corporation's limitations, it added another $1.5 billion ($22 billion) in lending authority to the RFC. Jones downplayed the changes, saying, "We're going to be doing more of what we've already been doing. The new law was asked to iron out some of the red tape."[39]

Circumstances dictated Congressional acquiescence to requests like Jones's. Hitler nearly a year before had made his intentions for Jews clear when a prominent German newspaper declared, "As soon as the last Jew is driven out of Germany, the rest of Europe, which is awaiting a German peace, may know this peace must be one without Jews."[40] The news was bad throughout Europe. Newspapers reported, "Only 42 of Belgium's 2,671 cities, towns, and villages escaped damage from bombs, artillery fire, or flames during the German army's swift conquest of that little nation."[41] The Atlantic had turned into a battlefield and a graveyard as Germany's growing submarine fleet continued to sink U.S. ships carrying military equipment to Britain, diminishing the benefits of "Lend-Lease." Prime Minister Winston Churchill warned that Britain's survival was hanging by "a slender thread."[42]

The United States began taking measured political action. It ordered all German consulates closed on June 16 because, said Undersecretary of State Sumner Welles, "of activities inimical to the welfare of this country."[43] Five days later, Italian consulates were ordered closed because,

39. *Houston Chronicle*, June 15, 1941.
40. *Houston Chronicle*, August 7, 1940.
41. *Houston Chronicle*, January 18, 1941.
42. Kennedy, *Freedom from Fear*, 454.
43. *Houston Chronicle*, June 16, 1941.

the official letter to the Italian ambassador said, they "serve no desirable purpose."[44] Then on June 22, to great surprise, Germany attacked Russia.[45] Congress responded with "the biggest cash appropriation bill in the nation's history, a gigantic $10,384,821,624 [$150 billion] item for the army."[46] Things quickly went from bad to worse. Radio intercepts revealed Japan was about to move into southern Indochina, British Malaya, and the Dutch East Indies. On July 25, one month after Germany invaded the Soviet Union, Japan seized naval and air bases in French Indochina. The next day Roosevelt froze all of Japan's U.S. assets, including those of the 70,000 Japanese immigrants and their descendents who lived in the country.[47] Within hours of Roosevelt's move, England froze Japanese assets throughout the British Empire.[48] The freeze turned into an embargo, depriving Japan of U.S. oil and removing the last restraint keeping it from invading the Dutch East Indies for petroleum.

As the global situation intensified, public opinion shifted, pressure mounted on politicians to protect the country, and criticism about ongoing national defense efforts increased. Mobilization was undefined and multilayered. The NDAC, for instance, had no chairman and its seven members acted independently of each other. Roosevelt abolished it at the end of 1940 and replaced it with the Office of Management Production (OPM). The OPM, like the NDAC, reviewed and approved requests for equipment and material and funneled many of them to the RFC.[49] Reliance on the RFC would only grow. In the beginning four agencies—the War and Navy Departments, the Maritime Commission, and the NDAC (now the OPM)—submitted requests to the RFC. By the war's end, nineteen government organizations would be pounding on the RFC's door for money.[50]

Roosevelt put two men in charge of the OPM: carmaker William Knudsen and labor leader Sidney Hillman. No one knew which of them actually called the shots, but at the very least industry, labor, and government were all at the same table. Roosevelt continued to add mobilization agencies, however, and confusion built up. After Germany attacked Russia, a House Military Committee issued a scathing report. It complained

44. *Houston Chronicle*, June 21, 1941.
45. *Houston Chronicle*, June 22, 1941.
46. *Houston Chronicle*, June 29, 1941.
47. Kennedy, *Freedom from Fear*, 510.
48. *Houston Chronicle*, July 25, 1941.
49. Culver and Hyde, *American Dreamer*, 258.
50. White, *Billions for Defense*, 57.

about the proliferation of agencies and boards, and said confusion had led to "major failures and delays" and a "serious lack of strategic materials." The report specifically said that supplies of aluminum were critically short "because of inadequate power and fabrication facilities." It also claimed that "rubber is not available in sufficient quantities primarily because of a lack of ships."[51] Some pointed a finger at Jones. Others slammed Roosevelt. Secretary of War Stimson in particular complained about the president, saying, "He has no system. He goes haphazard and he scatters responsibility among a lot of uncoordinated men and consequently things are never done."[52]

Undaunted, Roosevelt continued to establish agencies and boards as problems arose. He established the Economic Defense Board (EDB) on July 9 and put Vice President Henry Wallace in charge of international commercial activities, including imports, exports, and preclusive buying. On August 28 he established the Supply Priorities and Allocations Board (SPAB) to coordinate all mobilization efforts and, again, put Wallace in charge.[53] By having both organizations intersect directly with the RFC, Roosevelt lit the fuse to what would become known throughout Washington as the "war within the war."

Enabling Wallace to intrude into Jones's sacrosanct RFC domain was one of two moves by the president that would lead to deterioration in his and Jones's relationship. The other was Roosevelt's request that Jones buy the Empire State Building. On July 25 the president sent Jones a confidential memo with a handwritten note that said, "J. Jones, To put together & justify if possible." The memo itself said, "I have long felt that it would pay the Federal Government to put all of the Federal offices in and around New York City into one central building. We all know that the Empire State Building is a losing proposition, but on the other side, it is ideally located for a central Federal Office Building." The president continued, "I wish you would look into this whole subject, without passing it over to anyone else or speaking to anyone else about it. We can talk it over next week."[54] Jones, however, let the request sit without action for more than two years—a real test of the president's good will.

On August 20, 1941, however, relations were smooth enough to permit Jones to present the president with a new table for cabinet meetings.

51. *Houston Chronicle*, June 29, 1941.
52. Kennedy, *Freedom from Fear*, 485.
53. Culver and Hyde, *American Dreamer*, 256.
54. Franklin Roosevelt to Jesse Jones, July 25, 1941, Jesse H. Jones Collection [LOC].

Presidents since George Washington had sat at the head of their cabinet table.[55] Roosevelt's current table was almost fifteen feet long and five feet wide.[56] This made it difficult for those seated at the opposite end to hear the president. Jones solved the problem by designing an elongated octagon that was five feet wide in the middle and tapered to three feet at either end. Although not telling the president where to sit while conducting official business, Jones's design arranged for the president to sit at the side, in the middle of the mahogany table, rather than at one end. Jones had a second table made for the Senate Banking and Currency Committee, where he spent a lot of time offering testimony. Roosevelt's table, which was used for decades by other presidents, had a brass plaque at one end that said, "FRANKLIN DELANO ROOSEVELT, President of The United States of America, From his friend, Jesse H. Jones."[57]

Despite multiplying agencies and overlapping authority, and despite growing criticism, the militarization of U.S. industry was proceeding at a stupendous pace and the RFC was at the heart of it all. Jones announced huge transactions with Chile, Colombia, and Cuba. A *New York Times* article explained, "The tendency of the program is to build an economic wall around Latin America, creating a sort of embargo against all non-American purchasers. The instrumentalities for carrying out the program are mainly the Metals Reserve Company and Defense Supply Corporation."[58] Jones guaranteed Mexico that the U.S. would buy all of its surplus output, including every bit of copper, graphite, lead, mercury, tungsten, tin, and zinc that the country could produce.[59]

By September 1941 the DPC had spent more than $2 billion ($29 billion) to build plants that it then leased to companies to manufacture airplanes, ships, aluminum, steel, magnesium, ordnance, and machine tools. A $200 million ($2.9 billion) plant at Geneva, Utah, leased to United States Steel, was the DPC's biggest investment. The complex covered 1,600 acres and included coke ovens, blast furnaces, and eleven miles of railroad.[60] The Dodge-Chicago plant, built to manufacture engines for the B-29 Superfortress and B-32 Dominator airplanes, was the second costliest at $176 million ($2.5 billion). Jones said it was "the largest single industrial plant in the country," adding, "With its own steel forge and aluminum

55. Jones, *Fifty Billion Dollars*, 282.
56. A. R. Clas to Jesse Jones, August 8, 1941, Jesse H. Jones Collection [LOC].
57. Ibid.; Jones, *Fifty Billion Dollars*, 282.
58. *New York Times*, June 27, 1941.
59. *Wall Street Journal*, July 15, 1941.
60. White, *Billions for Defense*, 74.

foundry, Dodge-Chicago was the only factory which took in pigs of magnesium and aluminum and bars of steel at one end and turned out finished engines at the other."[61] The factory, which covered 145 acres, turned out more than 18,000 engines during the war.

The only tin smelter in the United States, under construction in Texas City, was scheduled to open that fall. Four synthetic rubber plants were also underway; Goodyear, B. F. Goodrich, Firestone, and U.S. Rubber had each agreed to operate one, but the process was still new. As a *Wall Street Journal* article said, "The synthetic rubber plants are being financed in order to give the companies experience in this new type of manufacture."[62] As he had before, Jones was using government as a catalyst to jump-start an industry and to spur development and progress. He also flexed the RFC's new muscle and offered loans to railroad companies for building additional cars to accommodate the growing loads of freight and soldiers being moved around the country. The Association of American Railroads projected it would need 270,000 new cars, over and above replacements, within the next two years.[63] Jones also was able to authorize tankers to carry larger loads to get more oil from the Gulf Coast to the thirsty east coast.[64]

And the British needed more cash. Under the RFC's new authority, Jones lent Great Britain $425 million ($6.1 billion) against $500 million ($7.2 billion) of the besieged nation's remaining U.S. assets. An official statement said that the loan was "authorized by the Reconstruction Finance Corp. with the approval of President Roosevelt and at the request of Jesse Jones, Federal Loan Administrator."[65]

Back in July, Jones had reported that the RFC had allocated $3 billion ($43 billion) toward "national defense"—by September, investments and loans had climbed to $4 billion ($58 billion). Jones asked for another $1.5 billion ($22 billion), testifying before a House Banking Committee, "We're about out of credit . . . We have authorized toward defense work $3.9 billion [$56 billion] odd . . . [and w]e've got a great deal more . . . to do."[66] When asked if new funds would be used for loans to Russia, Jones replied, "I'd be glad to help Russia in any way possible."[67] Two days later

61. Jones, *Fifty Billion Dollars*, 337.
62. *Wall Street Journal*, July 17, 1941.
63. *Wall Street Journal*, July 10, 1941.
64. *Houston Chronicle*, July 5, 1941.
65. *Houston Chronicle*, July 22, 1941.
66. *Houston Chronicle*, September 16, 1941.
67. Ibid.

he announced that the U.S. was buying $100 million ($1.4 billion) in strategic materials from the Soviets.[68]

Jones was also more than willing to help U.S. defense workers. In one of Pearson and Allen's kinder treatments, they reported, "In normal times, the Government brings to Washington as many as 2,000 new workers a year. Today the figure is 2,000 a month. Civil Service Commission estimates that in the next 16 months, 35,000 more defense workers will come to Washington. And most of them are women." The columnists continued, "Where will they sleep? A big man from Texas thinks he has the answer." They reported that the Defense Homes Corporation would build a dormitory near "Embassy Row on Sixteenth Street" with "750 rooms, some single and some double," that would house a thousand women. Pearson and Allen quipped, "Rules will be liberal in respect to using electric irons and electric toasters, but not in respect to entertaining young men. Jesse Jones will be protective god-father to all 1,000."[69] That was the nicest thing they would say about Jones for a long time.

Other reporters were beginning to turn on Jones for the RFC's supposed slowness to act. In October a *Wall Street Journal* article said, "Critics label Jones defense bottleneck no. 1: He dickers too long over financing new raw materials production, haggles even about which contractor will build the road to a new plant."[70] Another *Wall Street Journal* story said officials "claim that both defense and civilian production suffer because Federal Loan Administrator Jones has been slow to finance new facilities, especially . . . to expand production of basic material like steel, copper, aluminum, magnesium, and rubber." The reporter explained, "Where he admits delay, he is inclined to blame business men who aren't convinced that their industries should be expanded."[71] Some of the delay had to do with the contracts dealing with enormous projects too complex to fit the standardized DPC lease. A contract determined where a plant was located, who built it, how much it would produce, how much would be charged for the output, who would pay for it, and what would happen to the facility after the war. Producing what was required to defend human lives and preventing excess supply were the two compelling objectives guiding each negotiation.

One controversial lease resulted from negotiations with Alcoa for

68. *New York Times*, September 19, 1941.
69. Pearson and Allen, "Washington Merry-Go-Round," September 29, 1941.
70. *Wall Street Journal*, October 10, 1941.
71. *Wall Street Journal*, October 14, 1941.

three enormous aluminum plants. Pearson and Allen reported, "RFCzar Jones has just negotiated a contract with Alcoa whereby he hands them several million dollars to build new aluminum plants, and Alcoa, with absolutely no expense . . . writes its own ticket regarding their operation . . . [A] battle royal is being waged between Jones and Harold Ickes over this deal."[72] Interior Secretary Ickes, who had initiated the conversation with Alcoa and offered to provide the plants with electricity from the new Bonneville Dam in Oregon, asked Jones to look over the contract before it was signed. Jones and Arthur Davis, president of Alcoa, signed an amended contract before Ickes could reject what he thought was a government giveaway in its provisions. According to Pearson and Allen, the contract allowed Alcoa—already under investigation for being a monopoly—to set its own price, determine the amount it produced, and pay the government only fifteen percent of the net profits. They concluded, "For this, the RFC takes all the financial risk and Mr. Ickes supplies cheap electric power. Thus the Aluminum Corporation, with no risk, no money advanced, is not only guaranteed its expenses, but gets a tremendous profit."[73]

Congress stepped in. For the first time, Jones was under Congressional attack. Missouri Senator Harry S. Truman, who had established the Senate Committee Investigating National Defense, better known as the Truman Committee, to prevent fraud and waste during the industrial expansion, said that "Alcoa had put it over on Mr. Jones." The Senator complained, "This is just about the worst contract the government ever signed . . . I have read [it] at least a dozen times, and it has kept me awake nights because of my fears of what is going to happen to the government." Truman was mollified after an Alcoa representative explained that the contract did not give the company control over location or production and that [Alcoa] would receive no profit from the plant, only from its output.[74]

Jones was not satisfied with the rebuttal and he was furious about the "Washington Merry-Go-Round" column. Proving that he really was "thin-skinned," he wrote Hugh Baillie, president of United Feature Syndicate, listing three incorrect statements contained in the column about Alcoa and including content from the contract to counter them. Jones demanded, "As the distributor of the column . . . I deem it your responsibility to dis-

72. Pearson and Allen, "Washington Merry-Go-Round," October 25, 1941.
73. Ibid.
74. *New York Times*, October 31, 1941.

tribute . . . this letter to [subscribers] to this column . . . request[ing] that it be published in full as prominent[ly] . . . the column referred to as published."[75]

Four days later Jones's letter appeared as that day's "Washington Merry-Go-Round" column. Pearson responded with an exhaustive letter that admitted to only a typographical error. At the beginning of November, the columnists mentioned this typo and wrote, "Our apologies to Jesse on this point," but made no reference to Jones's major objections.[76] Jones protested to Baillie, "The statement inconspicuously appearing in a subsequent publication of the column that one of the statements in the earlier column was a 'typographical error' is not correct or a retraction."[77] Jones was still fuming ten days later, writing to Garner's wife that the story was "slanderous" and that Pearson and Allen are "a contemptible pair."[78]

Jones gave an Armistice Day speech to iron and steel company executives on November 11. This time he did not hesitate to say the U.S. was at war and began, "As much as the American people abhor war, and dread war, in their hearts they are now at war, at war with a monster . . . creeping over the continent of Europe as a hungry animal devouring all that is unable to resist it. We are not yet face to face with this monster, but millions . . . are, and have been; millions have already succumbed, and unless he can be stopped, we will face him as sure as the sun rises in the East." Jones defended himself saying, "We have undertaken to help those who are . . . fighting this monster, and there must be no hesitation, no slowing . . . no stopping, no haggling . . . We must furnish . . . the things that they do not have in sufficient quantity, and cannot get except through us." He explained, "We are helping Russia not because we like or embrace her form of government. We are helping England not because we approve everything that she does. We are helping China because we are against aggression. We are helping all of the people of the world that are fighting Hitler. We are doing this because we love liberty." Jones continued, "It is a terrible thing . . . spending our vast energies and resources, but there is no choice if we would avoid the fate that has already overtaken many peaceful nations."[79]

75. Jesse Jones to Hugh Baillie, October 29, 1941, Jesse H. Jones Collection [LOC].
76. Pearson and Allen, "Washington Merry-Go-Round," November 6, 1941.
77. Jesse Jones to Hugh Baillie, November 9, 1941, Jesse H. Jones Collection [LOC].
78. Jesse Jones to Mariette Garner, November 16, 1941, Jesse H. Jones Collection [LOC].
79. Jesse Jones, speech, Armistice Day, November 11, 1941, Jesse H. Jones Collection [UT].

On the same day, Jones received a draft of a new *Fortune* feature about him by Albert Furth. The author had written to Jones, "Naturally I cannot expect that you will like every bit of the story . . . but I am determined that you will not have grounds for considering it anything but fair." Furth added, "I don't think I have ever tackled a subject with such a multitude of angles."[80] Publisher Henry Luce also wrote to prepare Jones for what he would read, "There has been a great deal of discussion as to whether or not you have done a 100% job on all-out 'defense'—just as there has been the same discussion with regard to everyone else of importance from Franklin D. Roosevelt down . . . The *Fortune* story answers that question, it seems to me, fairly, factually, and in a manner to do you no discredit whatever in the light of general U.S. policy and the uncertain will of the American people." Luce continued, "It is not to be thought that you will like the story. But if you will be good enough to forget the 'grief' of its making, I believe you will agree it is a fair account of the question it undertakes to discuss."[81]

Jones went through the draft and corrected figures, changed words— he preferred to be called a "lender" rather than a "banker"—and suggested additions. He inserted sentences that accused Ickes and Truman of "deep laid plans . . . to make a record by questioning the acts . . . of some high officials in the defense program." He also rewrote the paragraph about Schram's departure from the RFC and removed sensitive information about overseas preemptive buying. The review process, however, was not as congenial nor as smooth as it had been when the first *Fortune* article appeared. Luce wrote Jones after receiving his comments, "I regret to say that I just could not see my way clear to insisting on changes in the substantive points—such as regards Schram . . . I'm sorry this was such a headache for you. It was also a headache for several people here."[82] Jones responded, "The story has been greatly improved, and while it contains a great deal of unwarranted gossip, I appreciate the improvement and attention you gave to it."[83] He later solicited a promise from Luce to print his statement if "any of the story . . . is mistaken in fact or interpretation."[84] The article was published much as it was originally written.

It began not with a full color portrait of Jones as it had last time, but with an illustration of the Secretary of Commerce as a multi-armed

80. Albert Furth to Jesse Jones, October 30, 1941, Jesse H. Jones Collection [UT].
81. Henry Luce to Jesse Jones, November 11, 1941, Jesse H. Jones Collection [UT].
82. Henry Luce to Jesse Jones, November 12, 1941, Jesse H. Jones Collection [UT].
83. Jesse Jones to Henry Luce, November 12, 1941, Jesse H. Jones Collection [UT].
84. Jesse Jones to Henry Luce, November 17, 1941, Jesse H. Jones Collection [UT].

deity, seated in full lotus on top of a pillar etched with Washington's mantra, "You'd better see Jesse." Hordes of tiny supplicants pleading for attention were shown surrounding the base of the enormous statue, which was detailed with factories, houses, continents, and the names of all the agencies under Jones, who wore a crown topped with a huge dollar sign. Trying to put his extraordinary position into words, the caption explained, "Though Mr. Jones's detractors might not concede him the quality of divinity, there is no doubt that his duties and powers approach the divine."[85]

Criticism of Jones was so unusual that the article's first lines took note, saying, "This autumn Jesse Holman Jones found himself undergoing a new and scarcely pleasant experience. For the first time in his national career, in any important way, he was getting a bad press. It seemed to happen all at once." The critics, according to Furth, were mostly "buck passers in OPM" and "all-outers in the New Deal." While Jones was reported as calling it a "smear campaign," the *Fortune* article countered, "Far from being a smear campaign, it was essentially a maneuver to arouse Jesse Jones to a full sense of the country's dependence upon him in its emergency." Then the magazine asked, "Is Jones of Texas a great national asset or is he in fact a bottleneck?"[86]

Assessing his stature, Furth reported that Jones had seven more lines in the Congressional Directory than President Roosevelt, and that the RFC was the "first government agency [to be] exempted from scrutiny by the Comptroller General." The article described his seeming omnipotence: "In 1940 the House of Jesse was enlarged to embrace the financing of U.S. rearmament and hemisphere defense." To make anything happen, "practically all of Washington . . . considers it essential to 'see Jesse.'" Furth continued, "The greatest part of Jesse Jones's show is now Defense Plant Corporation, the nearest thing yet to government in big business." The writer listed "such staggering items as $829 million [$12 billion] for expansion of the aircraft industry; $223 million [$3.2 billion] for . . . machine tools; and $114 million [$1.6 billion] for ships and shipyards." He revealed, "Jones has become the sole buyer of rubber for the entire U.S.," and described how he and "that other famous Texan, Will Clayton, the cotton man," were "busy buying up critical and strategic materials wherever in the world they can still be obtained." According to Clayton, the article said, "The U.S. and Great Britain have now cornered about 98 per-

85. Furth, "The War Goes to Mr. Jesse Jones," 91.
86. Ibid.

A 1941 *Fortune* magazine cover story featured Jesse Jones as an omnipotent deity. Courtesy *Fortune*, PARS International.

cent of the exportable output of essential materials" from Latin America. Then Furth asked, "All of the foregoing sounds very much like another glorious chapter in the old story of Jesse Jones, the busiest man in the U.S. and one of the most effective. What, then, is all the shooting about?"[87]

The magazine admitted that "much of the criticism of Jesse Jones goes

87. Ibid., 187.

wide of the mark," because the "RFC is the last stop on the tortuous route of a defense project from idea to reality." Furth reported, "projects are fussed with by other agencies" months before they reach the RFC, and they frequently arrive in "such untidy condition," according to Jones, that time is required to fix them. On the other hand, Furth said, Jones "is trying to arrange the financing of the U.S. arms program by the fine old practice of horse trading, conducted almost entirely by himself . . . As put by those who raised it, the issue is whether or not such horse trading can get both the best and the fastest defense deals for the country."[88]

Then the magazine turned to Schram and the DPC lease. Furth wrote that manufacturers rejected the OPM's Emergency Plant Facilities contract because "the working details [were] impossibly cumbersome." They instead preferred the DPC arrangement—the DPC worked out all of the details for the complex plants, paid to build them, took title to them in the government's name, and leased the finished facilities to manufacturers for a period of four to seven years. As Furth explained, "The government would own the plant unless the manufacturer exercised an option to buy," and he noted that the first DPC leases were accomplished with such nonchalance and so little publicity that "hardly anyone was conscious that the government had taken a momentous step toward extensive plant ownership." Controversy came from the difference in approach, whether "negotiating the deals in standardized form or dickering each one individually," would give the best result. According to the magazine, Schram contended that when using the standardized DPC lease, "nine cases out of ten, the manufacturer went along, and the deal was settled in a matter of a day or so; in many instances machinery for the new plant would be ordered at once, and ground broken the very next day." The magazine said, "In this way DPC struck an even stride that was not broken until Emil Schram departed for the New York Stock Exchange . . . The clear impression . . . was that RFC was not big enough to hold both Jesse Jones and Emil Schram." Furth added wryly, "To ask Jesse Jones to abstain from trading was like asking a whippet please to refrain from annoying the rabbits."[89]

The article gave Jones his due, listing all of the RFC's defense-related accomplishments in plant construction and material accumulation. Furth then concluded, "Jesse Jones is a great operator with a profound confi-

88. Ibid.
89. Ibid., 189.

dence in his long-accustomed way of doing business and a reluctance to overstep the provincial limits of his specific job. Both of these characteristics bear sharply on his relationship to the defense program and on the progress of defense itself." Jones wrote in his unpublished revisions that he was simply "playing by the rules." The article pointed out, "To be sure, he is a Texan, and Texas is whole-souled interventionist." Furth also acknowledged that the "mood of the country has been . . . ambivalent" and has not shown "any particularly readiness to upset and forgo its easy way of life or its way of doing business,"[90] which meant leaving Jones in charge.

The magazine hit the stands at the end of November. One week later the "ambivalent" mood that Furth had reported abruptly changed. In a surprise attack on Pearl Harbor on December 7, 1941, hundreds of Japanese aircraft descended on the Hawaiian island and in less than three terrorizing hours sank battleships, destroyed hundreds of airplanes, and killed 2,403 soldiers, almost half of them on the battleship *Arizona*, which plunged to the ocean floor after it was bombed. The only salvation was that the Japanese raiders failed to destroy the repair shops or the oil storage facility, which was filled to the brim with precious fuel, and no aircraft carriers, among the most vital vessels of the war, were docked at Pearl Harbor on that fateful day.[91]

Roosevelt declared December 7 a day "which will live in infamy" and reported that the Japanese had also attacked Malaya, Hong Kong, Guam, the Philippines, Wake Island, and Midway Island. On December 8, the U.S. Congress declared war against Japan. Three days later Germany and Italy declared war against the U.S., and the U.S., in turn, recognized a state of war with the two nations.[92] World War II had officially begun.

Jones said in his statement, "The nation's only objective now is victory over its enemies . . . Whatever government financing is needed for defense activities to supplement private credit will be available . . . Our tremendous business machine is ready for defense, but it must work night and day to supply our military needs until peace has been restored to a war torn world."[93] Less than one week after the Pearl Harbor attack, the RFC established the War Insurance Corporation to insure property

---

90. Ibid., 203.
91. Kennedy, *Freedom from Fear*, 522.
92. Ibid., 524.
93. Jesse Jones, statement on declaration of war, December 9, 1941, Jesse H. Jones Collection [UT].

owners against loss from enemy attack, including air raids. Private insurance companies could not agree on premiums and would not offer coverage.[94]

Schram wrote how much he appreciated Jones's "admirable courage and wisdom" in discharging his "grave responsibilities" now that the U.S. was at war. Schram continued, "I have read the recent article about you . . . in the December issue of *Fortune* magazine, and . . . observed with some dismay the particular references to our personal relationship during my tenure of office as Chairman. You and I know, of course, that any suggestion of incompatibility between us is a plain distortion of the truth." Schram concluded, "I earnestly hope that the real . . . respect and understanding that exists between us will continue . . . and . . . not . . . be impaired by such uninvited and unwarranted comments."[95] Jones replied, "You and I know that there has never been the slightest difference between us—I doubt even in opinion—as to our work here in the RFC." He continued, "It seems, however, that we must submit to a certain amount of unreliable . . . gossip, and . . . too many publishers are willing to print and circulate unfounded . . . stories, gossip and innuendo in the belief that it increases their circulation and profits."[96]

The Joneses usually went home to spend the holidays with family and friends, but this year, as he had before when he could not go home, Jones published a message on the front page of the *Houston Chronicle* that said, "Mrs. Jones and I would be with friends, associates, and relatives in Houston today if circumstances had not made it impractical for us to leave Washington at this time. We do extend warmest Christmas greetings to all, in the full confidence that the strength and determination of our moral and armed forces will preserve that freedom and independence for which every patriotic American is willing to lay down his life."[97]

94. *Houston Chronicle*, December 13, 1941.
95. Emil Schram to Jesse Jones, December 16, 1941, Jesse H. Jones Collection [UT].
96. Jesse Jones to Emil Schram, December 17, 1941, Jesse H. Jones Collection [UT].
97. *Houston Chronicle*, December 25, 1941.

1942

◈

A Material More Precious Than Gold

THE UNITED STATES OF AMERICA was at war. President Franklin Roosevelt asked each of his cabinet members to issue a statement about the pact formed among the Allied nations against the Axis powers. Jones released the following: "The determination of twenty-six countries to employ their full resources, military and economic, to preserve human rights and justice for all the peoples of the earth, and their agreement to stick together until Hitlerism is destroyed, is a new Magna Carta for the world."[1] In the coming years, Jones and the Reconstruction Finance Corporation would empower many of the Allied nations, particularly his own, to "employ their full resources" to prepare for and win World War II.

Since its 1934 inception, more than half of the Export-Import Bank's loans of $1 billion ($13 billion in current dollars) had gone toward stimulating development in Latin America. To counter Germany's overtures in the region, in 1941 the EIB had made loans only to Latin America. These influential loans helped develop highways, railroads, water systems, power plants, mining operations, and rubber plantations in Central and South America. Cuba, for instance, received loans to build roads and to

---

1. *New York Times*, January 2, 1942.

399

store sugar. EIB President Warren Pierson said the loans to Latin America "constituted vital links in hemisphere defense." Channeling Jones, he said, "Not a single item is in default."[2] In early 1942 Jones reported to the president, "We are buying and will continue to buy every exportable commodity produced in Latin America."[3]

Speaking to a *New York Times* reporter at the first of the year about the war agencies, Jones said, "The thing I feel about the Defense Plant Corporation, as well as nearly all the other branches of the Federal Loan Agency, is what a blessing it is that we had it when war came upon us. The war found us already in good working order."[4] In the year and a half before Pearl Harbor, the DPC had already spent more than $2.5 billion ($32.5 billion) on new factories. Spending accelerated rapidly to $4.2 billion ($55 billion) in the first six months of 1942.[5] Jones explained the reason for the RFC's early role in the military buildup: "The armed services cannot spend money without an appropriation, and that takes time. So, often when they knew they were going to need something very badly and must act swiftly in order to get production started, they have asked us to intervene."[6] The RFC circumvented Congress and provided an alternate source of funds for the war, just as it had funded New Deal programs during the Great Depression.

Jones added, "Although I am the person who is building the new plants, I would rather see us convert the old ones. It not only is speedier, but it will be better for industry when the war is over."[7] Even though most existing plants were too small and antiquated to manufacture the new modern military machinery, they were still idle from the Great Depression, so they were converted and expanded as the country turned from economic recovery to global war. The unemployed found jobs as factories reopened and as new ones were built. Resources, manpower sidelined by the Great Depression, and the RFC's early intervention allowed the United States to rapidly industrialize for war.

Jones also told the *New York Times* reporter that the commercial banks are "in good shape," that the railroads "are making money now and don't have to come to us," and that the RFC is operating "now almost completely

---

2. *New York Times*, January 1, 1942.
3. Jesse Jones to Franklin Roosevelt, February 16, 1942, Jesse H. Jones Collection [HE].
4. *New York Times*, January 1, 1942.
5. White, *Billions for Defense*, 37.
6. *New York Times*, January 1, 1942.
7. Ibid.

on a war basis." He said new factories to manufacture the magnesium, aluminum, and steel needed to produce ships, airplanes, tanks, and guns were up and running, and bigger ones were on the drawing boards.[8]

All of the RFC's wartime corporations were in full swing. The Metals Reserve Company had already spent nearly $1 billion ($13 billion) to acquire and store strategic metals and materials, including bauxite, mercury, chrome, diamonds, tungsten, and wolfram. The Defense Supplies Corporation had accumulated 250 million pounds of wool for uniforms, socks, blankets, and caps, and was beginning to produce millions of gallons of 100-octane gasoline for the tens of thousands of airplanes that would soon start to roll off assembly lines at the brand new DPC manufacturing facilities, employing thousands of men and women. The transition from a financially prostrate, economically contracting, and demilitarized nation into an industrialized, expanding behemoth, where machines mattered as much as manpower, promised to reach a crescendo in 1942.

Then a rubber shortage threatened to stop everything.[9] The crisis gave Jones one of the biggest headaches of his public career. The Rubber Reserve Company was the first wartime agency established after the 1940 legislation gave the corporation what Jones called "the dictionary." At the time, synthesizing rubber was still experimental, so only the natural resource was available. Much of it came from the Pacific Islands through a Dutch and British cartel that controlled most of the world's supply. When Jones presented the president's request that they stockpile rubber, the heads of the leading rubber corporations were unwilling to bear the cost; furthermore, they thought massive buying would inflate prices. Jones always gave private business first choice, but he knew it was unrealistic to rely on industry to purchase and store the largest accumulation of rubber ever assembled by one nation. Consequently, the Rubber Reserve Company became the sole purchaser and distributor of crude rubber for the country. Industry was not left out, however. The president of the Rubber Manufacturers Association and representatives from the five largest companies made the purchases from the Anglo-Dutch cartel on behalf of the Rubber Reserve Company. The company then sold the rubber to U.S. manufacturers in limited amounts for civilian uses. Most went to companies manufacturing for the military; it stored the rest. During the eighteen months before Pearl Harbor, the Rubber Reserve Company accumulated

8. Ibid.
9. Kennedy, *Freedom from Fear*, 619.

more than 600,000 tons of rubber, which was barely enough to last one year during peacetime.[10]

As the nation shifted to a wartime footing, people became aware of the dire rubber situation. Some accused Jones of not accumulating enough, while others were angry that he had not aggressively pursued the development of synthetic rubber. After Japan conquered Malaya and Java, taking over most of the world's natural rubber supply, the anger turned to near panic. When the production of passenger cars and trucks was banned at the first of the year mainly to save rubber, it also freed up factories to make planes, tanks, jeeps, and guns. One U.S. senator said, "I think it's about time we had a show down."[11]

As the debilitating shortage of rubber loomed, Jones was in trouble. The four small, experimental synthetic rubber plants were nowhere near complete. Their projected output had been expanded from 40,000 tons to 100,000, but that was miniscule compared to the need. The Germans, who had run short on rubber during World War I, had been experimenting ever since. The small amounts of rubber they synthesized from coal had helped them roll their forces across Europe. With the pressure on and the need urgent, Roosevelt and Jones put aside their skepticism about the experimental process. Jones announced that the Rubber Reserve Company would invest $400 million ($5.2 billion) to expand synthetic rubber production to 400,000 tons, even though no one at this point was quite sure how to do it. Jones hoped to have the initial four plants going in a matter of months with new larger plants in operation by the middle of 1943. He claimed that the rubber supply on hand and whatever was gained from a new public campaign to "reclaim and rework" used rubber would be sufficient until then.[12] Some vehemently disputed his optimistic forecast, but most everyone agreed that the development and production of synthetic rubber was essential to successfully wage war and to eliminate U.S. dependency on other nations for this vital commodity.[13]

What followed was one of the war's more miraculous feats. Jones got the rubber and oil company executives to pool their research, patents, and resources, and work with the government, through the RFC, to create an indispensable industry. The day after the announcement about the promised increase in synthetic rubber production, Lord Beaverbrook,

10. Jones, *Fifty Billion Dollars*, 396–400.
11. *New York Times*, January 9, 1942.
12. *New York Times*, January 12, 1942.
13. *Houston Chronicle*, January 13, 1942.

England's minister of supply, reassured British Prime Minister Winston Churchill that Jones had agreed to provide Britain with 50,000 tons of synthetic rubber a year once production commenced. Beaverbrook explained his confidence with, "It is a Jesse Jones business."[14]

In his annual report to Congress, Jones said that the past year had represented "largely an organizational stage" and that the current flow of armaments was "just beginning to give evidence of the huge output to follow."[15] The RFC's record was impressive, and its unprecedented spending accounted for a huge portion of the industrial buildup for war. Even though Jones was still in the doghouse with some lawmakers over rubber, Congress did not refuse when he asked for an additional $2.5 billion ($33 billion) in borrowing and lending authority so the RFC could buy Cuba's entire sugar crop, build more airplane factories, and fund the new synthetic rubber program.

Despite the rubber problem, the Empire State Building, and the tensions from Vice President Henry Wallace's encroachment on RFC territory, Jones and President Roosevelt still enjoyed a pleasant relationship. They exchanged gifts during Christmas and warm thank-you notes in January. In one, Jones thanked the Roosevelts for a poinsettia plant. In another he said, "I greatly appreciate the autographed book of your addresses . . . sent to me at Christmas."[16] For his part, Roosevelt wrote, "I am enchanted with that barometer-thermometer-clock-calendar-hygrometer combination which you gave me at Christmas time. Thank you ever so much—I shall enjoy keeping track of things with it!"[17] The president also wrote a little later, "Just a little personal note to thank you for that nice birthday greeting. It warmed my heart."[18]

Although he worked seven days a week, Jones occasionally enjoyed a game of bridge and a bit of official social life with his wife. At the first lady's invitation, he and Mary attended a White House dinner for the cabinet on January 22.[19] Five days later they went to New York for the Red Cross War Fund benefit at the Metropolitan Opera, where, according to the *New York Times*, "Mrs. Franklin D. Roosevelt heads a distinguished list of patrons." The paper also reported, "Mrs. Woodrow Wilson and Mrs.

14. Jones, *Fifty Billion Dollars*, 407.

15. *New York Times*, January 27, 1942.

16. Jesse Jones to Franklin Roosevelt, January 7, 1942, Jesse H. Jones Collection [LOC].

17. Franklin Roosevelt to Jesse Jones, January 12, 1942, Jesse H. Jones Collection [LOC].

18. Franklin Roosevelt to Jesse Jones, February 4, 1942, Jesse H. Jones Collection [LOC].

19. Eleanor Roosevelt to Mary Gibbs Jones, January 14, 1942, Jesse H. Jones Collection [HE].

Jesse Jones are expected to arrive today from Washington and will be at Mayfair House."[20] The reporter did not mention that Jones owned the famous hotel.

Mary appeared to enjoy life in Washington. A picture of her sitting next to Lt. Douglas Fairbanks and his wife at a birthday party for the president showed up in the *Washington Star*.[21] A gossip columnist later spotted her enjoying the first "at home" hosted by "Mme. Ivy Low Litvinoff, the English-born wife of the Soviet Ambassador," whose gatherings attracted "capitalists, diplomats, and official Washington." The columnist identified Mary as "Mrs. Jesse Jones, whose husband as head of the Federal Loan Corporation had approved Josef Stalin as a $1,000,000,000 risk."[22] Months before, Jones and the Soviet diplomat Andrei Gromyko had arranged for the RFC to lend the USSR funds to buy arms made in the U.S.

The Joneses also made time for family. Pearl Harbor shook up everyone, and Jones reassuringly wrote his granddaughter at the University of Texas at Austin, "You should give your undivided attention to your studies and prepare yourself to take your place in the life of our country in the full confidence that nothing will prevent your generation from a normal, natural life. Muna and I are looking forward to seeing you when it is convenient to come." He closed, "Worlds of love," and signed it, "Jesse H. Jones."[23] At around the same time, Jones wrote to his nephew, John, his brother's only son who had enlisted in the Army some months before, "I should like to have a line from you as to how you are getting along in the Army. Also if you have a few days' leave and no better place to go, Mrs. Jones and I would love to have you as our guest here. With love and best wishes from both of us, Your devoted uncle, Jesse H. Jones."[24] His engagement with younger family members was openhearted and formal all at the same time.

Most people still thought Jones was a "miracle man," despite the rubber problem.[25] Roosevelt had called for 185,000 planes, 120,000 tanks, and 55,000 anti-aircraft guns, plus uniforms and supplies for millions of U.S. soldiers.[26] The RFC, with massive new plants and factories, and its

20. *New York Times*, January 27, 1942.
21. *Washington Star*, January 25, 1942.
22. *New York Times*, February 13, 1942.
23. Jesse Jones to Audrey Jones, January 10, 1942, Jesse H. Jones Collection [HE].
24. Jesse Jones to John T. Jones Jr., February 13, 1942, Jesse H. Jones Collection [HE].
25. *New York Times*, January 18, 1942.
26. *Houston Chronicle*, February 17, 1942.

Jesse Jones's nephew, John T. Jones Jr., who was captured as a prisoner of war in North Africa in 1943.

worldwide buying program, would not only help meet, but exceed those towering goals.

The RFC did more than build factories and procure materials. It also handled support services and peripheral wartime needs. It constructed housing for defense workers, the most recent of which was a "hotel for negroes" in Washington, D.C. It established flight schools across the nation to train pilots to fly all the new airplanes being manufactured at breakneck speed. And it continued to offer every bank in the country assistance with loans to small businesses. Jones wrote to the bankers, who after ten years had become accustomed to receiving mail from him, that including "smaller enterprises" in the buildup for victory was "a definite Administration policy."[27]

In February, the RFC established another corporation. In his request, Jones wrote Roosevelt, "On urgent recommendation of the State Department, War Production Board, and Bureau of Economic Warfare, we have

27. *Wall Street Journal*, January 8, 1942.

agreed to undertake preclusive buying of strategic and critical materials on a highly non-commercial price basis, to prevent such materials reaching Axis countries." In true fashion, Jones wanted to separate an intentionally money-losing enterprise from other RFC business. To that end, he proposed forming the United States Commercial Corporation (USCC) to keep essential materials from the Nazis no matter the cost. Jones continued, "Some of these products, notably tungsten, have been driven to price levels far beyond world market prices, reflecting [the] urgent need of Germany for such materials." As was their custom, the president wrote, "I approve, FDR," by hand on the letter and returned it to Jones.[28] The USCC—with Jones's and Roosevelt's knowledge and approval—would later be used as a cover for secret service agents operating in other nations.[29]

The RFC war agencies initiated no projects on their own, instead organizing and financing projects requested by others, primarily the War Department, the Navy Department, the Maritime Commission, and the War Production Board, which was the successor to the National Defense Advisory Council, Office of Management Production, and Supply Priorities and Allocations Board—three of Roosevelt's earlier attempts to coordinate military mobilization. Each RFC project, no matter how enormous or tiny, had its own sponsor, and as 1942 wore on, orders multiplied.[30]

Unfortunately, the rubber shortage continued to tarnish Jones's "miracle man" reputation. He testified about it before the House Interstate and Foreign Commerce Committee, where newspapers reported he "disclaimed with some heat his responsibility for failing to obtain a greater stockpile of rubber before the war." Congressmen, who for ten years had only tossed a few softball questions his way before giving Jones whatever he wanted, were not so easygoing now. Neither was Jones. He asked those on the committee to raise their hands if they had anticipated the recent conquest of the entire Pacific by the Japanese. No one did. When a representative then asked Jones who should be blamed for the rubber shortage, Jones easily tossed back, "Well, Congress might take the responsibility if it wanted to. It did not start very early [to prepare for war]." In response to a question about synthetic rubber, Jones said, "Neither the president nor Congress ever gave me the authority to spend $500 million [$6.5 billion] for synthetic rubber production before January 10."[31]

28. Franklin Roosevelt to Jesse Jones, February 23, 1942, Jesse H. Jones Collection [LOC].
29. Jesse Jones to Franklin Roosevelt, November 6, 1942, Jesse H. Jones Collection [LOC].
30. White, Billions for Defense, 55.
31. New York Times, February 27, 1942.

In the end, Jones assured the committee, "I am convinced that if we use what we have carefully and sparingly, we will have enough for the war program with some to spare for essential civilian needs." The committee chairman was conciliatory in his reply, saying, "I am sure that the committee members feel that you have done everything possible to speed this program under the circumstances."[32]

Columnists and Jones antagonists Drew Pearson and Robert Allen were less appeased. They wrote after the hearings, "Few people realize how important loans are to the American war machine—and even less do they know what a throttlehold the man who controls those loans has upon war production. Reason is that most of the companies manufacturing war supplies have to receive loans from the Federal Treasury. Even such giant companies as Curtis, Packard, and General Motors have received war loans from the government." Most government loans were made through the RFC and Jones. They continued, "The speed of granting those loans, and the decision as to who gets them, not only means defeat or victory, but vitally affects the future economy of the United States." Repeating what they and others had said throughout the Great Depression, Pearson and Allen concluded, "That is why Jesse Jones today, as Federal Loan Administrator, is more powerful than the Chief of Staff, the Commander of the Fleet, the War Production Board, the Secretaries of War and Navy—in fact everyone in Washington save the President of the United States." As usual, they said Jones had too much power and was moving too slowly.[33]

Jones took matters in hand and released his own report to the president. Syndicated columnist Frank Kent of the *Baltimore Sun* said the report was "extraordinary" simply because it was "freer from the flub dub of the press agent than any that can now be recalled." He explained, "The Jones report is an accounting for the loans and commitments in connection with the war, amounting to the stupendous sum of $11½ billion [$150 billion] . . . Of particular interest, because of the criticism directed at him, is the chapter on rubber." Kent added, "Mr. Jones does not refer to the attack or defend himself."[34] Instead Jones laid out the facts as he saw them.

In the section that addressed rubber, Jones explained that four days after the original June 1940 legislation was passed that allowed the RFC to build plants and accumulate material for national defense, he signed

32. *Houston Chronicle*, February 26, 1942.
33. Pearson and Allen, "Washington Merry-Go-Round," March 6, 1942.
34. *Wall Street Journal*, March 26, 1942.

an agreement with the British and Dutch rubber cartel to buy everything available now and into the future. The four experimental synthetic rubber plants were approved six months later, and by May 1941 projected annual capacity was increased from 40,000 tons to 100,000 tons. After Pearl Harbor took everyone by surprise, plant capacity was multiplied to produce 400,000 tons, and expanded again to 700,000 tons after the fall of Singapore in February 1942. Jones said that the nation had a larger supply of rubber than ever before and that, in addition to fulfilling its own vital needs, the U.S. had to provide for other Allied nations, notably the British and the Russians. Kent concluded, "It is difficult to see wherein Mr. Jones lagged, or why he should have to 'take the rap.'"[35]

Even in the midst of Congressional hearings, Jones kept tabs on Texas doings, stepping in to help the president's son out of a financial jam. Elliott Roosevelt and his wife had owned a chain of twenty-three small radio stations throughout Texas, but by 1942 they were down to four, and those were losing money.[36] Elliott owed approximately $280,000 ($3.6 million), including $200,000 ($2.6 million) to John Hartford, president of the giant A&P grocery store chain, who had loaned him the money to buy the majority of the radio company stock. Sid Richardson, a mighty Texas oilman who had also invested in the radio company, persuaded Roosevelt to call Jones for help.[37] As Jones recalled, "In December 1941 the president asked me, as a personal favor to him, to look into Elliott's financial difficulties and see if anything could be done about them . . . Elliott had gone into the Army and had no way of paying his debts."[38]

Hartford met with Jones and said, "Candidly, I would rather not have Elliott Roosevelt's notes in my estate while I am living or after I am dead." Jones offered $4,000 ($52,000) to settle the debt and to buy back Elliot's pledged stock. It was the maximum one could give without incurring a gift tax. Jones counted the $4,000 as a gift, either to the president or to Elliott. Hartford gladly accepted, and on April 2, 1942, Jones delivered Elliott's stock and the cancelled note to the president.[39]

A few days later, the Truman Committee summoned Jones to testify about rubber shortages. Taking his seat, Jones rested his pince nez glasses on his thumb, leaned back and reported that the nation had a

---

35. Ibid.
36. Elliott Roosevelt to Charles Harwood, January 19, 1942, Jesse H. Jones Collection [HE].
37. Jones, *Fifty Billion Dollars*, 293–94.
38. Jesse Jones, testimony to the IRS, July 9, 1945, Jesse H. Jones Collection [HE].
39. Jones, *Fifty Billion Dollars*, 295.

President Franklin Roosevelt with his son, Elliott (left), whom Jones rescued from a
bad debt as a favor to the president, and Texas Governor James Allred (far right).
Courtesy Corbis.

stockpile of 700,000 tons of natural rubber and anticipated synthetic
rubber production of 300,000 tons in 1943 and 700,000 tons in 1944. He
told the committee that he frequently prodded cartel representative Sir
John Hay to increase raw rubber shipments by reminding him that development and production of synthetic rubber could be "undertaken here
on a large scale," in time eliminating the need for the cartel's product.
When Truman charged that a reliable source had accused the cartel of
pressuring Jones to abandon the synthetic rubber program all together,
Jones responded, "I doubt if he knew what he was talking about."[40]

He explained that manufacturing synthetic rubber on a large scale
was an "experimental field," in which "it was necessary for us to learn
how to do what we had to do while we were doing it." He said there were
many ways to produce synthetic rubber as well as various types, and that
up to now "large-scale commercial units have not been operated in this
country." Jones pointed out that he and the president had approved the

40. *Houston Chronicle*, April 7, 1942; *New York Times*, April 8, 1942.

experimental synthetic rubber program that Edward R. Stettinius and William L. Batt of the NDAC had brought to the RFC in September 1940. He added that they had "left a baby on our doorstep which hadn't been cleaned or washed." Or that was the way the *New York Times* reported it. The *Houston Chronicle* claimed he said, "The baby that was left on our doorstep had not been cleaned—if you know what I mean." Either way, the colorful remark evoked roars of laughter from the men on the committee. After testifying for more than two hours, the *Houston Chronicle* reported, "He was congratulated by Chairman Truman and other committee members."[41]

Eugene Meyer's *Washington Post* editorial about Jones's testimony was not so kind. Meyer and Jones had known each other since Woodrow Wilson's administration, when Meyer ran the War Finance Corporation, an early model for the RFC. He was serving as chairman of the Federal Reserve in 1932 when Herbert Hoover asked him to head the RFC, an organization and remedy Meyer himself had proposed. Jones, a Democratic member of the original bipartisan RFC board, and Meyer subsequently clashed over policy, particularly over publicizing loans and lending to municipalities and industry. (Jones was for both, and Meyer was against.) After Roosevelt became president, Meyer resigned from government and bought the *Washington Post*, rescuing it from bankruptcy. Jones's later remarks in speeches and broadcasts about the RFC's early days must have galled Meyer, especially when Jones said that the initial RFC board had been "entirely too timid," and that if it had judiciously loaned and invested more, much of the Great Depression would have been avoided. Ten years later, it was Meyer's turn.

A *Washington Post* editorial that focused on Jones's testimony before the Truman Committee accused him of hiding behind the "President, the British, and the Dutch," instead of accepting blame for the rubber shortage. It said, "The plain truth is that Mr. Jones fell down rather badly on the job of acquiring and producing sufficient rubber to meet an emergency that we should have foreseen." It explained, "The chief reason for his failure is a boundless ambition for power that has led to his taking on more jobs than he can successfully manage . . . Blaming the other fellow is a confession of defeat—not a mark of merit." With a final blow, it said, "The proof of an official's worth to his country lies in his ability to meet and conquer the kind of obstacles of which Mr. Jones complains."[42]

41. Ibid.
42. *Washington Post*, April 9, 1942.

That evening the Alfalfa Club—supposedly named for a plant that "does anything for a drink"—held a dinner at the Willard Hotel. Jones, Meyer, a few Supreme Court justices, and many influential politicians and businessmen attended. The event made front-page news the next day, but not because of anything said in a speech or divulged off the record. Instead, newspapers reported how toward the end of the evening, the usually unflappable Jones accosted Meyer, grabbed him by the lapels, and demanded a retraction. The exchange turned into a brawl. Columnist George Dixon of the *Washington Times-Herald* offered a tongue-in-cheek account. He reported, "A high-class ringside crowd . . . saw the administration's No. 1 money man, Jesse Jones, shake the daylights out of Eugene Meyer, multimillionaire Washington publisher, and then saw Eugene Meyer swinging like a maddened walrus in attempts to connect with the Jonesian chin." Dixon said Meyer "missed with a right and two lefts— which was all the swinging he had time for, considering that Jones had him by the lapels and practically lifted him off the floor—all the while rattling the publisher about like an empty barrel."[43]

Jones had a clear advantage in height and weight. *Time* magazine, which also covered the contretemps, described Jones as "hulking . . . 68, 6 ft. 3, 220 pounds" and Meyer as "trim . . . 66, 5 ft. 10, 186 pounds, who took boxing lessons for two years from Heavyweight Champion James J. Corbett."[44] One wag claimed Meyer missed his target because he "[was] so conservatively Republican that he found difficulty in moving to the left."[45] Dixon continued with his fun and wrote that the two statesmen "were pulled apart and lugged to neutral corners for a fanning." He said the "set to . . . had half official Washington in a shocked condition by midnight—by which time the news was around." Dixon wrapped up his nationally syndicated story saying that the "two battlers . . . were hustled by friends out into the night" and telling readers, "This just gives you a rough idea of the things that go on here in Washington."[46]

Roosevelt was "smilingly noncommittal" when asked about the dustup during a press conference.[47] But less than a week later, the president issued an executive order to shift responsibility for stockpiling from Jones to Vice President Wallace and the Bureau of Economic Warfare. Jones and Wallace had been at opposite ends of recovery policies from the start

43. *Washington Times-Herald,* April 10, 1942.
44. "Jesse Gets Ruffled."
45. *Houston Chronicle,* April 10, 1942.
46. Ibid.; *Washington Times-Herald,* April 10, 1942.
47. *New York Times,* April 10, 1942.

(left to right) Edward J. Flynn, Democratic National Committee chair; William S. Knudsen, Office of Production Management director; Jesse Jones; Jack Major; Vice President Henry Wallace; Associate Supreme Court Justice Robert H. Jackson; and U. S. Army Chief of Staff George Catlett Marshall at a Business Advisory Council Dinner hosted by Jones at the Shoreham Hotel.

of Roosevelt's first administration, when Wallace served as Agriculture Secretary. In 1940 Wallace became the most powerful vice president in history when Roosevelt gave him specific jobs to do that included taking charge of the SPAB and later the BEW. Like the RFC, both organizations were responsible for exports, imports, preclusive buying, and stockpiling. The competing organizations were an example of the confusion and resentments created by Roosevelt's predilection to assign the same responsibility to multiple parties. That tendency would lead to an explosion of epic proportion within his government.

The RFC was the original wartime agency. But since it had begun building plants and stockpiling in June 1940, Roosevelt had established thirty-five other agencies to coordinate and promote industrialization and militarization.[48] He abolished some —the NDAC, the OPM, and more re-

48. Culver and Hyde, *American Dreamer*, 257.

cently Wallace's SPAB—but would often replace them with new ones. The War Production Board, headed by Sears and Roebuck executive Donald Nelson, was one of the newest. William Knudsen was unceremoniously pushed aside when Nelson's WPB was given complete responsibility for production, despite the fact that Jones regarded Knudsen as one of the most effective figures during that crucial period. And now Wallace's BEW had been put in charge of procuring all of the materials needed for that production. Jones's RFC was only there to write the checks.

The prediction of Jones's demise was immediate. The day after Roosevelt announced the shift of responsibilities, the *St. Louis Post-Dispatch* referred to the "crumbling empire of Jesse H. Jones."[49] A *Wall Street Journal* reporter wrote, "Yesterday appears to have marked the fade-out of Jesse H. Jones as financier-in-chief of the war production program." He said that Jones had "apparently vanished." In addition to granting the BEW enormous new power, the article explained, Roosevelt had given the Army, Navy, and Maritime Commission the ability to arrange their own financing.[50] They would no longer need to go to Jones and the RFC for funds. Plant construction and stockpiling—Jones's two main responsibilities—had been taken from his hands. Or so it seemed. Almost as an aside, the *Wall Street Journal* reporter noted, "Although Mr. Jones apparently can act only as BEW tells him to, he still must sign the checks." The reporter pointed out that the RFC had the best terms and least complicated process for financing and constructing facilities and procuring materials.[51] The armed service chiefs knew that and, for the most part, continued to use the RFC instead of financing and planning their own projects.

Jones was more than miffed. He wrote Roosevelt that he intended to "cooperate in the new program," but, "In the interest of the work that is being done, and well done, I respectfully suggest that it would not be in the national interest to allow confusion, delay, and unnecessary waste to result from the manner in which the Executive Order is interpreted and administered." Next, probably referring to Knudsen, Jones added, "Nor would such course be fair to the loyal, patriotic, and capable men who are unselfishly consecrating their lives to this work without any hope of reward except an opportunity to serve their country and you faithfully." Many of them, he said, were "experienced in business and foreign

49. Ibid., 272.
50. *Wall Street Journal*, April 15, 1942.
51. Ibid.

Jesse Jones, Milo Perkins, and Henry Wallace, the primary players in Washington's war within the war. Courtesy Jesse Holman Jones Papers, Dolph Briscoe Center for American History, University of Texas at Austin.

commerce" and were "working without compensation."[52] Behind the diplomatic language, the message was clear. Jones did not like the situation or the results.

Two days later, he delivered another letter to Roosevelt in which he explained that the Metals Reserve Company, the Rubber Reserve Company, the Defense Supplies Corporation, the United States Commercial Corporation, and the Export-Import Bank were all very actively engaged in "buying, financing, transporting, storing, and distributing strategic and critical materials . . . in some 33 countries." He said, "There are well over 100 separate and distinct negotiations now in progress." Jones complained that Milo Perkins, Wallace's chief assistant, insisted on BEW participation in all contract negotiations, amendments, and conclusions.[53]

52. Jesse Jones to Franklin Roosevelt, April 21, 1942, Jesse H. Jones Collection [HE].
53. Jesse Jones to Franklin Roosevelt, April 23, 1942, Jesse H. Jones Collection [HE].

As luck would have it, Perkins had been in business years before in Houston and had been mixed up with a religious group that held services for a time in his attic. Even though he was also an extremely effective administrator and tactician, Jones disliked and distrusted him. Jones continued, "This means that every agreement, however simple, will have to be negotiated by two departments of the government, and finally approved by executives of both departments. This procedure will . . . greatly slow down this highly important war work."[54] As the bureaucratic wrangling went on, Jones conducted RFC business as usual and withheld funds from the BEW whenever he did not approve of its contracts and programs, which, of course, infuriated Wallace and Perkins.

Attacks against Jones and RFC's war agencies continued. A Democratic senator accused Jones of "paying tremendous amounts for know-how" and making "miserable progress" on an enormous $73 million ($950 million) DPC magnesium plant in Nevada, whose construction had brought almost 7,000 jobs to the area. Jones responded flatly, "The very serious charge of malfeasance against officials of DPC is completely refuted by the facts . . . , is false and misleading . . . , and is unworthy of a United States senator." Jones included a detailed accounting of the plant and had his statement to the committee filed by its chairman, Truman.[55] The accusations offended Jones, but responding to them was like swatting at flies—there were always more.

Jones defended his record and at the same time rose above the fray in a rousing speech at the 30th annual meeting of the U.S. Chamber of Commerce. He told the crowd in Chicago that the way to "win the war in the shortest possible time . . . is work and production, with no time out." He said, "Converting our industrial energies and our technical skill into war work, . . . with our support of . . . other United Nations that are at deadly grips with the enemy, has already upset the time-table of Mr. Hitler." Jones pointed out, "Miracles [are] being performed daily in American shops and factories," and he predicted that the "German people are losing confidence, are getting tired of the war, that they see the handwriting on the wall." He declared, "As Secretary of Commerce and Federal Loan Administrator, I see business and government working together, hand in hand, in the greatest effort the world has ever known."[56]

54. Ibid.

55. *Houston Chronicle*, April 24, 1942.

56. Jesse Jones, speech, U.S. Chamber of Commerce, Chicago, April 30, 1942, Jesse H. Jones Collection [UT].

Just as he had once recited the mind-numbing list of RFC investments in banks, houses, farms, and railroads during the Great Depression, Jones laid out an even more impressive array of facts and figures about the Corporation's ever-increasing investment in industrialization and militarization. He described how aluminum production was projected to increase seven times, magnesium output to jump twenty times, and synthetic rubber to go from virtually zero to 800,000 tons inside of two years. Jones talked about the $1.4 billion ($18.2 billion) spent on supplying machine tools to factories across the nation, about the opening of the Texas City tin smelter—the nation's first—and about the way the RFC was "buying everything needed in the war effort from A to Z, from antimony to zirconium." He said that the RFC had "bought practically all the private airplanes in the country and turned them over to the Army and Navy," and that it had financed forty-eight flight schools to train pilots to fly the tens of thousands of new fighter planes pouring out of RFC-financed factories.[57]

The RFC's investment in aviation was truly monumental. Fourteen of the fifteen largest new engine plants were wholly or partially owned by the DPC. The DPC and other RFC corporations were behind the factories that manufactured the aluminum, magnesium, and steel required for the airplanes and their bombs, built the airplane engines, supplied the 100-octane gasoline to fuel the engines, supplied the rubber for the tires, and assembled everything into finished airplanes. They also operated training schools where most U.S. pilots and thousands of British pilots learned how to fly.[58]

Jones concluded, "We have built or put equipment in approximately 1,000 plants for the production of war material." As he had during the Great Depression, he recognized his colleagues, particularly the president, acknowledging the efforts of "Secretary Stimson and Under Secretary Patterson of the War Department . . . [and] Frank Knox and Jim Forrestal of the Navy," as well as Nelson, Knudsen, Leon Henderson, and Paul McNutt—all important contributors to domestic mobilization—and "above all . . . the man who has the final responsibility, our great President, Franklin Delano Roosevelt."[59]

Jones's speech was widely covered. One might think a public relations

57. Ibid.
58. White, *Billions for Defense*, 68–71.
59. Jesse Jones, speech, U.S. Chamber of Commerce, Chicago, April 30, 1942, Jesse H. Jones Collection [UT].

campaign had been started to restore his reputation. Soon after his highly publicized testimony and speech, Jones's granddaughter, Audrey, launched a Liberty Ship, the *Matthew Maury*, at the Houston Shipbuilding Corporation on the Ship Channel.[60] Noted journalist George Creel published a pro-Jones article about the rubber shortage in *Collier's*, a hugely popular magazine with a circulation of 2,500,000, the gist of which was excerpted in many of the nation's papers. Creel cited the evidence and concluded, "There is a fairly general belief carefully fostered in certain Washington circles that the ice-eyed Texan, jealous of his reputation as a shrewd bargainer, delayed negotiations by haggling and 'horse-trading.' On the contrary, the record shows that Jones acted with a speed that must have jarred his cautious soul to the depths." After carefully analyzing the synthetic rubber situation, Creel reported, "Both the president and Mr. Jones looked to have the right to exchange congratulations."[61]

According to Jones, they could also pat themselves on the back about aluminum. He testified before a Senate Banking Subcommittee, saying, "It looks like we are going to have ample aluminum." He remarked, "We've done a lot of interesting things, all of which cost money," and then recited what the RFC had committed to defense: $2 billion ($26 billion) for airplanes, $700 million ($9.1 billion) on synthetic rubber, $734 million ($9.6 billion) on steel, and $182 million ($2.4 billion) on shipyards. He even described how an RFC subsidiary had purchased six million animal hides and had another six million on the way. Then Jones asked for $5 billion ($65 billion) more in borrowing and lending authority. He said that would suffice for now, but added that it may be necessary to ask for more.[62]

As Jones's request was winding its way through Congress, Firestone Tire and Rubber announced it had produced the first synthetic rubber from one of the new plants and that it would be used "in making the latest type combat tire for military vehicles."[63] Later in the month, Jones told the House Interstate Committee that "two or three [synthetic rubber] plants are coming into production in a small way," but by the end of the year, output would be 100,000 tons. Because many committee members had questions about supposed delays, Jones added, "Only a few are very far along because the engineering is the most difficult part." It was also hard to get scarce construction materials. But, Jones said, "We are now

---

promised the highest priorities for the materials necessary to build these plants."[64]

More than building materials were hard to get. Butter, coffee, sugar, and coal—everything was scarce because wartime demand was so extraordinarily high. To contain inflation, Roosevelt had frozen all retail prices at their March high in a program called the General Maximum Price Regulation, or "General Max."[65] Inflation was thus added to threats against the nation and to the RFC's list of critical issues to handle. Jones intended to use part of the requested $5 billion ($65 billion) to maintain these newly imposed price ceilings on commodities by paying subsidies to producers and processors. As a result, Jones's power was not diminishing, but increasing.[66] As Owen L. Scott, a *Washington Star* columnist, observed, "A few short weeks ago there were those who saw Mr. Jones edged out of the center of things . . . Yet today Mr. Jones is in the picture more than ever." He explained that one of Jones's "new tasks is to backstop the government's new system of price control, which reaches to the heart of the economic system. It is a task of immense difficulty . . . a job that requires much wisdom and experience."[67] Leon Henderson, in charge of the program to set and maintain maximum prices for commodities and consumer products, turned to Jones.

John Kenneth Galbraith, who worked with Henderson, met with Jones about subsidizing the price of coal. As Galbraith recalled, "Jesse—Uncle Jesse we called him—was our avenue to the financial world . . . particularly on the whole matter of subsidies to hold down prices." Galbraith explained that German submarines were sinking transport vessels traveling along the east coast. He said, "No sooner had we set [the price of coal than] word came that all . . . shipments . . . were going to have to go by rail because of the submarine menace. That, of course, cost a lot more money for utilities and consumers. So here we [had] proclaimed our intention of setting all prices, and suddenly we were faced with an absolute necessity to raise them." Galbraith continued, "So one afternoon . . . we went to see, out of desperation, Jesse Jones and Will Clayton, another noted Texan, and explained the situation we were in. We had set all [the] prices and now we had to raise [the price of coal,] a very important segment. Will Clayton listened, and Uncle Jesse listened, and they gave us

64. *Houston Chronicle*, May 28, 1942.
65. Schwarz, *Speculator*, 390.
66. *Houston Chronicle*, May 26, 1942.
67. *Washington Star*, May 31, 1942.

Jesse Jones and Leon Henderson, head of the Office of Price Administration, leave the White House on May 22, 1942, after talking about oil pipelines with President Franklin Roosevelt. Courtesy Corbis.

$10 million [$130 million] as [a] subsidy to hold the price of coal in the east. I remember to this day what a relief it was to know that we had established the principle of price stability for the war."[68]

The German submarines, or U-boats (for *unterseeboot*), were lethal. Before Pearl Harbor, the swarms of U-boats largely kept to Europe's Atlantic coast where they torpedoed ships carrying supplies and arms to the Allied nations. Churchill wrote, "The U-boat attack was our worst evil, the only thing that ever really frightened me during the war."[69] After the U.S. entered the war, the U-boats' territory expanded and they now lurked along the Atlantic coasts of South, Central, and North America. Tankers loaded with petroleum going from the Gulf Coast to the northeast were their favored targets. Karl Donitz, head of Germany's U-boat division, declared, "By attacking the supply traffic—particularly the oil—in the U.S. zone, I am striking at the root of the evil, for here the sinking

68. John Kenneth Galbraith to Steven Fenberg, November 22, 1996, Oral History Project [HE].
69. Kennedy, *Freedom from Fear,* 571.

of each ship . . . deals a blow at the source of his shipbuilding and war production."[70] In the first half of 1942, Nazi U-boats sank 171 ships traveling between Florida and New York, and sixty-two in the Gulf of Mexico. Delivery of oil and fuel stocks to the east coast fell by ninety percent.[71]

In response to the U-boats and with approval of President Roosevelt and Interior Secretary Harold Ickes, who was petroleum coordinator, Jones announced the construction of a massive twenty-four-inch pipeline to carry oil from Texas to Pennsylvania and New Jersey. Jones told W. Alton Jones, of Cities Services who represented the east coast oil companies, "It is understood that the oil industry will supply the necessary personnel, which shall be satisfactory to us, to construct and operate the lines."[72] The DPC would fund and own the pipeline; the DSC would supervise the oil industry's management.[73] This pipeline was as significant, if not more so, than the aqueduct that the RFC built during the Great Depression to take water from Colorado to California. Most oil pipelines in the U.S. were no more than eight inches in diameter, and all of them were much shorter than the 1,300 miles between east Texas and the east coast. Hundreds of thousands of contiguous transcontinental acres had to be assembled, surveyed, and cleared, and miles of tunnels had to be dug under the Mississippi River and two hundred other bodies of water to accommodate the "Big Inch" pipeline. The first pipes were laid less than two months after Jones made his announcement. From there on out, miles of pipe each day were installed on the $100 million ($1.3 billion) project.[74]

With pipeline construction just started, Henderson faced the same problem with oil that Galbraith had with coal. He wrote Jones that the oil industry was on the verge of collapse because of the exorbitant costs associated with moving petroleum by rail. He explained that the east coast required about "1,500,000 barrels daily, of which 95 percent in past years has been shipped in tankers." Henderson wrote that the extra transport cost "would require price increases of such magnitude as to imperil the entire price stabilization program . . . I am, therefore, asking, as an emergency war measure, . . . to make funds available through the Reconstruction Finance Corporation to meet the additional costs of transportation." Henderson concluded, "If sufficient funds are not forthcoming promptly,

70. Ibid., 566.
71. Burrough, *Big Rich*, 148.
72. *New York Times*, June 12, 1942.
73. Jones, *Fifty Billion Dollars*, 344.
74. Burrough, *Big Rich*, 150.

I am fearful that the petroleum supply program of the Atlantic Coast will collapse."[75]

Congress and the president were acutely aware of the problem. On June 6 President Roosevelt signed a bill that added $5 billion ($65 billion) to Jones's RFC bank account to address these needs.[76] The president wrote, "I am anxious that every possible administrative step be taken to maintain the price ceiling established under the General Maximum Price Regulations." Knowing Jones's reluctance to take a deliberate loss, the president pushed him to do so "in those instances in which the situation is so critical that some sort of action needs to be taken." Acknowledging Jones's power, Roosevelt closed, "You should . . . promptly advise congressional leaders of your plans in order to be assured that they have full understanding of the program and will facilitate legislation necessary for its success."[77]

U-boats, inflation, oil and coal transport, and rubber shortages threatened the home front. On the strength of the president's handwritten approval at the bottom of his letter, Jones instructed the RFC to start buying scrap rubber from the public above the ceiling price. Jones hoped to bring in 300,000 tons of scrap each year by offering a more attractive price than was currently legal. Roosevelt delivered a national radio address and urged people to turn in "every bit of rubber you can possibly spare" to any of the country's 400,000 gasoline stations. Patriotic citizens would be paid one cent for every pound they brought in as a contribution to the war effort. Through everyone's efforts, there would be "enough rubber to win this war." The president also asked listeners to drive less and slower to save rubber.[78]

Despite losing nominal authority to Wallace's BEW, Jones was still very much in the driver's seat. And he continued to be honored. Along with Pulitzer and Nobel Prize-winning author Pearl S. Buck, Jones received an honorary law degree from St. Lawrence University on June 8, and another one from Northwestern University on June 15. Jones had now accumulated eleven honorary degrees. From the graduation in Chicago, the Joneses went to Houston, where Audrey was getting married. About the only thing that could have pried Jones away from official business was his beloved granddaughter's wedding to John Albert Boehck, a lieuten-

---

75. Leon Henderson to Jesse Jones, June 5, 1942, Jesse H. Jones Collection [HE].

76. *New York Times*, June 7, 1942.

77. Franklin Roosevelt to Jesse Jones, June 19, 1942, Jesse H. Jones Collection [HE].

78. *Houston Chronicle*, June 13, 1942.

Pulitzer and Nobel Prize-winning author Pearl S. Buck and Jesse Jones receive honorary law degrees from St. Lawrence University on June 8, 1942. Although Jones had only an eighth-grade education, he accumulated eleven honorary degrees during his lifetime. Courtesy Briscoe Center for American History, University of Texas at Austin.

ant serving in the Naval Reserve at the new base in Corpus Christi, where John and Audrey had met during the opening of the Officer's Club.[79] The Joneses arrived in Houston on Thursday, June 18, were met at the train station by the usual mix of family, friends, and press. Jones spoke briefly to the reporters, saying, "The war production program is proceeding excellently. It couldn't be better," then he left with Mary for the Lamar Hotel.[80]

Jones mixed business with pleasure the next day by attending the launch of the Victory Ship *Mirabeau B. Lamar* at the Houston Shipbuilding Corporation yard, where each of the sixty-nine ships produced there was named for a Texas hero. Thousands of workmen and a few dignitaries attended the ceremony, where Jones spoke. "You men in overalls are just as important as the men in khaki," he acknowledged. "Every time you strike a blow on one of these ships, you strike a blow for the boys in the armed forces in all corners of the earth." Jones recounted, "Not all of the people thought that it was our war or that we should take part in

79. The couple eventually shortened their name to Beck.
80. *Houston Chronicle,* June 19, 1942.

On June 19, 1942, Jesse Jones attended the launch of the *Mirabeau B. Lamar* victory ship at the Houston Shipbuilding Corporation yard and told the workers during his speech, "You men in overalls are just as important as the men in khaki" (*Houston Chronicle*, June 19, 1942).

this war. Others who thought we should take part in the war didn't know what part." Then he said, "After Pearl Harbor, every man, woman, and child got fighting mad and will continue to be fighting mad until this war is won."[81]

On Saturday night at his granddaughter's wedding, Jones stood up as John Boehck's best man. Audrey's father, Tilford, walked her down the flower-lined aisle and through the packed Christ Church Cathedral before handing her to the groom. A full-page *Houston Chronicle* wedding announcement gushed, "The ballroom at the Rice Hotel was transformed

81. Ibid.

Jesse Jones with his granddaughter, Audrey, and her husband, John Boehck (later Beck). The Becks accumulated a renowned collection of Impressionist and Post-Impressionist paintings, which Audrey donated to the Museum of Fine Arts, Houston, after John's death in 1973. The John A. and Audrey Jones Beck Collection is housed in the Audrey Jones Beck Building at the Museum of Fine Arts, Houston.

into a veritable garden for the reception which followed the ceremony." The article also noted, "Lieutenant and Mrs. Boehck have gone to Fort Worth for a brief stay, after which they will motor to San Pedro, California, where they plan to be located for a year."[82] John flew airplanes fresh from the factory to wherever they needed to go.

A lot had happened in Houston during Jones's absence. Annual bank transactions passed $3 billion ($39 billion) for the first time in the city's history. Like most everywhere else, the jump came from the construction

82. *Houston Chronicle*, June 21, 1942.

and operation of new defense plants.[83] Furthermore, Houston's record-breaking transactions were calculated before it was announced the DPC would build for $32 million ($417 million) two plants in the area to produce rubber ingredients and lease them to the Humble Oil and Refining Company to operate.[84] Soon almost every major oil, chemical, and rubber company would be involved in the synthetic rubber industry. In addition to its industrial expansion, the city had sold a 134-acre tract of land south of downtown for a medical center that would include a hospital and research center for cancer, a children's hospital, a public clinic, and an institution to treat tuberculosis. These facilities would grow eventually into the world-renowned Texas Medical Center. According to the *Houston Chronicle*, the city had originally purchased the land in 1923, "on time payments, for $293,000 [$3.8 million]."[85]

The Joneses barely had time to enjoy Houston or Audrey's wedding. The press of duties waiting in Washington was unyielding. Inflation was still at the front of Jones's mind. As if the Nazis and Japanese were not scary enough, Jones delivered a national radio address titled "The Dangers of Inflation" to help Roosevelt sell his program to fix prices. Roosevelt frequently turned to Jones's power of persuasion, his straightforward language, and his credibility to push his policies with the public. Jones began, "Inflation once out of control definitely means disaster." He explained, "War has removed from the market many necessities and other things to which we have become accustomed. If they are not missing entirely . . . they will be scarce, and without effective control, prices will get out of bounds, and we will all be wrecked on the rock of inflation." Jones told his listeners, "The American people will have over thirty billion dollars more income in 1943 than the value of things for which the money can be spent. This is a potential 'inflationary gap' greater than any the world has ever known."[86]

He asked, "What shall we do, then, with this extra thirty billion dollars?" Encouraging responsibility, he said, "The answer is, share the cost of war through taxation, pay our debts, and put the balance in war bonds and stamps to help pay the cost of the war and to accumulate savings that we will need when the war is over. This is both prudent and patriotic." Jones closed the sale with, "If we can come out of this conflict with our

83. *Houston Chronicle*, January 1, 1942.
84. *Houston Chronicle*, June 3, 1942.
85. *Houston Chronicle*, March 18, 1942.
86. Jesse Jones, Mutual Broadcasting System radio address, "The Dangers of Inflation," July 8, 1942, Jesse H. Jones Collection [UT].

private debts greatly reduced and with a substantial investment in our country's future in the form of war bonds, we will be in a better position to undertake conversion from war to peace . . . When the war is over, we will have productive capacity far beyond any that either we or the world has ever known." He continued, "This great productive capacity can, however, be a Frankenstein if . . . people are not prepared and equipped to buy what our factories can produce [after the war]. That is why it will be wise not to spend unnecessarily now."[87] While Jones was asking the public to delay gratification to prevent inflation, he was also sowing policy seeds for a postwar economic and consumer boom.

In case he had not convinced his millions of listeners of the importance of keeping inflation down, Jones added, "Hitler would like to see inflation in the United States because he knows it would destroy confidence, create confusion, discord, and discontent, and make it more difficult for us to fight the war." Jones quoted the president, who had said fighting inflation is "the only front and [the] one battle where everyone in the United States—every man, woman, and child—is in action and will be privileged to remain in action throughout the war." Jones closed, "So let us see to it that all who are not in uniform enlist with the President in the battle against inflation. We can no more afford to lose this battle than we can afford to lose the war."[88] Jones told the nation to spend less, save more, and get ready for an abundant future. Soon he would also have to tell them to quit driving.

But first he had to tell the president not to buy the Empire State Building. He had avoided the issue for a year and in a letter to the president, Jones explained his slowness to take action, saying that "the price they are asking for the Empire State Building cannot, in my opinion, be justified."[89] By "they" he meant John J. Raskob, a former chairman of the Democratic National Committee who owned eighty-two percent of the Empire State Building Corporation, and former New York Governor Alfred Smith, who owned ten percent and managed the building. Both men had been instrumental in persuading Roosevelt to run for governor of New York in 1928, his stepping-stone to the presidency. Smith had supported Roosevelt's political aspirations, nominating him for president at the 1932 national convention, a time when Raskob had been Democratic

87. Ibid.
88. Ibid.
89. Jesse Jones to Franklin Roosevelt, July 29, 1942, Jesse H. Jones Collection [LOC].

National Committee chairman. Jones knew Roosevelt wanted to help his old party compatriots.

Jones said that the building had been completed in 1931 and, with land, had cost $48.4 million ($630 million) to build; the asking price was $45 million ($585 million). He said the building was worth about $27 million ($351 million), adding, "In these figures I have deducted nothing for the extraordinary cost of operating the Empire State Building due to its abnormal height, as compared to buildings of normal height, say 20 to 30 stories." Added to the high price and costs, Jones said that the building was losing money and the rep who was pushing the sale would receive $1 million ($13 million) in commission if the building sold at the asking price.[90] According to Jones, Roosevelt responded, "Yes, Jess, all that is probably true, but I would like to do something for Al Smith. He is broke and has an expensive family."[91] Jones didn't think that was reason enough for the government to pay such a high price for the building. When Governor Smith found out about Jones's position on the property, he stiffly told the president he would prefer to negotiate with someone else, and Roosevelt asked Jones to return the Empire State Building files, which he gladly did. The issue was far from resolved, however, and continued to sour Roosevelt's relationship with Jones.

The problem with rubber was also far from resolved as restrictions on civilian use escalated and supplies continued to shrink. Trucks delivering soft drinks, hard drinks, and other "nonessential materials" were prohibited from buying new tires.[92] Disputes over whether to make synthetic rubber from grain or petroleum added to the problem. Roosevelt created a committee to get a grip on the dire situation. He appointed Bernard Baruch as chair and asked Harvard University President James B. Conant and MIT President Dr. Karl T. Compton to assist with the study.[93] Within five weeks, Baruch, Compton, and Conant had delivered their report, written for them by journalist Sam Lubell, who had authored the critical two-part article on Jones in the *Saturday Evening Post* two years ago.

They said, "We find the existing situation to be so dangerous that unless corrective measures are taken immediately, this country will face both a military and a civilian collapse. The naked facts present a warning that

90. Ibid.
91. Jones, *Fifty Billion Dollars*, 460.
92. *Houston Chronicle*, July 25, 1942.
93. *Houston Chronicle*, August 6, 1942.

dare not be ignored." They documented how much rubber was on hand and how much was required, and warned that the nation was quickly facing a shortage of 211,000 tons. They reported that "unless adequate new supplies (natural or artificial) can be obtained in time, the total military and export requirements alone will exhaust our crude stocks before the end of next summer." The committee said the first priority should be the "maintenance of a rubber reserve that will keep our armed forces fighting and our essential civilian wheels turning. This can best be done by 'bulling through' the present gigantic synthetic program and by safeguarding jealously every ounce of rubber in the country." The committee recommended implementing a nationwide thirty-five-mile-per-hour speed limit, restricting civilian driving to five thousand miles per year, and rationing gasoline. They explained, "Gas rationing is the only way of saving rubber . . . The limitation [we propose] in . . . gasoline is not due to a shortage of that commodity—it is wholly a measure of rubber saving. That is why the restriction is to be nationwide. Any localized measure would be unfair and futile." They added, "Each time a motorist turns a wheel in unnecessary driving, he must realize that it is a turn of the wheel against our soldiers and in favor of Hitler." The committee allowed, "This [one] note of optimism is permissible: If the synthetic program herein outlined will fulfill reasonable expectancy, it will be possible to lessen this curtailment before the end of 1943. But until then, any relaxation is a service to the enemy."[94]

The report's writers glanced only briefly into the past and blamed no one in particular for the shortage. They said instead, "These errors, growing out of procrastinations, indecisions, conflict of authority, clashes of personalities, lack of understanding . . . are not to be recounted by us." What they recommended was the appointment of a "Rubber Administrator" to coordinate and control the entire effort. The investigators complained that not enough technical and scientific advice had been sought, and that the Russians should have been consulted about their own "synthetic system." But they added reassuringly, "The committee has investigated the status of the present government program for the production of synthetic rubber and believes that every one of the processes is technically sound and ultimately will work." In bold letters, the report concluded, "THE COMMITTEE RECOMMENDS THAT THE PRESENT PROGRAM BE PUSHED FORWARD WITH THE GREATEST POSSIBLE SPEED, WITHOUT

94. Bernard Baruch, James Compton, and Karl Conant, report to the president, September 10, 1942, Jesse H. Jones Collection [HE].

FURTHER CHANGE, EXCEPT THAT IF NEW PROJECTS ARE ADOPTED, THEY BE MADE ADDITIONS TO THE PRESENT PROGRAM." Baruch, Compton, and Conant ended by writing, "In drawing up these recommendations, the Committee has sought to find a basis upon which the entire nation can go forward together, uniting our energies against the enemy instead of dissipating them in domestic wrangling."[95]

Jones took comfort in the report's conclusions, but it was not in his nature to allow remarks about the lack of technical advice and Russian expertise to pass without comment. He sent the president three letters in a row after the Baruch report was released. The first gave the report a positive spin: "As I understand the Baruch Committee report, the present program is given unqualified approval." Jones then began angling for control. He reminded the president about an earlier conversation, "As [I] mentioned to you yesterday afternoon, a new administrator, unfamiliar with what has been done, is apt to slow the program down, particularly if he sets up a new organization." Then he proceeded to recommend a number of people for the position, including the president of Studebaker, president of the U.S. Chamber of Commerce, and president of Proctor & Gamble, adding in a handwritten postscript, "There are, of course, many more."[96]

After Jones had had time to digest the complete document, he sent Roosevelt a five-page letter crammed with his observations and opinions about every point made in the report. Jones particularly liked when Baruch and his group said that creating the synthetic rubber industry, one of the largest industries in the country, normally "would require a dozen years." It gave context to his own "slow" progress when they said, "To compress it into less than two years is almost a superhuman task." He reviewed his "superhuman" accomplishments, writing, "As you know, RFC was authorized to create a stockpile of crude rubber on June 28, 1940 . . . We acquired every ton of rubber that we could purchase until the sources of natural rubber were cut off by enemy action . . . We were able to accumulate more than 634,000 tons of rubber, by far the largest rubber stockpile ever possessed by any nation in the world." As for the lack of technical advice noted in the report, Jones countered that the program's chief advisor had collaborated with "one hundred and eighty-four technicians working together and with him in the rubber program." He returned to the point in another part of the lengthy letter, noting that he and others

95. Ibid.
96. Jesse Jones to Franklin Roosevelt, September 12, 1942, Jesse H. Jones Collection [HE].

had worked with "technicians from the automobile, rubber, and chemical industries," who had "investigated many different possibilities."[97]

Jones tended to take any hint of criticism to heart. More than a dozen years later, in his book about the RFC, he once again brought up the Baruch report, repeated his counter to the technical support charge, and addressed the accusation that he had not contacted the Russians. He wrote that a mission went to Russia and had come back with "no information that could make any contribution to the American synthetic rubber program." For emphasis, he put in italics, *The commission never got inside any Russian plants.*[98]

Toward the end of his letter, Jones complimented the committee's work, writing, "The report should go far toward answering questions that naturally arise in the minds of people all over the country who have been confused by conflicting statements, many of which have been false, misleading, and self-serving." Noting that the survey said the U.S. had "a good rubber program," he promised to "cooperate wholeheartedly with WPB, the new administrator, and anyone else that may be designated to have a part in the rubber program." He then attached an extremely long report detailing the location, capacity, cost, and completion date of the forty-one RFC synthetic rubber plants.[99]

The last letter was in the form of a memo that Jones hand-delivered to Roosevelt, right before the president's press conference. He wrote, "I think it a great mistake to allow the country to get the impression from the Baruch report that a great deal has not been accomplished in the rubber situation, both crude and synthetic. About all has already been done toward synthetic rubber that the Baruch report recommends, and the balance can be contracted within a few days if the critical materials can be spared."[100] Jones sat behind the president as he spoke to the reporters, but to his disappointment Roosevelt said nothing about the Baruch report or Jones's role in rubber.

Jones gave the report further thought over the years. He would later recall, "In making his report, my friend Baruch was willing to give me a little dig—for reasons of his own, maybe." He added, "Baruch . . . like some other Wall Streeters, [was] none too pleased that the RFC, the biggest banking and industrial corporation in history, could be run without

97. Jesse Jones to Franklin Roosevelt, September 13, 1942, Jesse H. Jones Collection [HE].
98. Jones, *Fifty Billion Dollars*, 414.
99. Jesse Jones to Franklin Roosevelt, September 13, 1942, Jesse H. Jones Collection [HE].
100. Memo, September 15, 1942, Jesse H. Jones Collection [HE].

calling on [him]."[101] Nonetheless, Baruch's clear intention was to serve the country and to get the people rallying behind rationing and conservation. His report worked. According to a Gallup Poll survey, forty-nine percent were in favor of gasoline rationing before the Baruch report was released; afterward, seventy-three percent thought it was a good idea.[102] One month after the report, a thirty-five-mile-per-hour speed limit was imposed on drivers of privately owned cars.[103]

In the end William Jeffers, president of Union Pacific Railroad, was selected as the new "Rubber Czar." A press report said, "Jeffers is expected to become, in effect, complete boss over the rubber reserve company and all other government agencies in matters affecting the rubber program." Jeffers was quoted as saying, "This means I have a tough job . . . The biggest stock pile of rubber we have is on the wheels of our automobiles. I ask every motorist, every truck driver, everybody who runs a car, to remember that he is now the custodian of a material more precious than gold."[104]

While Jeffers may have been officially in charge of rubber, he knew who paid the bills and whose back to scratch. Jeffers met with the Texas Congressional delegation almost immediately after his appointment and said, "I don't know what shape this country might have been in if we hadn't had Mr. Jones in there for the last 10 years. He is second only to President Roosevelt." Jeffers added, "The rubber situation is in a lot better shape than we have heard." The Texas congressmen appeared to be more concerned about gasoline rationing in their spread-out state than about Jones's reputation.[105] Jones didn't give Jeffers much due in later years. "Under his direction we continued our rubber program and carried it out and completed it 97 per cent as we had planned it . . . ," Jones recalled. "Mr. Jeffers directed us to do a few things which the Baruch committee had recommended . . . but soon rescinded most of those orders. As for natural rubber, he made no suggestion to us." Jones said Jeffers's largest contribution was "hammering away at getting materials for the construction of the synthetic rubber plants. He was continually at cross purposes with the War Department in fighting for materials." In a complimentary aside to Jeffers, Jones said, "We got them."[106]

Jeffers's role in the rubber program gave Jones time to focus on other

101. Jones, *Fifty Billion Dollars,* 412.
102. Schwarz, *Speculator,* 395.
103. *Houston Chronicle,* October 1, 1942.
104. *Houston Chronicle,* September 16, 1942.
105. *Houston Chronicle,* October 8, 1942.
106. Jones, *Fifty Billion Dollars,* 412–13.

Jesse Jones and William Jeffers (far right) inspect a piece of synthetic rubber.

demands. In a *Life* magazine photo spread of important wartime figures, Jones was shown at his desk, on his phone, eating lunch. The description read, "Jesse Jones eats in his own office every day, usually having soup, lamb chop, lettuce and tomato salad, rye crisp, butter, and coffee." Then the short paragraph said, "To define Jones's responsibilities would be to list virtually every organization within the national Government. Essentially, as Federal Loan Administrator, it is his job to finance the industrial plant expansion for waging war."[107]

Helping people understand the war effort and bringing them into it was also part of his job. In the fall Jones was on national radio to talk about the new "Air Age," which the RFC had helped create through its investments in aviation. Jones began, "For thousands of years, ever since the days of the Greeks and the Hebrew prophets, men have been dreaming of the day when they would fashion themselves a pair of wings and go flying through the skies with the freedom of a bird. That day has dawned . . .

107. *Life* (October 5, 1942).

In a photo spread of important wartime figures, *Life* magazine featured Jesse Jones among others, and said, ". . . it is his job to finance the industrial plant expansion for waging war" (*Life*, October 5, 1942). Courtesy Getty Images.

the sky is the new frontier waiting to be explored and conquered." He told listeners about the "nation-wide educational program" sponsored by the Commerce Department's Civil Aeronautics Administration, where in school "many boys and girls . . . have begun to learn for the first time more about airplanes, what makes them go, their place in modern life." He described the civilian training program that "has produced some 80,000 pilots, more than 30,000 of whom are now serving in the armed forces." Jones predicted, "After this war there will be a phenomenal boom in flying for all purposes—as phenomenal as the growth of the automobile and truck after the last war." He added, "There can be no doubt that our future strength lies in air power and our ability to make use of it . . . In the future it will mark our progress, measure our welfare, and will be our most effective aid in maintaining the just peace for which we are now

A Boeing aircraft plant during World War II. The RFC invested ten times more in aviation than the industry, until then, had spent on itself during its entire history.

fighting."[108] The RFC had invested ten times more on aviation than the industry had spent on itself during its entire history. As a result, Jones and the RFC profoundly influenced air transportation, defense, and science in the United States and around the world.

Jones's naysayers had settled down. Even Pearson wrote, "Jesse Jones and a German Jew named Hochschild are doing a good job on tin . . . Hochschild provides the ore and Jones does the smelting." He continued, "Jones was highly criticized at the beginning for his delays in establishing the smelter, and then waiting priceless months while he picked a site near his hometown of Houston. But now the plant is turning out metallic tin at high speed."[109] Jones was proud of the tin production as well. After the

108. Jesse Jones, radio address, "Air Age," September 10, 1942, Jesse H. Jones Collection [UT].

109. Pearson, "Washington Merry-Go-Round," September 27, 1942. Robert Allen had left the column to serve in the armed forces.

smelter first produced tin in May, he wrote the president, "I enclose the 'Roosevelt tin dollar,' made from the first run of fine tin smelted at the government's wholly owned tin smelter at Texas City on . . . May 5th. We have an excellent tin smelter that will have an annual capacity of 50,000 tons of fine tin."[110]

Meanwhile, synthetic rubber plants were finally coming on-line even as manufacturers were turning citizens' scrap rubber into urgently needed tires. Goodyear announced it was about to start producing "war tires" from reclaimed rubber that would be good "for 10,000 miles if not driven above 35 miles an hour." B. F. Goodrich made a similar announcement at around the same time.[111]

Metals were almost as scarce as rubber, and the Metals Reserve Company began buying and recycling "old bridges, abandoned buildings, household scrap, and any other metal that the general public, industry, or municipalities can provide." Jones, who appeared to be everywhere and involved with everything, said the program's success depended on the cooperation of the iron and steel industries and the participation of "everyone who is in possession of scrap metals or objects containing iron and steel which are serving no useful purpose." Jones and the WPB aimed to collect and reuse five million tons of scrap to help satisfy the war machine's unquenchable thirst for metal.[112] Between rubber and metal, the RFC was the nation's number one scavenger and recycler.

During the November midterm elections, the public's fears of inflation, rationing, and price and wage controls, as well as public infighting among the country's leaders, pushed voters toward the Republicans. The Democrats lost fifty-five seats in the House and nine in the Senate, but retained small majorities in both houses of Congress. Roosevelt knew public battles among members of his administration had hurt not only the Democrats' political standing, but also the war effort. Back in August the president had sent a letter to "the responsible head of each department and agency of the Federal Government," Jones among them. He said, "Too often in recent months, responsible officials of the government have made public criticism of other agencies of the government and have made public statements based either on inadequate information or on failure to appreciate all the aspects of a complex subject which is only

110. Jesse Jones to Franklin Roosevelt, July 12, 1942, Jesse H. Jones Collection [HE].
111. *Houston Chronicle,* September 25, 1942.
112. *Houston Chronicle,* August 28, 1942.

partially within their jurisdiction. This is inadvisable at any time. But in times of war it is particularly contrary to public policy."[113]

The president said these "divergences . . . are a direct and serious handicap to the prosecution of war" and leave the public feeling that its government is "uncertain as to its objects and general method, and that it does not know its job." Roosevelt went on, "[We] ought to be making trouble for the enemy and not for one another . . . Where honest differences of opinion exist, no one would propose to suppress them . . . But it is no solution to argue it out in public." Then he instructed his government heads, "Disagreements either as to fact or policy should not be publicly aired, but are to be submitted to me by the appropriate heads of the conflicting agencies. The policy of the government should be announced by me, as the responsible head thereof."[114] Jones and Wallace must have misplaced the president's letter.

At the first of December, Jones asked Congress for another $5 billion ($65 billion) for war purposes. In anticipation, the Senate Committee on Banking and Currency had asked Jones for a report on the "war activities of the government's lending agency."[115] According to the report Jones produced, the Metals Reserve Company had accumulated more than $3.2 billion ($42 billion) in strategic and critical metals and materials from around the world, and had standing contracts with many Latin American countries to buy all of their exportable minerals. That was just the opener. The report also said that in a little more than two years, the RFC and its subsidiaries had built 1,337 defense plants to manufacture everything from bombers, tanks, trucks, cargo planes, and ships to ball bearings, penicillin, guns, gasoline, and rubber. The DPC had built most of the new manufacturing capacity, and more than sixty percent of the plants were in full or partial operation. Nine of the twelve new, gigantic aluminum factories were running at full capacity, and another forty-eight were on the drawing boards. Twelve of the sixteen magnesium plants were churning out metal and eighty-three different companies now operated 144 new steel plants.[116]

Jones had told the press that synthetic rubber production would most likely exceed one million tons by next year.[117] When he testified before the committee, he made sure to point out that the synthetic rubber program

113. Franklin Roosevelt, August 20, 1942, Jesse H. Jones Collection [LOC].
114. Ibid.
115. *New York Times*, December 3, 1942.
116. Ibid.
117. Ibid.

had been arranged "prior to the appointment of the rubber director."[118] Under questioning, he also explained that the president's April executive order gave Wallace's BEW jurisdiction over all overseas purchases and removed the RFC's power to prohibit loans for those purchases that did not meet with its approval. Jones then noted that of all the agencies that submitted orders and contracts to the RFC for funding, the BEW was the only one that interfered with its international negotiations. One senator suggested amending the president's executive order by giving the RFC veto power over the BEW. Jones demurred, "I think I would not care to discuss that," though he later said that the situation "could be improved."[119] Wallace appeared before the committee the next day with his side of the story, complaining about his inability to get funds out of the RFC for his projects. He testified that the BEW made purchases only for war purposes, not to "influence or create social or industrial reforms in other countries," and that Jones was purposely withholding funds and delaying progress.[120]

Jones admittedly employed delaying tactics whenever he disagreed with BEW contractual provisions, particularly those that imposed social programs on foreign nations or that proposed to import unfamiliar food, farming methods, and health care to improve life for tribal people and consequently their productivity while working on rubber plantations in the Amazon basin. Jones later explained, "While the President had directed the RFC to follow the orders of the BEW and to pay out money on its orders, we nevertheless felt a responsibility to Congress for the money appropriated to us. We didn't have the same confidence in Henry that the President had. When we were told to do something by the BEW, we wanted to know what it was all about. In taking time to make such inquiries, no war effort was delayed, because we were already buying all over the world and had been for a year." Jones continued, "Our attitude was resented by Mr. Wallace and his super smart gang. They accused us of obstructing their outfit (which we did) and of hampering the war effort by failing to buy materials . . . (which we did not). What we actually obstructed were their efforts to throw money away to no good purpose."[121]

Despite the president's request to keep policy disputes private, the growing conflict between Jones and Wallace, and the animosity displayed

118. *Houston Chronicle,* December 16, 1942.
119. Ibid.
120. *New York Times,* December 16, 1942.
121. Jones, *Fifty Billion Dollars,* 489.

during their testimonies, was splashed all over the press. Meyer published an editorial titled, "Mr. Jones Rides Again" and accused him of promoting the proposed Congressional amendment to give the RFC veto power over the BEW and of trying to grab more authority.[122] Jones told Meyer that the editorial was "further evidence of your purpose to use your newspaper to malign me personally, as well as my work as a public official." He informed Meyer, "At no time did I or anyone connected with the Department of Commerce or the RFC inspire, suggest, or consent to any amendment to the bill as introduced."[123]

Jones wrote another letter in response to the influential newspaper's accusations that he gave "insufficient" answers when testifying: "You did not publish my answers in full, but picked out certain portions to suit your own purpose. Evidently you were afraid to let the readers of your paper form their own conclusions." Then he threatened to issue his own press release if Meyer did not print his current letter in full.[124]

Meyer wrote back that the paper never reveals its sources, that the senate committee was convinced it would be a mistake to give him control over the BEW, that the paper never prints committee hearings in full, and that his letter would not be published "because, in my judgment, the public is not interested in petty quibbling." Then Meyer told Jones to "spend more time in expediting the war effort and less time in writing letters."[125]

All the major papers covered the battle between Jones and Wallace, some being nicer than others. The *Wall Street Journal* reported that Jones's $5 billion ($65 billion) request was delayed because "of a controversy over the method by which the BEW obtains funds . . . from the RFC."[126] The manager of the Los Angeles RFC office sent Jones a clipping from the *Pasadena Post*, which said about his relationship with Congress, "Despite some small squabbles between him and FDR, no other cabinet member commands so much support and confidence at the eastern end of Pennsylvania Avenue." As evidence, the reporter pointed out that the committee members responsible for the pending RFC funding "gave up their vacations at the request of the Secretary of Commerce" and returned to Washington to consider the legislation. He continued, "There is not another member of the Presidential family who could have persuaded the

122. *Washington Post*, December 9, 1942.
123. Jesse Jones to Eugene Meyer, December 10, 1942, Jesse H. Jones Collection [LOC].
124. Jesse Jones to Eugene Meyer, December 17, 1942, Jesse H. Jones Collection [LOC].
125. Eugene Meyer to Jesse Jones, December 21, 1942, Jesse H. Jones Collection [LOC].
126. *Wall Street Journal*, December 17, 1942.

absentees to return . . . for such a purpose."[127] Jones's power, despite the controversies, was still intact.

The Joneses this time were able to go to Houston for the holidays. And like their visit in June for their granddaughter's wedding, Jones mixed business with pleasure. He took time out from celebrating with his family to present $86 million ($1.1 billion) to Navy Secretary Knox for a new cruiser to replace the USS *Houston* that ten months before had been torpedoed and sunk at sea by the Japanese. Houstonians had lobbied Congress in 1927 to name a cruiser for their city and port, and after it was launched, they followed the ship with interest as it traveled the globe. President Roosevelt used it for at least four official trips, including voyages to Haiti, the Virgin Islands, Puerto Rico, and the Galapagos Islands. It became the flagship of the Asiatic fleet after Pearl Harbor, and in March, as it headed through the Sundra Strait on its way to the Indian Ocean, the revered ship was blasted and sunk by a group of Japanese destroyers, cruisers, and torpedo boats. Only 368 of the 1,068 crewmembers survived, and they went on to endure brutal treatment by the Japanese as prisoners of war.

Two months after the ship went down, more than a thousand men rallied on Houston's Main Street, where they enlisted on the spot to replace the crew of the USS *Houston*. Public fervor over the ship remained high when, through a three-week bond sale campaign, the citizens of Houston collected almost $86 million ($1.1 billion) to build a new ship, more than double their $36 million ($469 million) goal. On December 21 the *Houston Chronicle*'s front page reported, "The successful conclusion of the campaign will be celebrated by the launching of eight ships, a parade, and a gigantic rally in the Sam Houston Coliseum. Secretary of the Navy Frank Knox and Secretary of Commerce Jesse Jones will be the leading figures at the celebration." The daylong celebration, the newspaper story indicated, would "begin with the launching of a merchant vessel at the Houston shipyards at 6:30 a.m. with Mrs. Jesse Jones the sponsor."[128]

Thousands of Houstonians filled the Coliseum and adjoining Music Hall, and packed the streets for the evening rally. Hundreds of officials attended, including Governor Coke Stevenson, Speaker of the House Sam Rayburn, and former Governor Hobby and his wife, Oveta Culp Hobby, who had recently become director of the Women's Army Corps.[129] Generals, admirals, and hundreds of enlisted men were there, along with

---

127. *Pasadena Post,* December 9, 1942.
128. *Houston Chronicle,* December 21, 1942.
129. Bill Hobby with Saralee Tiede, "How Things Really Work," 16.

More than a thousand Houstonians enlisted at a ceremony on Main Street in front of Jesse Jones's Lamar Hotel to replace the crew of the USS *Houston* that was torpedoed and sunk at sea by the Japanese. Courtesy Houston Public Library.

hundreds of uniformed Houstonians serving in local volunteer patrols, emergency corps, and auxiliary groups. It looked like wartime in Houston. After the dignitaries took their seats, a naval band played "Anchors Aweigh," and a choral group followed with a rousing rendition of "Praise the Lord and Pass the Ammunition."

Countering recent reports of racial tension, the *Chronicle* reported, "Persons who worry about the racial question would have felt as small as Tom Thumb Monday night. When John W. Rice, Negro professor, spoke, the crowd listened intently and frequently broke into his speech with prolonged bursts of applause. The same was true when the Negro chorus sang and again when Secretary Knox lauded the efforts of the Negroes."[130] Black Houstonians may have had a presence in the celebration, but they were still seated in a separate section.

After the singing, thunderous applause filled the immense auditorium as Jones approached the podium. He waited for silence and began, "As a

130. Ibid.

Houstonian, I take great pride in what we have done. My heart swells as I contemplate the patriotism that our citizens have shown. I am glad to be a Houstonian, and to have a part in these ceremonies." He announced that the money raised will "not only pay for the cruiser *Houston*, but will also cover the cost of an aircraft carrier," and he suggested it be called the *San Jacinto*. Then Houston's first citizen read a congratulatory telegram from President Roosevelt and introduced Secretary Knox. Handing a document to Knox, Jones said, "I now have the pleasure of presenting this certificate for $85,749,884.24, representing more than 250,000 individual purchasers of government bonds and stamps, ranging from school children to millionaires."[131] Humble Oil and Refining had led the effort by purchasing $5 million ($65 million) in war bonds for the new ship; Shell Oil bought $3.25 million ($42 million), and oilman Hugh Roy Cullen purchased $1.1 million ($14.3 million).[132]

Jones said, "Mr. Secretary, we were proud of the *Houston* when it rode the waves. We were desolate when it was lost in battle. But here's our pledge that there will always be a cruiser *Houston*."[133] According to the *Chronicle*, "the program was brought to an impressive close when lights were turned out for the benediction and the crowd held up burning matches as a symbol of a candle burning for those who have given their lives for freedom."[134] In addition to the hundreds who had lost their lives on the USS *Houston*, more than 10,000 U.S. soldiers had died so far during World War II.

Once his official duties were complete, Jesse turned his attention to family. The Joneses had established trusts for each family member in 1923 and had periodically added to them since then. They added to them again while they were home, and Jones wrote letters to his nephews, nieces, sisters, brother, and in-laws to tell them about it. He had exchanged a few letters throughout the year with his nephew John, who last wrote from Northern Ireland, where he was a first lieutenant in the Army. A letter from him dated December 25 arrived for the Joneses while they were in Houston.

John began, "My apologies for the stationery. It's the best available." He wrote on lined tablet paper that "It has been a pretty good Christmas . . .

131. Jesse Jones, speech, Sam Houston Coliseum, December 21, 1942, Jesse H. Jones Collection [UT].

132. *Houston Chronicle*, December 21, 1942.

133. Jesse Jones, speech, Sam Houston Coliseum, December 21, 1942, Jesse H. Jones Collection [UT].

134. *Houston Chronicle*, December 21, 1942.

As good a Christmas as you could expect so far away from home." Then, "I don't suppose there is anyway you could have known, as we were only given permission to write about our location a few days ago, but I'm now stationed in North Africa." Trying to be lighthearted, John said, "So far, I've managed to see quite a bit of the world while working for Uncle Sam. Of course, the part of the world that would look best will have to wait. I mean New York Harbor." He wrote that the area resembled "the Texas Big Bend Region," and observed, "If it weren't for the Arabs, Bedouin, [and] Berbers wandering over the countryside, you would be hard pressed to tell the difference." After sharing a few more details about the area, he closed, "Well, here's wishing you both a happy & prosperous New Year, and all the best of everything."[135]

135. John T. Jones Jr. to Jesse and Mary Gibbs Jones, December 25, 1942, John T. Jones Collection [HE].

1943

◈

Ask God to Stop Him from Lying

JESSE JONES WAS HOPING FOR A GOOD YEAR. He had been attacked, belittled, embattled, and bruised during the last one, which had been the most intense and challenging of his public career. It had also been one of the most productive. Jones recounted what the government had accomplished during the past twelve months in an article that was published in papers across the nation on January 3.

He began, "In a million American homes and hundreds of thousands of American factories and farms, the United States is today fashioning the noose with which the barbaric ambitions of the Axis powers will be strangled . . . What the United States has done in twelve months surpasses any similar endeavor in human history." He compared 1941 with 1942, showed how the defense budget had almost tripled to $62 billion ($761 billion in current dollars), how war bond purchases had increased from $1.8 billion ($22 billion) in one year to $12 billion ($147 billion) in one month, and said that the "goals for 1943 are even higher. It is estimated that, in the coming year, we will spend $88 billion [$1.07 trillion] for war purposes."[1] In fact, Roosevelt's new military budget would be $100 billion

1. *New York Times*, January 3, 1943.

443

($1.23 trillion).[2] Comparatively, 1939 federal expenditures, including New Deal programs, were less than $10 billion ($123 billion).

The enormous new expenditures would go toward purchasing new military equipment instead of building more new plants. Construction was nearly complete, and the plants were ready to produce. Jones said in the article that, in 1943, more planes would be built "than all the warring nations had in service prior to our entry into the hostilities." He said, "We will build more ship tonnage than we had afloat prior to Pearl Harbor. We will more than double the existing number of tanks and increase the weight of our artillery fire power beyond the combined total of the Axis nations."[3] The Defense Plant Corporation and other RFC subsidiaries had built many of the factories and acquired most of the materials that allowed this extraordinary production of war materials. Half of the DPC's five-year wartime investments were made in 1942; it would spend only fifteen percent of that in 1943, and outlays would continue to decline until the end of the war.[4] Now it was up to the private companies that operated the factories to fill the orders. The 1943 U.S. military budget would be larger than those of all other nations combined.

Marking the sea change in the nation's industrial base, Jones declared, "A factor which became an actuality in 1942 and which some Americans fail to take into account is that this country at present is—in fact and not just in theory—the storehouse of freedom. The United States is now the only place to which the United Nations can look for many absolutely essential war supplies." (The Allied forces were called the United Nations well before the international organization was established in 1945.) Looking forward, he called 1942 "only a curtain raiser" and said that "Today, on many fronts, the strategy of the United Nations has changed from defensive warfare to offensive action. The road signs now point to Berlin, Tokyo, and Rome—not away from them."[5] Weeks later, U.S. airplanes for the first time began to bomb Germany. Backed by Britain's Royal Air Force, U.S. pilots specifically targeted U-boats in German ports.[6] Soon, a full week would pass without the loss of a boat or a sailor in the Atlantic, a respite unknown since Pearl Harbor.[7]

On the home front, if 1942 had been all about rubber, then 1943 would

2. *Houston Chronicle*, January 1, 1943.
3. *New York Times*, January 3, 1943.
4. White, *Billions for Defense*, 69.
5. *New York Times*, January 3, 1943.
6. *Houston Chronicle*, January 29, 1943.
7. *Houston Chronicle*, February 22, 1943.

be all about Jones's rivalry with Henry Wallace. In mid-January Franklin Roosevelt left the country for the first time during his presidency to confer and strategize with Winston Churchill in Casablanca. During the president's absence, Wallace issued an executive order removing the authority to make foreign purchases from all RFC subsidiaries, including the DPC, the Metals Reserve Company, and the United States Commercial Corporation. William Jeffers, exerting authority as "Rubber Czar," intervened and boldly overrode the vice president. Jeffers directed Wallace's Bureau of Economic Warfare to submit foreign purchase proposals to him. If he approved them, he would instruct Jones, through an RFC subsidiary, to begin negotiations. The *Wall Street Journal* reported, "Mr. Jeffers's action was widely interpreted as a setback for BEW and its chairman, Vice President Wallace."[8] But, to echo Jones, that was "only a curtain raiser."

At the time Jones had other things to worry about. The war became very personal when his brother, John, received a telegram that said, "First Lieutenant John T. Jones Junior has been reported missing in action in North Africa since February 14."[9] John phoned his brother immediately. Jones was stricken; as Mary wrote to Margaret, John Jr.'s mother, "I have never known Jess to go to pieces as he did . . . when he talked to John Sr." She added that he "has talked to everyone who could have the least idea how to go about getting any information for us, and so many are working on it, I know we will hear good news soon. We must."[10]

As word spread, friends and family reached out to John Jr.'s parents. Amon Carter wrote, "I have just learned from the newspapers that Johnny is reported missing in action. I received [a] similar message Thursday about Amon Jr." Carter's son had been in Tunisia with John. He explained, "These boys were spread out too thinly over too much territory and were surrounded in a surprise attack." He said that only a small percent had been reported wounded or dead, and "with over 2,000 taken prisoner, I am confident that our boys are either German or Italian prisoners."[11]

Letters and cables poured in to John and Margaret, some from friends and colleagues of Jesse's. Emil Schram sent condolences on New York Stock Exchange stationery.[12] Congressman Lyndon Johnson wrote, "I know that the anguish and worry you are going through today cannot

8. *Wall Street Journal*, January 22, 1943.

9. Adjutant General Ulio of the United States to John Jones Sr., March 13, 1943, John T. Jones Jr. Collection [HE].

10. Mary Gibbs Jones to Margaret Jones, March 21, 1943, Jesse H. Jones Collection [HE].

11. Amon Carter to John T. Jones Sr., March 14, 1943, John T. Jones Jr. Collection [HE].

12. Emil Schram to John T. Jones Sr., March 17, 1943. John T. Jones Jr. Collection [HE].

be helped by any words of mine, but I just want you to know that my thoughts, my prayers, and my hopes are with you."[13] Family wrote too. Cousin Jeanette sent her "thoughts and prayers" to Margaret from New York.[14] John Boehck, Audrey's husband, wrote from California, "I'm hoping with everyone else that the next news you hear from North Africa will be directly from your son."[15] But life had to go on. Hoping to divert her a little, Mary wrote to Margaret, "Audrey Louise is here on a little visit and keeps us interested every minute . . . She is such good company and so gay." Mary said she hoped Audrey's "husband will be able to stop over when he flies to Norfolk . . . We do not feel that we know him at all as we only saw him for a few minutes at the wedding, but everyone speaks so well of him."[16]

Everyone needed a break from the war's traumas and demands. Two nights after learning that John Jr. was missing in action, Jones was at the Stage Door Canteen where it was "Texas Night." He donned an apron, waited tables, served hundreds of Texas soldiers, and sang along with Richard Kleberg, congressman from Corpus Christi, who reportedly "dressed in cowboy boots, silk shirt, and fancy bandana, played the accordion and sang cowboy songs."[17] Jones also found a reprieve in the occasional card game. Drew Pearson wrote, "Favorite pastime of Jesse Jones is playing bridge at the Brazilian Embassy. Sometimes he interrupts his bridge game long enough to peer down at the samba dancers, but never joins them."[18] A break from war was rare and needed.

The number of operating RFC plants continued to rise. On March 20 Jones reported, "Of the 1,479 war-plant projects owned by the government's Defense Plant Corporation, 1,022 have gone into operation." He added that, of the $9.2 billion ($113 billion) invested in new plants and equipment, $2.7 billion ($33 billion) had been spent on aviation. Jones said, "The Corporation will have invested in aircraft and aircraft accessory plants alone . . . about ten times the entire assets of all aircraft manufacturers before the war."[19] Even so, for all the attention on militarizing

13. Lyndon Johnson to John T. Jones Sr., March 17, 1943, John T. Jones Jr. Collection [HE].

14. Jeanette Jones to Margaret Jones, March 31, 1943, John T. Jones Jr. Collection [HE].

15. John Beck to Margaret Jones, March 18, 1943, John T. Jones Jr. Collection [HE].

16. Mary Gibbs Jones to Margaret Jones, March 21, 1943, John T. Jones Jr. Collection [HE].

17. *Houston Chronicle*, March 17, 1943.

18. Pearson, "Washington Merry-Go-Round," March 18, 1943.

19. *New York Times*, March 21, 1943.

Jesse Jones entertained troops from Texas at the Stage Door Canteen on March 16, 1943, two days after he was informed that his nephew, John T. Jones Jr., was missing in action. Courtesy Library of Congress.

U.S. industry, Jones never lost sight of the challenging task of returning to peacetime status. Fifteen months after Pearl Harbor (but still fifteen months before D-Day), conversations about converting the nation's industrial base from war to peace, and from public to private, were as urgent as those pertaining to production. Machine tools help explain why.

Jones wrote an article for *American Machinist* in March. In addition to raising the issue of economic conversion, the article showed the fundamental role that the RFC played in building and militarizing U.S. industry. Mass production cannot occur without saws, lathes, drills, shapers, and gauges, or as Jones explained, "but for machine tools, industry would still be dependent upon custom-built products." Almost as soon as it began accumulating raw rubber in 1940, the RFC began financing the production of machine tools used to build planes, jeeps, and other military equipment. He wrote that within two years, "more machine tools were built than in the preceding twenty years." Jones gave the rationale for the jumpstart: "It was believed that unnecessary delays could be avoided if such machinery and equipment could be manufactured before the war plant in which it would ultimately be used had even been planned specifically."[20]

Toward the end of the article—which, as usual, bulged with huge dollar amounts, projections, and accomplishments—Jones offered, "Producers of machine tools . . . must wonder what the post-war picture in their industry will be like. We will then have a larger reservoir of machine tools and precision instruments than ever in our history." He asked, "What are we going to do with them?" and suggested machine tools would be needed to repair "the material damage of war" in other nations, while "precision instruments can be utilized just as well for civilian production as for the making of armament." He concluded, "Economic experts are in apparent agreement that, after the war, the United States must have a high level of production, in order to maintain employment and prevent a . . . depression . . . We cannot do this without mass production and mass production needs precision instruments." Jones told "the tool builders of the country" that they "need not [feel] too much anxiety [as] to their place in the industrial picture of the future."[21]

Despite Jones's confidence, the peacetime direction of U.S. industry at this point was uncertain. Government was still deeply enmeshed in many areas of production: the RFC controlled ninety-six percent of the nation's synthetic rubber output, ninety percent of the capacity to manufacture magnesium, seventy-one percent of the aircraft industry, and half of the aluminum factories.[22] With firsthand knowledge about the country's growing industrial capacity, Jones and others knew that plans had to be devised to prevent economic catastrophe once the war ended and its demands dropped, in order to preserve capitalism, eliminate government ownership of private industries, and ensure an orderly transition to peace.

Toward that end, a group of leading industrialists and financiers formed the Committee for Economic Development. Paul Hoffman of Studebaker; Owen D. Young of General Electric; Marion Folsom of Eastman Kodak; Harrison Jones of Coca-Cola; and Thomas Lamont of J. P. Morgan were among the founding members who attended the first general meeting on April 14. Jones, who had known most of the members for years and had

20. Jesse Jones, article written for *American Machinist* (March 1943), Jesse H. Jones Collection [UT].
21. Ibid.
22. Jones, *Fifty Billion Dollars*, 316.

helped form the group, delivered a speech. He began, "My associates and I in the Department of Commerce have been privileged to meet with the Committee for Economic Development a number of times in the initial stages of your program, and I am glad to [be] at your first general meeting . . . We in the department regard the work of this committee as of paramount importance to the future of business and the economic security of the nation." He pushed [them] to make preparations now, saying, "Private initiative must be ready to occupy its rightful place when the war is over. It should be ready to take hold as government withdraws from the field of war production. If it is to do this, it must have plans even though they may be imperfect." Always conscious of the underdeveloped and cash-strapped South and West, and still trying to erase "sectional lines," he said that "every section of our . . . country should be included in the planning." He told them that maintaining high levels of employment and production, and finding markets for the enormous output from unprecedented industrial expansion were essential "if we are to avoid another postwar depression such as the one that engulfed us in the late twenties."[23]

Assuming partial responsibility for the nation's transformation, Jones shared, "The vastness of our post-war problem may seem more real to me because, through the Reconstruction Finance Corporation and other agencies under my supervision, much of the governmental expansion of industrial facilities has been done." He continued, "In some fields, such as aluminum, magnesium, and rubber, government will at the end of the war have a much greater capacity than private industry. In some lines, such as aircraft and airplane parts, government will own many times what private industry has built . . . Congress will have to decide how these government properties are to be operated in peacetime, and it will need the advice of every thinking man." Speaking from experience, he said, "In my view, Congress can be relied upon if those of us in business will be honest and frank with Congress." He warned, "It will be bad for the country, and each and every one of us, if any group attempts to take selfish advantage in the transformation we will have to face. It is, however, possible, if business and industry seek to cooperate wholeheartedly with government, that much of the war expansion can be put to work usefully for the United States and for many parts of the world. Certainly there will be an opportunity for private initiative and private capital to replace

23. Jesse Jones, speech, Committee for Economic Development, April 14, 1943, Jesse H. Jones Collection [UT].

government in business. It is your responsibility to see that this opportunity is not missed."[24]

As always, the business community got the first chance, but Jones added that if the committee and others did not come up with "concrete, practical suggestions for the conversion of industry from war to peace, government will have to make the decisions." Encouraging these leaders to seize the moment, he said, "Under such circumstances what the government does may not be to your liking. In that event we would have only ourselves to blame, for . . . if the past 10 years have taught us anything, it is that business cannot merely express dislike for what government does. It must be prepared to offer practical solutions based not on privilege, but service and the common welfare."[25]

Brimming with optimism, he said there "will be many opportunities for our farms and factories, our man-hours and money. Many parts of the world will have to be rehabilitated both physically and materially. This will greatly increase our foreign trade." He continued, "The problems will be to fill . . . orders, not to get them. In the United States alone, the consumer demand will be tremendous, and . . . war savings should release money enough to provide a substantial demand." Jones followed, "It is a big job to mobilize every company in America to prepare for high levels of employment and productivity. This is what I understand the Committee for Economic Development is attempting to do. It has never been tried before, and that constitutes a challenge to you." With his missing nephew never far from his mind, he concluded, "We at home must carry on with the determination to have ready for our boys, when they come back—a world where opportunity still exists, and [where] rights and privileges our generation has enjoyed are [still] available to them."[26]

Later that evening, Jesse's brother received another telegram. It said, "Your son First Lieutenant John T. Jones Junior reported a prisoner of war of the German government."[27] The excruciating month-long wait was over. John Jr. was alive and in a German prisoner-of-war camp designated, in accord with Geneva Conventions, for military officers. Amon Carter Jr. was there, too. Both had been captured in February as the Germans swept

24. Ibid.
25. Ibid.
26. Ibid.
27. Adjutant General Ulio of the United States to John T. Jones Sr., April 14, 1943, John T. Jones Jr. Collection [HE].

through the Faid Pass in Tunisia, where John Jr. was a tank officer with the American Expeditionary Force.[28]

Jones wrote his sister-in-law, Margaret, the next day, "I was glad to talk with you and the rest of the family last night about John." He said, "Adjutant General Ulio told me that the notice had gone to you automatically, and I am sure you have it by this time. The General has been very considerate." The next step, he wrote, is "get[ting] some things to John through the Red Cross, and I am taking it up with them." He thanked Margaret for remembering his sixty-ninth birthday on April 5 and closed, "With much love to all the family," then instead of formally writing out his full name as usual, he simply signed it, "Jesse."[29]

Mail from John Jr. finally began to arrive. He wrote his aunt and uncle, knowing they were more likely to receive mail than anyone, and reported, "I am quite safe and well both of mind and body. I wish you would contact Dad and let him know in case he has not yet received any word from me."[30] Jones had the telegram "photostatted" and sent to every member of the family.[31] A week after learning of John Jr.'s internment, Jones received a detailed letter from Norman Davis, chairman of the International Federation of Red Cross and Red Crescent Societies. Davis explained that prisoners received Red Cross food parcels and "clothing and comfort articles" once a week. He assured Jones that a Red Cross representative will "get in touch with your nephew to determine whether he has any particular requests to make." Davis reported that a delegation had visited the Oflag IX A/Z camp, where John was being held, and found an "excellent infirmary, . . . a good library and theater, but no sports ground." Davis closed, "Please be assured of my continuing interest in your nephew's welfare. Any further information that is received by our representative in Geneva will be immediately forwarded to you."[32] John Jr. was able to get quite a lot of mail out to his family in Texas. He wrote his cousins toward the end of April, "Amon Carter is here with me, and every day we compare Heaven and Texas. As we have neither been to Heaven, I'm afraid it comes out second best every time."[33]

28. *Fort Worth Star-Telegram*, April 15, 1943.

29. Jesse Jones to Margaret Jones, April 15, 1943, John T. Jones Jr. Collection [HE].

30. John T. Jones Jr. to Jesse Jones, March 18, 1943, John T. Jones Jr. Collection [HE].

31. Gladys D. Mikell to John T. Jones Sr., April 24, 1943, John T. Jones Jr. Collection [HE].

32. Norman Davis to Jesse Jones, April 23, 1943, John T. Jones Jr. Collection [HE].

33. John T. Jones Jr. to first cousins Jessie and Bill, April 10, 1943, John T. Jones Jr. Collection [HE].

Meanwhile Texas was planning "American-Made Rubber Day." A *Houston Chronicle* editorial proclaimed, "Whereas on Pearl Harbor day only a handful of chemists and industrialists were confident that America's then infant rubber industry would supply any great part of our rubber needs within less than several years, seventeen months later large plants are in operation, and within a few months we will be producing the artificial elastic at a rate surpassing our peacetime imports from Malaya." According to the editorial, Governor Stevenson said, "Texas gasoline is keeping our planes in the air and our tanks and jeeps and trucks in action. This year Texas adds one more great contribution to its war record. This year, all over Texas, plants will begin to turn out American rubber, made from Texas oil. Our state will lead all the nation in rubber production."[34] The governor proclaimed June 28 "American-Made Rubber Day in Texas" to recognize the new industry and to celebrate opening the first of four huge synthetic rubber plants in the Lone Star State.

On American-Made Rubber Day, a *Houston Chronicle* article described the new Baytown plant as a "massive engineering feat of steel, masonry, and intricate machinery . . . built with government money by the Good Year Tire and Rubber Company . . . It will be operated by the General Tire and Rubber Company." Other plants had been built to supply ingredients, such as "styrene and butadiene from plants of the Humble Oil and Refining Company at Baytown and the Monsanto Chemical Company at Texas City." The article said forty percent of the nation's synthetic rubber supply would come from four plants in Texas. It concluded, "With this enormous production in sight, it may be understood why the eyes of the rubber industry [are] focused on Houston and Baytown."[35] Synthetic rubber and related industries were largely responsible for adding "chemical" to Houston's designation as the petrochemical capital of the world.

Oil, chemical, and rubber company executives poured into Houston for the celebration, and their companies filled the local papers with full-page ads. Above a huge test tube, Goodyear's ad proclaimed, "In unity America has found rubber," and said, "Not one of these plants was in existence a year ago. This is the greatest industrial development in Texas since the discovery of oil." B. F. Goodrich showed Uncle Sam behind the wheel of a convertible speeding across a map of the United States on "American-made rubber" tires and recognized the nation's freedom from foreign

---

34. *Houston Chronicle*, May 1, 1943.
35. *Houston Chronicle*, June 28, 1943.

supplies with its headline, "Texas helps America write a new Declaration of Independence."[36]

The opening of an elaborate synthetic rubber exhibition in the morning kicked off American-Made Rubber Day. Housed in the lobby of a Houston office building owned by Jones, it showed off synthetic rubber gas masks, life rafts, and tires, including one driven "50 miles an hour for approximately 11,000 miles." According to the manufacturer, it still had 15,000 more miles to go. Wads of the miraculous substance were given to those who attended the first day of the weeklong exhibition. A piece of rubber was also put into a leather box with a gold plaque that said, "First synthetic rubber made in Texas presented to Jesse H. Jones by the Goodyear Tire and Rubber Company, June 28, 1943."

Jones was unable to attend the festivities and, instead, delivered a speech over the phone to the luncheon crowd, who had just returned from the Baytown plant's dedication. Jones's remarks were part congratulations and part defense. He began, "Texas has long been first in cattle, first in cotton, first in petroleum, and first in natural gas . . . Now comes rubber, which is of equal importance in our present-day economy. Because we in Texas have more of the necessary raw materials, which can be produced at the lowest cost, Texas will be first in rubber." He declared, "By the end of this year, we will have our own rubber industry, capable of meeting all essential needs, both for war and for civilian requirements."[37]

He made a point, "With the exception of a few small refinery conversions, our program for the production of rubber—from raw materials to the finished product—is being completed under the direction of Rubber Director William Jeffers in accordance with plans and contracts developed by the RFC and its subsidiaries . . . It is the industry which the men at RFC . . . brought into being, and they take pride in its approaching completion."[38] The alternative substance had gone from the lab to mass production in less than two years.

Jones closed by reading a letter from President Roosevelt: "The establishment of an industry of this magnitude, in so short a period, is in full keeping with the tradition of our people in meeting any emergency. All who have part in the manufacture of synthetic rubber have just cause to feel they are making a real contribution to the war effort."[39] At one of

36. *Houston Chronicle*, June 20, 1943.
37. Jesse Jones, speech, American-Made Rubber Day, June 28, 1943, Jesse H. Jones Collection [UT].
38. Ibid.
39. Ibid.

the day's events, William O'Neil, president of General Tire and Rubber, praised Jones's role in developing synthetic rubber: "Today is a tribute to Jesse H. Jones, secretary of commerce." O'Neil explained that without Jones's leadership, "this celebration would never have been possible." He recalled how in 1940 Jones had called "the heads of the major rubber companies to Washington and enlisted their support in a long range program for the accumulation of a national stock pile of crude rubber." He told how people became aware of the importance of rubber only after Pearl Harbor, and said, "While all the bickering . . . was raging, Mr. Jones was quietly sawing wood. His synthetic program was taking shape." He explained, "It was not a job that could be done overnight. We had had no large-scale experience in synthetic rubber production." O'Neil closed, "This is not just another in the long list of important contributions which Jesse Jones has made . . . It may mean the difference between winning and losing the war."[40]

Any feeling of vindication and fulfillment Jones may have felt from American-Made Rubber Day would not last long. After the celebration, Vice President Wallace publicly accused Jones of "obstructionist tactics," of delaying the war effort and creating "false impressions" about the BEW. Originally intending to make his accusations as testimony before a Senate committee, and despite the president's request to keep such disputes private, Wallace decided to release his statement to the press. He explained, "There are times when the sense of public duty outweighs the natural, personal reluctance to present facts of this nature. This is such a time."[41] Thus began Washington's war within the war, a visible and dramatic battle between two top officials—the vice president of the United States and an appointee who many considered, next to the president, the most powerful person in the nation. Wallace's public announcement took everyone by surprise, supposedly even the president.

Wallace said, "Although the president, on April 13, 1942, transferred full control over the programming of imported strategic materials from the Reconstruction Finance Corporation to the Board of Economic Welfare . . . Mr. Jones has never fully accepted that authority." Wallace, who had been stewing for more than a year, continued, "He and his personnel . . . have thrown a great many obstacles in the way of our exercise of the powers given us to carry out wartime assignments."[42] He said the RFC

40. Ibid.
41. *New York Times*, June 29, 1943.
42. *Houston Chronicle*, June 29, 1943.

had "failed dismally" in executing its responsibilities and that Jones had "done much to harass [BEW employees] in their . . . effort to . . . secure adequate stocks of strategic materials." He said, "Jesse Jones and Will Clayton stalled for months" on the South America rubber program and the accumulation of quinine. Wallace detailed BEW attempts to secure scarce resources and declared, "We are helpless when Jesse Jones, as our banker, refuses to sign checks in accordance with our directives." Wallace said, "All this, and I want to emphasize it, is bureaucracy at its worst; it is utterly inexcusable in a nation at war." Then he asked for direct BEW funding.[43]

These were fighting words. The press became the combatants' boxing ring, giving a worldwide audience ringside seats to the brawl. Within hours, Jones had punched back with a preliminary statement, "The release given out by Mr. Wallace today is filled with malice and misstatements." Jones briefly castigated BEW's record and process, and refuted Wallace's two main charges: the RFC's failure to adequately purchase and stockpile strategic materials, and the RFC's obstruction of BEW initiatives. Jones said, "I will answer the statement in detail and be glad to have a committee of Congress fully investigate the facts."[44]

At a press conference that same day, Roosevelt said Vice President Wallace's statement came as a surprise to him, and he wished that government officials would follow his "polite suggestion of last August" to keep disputes private. A reporter asked the president if the turmoil meant the war was going well overseas, but not at home. Roosevelt told the reporter to take a trip across the country and see for himself.[45]

At Roosevelt's request, James Byrnes, also known as "assistant president," called Jones and Wallace to the White House for a powwow. Byrnes had begun his political career as a U.S. representative from South Carolina in 1910. He was elected to the Senate in 1930 and appointed to the Supreme Court by Roosevelt in 1941. In 1942 Roosevelt asked him to resign from the Court to run the Economic Stabilization Office, the organization responsible for preventing runaway inflation. Then, a month before the Wallace-Jones dispute, Roosevelt created a "super agency," the Office of War Mobilization, and put Byrnes in charge. Byrnes had complete control over war production, as well as the power to settle disputes. His position and organization eclipsed Nelson's War Production Board and

43. *New York Times*, June 29, 1943.
44. Ibid.
45. Ibid.

gave Byrnes presidential-level jurisdiction over the home front while Roosevelt focused on the European and Pacific wars.

Jones's well maintained, warm, and financially beneficent relationships with his countless Capitol Hill friends worked in his favor in times like these. Wallace's aloof personality did not. Byrnes, like every other member of Congress, had been a recipient of Jones's largess. Most recently they had worked together on subsidies, one of the Defense Supplies Corporation's largest expenditures.[46] The RFC was already subsidizing coal and oil to keep prices down because of escalating shipping costs. As consumer goods became harder to get, prices skyrocketed and threatened to break through mandated price ceilings. Congress was divided over subsidies, and as often happened where money was involved and speed was essential, it was bypassed in favor of Jones and the RFC. On May 7 Jones had received a directive from Byrnes to subsidize meat, butter, and coffee, which he did "with the approval of the president." The RFC began paying subsidies to producers, packers, and manufacturers to stabilize prices so people could afford to eat.

Not long after, Jones and Wallace—two extremely agitated public figures—were in Bynes's office to resolve their dispute and end a very embarrassing situation. According to the *New York Times*, "An attempt by the War Mobilization Director, James F. Byrnes, to harmonize the differences between Vice President Henry A. Wallace and Secretary of Commerce Jesse H. Jones failed today after he had summoned them to his office for a two-hour discussion this afternoon."[47] Versions varied, depending on the source. One news release said the meeting was "fairly friendly, with Jones and Wallace talking with each other quite peaceably, though very frankly."[48] But a Byrnes biographer wrote, "Byrnes broke up the meeting when he feared Jones would physically assault the vice president."[49]

In his 1951 book about the RFC, Jones wrote about the meeting in a chapter titled "How Henry Wallace Missed the Presidency." Jones admitted to initial stiffness: "When I stepped inside the door leading to Mr. Byrnes' office, Mr. Wallace said, 'Hello, Jesse.' I did not return his greeting." Jones then recalled that Byrnes spoke at length about the damage the "quarrel" was doing to the administration and to the war effort. It did

46. Jones, *Fifty Billion Dollars*, 372.
47. *New York Times*, June 30, 1943.
48. *Houston Chronicle*, July 1, 1943.
49. Robertson, *Sly and Able*, 328.

not matter. According to Jones, he told Wallace that "when he said his prayers that night, he should ask God to stop him from lying." Jones remembered, "As soon as convenient, [I] excused myself and left the meeting. Nothing was accomplished, and I was determined nothing should be until I had answered the malicious diatribe which Wallace had released to the press."[50] Both men released statements after the meeting.

The press went wild. Hundreds of reporters and onlookers crowded the White House east gate to catch a glimpse of the notorious figures as they arrived and left the meeting. A popular cartoonist showed Wallace tied up like a calf on the ground with towering, chaps-wearing cowboy Jones looming over him with a fire-hot brand that had just imposed the sizzling word "Liar" on the vice president's behind. Wallace's caption read, "Every time I throw a charge, it boomerangs!" Jones's response was, "Aw, it'll cool off after a spell, son."[51]

Wallace's statement said he and Jones had come to a temporary agreement and that he wanted the BEW to have its own funds. He also said he "intended to assert that the . . . RFC . . . had delayed the war effort," not that Jones had a "personal motive" or that he was deliberately or intentionally delaying the war effort. Wallace said, "Our difficulties have had to do with strong differences of opinion with regard to the quantities of various products to be obtained at a given time and place."[52]

Jones would have none of it. He responded and said he would speak for himself. He declared, "Mr. Wallace tonight repeats that delays of the Reconstruction Finance Corporation have retarded the war effort. This dastardly charge is as untrue as when he first made it."[53]

Jones and Wallace had butted heads since the beginning of the New Deal. For example, Wallace, an acclaimed agriculturist, had wanted synthetic rubber made from corn, wheat, or molasses, not oil.[54] And personally, Wallace was a sharp contrast with Jones. He did not drink, did not swear, and was introverted and cerebral. He liked to garden and to play tennis.

Wallace, whose father had served in Harding's and Calvin Coolidge's cabinets as Secretary of Agriculture, had been a solid Republican until he switched parties in the 1930s. He was almost evangelical in his promulgation of the United States' values and purposes, especially those that

50. Jones, *Fifty Billion Dollars*, 495–98.
51. Ibid., 497. The cartoon by Cal Alley was called "Texas Branded."
52. *Houston Chronicle*, July 1, 1943.
53. Ibid.
54. Culver and Hyde, *American Dreamer*, 288.

"Branded," by Cal Alley, a typical political cartoon of the time, depicts the Jesse Jones/Henry Wallace feud. Courtesy Jesse Holman Jones Papers, Dolph Briscoe Center for American History, University of Texas at Austin.

supported and uplifted the "common man," whether he lived in Kansas or Peru. Longtime Democrat Jones just wanted to get the job done at the least cost to the U.S. taxpayer. There was nothing wrong with either approach to policy making; they simply did not mix. Roosevelt had only himself to blame for the remarkable bout between Jones and Wallace, having set the stage when he established the BEW with Wallace at its head and, effectively, put both men in charge of the same thing. A run-in was inevitable.

Jones released a formal statement a few days later. Wallace's statement was twenty-eight pages long, Jones's was thirty-six pages, not including a five-page cover letter to Carter Glass, chairman of the Senate Committee on Appropriations. Jones told Glass that during eleven years as a public servant, he had refrained from criticizing colleagues, but, Wallace's "tirade is so filled with malice, innuendo, half-truths, and no truths at all, that considerations of self-respect and of common justice to my associates force me to expose his unscrupulous tactics." But Jesse was just winding up and continued, "Mr. Wallace's statement that I have harassed administrative employees of BEW . . . is as silly and ridiculous as it is false." During the past fifteen months, he said, "BEW has frantically sent at great expense many 'missions' composed mostly of inexperienced men to all parts of the world." Jones continued, "A few well-selected men, under proper leadership, can accomplish much more in foreign countries, utilizing the citizens of such countries as much as possible . . . The foreign purchase program of the RFC has been conducted under . . . W. L. Clayton, who has had wide experience in the field of foreign trade for many years." Putting his position in a nutshell, Jones added, "Our immediate efforts in the foreign field should be concentrated on war procurement needs, and not on post-war ideologies."[55] Just as they had during the New Deal, Jones and Wallace personified opposing forces.

According to John Kenneth Galbraith, "The BEW was a liberal organization, strongly liberal in its motivation. It was a coalition of New Dealers, as was the Office of Price Administration, where I was." He continued, "There was a certain sense of conflict between a presumed conservative— Jesse Jones—and the liberals of the BEW. It may be that the BEW, which . . . I never regarded as a particularly effective organization, blamed some of its own failures on the RFC as the natural escape from its own inadequacy. It was not a good organization."[56]

Jones would have agreed. In his letter to Glass, he said "As for the charge which Mr. Wallace appears to regard as a major crime, that I have attempted to safeguard the taxpayers' money, I must plead guilty. Squandering the people's money even in wartime is no proof of patriotism." As if he were talking about buying bricks for a new building in Houston, Jones said, "The RFC does not pay $2.00 for something it can buy for $1.00. Maybe no one does, but the point is that some men know when you can buy it for $1.00, some don't know, and some don't care as long as

55. Jesse Jones to Carter Glass, July 5, 1943, Jesse H. Jones Collection [UT].
56. John Kenneth Galbraith to Steven Fenberg, November 22, 1996, Oral History Project [HE].

they are spending other people's money." Jones closed, "I will appreciate your placing this letter and my accompanying statement in the official record."[57]

The thirty-six-page statement's introduction continued where Jones's letter left off. It began, "RFC is purchasing 37 different metals. Mr. Wallace confines his discussion to six, with a reference to two others. The 29 metals which are not mentioned account for 97 percent of RFC's dollar commitments and 99 percent by weight." Jones claimed many of Wallace's statements "are false; others are purposely misleading. The net effect of these statements is to create the impression that failure to obtain these materials in larger quantities, or more promptly, has impeded the war effort. This implication is maliciously false." True to form, Jones then listed every metal, fiber, medicine, oil, and wood product purchased by RFC subsidiaries, described the status of each, and refuted every one of Wallace's charges.[58]

Shortly after Jones submitted his statement to Congress and the press, John Nance Garner wrote from Uvalde, "I know you are not running away . . . Politically speaking, it is more honorable and the better policy to stand up and be shot than to surrender. My suggestion is to stay with the ship. Stand your ground even if your head comes off by force."[59] Jones responded, "I had a great many calls from the boys on both sides of the aisle, but counseled them against making any speeches. I was assured by a number of them that the House believed in the way I had administered the RFC." He also told Garner, "I am reliably informed that the Wallace release was entirely unknown to the President, and obviously after its release there was but one course for me to pursue, regardless of the consequences."[60]

According to Pearson, Roosevelt did know about Wallace's intention but did "not appreciate how strong the statement was going to be." The columnist revealed, "The blast caught the President off base and he was irked."[61] Before Congressional investigations could get underway, and after Wallace delivered an ultimatum to the president to either remove him or give him the power he wanted, Roosevelt finally took the situation away from Byrnes. He abolished the BEW, then took the four agencies dealing with foreign purchases away from Jones and placed them in

57. Jesse Jones to Carter Glass, July 5, 1943, Jesse H. Jones Collection [UT].
58. Jesse Jones, rebuttal statement, July 5, 1943, Jesse H. Jones Collection [UT].
59. John Nance Garner to Jesse Jones, July 9, 1943, Jesse H. Jones Collection [LOC].
60. Jesse Jones to John Nance Garner, July 14, 1943, Jesse H. Jones Collection [LOC].
61. Pearson, "Washington Merry-Go-Round," July 22, 1943.

another new organization—the Office of Economic Warfare (OEW)—of which Leo T. Crowley was in charge. Crowley, one of Roosevelt's "favorite friction removers," had served as chairman of the Federal Deposit Insurance Corporation (FDIC) since 1934.

It appeared to be a defeat for Wallace and a victory for Jones. Pearson, hardly a Jones fan, revealed, "Harry Hopkins, Judge Sam Rosenman, and Byrnes all voted against the Vice-President . . . In the end, FDR himself decided to oust Wallace."[62] The *Wall Street Journal* reported, "Mr. Crowley has the added advantage of being on the right side of Jesse Jones. The Jones-Crowley friendship goes back for ten years to the time of the bank rehabilitation program in 1933 and 1934. The fact that Mr. Jones still has some grasp on government purse strings is not expected to stand in Mr. Crowley's way."[63] Quite to the contrary, it seemed that putting Crowley in charge of foreign purchases was like putting Jeffers in charge of rubber: nothing changed in terms of Jones's control. He still had the checkbook, or as he recalled, "Mr. Crowley and I went on working together in harmony. He made no changes in what we were doing abroad." Jones continued, "Mr. Wallace was out of a war job. He was once more just the Vice President, with little to do but wait for the President to die, which fortunately did not occur while Henry was Vice President."[64] Wallace's future on the 1944 ticket was ended in large part by his public feud with Jones.

In addition to abolishing the BEW and creating the OEW, Roosevelt sent a letter to the heads of all government departments and agencies. He told them that if they released a statement to the press about a government dispute without submitting it to either him or Byrnes first, "I ask that when you release the statement for publication, you send me a letter of resignation."[65] War was on, and it didn't help that it looked as if his government was in complete disarray. Jones issued a press release in which he said, "I concur most heartily in the President's determination to have harmony and cooperation between government officials and agencies in the war effort. The Department of Commerce and the Reconstruction Finance Corporation and its subsidiary corporations . . . will render every possible assistance to the new Director of Economic Warfare."[66] Wallace

62. Ibid.
63. *Wall Street Journal*, July 17, 1943.
64. Jones, *Fifty Billion Dollars*, 503.
65. Ibid., 506.
66. Ibid.

graciously conceded, saying, "In wartime no one should question the overall wisdom of the Commander in Chief."[67]

Despite visible in-fighting, production forged ahead. That spring Secretary of the Navy Knox said the nation "had arrived at the peak period," that plane and ship output had set new records. Rear Admiral Emory Land, chairman of the U.S. Maritime Commission, reported yards "are building more ships than all the rest of the world combined."[68] At the same time, Bill Knudsen, now in charge of production for the Army, predicted the U.S. would reach its goal of manufacturing 90,000 airplanes in 1943.[69] And on July 19, Interior Secretary Harold Ickes dedicated the longest, largest pipeline in the world after it received its final weld.

The DPC-financed "Big Inch" pipeline was built by the oil industry using, according to Jones, "the best pipeliners in the country." Texas oilmen and 15,000 roughnecks from around the nation put the enormous pipeline together.[70] They finished the 1,251-mile long, one-of-a-kind War Emergency Pipeline in 350 days and brought it in under its $100 million ($1.23 billion) budget. The oil that began to flow every twenty-four hours from Texas to refineries in New Jersey and Pennsylvania would have required 25,000 railcars constantly on the move to accomplish the same feat.[71] The "Little Inch"—a parallel twenty-inch pipeline—also financed by the DPC, would soon carry gasoline and light heating oil along the same route.[72] During the war, the Axis powers produced approximately 276 million barrels of oil; Texas alone produced more than 500 million. Joseph Stalin reportedly said to Churchill, "This is a war of engines and octanes. I drink to the American auto industry and the American oil industry."[73]

Nelson of the War Production Board reported to the president that the U.S. was on track to spend approximately $106 billion ($1.3 trillion) in 1943. He said production goals for 1942 had been unrealistically high, but "in the main production met the requirements of our war strategy . . . and will realize to the full the tremendous potential of American industry." Nelson also beseeched the president to begin "planning the transition back to a peacetime economy after the war."[74]

67. Culver and Hyde, *American Dreamer*, 310.
68. *Houston Chronicle*, April 27, 1943.
69. *Houston Chronicle*, April 1, 1943.
70. Jones, *Fifty Billion Dollars*, 343; Burrough, *Big Rich*, 149.
71. *New York Times*, July 20, 1943.
72. *New York Times*, April 30, 1943.
73. Burrough, *Big Rich*, 150.
74. *Houston Chronicle*, June 12, 1943.

With the Wallace imbroglio only days behind him, and at Roosevelt's request, Jones continued to prepare the nation for its conversion from war to peace even though D-Day was months away. He delivered a radio speech on July 21 to "discuss some of our present-day problems . . . and, more particularly, some that will confront us when the war has been won." He said, "The wisdom with which we consider and determine the future utilization of . . . government-owned plants will have a great influence on our economic future . . . The responsibility of the RFC, because of the 1,500-odd plants . . . which it has built and financed, will be very great . . . When peace comes, these plants, with the millions of service men and women and war workers, will constitute the principal problem in our post-war economy." Jones added, "Many of my listeners probably do not realize the extent to which government has financed expansion in many industrial fields."[75] Then he told them.

The RFC owned huge amounts of the nation's steel, aluminum, magnesium, rubber, and machine tool industries, and he used aviation to make his point: "Our biggest investment in manufacturing facilities for a single industry is that of aviation. We have built and own 521 plants for [the] production of aircraft, aircraft engines, parts, and accessories, at a total cost of $2.7 billion [$33 billion]. This is ten times the value of privately owned investments in this industry." Jones also told his audience about the twenty high-octane gasoline plants and the 3,800 miles of pipeline. Jones said the "Big Inch" pipeline, "the most important . . . is owned by the RFC and operated . . . by men in the oil industry."[76]

Ownership was one issue; capacity was another. Driving home that point, Jones said the synthetic rubber factories would produce "one-third more rubber than we have ever used in peacetime." No one knew exactly what to do with all of the government-owned capacity, but the alternatives were endless. Some wanted the largest plants split up and sold in pieces to give small businesses an opportunity to participate. Some wanted the government to keep the plants to compete with and control private industry. There were those who wanted the plants destroyed altogether to prevent unfair competition. Always wary of ideology, Jones warned, "We should, of course, be on guard against undue pressure from any of these groups, for if there ever was a question which must be settled in the national interest, it is the future utilization of this vast new industrial

75. Jesse Jones, radio address, *Washington Evening Star* Radio Forum, July 21, 1943, Jesse H. Jones Collection [UT].

76. Ibid.

empire." He suggested, "Where any industry is able to absorb government facilities in its line, on a basis fair to government, that policy should be adopted." He continued, "In those industries where government facilities approximate or far exceed those in private hands, the solutions will be more difficult. For example, we very easily could destroy private investments in the aviation industry, but certainly we should not, and will not." He continued, "And then there is synthetic rubber. We will own all of this industry, and Congress must determine how much of it we will maintain." The same way others in the future would talk about oil, Jones counseled, "Certainly, we should never again be entirely dependent upon foreign sources of rubber."[77] Jones and Roosevelt had ample opportunity to nationalize significant parts of the nation's economy: first banks, then industries. But that was never their intention. At all cost, they endeavored to preserve and strengthen the country's capitalist system.

Although Jones spoke as if victory were assured, he warned his listeners about "complacency" and "over-confidence." Jones said, "It is true that our fighting forces have given us good news in recent weeks, but in reality . . . the war is just beginning. After 19 months of fighting, we have not yet set foot on Continental Europe, and we are far from Tokyo."[78] When Jones spoke on July 21, the Allied forces had only days before invaded Sicily from North Africa and opened the way into Italy. Mussolini would be ousted and arrested within days.

Jones explained that supplying the fighting forces with food and equipment "will cause those of us at home to tighten our belts and get along on much less than we have been accustomed." He said, "Our sacrifices, insignificant as they are compared to those of the men who bear arms for us, may have to last for a long time yet, and be borne cheerfully. We cannot pamper ourselves without depriving our military forces." Then he spoke about rationing, price controls, and subsidies. He said, "That there could be shortages in our land of plenty is not easy to realize. Rationing turns our world upside down. Price controls strike us as economic heresy. Subsidies shock us. Yet without these we would have more disorder than any of us can well imagine." For Jones common sense trumped ideology almost every time. He continued, "Each new control . . . has annoyed us, and our first cry is that it won't work, that it is not necessary, but control, even though imperfect, has helped to make our available supplies go

77. Ibid.
78. Ibid.

around and has contributed to hold down inflation." Jones referred to the "millions of wage-earners . . . whose salaries are fixed by law and cannot be raised," and explained, "These people have no room in their budgets for increased costs . . . Subsidies, in so far as they serve to keep prices in line, will benefit those who cannot pay more, as well as those who can, and the cost will be relatively small." He added, "Subsidies on a few foods necessary to a sustained diet would make it possible for those low income groups to get along much better."[79]

Jones covered much ground, trying to reassure the anxious nation. He finished by sharing his priorities, which the public assumed would be translated into policy. Jones said, "All such problems—and there will be many others—must be decided in the light of two considerations: the over-all common good and victory."[80]

The Joneses, like everyone else, used rationing coupons for food and gas. A magazine series titled "Wives of Prominent Washingtonians" in *Woman's Home Companion* focused on six women. The installment devoted to Mary began, "Everyone of our sextette from Washington is limited to an A gas ration. Mrs. Jesse Jones . . . has given up a car altogether." The article's author, Edith Stern, said about Mary, "All the morning I spent with her, she was knitting for the Red Cross . . . But her main activity, she told me, is looking after one Jesse Jones who is so absorbed in work that he doesn't properly look after himself." Mary "lays out all of his clothes," and Jones "doesn't know what he eats, so she's very careful to have well balanced meals; with rationing, she feels this responsibility the greater." She did not handle this effort alone, however, since the Joneses had a cook six days a week. Stern also wrote, "She attends to all household business and finances, never carries little domestic disturbances to him . . . She reads and blue pencils books, clips the Houston papers her husband hasn't always time to read. She does all his shopping." Mary was then quoted as saying, "In fact, the only thing I don't do for him is to have his suits fitted on him!" Stern observed, "Her psychological handling of an all-business husband is common-sensible." Mary revealed, "I used to worry about his not taking proper care of himself. First it was a six-day week. Then a few hours added every Sunday. Now it's all day Sundays, too. But now I've stopped working at him. I [realized] that I wasn't getting results and that I was the only one who was

79. Ibid.
80. Ibid.

Mary Gibbs Jones and Jesse Jones at home. Mary once claimed, "The only thing I don't do for him is to have his suits fitted on him" (Interview of Mary Gibbs Jones by Edith Stern, transcript, August 4, 1943, Jesse H. Jones Collection).

suffering." Mary offered her secret to success, "My husband is simply the kind of man who can't leave anything undone, and since I've accepted that fact, we are both much happier."[81]

Stern said that the Joneses lived in an "apartment at the Hotel Shoreham, with occasional tables and trinkets imported from [their] home in Houston that take away the hotel furniture look." She added, "The Joneses expected to be in Washington a few weeks, have been there eleven years." Referring again to rationing, Stern closed, "Once in a while, Jesse Jones wants to bring someone home for dinner so he can talk business quietly. Whether he can or not all depends on those little coupons." Stern wrote, "The other night, in husbandly fashion, he called at 6:45 to ask, 'Can I bring a man home to dinner?' 'Who and how big?' his wife inquired. 'Lord

81. Interview of Mary Gibbs Jones by Edith Stern, transcript, August 4, 1943, Jesse H. Jones Collection [HE].

Beaverbrook—about 180 pounds,' he answered. She thought she could manage that," said Stern.[82]

With Mary's support, Jones had managed his own job well enough that, for all intents and purposes, mobilization's construction phase was practically done. The U.S. government had spent approximately $15 billion ($184 billion) just on new plants and factories to manufacture arms for the war; most were up and running. More than $9 billion ($110 billion) of the investment came from the DPC; the rest came primarily from other RFC subsidiaries, the Navy, the Army, and the Maritime Commission. Private business had invested $5 billion ($61 billion) on top of the government's $15 billion ($184 billion) for a total of about $20 billion ($245 billion) in new factories that were disgorging huge amounts of military equipment and material.[83] As extraordinary as that figure was, it did not include the purchase and accumulation of vast amounts of natural resources from around the globe or the enormous inventory of armaments that was growing every day.

Rubber Czar Jeffers resigned in September and told Roosevelt that the "big job" was complete. He said, "The problem of taking care of the requirements of the armed forces and keeping the country on rubber . . . is well in hand," and that all of the synthetic rubber plants were "either completed or substantially so." Jeffers also reported that he expected to have five million synthetic rubber tires available for civilian purchase by the end of the year and as many as thirty million ready for sale in 1944.[84]

Similar reports came from every direction. In 1940 the Navy had around 1,000 vessels—now it had 14,000, and almost 13,000 of them were landing boats.[85] Many more were on the way. One of the newest ships was the USS *San Jacinto*, the aircraft carrier paid for by the citizens of Houston some months before. Mary christened the ship in a ceremony in a New Jersey shipyard that "was kept at a wartime minimum." That meant no big ceremonies and no bands, but there was still a crowd from Houston and Texas. Governor Stevenson, Senator and Mrs. Tom Connally, Houston Mayor Otis Massey, Mr. and Mrs. James A. Baker Jr., A. D. Simpson from the bank, W. N. (Bill) Blanton from the Chamber of Commerce—all were there, along with a hundred more. The *San Jacinto* and the new cruiser *Houston* were both bound for the Pacific.[86]

82. Ibid.
83. *Houston Chronicle*, August 6, 1943.
84. *Houston Chronicle*, September 5, 1943.
85. *Houston Chronicle*, September 20, 1943.
86. *Houston Chronicle*, September 27, 1943.

Placing the nation's massive new industrial power into the right hands after the war was replacing production as the next big issue. Jones talked about it in all of his speeches. On September 30, he gave an address before the New York Board of Trade titled, "Post-War Problems." He told the commodity traders that the enemy was "on the defensive" and "the day of peace will come." Jones said, "We must be prepared to give jobs to the men and women now in the armed forces, and others engaged in war work. That is what I mean by post-war planning." He offered, "There is no mystery about it. It is just as necessary to prepare for peace, as it is to prepare for war."[87]

Jones explained, "The RFC has authorized the expenditure of more than $24 billion [$294 billion] for purely war purposes, building plants of all character, and buying critical and strategic materials in all parts of the world." Then, quantifying his point with an array of numbers, he broke down the 1,753 plants according to fifteen different industries: 116 plants for machine tools, 98 plants for radio equipment, 164 plants for iron and steel, 84 aluminum plants, 43 plants for hemp and rope fiber . . . and kept going. After reading the entire list, he said,"I enumerate these to indicate the extent to which government is in business, and some of the industries in which it has a large stake." He followed, "It is clear that government and business must find a solution which will be fair to both." Jones declared, "When the war is over, government should get out of active industry as soon as it can," and like a comedian delivering a well-timed punch line, he added, "without too much unnecessary loss." The national conundrum was that, "The future of our economy will depend, in substantial measure, on how the post-war world is organized."[88]

Jones primarily wanted to prevent monopolies, eliminate government control, develop foreign markets, and encourage free enterprise and full employment. He felt local businesses should have first crack at government facilities in their areas, and he had said in House testimony, "Local people should have the first call. I don't think we should permit the war to further concentrate our economy into big units. We're better off with small units."[89] Other government honchos had their own dogs in the hunt, and each had an opinion and agenda. Byrnes asked Bernard Baruch to form a committee to figure out what to do.

87. Jesse Jones, "Post-War Problems," speech, New York Board of Trade, September 30, 1943, Jesse H. Jones Collection [UT].
88. Ibid.
89. *Wall Street Journal*, September 28, 1943.

During this time, the proposed Empire State Building purchase bounced back to Jones from the Public Building Administration and Budget Director Harold Smith. Agreeing with Jones, Smith had told the president, "Little more than one-half of the total available space would be required" for government workers and "the suggested price of $38 million [$466 million] . . . was not economically justified." (The price had fallen from $45 million [$552 million] since Jones had first been involved.) Neatly handing off the hot potato, Smith told Roosevelt to let the RFC "continue discussion with the owners."[90] Roosevelt returned the file to Jones and asked him to try again. Jones said later, "I did nothing further about it, and the President never again mentioned the matter to me . . . I am sure he was displeased that I had not carried out his wish to buy the property and that he never forgave me for not doing it." Showing his power and restraint, he continued, "We had no direct authority to buy the building, but he thought I could do it if I wanted to. I probably could have but did not think I should."[91]

Jones did, however, think the RFC should be charged with disposing of the government's plants. As competing agencies and individuals jockeyed for position, he said to a Senate committee, "I should think you could take the RFC because it is a business agency, built the plants, knows the people." Jones warned, "It will take careful handling [of these properties] to not destroy private industry [after the war]."[92] When Jones was asked about the conversion issue, Pearson reported, "The big Texan leaned back in his chair and spun a story." According to the columnist, Jones said, "When I was a youngster back home, my father used to hitch up the horse and buggy every Sunday and drive the family over to my grandfather's place for Sunday dinner. But one day the horse ran away, and we lost it. There was a half-wit boy on the next farm who set out to find it. He was gone two days and finally came back with the horse." Jones continued, "Well, we asked him how he managed to find that horse, and he said, 'I just thought to myself, what would you do if you was a horse? And then I set out and found him.'" Jones said, "And that's just the way it is with this problem. When I tackle the problem of reconversion, I just use a little horse sense." Pearson concluded, "Jesse Jones has never cared much for

90. Harold Smith to Franklin Roosevelt, November 4, 1943, Jesse H. Jones Collection [LOC].
91. Jones, *Fifty Billion Dollars*, 464.
92. *Houston Chronicle*, December 4, 1943.

the government's economists. He thinks that a half-wit with a little horse sense can do better."[93]

Toward the end of the year, Jones had an opportunity to have some fun. At a gala event on December 17, he honored Orville Wright and recognized the fortieth anniversary of the Wright Brothers' flight at Kitty Hawk. More than eight hundred people attended, and many made speeches. Others sent messages if truly urgent matters kept them away. Soviet Ambassador to the U.S. Andrei Gromyko wrote Jones his regrets, "I have to leave for Cuba to present my Letter of Credence to President Fulgencio Batista as Minister of the Union of Soviet Socialist Republics to Cuba."[94] In Gromyko's place, the first secretary of the Soviet embassy read a statement from the people of the U.S.S.R. Jones spoke for President Roosevelt, who had just returned from the Tehran-Cairo conferences where he, Stalin, and Churchill had met for the first time to plan the D-Day invasion of Western Europe.

With Orville Wright at the head table—Wilbur had passed away in 1912—Jones, who frequently stood in for the president, read Roosevelt's statement. He began, "Today, man's imagination has difficulty in keeping pace with the everyday achievements of flying. The gift to the world by Orville and Wilbur Wright has made a broad highway of the skies over which time and distance are cut a hundred-fold. It is our duty to keep these air highways free and open, in order that all peoples of the world may more and more become good neighbors—better neighbors—and that the instrument of flying shall serve to keep the peace once it has again been achieved." The president said, "When the war is won, it will be our obligation to convert to peaceful pursuits the gains in the field of aviation that war has brought . . . The great capitals of the world will, with the dawn of peace, be as accessible by air as any point in the United States is now by rail." Alluding to the gargantuan RFC investment in aviation and other industries, the president said, "Experiments which would have required decades will have been accomplished in a few years, and if we will, we can use all of these advances for a lasting peace. God willing, we will." Still reading Roosevelt's letter, Jones told the crowd and the nation about the imminent return of a revered relic, "Orville Wright is going to bring the Kitty Hawk plane back from England where it has been in

93. Pearson, "Washington Merry-Go-Round," November 28, 1943.
94. Andrei Gromyko to Jesse Jones, December 16, 1943, Jesse H. Jones Collection [LOC].

Captain Eddie Rickenbacker, Eastern Airlines president and a celebrated World War I pilot, shakes hands with Orville Wright at the 1943 dinner arranged by Jesse Jones to honor the fortieth anniversary of the first Wright Brothers' flight, and to announce the return of the *Kitty Hawk* from England to the United States. Courtesy AP/Wide World.

the British Museum. The Nation will welcome it back as the outstanding symbol of American genius."[95]

Roosevelt wrote Jones after the dinner, "I do not need to tell you how sorry I was to miss the Wright dinner. I am sure, however, that you appreciate what a pile of work was waiting for me when I returned from the Cairo-Tehran meetings the very morning of December seventeenth." The president continued, "I am glad to know the dinner was such an outstanding success. In that, however, it merely fulfilled the expectations of those who knew of the painstaking work you put into the preparation. It was a fitting observance of a notable anniversary. I am genuinely sorry to have missed it."[96]

Jones honored another hero that month, his dear friend Will Rogers, who had died eight years before. With Betty Rogers's approval, the board

95. Franklin Roosevelt, statement prepared for Orville Wright dinner, December 17, 1943, Jesse H. Jones Collection [UT].

96. Franklin Roosevelt to Jesse Jones, December 27, 1943, Jesse H. Jones Collection [LOC].

of the Will Rogers Memorial Commission decided to distribute the last of the $2.1 million ($26 million) that had been collected mostly from contributors attending movie theaters across the nation since Rogers's untimely death. Adding to earlier scholarships given to the University of Texas, the University of Oklahoma, and the University of California, the commission now gave $75,000 ($920,000) to Texas A&M University for scholarships to help handicapped students; $25,000 ($307,000) to the Rogers memorial at Claremore, Oklahoma; and $25,000 ($307,000) to the Murrow Indian Orphan Home. Arrangements were also made to maintain the Saranac Lake hospital in New York that provided care for stage and screen actors.[97]

It looked as if the difficult year might end on a high note. In mid-December the *Saturday Evening Post* published a feature-length article by Pulitzer Prize-winning biographer Henry F. Pringle titled, "Biggest Big Shot: Uncle Sam," in which he identified the U.S. government as "the greatest industrial magnate in the history of the world." Throughout the article Pringle used the DPC to make his point and tagged Jones, under his half-page picture, as "Uncle Sam's manager for about half of the government's war properties." For perspective, Pringle said, compared to the DPC's collection of factories and refineries, "Henry Ford is a small businessman and the United States Steel Corporation a rather prosperous company trying to get along." He wrote, "Uncle Sam . . . has slight idea of what he will do with them when the war is over," and added, "Their output has changed the face of the nation, for steel is being manufactured on Western deserts, magnesium on the Texas gulf coast, and artificial rubber in Louisiana. Their postwar potentialities can alter radically the economics of the entire world."[98]

Pringle pointed out, "Uncle Sam is not only the biggest industrial magnate in history; he is also the most versatile." He described the variety of investments the government had made in every imaginable industry. For instance, he reported that the DPC had invested $45,000 ($552,000) in a small company to manufacture forceps so dentists could fix the teeth of millions of enlistees as they passed through the induction process; many had never been to a dentist before. The DPC goosed production of the recently discovered wonder drug, penicillin, by providing $590,000 ($7.2 million) to Cutter Laboratories. It had even supplied funds to build two churches in Las Vegas, and to enlarge an ice factory in Oregon, to pre-

97. *Houston Chronicle*, December 21, 1943.
98. Pringle, "Biggest Big Shot," 26.

vent "lowered morale among the hundreds of thousands of war workers" in each area. Pringle also wrote about the unique synthetic rubber factories, the enormous aviation investments, the $190 million ($2.33 billion) steel mill in Utah, the worldwide mining operations, and the $41 million ($503 million) that the DPC had spent on sixty-two flying schools, including "one, at Sweetwater, Texas . . . to train women pilots." One of Jones's favorite transactions was a $71 million ($873 million) loan to the Army Post Exchange Service to establish and operate PXs where soldiers could buy items like ice cream, soft drinks, beer, and cigarettes.[99] Jones noted later that this particular loan was paid back in full and said, "I like to think it helped bring some joy and comfort to every soldier who served in the army at home and overseas."[100]

Pringle wrote, "The holdings of the Defense Plant Corporation illustrate vividly the complexities of modern war." He stated, "It is not too much to say that none of the production goals set by President Roosevelt in January 1942 could conceivably have been met had it not been for the creation of the [DPC] . . . on August 22, 1940. When the Japanese struck at Pearl Harbor, the nation's war-production machine was already in high gear." Pringle referred to World War I, the Great Depression, and the initial work of the RFC to explain the growing acceptance of government ownership and control. He noted that plants expanded with private capital during the last war had become worthless after the armistice, and that the Great Depression's devastation had tempered "traditional prejudice against government participation." By putting Jones at the center of this evolution in attitude, Pringle wrote, "it caused hardly a ripple when the RFC actually purchased the stock of embarrassed banks instead of merely making tide-over loans . . . From this it was not too long a step to Government ownership of steel plants, copper mines, and aircraft factories."[101]

Joining the conversation about peacetime conversion, Pringle wrote, "No organization and no individual has yet reached a conclusion, but the goal is clear enough to everybody concerned—that the Government plants shall be operated so as to insure maximum employment after the war, that they shall not be operated to the detriment of private business." Pringle ventured that some plants would close, most would be taken over by industry, and some might be dismantled and shipped abroad to help with reconstruction. Pringle said surveys showed that "most of the manu-

99. Ibid.
100. Jones, *Fifty Billion Dollars*, 379–80.
101. Pringle, "Biggest Big Shot," 27.

facturers now operating DPC plants expect to run them after the war."
He suggested that some would scrap their prewar plants and use "only
the more modern, more efficient ones built with government funds." The
option to buy into the DPC leases motivated operators to build and maintain efficient plants. Still, Pringle noted, no matter how big or small,
every DPC installation across the nation boasted a durable metal plate
that said, "Property of the Defense Plant Corporation, an Instrumentality
of the United States Government."[102]

Jones had denounced the *Saturday Evening Post* article by Samuel Lubell.
As evidence, he had refused to order or distribute any copies. This time,
though, Bill Costello, Jones's chief assistant, notified all thirty-two RFC
branch managers about the December article. He wrote, "If you have
not already done so, you will want to read it and draw it to the attention of the employees in the Agency, as well as the Advisory Committee
members."[103] Tributes poured in to Jones from the RFC, friends, family,
and the public. In a typical letter, an advisory committee member from
the Oklahoma City RFC office wrote, "I can only say that I hope, when the
so-called 'Post-War Era' starts in, that they let Jesse Jones keep his hands
on the works, as I do not believe anyone else in the country can keep all
these billions of plants straightened out or handled where they will do
the ordinary, common folks . . . the most good."[104]

At the end of 1943, Jones commemorated national heroes, received
very good press, and went home for the holidays. Jesse and Mary arrived
in Houston on December 22 and went to dinner with friends the next evening. On the way their driver got lost. Jones got out of the car and crossed
the dark street to ask directions. On his way back, an oncoming car hit
him, breaking one of his legs and straining muscles; he was badly cut and
bruised all over. All of a sudden, Jones found himself laid up in his Lamar
Hotel penthouse. Then he came down with the flu.[105]

102. Ibid., 63.

103. William Costello to Herbert S. Daniel, December 15, 1943, Jesse H. Jones Collection [UT].

104. J. C. Eagen to H. W. Gibson Jr., December 21, 1943, Jesse H. Jones Collection
[UT].

105. *Houston Chronicle*, January 14, 1944.

1944

◈

Jump When the Gong Sounds

NEWS ABOUT JESSE JONES'S ACCIDENT and illness spread fast. The branch manager of the Tennessee Reconstruction Finance Corporation wrote Bill Costello that he had heard about the accident over the radio, "It would certainly be a calamity for him to be out of commission at this crucial time." More personally, he told Costello to warn Jones about "slipping or falling again, especially in view of the fact that he is a man of much weight."[1]

President Franklin Roosevelt, who also started the year with the flu, wrote, "I am awfully sorry about the accident. People in Texas must live in a very dangerous part of the world. First, you have a bout with an airplane and now you try to throw an automobile! Perhaps when you get to my age, you will take on nothing heftier than a long-horned cow."[2] Roosevelt was sixty-two. Jones was almost seventy.

Jones responded with congenial banter, "I note you refer to Texas being a dangerous part of the world and am prepared to agree. Having survived the airplane accident and the automobile . . . I hope to dodge the longhorn. He might be really rough." Jones told the president that he had

1. J. M. Gardenhire to William Costello, January 21, 1944, Jesse H. Jones Collection [UT].
2. Franklin Roosevelt to Jesse Jones, January 14, 1944, Jesse H. Jones Collection [LOC].

dressed for the first time since the accident to follow his custom of buying the first ticket in Houston to the President's Birthday Ball, a fundraiser for Roosevelt's Georgia Warm Springs Foundation, which he had established in 1926 to fight polio.[3] Jones paid $1,000 ($12,000 in current dollars) for the $1 ($12) ticket and so did Will Clayton.[4] Jones also reported, "The following day I dressed and entertained some wounded soldiers . . . gave them some eats and refreshments, and enjoyed visiting with them. They were typical country boys, all Texans." Jones added, "I tried to assure them that the government was preparing to do everything possible . . . to fit them back into civil life with a means of making their own way."[5]

Jones reassured Roosevelt, "I am in daily contact with the office . . . We have fine organizations in both the RFC and Commerce. They know how to work together and also understand government service. Both of these factors are very important when there is so much to do." He closed, "Mrs. Jones wishes to be remembered to you and your Missus, and please take care of yourself."[6] It took more than a month for Jones to recover enough to return to Washington.

A broken leg and fever, however, did not stop him from accomplishing things. He had prepared an article for the January issue of *Domestic Commerce,* a monthly publication. The article was either summarized or printed in full in papers across the nation at the first of the year. He began, "As we enter the new year and our third year of active participation in World War II, the need for preparing for the reconversion period by all segments of business grows daily."[7] Military brass recoiled at the mention of "reconversion." The discussion was premature and inappropriate, they blasted, and would lead to public "complacency" before the U.S. had fought its first major battles against the Germans and the Japanese. General Brehon Somervell, commanding general of the Army Service Forces, said civilians calling for reconversion "have never been bombed . . . have little appreciation of the horrors of war and only in a small percentage . . . do they have enough hate."[8] But away from the battlefield, the writing was on the wall. In some instances, plants were producing too much material, even for global war. Steel and aluminum plants on the drawing boards were cancelled as new plants came on-line and added to the already mas-

3. Jesse Jones to Franklin Roosevelt, January 20, 1944, Jesse H. Jones Collection [LOC].
4. *Houston Chronicle,* January 18, 1944.
5. Jesse Jones to Franklin Roosevelt, January 20, 1944, Jesse H. Jones Collection [LOC].
6. Ibid.
7. *New York Times,* January 2, 1944.
8. Kennedy, *Freedom from Fear,* 655.

sive output. Houston Shipbuilding Corporation reported that a Liberty ship "slid down the ways . . . at an average rate of one every five days during 1943." Even that impressive production placed the shipyard only fifth nationally.[9] In 1944 almost 100,000 new military aircraft would roll off assembly lines, exceeding everything produced by Germany, Japan, and Great Britain combined.[10] The enormous butadiene plant in Port Neches, Texas—the largest single plant in the synthetic rubber program—was about to open and would expand supply by more than ten percent.[11]

Jones continued, "War has created an abnormal economy. Production of machines of destruction and equipment for our fighting forces has superseded everything else. More than that, it has been necessary to leap far past what we ordinarily considered our capacity."[12] In an interview a month earlier, scientist and Goodyear executive R. P. Dinsmore had anticipated the problem and turned it into an opportunity. He predicted that one day shoes would come "with rubber soles and heels for longer wear," that engine vibration would be reduced with rubber mounts, and that automobile tires would be "far superior to any in use [now] or before the war." He also noted that the "thin line" between producing rubber and producing plastic "is getting fainter and fainter." He explained, "All the compounding and processing steps . . . are now available. Many plastics are created by the same or similar polymerizing processes for synthetic rubber." Dinsmore said the synthetic rubber industry would "continue to . . . progress in many ways, which the future undoubtedly will reveal to us."[13]

To avoid past mistakes and to create stability, Jones and others knew plans had to be made now. He wrote, "The precise day, month, or even year when peace will be declared is not for us to predict. But . . . it will come and . . . we will be among the victors." He continued, "It is possible that this most disrupting of all wars will end suddenly. There will be no time then to plan calmly and intelligently for a smooth transition from a war to a peacetime economy."[14] Whether the military liked it or not, Jones presciently pushed reconversion, and the RFC began to approach private operators of government plants about purchasing them with RFC financing. To that end, an inventory of the government's plants was being

9. *Houston Chronicle*, January 2, 1944.
10. Kennedy, *Freedom from Fear*, 654.
11. *Houston Chronicle*, February 24, 1944.
12. *New York Times*, January 2, 1944.
13. *Houston Chronicle*, December 19, 1943.
14. *New York Times*, January 2, 1944.

assembled. Some machine tools were already being declared "surplus," moved out of factories, and put up for sale by the RFC. But no one had been appointed to lead the overall effort. Measures were needed to prevent the large corporations that had grown out of huge government outlays from smothering small business and labor.

Jones explained, "[M]ajor production and . . . the larger share of profits are in the hands of big business. These facts are perfectly natural in a wartime economy. Only the highly organized large industries of our country could have wrought the conversion and production miracles that we are already taking for granted."[15] Indeed, out of $9.2 billion ($111 billion) invested by the Defense Plant Corporation, $4 billion ($48 billion) went to the nation's twenty-five largest corporations.[16] The three top recipients were Alcoa, General Motors, and U.S. Steel. The 350 investments of $100,000 ($1.2 million) or less in small companies paled in comparison.[17] The peacetime playing field would be beyond uneven.

Jones said small businesses were essential because of the thousands of people they employed, because the economy depended on businesses of all sizes to function smoothly, and because small communities depended on small business. Jones declared, "Small enterprises must be maintained because they are the essence of democracy." Wanting government out of business as soon as possible, Jones once more put the ball in business's court and said, "[G]overnment and business leaders and private organizations can formulate the plans, but to make them work, there must be a virile, courageous, and revitalized upsurge of private initiative."[18]

Rumor had it that Jones would lead the reconversion. A *Wall Street Journal* article predicted as much, noting, "Secretary of Commerce Jesse Jones is far in front in the running for this key job, and his formal appointment may come within the next week or two."[19] But in mid-February Bernard Baruch issued his report recommending that Jones's close colleague DSC Director Clayton be appointed as surplus war property administrator to oversee the economic reconversion. The Baruch report, which attempted to cast "reconversion" as "readjustment," also recommended quick disposal of war surplus, sales at fair market prices, equal opportunities for purchases (with a slight preference for local ownership), no subsidies, and a transparent process. The Baruch report opposed monopolies,

15. Ibid.
16. Jones, *Fifty Billion Dollars*, 338.
17. White, *Billions for Defense*, 48–49.
18. *New York Times*, January 2, 1944.
19. *Wall Street Journal*, January 12, 1944.

destruction of useful property, government operation and control of plants, and imposition of social change policies in decisions and actions.[20] It also recommended that the RFC consolidate its subsidiaries and dispose of its own property.

Four days after Baruch submitted his plan, Roosevelt issued an executive order to establish the Surplus War Property Administration (SWPA). James Byrnes, head of the Office of War Mobilization, appointed Clayton as SWPA's director. Resigning from the RFC, Clayton moved to the OWM in his new position. As if he were growing tentacles, Jones saw another top lieutenant ascend to a new place of power. The first SWPA meeting was held in the RFC boardroom on March 2. DPC President Sam Husbands and DPC Vice President Hans Klagsbrunn were put in charge of the RFC's surplus property, which accounted for the bulk of the government's holdings that could be converted to peacetime use. Through his RFC colleagues and relationships with Clayton and "assistant president" Byrnes, and despite his ongoing differences with Baruch, Jones would have a hand in converting the economy he had helped save during the Great Depression and that he had helped build during the war.

Clayton was more than a lieutenant; in many ways he was Jones's surrogate. He had often acted as mediator and messenger between Jones and Wallace as the two men feuded. Clayton liked Wallace and admired his ideals, but often rejected his policies and practices, especially those that combined social programs with overseas purchases and those that included attacks on his friend and boss. Indeed, Clayton and RFC President Howard Klossner had worked with Jones to compose the lengthy rebuttal to Wallace's onslaught back in June.[21] Press coverage of Clayton's appointment as SWPA director recognized the tight relationship. The *New York Times* identified him as the "right-hand man of Secretary of Commerce Jesse Jones."[22] The *Wall Street Journal* revealed, "Mr. Clayton, one of the world's biggest brokers in international cotton transactions . . . has been intimately associated with Mr. Jones in the direction of RFC's war procurement and war credit subsidiaries." The article did not mention that the Joneses and the Claytons also played bridge together at least two evenings a week, but the *Wall Street Journal* did report, "[Clayton] will have complete control of the policy and administration governing disposition of the [billions of dollars worth] of surplus war property expected to be in

20. White, *Billions for Defense*, 92–93.
21. Fossedal, *Our Finest Hour*, 100.
22. *New York Times*, February 11, 1944.

Susan Vaughn Clayton and Mary Gibbs Jones, who sold war bonds from a desk in the RFC building's lobby, sell bonds to their husbands, Will Clayton (left) and Jesse Jones. The Claytons and the Joneses played bridge together two to three times a week. Clayton worked with Jones to accumulate strategic materials from around the globe for the war effort. He later became Undersecretary of State and was instrumental in formulating the Marshall Plan. Courtesy Briscoe Center for American History, University of Texas at Austin.

the government's possession by the end of the year."[23] No war plant had yet been declared "surplus" by a sponsoring agency, which was a primary requirement for disposal.

The day Baruch's report came out, Jones appeared before the House Banking and Currency Committee to speak in favor of the SPWA and Clayton's appointment. He also called for the government to continue to operate the synthetic rubber plants to prevent cartel control over supplies and prices, expressed his opposition to Baruch's recommendation of selling or leasing properties at uniform prices, and announced that the RFC would provide loans to returning servicemen to help them reestablish businesses they had lost when they answered the call of duty.[24]

23. *Wall Street Journal*, February 26, 1944.
24. *Wall Street Journal*, February 15, 1944.

Reconversion may have been the hot topic in Washington and in the corridors of Congress, but the war was front-page news. By mid-April thousands of British and U.S. aircraft were on daily runs to bomb and destroy factories, bridges, and rail yards both in Germany and in occupied France, Holland, and other countries as part of a "preinvasion air offensive." In 1943, sending 200 planes on a mission had been a big deal; now groups of 1,000 or more were taking off day and night and dropping thousands of tons of bombs on Axis targets. Millions of soldiers and tons of military machines were massing on England's south coast.

Between 1940 and the spring of 1944, the U.S. armed forces had grown from a meager band of around 200,000 men to 10 million men and 500,000 women. Many of them were now in England; for more than a year, they had been pouring into the country at about 150,000 per month. Tens of thousands of U.S.-made airplanes, tanks, trucks, and ships, along with millions of bullets, tons of bombs, and mountains of food, clothing, and medicine—much of it from RFC-financed factories—covered vast fields, packed warehouses, and jammed ports and piers.

On the morning of June 6, more 5,000 landing craft carried 75,000 British and Canadian soldiers and 57,000 U.S. soldiers with all of their motorized equipment and modern weaponry across the English Channel to invade France on the Normandy coast. Another 25,000 soldiers—15,000 from the U.S. Airborne Division—parachuted into France from airplanes. Warships and aircraft provided cover as the loaded vessels crossed the treacherous channel. As many as 9,000 Allied soldiers were killed or wounded on D-Day, but more than 100,000 brave men were now on the European continent; with the mass of men coming up from Italy and Russians coming from the east, they were on their way to surrounding and defeating Hitler.[25] The RFC and its subsidiaries had made an enormous contribution to this historic effort with the output from its factories and shipyards, and through the rubber plants that supplied the tires and other components for the amphibious vehicles, aircraft, trucks, and tanks, which were necessary for victory.[26]

Jones, like most everyone else in official Washington, had little time for a personal life. His sister Lizzie passed away in May and Jones was unable to return to Houston to attend her funeral. In the last part of her life, Lizzie had lived at the Lamar Hotel. Jones philosophically wrote to one of Lizzie's friends, "No one knows better than you that she had not

25. Kennedy, *Freedom from Fear*, 722, 738, 741, 745.
26. Ibid., 715.

been well for the past few months and, under such circumstances, is better off. After all, she had had more than her allotted span, three score and ten, and most of her life had been happy."[27] Always generous, Jones wrote to one of Lizzie's two sons who, with his wife, had lived with his mother at the hotel, "Please do not be in too big a hurry about giving up the apartment. You can keep it as long as you want it."[28] Despite the demands of the day, Franklin Roosevelt took time to write Jones, "I was so sorry to hear of the death of your sister. This is just a line to let you know that I am thinking of you."[29]

Jones also hardly had time to correspond with his nephew, who was still interned in a German prisoner-of-war camp. Giving him a nudge, Jones's brother, John, sent him a copy of a recent letter from John Jr. and wrote, "I am enclosing an addressed envelope to John, thinking you might probably like to write him a letter."[30] Jones wrote to assure his nephew that he had been kept current on his situation through the family, then admitted, "I have been negligent in writing." He shared, "You have [heard] or will hear that your Aunt Elizabeth passed on last week, and since she had been failing badly, . . . she is much better off." Jones also reported, "Your Aunt Mary and I are both well, though an automobile ran over me at Houston [on] December 23rd and kept me laid up for six weeks. No permanent injury." Jones sent his nephew "love and best wishes" from both him and Mary, then wrote in longhand at the bottom of the letter, "Audrey paid us a visit recently—she looks well & is I am sure quite happy."[31]

Meanwhile, another relative was causing a ruckus in Democratic politics and affecting Jones's relationship with President Roosevelt. George Butler—who had married one of Jones's nieces and worked as one of his attorneys—belonged to the Texas Regulars, a well-organized branch of the state Democratic Party. At the state-level convention in May, the Regulars denounced the New Deal, labor unions, Roosevelt's run for a fourth term, and most particularly Vice President Wallace. Butler, chairman of the Texas Democratic executive committee, called for the Texas delegation to attend the upcoming national convention "uninstructed as to whom they shall vote for as the presidential nominee and vice presidential nominee." He also urged them to work and vote for restoration of a rule that required a two-thirds majority of convention delegate votes

27. Jesse Jones to M. Watson, May 22, 1944, Jesse H. Jones Collection [LOC].
28. Jesse Jones to Milton Farthing, May 12, 1944, Jesse H. Jones Collection [LOC].
29. Franklin Roosevelt to Jesse Jones, May 2, 1944, Jesse H. Jones Collection [LOC].
30. John T. Jones Sr. to Jesse Jones, March 21, 1944, John T. Jones Jr. Collection [HE].
31. Jesse Jones to John T. Jones Jr., May 14, 1944, John T. Jones Jr. Collection [HE].

to elect the party's nominees.[32] Furthermore, the Regulars were telling its members not to vote for Roosevelt even if he ended up on the ticket. Lamar Fleming, who was head of Anderson, Clayton & Co., and John H. Crooker, who was Clayton's personal attorney, also belonged to the Texas Regulars. In short, close aides to two of President Roosevelt's principal collaborators were publicly opposing his presidency as the national conventions approached in July.

The press went to work. Drew Pearson in particular sank his teeth into the controversy. One week after D-Day and a month before the convention, he wrote, "The president's political advisers aren't shouting about it, but they have now received a 20-page report on the Texas 'revolution.'" Pearson averred, "[It] appears to confirm . . . that Jesse Jones and Will Clayton forces were behind the move in the Texas Democratic convention to instruct electors to . . . not necessarily vote for the winner next November." Pearson identified George Butler as "Jesse Jones' nephew and attorney for 'Jesse H. Jones interests'" and reported, "The White House has been informed that Butler has the reputation in Houston of never doing anything without consulting Uncle Jesse." On this basis, Pearson concluded, "It is inconceivable that he would act without Jesse's approval." Pearson said that Crooker, "[an] attorney for Will Clayton, the man who sits at FDR's right hand when it comes to post-war liquidation," organized the revolt against Roosevelt. Further, "Working with Crooker was Lamar Fleming, head of the giant Anderson, Clayton & Company, biggest cotton broker in the world, of which Will Clayton is a partner. Both Fleming and Crooker came to Austin in advance of the [state] convention to spearhead the drive against Roosevelt." Pearson ended, "So far, the President has been too busy with the invasion to have any showdown with his Secretary of Commerce and Will Clayton."[33]

The next day Pearson reported that Butler and the Regulars were "more interested in keeping Henry Wallace off the ticket than in putting Roosevelt on."[34] Four days later he continued, "Around the White House these days, the seething ire at Jesse Jones is getting funny . . . Inside fact is that . . . Jones and Will Clayton, the Santa Claus for surplus war goods, were behind the Texas Roosevelt-haters." Pearson revealed, "Democratic National Chairman . . . Bob Hannegan went to see Jesse Jones. Jesse looked very naive . . . and said he didn't know a thing about the Texas revolt until

32. *Houston Chronicle*, May 5, 1944.
33. Pearson, "Washington Merry-Go-Round," June 13, 1944.
34. Pearson, "Washington Merry-Go-Round," June 14, 1944.

he read about it in the newspapers. [He] was charming, delightful, and, oh, so very ignorant about the whole thing."[35]

The press would not let it go. Pearson wrote something almost every day. *Washington Post* owner Eugene Meyer questioned Jones's loyalty to the president in a June editorial. Mindful of the president's directive about publicizing responses in the press, Jones wrote Roosevelt somewhat after the fact, "I am enclosing a copy of a letter which I have sent to Eugene Meyer. As I have already told you, I hope to be helpful in suggesting a solution."[36] In the letter to Meyer, Jones stated, "So that the inferences and innuendoes of that editorial, in so far as they apply to me and Texas, may be stamped as the lies that they are, I will say that I had no part, either directly or indirectly, in the plans for, or proceedings of, the Texas State Democratic Convention. I was not consulted, directly or indirectly, on the choice of delegates to the National Convention or the electors of the State of Texas. I had no foreknowledge of the resolutions to be offered at, or adopted by, the Texas State Democratic Convention."[37]

Jones took matters further and issued a statement on the front page of the *Houston Chronicle*. He questioned "the wisdom of some of the [state] convention's actions" and said they "went much further than many" realized. The Regulars wanted Roosevelt's name off the ballot in Texas, no matter who was selected at the national convention. Jones, who did endorse the two-thirds rule, thought they were going too far and declared, "A qualified voter has a right to cast his ballot for the candidate of his choice." He instructed, "For voters who do not wish to support the nominees of the two major parties, provision is usually made on the ballot." Then he warned, "Many Texans are now threatened with the loss of this right. Voters of the state of Texas, which gave President Roosevelt a greater majority in 1940 than . . . any other state in the Union, may be prevented from voting for him in 1944 if he is the nominee of his party." Jones said, "As it appears today, Texas Democrats may be effectively prevented from casting their vote for the party nominee."[38]

Pearson did not buy it. Three days after Jones published his statement, Pearson reported, "Inside the Cabinet, they are facetiously saying that, for FDR, July is 'Jesse Jones Month.'" He explained, "Exactly one year ago, the President was confronted with an open, vitriolic row between his

35. Pearson, "Washington Merry-Go-Round," June 18, 1944.
36. Jesse Jones to Franklin Roosevelt, June 27, 1944, Jesse H. Jones Collection [LOC].
37. Jesse Jones to Eugene Meyer, June 26, 1944, Jesse H. Jones Collection [LOC].
38. *Houston Chronicle*, July 5, 1944.

Vice President and his Secretary of Commerce, which he solved in favor of Jones. Today he has a Southern revolt on his hands, which he has told insiders he blames partly on Jesse Jones. So the question is: What is he going to do about it?" Pearson thought that the rebellion might spread if Roosevelt did not take decisive action. He said Jones had not been fired because he "has more power on Capitol Hill than any other Cabinet member." Pearson wrote, "Jones has loaned money to the constituents of more Congressmen than anyone in history." Pearson claimed that Clayton had disavowed any knowledge of the rebellion and offered to resign, but that Roosevelt had believed him and refused his offer. Pearson surmised, "The incident was embarrassing to Jones, however, because (1) he did not submit his resignation, and (2) he did not immediately denounce the Texas revolt." Then Pearson suggested Jones was angling for a slot on the ticket as vice president.[39]

Without naming names, Jones later recalled, "Certain troublemakers in Washington tried to make it appear to the President and others . . . that I had encouraged the action taken by the Regulars. This was due to the fact that George A. Butler, the husband of one of my several nieces, took a prominent part in the Regulars movement." Discussing the matter with the president, Jones told Roosevelt that he controlled his family about as well as the president controlled his, and reminded him that his son Elliott had tried to get Jones nominated for vice president at the 1940 Chicago convention even after the president had chosen Wallace. As evidence of his loyalty to the president and his rejection of the Texas Regulars, Jones wrote, "According to my code, I could not remain in his Cabinet and not support him."[40] Jones suspected, however, that Roosevelt never quite believed him.

Roosevelt declared his intention to run for a fourth term less than a week before the 1944 convention began in Chicago on July 17. He did not publicly endorse Wallace as his running mate and made it appear that he was leaving the decision about the vice presidential nominee to the delegates. Wallace and Byrnes each arrived at the convention with assurances from Roosevelt that they had his support and the nomination was wrapped up. Neither knew that the president had indicated to Hannegan, chairman of the Democratic National Committee, that he would "be very glad to run with" either Missouri Senator Harry Truman or Supreme Court Justice William O. Douglas. Byrnes was still a possible

39. Pearson, "Washington Merry-Go-Round," July 8, 1944.
40. Jones, *Fifty Billion Dollars*, 275–76.

candidate, but Wallace had been rejected months before because of his liberal leanings and the fallout from his feud with Jones.[41] This shouldn't have been a surprise. When talk about the ticket began in the spring, a *New York Times* reporter had written, "Many . . . practical politicians . . . recalled the President's criticism of Mr. Wallace in ending the Vice President's feud with Secretary Jesse Jones over the Board of Economic Warfare and were inclined to count the Iowan out of the picture."[42]

President Roosevelt was easily renominated on July 20. The Convention was being held as he headed to Hawaii to plan Pacific strategy, so he delivered his acceptance speech from his train in San Diego. More than 40,000 conventioneers listened and cheered in the hall overlooked by Roosevelt's huge spotlit portrait as they heard the president's reassuring voice. He called for a fast and powerful end to the war, for the establishment of international organizations for stabilization and security after the war, and for an economy that provided employment and a decent standard of living for all. As soon as the president finished speaking, and the cheering and organ music quieted down, chants of "We want Wallace" filled the Chicago stadium.

Earlier that afternoon, knowing he had nothing to lose, the vice president had delivered a groundbreaking speech, holding back nothing. Wallace told the packed stadium, "The future belongs to those who go down the line unswervingly for the liberal principles of both political democracy and economic democracy regardless of race, color, or religion. In a political, educational, and economic sense, there must be no inferior races. The poll tax must go. Equal educational opportunities must come. The future must bring equal wages for equal work regardless of sex or race." He continued, "Roosevelt stands for all this. That is why certain people hate him so. That also is one of the outstanding reasons why Roosevelt will be elected for a fourth time."[43] Wallace used the words "liberal" and "liberalism" eleven times in what was a relatively short speech. One columnist, moved to tears, said it was magnificent, then added, "But, goddam it, it isn't smart politics." *Time* magazine reported, "It was blunt, grave, tactless. It easily explained why Henry Wallace was the best loved and the best hated man in the stadium."[44]

41. Culver and Hyde, *American Dreamer*, 353.
42. *New York Times*, April 15, 1944.
43. Culver and Hyde, *American Dreamer*, 360–61.
44. Ibid.

The demonstration for Wallace surged after Roosevelt spoke, and party leaders panicked. If the vote were taken now, Wallace would win the nomination. Senator Claude Pepper from Florida did all he could to be recognized so he could nominate Wallace then and there: he jumped up and down on his chair, shouted at the top of his lungs, and finally began to fight through the crowd to the podium. As he reached the stairs, Chairman Samuel D. Jackson purposely banged his gavel and adjourned the session. The next morning Jackson apologized to Pepper saying, "I hope you understand." Pepper recalled, "What I understood was that, for better or worse, history was turned topsy-turvy that night in Chicago."[45] The party machine, President Roosevelt, and the public fights with Jones conspired to prevent Wallace from obtaining the nomination and from later becoming the president of the United States. That afternoon, Truman was nominated for vice president on the second vote.

Wallace and his wife, Ilo, received a telegram from Roosevelt that evening. "You made a grand fight and I am very proud of you," wrote the president. He also suggested there would be a place for Wallace in his administration by adding, "Tell Ilo not to plan to leave Washington next January."[46] Jones, who was in bed with pneumonia, did not attend the convention. He was unaware of how Wallace's defeat and Roosevelt's response to it would upend his life after the Chicago convention.

Right before the convention, Clayton had given the DPC power to dispose of all government surplus war plants and property. According to the *Wall Street Journal*, "Establishment of this basic policy adds another responsibility to the surplus-disposal duties of the RFC under the direction of Secretary of Commerce Jesse Jones." Jones and the RFC were already working to convert their own facilities; Clayton's move added the Army and Navy's surplus plants and real estate, including their bases, to that task. After twelve years in government service, and despite all manner of power plays at the highest levels, Jones was still accumulating power. The reporter said, "Shifting responsibility for disposing of Federally-owned wartime real estate and buildings to the RFC and the Defense Plant Corp. was explained by . . . the Surplus Property Administration Agency as 'one more step toward getting surplus disposal into . . . action . . . stage.'" Clayton's organization was operating under executive order and the article noted that Congress "has not yet passed comprehensive legislation

45. Ibid., 363–64.
46. Ibid., 367.

governing the policies and procedures for disposing of unneeded war materials."[47]

At the end of July, Jones reported that the RFC had reached the half-way point in its survey of all government property, that prospective purchasers should expect "fair prices," but not bargains, and that the RFC might furnish financing and extend leases to facilitate putting plants into civilian hands. He went into some detail about how he would determine a property's price, explaining that values would be determined by current replacement and adaptation costs. Jones took the middle between those who wanted all the surplus plants destroyed to prevent government competition and those who wanted the government to own and operate the plants to control competition. And he promised to make the best deal for taxpayers while protecting the common good.[48]

In a speech to a group of financial reporters and writers, he repeated the warning, "It would not be to the best interests of the country if all . . . government plants got into the hands of big business and . . . further increased monopolistic tendencies. We should not permit the war to further concentrate our economy in big units. The country is better off with smaller units, even if not always as efficient." Jones also said, "If our country can finance and win a $250 billion [$3 trillion] war, sending men and materials in unprecedented numbers and quantities all over the world, we are not going to let conversion to peace get us down."[49]

That summer, as RFC, Navy, and Army plants poured forth arms and equipment, contracts for new plants slowed to a relative trickle. Tin and paper shortages occasionally cropped up, but in late July, for the first time since World War II began, the director of a war agency voluntarily resigned and dissolved his organization because it was no longer needed. Bradley Dewey had succeeded William Jeffers as "Rubber Czar," and he announced the dissolution of his bureau, saying the synthetic rubber program was complete and producing as much, if not more, than Baruch's committee had recommended two years before. Dewey said the industry would survive after the war because, "I cannot see any capitalist planting rubber trees and waiting seven years for them to grow."[50] He was right. The synthetic rubber industry would thrive after the war, and those factories would be attractive assets. The same would be true for the "Big Inch"

47. *Wall Street Journal*, July 11, 1944.
48. *New York Times*, July 24, 1944.
49. Jesse Jones, speech, New York Financial Writers Association, June 3, 1944, Jesse H. Jones Collection [LOC].
50. *Houston Chronicle*, July 26, 1944.

and "Little Inch" pipelines built and owned by the RFC. Proposals from various corporations to transport natural gas through them from Texas to the east coast were already coming in.[51]

While the scope and pressures of his job expanded, Jones was struggling with his health. Within a six-month period he had been injured in a car accident, had developed flu and pneumonia, and recently had undergone foot surgery. In early August he and Mary went to the Thousand Islands Club to recuperate, rest, and fish. The luxurious marina on remote Wellesley Island sat on the St. Lawrence River upstream from Lake Ontario. It was one of the Joneses' favorite spots. Finally with a little time on his hands, Jones caught up with family and friends. He wrote to John Nance Garner, "I had seven weeks in bed, about three of which with a light case of pneumonia and the balance due to a slight operation. I am up now, but am a little weak and wobbly." In a light vein, he wrote, "Fishing is good, but we haven't been out yet. We usually get bass from 3/4 of a pound to 3 pounds. We fish with minnows, sometimes small frogs. It is good fun, but neither of us have felt like going out yet." He said, "Mrs. Jones got pretty well run down looking after me, although we had nurses and doctors."[52]

Then he got down to the real business "I am sure you have heard all about the Convention. I listened to it on the radio, night and day. I am sure that Jimmie Byrnes feels badly hurt, although he will stick around and do what he can. There is no choice in wartime. A man can't quit." He reported to Garner that "The RFC has done a tremendous amount of work in the war, and has done it as well and as business-like as possible . . . It has built some 2,000 plants of all kinds at a cost of between 8 and 10 billion dollars [$96 and $120 billion]. It has bought several billion dollars of raw materials and supplies from all over the world. While there have been a few tight spots here and there on some materials, no war activity has ever been held up for a lack of raw materials, metals, and what-not. We will write it up some day and put it in the Congressional Record." Still looking back, he confessed, "The only conflict we have had with any war agency was with BEW under Mr. Wallace." He couldn't resist sharing some gossip, writing, "Ickes is, of course, nasty when he can be, but that is to be expected, and we pay no attention to it. I am told that he, Tom Corcoran, and Francis Biddle tried very hard to maneuver Truman out and Douglas

51. *Houston Chronicle*, July 6, 1944.
52. Jesse Jones to John Nance Garner, August 14, 1944, Jesse H. Jones Collection [LOC].

in." Finally he admitted, "Personally, I am very much pleased that Wallace was displaced." He signed his letter, "Affectionately, Jesse."[53]

Jones wrote Audrey a couple of days later, noting, "It has been too hot to do much fishing. We were out a little today for the first time. Muna caught the big fish."[54] In another letter he began, "Dear Baby," and reported, "My feet have always been a problem, that is, of getting enough shoe leather to cover them." He sent regards to her new husband and lightheartedly signed his letter, "With worlds of love to both of you, As ever, Jesse Bods Jones."[55]

By the end of August, Jones, still a little weak, was back at work. The presidential campaign was heating up and so was the war. U.S. battle-field casualties now stood at 54,000. More than 91,000 U.S. soldiers had been wounded, almost 122,000 were missing, and 93,000 were prisoners of war.[56] Worldwide, many millions had been killed since the war began, including the millions of Jews and others in Hitler's ovens and concentration camps.

The Russians had lost millions of countrymen as they fought through Romania, Bulgaria, Hungary and into Poland. They were not far from Berlin when U.S., British, and Canadian troops began to penetrate German-held Dutch and Belgian borders. The D-Day campaign and the Normandy invasion reached a victorious climax on August 25 when the Germans surrendered Paris to the Allied forces. The people of France greeted U.S. soldiers as "liberators" in parades and parties. Charles De Gaulle, president of the provisional government of the French Republic, who took over the War Ministry after the Germans surrendered, said, "The enemy staggers, but he is not vanquished yet." He added that it was not enough to "chase him from our home . . . with the help of our dear and admirable allies." DeGaulle declared, "We want to enter his territory, as is fitting, as victors." At that point, the Allies had a three-to-one advantage in munitions and arms over the Axis powers.[57]

In the Pacific war, the U.S. Marines recaptured Guam in August and began building air bases there to accommodate the B-29 bombers that would soon head for Japan. During the battle 1,700 U.S. soldiers lost their lives, but Japan lost 18,000. By then each U.S. soldier in the Pacific had the equivalent of four tons of supplies, airplanes, and aircraft carriers behind

53. Ibid.
54. Jesse Jones to Audrey Jones Beck, August 17, 1944, Audrey Jones Beck Collection [HE].
55. Jesse Jones to Audrey Jones Beck, August 3, 1944, Audrey Jones Beck Collection [HE].
56. *Houston Chronicle*, July 14, 1944.
57. Kennedy, *Freedom from Fear*, 668.

him, compared with only two pounds of war material backing each Japanese soldier.[58] During 1944 U.S. submarines sank 600 Japanese vessels, depriving the aggressor nation of oil, men, battleships, aircraft carriers, and airplanes. Forging a deadly path, the U.S. was hopscotching its way across the Pacific, island by island, to Tokyo.

Jones sent letters to 370 corporate heads, asking what they intended to do with their 586 DPC-owned factories. He wrote, "While we do not know how soon the Defense Plant Corporation buildings which you are leasing will become surplus to the war effort, we would like to know whether or not you contemplate acquiring the property for postwar civilian activities, either under your option or through negotiation." Jones had to offer an opportunity to haggle. He prodded, "I am sure you can understand the problems which will confront all of us and that you want to . . . prevent unemployment in the reconversion period. We will greatly appreciate your co-operation by advising us as quickly as possible."[59] Unlike rebuffs by recalcitrant bankers from years before, Jones received 332 replies to his 370 requests within two weeks.

Sixty-six percent of the respondents wanted to negotiate a purchase or a lease; twenty percent could not decide; ten percent were not interested; and three percent said they were interested in leasing only. One respondent did not understand the question. Jones reported to Sam Rosenman, special counsel to the president, "We will probably be able to sell a good many buildings at fair prices, but not so [the] special equipment for war production." Repeating his position, he concluded, "I am strongly of the opinion that the plants should not be sacrificed."[60] Plants had been built in every state. How they were used after the war, and who operated them, would influence the economic and social future. The bulk of the new manufacturing capacity was in the hands of the country's largest corporations. General Motors alone had manufactured ten percent of the nation's output for war. More than two-thirds of all military contracts went to just one hundred corporations.[61] That's why Jones and others were concerned about monopolies.

The DPC accounted for more than 30 percent of all new facilities built across the nation. Most of them, unlike the Navy and Army's munitions plants, could be converted to peacetime use. They were geographically

58. Ibid.
59. *Houston Chronicle*, September 7, 1944.
60. Jesse Jones to Sam Rosenman, September 22, 1944, Jesse H. Jones Collection [HE].
61. Kennedy, *Freedom from Fear*, 621.

dispersed—for policy and security's sake, a single specific industry could not be concentrated in one area. Of the six states receiving the largest DPC investments, five were in the North and one was in the South. The DPC invested $1.4 billion ($16.8 billion) in 463 plants in Ohio and Michigan because of the automobile industry. Texas was third, with $650 million ($7.8 billion) invested in 108 facilities. Illinois, Pennsylvania, and New York followed. In the west, California received the most, coming in eighth. At the low end of the spectrum, the DPC invested $156,000 ($1.87 million) in a single Idaho project.

The South had made substantial economic gains. War Production Board Chairman Donald Nelson predicted that industrial and social development in the South "will astound the world," saying that, "Largely as a result of war, it has industrial know-how on a large scale and substantial accumulations of regional capital." Like Jones, businessmen in the South and West had dreamed of the day when they no longer depended on east coast banks to fund huge regional commercial projects. Nelson continued, "Within the lifetime of the next generation, the contribution of Southern resources . . . industrial skills, and . . . capital will bring the South into the vanguard of world industrial progress."[62] Texas had received more New Deal allocations than any other southern state, and more in war agency investment than others in the South during World War II. In years to come, it would be the only southern state where per capita income exceeded the national average.[63]

Legislation for peacetime conversion had been submitted to Congress, and in late September both houses hammered out their differences over surplus war property and sent the bill to Roosevelt. It would supersede the executive order he had issued in February and displace Clayton as sole director with a board of three. Before Roosevelt signed, Jones sent a letter to add his two cents' worth. He called the bill "not ideal by a great deal" and held out hope that changing it after it was enacted might help. Then he bowed to reality and covered his bases by suggesting names for the new board. He pointedly reprised the president's previous position as he wrote, "As you have often said, as many . . . plants as possible should be converted to domestic production, others . . . retained as standby, and some . . . will, of necessity, have to be scrapped." He added, "I should like to emphasize that disposing of government plants and facilities, includ-

---

62. Editorial quoting Donald Nelson in *American Mercury* (October 1944), *Houston Chronicle*, September 26, 1944.
63. Schwarz, *New Dealers*, 322.

ing stockpiles, is not a job that can be hurried unless we are willing practically to give them away. This would injure our whole economy." Jones pointed to a provision in the bill that permitted transferring RFC plants to other agencies without reimbursement, something he strongly opposed. Always protecting the bottom line, even during war, he wrote, "We will either have to be reimbursed for any properties transferred to other departments . . . or ask Congress to cancel our notes to the Treasury to cover such investments." Jones wrote, "I asked the conferees to include such provision in the Bill, but they did not do it."[64]

President Roosevelt signed the Surplus Property Act on October 3, 1944, but expressed reluctance to fully embrace the bill. He said he was "in full accord with the declared objectives" of reconverting "from a war to a peace economy and to facilitate the orderly disposal of surplus property," but he was concerned that "the elaborate restrictions imposed by the bill" will cause delay and confusion "rather than expedite reconversion and reemployment."[65] The president signed anyway, expecting that Congress would improve it after it was put into law.

Time magazine reported, "Congress last week passed a surplus property bill which clipped Mr. Clayton's power. Where he [had] ruled alone, a three-man board will henceforth dispose of the estimated $100 billion [$1.2 trillion] in surplus war goods." The magazine reported that Clayton planned to quit because he felt Congress had "turned surplus property disposal into a political grab bag," where valuable assets would "be parceled out among Government agencies by a political board with divided authority." According to *Time*, "Will Clayton was not alone in this view: Jimmy Byrnes was dead-set against the three-man board, and Elder Statesman Bernie Baruch has personally phoned Congressmen, begging them to drop it." The article concluded, "As the uproar swelled, the homeward-bound Congressmen wearily realized that the price for getting rid of Will Clayton had been too high. One of their first jobs after the election recess will probably be to patch up the bill."[66] In the end, the complicated legislation, which had created a circuitous route for each property and item to follow until it got back to the RFC for disposal, was never put into effect. Redistributing the nation's industrial might was still in the RFC's (and Jones's) hands.

---

64. Jesse Jones to Franklin Roosevelt, September 24, 1944, Jesse H. Jones Collection [LOC].
65. Roosevelt, "On Signing the Surplus Property Act of 1944."
66. "U.S. at War: The Surplus Surplus Bill."

Two weeks after the Surplus Property Act passed, the DPC sent a booklet it had been busy preparing to every bank, railroad, and chamber of commerce in the country. The "Briefalogue" described 879 DPC plants and pieces of its real estate that were projected to go on sale in forty-one states, as well as ninety-four additional properties owned by the War Department. The Briefalogue included Chrysler's five million-square-foot Dodge-Chicago plant where B-29 and B-32 engines were manufactured, and Ford's enormous Willow Run plant in Ypsilanti that made B-42 bombers. Jones explained that the booklet was intended to give "advance information as to the size, character, and location of [the] plants so that when any of them are declared surplus . . . they can be converted to civilian production through lease or sale with all possible speed and the least possible loss of employment." The Briefalogue promoted the properties as "the most modern in the country" with the "latest equipment."[67]

Just as when he had pushed small business, real estate, and long-term loans to banks during the New Deal, Jones sent a letter and copy of the Briefalogue to every bank president in the nation, asking for their participation. He wrote, "As you know, we have always stressed that we are not in competition with private lending institutions. However, we do stand ready to . . . participat[e] with you in loans that you may make in . . . financing the purchase or operation of these plants." The RFC had become a fixture over the past twelve years, which was evident as Jones continued, "You are familiar with this participating program, and the manager of the Reconstruction Finance Corp. loan agency serving your territory will be very glad to cooperate with you in every way possible."[68]

Meanwhile, election day was drawing near. When Roosevelt asked Jones to deliver a radio address to help the campaign, he agreed, despite another bout with the flu and the rumors flying about the Texas Regulars and his future in Roosevelt's cabinet. New York Governor Thomas E. Dewey and Ohio Governor John W. Bricker were the Republican opponents. Dewey was an internationalist who had favored many of Roosevelt's New Deal programs. The war was going well enough: right before the election, General Douglas MacArthur famously waded ashore in the Philippines after defeating the Japanese there, and the first U.S. troops had just entered Germany.[69] Nor did the domestic economy offer Republicans a political edge: annual national income had surged to more than $180 billion ($2.2 tril-

67. White, *Billions for Defense*, 100.
68. *Wall Street Journal*, October 17, 1944.
69. Kennedy, *Freedom from Fear*, 793.

lion). So Dewey was left to level charges against Roosevelt of communism, bad health, old age, and turmoil within his government. He frequently used the Jones-Wallace battle as evidence. In one blast, Dewey said, "For twelve straight years the New Deal has given this country a continuous demonstration of quarreling, dissension, and disunity." He cited "the long quarrel between the Vice President and the Secretary of Commerce, in which they publicly called each other obstructionist and liar."[70]

Not surprisingly, Pearson targeted Jones as a political liability for Roosevelt, chiming in, "Democratic leaders have been surprised and pleased that Dewey has not jumped on the record of [the] Secretary of Commerce in regard to rubber. They are not sure whether Dewey is pulling his punches because so many Republicans like Jesse Jones and because [his] nephew has been leading the anti-Roosevelt revolt in Texas, or whether it's because Dewey doesn't know all the facts."[71]

Jones gave the requested radio address during prime time on October 31. He was ill, but later recalled, "I could not, of course, decline to make the speech when requested by the President, without its being misunderstood." Jones took RFC general counsel John Goodloe with him in case he could not finish his speech.[72] His address, titled "Government and Business," was as much a declaration of his own record as it was of Roosevelt's. Jones may have had an inkling that his political life, not to mention his health, was in jeopardy and that he might have only one chance to set the record straight.

Jones started, "I have been associated with the President in the business end of government ever since he has been President. I was here in 1933, as a Democratic member of the bipartisan Board of the Reconstruction Finance Corporation, appointed by President Hoover, February 1932." He described the nation's decrepit condition, noting that national income had fallen from $80 billion ($960 billion) in 1929 to $40 billion ($480 billion) in 1932, and that "People all over the country were in a state of panic." He said, "It took a new and courageous point of view, a new and bold philosophy of government, to meet the situation." Jones noted that Roosevelt signed legislation after his first inauguration that allowed the RFC to buy stock in banks. Saying, "We put $1.17 billion [$14 billion] in the capital of 6,160 banks," he reminded his listeners, "Without this new government capital, there would have been few banks left . . . Putting a

70. *New York Times*, September 20, 1944.
71. Pearson, "Washington Merry-Go-Round," October 7, 1944.
72. Jones, *Fifty Billion Dollars*, 276.

solid foundation under our banking system was the first step in rebuilding our economy."[73]

Jones then talked about RFC's Depression-era loans to industry, agriculture, the railroads, and homeowners, and their positive impact. He told about the bridges, tunnels, aqueducts, and dams the RFC had built, and described how it helped bring electricity to rural areas. Jones said, "Most of [these] were new for government, but all were good for private business." He said he could not think of "one of them that should not have been undertaken."[74] And Jones reminded his listeners that these far-reaching and life-changing programs had cost taxpayers nothing.

Halfway through his speech, Jones turned to the war. He recalled how the RFC had started to build plants and stockpile critical materials eighteen months before Pearl Harbor. He pointedly said, "We were fortunate . . . to accumulate a large stockpile of rubber, enough to last us until we could build our synthetic rubber industry of 51 plants costing $700 million [$8.4 billion]—another Herculean task." He continued, "We were soon buying from all parts of the world many kinds of necessary critical materials . . . [W]hile there have been tight places here and there, no war effort has ever been delayed for lack of raw materials to manufacture fighting equipment, ships, guns, planes, or ammunition." Jones stated, "We could not have met this demand if we had not started well in advance of Pearl Harbor." Summing up the RFC's singular role, Jones said, "We built new plants and enlarged existing plants. We supplied machine tools. We built pipe lines and did countless other things necessary to our national defense and to war, and also to the maintenance of our domestic economy."[75]

Jones recognized others who had made significant contributions and acknowledged the industrial leaders who had come to Washington to help win the war. He said, "Most of these men gave up large salaries to work . . . at small pay, and were glad to do it. Without the drive and initiative of our industrialists—men accustomed to mass production—[and] without the great cooperative partnership between these men and . . . millions of American working men and women, we could not have produced our war requirements." Jones continued, "[F]uture historians . . . will find that the determining element which brought victory to the Allies

73. Jesse Jones, "Government and Business," CBS radio address, October 31, 1944, Jesse H. Jones Collection [UT].

74. Ibid.

75. Ibid.

was the productive power of the United States of America. It is a little short of miraculous and could only have been accomplished through co-operation between government, management, and labor. All have done a good job."[76]

Then Jones warned, "The war is far from over," saying, "We must continue to produce and to fight and to sacrifice. Every hour that the war is prolonged will be measured by the lives of our fighting men." He recognized "the men who offer their lives and those in the supply services who have kept them armed, fed, and clothed" and explained that "maintaining, servicing, and supplying five million fighting men overseas, and supplying our Allies at the same time, is almost beyond comprehension. Yet we are doing it and will continue to do it until the war is won, without any serious inconvenience to those of us at home. No country has ever equaled that remarkable record, and no country ever will."[77]

Jones got to the intent of his speech, declaring, "Credit for that, and for all the top planning in this war, is due to the President as Commander in Chief—and to his Chiefs of Staff and their associates." He concluded, "It is my considered opinion that the best interests of the United States, and of the world, call for the continuance in office of Franklin D. Roosevelt at this time. He led us out of the worst depression in our history. He is leading us to victory in the war and will be needed to establish a lasting peace."[78]

On the Sunday before the election, Jones's newspaper endorsed Roosevelt, as it had in the past. The editorial stated, "The Chronicle is convinced that the record of the past, the needs of the present, and the best interest of the nation and world in the period ahead . . . call for the re-election of President Roosevelt and . . . Senator Harry S. Truman as vice-president."[79] Because of the Texas Regulars, Jones may have felt added pressure to profess and prove allegiance to the president.

In his narrowest win yet, Roosevelt won with 25.6 million popular votes and 432 Electoral College votes; Dewey received 22 million votes and 99 electoral votes. The Democrats gained twenty House seats, maintaining its majority and Texan Sam Rayburn as Speaker, and, with fifty-six seats, maintained its majority in the Senate.[80] In the more than a million votes cast in Texas, a little more than seventy-two percent went for

76. Ibid.
77. Ibid.
78. Ibid.
79. *Houston Chronicle*, November 5, 1944.
80. Kennedy, *Freedom from Fear*, 793.

Roosevelt; sixteen percent went for the Republicans, and eleven percent voted with the Texas Regulars, who endorsed Senator Harry F. Byrd for president.

George Cottingham, editor of the *Houston Chronicle,* enthusiastically wrote Jones that the paper's staff "got particular satisfaction out of the good Roosevelt showing in Harris County, right here in Houston." He admitted, "Of course, I know that a newspaper doesn't win a campaign . . . but where there is a newspaper to speak for a cause, the cause is benefitted, and so we have a right to believe that The Chronicle was partly responsible for the fine Roosevelt vote in this county." Referring to the Texas Regulars, Cottingham said that "the best service The Chronicle rendered . . . was the publication of your front page editorial in July, recognizing that the Democrats of Texas could not let anybody read out of the party those who would want to vote for Roosevelt. Your editorial was widely copied and the position was widely followed by editors."[81] One might wonder if Cottingham's letter was meant for Jones or for Roosevelt.

Jones wrote to Roosevelt after the election, "I extend you my heartiest congratulations upon the vote of confidence the people gave you yesterday . . . Your policies and leadership have been approved, and I believe the new Congress . . . has a mandate to cooperate with you in shaping our . . . participation in world affairs . . . [so] that we may have a lasting peace. At least I hope so." He signed it, "With all good wishes always, Jesse H. Jones."[82]

Two weeks later, Roosevelt briefly responded, "My warm thanks to you for your fine note of congratulations. Your good wishes are sincerely appreciated." He signed it, "Affectionate regards, FDR."[83] At the end of November, he sent a much longer letter to thank him for the *Houston Chronicle's* support. The president said that in addition to "fighting for those policies which you and I believe are in the nation's best interest," the *Houston Chronicle* "was pointing . . . to a new and stronger national unity which our country must achieve to . . . surmount the problems that lie ahead of us." Roosevelt wrote, "I believe America will achieve that essential unity [and] I think we have made a fine start—thanks to The

81. George Cottingham to Jesse Jones, November 14, 1944, Jesse H. Jones Collection [HE].

82. Jesse Jones to Franklin Roosevelt, November 8, 1944, Jesse H. Jones Collection [LOC].

83. Franklin Roosevelt to Jesse Jones, November 21, 1944, Jesse H. Jones Collection [LOC].

Chronicle and those newspapers and spokesmen fighting side by side with it regardless of party leanings." Then he closed, "Let us keep up the good work together."[84] Jones must have scratched his head because, by then, newspapers teemed with stories about Wallace's future and the makeup of Roosevelt's next cabinet. One week after the election, and weeks before Jones received the letter about working together, Pearson wrote, "White House aides say FDR plans real cabinet clean-out this time," and that Jones had made the president "sore."[85] Three days later he wrote, "Speculation is red hot as to whether FDR will retain Jesse Jones, the man whose nephew led the anti-Roosevelt faction in Texas; also what he will do with Vice President Wallace, Jones' chief Cabinet enemy, who was FDR's chief support during the campaign."[86]

Jones had survived power plays before and despite Pearson's predictions, he appeared to be conducting business as usual. Whether for public relations purposes or by coincidence, official announcements about RFC activities and accomplishments appeared daily following the election. Jones released information about the "Big Inch" and "Little Inch" pipelines, stating they had "nearly halved the cost of moving oil from Texas to the Eastern Seaboard." He said that they "would be able to operate after the war in competition with ocean tankers and other transportation facilities" and that it "should be possible to sell [them] to private industry."[87]

Papers reported that payments of $134 million ($1.6 billion) on the $425 million ($5.1 billion) loan to "the United Kingdom of Great Britain and Northern Ireland had been made to the Reconstruction Finance Corporation, Jesse Jones, Secretary of Commerce, said today."[88] Soon after, a front-page, above-the-fold *New York Times* story reported that the RFC was mounting "the greatest merchandising job on record" by erecting "a vast chain of warehouses . . . throughout the nation . . . to provide storage space for commodities and machinery that already are beginning to pile up." The article cited Costello, "special assistant to Jesse Jones," as saying the "showrooms" would be built to hold the "tremendous weight of heavy industrial products and machinery . . . where prospective buyers may examine the goods." These included locomotives, airplanes, and

84. Franklin Roosevelt to Jesse Jones, November 29, 1944, Jesse H. Jones Collection [LOC].

85. Pearson, "Washington Merry-Go-Round," November 15, 1944.

86. Pearson, "Washington Merry-Go-Round," November 18, 1944.

87. *Houston Chronicle*, November 12, 1944.

88. *New York Times*, November 14, 1944.

machine tools, and the seven New York showrooms would serve as "the pattern for many others to be erected elsewhere in the country."[89] Jones was popping up everywhere.

Liberty magazine, a popular weekly in competition with the *Saturday Evening Post*, published a lengthy and informative interview with Jones. The caption under his half-page picture predicted, "Secretary of Commerce Jesse Jones will have a large share in settling the problems of reconstruction." Author Betty Milton Gaskill began by getting out of the way what was accepted by most, which was that Jones "has probably wielded more power in the last five years than any man in the country, barring Franklin Roosevelt." Jones then described the factions fighting over reconversion. He described one set as those who used "the success government has had with industry during the war to advance economic theories which . . . this country should adopt." On the other hand, were those who "have magnified the plight of industry and the difficulties they foresee in the conversion period." He warned, "We should, of course, be on guard against undue pressure from any . . . groups . . . ," and in typical fashion, ignored ideology by saying, "Let us examine some of the realities of the situation."[90]

Sticking to facts, Jones explained that the government owned "more than 5,000 plants and projects . . . ," and about 2,000 belonged to the DPC. The rest belonged to the Navy and War Departments and the Maritime Commission. Once a wartime agency declared its property surplus, for the most part the RFC took control. Referring to manufacturing plants and real estate, Jones tried to put that into perspective by explaining that $25 billion ($300 billion) was "now generally accepted" as the figure "with which we must deal in putting our economic house in order." However, "Only eight billion dollars' [$96 billion] worth of government plants and facilities will probably constitute our reconversion problem." Jones explained that around forty percent of government's expenditure on "plants and projects" had been for "camps, airfields, [and] supply depots." He said they "will not have great recovery value and certainly will not enter into the competitive industrial situation in time of peace." Another twenty percent had gone toward "manufacturing facilities for explosives, ammunition, guns, [and] combat vehicles." He said, "Some . . . should be retained as stand-by; others . . . may be scrapped." Jones summed up, "Thus, the eight-billion dollars[$96 billion] . . . [in] plants and facilities

89. *New York Times*, December 12, 1944.
90. Gaskill, "What Will We Do?" 17.

which remain are nowhere nearly so big a problem as we have been led to believe by those who toss around the twenty-five-billion-dollar [$300 billion] total."[91]

Jones patiently repeated important points. He said plants that "can be used should be fitted into our economy. Many should be kept as stand-by facilities. The others will be chargeable to the cost of war, and the salvage will not be great." He emphasized that "no formula can be evolved for disposing of these properties" and said this "is not a job that can be hurried, unless we . . . practically . . . give [the plants] away." Jones also cautioned, "We should not permit the war . . . to concentrate our economy in big units." He explained that twenty DPC plants had cost more than $100 million ($1.2 billion) each and that "these are not the sort of operations that little business can handle." While advising caution, he also communicated a sense of urgency, saying, "No government operation created for war . . . should be maintained a day after its functions have been fulfilled . . . It will be just as necessary [for] government [to] convert its activities after the war as for business and industry to jump when the gong sounds."[92]

Even though Jones whittled the reconversion nut down to $8 billion ($96 billion), he did not discount its impact, especially in industries where the RFC dominated the field. To illustrate the sheer size of RFC holdings, he used the 521 RFC aviation facilities, saying the "total square feet of airplane-plant space alone would cover a solid city block 200 feet wide and thirty-three miles long." At one point, he said, "If there ever was a question which must be settled in the national interest it is the future utilization of this vast new industrial empire."[93]

While Jones was planning the economy's future, Roosevelt was planning his administration's future. In late November, he replaced Cordell Hull as Secretary of State with Edward R. Stettinius Jr., who had served as chairman of the board of U.S. Steel and had held leadership positions in the Office of Management Production, with the "Lend-Lease" program, and most recently as Undersecretary of State. According to a *Wall Street Journal* article, "New Dealers" had wanted the post for Wallace. "The State Department appointment [going to Stettinius]," the paper went on, "[raised] the hopes of the left wingers for control of the Commerce Department, which can have considerable influence on domestic policies.

---

91. Ibid., 18.
92. Ibid., 68.
93. Ibid., 18.

The theory here is that Mr. Roosevelt would not turn the liberals down twice in a row." The reporter flatly said, "Mr. Wallace is the left wing candidate for the Commerce Department post."[94] The article appeared the day before Roosevelt wrote Jones about keeping "up the good work together."

Right after Stettinius's appointment, rumors surfaced in early December that Clayton would soon be selected as Assistant Secretary of State with control over all foreign economic policy. Jones's *Houston Chronicle* reported, "Clayton's scheduled appointment definitely scotches all reports that he was in any way connected with the Texas Democratic revolt . . . this summer, or that the president ever believed that he was."[95] Evidently that was not the case with Jones. A week later, the *Wall Street Journal* revealed, "Lame Duck Henry Wallace has been offered Jesse Jones' Commerce Secretaryship. The Texan hasn't been formally asked to leave, but insiders say he will be 'euchred out' if he doesn't quit."[96] A few days later, Raymond Moley, a former Roosevelt speechwriter and now a *Newsweek* columnist opposed to Roosevelt and the New Deal, reported that Jones was "high on the black-list" of a "strong-arm squad" of New Dealers. Moley wrote, "Age and somewhat impaired health are on the side of the purgers here. Mr. Jones has resisted all efforts to drive him from office over many years. But his enemies are persistent. They have few scruples about method." He added, "Rumor has it that the Vice President got some assurance of a selection of jobs."[97] Indeed, he had.

Months before, on August 29, Wallace and Roosevelt met over lunch. Roosevelt tried to soothe Wallace's hurt feelings over the way he and the party had treated him at the Convention. The muscling out had been so blatant, even conservative columnists had come to Wallace's defense. Frank Kent of the *Baltimore Sun*, wrote, "Beyond a doubt Mr. Wallace would have been renominated but for the active opposition of Mr. Roosevelt . . . No man in politics has been given shabbier treatment, with less reason, in a long time."[98] Roosevelt began their luncheon conversation by asking Wallace if he had shared the telegram with his wife, Ilo, in which the president asked her not to leave town after her husband left office in January. Roosevelt beat around the bush with other issues, but finally told Wallace

94. *Wall Street Journal*, November 28, 1944.
95. *Houston Chronicle*, December 1, 1944.
96. *Wall Street Journal*, December 8, 1944.
97. *Wall Street Journal*, December 11, 1944.
98. Culver and Hyde, *American Dreamer*, 370.

that he wanted him to be a part of his administration and that he could have, except for Secretary of State, any job he wanted.

Wallace would later recount that Roosevelt said he was going to get rid of "Jesus H. Jones" after the election. He said, "Well, if you are going to get rid of Jesse, why not let me have Secretary of Commerce, with RFC and FEA [Foreign Economic Administration] thrown in? There would be poetic justice in that." According to Wallace, Roosevelt replied, "Yes, that's right." Wallace afterward said, "I took the [Commerce Department job] because I didn't think I could take less than a cabinet post, and I didn't want to cut the throat of anyone that the president wanted to keep in. The only one that he'd indicated he was going to get out was Jesse Jones."[99] All this took place in August, before Jones gave speeches and wrote editorials supporting the president, and well before Roosevelt wrote the post-election letter that led his Commerce Secretary to believe he wanted them to work together. Growing uneasy after Roosevelt appointed Stettinius as Secretary of State in late November, Wallace sent a telegram to remind the president about their August conversation. He wrote, "My interest in poetic justice is stronger now than ever . . . My job now seems to be Commerce . . . Thanks if I may serve."[100]

Still, Roosevelt would not play his hand. In mid-December, Jones sent the president a letter outlining postwar plans for the Commerce Department. He said, "The field of foreign trade . . . needs considerable strengthening." He also suggested enlarging field services "to provide management advice and counsel to business—particularly small business." Never denying a constructive role for government, he explained, "It is our conviction that, when the returning veterans and those who have been engaged in war work begin to set up their own business establishments, government must make available the knowledge and experience it has gained in order to minimize the mortality rate of such ventures."[101]

Pearson wrote at the end of the year, "Friends of Jesse Jones have been chortling gleefully over the way the President has kept Vice-President Wallace dangling . . . for months with a Cabinet job just out of reach, promising him everything but never quite coming across." Pearson explained, "Sitting at FDR's right hand in the White House [is] Harry Hopkins, bosom pal of Jesse Jones. And every time the President gets tender-hearted

99. Ibid., 373.
100. Ibid., 377.
101. *Houston Chronicle*, December 25, 1944.

about offering Wallace something important, Harry jogs his elbow."[102] Pearson must not have known that just before Christmas the president had responded to Wallace's telegram, about their August agreement, telling Wallace that the Commerce Department was his and so was the RFC. If anyone asked about their conversation, Roosevelt told Wallace to say they had talked about reforesting Iran.[103]

The Joneses did not go to Houston for the holidays as usual, possibly because of Jones's precarious health, but more likely so Jones could stay on top of events as they unfolded.

102. Pearson, "Washington Merry-Go-Round," December 30, 1944.
103. Culver and Hyde, *American Dreamer*, 377.

1945

◈

A Very Difficult
Letter to Write

OVER THE HOLIDAYS, Jesse Jones stayed in touch with family. He wrote Margaret, whose son John was still a prisoner of war, "I deeply appreciate the beautiful embroidered handkerchiefs you sent me for Christmas," and shared, "Mary and I were quite disappointed not to get home for Christmas this year, but circumstances made it impractical for us to make the trip." He continued, "We are both well and hope that all of the members of all the families there are too."[1] Evidently the Joneses had not stayed in Washington for reasons of poor health.

As they had done for years, Jones and the president corresponded about Christmas gifts. Franklin Roosevelt wrote Jones, "Ever so many thanks for that fine old bourbon which you gave to me for Christmas. It is a most welcome gift and I am appreciative of your thought of me." He closed, "With all good wishes to you and Mrs. Jones for the New Year, Always sincerely, Franklin Roosevelt."[2] A few days later, Stephen Early, the president's secretary, sent the Joneses an invitation to "a service of intercession in the East Room of the White House at 10:00 A.M. on

1. Jesse Jones to Margaret Jones, January 1, 1945, John T. Jones Jr. Collection [HE].
2. Franklin Roosevelt to Jesse Jones, January 9, 1945, Jesse H. Jones Collection [LOC].

Saturday, January twentieth next."[3] They accepted "with honor" and made plans to attend the private event that would take place before Roosevelt's fourth inauguration.[4] It appeared to Jones that he had a job until January 20 at least.

News reports about RFC subsidiaries began again to appear, one after the other, as if by plan. On January 5 newspapers reported that the Defense Plant Corporation had disbursed $7.1 billion ($84 billion in current dollars) for "war plants, facilities, and machine tools."[5] A few days later, the Defense Supplies Corporation announced it had spent $3 billion ($35 billion) to produce "aviation gasoline" and more than $1 billion ($11.8 billion) to subsidize meat, coffee, and butter prices for the public.[6] On January 13, the New York Times reported that the Metal Reserves Company had "made commitments to buy supplies of strategic and critical metals and minerals amounting to $5.17 billion [$61 billion] between 1940 and the end of 1944," attributing the statement to "Jesse Jones, Secretary of Commerce and head of the RFC."[7]

The flow continued. Two days later, the Wall Street Journal reported, "The War Damage Corp. has issued more than 6.5 million insurance policies and 2.2 million renewals, Secretary of Commerce Jesse Jones announced." The Corporation, according to the paper, "insured against loss resulting from enemy attack—or from action of American forces in resisting enemy attack."[8] When private insurance companies had declined to assume the risk, the RFC, as usual, had stepped in. Saving the best for last, Jones announced that the synthetic rubber plants "now are capable of producing 1 million tons a year," and that some plants were producing the substitute for less per pound than the prewar cost of natural rubber.[9]

Finally, the cascade of information was brought together when Jones released the RFC's annual report to the president, Congress, and the press. It detailed the monumental contribution the RFC had made to the war and included information that had been released, perhaps strategically, in bits and pieces during the past few months. In all, the report said that the RFC had been authorized to spend more than $32 billion ($377 billion) for war purposes, that it had disbursed $18 billion ($212 billion) so far, and

3. Stephen Early to Jesse Jones, January 13, 1945, Jesse H. Jones Collection [LOC].
4. Jesse Jones to Stephen Early, January 16, 1945, Jesse H. Jones Collection [LOC].
5. Wall Street Journal, January 5, 1945.
6. Wall Street Journal, January 9, 1945.
7. New York Times, January 13, 1945.
8. Wall Street Journal, January 15, 1945.
9. Wall Street Journal, January 17, 1945.

that $9 billion ($106 billion) had been returned in rents, loan payments, and proceeds from the sale of equipment and materials manufactured in RFC plants. As he had done when counting the pass-through appropriations the RFC made during the Great Depression, Jones pointed out that $1.4 billion ($17 billion) of the wartime disbursements had gone toward subsidy payments under the Price Control Act.[10]

The day after the report's release and two days before Roosevelt's inauguration, James Reston reported in the *New York Times* on the RFC's $32 billion ($377 billion) bank account, writing, "It is this authorization power which is respected in the capital as a source of power, more than the Cabinet rank . . . and it is this power which Mr. Jones is said to be most eager to retain." Reston also reported, "President Roosevelt is understood to have told some of his colleagues that he will appoint Vice President Henry A. Wallace to replace Jesse Jones as Secretary of Commerce . . . The impression in the capital is that Mr. Jones will retain control of the Reconstruction Finance Corporation and its several satellite financial agencies." A Congressional delegation had visited Roosevelt the day before to urge him on in that direction, even though putting Wallace at Commerce and Jones at the RFC would set up a repeat of the BEW versus RFC fiasco. Reston claimed, "Mr. Jones has not yet been informed of the change."[11]

Jones had not been told officially, but he knew. He recalled, "Soon after the election, there was gossip in Washington that the President would probably replace me in the Cabinet. Two or three of my close friends, including Harry Hopkins, told me as much. Harry said that Henry Wallace was insisting to the President on having my job."[12] In addition, any member of Congress speaking on Jones's behalf to the president would most likely have conferred with Jones at length. And Jones read the newspapers. Reston's article concluded that everything would "be clarified within the next few days. Mr. Wallace's term as Vice President ends at noon on Saturday."[13]

Knowing something was coming, Jones began to tie up loose ends with the president. On the day of Reston's article, he sent Roosevelt a letter about Crumwold Farms, a 741-acre tract next to Roosevelt's Hyde Park estate that the RFC had bought at the president's request in 1942 to prevent Father Divine, a popular and controversial black spiritual leader

10. *New York Times*, January 17, 1945.
11. *New York Times*, January 18, 1945.
12. Jones, *Fifty Billion Dollars*, 277.
13. *New York Times*, January 18, 1945.

who already had property in the area, from moving in next door. Because Jones had purchased the property through a private insurance company the RFC had rescued during the Great Depression, ownership was indirect and, hence, vulnerable. Jones suggested transferring ownership of the property to the War Department since it was using the land as a camp for training military police.[14] It is also possible he wanted to remind Roosevelt of one of the many, sometimes controversial, favors he had done for him in the past.

The next day, Jones attended the first cabinet meeting Roosevelt had held in quite a while. He recalled, "Because of the state of the President's health, I had not seen him very much for several weeks, as Cabinet had not been meeting." Roosevelt had noticeably deteriorated. He was pale and gaunt, and had dark circles under his eyes; his shirt collar no longer fit and hung below his neck like a loosened noose. Jones continued, "During the session the President remarked that, although Henry Wallace would cease to be Vice President on the morrow, he would still be with us. He did not say in what capacity."[15]

Jones customarily stayed behind after cabinet meetings to discuss matters one-on-one with the president. He did so this time and handed Roosevelt a letter with details about an aluminum issue as well as a three-page letter listing all of the Commerce Department's bureaus and what each had done during the war. The letter ended with, "I should like to commend the heads of the various Bureaus in the Department and their respective organizations. They have all been prompted by a fine sense of patriotism and have done their jobs well."[16] Jones remembered, "After that Friday Cabinet, as was my custom, I discussed some RFC matters with the President with only the two of us present. He said nothing about replacing me." Jones also recounted, "That particular meeting with the President was the first time I had noticed the deterioration of his mind. The matters I discussed were not new, but he had no recollection of them whatever."[17]

On Saturday morning the Joneses attended the private White House religious service. Afterward, the inauguration ceremony was held on the south portico of the White House instead of the customary south steps of the Capitol. The weather was nasty and cold, the president was not well,

14. Jesse Jones to Franklin Roosevelt, January 18, 1945, Jesse H. Jones Collection [HE].
15. Jones, *Fifty Billion Dollars*, 278.
16. Jesse Jones to Franklin Roosevelt, January 19, 1945, Jesse H. Jones Collection [LOC].
17. Jones, *Fifty Billion Dollars*, 278.

and it was wartime. Bunting, parades, and festivities were absent. There was only snow and a wet, cold wind.

William and Oveta Culp Hobby were in town for the inauguration and to see their son, who was attending school in Washington. Jones asked his good friend to join him at the inaugural ceremony after the morning service. Hobby's son, Bill Jr., remembered, "It was a cold, miserable rainy day . . . My parents at that time always stayed at the Washington Hotel . . . and you could actually from the roof of the hotel see the back portico of the White House." Hobby continued, "My mother and I were up on the roof of the Washington Hotel, seeing what little we could of the ceremony, waiting for my father to come back and join us for lunch. In due course, my father called and said he was going to the Shoreham Hotel to have lunch with Mr. Jones. Mr. Jones [had] stopped at the hotel desk to pick up his mail, and he had a letter from President Roosevelt."[18]

At some point before his inauguration that day, Roosevelt had dictated and sent a letter by messenger to the Shoreham Hotel. The president wrote,

Dear Jesse,

This is a very difficult letter to write—first, because of our long friendship and splendid relations during all these years, and also because of your splendid services to the Government and the excellent way in which you have carried out the many difficult tasks during these years.

Henry Wallace deserves almost any service which he believes he can satisfactorily perform. I told him this at the end of the campaign, in which he displayed the utmost devotion to our cause, traveling almost incessantly and working for the success of the ticket in a great many parts of the country. Though not on the ticket himself, he gave of his utmost toward the victory, which ensued.

He has told me that he thought he could do the greatest amount of good in the Department of Commerce, for which he is fully suited, and I feel, therefore, that the Vice President should have this post in the new Administration.

It is for this reason only that I am asking you to relinquish this present post for Henry, and I want to tell you that it is in no way a lack of appreciation for all that you have done, and that I hope you will continue to be a part of the Government.

During the next few days I hope you will think about a new post—there

18. William P. Hobby Jr., to Steven Fenberg, February 16, 1996, Oral History Project [HE].

are several Ambassadorships which are vacant—or about to be vacated. I make this suggestion among many other posts and I hope you will have a chance, if you think well of it, to speak to Ed Stettinius, who will not leave to join me for several days.

Finally, let me tell you that you have my full confidence and that I am very proud of all that you have done during these past years.

With my warm regards, always sincerely, Franklin Roosevelt.[19]

Grace Tully, the president's assistant, called Jones that Saturday to schedule an appointment for noon the next day. Jones recalled, "I met [the president] at twelve o'clock in the Oval Room where we had had many pleasant and constructive meetings over the twelve-year period I had served under him." This meeting would not be so nice. Roosevelt again encouraged Jones to become the French ambassador and to use his unique skills to help restore the war-ravaged nation. Roosevelt also mentioned the Court of St. James, suggested that Jones chair the Federal Reserve, and even offered to create by executive order an organization where Jones could oversee reconversion. Jones was not at all interested. He remembered, "After twelve years of close association, to be dismissed in such a manner and for the reasons he gave, I could no longer have respected him or worked with him."[20]

Jones asked the president when he wanted him to leave office. Roosevelt replied that he was sending Wallace's name to the Senate the next day and wanted Jones to stay in office until he was confirmed. Roosevelt pressed him to come up with something he would like to do and to approve Wallace's appointment. Jones recalled, "This I could not do. I told the President that I thought Henry was totally unqualified for the position."[21]

As Jones and Roosevelt shook hands and parted, the president said, "It's not goodbye; I'll see you when I get back." Jones replied, "Mr. President, I think it is goodbye." Jones wrote later, "Our last meeting was probably a mistake. Better he had let it go with the letter of dismissal, because it was not a happy occasion for either of us. My long association with him had been pleasant, and to have it end in the manner it did was a disappointment to me and not pleasant for him." Jones then added, "I shuddered at the thought of the President, weakened mentally and physically

19. Franklin Roosevelt to Jesse Jones, January 20, 1945, Jesse H. Jones Collection [LOC].
20. Jones, *Fifty Billion Dollars*, 280.
21. Jesse Jones, memo on January 21 meeting with Franklin Roosevelt, March 20, 1945, Jesse H. Jones Collection [LOC].

as he obviously was, leaving that week for Yalta to meet Stalin and his horde."[22]

Roosevelt had dictated his letter dismissing Jones to Tully. She recalled in her memoir, "My personal feeling at the time was that it was neither a good letter nor the best way in which to handle a difficult situation." Tully asked the president whether Sam Rosenman and Early should review the letter before it was sent. She remembered, "The Boss replied rather abruptly that he wished it sent immediately and by hand to Mr. Jones's apartment." Tully also recalled, "The meeting between the two men . . . was not a long one and it was anything but agreeable. Mr. Jones looked grim when he arrived and grimmer when he left." She described how Roosevelt pushed things around on his desk when he was nervous, and then observed that he "did so to a particular degree this time. He looked tired, unhappy, and annoyed."[23]

With the help of his colleagues, Jones had started composing a response to the president's letter almost as soon as he finished reading it. He completed his response and sent it to Roosevelt after their noon meeting on Sunday. He informed the president in the cover letter, "Inasmuch as you are sending Mr. Wallace's name to Congress tomorrow, I am releasing your letter to me and my reply. I have eliminated from your letter any reference to your trip."[24]

In his formal letter to the president, Jones wrote:

I have your letter of today, asking that I relinquish my post as Secretary of Commerce, which carries with it the vast financial and war production agencies within the Reconstruction Finance Corporation and its subsidiaries, so that you can give it to Henry Wallace as a reward for his support of you in the campaign.

You state that Henry thinks he could do the greatest amount of good in the Department of Commerce, and that you consider him fully suited for the post. With all due respect, Mr. President, while I must accede to your decision, I cannot agree with either of you.

You refer very kindly to our long friendship and our splendid relations during all the years, and state that you appreciate my splendid services to the government and the excellent way I have carried out the many difficult tasks during these years. You are also good enough to say that I have your full

22. Jones, *Fifty Billion Dollars*, 280–81.
23. Tully, *F.D.R. My Boss*, 188–91.
24. Jesse Jones to Franklin Roosevelt, January 21, 1945, Jesse H. Jones Collection [LOC].

confidence, and that you are very proud of all I have done during these past years, and that you hope I will continue to be part of the government, probably in a diplomatic post. It is difficult to reconcile these encomiums with your avowed purpose to replace me. While I want to be of any further service that I can, I would not want a diplomatic assignment.

I feel and have felt a great sense of responsibility to the Congress and to you for the proper administration of the laws with respect to the RFC that have been passed in the expectation that they would be administered by me or someone experienced in business and finance.

I have had satisfaction in my government service because I have had the confidence of the Congress, as well as your own. I have had that confidence because I have been faithful to the responsibilities that have been entrusted to me. For you to turn over all these assets and responsibilities to a man inexperienced in business and finance will, I believe, be hard for the business and financial world to understand.

I appreciate the opportunity you have given me to serve my country through the depression and in time of war. My 13 years of government service are ample evidence of my desire to be of any assistance I can to the government. I can best be helpful in the line of my life's work—business and finance—but I seek no job.

With best wishes, Faithfully yours, Jesse H. Jones.[25]

Before leaving his office that Sunday night, Jones submitted to RFC Chairman Charles Henderson his resignation as chairman and director of all the subsidiaries. He wrote Leo Crowley and resigned from the Export-Import Bank as a trustee and sent a letter to Commerce Undersecretary Wayne Chatfield Taylor, asking him to assume the duties of secretary and federal loan administrator until his successor was confirmed. As a final act, Jones publicly announced his own termination by releasing the president's letter and his own to the press and effectively resigned from public service.[26]

Jones's dismissal, Wallace's nomination, and a bill to separate the RFC from the Commerce Department greeted Vice President Harry Truman when he assumed the chair as president of the United States Senate for the first time on Monday morning.[27] Roosevelt had fired one of the most trusted and powerful men in government, placed the enormous economic

25. Jesse Jones to Franklin Roosevelt, January 20, 1945, Jesse H. Jones Collection [LOC].
26. Jones, *Fifty Billion Dollars*, 284.
27. *New York Times*, January 22, 1945.

Dealing with Jesse Jones's dismissal and Henry Wallace's appointment as Secretary of Commerce greeted Harry Truman when he first assumed the vice presidency. Courtesy AP/Wide World.

clout of the RFC into the hands of one of the nation's most controversial figures, and, in doing so, brought the press, the public, and Congress to their feet voicing an almost unanimous shout of protest.

The *New York Times* stated, "For the personal integrity of Henry Wallace, the courage of his position on international affairs, and the broad and generous sympathies which he has displayed throughout his career, we have great respect. Surely there is a useful place for a man of such interests and such talents in this Administration. But surely the one place above all others into which Mr. Wallace does not fit is the place to which Mr. Roosevelt has now appointed him—the post of Secretary of Commerce—particularly if that post is to continue to carry with it control of the vast financial and war production agencies within the Reconstruction Finance Corporation and its subsidiaries."[28] Many newspapers across the nation echoed this opinion. Some, like the *Cleveland News*, thought the appointment was a "cynical and shocking payoff by President Roosevelt"

28. *New York Times*, January 23, 1945.

for Wallace's support during the recent campaign.[29] Others blamed the Texas Regulars: the *St. Louis Post-Dispatch*, one of the few major papers that supported Wallace, offered, "The president may have acted primarily because he suspects Jones of collusion in Texas' plot to throw part of the electoral college away from the party's candidate and because Wallace stuck by him." The paper added, "He could have acted because of the two men, one deserved on merit. That man is Henry Wallace."[30]

Eugene Meyer's *Washington Post* disapproved of the process, but not the outcome. It said, "Those who think Mr. Roosevelt is a good politician doubtless will revise their opinion in the light of the dismissal of Secretary of Commerce Jesse H. Jones. The dismissal takes place on the eve of the Big Three meeting . . . when the solidarity of legislature and people is required for the strengthening of the presidential hand. Yet this step is bound to rock Capitol Hill. The whole business is a disheartening tale of a pay-off." Unsurprisingly, the paper continued, "The Post will not shed any of the crocodile tears that the president lavished on the departing Mr. Jones. His dismissal, in our view, is long overdue."[31]

Members of Congress were outraged. Joseph W. Martin, the House minority leader, said about Jones, "If ever there was a time when we needed a man of great experience and ability it is now. His removal is a serious blow to the country and will be felt especially in the post-war period."[32] Republican Senator Robert Taft, who had spoken on Jones's behalf over the years, said his removal was a "very unwise change for the President to make, particularly with reference to the post-war period and the desire to further private enterprise."[33] But that position was not unanimous. William Langer, Republican senator from North Dakota, favored Wallace's appointment and said, "In my opinion he is in every way qualified for the position and will be the outstanding member in the cabinet to fight monopolies and cartels."[34] Similar endorsements, however, did not stop Senate Finance Committee Chairman Walter F. George from introducing a bill to separate the lending agencies from the Commerce Department. He said, "With respect to . . . the RFC and all the rest, . . . I have been willing to give these agencies extensive powers solely because I had confidence in the business experience and business judgment of Mr. Jones." He said he

29. Reprint of *Cleveland News* article, *Houston Chronicle*, January 23, 1945.
30. Reprint of *St. Louis Post-Dispatch* article, *Houston Chronicle*, January 23, 1945.
31. Reprint of *Washington Post* article, *Houston Chronicle*, January 23, 1945.
32. *New York Times*, January 21, 1945.
33. *New York Times*, January 23, 1945.
34. *Houston Chronicle*, January 22, 1945.

would not object to Wallace's appointment as Secretary of Commerce as long as the lending agencies were removed from his department.[35]

In addition to its pro-Jones editorial, the New York Times reported in a news article that "the bulk of the comment on Capitol Hill today was opposed to giving Mr. Wallace these responsibilities." In public, politicians accused Wallace of not having enough business experience, but behind closed doors, they feared his "alleged ideological opposition to the private enterprise system."[36] Ironically, Wallace's Pioneer Hi-Bred Company, which he had started from scratch to develop high-yield seeds, had generated more than $4 million ($48 million) in annual sales in 1944, proving, contrary to popular belief, that he did have firsthand experience with the intricacies and challenges of successfully operating a business.[37] As Secretary of Agriculture, he had managed thousands of employees and a multibillion dollar annual budget. Nonetheless, Wallace and Jones had always personified the two opposing ideological forces of Roosevelt's presidency, and, as usual, most of those in Congress lined up behind "Uncle Jess." Whether Wallace's nomination or the George bill would be considered first was the burning question. If the enormous lending agencies were not removed from the Commerce Department first, then Wallace's nomination was doomed.

Events happened fast. Roosevelt fired Jones on Saturday, and Jones released their letters to the press on Sunday. On Monday, Wallace's nomination and the George bill were introduced in the Senate. Senator Claude Pepper said the George bill was a "slap in the face for Wallace . . . and another way of undercutting the president and glorifying Jesse Jones."[38] That evening Roosevelt quietly departed for Yalta to meet with Joseph Stalin and Winston Churchill, leaving Wallace to his own devices. On Tuesday North Carolina Senator Josiah Bailey announced that the Commerce Committee would begin hearings on the George bill the following day, and that Jones would be on hand to testify about the merits of separating the federal lending agencies from the Commerce Department and operating them as an independent organization. Wallace would appear the following day. Bailey, who chaired the Commerce Committee, had pleaded with Roosevelt earlier in the week to keep Jones in place, at least as federal loan administrator.

35. New York Times, January 22, 1945.
36. Ibid.
37. Culver and Hyde, American Dreamer, 382.
38. Houston Chronicle, January 24, 1945.

On Wednesday morning the Senate chamber was packed with eager reporters, whirring movie cameras, hot klieg lights, and hundreds of anxious politicians. One reporter claimed the hearings "drew one of the biggest audiences in U.S. Congressional history."[39] Senator George went first; before testifying, he offered an amendment to his bill that would prevent Roosevelt from reuniting the lending agencies with the Commerce Department after Wallace was confirmed. He wondered aloud if Jones might head the new independent agency once everything had been settled. Jones entered while George was testifying, and everything came to an abrupt halt.[40] As one reporter observed, "the Texas banker clearly regarded the hearing as Jones Day on Capitol Hill. He arrived in the middle of George's testimony and stopped the talk for nearly ten minutes as photographers clustered around him. He waved to newspapermen and friends in the audience, gripped George's hand, [and] chewed gum expressionlessly while George finished speaking."[41] When Jones took the witness chair he asked Senator Bailey for permission to say something off the record. After Bailey conceded, Jones scanned the crowd and quipped, "I'm just wondering who gets the gate receipts." The crowd cracked up laughing.[42] Many of them had enjoyed a drink, a colorful story, or a game of cards with the affable and uniquely powerful public servant, or felt his arm around their shoulders. Jones had distributed the RFC's largesse during the Great Depression and World War II to practically every politician in the room. After he claimed the crowd, Jones launched into his prepared remarks.

He got right to the point, beginning, "The RFC and its subsidiaries conduct the most gigantic business enterprise . . . that the world has ever known . . . Individually and collectively, they affect the entire economy of this nation. The way in which they are administered from now on is even more important . . . if that is possible, than their administration in the past, since the postwar adjustments will need to be most carefully handled in order not to destroy our entire business and financial structure." He continued, "The man who is given the vast responsibilities contained in the RFC act should [have] proven and sound business experience." Without out naming names, Jones explained that the RFC mandate "could easily be abused, either by inexperience, visionary planning, or a disregard of

---

39. *Philadelphia Morning Public Ledger*, January 25, 1945.
40. *Houston Chronicle*, January 25, 1945.
41. James A. Wechsler, "The Nation" column, January 25, 1945.
42. Culver and Hyde, *American Dreamer*, 381.

the taxpayers' money." He pointedly said, "Certainly the RFC should not be placed under the supervision of a man willing to jeopardize the country's future with untried ideas and idealistic schemes. The lending agencies of the government can be administered, as they have been . . . for the benefit of all the people, or they can be used to destroy what we have built up . . . in 170 years of independence. That, to my mind, is the issue which this committee and the congress must decide."[43]

Senator Pepper asked Jones if it was possible for one man to administer both the Commerce Department and the Federal Loan Administration. Jones replied, "If you're trying to ask me if Henry Wallace is qualified for both jobs, I'd say no." Pepper talked about the rights of the accused and pressed Jones for facts to support his claim that Wallace was "incompetent." Jones shot back, "You talk too much at one time. I didn't say he was incompetent. Stick to the text." Jones explained, "The RFC can lend anything, any time, at any rate of interest, to anybody." He said some of the smartest men in the country seek loans because, "Where the honey is, the flies are. Where the money is, the moochers are." Jones declared he was unwilling to entrust taxpayers' money to someone who was a "visionary planner," someone who wasted taxpayers' money on "amateur experiments." Jones advised that men who have "no plans for remaking the world" should operate the lending agencies, and added, "It is my firm conviction that the government's investment in plants and facilities, and in raw materials of all sorts, represented by billions of the taxpayers' money, should not be made the subject of careless experimentation." Pepper asked once more if Jones thought one person could hold both jobs. Jones said, "I think it is possible if he'll work hard enough and enough hours, but I doubt if you would find many besides me who is fool enough to do it."[44]

Wallace had his turn the next day. Like Jones, he entered a standing room only chamber and received a thunderous standing ovation as he walked to his chair. Wallace testified for more than five hours, during which he called for a Congressional investigation of the RFC and said he would still serve as Secretary of Commerce if the lending agencies were removed, but only until war's end. In his testimony, Wallace said that the government should initiate programs if employment fell below a certain level and that it should continue to build public facilities and roads to keep jobs available after the war. Wallace called for guaranteed annual

43. *Houston Chronicle*, January 25, 1945.
44. Ibid.

wages and for "an adequate floor" on farm prices. He also called for a comprehensive federal health care program that would give every person "the right to the doctor and hospital of his own choosing."[45]

Addressing his supposed lack of business experience, Wallace said, "It is not a question of lack of experience. Rather it is a case of not liking the experience that I have had." He continued, "The real motive . . . for stripping the Department of Commerce of its vast financial powers has, of course, nothing to do with my competence . . . The real issue is whether or not the powers of the Reconstruction Finance Corporation and its giant subsidiaries are to be used only to help big business or . . . also to help little business and to help carry out the president's commitment to sixty million jobs."[46]

Within days, the George bill was sent to the full Senate for a vote. It removed the RFC and other lending agencies from the Commerce Department and passed, seventy-four to twelve. Two weeks later the House passed it with only two opposed. The legislation was ready for Roosevelt's signature after his return from Yalta and before Wallace's nomination as Secretary of Commerce was put to a vote on March 1.

On that day President Roosevelt reported to Congress about his meeting with Churchill and Stalin at Yalta. He apologized for delivering his remarks while seated, and said, "I know you will realize that it makes it a lot easier for me not to have to carry about ten pounds of steel around on the bottom of my legs."[47] After Roosevelt finished his speech, the Senate went into session. With the George bill already approved, the members voted fifty-six to thirty-two to make Wallace Secretary of Commerce. Wallace got the position, but not the power.

The next day Wallace was sworn in as Secretary of Commerce by Associate Justice Hugo L. Black, who, with a slap on Wallace's back, summed up the nation's relief and exclaimed, "You're in!" Wallace's new office was filled with family members, most of Roosevelt's cabinet, Vice President Truman, and many members of Congress, including Senators Bailey and Pepper. Jones was noticeably absent. He was reportedly at his RFC office packing and getting ready to move to a space in the Statler Hotel.

Later that day President Roosevelt was asked at a press conference if Jones would remain as federal loan administrator until someone else was named to the post. Roosevelt said no. To make sure he had heard right, the

45. Ibid.
46. Culver and Hyde, *American Dreamer*, 382.
47. Franklin Roosevelt, Address to Congress, March 1, 1945.

reporter asked, "Then he is no longer Loan Administrator?" Roosevelt responded, "That is right."[48] Speculation was already swirling about Jones's future. On the day Wallace was sworn in, the *New York Times* reported, "Washington was talking a good deal this afternoon about the future of Jesse Jones. It was understood he proposed to spend more time at his Houston home, but would also maintain headquarters in the national capital. His answer to questions was 'no comment.'"[49]

Four days after Wallace was sworn in, the Senate Banking Committee unanimously approved Fred M. Vinson as federal loan administrator to head the new independent lending agency.[50] Vinson, one of Truman's closest friends, had served as a representative from Kentucky, and then as a federal judge, before he had become director of economic stabilization in 1943. Vinson would last as federal loan administrator for less than one month before Roosevelt moved him to James Byrnes's position as director of War Mobilization and Reconversion. Byrnes, the "assistant president" who had just accompanied Roosevelt to Yalta and who felt the war was coming to an end, was ready to retire.

At the end of March, Roosevelt went to Warm Springs to rest and regain his strength and health. On April 12 at around noon, the president was sitting at his desk, first to pose for a portrait, then to begin going through mail and signing documents. He signed legislation extending the Commodity Credit Corporation—one of the first RFC agencies established by Jones to fight the Great Depression—before he rubbed his forehead several times, slumped forward, and complained about a tremendous headache. At 3:30 that afternoon, the president who brought the nation through the Great Depression and World War II died from a massive cerebral hemorrhage. He would not live to see Germany's defeat in the next month or Japan's surrender in August.[51] Truman was sworn in as president at 7:00 that evening. If Wallace had not battled so publicly and bitterly with Jones, perhaps he would have been the one taking the oath of office that night.

One of Roosevelt's last official acts was to extend an agency started by Jones in 1933. Jones was involved with Truman's first acts as vice president—in his capacity as president of the Senate—and he was involved almost immediately when Truman became president. Two days after

48. *New York Times*, March 2, 1945.
49. Ibid.
50. *Houston Chronicle*, March 6, 1945.
51. Goodwin, *No Ordinary Time*, 602.

Truman took the oath of office, he made John Snyder federal loan administrator and phoned Jones to tell him about the appointment.[52] Snyder had managed the RFC branch office in St. Louis and then had become vice president of the RFC and a director of the DPC in 1940. He was another of Truman's closest friends, an RFC insider, and a Jones colleague. Jones fully approved, saying, "President Truman could not have made a better appointment."[53]

The night after Snyder's appointment, the Business Advisory Council honored Jones with a dinner that William Knudsen, Emil Schram, and four other men had been planning for more than a month.[54] The nation's business leaders graced Jones with admiring speeches and presented him a silver tray from Cartier engraved with each council member's signature. Jones, who had endured months of turmoil and still harbored hurt feelings over his treatment by Roosevelt, was overcome. He began his remarks by admitting, "I feel much more like crying than making a speech." About the past thirteen years he shared, "I have loved my RFC work. My whole life has been devoted to business and finance. The RFC is business and finance on a broad scale." The president had passed away only days before, and despite his bitterness toward Roosevelt, Jones said with genuine gratitude and reverence, "President Roosevelt pulled us through the depression and was a great leader in war. We have lost a great man in his death, which we all deplore, but the country will go on. You could not be associated with Franklin Roosevelt as long as I was without loving the man, whether you agreed with him always or not."[55] He would not always be so kind.

Jones deeply appreciated the businessmen's tribute. He wrote Thomas McCabe, the Council's chairman, the next day, "My emotions were so affected last night that I am perfectly sure that I did not adequately express my appreciation to you for the great honor you paid me."[56] McCabe sent a copy of Jones's letter to each council member. Jones wrote Knudsen a similar confession, "Because of my emotions, I do not remember much that I said." Referring to their collaboration during the early part of the war, Jones recalled, "Of the billions that we spent at your request, we always felt that you knew the score. I shall always look back on that expe-

52. McCullough, *Truman*, 357.
53. *New York Times*, April 17, 1945.
54. Walter White to Jesse Jones, March 16, 1945, Jesse H. Jones Collection [LOC].
55. Jesse Jones, speech, Business Advisory Council testimonial dinner, April 17, 1945, Jesse H. Jones Collection [LOC].
56. Jesse Jones to Thomas McCabe, April 18, 1945, Jesse H. Jones Collection [LOC].

rience with great satisfaction."[57] During his speech to the council, Jones had reminded the business titans that Knudsen had blazed "the trail in the vast plant construction and the production of war material." Jones called him a "really great man, simple and direct."[58]

The testimonial dinner capped three months of anguish that drew expressions of admiration and regret from the press, the military, Congress, family members, strangers, and dear friends. Blanche Babcock sent a note of sympathy. Jones replied, "I would have been terribly disappointed if you had not written me on the occasion of the recent happenings . . . My friends, as well as many with whom I have no personal acquaintance, have been generous in their expressions of confidence in my public service. That confidence and appreciation is ample compensation for the effort I have made on behalf of our government these thirteen fateful years."[59]

Jones had helped save the nation's financial system, along with thousands of farms, homes, banks, and businesses, and had improved the country's infrastructure during the devastation of the Great Depression; in doing so, he showed how government can help people and make money at the same time. He helped militarize industry in time to win World War II and showed that business and government can cooperate and quickly build entire industries to protect the public, benefit the common good, nurture private enterprise, and overcome dependence on other nations for vital resources. Jones helped define Roosevelt's presidency as one that in many instances provided positive, profound, and enduring results for the nation in a financially astute and responsible manner. Despite Roosevelt's clumsy and politically expedient dismissal of Jones, both men were pivotal, heroic, and successful in their efforts to preserve capitalism and democracy during two of the most tumultuous and dangerous episodes in United States history.

Throughout his demanding public life in Washington, Jones always kept one foot in Houston. With no official position or responsibility in the federal government, his flourishing hometown pulled at him like a magnet. But Jones could not abruptly sever his ties to the power center of the nation. Protecting taxpayers' money, getting the best price possible for the factories, equipment, and materials owned by the RFC, putting

57. Jesse Jones to William Knudsen, April 25, 1945, Jesse H. Jones Collection [LOC].

58. Jesse Jones, speech, Business Advisory Council testimonial dinner, April 17, 1945, Jesse H. Jones Collection [LOC].

59. Jesse Jones to Blanche Babcock, February 4, 1945, Jesse H. Jones Collection [LOC].

the economy back into private hands, and setting his own record straight were urges as natural and as automatic as breathing for him. The RFC's staff had not changed much since his departure, and Snyder—a Jones loyalist—was running the show. Most of the wartime corporations, including the DPC, the DSC, the Metals Reserve Company, and the Rubber Reserve Company, had been dissolved and folded back into the RFC.[60] Jones was intimately familiar with almost every detail of the gargantuan government empire he had built, and because of his experience, connections, and stature, he could still make things happen. Even in Washington, trust, confidence, respect, and loyalty transcended official status. After the dust settled, Jones was still the go-to guy when it came to "reconversion." Jones confided to John Nance Garner, "I am making myself available to the boys in the RFC. Have comfortable offices in the Statler Hotel, watching the world go by. My own business has gotten along so well without me, that I am afraid to go home, but probably will return in the fall."[61]

Drew Pearson reported, "Jesse Jones, the man whom Franklin Roosevelt kicked out of the Cabinet, is now the man who really runs his old job of Federal Loan Administrator—backstage." He continued, "President Truman has closed his eyes to it, but Jones's position in Washington today is just about as powerful as ever. He operates from room 450 in the Statler Hotel, and his phone is so busy that not even his wife can reach him . . . If you want to buy a jeep, a truck, a factory, an oil refinery, or some old tires, it's Jesse Jones's old outfit which handles it."[62]

Stuart Symington, another friend of Truman's and a successful St. Louis entrepreneur, ran the Surplus Property Board—the reconversion organization that had succeeded the Surplus War Property Administration. Symington was eager to get plants and machinery into private hands and to consolidate all reconversion activities into one agency. The RFC was the natural choice.[63] One Congressional report claimed the RFC "had the best information in Washington" when it came to reconversion. Indeed, its DPC had fielded the best engineers in 1944 to survey each of its plants in preparation for the Briefalogue. The Bureau of the Budget cited DPC's Hans Klagsbrunn for "giving considerable thought to arrangements for

60. *Houston Chronicle*, May 16, 1945.
61. Jesse Jones to John Nance Garner, June 11, 1945, Jesse H. Jones Collection [LOC].
62. Pearson, "Washington Merry-Go-Round," November 15, 1945.
63. White, *Billions for Defense*, 97.

disposal of plant and equipment that would protect the government's interest and promote the welfare of the civilian economy."[64]

The scope and impact of reconversion were enormous. First, machinery and tools had to be cleared away before factories and plants could be put up for sale. Between Germany's surrender in May and Japan's defeat in August, the Navy and War Departments released hundreds of properties to the RFC for disposal. Requests to clear plants quadrupled.[65] Storage became a huge challenge. By August the DPC had to publish a new, much larger Briefalogue to advertise the plants and equipment for sale. Jones's expertise was needed.

And yet Houston called. Jones's nephew wrote two days after Germany's surrender, "Dear Uncle Jess, I'm alive and quite well. I was liberated on April 21st by the Russians. Please let the folks know immediately. Hope to see you all soon. Love, John."[66] John, who had been a prisoner of war for more than two years, was on his way home to Houston. Jones was eager to follow him in rejoining his family, and he had reason to build again. Houston never stopped growing during the Depression and the war, but population positively swelled after the war. Out of government for only five months, he announced a fourteen-story addition to his National Standard Building on Main Street and installation of air conditioning throughout.[67]

Wildcatter Glenn McCarthy also had announced plans to build a grand multimillion dollar hotel at "the end of Main Street." Instead of blocks from Buffalo Bayou, the distance to his new hotel was measured in miles. By sticking to Main Street, McCarthy missed out on the new high-traffic growth areas along the city's expanding freeway system, but the Shamrock Hotel, rising five miles south of Buffalo Bayou, marked the beginning of downtown's disintegration and Houston's decentralization. Exodus from downtown would not be noticed for a while because Houston was at the start of an enormous boom.

64. Ibid., 98.
65. Ibid., 100–101.
66. John T. Jones Jr. to Jesse Jones, May 7, 1945, John T. Jones Jr. Collection [HE].
67. *Houston Chronicle*, June 30, 1945.

Home

1946–1956

It Has Grown
Out of Bounds

THE JONESES TOOK MORE THAN TWO YEARS to move completely from Washington back to Houston.[1] Toward the end of 1945, it appeared that Jones was still in charge of the Federal Loan Administration (FLA). John Snyder had lasted as administrator only a little longer than Fred Vinson, so no one was officially in charge. Drew Pearson, who still had not let go of Jones, reported that neither Vinson nor Snyder had made any changes to FLA operations and that both had "left behind the staff Jesse had appointed." Pearson concluded, "So today, Jones finds himself with his close friends running the Federal Loan Administration. And while he can't sign letters or give official orders, actually, by dropping a word here or a word there, he can indirectly run the show."[2] Stuart Symington, now in charge of selling the government's vast holdings of factories and equipment, had successfully abolished the ineffectual three-man board his predecessor, Will Clayton, had opposed, giving him singular authority over plant and material disposal.[3] He sought to accelerate reconversion, but within months of assuming the position, Symington resigned to

---

1. Allied Van Lines receipt, November 19, 1947, Jesse H. Jones Collection [HE].
2. Pearson, "Washington Merry-Go-Round," December 23, 1945.
3. White, *Billions for Defense*, 96.

become Assistant Secretary of War. General Edmund B. Gregory, a career military man who had no apparent business experience, took his place as surplus properties administrator.[4] With another new administrator and still no one in charge of the FLA, Pearson reminded readers, "From his hotel room, Uncle Jesse keeps a quiet finger in the pie and remains one of the most powerful financial figures in Washington."[5]

Most of the nation's wartime factories, equipment, and materials were owned by four agencies: the War Department, the Navy Department, the Maritime Commission, and the RFC—mostly through its Defense Plant Corporation. Nearly sixty percent of the DPC's investments had been made in aviation, which expanded more than a hundred times during the course of the war. Production in the massive factories, along with demand, plunged to next to nothing after the war.[6] In addition, the War and Navy Departments were stuck with nearly 30,000 surplus airplanes that they warehoused in crowded airfields across the nation.[7] In the end, George and Herman Brown, owners of an international construction company, would buy most of the planes, scrap them, and recover millions of pounds of aluminum and thousands of ounces of platinum and silver from the machines that had once been so vital to victory.[8]

The DPC was looking to sell or lease its enormous aviation plants to just about anyone. The aircraft engine plant in Chicago—the largest industrial plant in the nation—covered 145 acres and had cost $176 million ($1.9 billion in current dollars) to build.[9] The Tucker Corporation tried to build its new Torpedo car there, but sank in scandal and never got enough financing to get going.[10] Eventually Ford took over.[11] Henry Kaiser, who still owed the government $44 million ($478 million) for his wartime plants, bought the Willow Run plant for $10 million ($109 million) in 1946 to manufacture Kaiser-Frazer automobiles. Like the Tucker effort, Willow Run financing was thin. Jones had worked with Kaiser when the RFC financed his magnesium, steel, and shipbuilding plants. From the sidelines, he warned Kaiser in early 1946, "Your energetic activities are apt to require a great deal of money for which you will be trustee . . . I would not be your friend if I did

4. Ibid., 98.
5. Pearson, "Washington Merry-Go-Round," December 23, 1945.
6. White, *Billions for Defense*, 104–5.
7. Pratt and Castaneda, *Builders*, 99.
8. Ibid., 100.
9. Jones, *Fifty Billion Dollars*, 337.
10. White, *Billions for Defense*, 104.
11. Jones, *Fifty Billion Dollars*, 338.

not again sound this note of caution."[12] But Kaiser ignored the advice, and the Kaiser-Frazer car company went out of business within a matter of years. The financial troubles of both companies, along with the Playboy Motor Car Corporation, would contribute to the RFC's growing disrepute. Jones's influence had finally, and obviously, diminished.

Jones later recalled, "I would like to have remained in charge of the RFC and its subsidiaries . . . so as to have . . . recoup[ed] as much as possible from the vast investments we had made in plants and strategic materials." He self-assuredly wrote, "I could have saved the government many hundreds of millions of dollars in the preservation and disposition of these vast investments over what was realized by having them turned over to others who had no familiarity . . . and, as often as not, no great amount of business experience."[13]

A few RFC wartime investments, however, turned out well, most notably the synthetic rubber plants and the "Big Inch" and "Little Inch" pipelines. They were the RFC's most profitable wartime ventures and, possibly, most influential, particularly on the Texas Gulf Coast.[14] This region and other parts of the West and the South were industrialized during World War II, primarily to avoid attacks on factories sited along the Atlantic coast, but also to utilize abundant natural resources and available workforce. After the war, synthetic rubber, magnesium, steel, oil, and tin continued to pour out of the plants lining the Texas and Louisiana coasts. Nearly eighty-seven percent of the rubber consumed in the United States now came from the plants owned by the government, most located along the Gulf Coast. Noted author John Gunther visited the area after the war and was quoted as saying that the "entire region between Houston and Beaumont seems, in fact, to be a single throbbing factory."[15] Unlike airplanes, an almost unquenchable demand for oil, chemicals, and commodities rose after the war. People poured into the area as production and job opportunities soared.

Employment in Houston's chemical industries went from a tiny 180 to 20,000 during the 1940s. Annual industrial payrolls increased from less than $200,000 ($2.17 million) to more than $60 million ($652 million).[16] Houston's population swelled from 410,000 to 726,000.[17] In 1945 the city

---

12. Jesse Jones to Henry Kaiser, January 7, 1946, Jesse H. Jones Collection [LOC].
13. Jones, *Fifty Billion Dollars*, 286.
14. White, *Billions for Defense*, 109.
15. Carleton, *Red Scare!* 13.
16. Ibid.
17. Ibid., 14.

was behind only New York, Los Angeles, Detroit, and Chicago in new construction.[18] A Harris County survey determined that 550 new houses would need to be built each month for the next three years to accommodate the growth.[19] Developers rubbed their hands together as they envisioned new suburban shopping centers, movie theaters, housing developments, and freeways, many either planned or already well under way. Toward the end of 1945, Jones wrote Emil Schram, "I have just returned from a week in Houston—my first in a very long time. It has grown 'out of bounds.'"[20]

Indeed it had. In 1898, the city encompassed nine square miles; now it covered seventy-six square miles and would soon double in size again.[21] Even though the majority of his real estate investments relied on a vibrant urban core, Jones and his National Bank of Commerce did not resist Houston's growth and decentralization. For the first time, outside professional management was brought in to the bank to establish departments to procure and service oil, real estate, and international loans, all of which would help propel the city into a major metropolitan area and also make money for the bank.

The bank helped finance gas stations, apartment complexes, home mortgages, and the Gulfgate Shopping Center, Houston's first suburban mall, which was eight miles southeast of the Main Street corridor.[22] The bank supported the area's new petrochemical industries by lending for drilling, refining, production, and transportation. When petroleum engineer E. O. Buck became head of the bank's new oil lending department, he promised to leave in one year if he had not brought in $10 million ($109 million) in new loans. He brought in $18 million ($196 million), later remembering, "Out our window each morning were more opportunities than we could handle."[23] George Ebanks, who established the bank's international lending department, relied on Jones to reverse the more provincial loan committee's decisions on transactions that they did not understand or appreciate. Between 1946 and 1956, the bank's deposits doubled while the city continued to grow and spread.[24]

Jones built to accommodate growing demand for downtown office space and parking. The fourteen-story addition to the National Standard

18. *Houston Chronicle*, January 12, 1946.
19. *Houston Chronicle*, October 10, 1945.
20. Jesse Jones to Emil Schram, October 10, 1945, Jesse H. Jones Collection [LOC].
21. McComb, *Houston: Bayou City*, 199.
22. Buenger and Pratt, *But Also Good Business*, 164.
23. Ibid., 159.
24. Ibid., 166.

Houston skyline, 1950s.

Building was under way by early 1946, and several new projects were on the drawing boards. To provide parking for cars jamming downtown, Jones wrote his friend Chick Fisher in Detroit, "I am considering building a garage in an office building. I understand that the Fisher Building has garage facilities. If so, I would appreciate your asking some of the boys to send me a little sketch, if not too much trouble, of the plans—how it works, etc."[25] Typically, only office buildings, stores, restaurants, movie theaters, and hotels fronted Main Street and its parallel thoroughfares, but from now on, most new buildings would include multi-story garages that accommodated hundreds of cars.

As Jones's attention turned away from Washington, his life in public service gave way to philanthropy. Houston Endowment, the foundation established by the Joneses in 1937, had made, on average, donations of approximately $30,000 ($326,000) a year. His reverence for Wilson and his determination to expand people's world views prompted Jones to write John Lloyd Newcomb, president of the University of Virginia, in 1945 and offer to donate $300,000 ($3.26 million) to establish the Woodrow Wilson School of International Affairs. Jones explained that the school would "honor the memory of a great American statesman" and "help in giving coming generations of young Americans a livelier appreciation of the vital interests and heavy responsibility of the United States in the outside world."[26] The donation and new school were announced in the *New York Times*.[27]

25. Jesse Jones to Charles Fisher, September 30, 1946, Jesse H. Jones Collection [LOC].
26. October 23, 1945 [HE].
27. *New York Times*, November 4, 1945.

The Joneses were very aware of the importance of education. Jones had only an eighth grade education and, despite enormous accomplishments, felt forever handicapped. Mary, on the other hand, attended college when most women during her day hardly completed grade school. One week after the gift to establish the Woodrow Wilson School of International Affairs, Jones offered the president of the Texas State College for Women $5,000 ($54,500) annually for ten years "to assist worthy girls who want . . . an education but are not in a position to fully pay their way through college." The annual donation was enough to pay for room, board, books, and tuition for twenty girls each year. The scholarships were fashioned to support a girl through four years of college as long as she maintained good grades and a good reputation. Jones continued, "Mrs. Jones is particularly interested in helping girls who want to study home economics or music . . . I would appreciate it if the scholarships could be [named] the 'Mary Gibbs Jones Scholarship.'"[28] National newspapers reported that the board of regents had accepted the gift and identified the donors as "Mr. and Mrs. Jesse H. Jones of Houston and Washington."[29]

The Joneses' philanthropy accelerated the following year. Unusual for the time, especially in the segregated South, the Joneses—through Houston Endowment—established a ten-year scholarship program for Prairie View University, a black college near Houston. Jones wrote to Prairie View President W. R. Banks that the $25,000 ($272,000) donation was intended "for the creation and maintenance of scholarships for deserving Negro girls who want to specialize in Home Economics." Refining a template that the foundation would use for future scholarship programs at other colleges, Jones explained that recipients were not required to repay anything and he concluded, "Mrs. Jones and I have long been interested in Prairie View." Once again, he asked that the scholarships be named for Mary.[30]

Banks responded, "The announcement of this proposal to our people here has been received with great enthusiasm and it is indeed heartening. You will never know how far-reaching this generous expression of your interest in our people will be."[31] The grant, like the others, made news. The *Negro Labor News* in Houston devoted half of its June 8 front page to huge headlines, an article about the scholarship, and a picture of

28. Jesse Jones to L. H. Hubbard, October 31, 1945 [HE].
29. *Houston Chronicle*, November 3, 1945.
30. Jesse Jones to W. R. Banks, May 30, 1946, Jesse H. Jones Collection [HE].
31. W. R. Banks to Jesse Jones, May 31, 1946, Jesse H. Jones Collection [HE].

The first Prairie View University Mary Gibbs Jones and Jesse H. Jones Scholarship recipients celebrate with a float at a football game in 1946.

Jones handing the contract to Banks—this at a time when many southern white leaders would not associate with a black man, let alone be photographed with one. Jones sent a copy of that newspaper, along with a note, to Fannie Roots, his housekeeper in Washington. Jones wrote, "I am sending you a copy of the *Negro Labor News*, published in Houston, which carries a story about our creating the 'Mary Gibbs Jones Scholarships' for girls at Prairie View." He told her, "Prairie View is one of the outstanding Negro colleges in the United States" and he explained that one of its many prominent graduates was "Dr. Patterson, President of Tuskegee University, of which I am a trustee." Jones would soon accept an invitation from John D. Rockefeller to serve as a trustee of the United Negro College Fund. He closed, "I have stayed away much longer than I intended but hope to be home [in Washington] soon."[32] Thoughtful acts on Jones's part like this were common, and engendered deep loyalty and devotion among his employees, whether in Washington or Houston, and whether black or white. Jones frequently visited employees in the hospital and had

32. Jesse Jones to Fannie Roots, June 10, 1946, Jesse H. Jones Collection [LOC].

designated $300,000 ($3.3 million) in his will to be divided among his more than 2,500 employees.[33]

Jones was at least one step ahead of many civic and business leaders in the South. A few months after their first grant, the Joneses added $25,000 ($272,000) to the Prairie View fund to provide scholarships for young men interested in agriculture. The front page *Houston Chronicle* article about the new program explained that the Joneses believed too many young men were leaving farms and abandoning agriculture.[34] E. B. Evans, one of the school's top administrators, wrote Jones, "The faculty, students, and, I am sure, all Negroes join me in respectfully expressing genuine appreciation for the noble act of democratic philanthropy . . . By your foresight, the progress of Negroes will be greatly enhanced."[35] More than half of Prairie View's male students at that time studied agriculture. According to a report issued by the "subsistence department" at the school, the family incomes of the first scholarship recipients ranged from only $450 ($4,890) to $1,500 ($16,300) a year.[36] Poverty prevented many from graduating. The Joneses established similar scholarship programs in agriculture for young white men at the University of Tennessee and at Texas A&M University. Remembering his start in life, Jones wrote Texas A&M President Gibb Gilchrist, "I have had a feeling . . . that too many of our young men were being educated away from the farm, and it is our expectation that scholarships . . . will be awarded to young men who are interested in the study of agriculture and related fields, and who would expect to return to the farm."[37] Just as the scholarships for women had been named for Mary Gibbs Jones, the scholarships for men were called "Jesse H. Jones Scholarships."

Not all Houston Endowment grants were large or for scholarships. Each month, like clockwork, the Buckner Orphans Home in Dallas received a $50 ($540) donation. Perhaps Jones recalled his childhood, remembering the poverty he saw and the service Buckner delivered to the city. Small donations also went to Springfield, Tennessee, to help former neighbors, to rebuild the country church where he had prayed as a child, and to help kids with school and music lessons. And each year the foundation made generous donations to the American Red Cross, the United Jewish

33. Jesse H. Jones, will, December 7, 1950, Jesse H. Jones Collection [HE]; Jo Murphy to Steven Fenberg, December 11, 1996, Oral History Project [HE].

34. *Houston Chronicle*, October 31, 1946.

35. E. B. Evans to Jesse Jones, November 1, 1946, Jesse H. Jones Collection [HE].

36. R. W. Hilliard to Fred J. Heyne, August 13, 1946, Jesse H. Jones Collection [HE].

37. Jesse Jones to Gibb Gilchrist, June 7, 1946, Jesse H. Jones Collection [HE].

Appeal, the Houston Community Chest, the Museum of Fine Arts, Houston, the Houston Symphony, and dozens of other organizations, most of them serving Houston. Toward the end of 1946, Jones wrote Fred Heyne and offered to endorse all of his government paychecks, by now totaling $143,783 ($1.56 million), to Houston Endowment.[38] He had not cashed even one since 1932. Jones turned over the checks, let go of the past, and moved into the future.

Even so, Jones had not lost interest in national affairs, and he wanted to be included in the conversation. With no official standing or public platform from which to express his feelings and views, he used the *Houston Chronicle* as a forum. Jones reviewed, approved, suggested, or wrote many of the *Chronicle*'s editorials and because the paper was his, these positions were often reported in other papers. For instance, the *Chronicle* opposed a proposed $3.7 billion ($40 billion) reconstruction loan to Great Britain and wrote that it would lead the United States "down a financial road that is likely to lead to disaster." The paper suggested instead to increase the 1941 RFC loan to England, which had plenty of security, to $1 billion ($10.9 billion).[39] Jones's position was repeated in most of the nation's major papers. He still had a voice, he still wanted to protect taxpayers' money, and others still listened.

Jones's politics were more conservative than his philanthropy and business decisions, especially when it came to Communism. A Jones editorial published a month before the 1946 midterm elections said that Henry Wallace, Harold Ickes, and Henry Morgenthau were unqualified to hold cabinet positions in a "Democratic administration," and that they harbored illusions of assuming "the mantle of the former president." Jones still resented them because of his heartless dismissal and the installation of his arch rival, Wallace, in his position. The paper criticized them for attending a conference where "dissident elements . . . adopted a platform which should please most 'fellow travelers' for it absorbed [a] large portion of the current Moscow party line" of appeasement and disarmament. The editorial again castigated the British loan as well as Wallace's position on the atomic bomb.[40] Just as he had copied and distributed magazine articles and speeches in the past, Jones mailed copies of the paper to those he thought should know his opinion, including President Harry Truman and Bernard Baruch.

38. Jesse Jones to Fred Heyne, September 30, 1946, Jesse H. Jones Collection [HE].

39. *New York Times*, April 13, 1946.

40. *Houston Chronicle*, October 1, 1946.

Baruch was now the United States representative on the United Nations Atomic Energy Commission, and from that position, recommended to President Truman that the U.S. share atomic technology with other nations. Jones published an editorial opposing the report's position, sent it to Baruch, and initiated a round of correspondence similar to the one over campaign contributions in 1924, only this time it was friendlier. Baruch wrote Jones a short note to tell him he had received the editorial and asked just how long he thought such secrets could be kept. He lightly said, "I hope the world is going as well as it can be with old age creeping over you so fast. I speak from experience," signing it, "Bernie."[41]

Jones answered that he could not say how long the secret could be kept and countered that no one could inspect Russia accurately or trust its dictators to honor treaties. He warned, "Man has progressed, but he is still cruel. Bullies are still at large." He closed, "We will go on having wars and peace treaties [will be] broken. However, you and I will be looking down, or up, as the case may be, at the next one. Maybe we will be bulls in Montana."[42] Baruch replied that the secrets should be shared because of the "great pressure to develop atomic energy for peaceful purposes." He added, "Unfortunately, the difference between dangerous and non-dangerous activities is not clearly defined . . . Remember, we have pressure not alone from outside but terrific pressure from inside." Treading on sensitive territory, Baruch reminisced about the war and wrote that "wastes and mistakes" had occurred because "when we saw war coming, we did not get ready or arrange the organizations that would have helped us." Baruch went on, "We proceeded in a faltering manner in industrial mobilization . . . and stumbled on price control." Jones must have felt slapped in the face. Baruch concluded, "All of these things made it difficult when war started and great organizations like yours had to swing into action."[43]

Predictably, Jones followed with a response recounting the accomplishments of his entire RFC career. He reminded Baruch that the RFC had "authorized more than $2.5 billion [$27 billion] for the construction of plants prior to Pearl Harbor," and he wrote, "By Spring 1942, our plant authorizations exceeded $7 billion [$76 billion], and later $10 billion [$109 billion]. It is this jump on the Axis powers that I refer to as having shortened the war." Back to the bomb, Jones told Baruch that his "atomic

---

41. Bernard Baruch to Jesse Jones, July 31, 1946, Jesse H. Jones Collection [LOC].
42. Jesse Jones to Bernard Baruch, August 10, 1946, Jesse H. Jones Collection [LOC].
43. Bernard Baruch to Jesse Jones, August 21, 1946, Jesse H. Jones Collection [LOC].

formula . . . reads well, but is impractical because it cannot be enforced." Jones confirmed their friendship and wrote at the bottom of the letter, "Be well and don't weaken."[44] They continued to write back and forth about world affairs as if they were enjoying a game of chess by mail.

For the first time in fifteen years, the Democrats lost both houses of Congress in the 1946 midterm election. As Congressional committee chairs changed over to Republican, Jones's power base in Washington further evaporated. The old guard was fading. Earlier in the year, Harry Hopkins and Carter Glass, two of Jones's closest political associates, had passed away. After the election, Bill Costello, Jones's personal assistant throughout his thirteen years at the RFC, resigned from his position as vice president of the RFC mortgage company and as special assistant to the RFC board of directors.[45] The *New York Times* reported, "He will open offices in Washington and Houston for the J. A. Zurn Manufacturing Company of Erie, Pa., makers of building-plumbing drainage devices and fittings."[46] Through the natural passage of time, Jones's influence in Washington was shrinking.

So was his family in Houston. On August 15, 1946, his brother, John, passed away at the age of seventy-three. Jones flew to Houston to be with his brother in his final hours, telling a reporter, "When we were kids, John whipped all the boys too big and tough for me to handle."[47] In Houston, Jones wrote Mary, who was waiting at the Thousand Islands Club on Wellesley Island in upstate New York. He affectionately began, "Dear Sweetheart," and inquired about her comfort during her trip to the club. He then reported, "John passed away exactly at 11—the time of our arrival" at the "air park." He told her he had "found all the family at John's apartment" and "All agreed that John was much better off since he could not get well." Jones also told Mary who had served him breakfast that morning and that he had stayed in room 912 at the Lamar Hotel because, unlike their apartment, it was air-conditioned. He sent "worlds of love" to their Thousand Islands friends and "all the rest to you my sweetheart."[48]

Jones had taken care of his family, arranging jobs and setting up trusts for them, ever since he began to succeed in business. He provided his nieces and nephews with enough for shelter, food, and clothing, but success was their responsibility, even though many of the men had jobs with

44. Jesse Jones to Bernard Baruch, August 29, 1946, Jesse H. Jones Collection [LOC].
45. *Houston Chronicle*, December 2, 1946.
46. *New York Times*, December 2, 1946.
47. *Houston Chronicle*, August 15, 1946.
48. Jesse Jones to Mary Gibbs Jones, August 15, 1946, Jesse H. Jones Collection [HE].

the Jones Interests. Jones also saw that his remaining sister, Ida, and cousins, Augusta and Jeanette, had whatever they wanted and needed. Jones was the benevolent patriarch. He played a similar role with employees including, until recently, those at the RFC and the Commerce Department, and with members of Congress. He promoted kinship, loyalty, care, and support.[49] In that spirit, Jones asked Heyne in late 1946 to advance $500,000 ($5.4 million) to establish the Commercial and Industrial Life Insurance Company and explained, "My principal purpose in organizing this company is to provide life insurance and probably health and accident insurance for employees of our various interests."[50] Jones gave the company to Houston Endowment, appointed employee Milton Backlund as its president, and renamed the National Standard Building the C&I Life Building. The twenty-two-story skyscraper, with C&I Life in blazing red lights across the top, became a fixture of Houston's expanding skyline.

Jones had always made others feel included and part of something bigger than themselves. In February, he invited a group of recent Texas A&M scholarship recipients to Houston for a visit, and the boys, all from farms in rural Texas, joined Jones in his downtown Houston office for an hour-long visit. They gawked at the city's skyline from the top of the Gulf Building, had lunch at the Rice Hotel's Empire Room, and took a tour of the Houston Ship Channel, where for the first time they saw oceangoing vessels and huge, humming industrial plants.[51] R. Henderson Shuffler, the Texas A&M development director, wrote Backlund after the visit and thanked him for the opportunity to watch "four youngsters have the biggest time of their lives." He said, "Every one of these boys will dig in now with an even greater determination."[52]

The Joneses, through Houston Endowment, established other scholarship programs to recognize people they wanted to honor. They established a scholarship program in economics at Austin College in memory of John T. Jones Sr. and one for graduate students in engineering at MIT to honor Bill Knudsen.

Responding to a request from Herbert Hoover, Houston Endowment sent a donation to the Boys Club of America. Jones pointed to shared experience when he wrote the former president, "We have had the same number of birthdays and have both been busy from early boyhood." He

49. Buenger, "Between Community and Corporation," 483.
50. Jesse Jones to Fred Heyne, December 18, 1946, Jesse H. Jones Collection [HE].
51. *Houston Chronicle*, February 16, 1947.
52. R. Henderson Shuffler to Jesse Jones, February 20, 1947, Jesse H. Jones Collection [HE].

Texas A&M University scholarship recipients visit with Jesse Jones in his Houston office in 1947. A *Houston Chronicle* reporter observed during one of those visits that Jones was as "proud as a father" (*Houston Chronicle*, April 26, 1949).

continued, "I am glad to say that the most useful years of my life were spent in government, through original appointment by you, and I feel that you can take satisfaction in the operations of the RFC."[53]

Jones must have felt great satisfaction with the sale of the "Big Inch" and "Little Inch" pipelines to Texas Eastern, a new company formed by George and Herman Brown to make the purchase. Natural gas had gained wider acceptance as an efficient fuel to heat homes and to generate electricity, and the pipelines could be converted easily to transport gas instead of oil. With coal miners striking and bottling up other fuel supplies, the pipelines, which had been idle since the end of war, became hot properties. The Browns' bid of $143 million ($1.36 billion) beat all the others. When this was added to the $109 million ($1.04 billion) net profit the RFC had realized in transporting and selling oil to refineries during the war, the pipelines turned out to be one of the government's most profit-

53. Jesse Jones to Herbert Hoover, May 23, 1947, Jesse H. Jones Collection [LOC].

able undertakings during and after the war.[54] As more and more people switched from coal and oil to cheaper, cleaner natural gas, natural gas sales doubled between the end of the war and 1951. Pipelines began to crisscross the country, and Texas Eastern stock soared in value from $150,000 ($1.4 million) to $10 million ($95 million) in just one year.[55]

Not everything Jones and the RFC had done turned out as well. In 1947 Jones was called on to testify before Congress, either in writing or in person, about losses related to the RFC's $18 million ($171 million) investment in Howard Hughes's Spruce Goose airplane;[56] about forcing the B&O Railroad into bankruptcy allegedly to maintain jobs for RFC officials;[57] about lawsuits and commissions stemming from requests for RFC loans to King ibn Saud in Saudi Arabia that were declined;[58] and about Elliott Roosevelt's debt to Jones, which Congress investigated on grounds of tax evasion after Elliot's main lender wrote it off as a bad loan. When the loan was publicized, Elliott finally repaid Jones, writing "Uncle Jesse" that he was "extremely anxious" to pay the debt Jones had settled in his behalf and was willing to pay the entire amount plus six percent interest.[59] Jones sent a two-line response, specifying a total due of $5,741 ($55,000), which used the prevailing four percent interest rate, and forgoing the warm inquiries typical of Jones's correspondence.[60] Jones received payment the following week.

Baruch offered sympathy, "As the years go by, you will find that the nibblers will get less and less, and the job you did will become more important . . . don't let anybody make you cynical. You have had too much and done too much. All of the criticism will pass away, if you will just take it philosophically. I am inclined to believe that is the way you will take it."[61] Jones replied, "I appreciate your concern about my state of mind as regards recent criticism . . . Rest assured that it has not given me the slightest worry."[62]

Jones was more concerned about issues such as the World Bank, the Marshall Plan, and international lending. He did not limit himself to

54. White, *Billions for Defense*, 109.
55. Burrough, *Big Rich*, 152.
56. *New York Times*, February 11, 1947.
57. *New York Times*, May 19, 1947.
58. *Houston Chronicle*, November 4, 1947.
59. Elliott Roosevelt to Jesse Jones, July 1, 1947, Jesse H. Jones Collection [HE].
60. Jesse Jones to Elliott Roosevelt, July 5, 1947, Jesse H. Jones Collection [HE].
61. Bernard Baruch to Jesse Jones, May 8, 1947, Jesse H. Jones Collection [LOC].
62. Jesse Jones to Bernard Baruch, May 12, 1947, Jesse H. Jones Collection [LOC].

editorials in the *Chronicle,* but also wrote to President Truman. In one letter, Jones wrote, "I regard the selection of a new President for the World Bank to be of paramount importance." That Eugene Meyer had served as president only added to Jones's consternation and he warned against participating "until we can bring our own economy and debt situation into better control and balance." He told Truman, "Lending money, with the expectation of getting it back, is as much a specialty as any other calling . . . Making questionable foreign loans to create exports is a sure road to ultimate loss to the taxpayers." He concluded, "In the final analysis, whatever the exporter makes is apt to be at the expense of the taxpayer . . . I am in no sense against exports, nor am I against foreign lending when done on a practicable basis, and not in too large amounts."[63] In another letter, Jones said, "We should rub out and start over as far as the World Bank is concerned." He suggested using the Export-Import Bank instead, and speaking from experience with Wallace's Bureau of Economic Warfare, he noted, "One foreign lending agency should be sufficient to do everything that we can afford to do and what we should be expected to do."[64]

Despite Clayton's role in the Marshall Plan, Jones was not convinced about its particulars and in declining an invitation to join an organization to endorse and promote it, wrote Secretary of War Robert P. Patterson, "I am as anxious as anyone to help the distressed people of Europe."But Jones suggested an alternative: "We should give them food, clothing, and medicines to the extent that we can, say, for the period of a year, and take another look at the situation then."[65] He continued, "I think we should also assist them with agriculture and probably some other equipment that would enable them to work out their own problems." He knew that a prostrate people, unable to rebuild their lives or their nations, would be vulnerable to subversion, chaos, and collapse, but always with his eye on U.S. taxpayers, he was wary of the Marshall Plan's effect on the U.S. economy. A *Houston Chronicle* editorial said the $17 billion ($162 billion) four-year plan "must be weighed most carefully to determine whether or not it can operate without further and dangerously damaging our already unbalanced economy."[66] Even so, Jones wrote Lord Beaverbrook,

63. Jesse Jones to Harry Truman, December 10, 1946, Jesse H. Jones Collection [LOC].

64. Jesse Jones to Harry Truman, February 21, 1947, Jesse H. Jones Collection [LOC].

65. Jesse Jones to Robert P. Patterson, November 6, 1947, Jesse H. Jones Collection [LOC].

66. *Houston Chronicle*, December 20, 1947.

"I am sure that our Congress will vote substantial relief for Europe, and should."[67]

Wallace and his supposed Communist sympathies got the once-over at the end of 1947 when the former vice president announced that he would run for president as a third party candidate. Truman had removed Wallace from his cabinet several months before. The *Chronicle* editorialized, "The Communists now have Henry Wallace. He is their avowed leader." It continued, "The Iowa Republican and make-believe Democrat has been parroting more and more of the Moscow line . . . He has become convinced that he alone represents the road to peace, but in reality he is influenced by hatred of the man who asked for his resignation from the cabinet."[68]

Despite Wallace's campaign and an occasional Congressional hearing, Jones's RFC record remained unsullied. On December 10 more than three hundred former and current RFC employees gathered at the Waldorf-Astoria Hotel in New York to honor Jones at an "Old Timers' Reunion," organized by New York Stock Exchange President Schram, Treasury Secretary Snyder, and Stanley Reed, associate justice of the Supreme Court. Against doctor's orders, Hoover got out of bed to attend and deliver a short speech. He observed, "Jones never let politics interfere with his concept of public service, which constitutes the mark of a great American."[69] Truman sent a statement that recognized the "inspiring part that the RFC played in the rescue and stimulation of business during the depression years," and that congratulated the organization and Jones for the "development of production and the accumulation of critical and strategic supplies for the defense and war programs." He concluded, "It is fitting that those associated with Mr. Jones during those significant periods now do honor to their great leader, a tribute in which I heartily join."[70] John Nance Garner telegrammed from Uvalde, noting, "It was my opportunity to serve in Washington for 38 years, or one-fourth of the history of the Republic from its founding until the time I left Washington." He continued, "I had an opportunity to observe the work of many administrative officers in that time, and I place Jesse Jones at the top of them all."[71]

---

67. Timmons, *Jesse H. Jones*, 375.
68. *Houston Chronicle*, December 31, 1947.
69. *Houston Chronicle*, December 11, 1947.
70. Harry Truman to John W. Snyder, December 10, 1947, Jesse H. Jones Collection [LOC].
71. John Nance Garner to Emil Schram, December 9, 1947, Jesse H. Jones Collection [LOC].

After speeches, salutes, and songs by Morton Downey, Jones told his devoted colleagues, "You honored me first and most when you did the work that was assigned to you for your government so well and faithfully." Then, "We have all been given the great privilege of aiding our country in the two greatest periods of crisis . . . in modern times—the depression and the last war. Between us we did a good job." Jones shared, "I have not been a praying man, but I must confess that I prayed repeatedly that we would have the courage to do the job that we had to do in the depression. Then we passed on to the war period." He talked about the 1940 legislation that allowed the RFC to buy, accumulate, or build anything needed to defend the country, and said, "At that time President Roosevelt could not get appropriations directly for war work, [but] the RFC could get the funds and do what was needed . . . to get us ready for the greatest test that we have ever faced." Jones matter-of-factly declared, "The 17 months' jump that we got on Hitler . . . shortened the war considerably in my opinion . . . That is an accomplishment that all of us here share."[72]

Jones's connection to the RFC endured. A few days before the banquet, as Jones sat in on a Congressional hearing about RFC wartime expenditures, he told the chairman, "That's my baby. I want to see what you're doing with it."[73] At the end of the year, however, he and Mary closed their Shoreham Hotel apartment and moved back to Houston for good.

They found a relentless flood of people pouring into town. Builders constructed almost 13,000 homes in 1947—twice the projected 550 a month.[74] At the beginning of 1948, Jones, always looking ahead, and willing and able to call on his Washington connections, wrote the head of the Federal Communications Commission, "I am writing now particularly to get any thought you may have regarding television. How soon we may expect it in this section . . . I have thought as soon as the screens get large enough, that we would like to have it down here."[75]

Jones was back to building in Houston, which meant local political showdowns. He spent the first month of the year slugging it out with oil magnate and philanthropist Hugh Roy Cullen over proposed zoning laws. Jones and the *Chronicle* endorsed zoning to protect unrestricted residential areas "from undesirable [commercial] encroachments."[76] Cullen thought zoning laws were "un-American and German"; he finally sent a

---

72. *Houston Chronicle*, December 11, 1947.
73. *New York Times*, December 3, 1947.
74. *Houston Chronicle*, December 7, 1947.
75. Jesse Jones to Wayne Coy, January 22, 1948, Jesse H. Jones Collection [LOC].
76. *Houston Chronicle*, January 24, 1948.

disgruntled letter to the Houston papers that said in part, "It has been a pleasure to help build this city up to now, but Jesse Jones has been away from here most of the . . . last 25 or 30 years, and has come back . . . and decided, with the influence of the press here, and the assistance of a bunch of New York Jews, to run our city, so I am going to give our city to Jesse and his crowd." Cullen said he was resigning "as chairman of the board of regents of the University of Houston, as a member of the Medical Center, and every other organization of which I am a member."[77]

Jones ran Cullen's letter and his own response on the front page of his newspaper, two days before the city voted on zoning. He graciously complimented Cullen's civic generosity and pointed out that neither of them would be affected by zoning since "Mr. Cullen lives in River Oaks, which is highly restricted, and I live in a downtown hotel." (At the time, restrictions prohibited Jews and blacks from living in River Oaks, the city's poshest neighborhood.) Referring to Cullen's more inflammatory remarks, Jones only said mildly, "Since most of the large cities of our country have zoning, I see no justification for Mr. Cullen's statement that zoning is 'un-American and German.'"[78] Despite Jones's effort, zoning was defeated. It was a new world where Jones could not easily pull the strings to make things happen the way he wanted.

He did not appear to take the defeat too seriously. Jones reported to a friend, "We had a little fun election day—Roy and I and a few others— but all is well now. Roy is not resigning and we don't have zoning."[79] He seemed to be enjoying local matters. When he sent Miss Blanche the newspaper clippings containing Cullen's letter, he apologized for not corresponding more often, "My many interests and . . . civic responsibilities just steal the time away, and days have melted into weeks before I know it. As I approach the evening of life, there seems to be so many things to do and so little time to do them in." He said the city was "growing by leaps and bounds" and "big shots are constantly coming to look it over." Maybe missing Washington's nightlife, he told her that Edgar Bergen, Charley McCarthy, and Mortimer Snerd had been in town and "gave us a lot of laughs." He said he had donated some of the calves for the Calf Scramble at the Houston Fat Stock Show and noted that the boys then raised them to help "pay their way through college with the money they earn." Jones attended the rowdy competition, saying, "I enjoyed every minute of it."

77. *Houston Chronicle*, January 29, 1948.
78. Ibid.
79. Jesse Jones to Joseph W. Evans, February 10, 1948, Jesse H. Jones Collection [LOC].

He reminded her, "Keep as comfortable as you can and remember always that you are constantly in my thoughts and that I would do anything to make you more comfortable."[80] Later that year, he air-conditioned her house in Dallas.[81]

Jones was trotted out almost anytime anyone of importance came to town. His attendance added gravitas to any event, especially when he introduced the guest of honor, whether it was Eddie Rickenbacker from Eastern Airlines promoting service to the west coast or Treasury Secretary Snyder speaking at the annual Chamber of Commerce meeting. At this point, philanthropy seemed to consume most of his time and interest. Houston Endowment established a raft of its ten-year scholarship programs, seven of them to honor World War II military heroes and, according to the grant contract, "to offer . . . potential leaders an opportunity to secure the training which will fit them for military careers."[82] Jones hoped the "name the scholarships honor will serve as a lasting inspiration to the young men who benefit through the awards."[83] Scholarships honoring Fleet Admiral William F. Halsey Jr. and General Alexander Archer Vandegrift were established at Rice University. Scholarships in honor of General of the Army Dwight David Eisenhower and General George S. Patton were established at Texas A&M University. General Douglas MacArthur was honored with a scholarship at the New Mexico Military Institute, and Fleet Admiral Chester W. Nimitz and Fleet Admiral Ernest J. King were honored at the University of Texas at Austin.[84]

Repeating the credit line in articles whenever a new Houston Endowment scholarship program was announced, the *Houston Chronicle* reported, "These scholarships are in line with . . . Mr. and Mrs. Jones . . . making available to deserving young men and women in many institutions . . . the opportunity to obtain a college education."[85] In addition to the seven military scholarships and the programs earlier established, Houston Endowment created ten-year programs at Baylor University (to send local pediatric students to train at Harvard Medical School and at the Children's Hospital in Boston), and the University of Houston (to train nurses for the Texas Medical Center). Mary played an active role at

80. Jesse Jones to Blanche Babcock, February 10, 1948, Jesse H. Jones Collection [LOC].

81. Jesse Jones to John Carpenter, May 28, 1949, Jesse H. Jones Collection [LOC].

82. Contract between Houston Endowment and Texas A&M University, January 31, 1948 [HE].

83. *Houston Post*, January 25, 1948.

84. January 29, 1948 [HE].

85. *Houston Chronicle*, January 25, 1948.

the foundation, as did John Jr., who had become more involved with the family's interests since returning from the prisoner-of-war camps. Mary wrote John from the Thousand Islands Club, where the Joneses now spent each August, "Jess and I think the proposed agreement for the scholarships to the University of Houston well planned." Also, "The fishing has been very good, particularly now that we can enjoy the sport in much comfort in our new Chris Craft boat."[86] The thirty-four foot cabin cruiser was named *Audrey* after their granddaughter.[87] They were clearly enjoying life and helping others. In 1948, Houston Endowment donated more than $200,000 ($1.8 million) toward its grant commitments; of that, $116,000 ($1.02 million) went toward education.[88]

Life, of course, had its sad moments. Miss Blanche passed away in September. Jones wrote to her daughter, "I cannot readily accept the fact that Miss Blanche is no longer to be with us. I felt that she would live on and on. In truth, her spirit will."[89] But many happy events outnumbered the inevitable sad occasions. Right around Jones's seventy-fourth birthday, the Chinese government honored him in Washington. Chinese Ambassador Wellington Koo, whom Jones had met at the Paris Peace Conference after World War I, said on behalf of President Chiang Kai-shek, "As administrator of the Federal Loan Agency and secretary of commerce, he contributed a great deal in sustaining China in her resistance against aggression, and as publisher and owner of the *Houston Chronicle*, he always takes a sympathetic attitude toward the peoples who are struggling for freedom and liberty." Koo continued, "In recognition of his distinguished service in bringing about the Allied victory and especially in the promotion of co-operation between China and the United States, the national government of the Republic of China confers upon Jesse Holman Jones the decoration of the Order of Ching Hsin, auspicious star, with grand cordon." Accepting the honor, Jones said, "It afforded me the very greatest possible pleasure while in the government to be of assistance to your country."[90] Sweden also decorated Jones for his contributions during World War II.

This was a time of looking back. Baruch wrote Jones, "The other day I was in Washington, and as I was leaving my room, a man came up and asked if I were Jesse Jones. I had to inform him that unfortunately I was

86. Mary Gibbs Jones to John T. Jones Jr., August 20, 1948, Jesse H. Jones Collection [HE].
87. H. Newell to Rodi Towing Service, November 4, 1948, Jesse H. Jones Collection [HE].
88. Houston Endowment annual report for 1948 [HE].
89. Jesse Jones to Florence Roemer, December 27, 1948, Jesse H. Jones Collection [HE].
90. *Houston Chronicle*, April 10, 1948.

not." Referring to their differences over the years, he continued, "I just wanted to say that I am sorry there should be a cloud between us, even the size of a man's hand. I have only the best wishes for you and hope that there will be happiness and peace for you and yours."[91] In jest, Jones replied, "I have been taken for you on many occasions, the penalty we pay for being such handsome men. While I hold a score or two against you, and on a few occasions we have not agreed, there is no reason in the world why we should not be friends and wish each other well." He added, "I suppose we may be excused for the belief that we have each contributed something a little out of the ordinary and that we may take pride in the fact."[92]

Neither man attended the 1948 Democratic National Convention. Columnist James Reston reported, "The story of this convention is not in the Democrats who go by, but in those who do not; not in those present and accounted for, but in the great figures of the party who are . . . absent." Reston's number one absentee was "that historic and controversial figure—Franklin D. Roosevelt," who had dominated the last four conventions. He also counted as missing Hopkins, Garner, Wallace, and Eleanor Roosevelt and wondered, "Where are the brain-trusters—the Cohens and the Corcorans . . . ? Where are the former Cabinet members—Judge Hull . . . ; Jesse Jones, building his empire in Texas; Henry Morgenthau . . . and the rest?" Reston continued, "Where are the financial angels [like Baruch]?" Reston wrote, "When the roll of the illustrious is called, the old voices do not answer." He reported that one conventioneer said, "The Democratic party is breaking up before our eyes," but Reston countered, "It broke and scattered long ago."[93]

That is how Jones felt. In one of the biggest and most public decisions of his political life, Jones endorsed Republican candidates Thomas Dewey and Earl Warren for president and vice president on the front page of the *Houston Chronicle*. That same day Truman started a campaign tour, which included stops in Texas.

Jones's position was reported, discussed and dissected by every pundit and politician around. He said Truman had good intentions but had "not shown the leadership necessary for the successful management of our national and international affairs." Also, that "our federal government has become a stagnant and swollen patchwork of unnecessary

91. Bernard Baruch to Jesse Jones, June 8, 1948, Jesse H. Jones Collection [LOC].
92. Jesse Jones to Bernard Baruch, June 25, 1948, Jesse H. Jones Collection [LOC].
93. *New York Times*, July 13, 1948.

agencies and bureaus during 16 years of unchanged control," pointing to the $40 billion ($360 billion) annual budget and the 2,000,000 "persons on the federal civilian payroll" as evidence. Simply stated, "An overhauling is badly needed."[94] Jones's lingering bitterness over his dismissal was not mentioned.

His endorsement of the Republican ticket advised, "We Democrats can no longer . . . [take] refuge in the fact that we have always been of a particularly political faith; [or hold] that we are Democrats and can vote no other ticket." Jones, a pillar of the party, continued, "Tradition should not dictate our decisions. When we go to the polls to cast our votes . . . patriotism should tell us to forget party labels this year."[95] According to the *New York Times*, President Truman had "no comment" about Jones's editorial.[96] Later that month, the *Times* endorsed Dewey and Warren.

Once endorsements had been made by both papers, Jones wrote to Arthur Hayes Sulzberger, publisher of the *New York Times*: "My course was particularly difficult, and taken in genuine sadness, because of my personal relations and friendship with President Truman and Senator [Alben] Barkley, both of whom I hold in high esteem." He shared, "I have no acquaintance with either Governor Dewey or Governor Warren, but each has demonstrated his ability in public affairs by the successful administration of the affairs of their respective states." Dewey was governor of New York, and Warren governed California. Jones concluded, "That we need a change in our national leadership must be obvious to all who are not of some special interest group or who are not controlled by sentiments of tradition."[97]

The *Houston Chronicle* and many other major newspapers continued to editorialize against Truman right up to the election. No one expected him to win. *Newsweek* magazine polled fifty esteemed political writers and every one of them said Truman would lose. The magazine predicted, "The landslide for Dewey will sweep the country." It also predicted Congress would remain in Republican hands.[98] To almost everyone's great surprise, Truman won with 303 electoral votes and more than 24 million popular votes to Dewey's 189 electoral votes and 22 million votes. Strom Thurmond, who had run for president as a Dixiecrat and said integrat-

94. *Houston Chronicle*, September 17, 1948.
95. Ibid.
96. *New York Times*, September 18, 1948.
97. Jesse Jones to Arthur Hayes Sulzberger, October 4, 1948, Jesse H. Jones Collection [LOC].
98. McCullough, *Truman*, 694.

ing the armed services was "un-American," received thirty-nine electoral votes and a little over a million popular votes.[99] Wallace had run on the Progressive ticket, received no electoral votes, and slightly fewer popular votes than Thurmond.[100] In addition to Truman's unexpected victory, the Democrats recaptured both houses of Congress. The day after the election, the *Houston Chronicle* splashed "Hats Off to Mr. Truman" across the front page, congratulated him, and pledged, "Our best wishes are with you." In the *New York Times*, Jones said, "President Truman is a good American and with a Democratic Congress of good majorities in both houses, in my opinion, will give a good account of himself."[101]

At the beginning of 1949, in a letter to Cordell Hull, who had served as Roosevelt's Secretary of State from 1933 to 1944, Jones looked back at his endorsement."As you probably know, I advised the election of Dewey and Warren on the ground that I felt very keenly the need of a change, a house-cleaning in our national affairs. I like Truman personally and, of course, am very fond of Barkley." In a revealing statement, Jones shared, "I have always regarded myself a liberal, and except for . . . McKinley against Bryan, I have voted the Democratic ticket." Telling Hull about life in Texas he wrote, "Our section of the country continues to grow, and Houston along with it, due in large part to oil, gas and chemicals." He added, "I am now back building more buildings, which I enjoy, and trying to round up the herd, as my operations have extended into many fields." He also confessed, "It has not been a good year for me healthwise, and having always been able to work long hours, it is difficult to adjust myself."[102]

With the exception of friends and colleagues, Jones wrote politicians only when he was required to testify, when he had something to offer based on his knowledge and authority, or when an issue or opportunity might affect Houston and/or his businesses. He advised the House Banking and Currency Committee to suspend assessments that banks paid to the FDIC because the fund's current $1 billion ($8.9 billion) balance and the interest it generated could cover any current and future costs.[103] Jones's letter generated a tremendous amount of coverage in papers across the country, with the *New York Times* noting the interest Jones could still provoke: "The matter was brought into sharpest focus

99. Ibid., 667.
100. Shields-West, *Almanac of Presidential Campaigns,* 191.
101. *New York Times,* December 3, 1948.
102. Jesse Jones to Cordell Hull, January 5, 1949, Jesse H. Jones Collection [LOC].
103. Jesse Jones to Brent Spence, April 30, 1949, Jesse H. Jones Collection [LOC].

late last month, when Jesse Jones, former head of the Reconstruction Finance Corporation, asked Congress for suspension of the payments."[104] Politicians continued to court Jones, even those who entered office long after he had left Washington. Freshman Texas Representative Lloyd Bentsen Jr. sent Jones a copy of a bill to lower the FDIC assessment rate and wrote, "My interest in this particular piece of legislation was stimulated by a letter I received from you some time ago, and on investigation into the matter to which you referred, I introduced the bill."[105] Jones responded with practical interest, "Your formula is a little intricate and the percentage small." He advised him about an alternative and closed, "I appreciate your writing me as you did."[106]

Jones remained interested in national affairs and still had influence, but he savored the easier pace of life in Houston. He wrote Schram, "Mrs. Jones and I . . . expect to be coming East after a few weeks, 'though we are very comfortable at home with air conditioning, and only two blocks from office to home."[107] Plus there was enough going on to keep Jones engaged. For one thing, Main Street was changing before his eyes. Foley's new eight-floor department store was completely covered in smooth stone and had windows only on the ground floor. The resulting monolith covered the entire 1100 block of Main, sitting on the next street from the Lamar Hotel and the movie theaters Jones had built. On the opposite side of Main, Sakowitz had an elegant new building under construction, and Ben Wolfman had spent $1 million ($8.9 million) to remodel The Fashion, a department store that occupied what had been the Kirby Lumber Company Building. Like Foley's and Sakowitz, The Fashion also had windows only on the ground floor, reflecting the advent of air conditioning and the absence of the need to open windows for ventilation. For the next ten years, the number of dollars consumers spent downtown stayed about the same, while downtown's proportion of sales shrank from fifty-one percent to twenty-eight percent.[108] The influx of people into greater Houston still sustained downtown even as the city moved steadily outward.

The opening of Glenn McCarthy's $20 million ($178 million) Shamrock Hotel south of downtown on March 17, 1949, signaled the shift to a suburban lifestyle. For decades the city's social life had centered on the Rice

104. *New York Times,* June 5, 1949.
105. Lloyd Bentsen to Jesse Jones, October 3, 1949, Jesse H. Jones Collection [LOC].
106. Jesse Jones to Lloyd Bentsen, October 10, 1949, Jesse H. Jones Collection [LOC].
107. Jesse Jones to Emil Schram, July 5, 1949, Jesse H. Jones Collection [LOC].
108. McComb, *Houston: Bayou City,* 192.

Hotel and downtown. Now dozens of Hollywood's biggest stars, hundreds of reporters, and thousands of Houstonians flocked to the Shamrock Hotel for an opening night celebration that would live in legend for many years to come. Two thousand people were invited to attend, but three thousand showed up. The hotel was jammed from wall to wall, and no one could get through. Desperate to find their tables, the dressed-up mob began cutting across the Emerald Room stage while Dorothy Lamour was trying to conduct her nationally broadcast show. One woman, glittering in diamonds and wrapped in fur, grabbed the microphone from Lamour and shouted, "I don't give a damn about your broadcast! I want my dinner table!"[109] Even Jones could not get to his table in the dining room and neither could Mayor Holcombe. A *Chronicle* headline dubbed it "Bedlam in Diamonds."[110] It was everything McCarthy had hoped for. The gaudy, raucous event garnered national attention and showed that a new kind of Houston had emerged.

The next evening McCarthy premiered his new movie, *The Green Promise*, at Jones's Metropolitan and Kirby Theaters. As if paying homage to Houston's past, the forty or so stars McCarthy had brought in for the opening paraded from the Shamrock down the Main Street corridor in convertibles, heading toward the downtown theaters. The *Houston Chronicle* reported, "It was hard to tell who was the most thrilled, the thousands and thousands of people who lined the streets to see the parade and filled the Metropolitan and Kirby theatres, or the stars who were given an ovation greater than any they have ever received before."[111] Jack Paar served as master of ceremonies at the Metropolitan and introduced a steady stream of Hollywood glitterati, including Ginger Rogers, Van Heflin, Walter Brennan, Stan Laurel, Robert Preston, Maureen O'Hara, and child actress Natalie Wood.

Jones had magnanimously congratulated McCarthy in a full-page *Houston Chronicle* ad, but attending a meeting at the Shamrock the following week—one that included top officials from Mexico and the United States—must have galled Jones, or at least troubled him a little.[112] Earlier, that meeting and any coincidental entertainment undoubtedly would have occurred downtown at his Rice Hotel.[113]

Nonetheless, the Joneses were more interested in building Houston

109. Burrough, *Big Rich*, 182.
110. Ibid., 183.
111. *Houston Chronicle*, March 19, 1949.
112. *Houston Chronicle*, March 13, 1949.
113. *Houston Chronicle*, March 23, 1949.

for tomorrow than in wallowing in the past. In 1949 Houston Endowment donated $50,000 ($445,000) to the Methodist Hospital Building Fund, the first of many donations the foundation would make to the hospitals and schools in the nascent Texas Medical Center, which was budding at the end of Main Street across from McCarthy's new hotel.[114] That summer, W. W. Kemmerer from the University of Houston wrote Jones that the medical center needed "250 professional nurses annually to meet existing demands and 350 annually if all proposed hospitals are built." He added, "This is the most difficult task we have ever undertaken." Kemmerer proposed to meet that need, writing, "This training program for professional nurses will be on a four-year basis," and he estimated that $900 ($8,000) would cover "room and board, tuition, and books" per student for the first year.[115] Jones wrote Kemmerer four days later, "I have passed it along to the Trustees of Houston Endowment with the suggestion that they consider assuming some part of the program."[116] In less than two weeks, Houston Endowment had established the Jeannette Jones Scholarships in Nursing program at the University of Houston. Like most of the others, the scholarship funding was paid in equal installments over ten years and the program bore the name of someone the Joneses admired and cared about—in this case, Jesse's first cousin.[117] Instead of shaking hands with prominent statesmen and world leaders, Jones was now seen in newspaper pictures handing checks to young nurses in uniform.[118] He was also seen in the papers with another group of Texas A&M scholarship recipients. The caption under the picture of Jones with the eager students said, "Proud as a father."[119]

In an effort to "round up the herd" (i.e., to get his affairs in order), Jones had funneled most properties to the Commerce Company, his holding company. He transferred 5,000 shares to Houston Endowment, which gave the foundation controlling interest in the Houston Chronicle Publishing Company, KTRH radio, and the Rice Hotel.[120] Houston Endowment already owned the C&I Life Insurance Company. In 1950, Houston Endowment's board included Heyne, Backlund, George Butler, and sev-

---

114. Fred J. Heyne to Hines H. Baker, January 6, 1949 [HE].

115. W. W. Kemmerer to Jesse Jones, July 14, 1949, Jesse H. Jones Collection [HE].

116. Jesse Jones to W. W. Kemmerer, July 18, 1949, Jesse H. Jones Collection [HE].

117. Milton Backlund, interoffice correspondence, August 26, 1949 [HE].

118. *Houston Post*, September 4, 1949.

119. *Houston Chronicle*, April 26, 1949.

120. J. H. Creekmore to Frank A. Liddell, November 26, 1949, Jesse H. Jones Collection [HE].

eral Gibbs and Jones family members, including John Jr., who had also become president of the *Houston Chronicle*. The foundation had a governing board, but the Joneses gave it direction.

After Houston Endowment initiated a scholarship program at the University of New Brunswick to honor England's Lord Beaverbrook, Jones wrote to his World War II ally that the scholarship was established because of "the great service you have rendered your country and ours, especially in war, and particularly to me in building a fire that finally got rubber shipments to us from the Far East." Jones reported, "Our synthetic [rubber] industry developed more than 1,000,000 tons a year, and as you probably know, the product is continually being improved and is better for many purposes than natural rubber." To ensure that the armed services had an adequate supply of rubber, of particular importance during the subsequent Korean War, and until an appropriate divestiture plan could be implemented, the federal government retained possession of the synthetic rubber plants and continued to lease them to private operators. Jones also told Beaverbrook that he had been working on a book about his government service, and asked him to share some information about rubber and Winston Churchill with Edward Angly, his coauthor.[121]

The Joneses followed the nursing scholarships for the medical center with the establishment in 1950 of a Jesse H. Jones Fellowship in Cancer Education, honoring Dr. E. W. Bertner at the M. D. Anderson Hospital for Cancer Research. Bertner had come to Houston in 1913 to serve as the Rice Hotel's house physician. He then became M. D. Anderson Hospital's first director and, later, the first president of the Texas Medical Center. The $25,000 ($220,000) grant was made two months before Bertner passed away. Dr. R. Lee Clark Jr., Bertner's successor, wrote Jones, "That an educational project of this type . . . should be named for Doctor Bertner is indeed a tribute to his never-ceasing enthusiasm and accomplishments in the progress of medical science." He also wrote, "The grant . . . will enable physicians and scientists of ability to receive training . . . for devoting their lives to the care of the cancer patient, and to teaching and research in the field of the malignant disease."[122]

Jones drew on personal funds to take care of his family. He wrote Jeannette, who had moved to New York as a young woman and stayed, that the income from the stocks she held in his companies "will be ample to last you, as long as you live." He added, "When you need more just

121. January 19, 1950 [HE].
122. May 23, 1950 [HE].

write Mr. Heyne." With typical humor, he said, "Mr. Heyne . . . is guardian for all of us, and I do not expect him ever to die." He told her about the $275,000 ($2.4 million) gift they had made to Houston's Hedgecroft Clinic, "a small hospital for polio . . . [that] takes care of about 50 children at a time and is always full." Harris County had the second highest incidence of polio in the nation.[123] In keeping with their philanthropic priority to improve life for the people of Houston, the Joneses contributed another $100,000 ($882,000) the following year to enlarge the clinic. In his wide-ranging letter, Jones said if Jeannette did not have a television, he would send her one for Christmas, and that he liked a recent speech by Dewey better than one by President Truman.[124]

Even as he kept up with politics, he had little desire to get entangled again in Washington. He wrote a friend that Arkansas Senator Fulbright had asked him to testify about the future of the RFC, then said, "But I am not quite up to it." He lamented, "It is terrible, the things they are doing."[125] So instead of appearing in person, Jones offered Fulbright his unvarnished views in a four-page, single-spaced letter that he wrote on April 10, 1950, five days after his seventy-sixth birthday. Writing on *Houston Chronicle* letterhead, he began, "My views about the RFC are mixed," and said, "I have a great affection for the Corporation to which I devoted thirteen years of my life, and have pride in its accomplishments during that period." And he commented, "I have great affection for my associates who shared the responsibility with me, some of whom are still with the Corporation." Then he dropped the other shoe: "But [I] am saddened by the way [the RFC] is now being misused."[126]

Jones continued, "The Corporation was created as an emergency agency when millions of our people were on short rations, when there was no market for farm products and no demand for anything but a square meal." He reminded Fulbright that the RFC's powers had been expanded only to meet emergencies and to do "what private enterprise was not in a position to do." Jones explained that the RFC, "with its experienced personnel, was a 'natural' to take over war work." He stated frankly, "At the war's end, [with] our banking structure . . . fully restored and able to provide credit for all legitimate purposes, the RFC should have been placed in liquidation. That it was not is no credit to the government."[127]

123. Wooten, *Polio Years*.
124. Jesse Jones to Jeanette Jones, December 16, 1950, Jesse H. Jones Collection [HE].
125. Jesse Jones to Al Parish, April 24, 1950, Jesse H. Jones Collection [LOC].
126. Jesse Jones to J. William Fulbright, April 10, 1950, Jesse H. Jones Collection [LOC].
127. Ibid.

Jones was unstinting in his criticism of the RFC's ill-advised postwar loans, writing, "Excuses are found to make loans . . . that under no circumstances can be justified." He referred to several disastrous examples, including the Kaiser-Frazer loan to produce automobiles and the Waltham Watch Company loan. Jones had assiduously protected taxpayer money for thirteen years from dubious transactions, and had to ask, "If a concern as old and experienced as the Waltham Watch Company could not make a go . . . in such good times as we have been having since the war's end, the government certainly could not, so why the loan?" He concluded, "As for the future of the RFC, I think it should be given a decent burial, lock, stock, and barrel." If Congress was not willing to liquidate the RFC, he said, then at least close the thirty-two branches and limit the size of loans to business and industry, ensuring they are made only "in cooperation with banks and other financial institutions, which would make and administer the loans." Jones closed his letter, "I have made these observations, comments, and suggestions from my long experience . . . and wish to remind you that where the sugar is, you will always find the flies."[128]

Jones had a high opinion of Eisenhower. He had named a scholarship in honor of the celebrated general and had introduced him as the keynote speaker at Houston's Chamber of Commerce's annual dinner in 1949. Jones encouraged him to come back in 1950. In a letter to Eisenhower's office at Columbia University, where he was president, Jones wrote, "There are good reasons why you should be seen and heard occasionally around the country. People are worried."[129] Communism, Korea, inflation, and taxes were on people's minds. Eisenhower did come to Texas in 1950, delivering a speech at Texas A&M University in November. As usual, Jones offered feedback: "You made an excellent speech at A&M and it came over the radio perfectly." Jones confessed, "More than ever I want you to be President of the United States." With his typical personal touch, he closed, "Please let Mrs. Eisenhower know that Mrs. Jones and I asked about her and were sorry she could not have been with you."[130]

Jones told Eisenhower on one of his visits to Texas, "I am happiest when I am planning and building."[131] If so, he must have been almost delirious with joy. In July 1951 a local magazine reported that since his

128. Ibid.

129. Jesse Jones to Dwight Eisenhower, July 15, 1950, Jesse H. Jones Collection [LOC].

130. Jesse Jones to Dwight Eisenhower, November 10, 1950, Jesse H. Jones Collection [LOC].

131. Timmons, *Jones: Man and Statesman,* 379.

return from Washington, Jones had "spent more money in downtown Houston, built more buildings, provided more jobs and quarters for others to work in than any other Houstonian," then parenthetically added, "besides himself earlier." The article went on, "Just 'filling in' the chinks and crannies of his heart-of-Houston empire, Mr. Jones has built more than $15 million [$123 million] worth of buildings since 1946."[132] During that time, Jones filled up downtown blocks with multi-story annexes, additions, and garages, next to or on top of, the skyscrapers that he had already built. He also constructed a sixteen-story building for the telephone company and spent $3 million ($25 million) remodeling the Rice Hotel and reconfiguring its roof garden to accommodate Houston's growing oil industry and the Petroleum Club, whose members previously had met in a coffee shop.[133] The city may have been spreading out, but plenty was happening downtown. Jones wrote Jeannette, "Main Street is about as busy as Fifth Avenue, with no place to park."[134]

But nightlife in downtown Houston was starting to decline. Jones wrote Nicholas Schenck, the president of Loews Inc., to remind him that the leases on the Loews and Metropolitan Theaters were about to expire, prodding, "The ground has become so valuable that the improvements now on the property do not justify their continuance at the present income . . . The location is about the number 1 spot in Houston, and we are looking forward to improving the property in such a manner as to produce more commensurate revenue." Jones assured him, "We, of course, are in no jiffy about it, but wanted to bring it to your attention for your thinking."[135] Of the more than fifty movie theaters in the city, most were new and in the suburbs, including half a dozen drive-ins. Attendance at the Metropolitan declined from 1,126,849 in 1950 to 1,006,367 in 1951 and would continue to drop to 521,178 in 1960.[136]

As 1951 opened, Jones sold his twenty-two-story Commerce Building, its new annex, and a five-story garage to the Tennessee Gas Transmission Company for $11 million ($90 million). The *Wall Street Journal* said: "This [is] of one of the largest [sales] ever made in downtown Houston."[137] Jones wrote to a colleague, "I have been building business buildings for

132. Carroll, "Skyliner Jesse H. Jones," 12, 13, 34.
133. Chapman, "Swank Rice Hotel."
134. Jesse Jones to Jeanette Jones, July 6, 1951, Jesse H. Jones Collection [UT].
135. Jesse Jones to Nicholas Schenck, January 26, 1951, Jesse H. Jones Collection [HE].
136. Theater attendance statement, Jesse H. Jones Collection [HE].
137. *Wall Street Journal*, January 18, 1951.

43 years," and told him the buildings originally cost about forty percent of the $11 million ($90 million) sales price. Letting go of what he had built was new for Jones, who admitted, "It is the only building that I ever sold, and now I am having to take a vacation to recuperate."[138] Tennessee Gas—later known as Tenneco—had been a tenant in the Commerce Building since it started business in 1945.[139] The rapid growth of its business and of the natural gas industry enabled the young company very quickly to buy its own skyscraper.

Jones could "recuperate" because he had Heyne to oversee everything, R. P. Doherty and A. D. Simpson to handle business at the bank, and nephew John Jr. to run the *Houston Chronicle*. John was his eyes and ears and sent him reports about almost everything. Except for John, almost everyone in upper management was seventy to eighty years old. When Jones was vacationing at Saratoga Springs in New York, John reported on the Rice Hotel renovations, "The Petroleum Club is starting to show some of its final form, and I believe you will be pleased when you see it." Then he made a laughing reference to "two rather fantastic murals, which will either greatly stimulate the sale of drinks or cause the members to swear off completely." He also told his uncle, "On the *Chronicle* we have added three experienced men to our news staff that, I believe, have helped the paper materially." In the course of writing about the Worth Hotel and a new building and garage in Fort Worth, John conveyed warm greetings from Amon Carter and suggested that Jesse "talk to a few of the people around the Capitol" who could help them get a construction permit for a new television station. John suggested three names: one was Lyndon Johnson.[140]

Jones had first encountered Johnson at the back of a train when the congressman came to meet President Roosevelt after his vacation in Galveston. According to Johnson biographer Robert Caro, Roosevelt thought he was "a most remarkable young man." As Garner, Sam Rayburn, and Jones lost favor with the president during the mid-1940s, "Roosevelt was, more and more, making Johnson his man in that state: the individual through whom political matters relating to Texas were cleared." Part of Johnson's appeal, Caro explained, was that "with older men who possessed

138. Jesse Jones to Edward N. Maher, February 2, 1951, Jesse H. Jones Collection [HE].
139. *Houston Chronicle*, January 19, 1951.
140. John T. Jones Jr. to Jesse Jones, August 31, 1951, John T. Jones Jr. Collection [HE].

power, Johnson had always been 'a professional son'—utterly deferential ('Yes, sir,' 'No, sir')."[141] Johnson did the same with Jones.

Responding to a favorable *Chronicle* editorial, Johnson expressed his gratitude, and declared, "I will always appreciate your counsel and suggestions on how my services can be improved."[142] He courted the older man, even though Jones had admitted to Johnson in a previous letter, "While a lifelong Democrat, I did not support either President Truman or you in the 1948 election, [but] in neither case was it personal."[143] (Yet it probably was just a little personal, since Jones's break with the Democrats likely reflected lingering resentment of Roosevelt and anyone politically close to him.) Johnson wrote that he agreed with Fulbright's need to investigate the RFC and to tell him how much he appreciated a compliment Jones sent his way: "It gives me more encouragement than I can tell . . . that you think I am doing a good job. I am trying with every energy at my command . . . and I am sure that with . . . your advice and counsel I can come nearer to succeeding than would otherwise have been possible."[144]

In 1951 the RFC was still mired in scandal and Senator Fulbright led the charge to improve its operations. A soured $37 million ($302 million) loan to a bankrupt company that had produced pre-fabricated houses was all over the news. Senator Fulbright introduced a bill to abolish the RFC board and replace it with one administrator, to restrict its lending powers and to forbid secret negotiations. Truman had twice submitted nominees to the RFC board, but the Senate took no action to confirm them.[145] Asked about the proposed bill, Jones said the current personnel were not competent to make decisions, that the Corporation should have been dissolved after the war, and that reorganization would not help because "politicians won't keep their hands off of it." When asked who was responsible, Jones replied, "That is not for me to say," but he remarked that the structure of the organization was less important than the "caliber" of the people who ran it.[146] Against the examiners' advice, the RFC board had recently approved loans to the luxurious Saxony and Sorrento Hotels in Miami Beach.[147]

The RFC actions and Jones's comments shared headlines across the

141. Caro, *Path to Power*, 667–68.
142. December 28, 1950, Lyndon Baines Johnson Papers.
143. December 3, 1950, Lyndon Baines Johnson Papers.
144. April 17, 1951, Lyndon Baines Johnson Papers.
145. *Houston Chronicle*, January 17, 1951.
146. *New York Times*, March 4, 1951.
147. *New York Times*, March 24, 1951.

country. A Fort Wayne, Indiana, newspaper exclaimed, "Senators who want to abolish the Reconstruction Finance Corp. today hailed the renewed support of former Chairman Jesse H. Jones as a valuable weapon in their fight against the Government lending agency."[148] Virginia Senator Harry Byrd Sr. wired Jones, "It would be tremendously helpful if you could . . . testify on abolition of RFC. We have a very hard fight on hand but . . . can win by your appearance."[149] Jones declined, writing, "Circumstances . . . are such that I cannot testify at any . . . definite date." He enclosed a statement and, referring to the earlier letter to Senator Fulbright, said, "There is not much more that I could add," but managed to squeeze in these comments: "There is ample private credit available for all justifiable demands . . . [and] certainly no excuse for making loans . . . to manufacturing and carrying automobiles as in loans . . . to the Kaiser-Frazer Company . . . There is no excuse for government lending on hotels, as in the case of the Florida boom hotels and the Nevada gambling-house hotels. The[y] were made to bail out existing creditors that were well able to carry the loans, and did not increase or add dollars to business."[150]

Legislation was passed to reorganize the RFC, and Stuart Symington became the RFC director.[151] Jones wrote the president to compliment him on the "text and delivery" of a recent speech about foreign policy, then said, "While I am strong[ly] of the opinion that the RFC should be [liquidated,] I believe Stuart Symington will operate it . . . to avoid abuses, and I was very glad you appointed him."[152] Truman thanked Jones and told him the four speeches he enclosed "set out the policy of the Democratic Party."

The following month, Symington revoked the authority of the thirty-two RFC branches to approve and make loans except in cases of disaster. As they had under Jones, branch office staff now received and analyzed loan applications and forwarded recommendations to the Washington office for approval.

After leaving office in 1945, Jones had declined requests to testify before Congress whenever possible. He had not been heard on national radio for years. He expressed himself in written testimony, in letters to individuals, and through the editorial page of his *Houston Chronicle*. Otherwise, he had no platform unless the news services happened to spread

148. *Fort Wayne News-Sentinel,* March 24, 1951.
149. Harry Byrd to Jesse Jones, April 10, 1951, Jesse H. Jones Collection [LOC].
150. Jesse Jones to Harry Byrd, April 20, 1951, Jesse H. Jones Collection [LOC].
151. *New York Times,* April 17, 1951.
152. Jesse Jones to Harry Truman, May 9, 1951, Jesse H. Jones Collection [LOC].

what he had done or said. Feeling the need to set his record straight, Jones had begun writing with journalist Edward Angly a blow-by-blow account of his time in Roosevelt's administration. *Fifty Billion Dollars: My Thirteen Years with the RFC* was published in 1951.

Jones began the book with a dedication and a quote: "I dedicate this story to the memory of my father, William Hasque Jones, from whom I received the precepts which have guided my life, and to the men and women of the Reconstruction Finance Corporation who rendered a great service to our generation in the depression of the early 1930s and in World War II." The book's epigraph came from testimony he had given before a House subcommittee in 1939: "Things nearly always get better if you give them time. That is particularly true with collateral and properties and people."[153]

Then the book launched into a detailed account of just about everything the RFC accomplished during the Great Depression and World War II, including how much each effort cost, and how much each made or lost. Interspersed with the flood of figures that Jones so often recited in speeches and broadcasts were anecdotes, personalities, challenges, a little name-calling, and the author's trenchant opinions about Roosevelt and Wallace, as well as controversies where the writer almost always came out on top. Jones's goals were to record the RFC's accomplishments and settle old scores.

He called Wallace an "incompetent meddler" with "screwball ideas," and titled one chapter, "How Henry Wallace Missed the Presidency." Another was called, "FDR Asks Us to Buy the Empire State Building." In the chapter on "Relations with the Roosevelts, the Cabinet, and Truman," Jones disclosed, "My relations with Franklin D. Roosevelt were cordial from March in 1933—when he inherited me from the Hoover Administration as a director of the RFC—until the January afternoon in 1945 when he asked me to step aside . . . as Secretary of Commerce so that he could reward Henry A. Wallace—whom he had not been able to get renominated for the Vice Presidency at the National Democratic Convention."

Jones disclosed, "However, there were occasional irritations from 1942 onward."[154] Then he recounted all of them on the next fifty-six pages; he called Roosevelt a "total politician" who "changed his tactics whenever politics seemed to dictate, and with no intention of leaving the White House

153. Jones, *Fifty Billion Dollars*, v–vi.
154. Ibid., 255.

until voted out—or carried out."[155] Jones blamed Wallace on Roosevelt and vented, "He liked new ideas, even if they were radical—such as Wallace's plowing up every third row, to reduce agricultural production, and killing little pigs to make meat scarcer, so as to raise prices. I have always thought the reason he liked Wallace so well was that Wallace was always popping up with some new idea—many of them screwball."[156]

Jones was back. Practically every newspaper reviewed his book. Although the reviews came from diverse directions, they arrived at the same conclusions. Samuel Lubell, author of the 1940 *Saturday Evening Post* article that Jones disliked and of Baruch's 1942 rubber report, concluded, "Jones' handling of the RFC's bewilderingly varied operations . . . was certainly the outstanding administrative performance of the Roosevelt period and one of the most skilled in our history." On the other hand, he called Jones to task for claiming that he kept his agency "out of politics." Lubell commented, "Few persons in Washington were deeper in politics than he . . . He held the grandiose balance of power politics between Roosevelt and Congress. Jones, in truth, was the Great Compromise of the Roosevelt-Congress struggle." Lubell explained, "Emergencies kept popping up which required the broadest grants of executive authority. Congress resolved [the] dilemma by entrusting the powers and funds to Jones, setting him up as a parental check on the President." And he observed, "Jones was the leash on the Presidential collar." He said the book "show[ed] what was done and could be done again by government in overcoming economic adversities in a business like way." As a final note, "Jones gives himself the best of the disputes in which he was involved, nowhere confessing major error."[157]

Newsweek editor Raymond Moley—an original member of Roosevelt's "Brain Trust," who later turned against the New Deal and the president—prefaced his review, "In the first weeks of the Roosevelt regime, I met Jones almost daily at the White House and the Treasury." About Jones's independence, Moley wrote, "As his book amply proves, when Roosevelt . . . asked Jones to do something that might have ended in embarrassment or disaster, the master of the RFC shrewdly found ways either to sidetrack the idea or to accomplish the end in a safer, sounder way." Moley speculated, "Perhaps Roosevelt ultimately felt grateful for this means of saving

---

155. Ibid., 260.
156. Ibid., 261.
157. Lubell, "Plus $20 for a Barber," *New York Times*, October 21, 1951.

himself from his own folly, or perhaps he stored up smoldering resentment against Jones. [H]owever, he never risked . . . a break [until the end], for he knew very well that [it] would sweep away his influence with the most influential members of his own party in Congress." Moley stated, "The RFC was, in fact, the keystone of recovery and the foundation of the war effort." And like other reviewers, Moley also observed that, "Jones has the last and best word."[158]

John Kenneth Galbraith similarly observed: "It is Jesse Jones's view that the wisest and most important man in Washington during his years of service . . . was Jesse Jones." He mentioned Jones's battle with Henry Wallace and said, "The author is still very, *very* angry with Wallace and with all the people who worked for him." Galbraith, who had on occasion worked with Jones, marveled at his power, noting, "It came to pass eventually that the RFC could lend (or grant) any amount of money to anyone for anything. It must be conceded that some of FDR's proposals for using th[at] power were unusual." He mentioned the Empire State Building, saying, "Jones sat on the project long enough to allow the impulse to cool, and this was probably just as well."[159]

While Lubell called Jones "the leash on the presidential collar," Galbraith called him the "stubborn hand on the spigot" and claimed, "Not since the time of Charles I has such a power been granted so fully by an English-speaking legislature as . . . to Roosevelt by way of the RFC. This allowed for flexibility and especially for improvisation in fighting the Depression; it was, of course, indispensable for the war." He continued, "As a simple matter of political tactics, this delegation of power became possible because it was to be administered by the conservative and notoriously cautious Jones. But even assuming the power, especially in a liberal Administration, there [needed to] be a stubborn hand on the spigot." Galbraith elaborated on Jones's command of the purse: "For even the President to get money out of the RFC was a grueling task. For anyone else, it assumed the status of a campaign." Galbraith concluded, "[W]hile Jesse Jones may not have been the paragon of fiduciary and political wisdom that he unreluctantly hints, he was not the negative force that some of his Washington contemporaries were inclined to think. On the contrary . . . he was a very useful man even by New Deal standards. If he

158. *Houston Chronicle,* October 15, 1951.
159. Galbraith, *The Reporter,* October 30, 1951.

hadn't existed he would have had to been invented, and that would have been some job."[160]

Symington, the current RFC director, agreed. Jones saw Symington off at the Houston airport after he came to inspect the tin smelter that—like the synthetic rubber plants—was still owned by the government, but operated by a private concern. Symington had finished the first half of Jones's book and said to him in front of the reporters gathered at the airport, "I just don't see how you did it." To keep him off the hook, Jones interrupted and said that Symington did not need to make any more comments about the book. Symington then said to the reporters, "The only thing pertaining to world affairs I will comment on is Mr. Jones."[161] After publishing his detailed story, reading the reviews, and enjoying the success—the book sold by the thousands in Houston—and connecting with the current RFC administrator, Jones must have felt assured about his place in history and satisfied with his life, now devoted to his family, business, and philanthropy.

The following year, Houston Endowment added a scholarship program at Prairie View A&M to train nurses and scholarship programs at other schools to honor both Hoover and Garner. Jones wrote Garner, "Through our foundation, Houston Endowment Inc., we are contributing to the education of between 400 and 500 boys and girls at a dozen or more different colleges and schools throughout the country . . . We would like to create some John Nance Garner scholarships, probably in Public Affairs or Statesmanship [at] the school or college of your choice." Jones explained, "The college selects the students and Houston Endowment Inc. gives the money to the college for the school year."[162] The scholarship program honoring Garner was established at Trinity University in San Antonio. In response to the program in his honor, Hoover wrote, "I suggest that the scholarship should go to the Engineering School of the University of Nevada at Reno. This school is efficient, it is close to the grass-roots, and most of its boys work their way through."[163]

In Houston, the primary focus of their philanthropy, the Joneses donated $600,000 ($4.8 million) to build a library in the Texas Medical Center in 1952. Dr. M. D. Levy, president of the Houston Academy of

160. Ibid.
161. *Houston Chronicle,* October 18, 1951.
162. Jesse Jones to John Nance Garner, June 18, 1952, Jesse H. Jones Collection [HE].
163. Herbert Hoover to Jesse Jones, May 20, 1952 [HE].

Medicine, said at the groundbreaking ceremony, "This is something we have been looking forward to since the creation of our great medical center. [It] would not be complete without a medical library where we can all continue in our studies and keep posted on the latest advances and discoveries in medicine and surgery."[164]

Rabbi Schachtel said prayers, and Mary and Dr. Bertner's widow used shovels to turn the ground for the new building. Leland Anderson, president of the Texas Medical Center board of trustees, pointed out that the groundbreaking was the ninth since building began in 1946.[165]

Dr. William Fields played a key role in the library's development and took Jones on a tour before the building was completed. He remembered walking with Jones and Cameron Fairchild, the architect, into the men's room. Fields recalled, "Mr. Jones looked and realized that he could stand in front of the toilet and look right outside to the walkway. He turns to Fairchild and says, 'Fairchild, is this the way you have it at home?'" They all had a good laugh, and Fairchild quickly had a visual barrier installed across the front window.[166] The library was the only building in Houston that Jones would allow to carry his name during his lifetime.

In 1952, John Jones presented a Jesse H. Jones Scholarship in Journalism at the University of Texas at Austin during the opening of the school's new journalism building. The *Houston Chronicle* commemorated the school and the grant with an editorial, "Journalism School Is Weapon for Freedom," and as it often did, used the opportunity to discredit communism and foment fear about "red" infiltration. The editorial stated, "Public apathy toward incipient tyranny is a menace to freedom" and used Russia as an example of "where the Communists numbered only a relative few of the total population when they took over the country." It continued, "Newspapers form the first line of defense against totalitarianism" and concluded, "Every young person entering the field of journalism must become aware of this responsibility."[167]

All of the Houston newspapers demonized communism, but the *Chronicle* was perhaps a little louder. In his authoritative book, Don Carleton contends that Jones and the Hobbys, who published the *Houston Post*, were offended by Communism, but never anticipated a takeover of the country. Their virulent comments were more of a reaction to avid far left liberals

164. M. D. Levy, speech, Texas Medical Center library groundbreaking, October 15, 1952, Jesse H. Jones Collection [HE].
165. *Houston Chronicle*, October 15, 1952.
166. William Fields to Steven Fenberg, February 7, 1996, Oral History Project [HE].
167. *Houston Chronicle*, November 4, 1952.

and forced unionization, and an attempt to steer voters to Eisenhower.[168] The *Chronicle's* editor, Emmett Walter, was responsible for the content of the columns and Jones allowed him to publish them.

Judging by the *Chronicle's* editorial page, and by Jones's comments about Roosevelt and Wallace in his book and in letters, one might think he had become quite reactionary. However, Jones's hurt over Roosevelt and concerns about communism did not paint a complete picture. On other subjects, such as race relations (considering his time and place), he was fairly progressive.

In 1952, John Jones Jr. wrote a copy editor that "Mr. Jones has . . . made a suggestion relative to the editorial policy of The Chronicle." That meant, "Do this now." John instructed the editor to stop using "Negro" in headlines to identify perpetrators of crimes or victims of accidents, and he gave recent examples that were no longer acceptable, like "an attempted rape by a Negro man," and "four Negro children burned to death."[169] The two most enduring misconceptions about Jones—that he arrived in Houston with nothing and that he became a reactionary late in life—are both inaccurate.

A view of Jones's broadmindedness comes from Ann Holmes, the *Houston Chronicle's* longtime arts editor, who began working at the paper in 1942. In four years she moved from military editor to arts editor, the position for which she had originally applied. Holmes had only encountered Jones while walking through the Chronicle Building lobby and seeing "this giant of a man, with this white hair." She remembered, "He literally looked like Zeus! He was awesome." Holmes said he was also a little shy and looked around corners to see who was there and what they were doing. She added that the Joneses would often call the city desk "about small things." Holmes remembered, "Mrs. Jones would call and say, 'Where is that Louella Parsons column about Hollywood? I don't find it in the paper today.' It was nice that they had that personal touch. It was his newspaper after all."[170]

After becoming arts editor, Holmes wanted to apply to participate in a program that would allow her to travel in Europe for a year to observe how the top arts organizations were operated and why they thrived. Holmes wanted to bring the perspective back to Houston. She asked John, who

---

168. Carleton, *Red Scare!*, 74, 76.

169. John T. Jones Jr., memo, *Houston Chronicle*, November 25, 1952, John T. Jones Jr. Collection [HE].

170. Ann Holmes to Steven Fenberg, February 15, 1996, Oral History Project [HE].

A conference room wall in Jesse Jones's Houston office covered with pictures of people he had worked with and admired. Presidents Woodrow Wilson and Franklin Roosevelt are in the center and surrounded by the others. Another larger portrait of Wilson had a spot of its own and dominated the room.

said, "Well, Miss Annie, I think maybe you should go talk to Uncle Jesse about that." John arranged the appointment and she arrived somewhat nervously.[171] His office was cavernous. The walls of the simply furnished office were covered with copies of autographed political cartoons and signed pictures of notable people he had known, including an oversize picture of Franklin Roosevelt in the middle, indicating Jones had not turned completely away from his colleague of many years. A large portrait of Woodrow Wilson hung in a spot of its own and dominated the room, as did an illustration of downtown Houston's skyline with Jones's buildings colored in red. The bright color filled most of the picture.

Reaching Jones's desk, Holmes sat down and proceeded to tell Jones what she wanted to do. As always, Jones asked a few questions that quickly got to the point. Holmes said that as an arts editor, she felt "provincial." She told Jones, "I do not know enough and I need to go out and get smart."

171. Ibid.

In response, Jones told her to see Gladys Mikell, his secretary, grab a type-writer, and write a letter recommending herself for the program, and he would sign it. Flustered, Holmes left his office and told Mikell what Jones had said. According to Holmes, Mikell laughed and said, "Oh yes, I know that gambit. He does that sort of thing to people all the time. Don't worry, honey. Just write the finest things you can think of, because he's going to change it all anyway." To his staff's amazement, he signed the letter just as Holmes wrote it. With Jones's support, she was accepted and received a one year leave of absence to help Houston become "less provincial."[172]

Jones was anything but provincial. Unusual for the time, Houston Endowment scholarship programs were almost always divided equally between men and women. Even more unique, particularly in the segregated South, many were given to minority students. Replying to a 1952 inquiry from a reporter, Heyne sent a detailed account of the scholarship programs: "The 442 graduate and undergraduate students include 30 Negroes at Prairie View, 12 at Texas Southern University, and 8 at Tuskegee Institute."[173] Scholarships for minorities accounted for more than eleven percent of the total. Many scholarships went to train nurses, and they all reflected Jones's wishes.

Jones once shared, "Most of the appeals come to me direct and will probably as long as I am here. The directors, of course, have the authority, but . . . they will naturally look to me for suggestions." He backed the foundation with substantial resources and revealed, "For several years the Foundation has owned 60% of the capital stock of Commerce Company and is now a substantial stockholder in The National Bank of Commerce."[174]

Jones resisted pigeonholing—in 1952 he contributed to both political parties. In a statement about his contributions, which was published nationally, Jones explained, "I am contributing to the Democratic National Committee to help finance their campaign for Stevenson and to the Republican National Committee for Eisenhower. Because of my Washington service, I have friends in both parties and believe it is desirable that both parties have an opportunity to present their case to the people, all of which costs money."[175] Campaigns now cost more than ever because of the expense of television time and air travel. While Jones served on Houston's welcoming committees for both Stevenson and Eisenhower

172. Ibid.

173. Fred Heyne to W. Marvin Hurley, May 26, 1952, Jesse H. Jones Collection [HE].

174. Jesse Jones to A. C. Newlin, White and Case, April 28, 1953, Jesse H. Jones Collection [HE].

175. *New York Times*, October 29, 1952.

The Joneses with the Eisenhowers. Although he was a Democrat, Jesse Jones supported Republican candidate Dwight D. Eisenhower and wrote to him, "More than ever I want you to be President of the United States."

when they came to campaign, he personally rooted for the Republicans and corresponded with Eisenhower as he had with so many other world leaders. When Eisenhower was selected as the Republican candidate, Jones wrote, "We are all very happy at the outcome of the Convention."[176] After Eisenhower's landslide victory, Jones wrote to the new first lady, "In addition to congratulating the General and you, I just wanted to tell you that your being ever at his side with a beautiful smile and those 'nice bangs' won many votes." He continued, "With all of our modern facilities, gadgets, radio, television, and the airplane, it takes a robust character to go through one of these national campaigns." Jones then advised, "When he goes to Korea, you must see to it that he has two escort planes, and maybe go with him."[177]

The Joneses attended a Houston Symphony opening-night performance on election night. Decked out in gorgeous formal attire, they were featured the next day in the *Chronicle*'s society pages. Part of the caption under their picture said, "When asked how he happened to be at the

176. Jesse Jones to Dwight Eisenhower, July 17, 1952, Jesse H. Jones Collection [HE].
177. Jesse Jones to Mamie Eisenhower, November 5, 1952, Jesse H. Jones Collection [LOC].

symphony instead of by his radio, Mr. Jones smiled and pointed to Mrs. Jones. 'She's why,' he said."[178] Family trumped everything, including politics and business. The previous spring, family concerns had led Jones to reject an attractive offer for the LeRoy Sanitarium in New York because his cousin Jeannette was recuperating there after an accident. He wrote to her, "I decided . . . not [to] sell it because I was afraid it would disturb your peace of mind." He also gave her news about her sister, Gussie, who was now blind and living at the Lamar Hotel. Jones assured Jeannette that Gussie had access at all times to "a Cadillac limousine I used when in Washington."[179] Jones himself rode around in the back of a Ford convertible because, when the top was down, it was easier to get in and out with his bad back. It caused a bit of a spectacle whenever the dark green car pulled up in front of a building on bustling Main Street, the top folded back, and Jones stepped out.

Jones had a new generation to enjoy when his nieces and nephews began having children of their own. John Jr. had three children and named his first boy Jesse Holman Jones II after his uncle. He was called "Jay" for short. Jones wasted no time writing to young Jesse the day he was born, "I am pleased at your arrival and honored that you are to bear my name."[180] Jones also remained as close as ever with Audrey, who with her husband, John, doted on her grandparents. Jones sent her notes and articles about the dangers of smoking and continued to sign his letters "Bods."

In 1953, Jones made plans to demolish his first skyscraper, the Bristol Hotel, and to replace it with what would be his last building in Houston. At seventy-nine, he was busy negotiating deals with prime tenants for his latest building. He was, as he wrote one of his banker friends, ready to "clean up" the Bristol Hotel block, where he was already adding other new buildings and parking garages.[181] He was also corresponding frequently with Lyndon Johnson, now Senate minority leader, mostly about the rubber plants and the tin smelter near Houston. In March Jones wrote that he thought the plants should be sold, adding, "but we should not give the properties away for a few cents on the dollar, as most other plants we built in the war . . . were." Still sore about the RFC's poor record after he left, he continued, "Most of them were sacrificed . . . if they had been handled in a business-like manner . . . the Federal Treasury would be much better

---

178. *Houston Chronicle,* November 4, 1952.
179. Jesse Jones to Jeanette Jones, April 23, 1952, Jesse H. Jones Collection [UT].
180. Jesse Jones to Jesse Jones II, October 24, 1951, Jesse H. Jones Collection [UT].
181. Jesse Jones to W. P. Hamblen Sr., March 24, 1953, Jesse H. Jones Collection [UT].

off." As for the rubber plants, Jones directed, "When the plants are sold, the purchaser[s] should be required to continue them in operation to a substantial extent." He warned, "We should never be caught again like we were when it was necessary to build those plants."[182]

Johnson responded, gushing, "I am indebted and strengthened by your letter regarding the disposal of Government rubber facilities to private industry. My . . . personal study of the Government's rubber facilities, as well as its tin facilities, convinced me of two things: First, except for your extreme vision and foresight, as well as your prudent business judgment, the American taxpayers would have had to ante up many additional millions, and perhaps billions, in tribute to both the British Empire and the tin cartel, and Second, our defense posture would have been materially diluted except for these actions taken by you which have generally gone unnoticed."[183] Although they were not close, the following month Johnson wrote again, "Bird and I were . . . hoping you could be here this coming Friday for the party we are giving for the Hobbys and the Andersons."[184] Jones turned down the invitation, pleading poor health.

Since battling pneumonia in 1944, Jones had had bouts with the flu and seemed more susceptible to colds, but each time he got back up and kept going. In mid-July 1953, Jones was rushed to the hospital for emergency gall bladder surgery. This time he did not recover quite so fast.[185] Bascom Timmons reported that the surgery, a major procedure at that time, "was followed by a nip-and-tuck struggle for life."[186] Fields, the neurologist who had taken Jones on a tour of the library building, was called in to consult. He recalled, "I could hear this man actually shouting and bellowing in the next room. He was there in bed with his arms and legs tied down holding him, and there were several people in attendance. He was clearly out of his head." Fields realized Jones had a collapsed lung and immediately intervened.[187] Because of his diagnosis and action, Jones survived. At the end of July, among many other well-wishers, Senator Johnson wrote, "The news that you are out of the woods was the best I have had in a long time. I am delighted that you feel well enough to 'sit up and read the newspaper.'"[188]

182. March 13, 1953, Lyndon Baines Johnson Papers.
183. March 17, 1953, Lyndon Baines Johnson Papers.
184. April 13, 1953, Lyndon Baines Johnson Papers.
185. *Houston Chronicle*, July 12, 1953.
186. Timmons, *Jones: Man and Statesman*, 388.
187. William Fields to Steven Fenberg, February 7, 1996, Oral History Project [HE].
188. July 30, 1953, Lyndon Baines Johnson Papers.

(left to right) Senator Edwin C. Johnson of Colorado, Jesse Jones, and Senator Lyndon B. Johnson of Texas attend the Independent Natural Gas Association of America meeting at the Rice Hotel in 1950. Senator Lyndon Johnson treated Jones with great deference and respect. Courtesy *Houston Chronicle*.

Jones slowly resumed his activities and toward the end of the year honored his past with a $50,000 ($397,000) donation to help build a new hospital in Springfield, Tennessee. Earlier, he had sent a small donation to help the Hopewell Church; in responding to the request from a distant cousin, Jones wrote, "I am glad to know that Hopewell is still a church. My father took a great interest in it, and I recall it a little. In fact, I went to school at the little Hopewell schoolhouse." He continued, "You will be interested to know that my sister Ida Garrett is now in her 85th year . . . I guess we have all lived our full time."[189] He may have felt that way, but Jones continued to form new businesses and to look ahead.

In place of the Bristol Hotel, Jones built the eighteen-story Houston Club Building with an attached garage. Although new office buildings, bank buildings, and parking garages under construction by Jones and others made downtown look like a giant erector set, suburban houses and shopping centers accounted for the majority of the record-breaking

189. Jesse Jones to to Bela D. King, January 31, 1953, Jesse H. Jones Collection [UT].

number of building permits in 1954.[190] Jones also pursued his interest in television. In 1954, Houston had three television stations, including the University of Houston's KUHT, the first public station in the country. Four parties had been competing for years for the last VHF license in Houston, and they finally came together as one group to procure the last spot on the dial. The Jones Interests took a one-third ownership in the new station; by contract and through publicity it would become known as "The Chronicle Station."[191] Significantly, John T. Jones Jr.—not his uncle Jesse—had negotiated with the three other parties, and he became the new company's president.

Jones, however, was still in the saddle at the National Bank of Commerce. He wrote a letter to the shareholders in early 1954, exclaiming that 1953 had been "our best year from every standpoint—gross and net earnings, facilities offered, and customers served." He said, "This was our 32nd year of continuous dividends" and reported, "Benefits provided for our personnel include a Christmas bonus, group life, hospital, and health insurance, and a retirement plan."[192] Jones always looked out for his employees, one of many reasons why they were so loyal and devoted. When August Waites, a parking attendant and Jones's occasional driver, lost retirement benefits after he was transferred from a hotel garage to the bank garage, Jones wrote Heyne with a plan to renew his status.[193] On another occasion, after a Rice Hotel laundry staff member had been hospitalized and well cared for, the laundry manager wrote Heyne, "I wish to personally thank the Jones Interests for the nearly two hundred other employees here at the Rice Hotel Laundry who are so liberally protected and cared for . . . We are proud of the fact that no other laundry in the entire nation has a program for its employees that will come near ours."[194]

Jones remained in touch with Senator Johnson, who wrote more frequently as the RFC's termination date approached, and the status of the tin smelter and rubber plants became more pressing. He wrote Jones, "Your judgment would be deeply appreciated, because your opinion is worth more than that of any one in America."[195] Many wanted the government-owned smelter shut down. Johnson and Jones wanted it open until it could

190. *Houston Chronicle,* October 31, 1954.

191. "Proposed Consolidation," December 31, 1953, Jesse H. Jones Collection [HE].

192. Jesse Jones, National Bank of Commerce shareholders letter, January 8, 1954, Jesse H. Jones Collection [HE].

193. Jesse Jones to Fred Heyne, January 14, 1953, Jesse H. Jones Collection [HE].

194. L. R. Pell to Fred Heyne, September 16, 1953, Jesse H. Jones Collection [HE].

195. February 19, 1954, Lyndon Baines Johnson Papers.

be sold to someone who promised to keep it going. Johnson included a copy of the *Congressional Record* where his remarks and the Senate's resolutions concerning the smelter were published. In part, he said, "With the start of the Korean war in June of 1950, we were again faced with a serious tin crisis" as "foreign producers and smelters of tin engaged in a campaign to gouge the American taxpayer." He reminded the legislators, "Because we had the smelter . . . we were able effectively to stop the skyrocketing of tin prices and return them to a more normal level."[196]

Johnson then warned, "Today this country faces a critical situation in Indochina. What that situation will produce no one can predict . . . Asiatic countries normally produce 65 percent of the free world's tin supply. If Indochina falls, all of those countries will be threatened . . . In the face of these facts, we find government officials today planning to close the American tin smelter." Johnson concluded, "If Congress does not act promptly, the American smelter will be closed, and we will have lost our most effective force against the constant danger of price and production domination by the international tin combine. We will have lost the most effective tin weapon in our national security arsenal." Johnson submitted resolutions to keep the smelter open and for Congress to conduct a "study . . . of the desirability of a permanent domestic tin-smelting industry and the adequacy of our strategic stockpile of tin and emergency sources of supply."[197]

Johnson notified Jones that success seemed assured. Jones wrote back, "Your telegram received, and the news is excellent," and added by hand, "Keep up the good work."[198] On May 27 the Senate Armed Services Committee voted unanimously to continue operations. In anticipation of the RFC's June 30 dissolution, President Eisenhower subsequently transferred all of its operations and assets, including the rubber plants and the tin smelter, to the Treasury Department.[199] Upon the Corporation's demise, the new Small Business Administration took over lending operations where the RFC had left off. Jones and Johnson continued to exchange letters about tax policies, states rights, United Nations delegates, and obtaining direct air service from the east and west coasts to Houston.

Johnson wrote when Jones's picture appeared on the July 5 cover of *Newsweek* magazine when Houston's population had reached one million

---

196. Johnson, Speaking on smelter resolution on April 14, 1954.
197. Ibid.
198. May 27, 1954, Lyndon Baines Johnson Papers.
199. *New York Times,* June 30, 1954.

In its July 5, 1954, cover story, *Newsweek* magazine reported, "Without Jones, Greater Houston this week could not celebrate the arrival of its millionth citizen." Courtesy *Houston Chronicle*.

citizens. The picture placed Jones between a pretty young girl and an oil derrick. Jones showed his age, but he still looked robust and commanding, albeit like someone's grandfather. Through statistical estimates, the Houston Chamber of Commerce determined that July 3 was the big day when the one millionth person would move to town, and the city boosters planned events around "M Day" that included parties, parades, and a commemorative ceremony at Miller Outdoor Theatre in Hermann Park. The Chamber invited Jones to attend, writing, "In passing the million mark, Metropolitan Houston (Harris County) will be the first in the South and Southwest with that distinction . . . Your presence will add a great deal to the observance."[200] On the big day, Jones was interviewed on CBS's "News of America" radio program. He spoke from experience, noting, "From a city of 45,000 people 50 years ago, to a metropolis of 1,000,000 people is the story of Houston, which is being celebrated this week." Looking ahead, he said, "Now for another stretch of 50 years and, I hope, another

200. June 8, 1954, Jesse H. Jones Collection [HE].

progress report from my namesake, Jesse Jones II, now 2 years of age."[201] *Newsweek* reported, "Without Jones, Greater Houston this week could not celebrate the arrival of its millionth citizen. Without Jones, the city skyline might look more like some soft small bumps."[202]

That evening, thousands celebrated at the outdoor amphitheater, and Jones and other dignitaries presented flowers and an assortment of prizes to Barney Clifton McCasland Jr., identified as the one millionth citizen who had just moved with his wife and five children from Jackson, Mississippi, to take a job with Cities Service Oil Company. The Chamber gave the McCaslands groceries for a year, a trip around the United States, and a new Chevrolet sedan. Indicative of the times, McCasland said, "Wouldn't you know, I just went in debt for a new Ford station wagon." Later in the ceremony, Mayor Roy Hofheinz said, "It is the beginning of a new era."[203]

In the multi-page article, *Newsweek* focused primarily on the Houston Ship Channel, saying, "More ships pass through here than through the Panama Canal . . . It's an avenue of industry with 150 major plants, everything from steel to synthetic rubber." The magazine did not say that forty years earlier Jones had raised Houston's share of the funds to develop the channel in one of the first private-public partnerships with the federal government, and that he had been the first chairman of the Houston Harbor Board. The article recounted how natural gas had gone from a wasted by-product to the "sixth largest industry in the United States, edging close to oil and coal as a main fuel for power," but failed to mention the pivotal role the RFC's two "Inch" pipelines had played in the conversion. The article also declared, "Petrochemical is a word that meant nothing to Houston fourteen years ago." Again, the magazine did not recognize Jones's or the government's role when the DPC, Defense Supplies Corporation, Rubber Reserve Company, Metals Reserve Company, and other RFC subsidiaries commenced business fourteen years before. The article said that eighty-five percent of the nation's petrochemical plants and "90 producers of basic chemicals turning out 200 different products" were now based in the greater Houston area.[204]

Other national publications also carried stories about Houston's new status. The *New York Times* said, "There really doesn't seem to be a foreseeable end to the growth of Houston and environs so long as the indus-

201. *Houston Chronicle,* July 3, 1954.
202. "Special Report: Greater Houston."
203. *Houston Chronicle,* July 4, 1954.
204. "Special Report: Greater Houston."

tries keep on growing and new ones keep coming in." Like *Newsweek* and others, it reported that in natural resources, "the 200 or so miles along the Gulf Coast which contains Houston . . . is the richest area of its size in the world." The reporter also observed, "One of the striking things about Harris County, in which Houston is situated, is that it contains more cattle than any other of the 254 Texas counties."[205] That would not be the case for long. The week after "M Day," developer Frank Sharp announced a new subdivision of 15,000 homes on what had been the 4,000-acre Westmoreland Farm. More than twenty miles from downtown, Sharpstown was only one of many housing developments to come.[206]

When Jones first came to see his Uncle M. T. and Aunt Louisa and his cousins Jeannette, Gussie, and Will (with his then-wife, Mary) in the 1890s, he stepped off the train into a small town with horses and buggies plodding up and down the sometimes muddy downtown streets, lined with small business buildings and graceful mansions. By wielding the combined power of business, civic leadership, philanthropy, and government to create a community where people could thrive, Jones was instrumental in turning that village into a sprawling, vibrant metropolis with subdivisions, shopping malls, highways, and hundreds of thousands of cars. The *New York Times* reporter wondered who would lead Houston into the future and wrote, "Jesse Jones, who loves property that he can see and touch (that is why he became a real-estate millionaire instead of a really big oil millionaire), will have to stop work before much longer; indeed, he is already cutting down on his activities."[207]

Instead of his uncle, John Jones was center stage when KTRK-TV went on the air with a televised inaugural gala in November. John gave a speech; the Houston Symphony performed on television for the first time; Marguerite Piazza from New York's Metropolitan Opera and ventriloquist Señor Wences performed; and a group of thirteen dancers dressed as Channel 13's black cats danced between performances.[208] Extensive newspaper coverage about Houston's third commercial station never even mentioned Jesse Jones.[209] One article said, "John Tilford Jones Jr., youthful president of The Chronicle, was elected president by Houston Consolidated Television Co. in February, a month after several applicants for Channel 13 had merged to form the company that operates KTRK-TV." Another explained,

205. *New York Times*, August 1, 1954.
206. *Houston Chronicle*, July 10, 1954.
207. *New York Times*, August 1, 1954.
208. *Houston Chronicle*, November 17, 1954.
209. *Houston Chronicle*, November 19, 1954.

"The consolidation brought together the cream of Houston's business, financial, and civic leadership in a single enterprise." John was counted as a "chief figure."[210] Though his uncle was not mentioned at all, he had not been left out entirely—he had negotiated behind the scenes with the network presidents. But he had avoided partnerships throughout his business life, and at this point he was probably reluctant to become involved even though one of his companies owned the largest block of stock.

Jones was more focused on Main Street than he was on television. Main Street retail had conglomerated along downtown's southern edge and for all intents and purposes gone no farther south than eleven blocks from Buffalo Bayou. Jones and Stanley Marcus batted letters back and forth concerning Neiman-Marcus's purchase of the Fashion department store in Jones's Kirby Building in the 900 block. Marcus intended to keep the Fashion name on the store because, as he later recalled, after operating only in Dallas, "We didn't realize our own capability to open a store that would be accepted immediately by the public. We thought we needed something that was already existent. After about six months, we changed the name to Neiman-Marcus."[211] The exclusive store on Houston's Main Street was the retailer's first outside of the Dallas-Fort Worth area, but it would not be its last. During negotiations with Jones, Marcus also bought a twenty-two-acre tract of land far west of downtown in what would become known as the Galleria area.[212] Meanwhile, Sakowitz had moved its store south from Jones's Gulf Building to its own new, elegant building across from Foley's. In 1955 Neiman's, Sakowitz, and Foley's—three of the most sophisticated and up-to-date stores in the country—were clustered in downtown's south end. From the 12th block on, downtown practically ended.

Houston was changing and growing, and Jones was acutely conscious of the passing time. John Goodloe, who began work at the RFC in 1932 and eventually succeeded Jones as chairman, wrote his former boss about a get-together with some of the "old-timers" and told Jones his ears "should have been burning."[213] Jones thanked him for the letter and shared, "The years we have lived have been relatively happy ones, but with all the modern inventions, and talk about space stations and space travel circling the earth, our time may be regarded as pioneer days."[214] Jones's sister Ida

---

210. Ibid.
211. Stanley Marcus to Steven Fenberg, March 4, 1996, Oral History Project [HE].
212. *Houston Chronicle*, December 20, 1964.
213. John Goodloe to Jesse Jones, July 29, 1955, Jesse H. Jones Collection [UT].
214. Jesse Jones to John Goodloe, August 2, 1955, Jesse H. Jones Collection [UT].

(left to right) Milton Backlund, Fred Heyne, Jesse Jones, and John T. Jones Jr. in Jones's downtown Houston office. John T. Jones Jr. became president of Houston Endowment, the *Houston Chronicle,* and other Jones Interests entities. Jesse Jones gave all of his buildings and corporations to Houston Endowment; in response to the Tax Reform Act of 1969, they were sold and the proceeds were invested in securities. The 1987 sale of the *Houston Chronicle* to the Hearst Corporation completed the process. In 2011 Houston Endowment had assets of approximately $1.5 billion. Since its inception, the foundation has donated more than $1.5 billion primarily to organizations that serve the greater Houston area to help fulfill the Joneses' vision of a vibrant community where the opportunity to thrive is available to all.

was his last living sibling and the only one besides him who remembered their childhood days on the Tennessee tobacco farm. Along with Gussie, she was also one of the last family members living at the Lamar Hotel. On her eighty-sixth birthday at the end of December, Jones wrote, "I am reminded today that you are passing another milestone, but I am close behind and am apt to catch up if you don't walk a little faster. It has been a fine life for both of us and we should be thankful."[215]

As he turned eighty, Jones began tying up familial and philanthropic loose ends. Houston Endowment donated a block of land across the street from St. Paul's Methodist Church (where Bonwit-Teller had planned to build a store) for an activities and education center. Over the years, St. Paul's had built two sanctuaries and Jones had served as the building committee's chairman both times. As a commemorative plaque on the sanctuary's

215. Jesse Jones to Ida Garrett, December 20, 1955, Jesse H. Jones Collection [UT].

lobby wall testifies, his Aunt Louisa had donated the bells in the church tower "to the glory of God and in memory of Martin Tilford Jones."[216]

Houston Endowment also made a grant to Rice Institute to buy a rare collection of first edition eighteenth-century English plays in memory of Dr. Stockton Axson, the first head of Rice's English Department, Wilson's brother-in-law, and the Joneses' dear friend.[217] Rice President W. W. Houston explained to Jones that the collection, which "includes more than half the plays published in Great Britain between 1700 and 1800, would be of great value in scholarly work, and would put the Fondren Library on somewhat the same level in this field as the Huntington Library and the Harvard Library."[218] Jones had told Houston Endowment's trustees five years before that he was looking for a way to honor Dr. Axson, and he finally found an appropriate tribute.[219]

The city's growing universities provided him with the perfect way to honor his wife and Heyne, the man he called "his other self" who could sign his name as if it were Jones's. In late 1955, John T. Jones Jr. informed Heyne, "I have this week made an oral commitment to General Bruce on behalf of the trustees of Houston Endowment in the approximate amount of $1,000,000 [$7.9 million], this money to be expended for the construction of a college classroom building on the campus of the University of Houston . . . I have kept Mr. Jesse Jones informed of my actions in regard to the university and this grant, and he is in accord."[220] Jones subsequently instructed General A. D. Bruce, the university president, on the building's name, writing, "Our stipulation will be that the building be named for my associate of a half-century, Fred J. Heyne, without whose association I could not have spent thirteen years in public service in Washington."[221] To meet growing demand for classroom space, the foundation added $500,000 ($3.95 million) to the grant to enlarge the building before it was even under construction. According to a newspaper report, Heyne knew about the grant, but discovered the building would carry his name only after he read it on the front page of the *Houston Chronicle*.[222]

---

216. *Houston Chronicle*, April 24, 1955; St. Paul's Methodist Church, Jesse H. Jones Collection [HE].

217. *Houston Chronicle*, December 21, 1955.

218. W. W. Houston to Jesse Jones, December 13, 1955, Jesse H. Jones Collection [HE].

219. February 18, 1950, Jesse H. Jones Collection [HE].

220. John T. Jones Jr. to Fred Heyne, November 23, 1955, Jesse H. Jones Collection [HE].

221. Jesse Jones to A. D. Bruce, January 16, 1956, Jesse H. Jones Collection [HE].

222. *Houston Chronicle*, September 1, 1963.

To honor Mary, Houston Endowment made a $1 million ($7.9 million) grant for dormitories at Rice Institute that would allow women to live on campus for the first time since the university opened in 1913. George R. Brown, chairman of the board of trustees, said in a published statement about the new Mary Gibbs Jones College for Women, "Rice has been trying to obtain the money for the girls' dormitory since the school was founded." He also said the building's name was an "appropriate monument to this great lady."[223] The three buildings, arranged in a U-shape and connected by covered walkways, accommodated 210 girls. Each dormitory floor included a lounge area, a kitchen, and laundry facilities. One newspaper article exclaimed, "All buildings will be completely air conditioned."[224]

W. N. (Bill) Blanton had first met Jones when he boarded a train in east Texas to warn him about the crowds, banners, and bands waiting in the next town to thank him for bringing the 1928 Democratic national convention to Houston. Blanton had moved to Houston soon after, had become president of the Chamber of Commerce, and through the years had cultivated a warm, collegial relationship with Jones. After the Rice donation was announced, Blanton wrote Jones, "Rice Institute has long been in serious need of equal facilities for its young women. Generations of our citizens of the future will bless the memory of you and your wonderful wife for making possible a better world." He continued, "How truly it can be said that Mr. and Mrs. Jesse H. Jones found Houston a city of wood and dirt, and left it a metropolis of marble and beauty."[225]

As 1956 began, Jones continued to correspond with Marcus about reconfiguring the Main Street store. He also traded letters at least weekly with Jeannette, who lived at his Mayfair House in New York. He reported, "We are all fairly well here except that I cannot run as fast nor jump as high as I once could, but with Mr. Heyne and my own two efficient secretaries, I manage to get along very well."[226] In late February he wrote, "We were honored last night at the Rice, some ten or twelve hundred people. I was selected as the citizen that had done the most for the city the past year. So, today I am a little tired."[227]

In March, Timmons gave Jones the good news that Henry Holt & Company had agreed to publish his biography that Timmons had been

223. *Houston Chronicle,* November 17, 1955.

224. *Houston Chronicle,* December 30, 1955.

225. W. N. (Bill) Blanton to Jesse Jones, November 18, 1955, Jesse H. Jones Collection [HE].

226. Jesse Jones to Jeanette Jones, January 21, 1956, Jesse H. Jones Collection [HE].

227. Jesse Jones to Jeanette Jones, February 23, 1956, Jesse H. Jones Collection [HE].

working on for the past few years.[228] Later that month, Jones's life came full circle with the opening of the Jesse H. Jones Hospital in Springfield, Tennessee. His nephew John stood in his place at the ceremony, where more than six thousand people traveled in from their homes in the Tennessee hills and thronged the opening events. John unveiled a portrait of Jones for the hospital lobby and announced that, in addition to the $50,000 ($390,000) donation for the building, Houston Endowment had established a fund to assist indigent patients who needed treatment at the hospital. The fund was named in honor of Jesse's father, William Hasque Jones.[229] While visiting the family's old stomping grounds, John explored his roots, visited ancestral homes, and met and talked with people who knew his family. He took pictures and showed them to his uncle when he returned to Houston, describing what he saw, whom he met, and what was going on in Jones's rural childhood home from so long ago.[230]

On March 27, Lyndon Johnson wrote Jones a letter of thanks "for the fine editorial comments" about a bill he had recently sponsored.[231] Johnson received a reply on April 6, the day after Jones's eighty-second birthday, saying, "Your letter of March 27 to Mr. Jones has been received during his indefinite absence from the office. It will be brought to his attention upon his return."[232]

Jones's kidneys were failing and he was in the hospital.[233] On May 28, rumors surfaced of his condition. Lyndon Johnson received a memo from an assistant that said, "Jesse Jones will not likely live through the night" and that the Associated Press wanted "a statement from you this afternoon to use in the event he dies."[234] Anne Holmes recalled, "There was a death watch at the paper that was very sad because he was declining and everybody was just waiting for the word."[235] That word finally came. Jesse Jones died on June 1, at 8:30 p.m. in St. Luke's Hospital at the Texas Medical Center. The papers said the cause was "uremic poisoning," or kidney failure.

Jones's body was moved to the George H. Lewis Funeral Home, where his employees stood watch over their beloved boss around the clock from

228. Bascom Timmons to Jesse Jones, March 2, 1956, Jesse H. Jones Collection [HE].
229. *Robertson County Times*, March 29, 1956.
230. John T. Jones Jr. to Garner Fuqua, March 28, 1956, Jesse H. Jones Collection [HE].
231. March 27, 1956, Lyndon Baines Johnson Papers.
232. R. McKinnon to Lyndon Johnson, April 6, 1956, Lyndon Baines Johnson Papers.
233. Timmons, *Jones: Man and Statesman*, 390.
234. May 28, 1956, Lyndon Baines Johnson Papers.
235. Ann Holmes to Steven Fenberg, February 15, 1996, Oral History Project [HE].

Saturday morning until the funeral service on Monday, June 4. Milton Backlund sent John Jones a list of those who participated and said that they "considered it an honor and served on the watch with a great deal of affection and emotion."[236] During that time more than 1,500 people came to pay their respects.

Newspapers across the nation eulogized Jones and published tributes from Presidents Eisenhower, Truman, and Hoover. Eisenhower said, "Jesse H. Jones' life is a record of extraordinary achievement both as private citizen and public official. He will be . . . remembered as one of the great builders and philanthropists of the South and as a loyal and effective public servant to the nation."[237] Truman said, "I knew Mr. Jones well and liked him very much. He did an outstanding job as head of the Reconstruction Finance Corporation."[238] Hoover simply said, "I greatly grieve the loss of a personal friend of so many years."[239]

Vice President Richard Nixon got in on the act, perpetuating the most common misconception about Jones when he said, "From conditions of poverty, he rose to be one of the truly powerful men of this country." Complimenting Jones's clean record, Nixon also said (with unanticipated irony), "His lending of $50 billion [$390 billion] when he was chairman of the Reconstruction Finance Corp. without a breath of scandal is an epitaph in itself."[240] Timmons—Jones's biographer and a longtime Washington correspondent—reported, "Mrs. Woodrow Wilson, widow of the president who first called Jones to Washington, said Jones long had the confidence of the World War I president." She added, "He and Mrs. Jones have been my most devoted friends for years."[241] In an unlikely tribute for a southern white businessman, C. W. Rice, publisher of Houston's *Negro Labor News*, wired the *Houston Chronicle*'s editor, "The Negro citizens join the millions in mourning the death of Jesse H. Jones. His greatness was demonstrated by the interest manifested in the welfare of humanity regardless of race, creed, or station in life. Texas and the nation have truly lost a great citizen."[242]

Two thousand people filed by Jones's copper coffin at St. Paul's Meth-

236. Milton Backlund to John T. Jones Jr., June 4, 1956, Jesse H. Jones Collection [HE].
237. *New York Times*, June 3, 1956.
238. *Houston Chronicle*, June 2, 1956.
239. *New York Times*, June 3, 1956.
240. *Houston Chronicle*, June 2, 1956.
241. Ibid.
242. C. W. Rice to Emmett Walter, June 2, 1956, Jesse H. Jones Collection [HE].

odist Church to pay their last respects before the funeral service began.[243] The family requested charitable donations in Jones's memory instead of flowers, but an enormous arrangement from Edith Wilson and a small one from the Houston Street & News Boys' Club graced Jones's coffin. The family arrived in two limousines and went directly to a private office as mourners filled the thousand-seat sanctuary. Holmes recalled, "I couldn't even get in. It was . . . like a great affair of state, as it should have been."[244] The enormous pipe organ filled the church with "Oh, Come Let Us Adore Him" as the family filed into the first row. Mary was the last to enter. At Jones's request, the service was short and simple—over in fifteen minutes.[245] Family members, including John T. Jones Jr., John Beck, and George Butler, carried the casket to the hearse, and Mary, Audrey, and the Heynes followed it to Forest Park cemetery over roads that Jones had covered in shell fifty years before, passing through areas that had been dense forest when he first came to Houston in the 1890s. At the private graveside ceremony, the fifty or so family members and close friends could look west and see Jones's downtown skyline. To the east rose the growing metal mass of the petrochemical plants along the Houston Ship Channel. As Jones's coffin was lowered into the ground, St. Paul's Pastor Neal Cannon said, "We commit his body to its final resting place, but his spirit we commend to God."[246]

Lyndon Johnson said, "Texas will just not be the same with Jesse Jones gone. He caught the early vision of our State, and . . . helped in the building of it. He was part of it and of us. All of his labors were bent toward the building of a better Texas and a better America. We will miss his greatness, and we will miss his very genuine contributions to our country."[247]

Jesse Jones combined capitalism and public service to build a city, make money, and improve his community. As an appointed government official, he combined capitalism and public service to rescue his nation and to help save the world from facism and imperialism. During the Great Depression, Jones and the RFC bought stock in banks, recapitalized them, enabled them to lend again, and saved the nation's financial system from complete dissolution. When scared bankers would not lend their fresh capital, the RFC breathed life into the moribund economy by making

243. *Houston Chronicle,* June 5, 1956.
244. Ann Holmes to Steven Fenberg, February 15, 1996, Oral History Project [HE].
245. *Houston Press,* June 5, 1956.
246. Ibid.
247. Lyndon Johnson, statement on Jesse Jones, June 1, 1956, Lyndon Baines Johnson Papers.

loans to homeowners, farmers, businessmen, railroads, and disaster victims. When private business was unable or unwilling to function, Jones and the RFC filled the gap and typically generated profits for the government. In a shining example, the RFC helped bring electricity to rural areas; arranged for cash-strapped farmers to buy toasters, water pumps, fans, refrigerators, and radios on credit so they could use the new power and have better lives; helped local banks and retailers; and in the process, made money for the government.

After the Korean War, the synthetic rubber plants that the RFC built before Pearl Harbor were finally put up for sale by the government. The bidding process began in 1953 and concluded in April 1955 with the sale of twenty-four of the twenty-seven wartime plants. When title for the first three transferred to private hands, the *New York Times* reported, "The Government's second-largest industrial monopoly will start breaking up today," and added that the synthetic rubber initiative was "exceeded in magnitude only by the atomic energy program."[248] Proceeds from selling the plants, along with income from rubber sales during and after World War II, resulted in a handsome profit for the government, which had financed and nurtured the vital industry from infancy to mass production in less than two years. At the time of the sale, the plants were running at full capacity. And as Jones had wished, the United States no longer depended on foreign sources for the essential commodity.[249]

When Colonel Edward Mandell House first brought Jones to Woodrow Wilson's attention, he sold him as "the type of young Southern man we ought to interest in public service."[250] Jones's perspective, personality, and vision, along with his administrative and entrepreneurial skills, enabled him to build a thriving city, to help save his vulnerable nation, and to show that government works when a capitalist with his eye on the bottom line and on the common good is in charge.

248. *New York Times*, April 21, 1955.
249. White, *Billions for Defense*, 109.
250. Bascom Timmons to the *Houston Chronicle*, June 2, 1956, Jesse H. Jones Collection [HE].

Bibliography

Adams, Mildred. "The Man Who Lends Uncle Sam's Money." *The New York Times Magazine*, February 4, 1934.

Alter, Jonathan. *The Defining Moment: FDR's Hundred Days and the Triumph of Hope*. New York: Simon & Schuster, 2006.

American Red Cross Annual Report. Washington, D.C.: American Red Cross, 1918.

"American Red Cross Nursing: A Tradition of Service." Exhibition notes. Washington, D.C.: American Red Cross Museum, 2000.

"Angelina County." In *The New Handbook of Texas*, edited by Ron Tyler, et al. Austin: Texas State Historical Association, 1996.

Audrey Jones Beck Collection. Houston Endowment Archive, Houston.

Barnstone, Howard. *The Architecture of John F. Staub: Houston and the South*. Austin, Texas: University of Texas Press for Museum of Fine Arts, Houston, 1979.

Beck, Audrey Jones, comp. *The Collection of John A. and Audrey Jones Beck*. Houston: Museum of Fine Arts, Houston, 1998.

"Billions Wild." Editorial. *Saturday Evening Post* (December 7, 1940).

Blum, John Morton. Interview. In *Brother Can You Spare a Billion? The Story of Jesse H. Jones*. DVD. Directed by Eric Stange. Steven Fenberg, Executive Producer. Houston: Houston Public Television Home Video, 2000.

Brink, Wellington. "Jesse Jones: Chairman of the RFC." *Holland's: The Magazine of the South* (August 1934).

Buenger, Walter L. "Between Community and Corporation: The Southern Roots of Jesse H. Jones and the Reconstruction Finance Corporation." *Journal of Southern History* 56, (1990): 483, 491.

Buenger, Walter L. Interview. In *Brother Can You Spare a Billion? The Story of Jesse H. Jones*. DVD. Directed by Eric Stange. Steven Fenberg, Executive Producer. Houston: Houston Public Television Home Video, 2000.

Buenger, Walter L., and Joseph A. Pratt. *But Also Good Business: Texas Commerce Banks and the Financing of Houston*. College Station: Texas A&M University Press, 1986.

Burrough, Bryan. *The Big Rich: The Rise and Fall of the Greatest Texas Oil Fortunes*. New York: Penguin Press, 2009.

"Business and Government." Editorial. *Fortune* (May 1940).

Carleton, Don E. *Red Scare!: Right-wing Hysteria, Fifties Fanaticism, and Their Legacy in Texas*. Austin, TX: Texas Monthly Press, 1985.

Caro, Robert A. *The Path to Power*. New York: Knopf, 1982.

Carroll, Jim. "Skyliner Jesse H. Jones: The Autocrat of Main Street." *Preview of Texas* (July 1951).

Chapman, Betty. "Swank Rice Hotel Reflected Grandeur of Early Houston." *Houston Business Journal* (November 1–7, 1996).

Chapman, Betty Trapp. *Historic Photos of Houston*. Nashville, TN: Turner Publishing Company, 2007.

Creel, George. "Hard-Boiled Jesse." *Collier's* (February 1936).

Cox, Patrick. *The First Texas News Barons*. Austin: University of Texas Press, 2005.

Culver, John C., and John Hyde. *American Dreamer: The Life and Times of Henry A. Wallace*. New York: Norton, 2000.

Dallas Public Library Collection, Dallas, TX.

Davison, Henry P. *The American Red Cross in the Great War, 1917–1919*. New York: Macmillan, 1919.

Dingus, Anne. "Last Page." *Texas Monthly* (November 1996).

Dock, Lavinia L., et al. *History of American Red Cross Nursing*. New York: Macmillan, 1922.

Dulles, Foster Rhea. *The American Red Cross: A History*. New York: Harper, 1950.

Ellis, Edward Robb. *A Nation in Torment: The Great American Depression, 1929–1939*, rev. ed. New York: Kodansha International, 1995.

Fleming, Thomas. *The New Dealers' War: FDR and the War within World War II*. New York: Basic Books, 2001.

Flora, Joseph M., and Lucinda H. MacKethan, eds. *The Companion to Southern Literature: Themes, Genres, Places, People, Movements, and Motifs*. Baton Rouge: Louisiana State University Press, 2002.

Fossedal, Gregory A. *Our Finest Hour: Will Clayton, the Marshall Plan, and the Triumph of Democracy*. Stanford, Calif.: Hoover Institution Press, 1993.

Furth, Albert. "The War Goes to Mr. Jesse Jones." *Fortune* (October 1941).

Gaeddert, G. R. *The History of the American National Red Cross*, vol. 4. Washington, D.C.: American National Red Cross, 1950.

Gaskill, Betty Milton. "What Will We Do with Government War Plants?" *Liberty* (November 11, 1944).

Gaston, Kay Baker. "Robertson County Distilleries, 1796–1909." *Tennessee Historical Quarterly* 43 (1984): 49.

Gilbert, Martin. *The First World War*. New York: Henry Holt, 1994.

Ginsburg, David. Interview. In *Brother Can You Spare a Billion? The Story of Jesse H. Jones*. DVD. Directed by Eric Stange. Steven Fenberg, Executive Producer. Houston: Houston Public Television Home Video, 2000.

Goodwin, Doris Kearns. *No Ordinary Time: Franklin and Eleanor Roosevelt: The Home Front in World War II*. New York: Simon & Schuster, 1994.

"Green Diamond Creates Good Will on Tour." *Illinois Central Magazine* (May 1936): 3.

Heckscher, August. *Woodrow Wilson*. New York: Collier Books, Macmillan, 1991.

Henderson, Deborah Kelley. *Robertson County's Heritage of Homes*. 36–38. Springfield, TN: Robertson County Antiquities Foundation, 1979.

Hill, L. B., ed. *A History of Greater Dallas and Vicinity*, vol. 2. Chicago: Lewis Publishing, 1909.

Hobby, Bill, with Saralee Tiede. *How Things Really Work*. Austin: Dolph Briscoe Center for American History, University of Texas at Austin, 2010.

Houghton, Dorothy Knox Howe, Barrie M. Scardino, Sadie Gwin Blackburn, and Katherine S. Howe. *Houston's Forgotten Heritage*. Houston: Rice University Press, 1991.

Houston Endowment Grant Files. Houston Endowment Archive, Houston.

Ickes, Harold L. *The Secret Diary of Harold L. Ickes*. New York: Simon and Schuster, 1954.

In Flanders Fields Museum exhibition wall labels, Ieper, Belgium. Permanent exhibition.

"Jesse Gets Ruffled," *Time* (April 20, 1942).

Jesse H. Jones Collection [Rice]. Rice University Archive, Houston.

Jesse H. Jones Collection [UT]. Dolph Briscoe Center for American History, University of Texas at Austin.

Jesse H. Jones Collection [LOC]. Library of Congress, Washington, D.C.

Jesse H. Jones Collection [HE]. Houston Endowment Archive, Houston.

John T. Jones Jr. Collection. Houston Endowment Archive, Houston.

Johnson, Lyndon Baines. Speaking on smelter resolution on April 14, 1954, to the Senate Armed Services Committee, 83rd Congress, 1st sess. *Congressional Record* 100, pt. 5162: 76.

Johnston, Marguerite. *Houston: The Unknown City, 1836–1946*. College Station: Texas A&M University Press, 1991.

Jones, Jesse. "Billions Out and Billions Back," *Saturday Evening Post* (June 12, 1937): 5–63.

Jones, Jesse. "Love for Fellow Men Was Proven in Those Days." *Red Cross Courier*, April 1, 1927.

Jones, Jesse H., with Edward Angly. *Fifty Billion Dollars: My Thirteen Years with the RFC (1932–1945)*. New York: Macmillan Company, 1951.

Kennedy, David M. *Freedom from Fear: The American People in Depression and War 1929–1945*. New York: Oxford University Press, 1999.

Klaus, Ida. Interview. In *Brother Can You Spare a Billion? The Story of Jesse H. Jones*. DVD. Directed by Eric Stange. Steven Fenberg, Executive Producer. Houston: Houston Public Television Home Video, 2000.

Law, Henry L. *Tennessee Geography*. Oklahoma City: Harlow Publishing, 1954.

Leuchtenburg, William E. *Franklin D. Roosevelt and the New Deal, 1932–1940*. New York: Harper & Row, 1963.

Levin, Phyllis Lee. *Edith and Woodrow: The Wilson White House*. New York: Scribner, 2001.

Lindsley, Phillip. *A History of Greater Dallas and Vicinity*. Chicago: Lewis Publishing, 1909.

Lubell, Samuel, "Plus $20 for a Barber," *New York Times*, October 21, 1951.

Lubell, Samuel. "New Deal's J. P. Morgan." 2 parts. *Saturday Evening Post* (November 30, 1940, and December 7, 1940).

"Lumber Industry." In *The New Handbook of Texas*, edited by Ron Tyler, et al. Austin: Texas State Historical Association, 1996.

Lyndon Baines Johnson Papers. Lyndon Baines Johnson Library and Museum, Austin, Texas.

Macmillan, Margaret. *Paris 1919*. New York: Random House, 2001.

Mallon, Paul. "The Dough Doctor." *Today* (March 31, 1934).

McAshan, Mary Phelps. *On the Corner of Main and Texas: A Houston Legacy*. Houston: Hutchins House, 1985.

McComb, David G. *Houston: The Bayou City*. Austin and London: University of Texas Press, 1969.

McCullough, David. *Truman*. New York: Simon & Schuster, 1992.

McElhaney, Jacquelyn Masur. "Childhood in Dallas, 1870–1900." Master's thesis, Southern Methodist University, 1962.

McElvaine, Robert S. *The Great Depression, America, 1929–1941*, rev. ed. New York: Three Rivers Press, 1993.

McKean, David. *Tommy the Cork: Washington's Ultimate Insider from Roosevelt to Reagan*. Hanover, NH: Steerforth Press, 2004.

A Memorial and Biographical History of Johnson and Hill Counties. Chicago: Lewis Publishing, 1892.

"National Affairs: Jesse Jones's Friends." *Time* (January 25, 1937).

"National Affairs: The Cabinet—Emperor Jones." *Time* (January 13, 1941).

The National Archives, Washington, D.C. http://www.archives.gov/.

The National World War II Museum exhibition notes, New Orleans, Louisiana.

The New Handbook of Texas, edited by Ron Tyler, et al. Austin: Texas State Historical Association, 1996.

Olson, James S. *Saving Capitalism, The Reconstruction Finance Corporation and the New Deal 1933–1940*. Princeton, NJ: Princeton University Press, 1988.

Oral History Project. Houston Endowment Archive, Houston.

"Orange, Texas." In *The New Handbook of Texas*. Edited by Ron Tyler, et al. Austin: Texas State Historical Association, 1996.

Pearson, Drew, and Robert Allen. "Washington Merry-Go-Round," syndicated newspaper column. New York: United Feature Syndicate, Inc. See "Dates" at http://www.library.american.edu/pearson/biography.html.

Pearson, Drew. "Washington Merry-Go-Round," syndicated newspaper column. New York: United Feature Syndicate, Inc. See "Dates" at http://www.library.american.edu/pearson/biography.html.

Pistole, Alfred W. "A History of Hopewell Baptist Church, Robertson County: Springfield, Tennessee." Stored at Gorham MacBane Public Library, Springfield, TN, 1975.

Platt, Harold L. *City Building in the New South*. Philadelphia: Temple University Press, 1983.

Pratt, Joseph A., and Christopher J. Castaneda. *Builders: Herman and George R. Brown.* College Station: Texas A&M University Press, 1999.

Pringle Henry F. "Biggest Big Shot: Uncle Sam." *Saturday Evening Post* (December 18, 1943).

Ragsdale, Kenneth B. *The Year America Discovered Texas: Centennial '36.* College Station: Texas A&M University Press, 1987.

Reich, Robert B. *Aftershock.* New York: Alfred A. Knopf, 2010.

Reid, Daphne A., and Patrick F. Gilbo. *Beyond Conflict: The International Federation of Red Cross and Red Crescent Societies, 1919–1994.* Geneva: International Federation of Red Cross and Red Crescent Societies, 1997.

Reid, Yolanda G., and Rick S. Gregory. *Robertson County, Tennessee: Home of the World's Finest.* Nashville: Turner Publishing Company, 1996.

"RFC: The House of Jesse." *Fortune* (May 1940).

Robertson, David. *Sly and Able: A Political Biography of James F. Byrnes.* New York: Norton, 1994.

Roosevelt, Eleanor. *The Autobiography of Eleanor Roosevelt.* New York: Da Capo Press, 1961.

Roosevelt, Franklin Delano. "Address to Special Session of Congress, May 16, 1940." http://www.ibiblio.org/pha/7-2-188/188-16.html (accessed March 25, 2010).

Roosevelt, Franklin Delano. "Fireside Chat radio address, May 26, 1940." http://www.mhric.org/fdr/chat15.html (accessed March 25, 2010).

Roosevelt, Franklin Delano. "Inaugural Address of the President, March 4, 1933." http://www.archives.gov/education/lessons/fdr-inaugural/images/address-1.gif (accessed March 23, 2010).

Roosevelt, Franklin Delano. "1937 State of the Union Message." http://www.presidency.ucsb.edu/ws/index.php?pid=15336 (accessed March 25, 2010).

Roosevelt, Franklin Delano. "1939 State of the Union Message." http://www.presidency.ucsb.edu/ws/index.php?pid=15684 (accessed March 25, 2010).

Roosevelt, Franklin Delano. "1940 State of the Union Message." http://www.presidency.ucsb.edu/ws/index.php?pid=15856 (accessed March 25, 2010).

Roosevelt, Franklin Delano. "1941 State of the Union Message." http://www.presidency.ucsb.edu/ws/index.php?pid=16092 (accessed March 25, 2010).

Roosevelt, Franklin Delano. "On Signing the Surplus Property Act of 1944." http://www.presidency.ucsb.edu/ws/index.php?pid=16567&st=surplus+property+act&st1= (accessed March 26, 2010).

Roosevelt, Franklin Delano. "Third Inaugural Address, January 20, 1941." http://www.presidency.ucsb.edu/ws/index.php?pid=16022 (accessed March 25, 2010).

Schlesinger Jr., Arthur M. *The Crisis of the Old Order, 1919–1933.* Boston: Houghton Mifflin, 1957.

Schulman, Bruce R. "Interactive Guide to the World's Columbian Exposition 1996–2000." http://xroads.virginia.edu/~MA96/WCE/history.html

Schwarz, Jordan A. *The New Dealers: Power Politics in the Age of Roosevelt.* New York: Knopf, 1993.

Schwarz, Jordan A. *The Speculator, Bernard M. Baruch in Washington, 1917–1965.* Chapel Hill, NC: University of North Carolina Press, 1981.

Shields-West, Eileen. *The World Almanac of Presidential Campaigns.* New York: World Almanac, 1992.

Sibley, Marilyn McAdams. *The Port of Houston: A History*. Austin and London: University of Texas Press, 1968.

"Special Report: Greater Houston: Its First Million People—and Why." *Newsweek* (July 5, 1954): 38–45.

Stoltz, Jack. *Terrell, Texas 1873–1973: From Open Country to Modern City*. San Antonio: Naylor, 1973.

"Texas Titan," *Time* (January 22, 1934).

Timmons, Bascom. *Jesse H. Jones: The Man and the Statesman*. New York: Henry Holt, 1956.

"The Treaty of Guadalupe Hidalgo." http://www.loc.gov/rr/hispanic/ghtreaty/ (accessed March 25, 2010).

Tully, Grace. *F.D.R. My Boss*. New York: C. Scribner's Sons, 1949.

"U.S. at War: The Surplus Bill." *Time* (October 2, 1944).

Wakefield, Paul. "Jesse Holman Jones." Biographical sketch, 1928, Houston Endowment Archives.

"Waxahachie, Texas." In *The New Handbook of Texas*, edited by Ron Tyler, et al. Austin: Texas State Historical Association, 1996.

"Where Will the Next President Be Named?" *Literary Digest* (February 11, 1928).

White, Gerald T. *Billions for Defense: Government Financing by the Defense Plant Corporation during World War II*. Tuscaloosa: University of Alabama Press, 1980.

White, Graham, and John Maze. *Henry A. Wallace: His Search for a New World Order*. Chapel Hill, N.C.: University of North Carolina Press, 1995.

Will Rogers Museum, Claremore, Oklahoma.

Wooten, Heather Green. *The Polio Years in Texas: Battling a Terrifying Unknown*. College Station: Texas A&M University Press, 2009.

Index

A&P grocery chain, 408
Adolphus Hotel, 146, 268
Advertising Clubs of America, 258
Agricultural Adjustment Act (AAA),
    207–208
Alabama-Coushatta Indian tribe, 329
Alamo, restoration of, 259
Alcoa:
  contracted to build aluminum plants,
    390–391
  DPC investments, 478
  impact of loan to Reynolds Metal
    Company, 356, 369
Aldrich, Winthrop, 272
Alfalfa Club, 411
Allen, A. C., 46
Allen, J. K., 46
Allen, Robert:
  accusations of failing to save textile
    industry, 237
  Alcoa controversy, 391–392
  automobile competition and banking
    closures, 229

on delays in defense supplies, 383–384
on government reorganization, 328
Jesse's appointment to head of FLA,
    334
Jesse's desire to be Secretary of
    Treasury, 219, 220
on possibility of regional government
    banks, 305
predictions about RFC demise, 271,
    293, 296
relief for flood victims, 278, 306–307
RFC's lending policies, 311–312, 407
special legislation for Jones' two
    government posts, 359
U.S. lending during WWII, 345
Allred, James, 268, 285
Aluminum, RFC investment in, 417
American Airlines, 132–133
American Bankers Association, 212, 231,
    247, 320
American Expeditionary Force, 71, 451
American Federation of Labor, 354
American First Committee, 383

American General Life Insurance
Company, 110
American Legion's Armistice Day
Exercises, 318–320
American Machinist, 447
American-Made Rubber Day, 452–454
American Red Cross, 534
expanded role post-WWI, 81–82
increased membership after WWI, 68
Jesse's organization of, 3–4, 68
parades, 73–74
"Red Cross girls," 71
War Council, 69
disbanding of, 82–83
Jesse appointed to, 80
See also Department of Military Relief
(DMR); International Federation
of Red Cross
American Rolling Mill, 380
"America's Sixty Families," 300
Anderson, Clayton & Company, 183, 483
Anderson, Leland, 564
Andrews, Frank, 54–55
Angly, Edward, 553, 559
Anti-Comintern Pact, 338
Armstrong, Seph, 21
Army Post Exchange Service, 473
Association of American Railroads,
389
AT&T, 251
Atwater, Pierce, 290
Austin College, 538
Austin, Stephen F., 284
Aviation:
B-29 Superfortress, 388
B-32 Dominator, 388
RFC investment in, 416
WWII need for, 316, 338–339, 342, 351,
356, 361
Axson, Stockton, 74, 80–81, 94, 103–104,
111, 113–117, 249, 579

B. F. Goodrich, 389, 435, 452
Babcock, Blanche Aldehoff:
communications with Jesse, 50, 74,
288–289, 368
death of, 546

Jesse's comments, 146
relationship with Jesse, 14, 21
Bach Singers, 233
Backlund, Milton, 292, 538, 582
Bailey, Josiah, 246, 515
Baillie, Hugh, 391
Baker, James A., 47–48, 51, 182–183, 329
Baker, Newton D., 192
Ball, Thomas, 47, 155
Baltimore Sun, 407, 502
Bank of America, 189
Bankers Mortgage Building, 104–105,
131–132, 292
Banking Act of 1933, 214
Banking, state closures during Great
Depression, 182–184, 191–192,
199–200
Banks, W. R., 532–533
Barkley, Alben, 246, 353
Barnston, Henry, 154
Baruch, Bernard:
appointed to investigate grain-based
vs. petroleum-based rubber,
427–431
conflict with Jesse about campaign
contributions, 121–122
mends relationship with Jesse, 158,
546–547
mission in Europe, 315–316
Price Fixing Committee, 80
recommends that Truman share
atomic technology with other
nations, 536
report on post-war problems, 468,
478–479
solicits donations for Wilson's home,
104
United Nations Atomic Energy
Commission, 535
Batt, William L., 410
Battle Creek Sanitarium, 91
Baylor University, 545
Beaux-Arts buildings, 24
Beck, John, 583
Bell Telephone, 178
Belmont, August, Jr., 101–102
Bentsen, Lloyd, Jr., 549

Bethlehem Steel, 177
"Big Inch" pipeline, 420, 462, 463, 499, 529, 539
Binz Building, 36
Black, Eugene R., Sr., 212, 238
Black, Hugo L., 518
Black Monday, 277
Blaine, John J., 253
Blair, Emily Newell, 158
Blanton, W. N. (Bill), 138, 178, 295, 580
Blitz Orchestra, 54
Blum, John Morton, 202
Boehck, John Albert, 421–422, 423
Boeing Aircraft Company, 350
Bolling, Randolph, 114
B&O Railroad, 540. See also Railroads
Bowers, Claude G., 157
Boys Club of America, 538–539
Brashear, Samuel, 36
Brazil, U.S. loan to, 362–363
Brazilian Steel Plan, 362
Breadlines, 184
Brennan, Walter, 551
Bricker, John W., 494
"Briefalogue," 494
Bristol Hotel, 43, 46, 569
Broun, Heywood, 191
Brown, George, 528, 539, 580
Brown, Herman, 528, 539
Bryan, William Jennings, 51
Buchanan, James P., 280
Buck, E. O., 530
Buck, Pearl S., 421
Buckner Orphanage, 16, 534
Buenger, Walter, 63
Buffalo Bay, dredging of, 47
Buffalo Bayou, 36
    increased development after 1900 Galveston hurricane, 38
    geographic layout of, 46–47
Bulow, W. J., 144
Bureau of Economic Warfare, 411
    delaying tactics on social programs in foreign nations, 437–438
    Roosevelt abolishes, 460
    Wallace and, 412–413
    weakens RFC, 413, 414–415

Bureau of Foreign and Domestic Commerce, 381
Business Advisory Council, 520
Butler, George, 340, 482–483, 485, 583
Byrd, Harry, 276, 497
Byrnes, James, 455–456, 479

C&I Life Building, 538
C&I Life Insurance Company, 552
Campbell, Ben, 66–67
Campbell, J. Lee, 42, 55
Canadian National Opera Company, 55
Cannon, Neal, 583
Cape Lookout, 378
Carleton, Don, 564
Carnegie, Andrew, 35
Caro, Robert, 557
Carson, Mary, 110
Carter, Amon, 132–134, 151, 247
Carter, Amon, Jr., 450–451
Carter, S. F., 45
Catholicism, 106, 136, 144, 148, 158–159, 163, 190, 329
Centennial Exposition, 259
Central Republic Bank, 191–192
Cerrachio, Enrico, 234
Chandler, Harry, 249–250
Chase National Bank, 272
Chevrolet, 342
Chicago:
    as Jones' inspiration for Houston, 25, 112
    World's Fair, 23–25
Chicago Fire of 1873, 25
China:
    honors Jesse, 546
    U.S. loan to, 344–345, 362
Christ Church Cathedral, 423
"The Chronicle Station," 572
Chrysler, Walter P., 203
Chrysler Motor Co., 229
    Surplus Property Act and, 494
Churchill, Winston, 385, 403, 419, 515, 553
Cities Service Oil Company, 575
City Auditorium, 48, 55
"City Beautiful" movement, 24

Civil Aeronautics Administration, 433

Civilian Conservation Corps, 308, 378

Clark, R. Lee, Jr., 553

Clayton, Will, 138, 364, 380, 394–395, 459, 523
  to head reconversion as head of SWPA, 478, 479
  role in Marshall Plan, 541
  subsiding coal prices, 418–419

Clemenceau, Georges, 83

Cleveland News, 512–513

Coal, subsidizing price of, 418, 421

Coca-Cola, 448

Cohen, Ben, 223, 237

Colonel Edward Mandell House, 584

Columbia Broadcasting Company, 157, 247

Columbia Broadcasting System, 274, 574

Columbia University, 555

Columbus, Christopher, 23

Commercial and Industrial Life Insurance Company, 538

Committee for Economic Development, 448–449

Commodity Credit Corporation (CCC), 208, 310
  attempts to abolish, 327
  moved to Department of Agriculture, 348
  Roosevelt extends, 519
  success of, 230

Commodore Hotel, 241

Communism, 495, 535, 564–565

Community Chest, 181–182, 535

Compton, Karl T., 427–431

Comstock, William A., 199–200

Conant, James B., 427–431

Confederate guerillas, 10

Conscription, Woodrow Wilson and, 75

Consumerism, Great Depression and, 176

Convalescent House, 79

Coolidge, Calvin, 95, 457
  becomes president, 119–120
  vetoes McNary-Haugen bill, 147

Corcoran, Thomas, 190, 222–223, 237
  blames recession on monopolies, 300
  as Jesse's liaison to Morgenthau, 253
  lobbies for Roosevelt's desire to expand Supreme Court, 280–281

Costello, Bill, 249–250, 251, 303, 357, 537

Cottingham, George, 497

Cotton, surplus during Great Depression, 207–208

Couch, Harvey, 187

Coughlin, Charles, 339

Couzens, Jim, 200

Cox, James, 95

Cracker Jacks, 24

"Cradle of the Skyscraper," 25

Creel, George, 417

Crowley, Leo T., 238, 461, 512

Crumworld Farms, 507

Cullen, Hugh Roy:
  conflicts with Jesse, 543–544
  contributes to *USS Houston* replacement, 441

Curtis, Charles, 149, 192, 407

Cutter Laboratories, 472

Dalhart Hardware Company, 42

Dallas:
  1897 State Fair, 30
  Centennial Exposition, 259
  Jesse's developments in, 104

Dallas Club, 30–31

"The Dangers of Inflation," 425–426

Daniels, Bebe, 132

Daughters of the American Revolution, 156

Davies, John E., 293

Davis, A. W., murder of, 150

Davis, Arthur, 391

Davis, John W., 120, 121

Davis, Norman, 451

Davison, Henry P.:
  appointed War Council chairman, 69
  commitment to Red Cross, 70–71
  on role of Red Cross post-WWI, 80–81
  work with League of Red Cross Societies, 82–88

Dawes, Charles, 186, 190–191

"Dawes Loan," 192–193
De Gaulle, Charles, 490
Defense Homes Corporation, 363
Defense Plant Corporation (DPC), 356,
    379, 400
  preferred to NDAC's EPF, 361
  reconversion and aviation plants, 528
  utilizes lease agreement, 361
Defense Supplies Corporation (DSC),
    establishment of, 356
DeMille, Cecil B., 132
Democratic Party:
  1920 National Convention, 95
  1924 National Convention, 120–123, 142
  1928 National Convention, 4, 136, 137,
    141–143, 259
  1932 National Convention, 191–198
  1936 National Convention, 262–263
  1940 National Convention, 353–354
  1944 National Convention, 486
  1944 Texas Convention, 484
  1948 National Convention, 547
Department of Commerce and
    Reconstruction Finance
    Corporation, 461–462
Department of Military Relief (DMR):
  builds rehabilitation center, 79
  contributions of, 71
  Jones heads up, 69
  Motor Corps, 78
  See also American Red Cross
Department of Publicity and Promotion
    of the Exposition, 23
DePelchin Faith Home, 27, 96–97, 110,
    233, 289
Dewey, Bradley, 488–489
Dewey, Thomas E., 494, 547
Dickson Colored Orphanage, 96, 128
Didiot, Joe, 21–22, 50
Dinsmore, R. P., 477
Disaster Loan Corporation (DLC), 278–
    279, 308
Dixon, George, 411
Dodge, Cleveland, 69, 75, 113–117
Dodge-Chicago plant, 388–389
Doherty, R. P., 206
Domestic Commerce, 476

Donitz, Karl, 419–420
Douglas, Lewis, 201
Douglas, William O., 485
Downey, Morton, 543
Durr, Clifford J., 357
Dust Bowl, 236–237

Early, Steve, 357–358, 505
Eastern Airlines, 545
Eastman Kodak, 448
Ebanks, George, 530
Eccles, Marriner, 300
Economic Defense Board (EDB), 387
Economic Stabilization Office, 455
Edgewood Realty Company, 291–292
  establishment of, 41
  growth of, 43
Education:
  health issues and, 13
  RFC contributions to, 243
  segregated, 13, 532–534
Eisenhower, Dwight David, 545
  elected president, 568
  Jesse and, 555–556, 566–567
Electric Building, 127
Electric Home and Farm Authority
    (EHFA), 226–227, 243
  attempts to abolish, 327
  success of, 230
"Elements of Success," 129–130
Elkins, James, 138
Emergency Banking Act, 201–203
Emergency Plant Facilities Contract
    (EPFC), 356–357
Emergency Relief and Reconstruction
    Act, 194
Empire State Building, 387, 403, 426–
    427, 469, 560
Evans, E. B., 534
Eveready Hour, 157
Exchange Club, 146
Exchange National Bank, 32
Export-Import Bank (EIB), 230
  Brazil, 362–363
  loans to other countries, 230–231
  public fear of foreign conflict, 326–327
  WWII and, 343–344

ExxonMobil, 69
"The Eyes of Texas," 246, 260, 377

Fair Building, 169
Fairchild, Cameron, 564
Fair Department Store, 169
Fair Labor Standards Act, 312
Fall, Albert, 119
Famous Players-Lasky, 132
Fannie Mae, 303
Fannin, James W., 284
Farley, James, 192, 300
    endorses Jones as 1940 vice
        presidential candidate, 330–332,
        353
Farm Credit Administration, 263
Farm legislation, 160, 164
    AAA and, 207–208
    CCC and, 208–209
    Jesse on, 146–148
    Great Depression and, 176, 236
    See also specific crops
Farrar, R. M., 63, 182, 233
Farthing, J. B., 12, 23, 233
The Fashion, 550
Father Divine, 507–508
Federal Communications Commission,
    543
Federal Deposit Insurance Corporation
    (FDIC), 238, 461
    development of, 203, 213, 214
    public confidence in, 217
Federal Emergency Relief
    Administration (FERA), 237
Federal Housing Administration (FHA),
    239, 263, 382
Federal Loan Administration (FLA):
    Jesse appointed to head of, 333
    Roosevelt's plan to consolidate, 328
Federal National Mortgage Association
    (FNMA), 302–303, 305
Federal Reserve banks, 222–223–226
Federal Security Agency, 328
Federal Works Agency, 328
Ferdinand, Francis, 59, 89
Ferguson, Miriam Amanda ("Ma"),
    124–125

Ferris, Royal A., 31–33, 145, 146
Ferris wheel, first, 24
Fields, William, 564
Fifty Billion Dollars: My Thirteen Years
    with the RFC, 559–561
Finn, Alfred C., 105, 141, 270, 340
Firestone Tire and Rubber, 389, 417
First National Bank of Detroit, 203–204,
    229
First National Bank of Waxahachie, 23
Fish, Hamilton, 276, 326–327
Fisher, Charles T., 253, 353
Fisher, Chick, 531
Fisher, Fred, 288, 341
Fisher Body Works, 341
Fleming, Lamar, 482
Fletcher, Duncan, 221–222
Foley Bros., 73
Foley's, 550
Folsom, Marion, 448
Ford, Henry, 200, 229
Ford Motor Company, 342
    Surplus Property Act and, 494
Forestlawn Cemetery, 244
Fort Worth, Jesse's developments in,
    104, 125, 127–128, 169
Fortune:
    feature on Jesse, 346–349
    story on Jesse and defense spending,
        393–397
Foster, M. E., 44, 106–107, 124–125, 130
Franco, Francisco, 338
Frankfurter, Felix, 190
Franzheim, Kenneth, 141
Furth, Albert, 393–397

Galbraith, John Kenneth, 209, 264, 382,
    418, 459, 561
Galveston, 1900 hurricane, 38
Galveston Bay, 46–47
Galvez Hotel, 285
Garner, John Nance, 2–3, 165, 186
    1936 nomination for vice president,
        263
    advice to Jesse on Wallace dispute, 460
    attempts to run against Roosevelt for
        third term, 367–368

attendance at Jesse's 63rd birthday party, 281–282
conflict with Roosevelt, 280
elected vice president, 197
Jesse's friendship with, 228
Garrett, Daniel, 124
Gaskill, Betty Milton, 500
Gasoline, rationing, 428, 431, 464–465
General Electric, 36, 148, 448
General Maximum Price Regulation, 418, 421
General Motors (GM), 229, 341, 342, 407
  DPC investments, 478
  RFC and National Bank of Detroit, 203–204
  output for war, 491
  rehiring of employees and removal of pay cuts, 317
The General Theory of Employment, Interest, and Money, 301
General Tire and Rubber Company, 452, 454
Geneva Convention, 68
George, Walter F., 514
George bill, 515–518
George H. Lewis Funeral Home, 581
George Peabody College for Teachers, 226
Georgia Warm Springs Foundation, 476
Giannini, A. P., 189, 246
Gifford, Charles L., 238
Gilchrist, Gibb, 534
Ginsburg, David, 205
Glass bill, 308–309
Glass, Carter, 186, 305, 459, 537
Glass-Steagall Act, 214
Glenwood Cemetery, 33
Goebbels, Paul Joseph, 319
Gold:
  buying program, 209–211
  sterilized, 289, 294
Goldwyn, Samuel, 132
Goodloe, John, 495–497, 577
Good Year Tire and Rubber Company, 389, 435, 452
Green Diamond, 255–257
Gromyko, Andrei, 404, 470

Gulfgate Shopping Center, 530
Gulf Oil Company, 289
  Building, 169, 173–174, 175

Halsey, William F., Jr., 545
Harding, Warren G., 95, 107–108, 119
Hardin-Simmons College Cowboy Band, 377
Harriman, Averill, 257
Harriman, William Averell, 102
Harris, C. T., 26
Harrison, Benjamin, 23
Harrison, Pat, 161
Hartford, John, 408
Harvard Library, 579
Harvard Medical School, 545
Harvard University, 427
Hearst, William Randolph, 191
  Jones endorsement as 1940 presidential candidate, 353
  Landon endorsement, 264
Hedgecroft Clinic, 554
Hefley, Ed, 262
Heflin, Van, 551
Henderson, Charles B., 253, 278, 512
  appointed chairman of RFC, 384
  FNMA board, 303
  as president of Metals Reserve Company, 363
Henderson, Leon, 418
Henry Holt & Company, 580–581
Heyne, Fred, 69, 292, 340, 535, 557, 579
Highland Rim, 7
Hillman, Sidney, 386
Hill's Business College, 20
Hillsboro Mirror, 21
Hitler, Adolf, 313–314, 350
Hobby, Oveta Culp, 439, 509
Hobby, William P., 261, 509
Hoffman, Paul, 448
Hofheinz, Roy, 575
Hogg, W. C., 145
Holcombe, Oscar, 137, 138–139, 140, 234–235, 260
Holmes, Ann, 565–567, 581
Home Owners Loan Corporation, 239, 263

Hoover, Herbert, 538–539, 542
 approach to Great Depression relief
  efforts, 184–185
 "confidence campaign," 179–180
 RFC legislation, 192–194
 Roosevelt's criticism of, 263
 selected as 1932 presidential
  candidate, 192
 selected as 1928 presidential nominee,
  149
 setting precedence for New Deal, 194
 wins 1928 presidential election, 165,
  166
 See also Reconstruction Finance
  Corporation (RFC)
Hopewell Church, 571
Hopkins, Harry, 237, 294, 300, 503, 507,
 537
The Hospitality House, 149–150
House, Edward Mandell, 51
House, T. W., Jr., 45, 51
House Banking and Currency
 Committee, 480, 549–550
House Interstate and Foreign
 Commerce Committee, 406
Houston, Andrew Jackson, 261
Houston:
 decentralization, 523
 speed of development in, 35–36
Houston, Sam, 284
Houston, W. W., 579
Houston Academy of Medicine, 563
Houston Airport, 174–175
Houston Chamber of Commerce, 232–
 233
Houston Chronicle Publishing
 Company, 552
Houston Chronicle, 212, 213
 conflicts over position on "Ma"
  Ferguson, 124–125
 endorses 1948 Republican
  presidential candidates, 548
 endorses Roosevelt for fourth term,
  497, 498
 expansion of, 44
 Jesse's continued involvement after
  Washington career, 535

 as Jesse's platform for the Houston
  Ship Channel disputes, 97–98
 publishes series about Ku Klux Klan,
  106–107
 women's suffrage, 52
Houston Club Building, 571
Houston Community Chest, 128
Houston Daily Post, 33, 55, 56
Houston Endowment, 49, 291, 292, 531,
 534–535, 538, 545–546, 552, 579
Houston Fat Stock Show, 544
Houston Festival, 39–40. See also
 Notsuoh Deep Water Jubilee
Houston Harbor Board:
 Jesse appointed chairman, 52
 Jesse resigns, 67
 wharf controversy, 66–67
Houston National Bank, 182–183
"Houston Plan," 47–48
"Houston Platform," 160, 164
Houston Post, 98, 112, 113, 141, 146
Houston Properties Corporation, 127
Houston Ship Channel, 575
 combining capitalism and public
  service, 3
 community impact, 63
 controversy over wharves and
  warehouses, 97–99
 opening of, 59, 61
 public and private funding, 47–48
 steel plant along, 380
Houston Shipbuilding Corporation, 417,
 422, 476–477
Houston Street & News Boys' Club, 583
Houston Symphony Orchestra, 48, 67,
 535
Howard School, 12–13
"How Henry Wallace Missed the
 Presidency," 456
Hudson, Eugene A., 61
Huggins, W. O., 124–125, 181
Hughes, Howard, 312–313, 540
Hull, Cordell, 143, 230, 326, 501
Humble Oil and Refining Company, 146,
 289
 contributes to USS Houston
  replacement, 441

Jesse sells stock in, 69
to operate synthetic rubber plants,
425
supplies ingredients for synthetic
rubber plants, 452
Huntington Library, 579
Hurt, Nancy Jones:
becomes caregiver of Jones children,
11–12
death of, 124
named in Jesse's will, 42
Hurwitz, Ben, 174
Husbands, Sam, 363, 479
Hutcheson, J. C., 67
Hyde Park, 508

Ickes, Harold, 294
blames recession on monopolies,
300
Jesse's criticism of in *Chronicle*, 535
U-boats and, 420
Illinois Central, 255–257
Immigration, role in 1924 election, 120
Independent Petroleum Association of
America, 294–295
Industrial Revolution, 51
Inflation:
controlled, 207
Jesse on, 425–426
Roosevelt fights wartime, 418
Inter-American Highway, 231
Interest rates, cutting, 241, 254–255
International Federation of Red Cross,
451
Internationalism, role in 1924 election,
120

J. A. Zurn Manufacturing Company, 537
J. P. Morgan, 46, 448
Jackson, Samuel D., 487
Jackson Day Dinner, 302
Jacobs, William States, 152
Jeffers, William:
overrides Wallace's efforts to weaken
RFC, 445
role in rubber program, 431, 453, 467
Jefferson Davis Hospital, 150

Jesse H. Jones Aeronautical Beacon,
174–175
Jesse H. Jones Fellowship in Cancer
Education, 553
Jesse H. Jones Hall for the Performing
Arts, 49
Jesse H. Jones Hospital, 581
Jesse H. Jones Scholarship in
Journalism, 564
Jesse H. Jones Scholarships, 534
Johnson, Lyndon Baines, 280
Jesse's correspondence with, 333–334,
558, 569–570, 572–573, 581
relationship with Roosevelt, 285–286
Texas economy and, 380
Johnson Act, 385
Jones, Audrey, 234, 249, 569
attends University of Texas at Austin,
378
christens Green Diamond, 257
graduation, 329
launches *Matthew Maury*, 417
marries, 421, 423–424
relationship with Jesse and Mary,
109–110, 134
trip to Europe, 313–314, 315
at University of Texas at Austin, 404
Jones, Augusta, 37, 91
Jones, Carrie, 8, 23, 37
Jones, Eli, 7
Jones, Elizabeth, 8, 23, 38
death of, 481–482
Jones, Harrison, 448
Jones, Ida, 8, 23, 38, 571, 577–578
Jones, Jeanette, 37, 553, 556
Jones, Jesse:
63rd birthday party, 281
American Red Cross, fundraising for, 68
arts, involvement with the, 48, 55
banking
entrance into career, 42, 45
First National Bank of Waxahachie,
23
rescues Houston banks after 1929
crash, 182–184
boxing, 21
Communism and, 535, 542, 564–565

Jones, Jesse (*cont.*)
  Congressional attack, under, 391–396,
    408–411
  as "conservative force" of the New
    Deal, 206–207, 220
  criticism in *Saturday Evening Post,*
    368–371
  death of, 581
  Democratic Party
    credited with Houston getting 1928
      National Democratic Convention,
      137–138, 143–144
    finance chairman of 1924
      Democratic National Committee,
      120–123
    replaced as director of finance
      for 1928 Democratic National
      Committee, 163–164
    speaks at 1936 Democratic National
      Convention, 262–263
  education
    belief in importance of, 532
    brief career in, 20
    in Dallas, 14–15, 20
    receives honorary degrees, 129, 270,
      286, 421
    in Kentucky, 18
    leaves to pursue work, 18
    struggles with, 15
    in Tennessee, 12–13
  entry into business, 16–18
  father's influence, 20
  first banking account, 18
  first tobacco crop, 16–19
  inherits father's tobacco business, 23
  loan from Ferris, 32–33
  family
    financial responsibility for, 537–538
    marriage to Mary Gibbs Jones, 100
  FLA after leaving, continued influence
    on, 527
  Fortune feature article, 346–349, 371
  at George bill hearing, 516–517
  health issues, 475–476, 489, 494, 570
  Houston Chronicle, buys half interest
    in, 44
  Jesse H. Jones Day, 234, 268–269

lumber business
  exits, 50
  growing, 37–39, 41–42
  Manchester wharf funding
    controversy, 66–67
  myths surrounding, 23–24
  Order of Ching Hsin, receives, 546
  presidential candidacy, talk of a, 143–
    144, 144–145, 159–160
  reconversion from war to peacetime,
    476–479, 480–481
  Republican party
    contributes funds to both parties for
      1952 campaigns, 567–568
    endorses Republican candidate, 547
  RFC
    board of, 186–188
    praised for work with, 205–206
    public relations efforts on behalf of,
      194–195, 211–212, 223–225, 232
    publishes book about, 559–561
    resigns from, 512
  Rogers, relationship with Will, 244–
    245
  Roosevelt
    campaigns for fourth term, 264–269,
      365–367, 494, 495
    end of relationship with, 509–511,
      512
    professional and personal
      relationship with, 218–219
  rubber shortage, blamed for, 402, 403,
    406, 407–408
  as Secretary of Commerce, 357–360
  Texas Centennial, involvement with,
    257–259
  Wilson, Woodrow
    accompanies to Europe, 81–89
    contributes to pension for, 113–117
  See also specific businesses
Jones, Jesse Holman, II, 569
Jones, John T., Sr., 8, 37, 538
  death of, 537
  First National Bank of Waxahachie
    stock, 23
  inheritance, 23
  M. T. Jones Lumber Company stock, 23

named mayor of Dalhart, 42
oversees Jesse's Fort Worth
developments, 128
philanthropy, 564
president of Jesse's hardware
company, 42
Jones, John T., Jr., 110, 583
children, 569
enlistment, 404
Houston Endowment to honor Heyne,
579
MIA report, 445
POW, 450–451
return home, 523
success of, 557, 576–577
Jones, Laura Anna Holman, death of,
10–11
Jones, Louisa, 233
Jones, Martin Tilford (M. T.):
ambition, 27–28
community involvement, 27–28
death of, 33–34
distrust of Jesse, 26
establishes lumber business, 13
Jesse made executor of estate, 37
liquidation of estate, 63
as role model to, 27–33
as surrogate parent to Jesse, 26
See also M. T. Jones Lumber Company
Jones, Mary Gibbs:
American Red Cross, involvement
with, 68
background, 40–41
divorces Will, 91
Jesse's early interest in and
relationship with, 40–41, 42
journals, 100–102, 103, 108
life in Washington, 404
marriage to William, 29, 37
relationship with Edith Wilson, 103
Roosevelt, relationship with Eleanor,
371–372
Wilson, relationship with Edith,
371–372
Woman's Home Companion feature,
465–467
Jones, Thomas, 114, 116–117

Jones, Tilford, 37, 41, 340
at Audrey's wedding, 423
engagement, 92
enrollment at Cornell, 64
issues with Will, 92
Jones, W. Alton, 420
Jones, Will:
Deepwater farm issues, 91, 92
divorces Mary, 91
Jones, William:
community involvement, 19–20
death of, 23
imparts business ethic, 20
inheritance from father, 37
political views, 19–20
relationship with Jesse, 29
tobacco farm, 8
Joseph Meyer Interests, 183
Juicy Fruit gum, 24

Kaiser, Henry J., 379, 380, 528
Kaiser-Frazer car company, 528, 529, 554
Keep America Out of War Congress, 383
Kelly, Edward, 354
Kemmerer, W. W., 552
Kent, Frank, 407, 502
Keynes, John Maynard, 300–301
Kiest, E. J., 268
King, Ernest J., 545
Kinkaid School, 329
Kirby, John, 128
Kirby Lumber Company Building, 127
Kirby Theater, 127
Kitty Hawk, 470–471
Klagsbrunn, Hans, 357, 479
Klaus, Ida, 190
Klossner, Howard, 363
Knox, Frank, 262
Knudsen, William, 341–342
endorses Jones as 1940 presidential
candidate, 353
placed in charge of OPM, 386
scholarship program to honor, 538
Korean War, 553, 584
KPRC, 141–142, 373
Kristallnacht, 319
Krock, Arthur, 191, 237

Krupp and Tuffly, 169, 170
KTRH radio, 181, 552
KTRK-TV, 576
KUHT, 572
Ku Klux Klan, 8
  1924 Presidential election, 120, 122
  exposed in *Houston Chronicle*, 106–107
  "Ma" Ferguson and, 124
  See also Racism
Kuldell, R. C., 177
KXYZ, 290

LaFollette, Robert M., 120
LaGuardia, Fiorello Enrico, 227
Lamar, Mirabeau B., 373
Lamar Hotel, 134, 169
Lamont, Thomas, 448
Lamour, Dorothy, 551
Land, Emory, 462
Landon, Alf, 262
Langer, William, 514
Latin America:
  Roosevelt's desire to cultivate markets
    in, 363–364, 388
  stimulating development in, 399–
    400, 436
Laurel, Stan, 551
Law, Francis M., 231
League of Nations:
  establishment of, 84
  opposition to, 92–94
  withdrawal of Germany, 313
League of Red Cross Societies, 82–83
  Jesse's involvement with, 82–89
Leahy, William, 328
Lehman, Herbert, 163–164
Lehman Brothers, 163
Lehmann, Lotte, 372
"Lend-Lease" policy, 376, 383, 385, 501
LeRoy Sanitarium, 169, 569
Leviathan, 120
Levy, Abe and Haskell, 96
Levy, M. D., 563
Levy's Dry Goods, 169
Liberty, 500–501
Life, Jesse in, 432
Lindbergh, Charles, 339

Lippmann, Walter, 139, 191, 194
The Literary Digest, 140, 144, 266
"Little Inch" pipeline, 462, 529
Loew, Marcus, 132
Loew's State Theater, 134
Loews Inc., 556
Los Angeles Times, 249
Lovett, Edgar Odell, 93
Lubell, Samuel, 368–371, 427
Luce, Henry, 216–217, 393
Lumber, 13
  demand for Texas, 27
  "double-ender," 27–28, 41
  See also M.T. Jones Lumber Company
Lumberman's National Bank, 45

M. D. Anderson Hospital for Cancer
  Research, 553
M. T. Jones Lumber Company, 14, 15
  expansion, 27, 37
  Jesse's employment at, 21–23, 28–29
MacArthur, Douglas, 494, 545
MacKay Telegraph-Cable Company, 61
Majestic Theater, 55
Manufactures and Liberal Arts
  Building, 24
Maragliotti, Vincent, 174
Maritime Commission, 386, 406
Marland, E. W., 318
Marshall, George C., 378
Marshall Field, 127
Marshall Plan, 540, 541
Martin, Joseph W., 514
Mary Gibbs Jones College for Women,
  580
Mary Gibbs Jones Scholarship, 532, 533
Matthew Maury, 417
Mayfair House, 125–126
Mayflower Hotel, 372
McAdoo, William Gibbs, 52, 120, 191
McCabe, Thomas, 520
McCarthy, Glenn, 523, 550–551
McCarthy, Wilson, 187
McCasland, Barney Clifton, Jr., 575
McCormick, Cyrus, Jr., 114, 116–117
McDonald, Stewart, 305, 315
McIntyre, Marvin, 285

McNamee, Guy, 157
McNary, Charles, 353
McNary-Haugen bill, 147, 160, 353
"M Day," 574, 576
Medical Arts Building, 127
Melchior, Lauritz, 372
Memphis Tribune, 331–333
Mencken, H. L., 151, 191
Merriam, Carroll B., 252
Metal:
  essential to war effort, 362–363
  shortage, 435
Metals Reserve Company and Defense
    Supply Corporation, 352, 388, 401,
    435, 436
Methodist College, 40
Methodist Hospital Building Fund, 128,
    552
Metropolitan Opera House, 75, 372, 403
Metropolitan Theater, 132, 556
Meyer, Eugene, 185
  altercation with Jesse, 411
  attacks Jesse on BEW delays, 438
  comments on Jesse's dismissal as
    Secretary of Commerce, 514
  criticism of Jesse and rubber shortage,
    410
  questions Jesse's loyalty to Roosevelt,
    484
  resigns from RFC, 195
  selected as chairman of RFC, 186, 188
Midway, 24
Milbank, Jeremiah, 79
Military expansion, WWII and, 327–328
Miller Outdoor Theatre, 574
Mirabeau B. Lamar, 422
Missouri Pacific, 189
MIT, 427
Moley, Raymond, 221, 502, 561–562
Monopolies, Woodrow Wilson on,
    51–52
Monroe, James, 318
Monsanto Chemical Company, 452
Moody, Dan, 145
Moody, W. L., III, 182
Moore, W. W., 292
Morgan, J. Piermont, 126

Morgenthau, Henry, 209, 238
  advice on economic crisis, 300
  appointed to Secretary of the Treasury,
    219
  Jesse's criticism of in *Chronicle,* 535
  lobbying to abolish RFC, 253
  opposition to RFC, 276, 289
  perceived triumph over Jesse's RFC,
    293
Moscow Peace Treaty, 345
Munn's Department Store, 68
Murrow Indian Orphan Home, 472
Museum of Fine Arts—Houston, 67,
    128, 315, 535
Mussolini, Benito, 338, 464

N.V. Billiton-Maatschapij, 380
National Bank of Commerce, 63, 110,
    174, 175, 179, 183, 206, 530, 572
National Bank of Detroit, 204
National Broadcasting Corporation
    (NBC), 141, 148, 157–158, 247, 290
National Defense Advisory Council
    (NDAC), 356
  EPF vs. DPC's lease agreement, 361
  Office of Management Production
    (OPM) and, 386
  War Production Board and, 406
National Drainage Association, 252
National Housing Act of 1934, 302
National Paint, Varnish, and Lacquer
    Association, 247
National Press Club roast, 371
National Standard Building, 530–531,
    538
National Youth Administration, 378
National Youth Authority, 307–308
Native Americans, 10, 149
Natural gas, 539, 540
Nazi Party, 313
Negro Labor News, 532–533, 582
Neilson, P. R., 346
Neiman-Marcus, 577
Nelson, Donald, 413, 492
Neophogen College, 13
Neutrality Acts, 338–339, 343–344, 376
Newcomb, John Lloyd, 531

New Deal. *See specific programs*
New Mexico Military Institute, 545
New Rice Hotel Company, 50
"News of America," 574
Newsweek, 548, 573–574, 561–562, 575
New York Evening Sun, 139
New York Herald, 136
New York Southern Society, 297
New York State Bankers Association, 217
New York Stock Exchange, 149, 542
New York Times, 140, 161, 162, 400
  Clayton's SWPA appointment, 479
  endorses 1948 Republican
    presidential candidates, 548
  RFC report, 237
  Roosevelt replacing Jesse with
    Wallace, 515
  Wallace appointment to Secretary of
    Commerce, 513
The New York Times Magazine, 23
New York World, 106
New York:
  Jesse's construction projects in, 104,
    125–127, 169, 173
  Jones' stay in, 101–102, 105–106, 108
Nimitz, Chester W., 545
Nixon, Richard, on Jesse Jones, 582
Normandy, 315
Norris, George, 241
Notsuoh Deep Water Jubilee, 59
Notsuoh Festival, 39–40
Nuremberg Decrees, 313

O'Connor, J. F. T., 238
Office of Economic Warfare (OEW), 461
Office of Management Production
  (OPM), 386
  replaced by War Production Board,
    406
Office of War Mobilization, 455, 479
Oflag IX A/Z camp, 451
Oglethorpe University, Roosevelt's
  speech at, 196, 207, 210
O'Hara, Maureen, 551
Oil pipelines, 420, 462
Oil production, as a buffer for Houston
  economy in Great Depression, 179

Oil World Exposition, 294–295
"Old Timers' Reunion," 542
Olson, James, 223
O'Neill, William, 454
Orlando, Vittorio, 83
Osborn, William Church, 147–148

Packard Motor Car Company, 361, 407
Pact of Steel, 338
Panama Canal, 48
Paramount Studios, 132
Paris Peace Conference, 80, 83, 84, 149
Pasadena Post, 438
Pastoriza, Joseph, 67
Pattman, Wright, 380
Patton, George S., 545
Pavlova Ballet Company, 55
Peabody State Normal School, 13
Pearl Harbor, 3, 397
Pearson, Drew:
  accusations of failing to save textile
    industry, 237
  Alcoa controversy, 391–392
  automobile competition and banking
    closures, 229
  on delays in defense supplies, 383–
    384
  on government reorganization, 328
  Jesse's appointment to head of FLA,
    334
  Jesse's desire to be Secretary of
    Treasury, 219, 220
  Jesse's influence after leaving Cabinet
    position, 522, 526, 527
  on possibility of regional government
    banks, 305
  predictions about RFC demise, 271,
    293, 296
  relief for flood victims, 278, 306–307
  RFC's lending policies, 311–312, 407
  Roosevelt-Wallace-Jones conflict,
    503–504
  special legislation for Jones' two
    government posts, 359
  U.S. lending during WWII, 345
Penicillin, 472
Pepper, Claude, 333, 487

Perkins, Milo, 414–415
Pershing, John J., 71
Petroleum Club, 556, 557
Phelps-Dodge Copper Corporation, 69
Philadelphia Morning Public Ledger, 139
Pierce-Arrow, 63
Pierson, Warren, 400
Pig, surplus during Great Depression, 208
Pioneer Hi-Bred Company, 515
Pizzella, Edmond, 246
Playboy Motor Car Corporation, 529
Pomerene, Atlee, 195
"Post-War Problems," 467
Potter, Hugh, 282
Powell, Robert, 150
Prairie View University, 532, 533, 534
Pratt, Joe, 63
Preston, Robert, 551
Price Control Act, 506
Pringle, Henry F., 472–474
Proctor & Gamble, 429
Prohibition laws, 99
  Al Smith opposes, 161, 120
  repeal, 253
  role in 1924 election, 120
  role in 1928 election, 148, 164–165
Public National Bank, Jesse rescues, 182–183
Public Works Administration (PWA), 237, 253, 263, 289
  Roosevelt cuts spending, 294
  Roosevelt requests funds to renew, 307–308
Publix Theatre, 127, 132

Racism:
  1928 Democratic National Convention, segregation at, 162
  armed forces, segregated, 549–550
  labeling in newspapers, 565
  tensions in Houston after lynching, 150, 155
  violence and, 8
  See also Education, segregated; Ku Klux Klan
Radio. See specific stations

Railroads:
  competition with other forms of transportation, 241
  impact of Great Depression on, 179
  in trouble, 240–242, 247–248, 254–257
  in WWII, 389
Raskob, John J.:
  Empire State Building purchase, 426–427
  selected as chairman of 1928 Democratic National Committee, 163
Rationing, 464–465
Rayburn, Sam, 439, 497
RCA, 148
Reconstruction Finance Corporation (RFC):
  aviation, investment in, 416
  criticism of, 190, 192–193, 205, 238, 346–347
  efforts to rescue banks, 199–200
  finances production of machine tools, 447–448
  formation of, 186–196
  funds to start PWA, 237
  gold prices, raises, 209–210
  granted extension, 276
  instructed to stop lending, 292, 294
  investigation, 558–559
  Jesse and
    appointed to board, 1
    appointed to chairman, 2
    influence on board members, 252–253
    resigns from, 335–336
  legislation to make relief loans to states and cities, 193–194
  loans
    direct loans to businesses and industry, 222–226
    disaster, 276–277
    on inventory, 309
    post-war, 554
    to Russia and China, 209
    for useful public works projects, 308–309
  losses, 540

Reconstruction Finance Corporation (*cont.*)
  Mortgage Company, 240, 279, 305
  power to invest, 202
  profits from transporting and selling
    oil, 539–540
  purchases municipal bonds to help
    cities, 227
  railroads, aid for, 240–242, 247–248,
    254–257
  reauthorization, 237–240, 326–327
  reconversion, growing
    responsibilities for, 487–488
  Roosevelt once again makes loans
    available, 304–305
  rumors of dismantling, 271–273
  San Francisco Bay Bridge, funding
    for, 195
  subsidiaries announced, 506–507
  transition from war to peace, 463
  wartime organization, 363
  weakened by WWII agencies, 412–413
  See also Commodity Credit
    Corporation (CCC)
Red Crescent Societies, 451
Red Cross War Fund, 403
Red Roosters, 110, 111
Reed, Stanley, 208, 542
Republican Party:
  1924 National Convention, 120, 142
  1928 National Convention, 149–150
  1932 National Convention, 192
  1936 election, 269
  1940 presidential candidates, 353
  1944 Presidential candidates, 494
  regains control in 1946 midterm
    elections, 537
  views of Jesse, 220–221
Reston, James, 507, 547
Reynolds Lumber Company, 39
Reynolds Metal Company, 356, 369
Rhineland, 314
Rice Hotel, 56
  1928 Democratic National Convention
    and, 155
  Audrey's wedding, 423–424
  community impact, 63
  as home to Jones', 134

Jesse's first Houston home, 37
  remodeled, 556
  renovations to, 127
  rivaled by Shamrock, 550–551
Rice, C. W., 582
Rice, H. Baldwin, 33, 47, 48–50
Rice, John W., 440
Rice Institute, 50–51, 246, 270, 579, 580
Rice University, 74, 545
Richardson, Sid, 408
Rickenbacker, Eddie, 545
Ringling Brothers, 140
River Oaks Country Club, 156
Robertson County, 7, 10
Robinson, Joe, 186
Robinson, Joseph P., 156
Rockefeller, John D., 533
Rockefeller, Nelson, 364
Rockwell, J. M., 54
Rogers, Betty, 249, 250, 329
Rogers, Ginger, 551
Rogers, Jim, 245
Rogers, Will, 120
  1928 Democratic National
    Convention, 151, 156, 157–159, 162,
    166
  1929 Stock Market Crash, 175–176
  benefit concerts during Great
    Depression, 181
  death of, 244–245
  memorial, 247
  on RFC legislation, 193
  on Roosevelt, 191
  See also Will Rogers Memorial
    Commission
Roosevelt, Eleanor:
  at 1940 Democratic National
    Convention, 353, 355
  appeals to RFC for low-income
    housing projects, 204–205
  supports Jesse rather than Wallace as
    FDR's running mate, 354
Roosevelt, Elliott:
  Jesse pays debts, 408
  radio stations in Texas, 408
  repays loan to Jesse, 540
  support for Jesse, 330, 353, 485

Roosevelt, Franklin:
 1928 campaign, 130–131, 148–149
 1936 nomination for president, 263
 "Brain Trust," 238
 death of, 519
 Empire State Building, encourages
  Jesse to purchase, 387, 403, 426–
  427, 469, 560
 FDIC, opposition to, 214
 "Fireside Chats," 202–203, 337–338, 351
 governor of New York, 171, 191
 Jesse, relationship with, 403
  appoints to FLA, 333
  plans with Wallace to fire, 502–504
  replaces as Secretary of Commerce,
   509
  requests special legislation to hold
   two government jobs, 357–359
 "lending-spending campaign," 311
 loss of support for, 264, 317
 mental deterioration, 508
 national defense spending, appeals
  for increase in, 350–351
 Neutrality Acts, attempts to repeal,
  339
 presidential candidacy, 191–198
  elected president, 196–197, 269–270,
   367–368, 485–486, 497
  inauguration, 200–201, 377–378,
   509
  "spontaneous" nomination for third
   term, 353–354
 reorganization of government, 328
 RFC to raise gold prices, appeals to,
  209
 Supreme Court, seeks to expand,
  279–280, 317
 Texas Regulars, 482–485
"Roosevelt Depression," 301
Roots, Fannie, 533
Roper, Daniel, 230, 238
Rosenman, Sam, 491
Ross, Nellie Taylor, 159
Rough Riders, 262
Royal Air Force, 444
Rubber Manufacturers Association, 401
Rubber Reserve Company, 352, 401–402

Rubber:
 disputes over grain- vs. petroleum-
  based, 427–431
 essential to war effort, 361–363
 experimental plants, 402, 409–410,
  417
 four U.S. plants under construction in
  WWII, 389, 452–453
 Jesse on synthetic program, 436–437
 RFC to buy and stockpile, 355, 365, 380
 WWII shortage, 401–403, 406–410,
  421, 427–431
 See also Latin America
Rural Electrification Administration
 (REA), 243
Russell, Lillian, 24–25
Russian Symphony Orchestra, 48
Ryan, Thomas Fortune, 121

Sakowitz Brothers', 67, 171
Salary, limits on bank executive, 2
Salesmanship Club, 249
Salvation Army, Jesse's contributions
 to, 96
Sam Houston Coliseum, 271, 295
Sam Houston Hall, 140–141
San Francisco Bay Bridge, 195
San Francisco-Oakland Bay Bridge, 250
San Jacinto, 441
San Jacinto Battleground, 60, 259,
 260–261
San Jacinto Monument, 259, 282, 283,
 284–285, 373
The Saturday Evening Post, 500
 "Biggest Big Shot: Uncle Sam," 472–
  474
 feature on Jesse, 368–371
Schacher, Eugene, 262
Schram, Emil, 252, 278, 542
 approach vs. Jesse's bargaining, 384
 as president of DPC, 363
 FNMA board, 303
 in Fortune article about DPC lease, 396
 leaves RFC to become president of
  New York Stock Exchange, 384
 replaces Jesse as head of RFC, 333
Schwab, Charles, 177–178, 246

Schwartz, Jordan, 221
Scott, Owen L., 418
Scottish Rite Cathedral, 234
Seagraves, Odie, 182
Sears and Roebuck, 413
Seattle Times, 140
Senate Banking and Currency
    Committee, 221–222, 298, 306
Senate Committee Investigating
    National Defense, 391
Sevier, John, 14
Shamrock Hotel, 523, 550
Sharecropping, 16
Shearn Methodist Episcopal Church, 44
Shell Company, 289
  butadiene plant, 380
  contributes to *USS Houston*
    replacement, 441
Ships of All Nations Pageant, 60
Simpson, A. D., 203, 206
Simpson, Dee, 333
Sloan, Alfred P., 203
"Small Inch" pipeline, 499, 539
Smith, Alfred E., 120, 136, 266
  1928 presidential candidacy, 156,
    159–161
  Empire State Building purchase,
    426–427
Smith, Harold, 468
Snyder, John, 520
Social Security, 295–296
Socialism:
  criticisms of RFC and, 205
  New Deal critiques, 2, 266
Somervell, Brehon, 476
South Texas Commercial National
    Bank, 27
South Texas Lumber Company:
  establishment of, 39
  Jesse sells controlling interest, 50
South Texas Truck Company, 99
Southern Loan and Investment
    Company, 41
Southern Methodist University, 250
Southern Pacific Railroad, 61, 183
Southwestern University, 128
Spanish influenza epidemic, 77

Speed limits, implementing, 428, 431
Spindletop, discovery of oil at, 38
Spruce Goose, 540
St. Lawrence University, 421
St. Louis Post-Dispatch, 413, 514
St. Luke's Hospital, 581
St. Paul's Methodist Church, 27, 96, 233,
    578, 582–583
St. Paul's Sanitarium, 33, 34
Stage Door Canteen, 446
Stalin, Joseph, 462, 515
Stanford University, 250
Star-Telegram, 132, 134
Statler Hotel, 522
Staub, John, 134–135
Stephens, Hubert, 253
Sterling, Ross, 145–146, 182
Stern, Edith, 465–467
Stettinius, Edward R., Jr., 410, 501
Stevenson, Coke, 439
Stranded in Paris, 132
Studebaker, 429, 448
Sulzberger, Arthur Hayes, 548
Supply Priorities and Allocations Board
    (SPAB), 387
  replaced by War Production Board,
    406
  Wallace and, 412–413
Surplus Property Act, 493
Surplus Property Board, 522
Surplus War Property Administration
    (SWPA), 479
Symington, Stuart, 522, 526–527
  become RFC director, 559
  on Jesse's book, 562

T. W. House and Company: failure of, 45
Taber, Frederick H., 253
Taft, Robert A., 359, 514
Taft, William Howard, 100, 259–260
Tariffs, Woodrow Wilson on, 51–52
Taub, Sam, 54, 340
Taylor, Wayne Chatfield, 512
Taylor, Zachary, 285
Teapot Dome scandal, 119–120
Temple Beth Israel, 154
Temple University, 286–288

Tenneco, 557
Tennessee Gas Transmission Company, 556–557
Tennessee Reconstruction Finance Corporation, 475
Tennessee Valley Authority (TVA), 226–227
Texaco, 46
Texas A&M University, 270, 340, 472, 534, 545, 552
Texas Centennial, 257–259
The Texas Company, 289
    brings Texaco to Houston, 46
Texas Eastern, 539
Texas League of Women Voters, 128
Texas Medical Center, 425, 545, 552, 563, 564
Texas and Pacific Railroad, 26–27
Texas Portland Cement Company, 66
Texas Regulars, 482–485, 497, 514
Texas State College for Women, 532
Texas State Fair, 32
Texas State Hotel, 171, 290
Texas Transport Mail Line, 151
Third Ward School, 14
Thompson, Audrey, 92
Time, 3, 207, 215–217, 376–377, 493
Timmons, Bascom, 187–188, 244, 258, 303, 580–581, 582
Tin:
    RFC to buy and stockpile, 355, 365, 380
    smelt under construction in WWII, 389
Tobacco:
    Jones first crop, 16–17
    Tennessee economy, 7
    transportation, 18
Today, names Jesse the "Dough Doctor," 221
Todd Shipbuilding Corporation, 380
Toomey, Joe, 261
Traffic Club of New York, 241
Transamerica Corporation, 189
Traylor, Melvin, 191
Treaty of Guadalupe, 285
Treaty of Versailles, 89

Truman, Harry S., 232
    1944 candidacy for vice president, 487
    as potential running mate for Roosevelt's fourth term, 485
    relationship with Jones in first days of presidency, 519–520
    Truman Committee, 391, 407–408
    wins 1948 presidential election, 548–549
Tucker Corporation, 528
Tully, Grace, 510, 511
Tumulty, Joseph, 75, 92
Turning Basin, 97

U.S. Chamber of Commerce, 311
U.S. Department of Commerce, 174–175
U.S. Rubber, 389
U-boats, 419–420, 421
Union Bank and Trust, 42–43, 182
Union Guardian Trust Company, 200
Union Pacific Railroad, 431
United Jewish Appeal, 535
United Nations Atomic Energy Commission, 536
United Negro College Fund, 533
United States Bank, defaults after 1929 crash, 180
United States Commercial Corporation (USCC), 406
United States Steel Corporation (U.S. Steel), 472, 478
University of California, 472
University of Houston, 545, 546, 552, 572
University of Oklahoma, 329, 472
University of Tennessee, 534
University of Texas, 128, 246, 329, 472, 545, 564
University of Virginia, 531
USS George Washington, 82
USS Houston, 439
USS San Jacinto, 467

Van Swearingen, Oris and Mantis, 189
Vandegrift, Alexander Archer, 545
Vanderbilt University, 13
Versailles Peace Treaty, Hitler renounces the, 313–314

Victory Ship, 417, 422

Vinson, Fred M., 519

Waites, August, 572

Wall Street Journal, 344–345
  on Clayton's SWPA appointment,
    479–480
  reports of Jesse's demise, 413

Wall Street 1929 crash, 175–176. *See also*
  Great Depression

Wallace, Henry A., 207, 348
  criticism of, 355
  establishes SPAB, 387
  at George bill hearing, 517–518
  Jesse's rivalry with, 444–445, 454–461,
    507, 535
  New Dealers continued support for,
    501–502
  rejected as 1944 running mate, 485–
    486
  requests direct BEW funding, 455
  RFC and, 403
  Roosevelt and, 354, 460, 502–503
  speech at 1944 Democratic
    Convention, 486
  support for 1944 vice presidential
    nomination, 486–487
  takes charge of SPAB and BEW, 411–
    413

Walter, Emmett, 565

Waltham Watch Company loan, 554

Walton, T. O., 270

War Damage Corp., 506

"Warehouse War," 364

War and Navy Departments, 356, 386

War Finance Corporation (WFC), 185

War Industries Board, 80

War Insurance Corporation, 397

War Mothers of Houston, 154

War Production Board, 406, 413, 455,
    462

Warren, Earl, 547

"Washington Merry-Go-Round"
    column, 391–392

Washington National Cathedral,
    Woodrow Wilson at, 117–118

Washington Post, 410, 514

Washington Star, 418

WBAP, 132

Welles, Sumner, 385–386

Wellington Brink, 244

Wells, Orson, 55

West, J. M., 50

Westheimer Moving and Storage, 174

Whiskey, Tennessee economy, 7

The White City, 24

Wilkie, Wendell, 346–347, 353

Will Rogers Memorial Commission, 247,
    317–318, 329, 472

Will Rogers Memorial Hospital, 318

Will Rogers Memorial Museum, 318

Wilson, Edith:
  1928 Democratic National
    Convention, 152–160
  championed by Jones, 4
  comments on Smith's presidential
    candidacy, 165
  sends arrangement for Jesse's funeral,
    583
  Red Cross War Fund benefit, 403–404
  role after Woodrow's stroke, 95
  on Woodrow's pension, 115

Wilson, Woodrow:
  1928 Democratic National
    Convention, honored at, 152–153,
    157, 160
  advocates for unlimited draft, 75
  American Red Cross and, 3–4, 68,
    74–75
  brings Jesse to Washington, 68–69
  chosen as presidential nominee, 51–52
  death of, 117–118
  foreign policy of neutrality, 62–63
  health issues, 94–95
    kept from public, 102
  Jones gets pension for, 4
  opposition to Eighteenth
    Amendment, 99
  Paris Peace Conference, 83–84
  pension for, 113–117
  promotion of League of Nations,
    92–94

on Wall Street, 75, 76–77
WWI and, 64–66
"Wives of Prominent Washingtonians," 465
Wolcott, Jesse P., 276
Wolfman, Ben, 550
Woman's Home Companion, 465
Women, 4, 52, 79
Women's Army Corp, 439
Women's Co-Operative Home, 233
Women's National Democratic Club, 165
Wood, Natalie, 551
Woodin, William, 201, 219, 220
Woodring, Harry, 277
Woodrow Wilson School of International Affairs, 531, 532
Woodul, Walter Frank, 245
Wool, RFC buys and stockpiles, 380–381
Woolard, Louisa, 26, 52, 99–100
Works Progress Administration (WPA), 243–244, 253, 289, 378
  Roosevelt cuts spending, 294
  Roosevelt requests funds to renew, 307–308
World Bank, 540, 541

World War I, 275
  American entrance into, 64–66
  American Red Cross and, 3–4
World War II:
  causalities, 490
  Great Britain and France declare war on Germany, 337
  impact on U.S. economy, 382–383
  mobilization, 1
  rumors of "phony war," 350
World's Columbian Exposition, 30
  increases demand for Texas timber, 27
  Jones attends, 23–25
Worth Hotel, 127, 132
Worth Theater, 127
Wortham, Gus, 110, 232–233
Wright Aeronautical Corporation, 355–356
Wright Brothers, 470

Young Women's Cooperative Home, 27
Young, Owen D., 148, 448

Ziegfeld Follies, 151
Zukor, Adolph, 132